CRITICAL PRAISE FOR THE CURRENT AND PREVIOUS EDITIONS OF *ETHICS IN PSYCHOTHERAPY AND COUNSELING*

"I love this book! And so will therapists, supervisors, and trainees. In fact, it really should be required reading for every mental professional and aspiring professional.... And it is a fun read to boot!"

—Stephen J. Ceci, PhD, Cornell University

"A splendid book.... This is essential reading for all those in psychotherapy and related fields."

—Clifford Stromberg, Esq., Partner, Healthcare Law, Hogan & Hartson, Washington, DC

"It should be part of every therapist's basic library."

—Allen Webb, PhD, ABPP, Former President, American Board of Professional Psychology

"A classic must-have book for all psychologists that just keeps getting better with each edition...."

—Nadya Fouad, Distinguished Professor, University of Wisconsin; Editor, *Counseling Psychologist*

"Pope and Vasquez have done it again.... An indispensable resource for seasoned professionals and students alike."

—Beverly Greene, PhD, ABPP, St. John's University

"A wonderful, helpful guide to the complexities of modern-day ethics. As hard as it is to imagine, this revision by Drs. Pope and Vasquez of their landmark text is even more timely, insightful, and important."

—Patrick Deleon, PhD, Former President, American Psychological Association

"At last the working clinician has concrete, down-to-earth help to resolve issues of ethics and professional responsibility that one confronts daily. This book is a must for faculty ... should be required for all clinicians in training."

—Jerome Singer, PhD, ABPP, Yale University

"An updated version of a classic text on ethics in psychology. Drs. Pope and Vasquez provide the reader with an outstanding set of tools for enhancing ethical behavior in an increasingly complex professional world."

—Ronald F. Levant, EdD, Former president, American Psychological Association

"A wonderfully insightful and unique book for all therapists, supervisors, and students; an affirmation of our rich scientific and professional heritage and values."

—Jack Wiggins, PhD, Former President,
American Psychological Association

"A wise and useful book which should be in every practitioner's library and be required in all clinical and counseling training programs."

—David Mills, PhD, former Director, APA Ethics Office

"An excellent analysis of the meaning of ethics in the everyday life of practicing therapists."

—Patricia Keith-Spiegel, PhD, former Chair, APA Ethics Committee

"This third edition of the classic ethics text provides invaluable resources and enables readers to engage in critical thinking in order to make their own decisions. This superb reference belongs in every psychology training program's curriculum and on every psychologist's bookshelf."

—Lillian Comas-Diaz, PhD, Former President,
APA Division of Psychologists in Independent Practice

"Ken Pope and Melba Vasquez are right on target once again in the third edition, a book that every practicing mental health professional should read and have in their reference library."

—Jeffrey N. Younggren, PhD, Risk Management Consultant,
American Psychological Association Insurance Trust

"Drs. Pope and Vasquez have done a masterful job in their third edition in helping practitioners think through how to respond to complex ethical dilemmas and assume personal responsibility for their actions. This book also provides an excellent articulation of best practices in negotiating and clarifying complex ethical dilemmas. The authors explore the complexities of ethical decision-making in creative ways that encourage mindful awareness and continual inquiry. They use an active approach with scenarios followed by a set of questions to explore each topic. This is an essential book for every clinician—from trainees to seasoned practitioners. It will have a powerful impact on the field for many years to come by providing practitioners a solid foundation and road map upon which to provide competent and ethical treatment."

—Linda Garnets, PhD, UCLA

"This dynamic 3rd edition invites the reader into an active questioning process that goes well beyond ethics codes and standards. The engaging autonomy-based approach empowers practitioners to discover the most ethical and positive response to a unique client with unique needs and resources in a unique context."

—Carol D. Goodheart, EdD, 2010 President,
American Psychological Association

"The talents of Drs. Pope and Vasquez relative to their abilities to translate difficult and sensitive material into a user-friendly resource, continues to shine forth in this latest work. Their appreciation of the multiple contexts (multicultural, social, political, historical, and intra-personal) within which ethical decision-making is framed and their attention to the emotion-laden human component that fuels a professional's response to the ethical circumstances and dilemmas they confront adds a shining touch to their impeccable scholarship. This text represents an invitation to mental health professionals across levels of academic and clinical experiences to sharpen their service-provider talents and tools and a response in the affirmative to these distinguished authors is highly encouraged."

—William D. Parham, PhD, ABPP, President, Society of Counseling
Psychology, Division 17 of the American Psychological Association; Dean,
Graduate School of Professional Psychology, John F. Kennedy University

"An excellent blend of case law, research evidence, down-to-earth principles, and practical examples from two authors with outstanding expertise. Promotes valuable understanding through case illustrations, self-directed exercises, and thoughtful discussion of such issues as cultural diversity."

—Dick Suinn, Former President, American Psychological Association

"The Pope and Vasquez text will stand as a premier reference source for ethics codes, practice guidelines, and leading-edge topics of expanding practice. The authors do a masterful job of blending relational aspects of practice (e.g., power, trust, cultural and contextual differences, self-care, and boundaries) with areas of continuing competency development (e.g., practice in electronic services, evolving skills in assessment and evaluation, and procedures for responding to complaints). The result is a powerhouse of resources and tools for practice today and into the future."

—Linda Campbell, PhD, University of Georgia

"This unique volume provides invaluable ethical guidance for psychologists engaged in professional practice. The scenarios and accompanying questions added to most chapters will prove especially helpful to those who offer courses and workshops concerned with ethics in psychology."

—Charles D. Spielberger, PhD, ABPP; Former President,
American Psychological Association

"An outstanding book. The chapter on testing, assessment, and diagnosis is heartening; it identifies the ethical responsibilities as well as dilemmas and pitfalls we face as practitioners."

—Philip Erdberg, PhD, ABPP, Former President,
Society for Personality Assessment

"A comprehensive and practical guide for practitioners who strive to have an ethical, competent, and caring practice, this book is a practical resource those who aspire to be excellent psychotherapists and counselors. Useful and relevant, it will not gather dust."

—Jessica Henderson Daniels, PhD, ABPP,
Childrens Hospital, Boston; APA Board of Directors

"This is an excellent, well-written blend of scholarship, common-sense, and wise counsel that is easy to read and full of practical illustrations likely to benefit both the novice and experienced psychotherapist."

—Gerald Koocher, PhD, ABPP, Dean of the School for
Health Studies at Simmons College; Former President,
American Psychological Association

"A necessary book for those who want to take their risk-management strategies to the next level."

—Eric Harris, J.D., PhD, Risk Managment Consultant,
American Psychological Association Insurance Trust

"Useful to every psychologist. I expect it will land on everyone's bookshelf as a well-thumbed source of important information on such topics as working with suicidal clients. We will use it in training at our Center."

—Norman Farberow, PhD, ABPP, Co-Founder and
Co-Director, L.A. Suicide Prevention Center

Ethics in Psychotherapy and Counseling

A Practical Guide, Fourth Edition

KENNETH S. POPE
MELBA J. T. VASQUEZ

WILEY

John Wiley & Sons, Inc.

Published by John Wiley & Sons, Inc., Hoboken, New Jersey.
Published simultaneously in Canada.

Library of Congress Cataloging-in-Publication Data:

Pope, Kenneth S.

   Ethics in psychotherapy and counseling : a practical guide/by Kenneth S. Pope, Melba J. Vasquez. – 4th ed.
       p. cm.
   Includes bibliographical references and index.
   ISBN 978-0-470-63307-6 (pbk.); ISBN 978-0-470-91722-0 (ebk); ISBN 978-0-470-91723-7 (ebk); ISBN 978-0-470-91724-4 (ebk)
1. Counseling psychologists–Professional ethics.   2. Psychotherapists–Professional ethics.   3. Counseling psychology–Moral and ethical aspects.   4. Psychotherapy–Moral and ethical aspects.   5. Counseling psychologist and client.   I. Vasquez, Melba Jean Trinidad. II. Title.

   BF636.67.P67 2011

   174'.91583–dc22

                                                                                                2010019066

Printed in the United States of America

10 9 8 7 6 5 4 3 2 1

DEDICATION

To those whose kindness, integrity, courage, ethics, and love
keep showing me and others that life can be more than we thought,
and inspire us to do something about it;
Especially to Hanna, Phil, Utah (who made it my best birthday ever, but
whose Golden Voice of the Great Southwest is now silent), Judy, Ed, Pete,
and Mary Ann,
for decades of making me laugh, cry, sing, and dream;
And most of all to Karen, who knows why.

—Ken Pope

To my friends, colleagues, clients, students, and family,
from whom I have learned tremendously;
Especially my spouse and best friend, Jim H. Miller;
And mother, Ofelia Vasquez Philo.

—Melba Vasquez

CONTENTS

PREFACE

Welcome to those who are new to this book! To those who read the first, second, or third edition, welcome back!

The field of psychotherapy continues to evolve along with ethical theory, research, and practice. We updated all chapters to reflect those changes.

There are some new chapters. The first two chapters in the book are now "What Do I Do Now?" and "Ethics in Real Life."

There is a new chapter on technologies: "Therapy in the Digital World: The Ethical Challenges of the New Technologies."

Chapter 12, "Different Conclusions: Example from the Interrogation Controversy," which is another new chapter, provides an example of how people of good faith can think through an ethical issue and reach different conclusions about the most ethical approach.

The Appendices include the ethics codes of the American Psychological Association and the Canadian Psychological Association, as well as a list of over 100 other ethics codes and professional guidelines for therapy, assessment, counseling, and forensics.

BASIC ASSUMPTIONS

Although much of the material is new, this book's fundamental approach to ethics remains unchanged from the first edition. The approach is grounded in seven basic assumptions:

> 1. Ethical awareness is a continuous, active process that involves constant questioning and personal responsibility.

Conflicts with managed care companies, the urgency of patients' needs, the lack of adequate support, the possibility of formal complaints, mind-deadening routines, endless paperwork, worrying about making ends meet, exhaustion, and so much else can block our personal responsiveness and dull our sense of personal responsibility. They can overwhelm us, distract us, drain us, and lull us into ethical sleep. Our work requires constant alertness and mindful awareness of the ethical implications of what we choose to do and not do.

Ethical awareness includes taking into account our very human lack of perfection. All of us have weaknesses, vulnerabilities, and blind spots. The dramatic differences are not so much between those who have many human imperfections and those who have few but between those who are freely open—to themselves and others—about how their own shortcomings affect their work, and those who tend to see others as inferior versions of themselves. Chapter 6, "Competence and the Human Therapist," explores some of these themes.

Ethical awareness also depends on our ability to take care of ourselves, to recognize when fear, anger, boredom, resentment, sadness, hopelessness, or anxiety hurt work, and to do something about it. Chapter 7, "Creating Strategies for Self-Care," offers ideas on how we can recognize when our lack of enthusiasm, resilience, meaning, and joy makes us less effective and suggests the steps we can take to prevent that from happening or to turn things around it when it is happening.

> 2. Awareness of ethical codes is crucial, but formal codes cannot take the place of an active, thoughtful, creative approach to our ethical responsibilities.

Awareness of ethics codes is crucial to competence in the area of ethics, but the formal standards are no substitute for an active, deliberative, and creative approach to fulfilling our ethical responsibilities. Codes prompt, guide, and inform our ethical consideration; they do not shut it down or replace it.

Ethical practice never means following a code in a rote, thoughtless manner. Each new client, whatever his or her similarities to previous clients, is unique. Each situation is unique and constantly changing—time and events do not stand still. Our theoretical orientation, the nature of our community and the client's community, our culture and the client's culture, and so many other contexts shape what we see and how we see it. Every ethical decision must take these contexts into account. The codes may steer us away from some clearly unethical approaches. They may shine a light on important values and concern. But they cannot tell us what form these values and concerns will take. They may set forth essential tasks, but they cannot spell out the best way to accomplish those tasks with a unique client facing unique problems in a specific time and place with limited resources. Decisions about ethical behavior are the result of a process.

> 3. Awareness of relevant legislation, case law, and other legal standards is crucial, but legal standards should not be confused with ethical responsibilities.

A risk in the emphasis on legal standards is that adherence to minimal legal standards, which in some cases means finding ways around those standards, can become a substitute for ethical behavior. This trend has become increasingly prevalent in the political arena. A politician or political appointee holding a position of great public trust faces clear evidence that he or she betrayed that trust. When no other defense or justification is available, the politician insists that nothing wrong was done because no law was broken. (Even such desperate defenses hit a snag when it turns out that a law was broken; in those cases the individual stresses that there was a "technical violation of the law.")

An overly exclusive focus on legal standards can discourage ethical awareness and sensitivity. It is crucial to realize that ethical behavior is more than simply avoiding violation of legal standards and that one's ethical and legal duties may, in certain instances, be in conflict. Practicing "defensive therapy"—making risk management our main focus—can cause us to lose sight of our ethical responsibilities and the ethical consequences of what we say and do. Ethical awareness avoids the comfortable trap of aiming low, of striving only to get by without breaking any law.

Though often compatible, the legal framework is different from the ethical framework. Ethical awareness requires clearly distinguishing the two and alertness to when they stand in conflict. These conflicts are discussed in Chapters 9, "Codes and Complaints in Context," and Chapter 12, "Different Conclusions."

> 4. We believe that the overwhelming majority of therapists and counselors are conscientious, dedicated, caring individuals, committed to ethical behavior. But none of us is infallible.

All of us can—and do—make mistakes, overlook something important, work from a limited perspective, reach conclusions that are wrong, hold tight to a cherished belief that is misguided. We're aware of many barriers between us and our best work, but we may underestimate or overlook some of those barriers. Part of our responsibility is to question ourselves: What if I'm wrong about this? Is there something I'm overlooking? Could there be another way of understanding this situation? Are there other possibilities? Can I come up with a more creative, more effective, better way of responding?

> 5. Many of us find it easier to question the ethics of others than to question our own beliefs, assumptions, and actions. It is worth noticing if we find ourselves preoccupied with how wrong others are in some area of ethics and certain that we are the ones to set them right, or at least to point out repeatedly how wrong they are.

It is a red flag if we spend more time trying to point out other people's weaknesses, flaws, mistakes, ethical blindness, destructive actions, or hopeless stupidity than we spend questioning and challenging ourselves in positive, effective, and productive ways that awaken us to new perspectives and possibilities. Questioning ourselves is at least as important as questioning others.

> 6. Most of us find it easier to question ourselves on those intriguing topics we know we don't understand, that we stumble onto with confusion, uncertainty, and doubt. The harder but more helpful work is to question ourselves about our casual certainties. What have we taken for granted and accepted without challenge? Nothing can be placed off-limits for this questioning.

Certainties are hard to give up, especially when they've grown to be part of us. They become landmarks, helping us make sense of the world, guiding our steps. But perhaps an always-reliable theoretical orientation begins distorting our view of a new patient, leading us to interventions that make things worse. Or having always prided ourselves on the soundness of our psychological evaluations, we keep rereading our draft report in a case in which an unbiased description of our findings may bring about a tragic injustice, harming many innocent people, and begin to wonder if our feelings for the client led us to shade the truth. Or the heart of our internship has been the supervision, and we've made it a point to tell the supervisor everything important about every patient, except about getting so aroused every time with that one patient, the one who is not very vulnerable at all and doesn't really need therapy, the one we keep having fantasies of asking out after waiting a reasonable time after termination and then, if all goes well, proposing to.

We must follow this questioning wherever it leads, even if we venture into territories that some might view as politically incorrect or—much more difficult for most of us—"psychologically incorrect" (Pope, Sonne, & Greene, 2006).

> 7. As psychologists, we often encounter ethical dilemmas without clear and easy answers.

As we try to help people who come to us because they are hurting and in need, we confront overwhelming needs unmatched by adequate resources, conflicting responsibilities that seem impossible to reconcile, frustrating limits to our understanding and interventions, and countless other challenges. We may be the only person a desperate client can turn to, and we may be pulled every which way by values, events, limited time, and limited options. Our best efforts to sort through such challenges may lead us to a thoughtful, informed conclusion about the most ethical path that is in stark contradiction to the thoughtful, informed conclusion of a best friend, a formal consultant, our attorney, or the professional groups we belong to. Chapter 12 explores the ways in which a complex situation can lead people to very different conclusions about the most ethical response. In the midst of these limitations, conflicts, disagreements, and complexities, we must make the best choices we can. We must each answer the challenging question: What do I do now? And each of us must take responsibility for that decision. We cannot shift personal responsibility for our ethical decisions and acts to another person, group, law, code, or custom. *There is no legitimate way to avoid these ethical struggles. They are part of our work.*

A NOTE ON TERMINOLOGY

This book addresses ethical issues encountered by psychologists functioning as *psychotherapists*, other kinds of *therapists* (e.g., behavior therapists), and *counselors*. For the sake of brevity and convenience, we have often used just one of these terms—rather than some hyphenated form of all three—in a sentence. Similarly, some therapists identify those to whom they provide services as *clients*; others use the term *patients*. Again, for the sake of brevity and convenience, we have used these terms interchangeably throughout the book.

ACKNOWLEDGMENTS

We are deeply indebted to so many people who contributed directly or indirectly to this book. We are grateful to all but have space to mention only a few. We would never have obtained the multiyear actuarial data about malpractice suits, licensing board actions, and ethics complaints against psychologists in Canada and the United States without the generous help of the American Psychological Association (APA) Ethics Office staff, including Stephen Behnke, executive director; Sonia Wiggins, APA Membership Office; Karen Thomas, APA Office of Rights and Permissions; Steve DeMers, executive director, and Janet Pippin, staff of the Association of State and Provincial Psychology Boards; Bruce Bennett, CEO, APA Insurance Trust; Carole Sinclair, Canadian Psychological Association (CPA) Ethics Committee Chair; and John Service, former executive director of CPA.

Ray Arsenault, Stephen Behnke, Linda Campbell, Ursula Delworth, Barry Farber, Lisa Grossman, Tom Gutheil, Kate Hays, Gerry Koocher, Loralie Lawson, Karen Olio, and Janet Sonne are among those who read drafts of the current or previous editions and offered valuable suggestions for improvements.

We asked a number of prominent therapists with expertise in recognizing and responding to suicidal risk to discuss pitfalls of work in this area. Chapter 20 presents the advice that each of these experts gives to readers. We thank those who contributed discussions: David Barlow, Danny Brom, Marla Craig, Jessica Henderson Daniel, Norman Farberow, the late Erika Fromm, Rosa Garci-Peltoniemi, Jesse Geller, Don Hiroto, Nadine Kaslow, the late Helen

Block Lewis, Marsha Linehan, Ricardo Munoz, Michael Peck, David Rudd, Gary Schoener, the late Hans Strupp, and Danny Wedding.

We received exceptionally skillful and generous help from Rebecca McGovern and Xenia Lisanevich of Jossey-Bass Publishers in preparing the first edition; from Alan Rinzler, Katie Levine, Margaret Sebold, Joanne Clapp Fullagar, and Paula Goldstein of Jossey-Bass Publishers and Rachel Anderson of Satellite Publishing Services in preparing the second edition; from Alan Rinzler, Carol Hartland, Seth Schwartz, and Jennifer Wenzel of Jossey-Bass Publishers, along with Beverly Harrison Miller, in preparing the third edition; and from Patricia Rossi, Fiona Brown, and Kate Lindsay in preparing this fourth edition. We also wish to thank Joel Dvoskin for permission to cite his Division 41 presidential address in Chapter 12.

Chapter 1

WHAT DO I DO NOW?

What do I do now?

If I tell the insurance company this patient's actual diagnosis, the insurance company won't pay, and I'll be short the office rent this month.

My supervisor tells me to do things I know are wrong, but he's nationally known and I have to get a good recommendation.

This woman tells me I'm her last hope because her husband beats her, but there are no shelter beds open and she can't go to the police because her husband's a decorated police captain.

The physician down the hall is a quack, but as long as I refer my patients to him, he sends me enough referrals to pay my bills.

Doing psychotherapy confronts us with constant dilemmas. Each ethical dilemma, large or small, subtle or blaring, brings a tangle of questions. Is there a "right" thing to do? If so, how do I find out what it is? What makes it right? Who says so? If I do it, what will happen to the patient? to me? to innocent— and not-so-innocent—bystanders?

We wrestle with personal questions that are hard to admit to ourselves or others. What am I tempted to do? What could I get away with? Would doing the right thing cost too much? get people mad at me? get me sued? get me fired? Would doing the wrong thing be all that bad, especially if no one found out about it? What if I'm not strong enough, not "good" enough to do the right thing? Can I duck this one and palm it off on someone else?

These stinging questions always lead back to the basic question: What do I do now?

1

Ethics helps us answer that question. Ethical awareness lets us see more clearly how our choices affect the lives of our patients, our colleagues, and the public. It frees us from the confining webs of habit, fatigue, fallacy, dogma, carelessness, hurry, and daily pressures. It helps us see new possibilities, respond in new ways, and act with greater understanding.

This book's purpose is to help readers answer that basic question: What do I do now? Readers looking for a cookbook approach, one that authoritatively tells them the right thing to do in every situation, will be disappointed. We do not believe that approach works in the real world or that it serves therapists or their patients.

We hope this book helps you to strengthen your awareness of the ethical challenges, pitfalls, and opportunities in each unique, constantly changing situation and to make the best choices.

This chapter describes seven basic assumptions underlying our approach.

> Ethical awareness is a continuous, active process that involves constant questioning and personal responsibility.

Conflicts with managed care companies, the urgency of patients' needs, the lack of adequate support, the possibility of formal complaints, mind-deadening routines, endless paperwork, worrying about making ends meet, exhaustion, and so much else can block our personal responsiveness and dull our sense of personal responsibility. They can overwhelm us, distract us, drain us, and lull us into ethical sleep. Our work requires constant alertness and mindful awareness of the ethical implications of what we choose to do and not do.

Ethical awareness includes taking into account our very human lack of perfection. All of us have weaknesses, vulnerabilities, and blind spots. The dramatic differences are not so much between those who have many human imperfections and those who have few but between those who are freely open—to themselves and others—about how their own shortcomings affect their work and those who tend to see others as inferior versions of themselves. Chapter 6, "Competence and the Human Therapist," explores some of these themes.

Ethical awareness also depends on our ability to take care of ourselves, to recognize when fear, anger, boredom, resentment, sadness, hopelessness, or anxiety hurt work, and to do something about it. Chapter 7, "Creating Strategies for Self-Care," offers ideas on how we can recognize when our lack of enthusiasm, resilience, meaning, and joy makes us less effective, and details the steps we can take to prevent that from happening or to turn things around it when it is happening.

> Awareness of ethical codes is crucial, but formal codes cannot take the place of an active, thoughtful, creative approach to our ethical responsibilities.

Awareness of ethics codes is crucial to competence in the area of ethics, but the formal standards are no substitute for an active, deliberative, and creative approach to fulfilling our ethical responsibilities. Codes prompt, guide, and inform our ethical consideration; they do not shut it down or replace it.

Ethical practice never means following a code in a rote, thoughtless manner. Each new client, whatever his or her similarities to previous clients, is unique. Each situation is unique and constantly changing—time and events do not stand still. Our theoretical orientation, the nature of our community and the client's community, our culture and the client's culture, and so many other contexts shape what we see and how we see it. Every ethical decision must take these contexts into account.

The codes may steer us away from some clearly unethical approaches. They may shine a light on important values and concerns. But they cannot tell us what form these values and concerns will take. They may set forth essential tasks, but they cannot spell out the best way to accomplish those tasks with a unique client facing unique problems in a specific time and place with limited resources. Decisions about ethical behavior are the result of a process.

> Awareness of relevant legislation, case law, and other legal standards is crucial, but legal standards should not be confused with ethical responsibilities.

A risk in the emphasis on legal standards is that adherence to minimal legal standards, which in some cases means finding ways around those standards, can become a substitute for ethical behavior. This trend has become increasingly prevalent in the political arena. A politician or political appointee holding a position of great public trust must respond to clear evidence that he or she betrayed that trust. When no other defense or justification is available, the politician insists that nothing wrong was done because no law was broken. (Even such desperate defenses hit a snag when it turns out that a law was broken; in those cases the individual stresses that there was a "technical violation of the law.")

An overly exclusive focus on legal standards can discourage ethical awareness and sensitivity. It is crucial to realize that ethical behavior is more than simply avoiding violation of legal standards and that one's ethical and legal duties may, in certain instances, be in conflict. Practicing "defensive therapy"—making risk management our main focus—can cause us to lose sight of our ethical responsibilities and the ethical consequences of what we say and do. Ethical awareness avoids the comfortable trap of aiming low, of striving only to get by without breaking any law.

Though often compatible, the legal framework is different from the ethical framework. Ethical awareness requires clearly distinguishing the two and alertness to when they stand in conflict. These conflicts are discussed in

Chapter 9, "Codes and Complaints in Context," and Chapter 12, "Different Conclusions."

> We believe that the overwhelming majority of therapists and counselors are conscientious, dedicated, caring individuals, committed to ethical behavior. But none of us is infallible.

All of us can—and do—make mistakes, overlook something important, work from a limited perspective, reach conclusions that are wrong, hold tight to a cherished belief that is misguided. We're aware of many barriers between us and our best work, but we may underestimate or overlook some of those barriers. Part of our responsibility is to question ourselves: What if I'm wrong about this? Is there something I'm overlooking? Could there be another way of understanding this situation? Are there other possibilities? Can I come up with a more creative, more effective, better way of responding?

> Many of us find it easier to question the ethics of others than to question our own beliefs, assumptions, and actions. It is worth noticing if we find ourselves preoccupied with how wrong others are in some area of ethics and certain that we are the ones to set them right or at least to point out repeatedly how wrong they are.

It is a red flag if we spend more time trying to point out other people's weaknesses, flaws, mistakes, ethical blindness, destructive actions, or hopeless stupidity than we spend questioning and challenging ourselves in positive, effective, and productive ways that awaken us to new perspectives and possibilities. Questioning ourselves is at least as important as questioning others.

> Most of us find it easier to question ourselves on those intriguing topics we know we don't understand, that we stumble onto with confusion, uncertainty, and doubt. The harder but more helpful work is to question ourselves about our casual certainties. What have we taken for granted and accepted without challenge? Nothing can be placed off limits for this questioning.

Certainties are hard to give up, especially when they've grown to be part of us. They become landmarks, helping us make sense of the world, guiding our steps. But perhaps an always-reliable theoretical orientation begins distorting our view of a new patient, leading us to interventions that make things worse. Or having always prided ourselves on the soundness of our psychological evaluations, we keep rereading our draft report in a case in which an unbiased description of our findings may bring about a tragic injustice, harming many innocent people, and begin to wonder if our feelings for the client led us to shade the truth. Or the heart of our internship has been the supervision, and we've made it a point to tell the supervisor everything important about every patient, except about getting so aroused every time with that one patient, the one who is not very vulnerable at all and does not really need therapy, the one we keep having fantasies of asking out after waiting a reasonable time after termination and then, if all goes well, proposing to.

We must follow this questioning wherever it leads, even if we venture into territories that some might view as politically incorrect or—much more difficult for most of us—"psychologically incorrect" (Pope, Sonne, & Greene, 2006).

As psychologists, we often encounter ethical dilemmas without clear and easy answers.

As we try to help people who come to us because they are hurting and in need, we confront overwhelming needs unmatched by adequate resources, conflicting responsibilities that seem impossible to reconcile, frustrating limits to our understanding and interventions, and countless other challenges. We may be the only person a desperate client can turn to, and we may be pulled every which way by values, events, limited time, and limited options. Our best efforts to sort through such challenges may lead us to a thoughtful, informed conclusion about the most ethical path that is in stark contradiction to the thoughtful, informed conclusion of a best friend, a formal consultant, our attorney, or the professional groups we belong to. Chapter 12 explores the ways in which a complex situation can lead people to very different conclusions about the most ethical response. In the midst of these limitations, conflicts, disagreements, and complexities, we must make the best choices we can. We must each answer the challenging question: What do I do now? And each of us must take responsibility for that decision. We cannot shift personal responsibility for our ethical decisions and acts to another person, group, law, code, or custom. *There is no legitimate way to avoid these ethical struggles. They are part of our work.*

Chapter 2

ETHICS IN REAL LIFE

Even the simplest ethical concept, standard, or guideline can fool us. We hear it in class. We read it in the code. We understand and remember it. We could explain it on a test, give a lecture on it, or help a jury understand it during a cross-examination.

We know the concept, standard, or guideline, but it fools us when it shows up in the complex messiness of real life. It comes dressed in different clothes and we fail to recognize it.

Therapy offers countless challenges to recognizing when and where a specific ethical concept, standard, or guideline might be helpful or crucial. One reason is that concepts, standards, and guidelines tend to be abstract, are often very general, and may sometimes be ambiguous. Another reason is that psychotherapy can be such a complex set of interactions between two unique people. Yet another is that psychotherapy can serve as the intense focus of need, hope, risk, and expectation. Lives can be at stake.

Therapy holds out the promise of help for people who are hurting and in need. It can change lives.

Clients can discover their strengths. They can change course toward a more meaningful life. They can confront loss, tragedy, hopelessness, and the end of life in ways that do not leave them numb or paralyzed. They can discover what brings them joy and what sustains them in hard times. They can begin to trust, or trust more wisely. They can learn new behaviors in therapy and how to teach themselves new behaviors after therapy ends. They can question what they always believed was unquestionable. They can find out what matters most to them and stop wasting time. They can become happier, or at least less miserable. They can become better able, as Freud noted, to love and to work.

As therapists, we hold great responsibilities. What we do can make a difference in whether a client loses hope and commits suicide or chooses to live, whether a battered spouse finds shelter or returns to someone who may kill, and whether an anorexic teenager chooses health or starves to death. Even new therapists know that such dramatic examples tell only part of the story. So many people come to us facing what seem to be minor, hard-to-define problems, yet the hard, risky, unpredictable twists and turns of therapy can lead to more meaningful, effective, fulfilling lives.

In the midst of this work as it actually happens in real life, it is not always easy—to say the least—to recognize those moments when a specific abstract ethical concept, standard, or guideline is relevant.

The purpose of this chapter is to provide seven examples of those moments as they happen in the complex messiness of life. It is worth emphasizing a theme from the previous chapter: Ethical concepts, standards, and guidelines inform our judgment. They do not replace it. They do not relieve us of our responsibilities. They help us recognize, think through, and find or create a path to fulfill those responsibilities.

We created these fictional scenarios for ethics and malpractice workshops. None is based on a specific individual case (and none of the individuals is based on an actual clinician or patient), but all seven represent the kinds of challenges that therapists and counselors face.

In these scenarios, the clinicians were trying to do their best. Readers may disagree over whether each clinician met the highest or even minimal ethical standards, and such disagreements can form the focus of classroom, case conference, supervision, or related discussions. In at least one or two instances, you may believe that what the clinician did was perfectly reasonable and perhaps even showed courage and sensitivity. In some cases, you may believe that important information is missing. But in each instance, the professional's actions or failures to act became the basis of one or more formal complaints.

COMPUTER COINCIDENCES

What happened to these therapists was so traumatic that even though they are fictional characters and never existed, they fled into other lines of work, do not want to be recognized, and demanded anonymity in this hypothetical scenario. The catastrophes started when one of them hit the Send button on his computer.

For many years these therapists maintained a small and very successful group practice. Then they modernized, bringing in state-of-the-art computers, elegantly networked and equipped with wonderful software that made their work much easier.

Until one day the first therapist hit the Send button.

He had carefully collected all the electronic records of one of his patients, who was involved in litigation, to e-mail to the patient's attorney. He had assembled the billing records, results of psychological testing, records of therapy sessions, as well as the background records (employment, disability, and others).

The therapist gave one last look and then hit the Send button.

It was only after watching his computer send off the records that he realized he had used the wrong address on the e-mail. The patient records were on their way not to the patient's attorney but to a large Internet discussion list that was listed right next to the attorney in the therapist's address book. This unfortunate series of events led to a formal complaint against the therapist.

By a far-fetched coincidence typical of hypothetical scenarios, the second therapist walked into the first therapist's office just when the first therapist was hitting the Send button. The second therapist said: "Can you believe it!? I'm being sued, and it's all because of my computer! When my patient temporarily moved to the East Coast for a sabbatical, we thought it best to continue treatment, but because of the time difference and our heavy schedules, we couldn't find a time when we could both talk, so we decided to communicate by e-mail. But then she got mad at me about something and filed complaints against me *in the other state!* So now they're saying I was providing psychological services in that state without being licensed there and that I failed to follow that state's rules and regulations about…well, you'd have to read the complaints her attorney has filed with the licensing board, the courts, and the ethics committee. It's terrible!"

As if sensing that another wild coincidence was needed to keep the story moving, the third therapist rushed into the first therapist's office at just that moment and cried, "You won't believe what just happened! I just got a formal notice that I'm being sued! I just found out what happened: Somehow a virus or Trojan or worm or one of those things got into my computer and took my files—you know, all my confidential case files—and sent them to everyone listed in my address book and to all the other addresses in my computer's memory. What do I do now?"

On cue, the fourth therapist ran into the room and wailed, "Help! I'm in such trouble! One of my patients is involved in a nasty lawsuit, and I received a court order to produce all my records. The patient had given me consent to turn them over because she and her attorney believe they will be the key to their winning the case. So I sat down to print them out and . . . they're gone! My hard drive crashed, and when I hired a company to rescue what they could, they retrieved some records but all the files for that patient are gone. What do I do now?"

Although the room was getting crowded, the fifth therapist slouched in, collapsed in a chair, and announced, "I'm doomed. I kept all my records on my laptop. But while I was at lunch today, someone broke into my car and stole my laptop. Then I got worse news. I thought at least the files would be safe because I encrypted them, but a colleague just told me that since the program I used to encrypt and unencrypt them is on that computer and since many thieves have software that enables them to get past passwords and gain use of the encryption program, it would be pretty easy for a hacker to unencrypt my files."

When the final member of their group practice failed to show up with bad news, they grew concerned and went down the hall to her office. She was sitting at her desk with a big smile on her face. She chirped, "I can't tell you how good I feel! I've been so concerned about keeping records on my computer that I finally decided it just wasn't worth the worry. I printed out all my records, made extra copies that I put in my safe deposit box, and got rid of my computer. It was such a good move for me. I haven't felt this good in days."

It was only months later that she discovered, as she read the complaint filed against her, that she had done a poor job of trying to erase her hard drive before selling her computer. The person who had bought it had little trouble retrieving the supposedly erased files and reading all the details about her patients.

LIFE IN CHAOS

Professor Alvarez, a 45-year-old member of the physics department at the local university, has never before sought psychotherapy. He shows up for his first appointment with Dr. Brinks. Professor Alvarez says that his life is in chaos. He was granted full professor status about a year ago, and about a month after that, his wife suddenly left him to live with another man. He became very depressed. About four months ago, he began to feel anxious and have trouble concentrating. He feels he needs someone to talk to so that he can figure out what happened. Professor Alvarez and Dr. Brinks agree to meet twice a week for outpatient psychotherapy.

During the first few sessions, Professor Alvarez says that he feels relieved that he can talk about his problems, but he remains anxious. During the next few months, he begins talking about some traumatic experiences in his early childhood. He reports that he is having even more trouble concentrating. Dr. Brinks assures him that this is not surprising; problems concentrating often become temporarily worse when a patient starts confronting difficult issues. She suggests that they begin meeting three times a week. Professor Alvarez agrees.

A month later, Professor Alvarez collapses and is rushed to the hospital, where he is pronounced dead on arrival. An autopsy reveals that a small but growing tumor had been pressing against a blood vessel in his brain. When the vessel burst, he died.

Months after Professor Alvarez's death, Dr. Brinks learns that Professor Alvarez's relatives are pursuing a formal complaint against her with the state ethics committee. Furthermore, she is being sued for malpractice. The ethics complaint and the malpractice suit allege that she was negligent in diagnosing Professor Alvarez in that she had failed to take any step to rule out organic causes for Professor Alvarez's concentration difficulties, had not applied any of the principles and procedures of the profession of psychology to identify organic impairment, and had not referred Professor Alvarez for evaluation by a neuropsychologist or to a physician for a medical examination.

Therapists and counselors in ethics and malpractice workshops (who would probably not constitute a random sample of practicing psychologists) who have reviewed this scenario have tended to conclude that Dr. Brinks may have been practicing beyond the range of her competence and violated some of the fundamental standards of assessment (see Chapter 15).

EVALUATING CHILDREN

Ms. Cain brings her two children, ages 4 and 6, to Dr. Durrenberger for a psychological evaluation. She reports that they have become upset during the past few months. They have nightmares and wet their beds. She suspects that the problem may have something to do with their last visit with their father, who lives in another state.

Dr. Durrenberger schedules three sessions in which he sees Ms. Cain and her two children together and three individual sessions with each of the children. While preparing his report, he receives a subpoena to testify in a civil suit that Ms. Cain is filing against her ex-husband. She is suing for custody of her children. During the trial, Dr. Durrenberger testifies that the children seem, on the basis of interviews and psychological tests, to have a stronger, more positive relationship with their mother. He gives his professional opinion that the children would be better off with their mother and that she should be given custody.

Mr. Cain files an ethics complaint, a civil suit, and a licensing complaint against Dr. Durrenberger. One basis of his complaint is that Dr. Durrenberger failed to obtain informed consent to conduct the assessments. When Mr. and Ms. Cain had divorced two years previously, the court had granted Mr. Cain legal custody of the children but had granted Ms. Cain visitation rights. (Ms. Cain had arranged for the assessments of the children during a long summer visit.)

Another basis of the complaint was that Dr. Durrenberger had made a formal recommendation regarding custody placement without making any attempt to interview or evaluate Mr. Cain. Mr. Cain's attorney and expert witnesses maintained that no custody recommendation could be made without interviewing both parents. Furthermore, he mixed his roles as psychotherapist and custody evaluator. Dr. Durrenberger clearly had not reviewed the Guidelines for Evaluation of Child Custody in Family Law Proceedings (APA, 2009).

Although laws regarding rights of custodial and noncustodial parents differ from state to state and province to province, participants in ethics and malpractice workshops tend to conclude that Dr. Durrenberger had not fulfilled his ethical (and, in many states, legal) responsibility to obtain adequate informed consent from the relevant parent (see Chapter 14) and that he had failed to conduct an adequate assessment to justify his conclusions and recommendations (see Chapter 15).

THE FATAL DISEASE

When George, a 22-year-old college student, began psychotherapy with Dr. Hightower, he told the doctor that he was suffering from a fatal disease. Two months into therapy, George felt that he trusted his therapist enough to tell her that the disease was AIDS.

During the next 18 months, much of the therapy focused on George's losing battle with his illness and his preparations to die. After two stays in the hospital for pneumonia, George informed Dr. Hightower that he knew he would not survive his next hospitalization. He had done independent research and talked with his physicians, and he was certain that if pneumonia developed again, it would be fatal due to numerous complications and that it would likely be a long and painful death.

George said that when that time came, he wanted to die in the off-campus apartment he had lived in since he came to college—not in the hospital. He would, when he felt himself getting sicker, take some illicitly obtained drugs that would ease him into death.

Dr. Hightower tried to dissuade him from this plan, but George refused to discuss it and said that if Dr. Hightower continued to bring up the subject, he would quit therapy. Convinced that George would quit therapy rather than discuss his plan, Dr. Hightower decided to offer caring and support—rather than confrontation and argument—to a patient who seemed to have only a few months to live.

Four months later, Dr. Hightower was notified that George had taken his life. Within the next month, Dr. Hightower became the defendant in two civil suits. One suit, filed by George's family, alleged that Dr. Hightower, aware that George was intending to take his own life, did not take reasonable and adequate steps to prevent the suicide, did not notify any third parties of the suicide plan, did not require George to get rid of the illicit drugs, and did not use hospitalization to prevent the suicide.

A college student who had been George's lover filed the other suit. The lover alleged that he did not know that George had been suffering from AIDS. The suit claimed that Dr. Hightower, knowing that George had a lover and that he had a fatal sexually transmitted disease, had a duty to protect the lover, which superseded Dr. Hightower's principle of confidentiality.

This scenario has been one of the most agonizing and controversial for the psychotherapists and counselors who consider it at ethics and malpractice workshops. Some believe that Dr. Hightower acted in the most humane, sensitive, and ethical manner. Others believe that she was wrong to accept, without more vigorous challenge, George's decision to take his own life. In this sense, it illustrates the dilemmas we face when confronted with a suicidal individual (see Chapter 20). It also illustrates how issues such as confidentiality (see Chapter 19) have been challenged when a specific third party or the public more generally may be put at risk by a client (Kooyman & Barret, 2009).

Many would argue that the main goal of therapy when suicide is an issue is to defuse the potentially lethal situation. According to this view, we have a professional duty to try to prevent patients from harming themselves, a duty that may include in extreme cases taking steps to hospitalize patients against their will through civil commitment.

Others would argue that therapists must respect the client's autonomy even if that includes the client's decision to commit suicide. Some would accord this "right to die" to any client. Others would recognize it only in certain extreme situations (e.g., if the client is suffering from a painful and terminal disease). Some would draw the line at accepting a client's decision to commit suicide and taking no steps to interfere with the client's self-destructive acts. Others would consider actively assisting the person to die.

These agonizing, controversial issues have become especially difficult for some who provide mental health services to those with AIDS (Kooyman & Barret, 2009; see Pope & Morin, 1990), as in this vignette. As is so often the case, the ethical and clinical issues are interwoven with legal standards. Laws addressing assisted suicide raise complex issues and stir controversy (Bluestein, 2009; Carter, VandeKieft, & Barren, 2005; Curlin, Nwodin, Vance, Chin, & Lantos, 2008; Dickens, Boyle, and Ganzini, 2008; Downie, 2004; Fischer, Huber, et al., 2008; Ganzini, 2006; Gielen, van den Branden, & Broeckaert, 2008; Glascock, 2009; Gostin, 2006; N. G. Hamilton & Hamilton, 2005; Herlihy & Watson, 2004; Kleespies, 2004; Lyall, 2009; Lindblad, Lofmark, & Lynoe, 2008; Okie, 2005; Radtke, 2005; Rosenfeld, 2004; Werth & Blevins, 2006).

THE MECHANIC

Ms. Huang, whose family had moved from mainland China to the United States 15 years ago, is a 45-year-old automobile mechanic. She agreed, at the strong urging of her employer, to seek psychotherapy for difficulties that seem to affect her work. She shows up late at her job, often phones in sick, and seems distracted. She complains to her new therapist, Dr. Jackson, about how hard it is to cope with both psychomotor epilepsy, which has been controlled through medication, and her progressive diabetes, which also requires medical care.

Although she has no real experience treating those from the Chinese culture or those with chronic medical conditions such as epilepsy and progressive diabetes, Dr. Jackson begins work with Ms. Huang. She meets with her on a regular basis for three months but never feels that a solid working alliance is developing. After three months, Ms. Huang abruptly quits therapy. She has not paid for the past six sessions.

Two weeks later, Dr. Jackson receives a request to send Ms. Huang's treatment records to her new therapist. Dr. Jackson notifies Ms. Huang that she will not forward the records until the bill has been paid in full.

Sometime later, Dr. Jackson receives notice that the American Psychological Association (APA) Ethics Committee is investigating an ethics complaint against her and that she has been sued for malpractice. The complaints allege that Dr. Jackson had been practicing outside her areas of competence because she had received no education, training, or supervised experience in treating people from the Chinese culture or those with multiple serious and chronic medical diseases.

The complaints also alleged that Ms. Huang had never adequately understood the nature of treatment, as evidenced by the lack of any written informed consent. Finally, the complaints alleged that "holding records hostage" for payment violated Ms. Huang's welfare and deprived her subsequent therapist of having prompt and comprehensive information for Ms. Huang's treatment.

Participants in ethics and malpractice workshops, asked to assume the role of an ethics committee to review this scenario, often conclude that Dr. Jackson was acting without adequate competence to treat someone from a different culture (see Chapter 18) or with a chronic medical condition, had not obtained adequate informed consent in regard to a clear description and understanding of Dr. Jackson's fee structure (see Chapter 14), and had misused the power of her role as therapist in refusing to release records because of an unpaid bill.

THE POSTDOCTORAL EXPERIENCE

Dr. Larson is executive director and clinical chief of staff at the Golden Internship Health Maintenance Organization (HMO). For one year, he closely supervises an excellent postdoctoral fellow, Dr. Marshall. The supervisee shows great potential, working with a range of patients who respond positively to her interventions. After completing her postdoc and becoming licensed, Dr. Marshall goes into business for herself, opening an office several blocks from Golden Internship Health Maintenance Organization.

Before terminating her work at the HMO, Dr. Larson tells Dr. Marshall that she must transfer all patients to other center therapists. All of the patients who can afford her fee schedule, however, decide to continue in therapy with her at her new office. The patients who cannot afford Dr. Marshall's fee schedule are assigned to new therapists at the center.

Dr. Larson hires an attorney to take legal action against Dr. Marshall, asserting that she unethically exploited the HMO by stealing patients and engaging in deceptive practices. He files formal complaints against her with both the state licensing board and the APA Ethics Committee, charging that she had refused to follow his supervision in regard to the patients and pointed out that he, as the clinical supervisor of this trainee, had been both clinically and legally responsible for the patients. He refuses to turn over the patients' charts to Dr. Marshall or to certify to various associations to which she has applied for membership that she has successfully completed her internship.

Dr. Marshall countersues, claiming that Dr. Larson is engaging in illegal restraint of trade and failing to act in the patients' best interests. The patients, she asserts, have formed an intense transference and an effective working alliance with her; to lose their therapist would be clinically damaging and not in their best interests. She files formal complaints against Dr. Larson with the licensing board and the APA Ethics Committee, charging that his refusal to deliver copies of the patients' charts and to certify that she completed the postdoc violates ethical and professional standards.

Some of the patients sue the HMO, Dr. Larson, and Dr. Marshall, charging that the conflict and the legal actions (in which their cases are put at issue without their consent) have been damaging to their therapy.

Workshop participants often conclude that both Dr. Larson and Dr. Marshall have behaved unethically in terms of misusing their power (see Chapter 4), failing to clarify in advance the conclusion of Dr. Marshall's work with the patients (see Chapter 14), and neglecting to address these issues adequately in the supervision contract (see Chapter 21).

STAYING SOBER

In therapy for one year with Dr. Franks, Mr. Edwards is an alcoholic and drank heavily for four years prior to the therapy. Dr. Franks uses a psychodynamic approach and incorporates behavioral techniques specifically designed to address the drinking problem.

Two months into therapy, when it became apparent that outpatient psychotherapy alone was not effective, Mr. Edwards agreed to attend Alcoholics Anonymous (AA) meetings as an adjunct to his therapy. During the past nine months of therapy, Mr. Edwards had generally been sober, suffering only two relapses, each time falling off the wagon for a long weekend.

Now, a year into therapy, Mr. Edwards suffers a third relapse. He comes to the session having just had several drinks. During the session, Dr. Franks and Mr. Edwards conclude that some of the troubling material that has been emerging in the therapy had led Mr. Edwards to begin drinking again. At the end of the session, Mr. Edwards feels that he has gained some additional insight into why he drank. He decides to go straight from the session to an AA meeting.

One month later, Dr. Franks is notified that he is being sued. On his way from the therapy session to the AA meeting, Mr. Edwards had run a red light, hitting and killing a mother and her child who were crossing the street. The suit alleged that the therapist knew or should have known his patient to be dangerous and should have taken steps to prevent him from driving until his alcoholism no longer constituted a danger to the public.

Although workshop participants tend to fault Dr. Franks for not adequately assessing his client's condition and the danger that the client's driving in that condition would constitute for the public, there was a common empathic response, as with many of the other scenarios. Clinicians tended to identify with the fictional Dr. Franks and thought, "There but for the grace of God go I."

Struck by the enormous complexity and responsibilities the hypothetical clinicians face, we wonder if we would do any better if we were in their place.

Because this book's approach emphasizes personal responsibility and the need—as these seven scenarios illustrate—to think clearly about the responsibilities emerging in each new situation, Chapter 3 focuses on critical thinking.

ETHICS AND CRITICAL THINKING

The club of ethically perfect therapists—those with flawless ethical judgment and fallacy-free ethical reasoning—is snobbishly exclusive. So far, no one has qualified for membership.

Most of us accept that we're not cut out for that club. We realize the obvious: We all have weaknesses. We fail to see something in our ethical blind spots. We misjudge how an ethical principle applies to a specific situation. We rush past a red flag. Our ethical reasoning adds 2 plus 2 and comes up with 4,938. It happens to all of us from time to time.

We have weaknesses, but they can be strengthened. One good place to start is how we think about ethics. The more we notice how we think about ethics, the more we can think critically about our own ethical judgment, reasoning, language, and justifications. Learning to recognize major patterns and pitfalls can improve our approaches and avoid pitfalls (or at least recognize when we fall into pits). This chapter looks at common problems in judgment, reasoning, language, and justifications.

JUDGMENT[1]

Ethics requires judgment. Ethical issues as they occur in real life are rarely simple, obvious, and easy. As highlighted throughout this book, both client/patient and therapist are unique, their relationship is complex, and the situations they face are rarely static. Subtle ethical issues can sneak by unnoticed. Ethical crises can appear in a clash of competing needs, expectations, and values. Time and resources are often scarce. No one can effectively apply

---

[1] This section is adapted from "Fallacies and Pitfalls in Psychological Assessment." Copyright © 2003 by K. S. Pope, available at http://kspope.com.

the principles in the ethics code or other sources of guidance to real-life situations in an automatic, unthinking, or rote manner. There is no paint-by-numbers approach that works. This section explores three factors that influence our ethical judgment: cognitive commitments, authorities, and groups.

Cognitive Commitments

If we commit to an approach, theory, or idea, our commitment influences our judgment. Francis Bacon described this process in 1620 (1955):

> The human understanding when it has once adopted an opinion ... draws all things else to support and agree with it. And though there be a greater number and weight of instances to be found on the other side, yet these it either neglects or despises, or else by some distinction sets aside and rejects.... This mischief insinuate[s] itself into philosophy and the sciences; in which the first conclusion colors and brings into conformity with itself all that come after. (p. 472)

Evans (1989) noted that "confirmation bias is perhaps the best known and most widely accepted notion of inferential error." The notion "is that human beings have a fundamental tendency to seek information consistent with their current beliefs, theories or hypotheses and to avoid the collection of potentially falsifying evidence" (p. 41).

Cognitive and social psychology have explored how this influence takes different forms. Kurt Lewin (1976; see also Gold, 1999) examined how committing to a decision often seems to freeze the mind, hardening it against reconsideration. Ellen Langer (1989), summarizing the research she and her colleagues had conducted (e.g., Chanowitz & Langer, 1981), described the common process of

> forming a mindset when we first encounter something and then clinging to it when we reencounter that same thing. Because such mindsets form before we do much reflection, we call them premature cognitive commitments.... The mindless individual is committed to one predetermined use of the information, and other possible uses are not explored. (p. 22)

Leon Festinger's experiments focused on how commitment to an approach, theory, or idea leads to a screening out of any information that would lead to cognitive dissonance. The commitment means that there would be "less emphasis on objectivity and there is more partiality and bias in the way in which the person views and evaluates the alternatives" (1964, p. 155; see also Frey & Schulz-Hardt, 2001; Hill, Memon, & McGeorge, 2008; Munro & Stansbury, 2009; Tschan, Semmer, & Gurtner, 2009).

Our vulnerability to this bias creates a responsibility to question our own views, whether snap judgments or long-held beliefs. We can balance our loyalty to our judgments if we search relentlessly for facts that do not fit, listen openly to those who disagree, and constantly ask ourselves what the other possibilities are. Otherwise we can end up clinging so tightly to our ethical certainties that we do not notice contradictory information, better possibilities, and the consequences of our own missteps.

Authorities

When puzzling over an ethical dilemma, we often turn to authorities. The law, a supervisor, and the ethics code can provide invaluable help. We misuse these resources, however, if we use them to short-circuit our ethical judgment. We cannot avoid an ethical struggle by focusing only on the law and claiming "It violates no law [or the law requires it] so it must be ethical." We cannot shrug off ethical responsibility by explaining that we were just following what our supervisor told us to do. We cannot hide behind ethics codes as refuge from an active, creative search for the most ethical response.

Awareness of ethics codes is crucial to competence in the area of ethics. The codes prompt, guide, and inform our ethical consideration. They do not take the place of our thoughtful consideration. There is no way that the codes and principles can be followed effectively or applied in a rote, thoughtless manner. Each new client, whatever his or her similarities to previous clients, is a unique individual. Each situation also is unique and is likely to change significantly over time. Codes may prohibit some acts as clearly unethical. They may call our attention to ethical concerns in different areas of practice, but they cannot tell us how these concerns will manifest themselves in a particular clinical situation. They may set forth essential tasks that we must fulfill, but they cannot tell us how we can accomplish these tasks with a unique client facing unique problems. We cannot hide from these struggles.

Groups

Like authorities, groups are a valuable resource. They can provide support, diverse views, the opportunity to work together on an ethical dilemma, and relief from the sense of isolation. But—also like authorities—certain group processes can work to block sound ethical judgment. We get ourselves into trouble when we allow groups to shield us from ethical struggles and the sense of ethical responsibility.

Psychologist Paul Meehl (1977) wrote a fascinating essay we recommend to all of this book's readers, "Why I Do Not Attend Case Conferences." He pointed out the "groupthink process" (p. 228) that discourages sound judgment and may be familiar to all of us:

In one respect the clinical case conference is no different from other academic group phenomena such as committee meetings, in that many intelligent, educated, sane, rational persons seem to undergo a kind of intellectual deterioration when they gather around a table in one room. (p. 227)

Psychologist Irving Janis (1972) studied ways in which groupthink clouds our judgment. Janis and Mann (1977, pp. 130–131) identified the eight symptoms of groupthink, adapted next, to emphasize their effects on ethical judgment:

1. An illusion of invulnerability, shared by most or all members, which creates excessive optimism and encourages taking extreme risks
2. Collective efforts to rationalize in order to discount warnings
3. An unquestioned belief in the group's inherent high ethics, leading members to underestimate their ethical responsibilities or the negative consequences of their behavior
4. Stereotyped views of those who disagree about ethical issues, encouraging group members to disparage the motives, intelligence, heart, or good faith of those who disagree with the group's views
5. Pressure on any group member who dissents or raises serious questions about the group's views or behavior
6. Self-stifling of deviations from the group's approach; an inclination of each member to deny, discount, or minimize doubts or counterarguments
7. The illusion of virtual unanimity, created by self-stifling and assuming that silence means consent
8. Some members taking on the role of "mindguard[s]—members who protect the group from adverse information that might shatter their shared complacency about the effectiveness and morality of their decisions."

Making Better Ethical Judgments

We can make better ethical judgments if we remain aware of how cognitive commitments, authorities, and groups can serve us well—but also sweep us off course. Errors in ethical reasoning, the focus of the next section, can also send us in the wrong direction.

LOGICAL FALLACIES IN ETHICAL REASONING

Logical fallacies show up in camouflage. They hide in the background and blend in with some of our best reasoning. They fool us with misdirection. We often miss how they convince us in our ethical reasoning that adding apples and oranges equals somewhere in the neighborhood of green beans. Here are 22 logical fallacies, with a brief description and example of each, that can send ethical reasoning off track. No one is magically immune to them. They trip up all of us at one time or another.

1. Ad Hominem or Ad Feminam

The argumentum ad hominem or ad feminam attempts to discredit an argument or position by drawing attention to characteristics of the person who is making the argument or who holds the position.

Example: "The research and reasoning that supposedly supports (or that supposedly discredits) this intervention are a joke. The researchers are people who are not methodologically sophisticated and there have been rumors—I have no idea whether they're true or not—that they faked some of the data. The advocates (or opponents) of this intervention are the worst kind of sloppy thinkers. They are fanatical adherents who already have their minds made up; they've become true believers in their cause. They make arguments only a stupid person would accept, and mistakes in reasoning that would make an undergrad psych major blush. These are not the kind of people who deserve to be taken seriously."

2. Affirming the Consequent

This fallacy takes the form of:
If x, then y.
y.
therefore: x.

Example: "People who are psychotic act in a bizarre manner. This person acts in a bizarre manner. Therefore: This person is psychotic."

Alternate example: "If this client is competent to stand trial, she will certainly know the answers to at least 80% of the questions on this standardized test. She knows the answers to 87% of the test questions. Therefore she is competent to stand trial."

3. Appeal to Ignorance (ad Ignorantium)

The appeal to ignorance fallacy takes the form of:
There is no (or insufficient) evidence establishing that x is false.
Therefore: x is true.

Example: "In the six years that I have been practicing my new and improved brand of cognitive-humanistic-dynamic-behavioral-deconstructive-metaregressive-deontological psychotherapy (now with biofeedback!), which I developed, there has not been one published study showing that it fails to work or that it has ever harmed a patient. It is clearly one of the safest and most effective interventions ever devised."

4. Argument to Logic (Argumentum ad Logicam)

The argument to logic fallacy takes the form of assuming that a proposition must be false because an argument offered in support of that proposition was fallacious.

Example: "This new test seemed so promising, but the three studies that supported its validity turned out to have critical methodological flaws, so the test is probably not valid."

5. Begging the Question (Petitio Principii)

This fallacy, one of the fallacies of circularity, takes the form of arguments or other statements that simply assume or restate their own truth rather than providing relevant evidence and logical arguments.

Examples: Sometimes this fallacy literally takes the form of a question, such as, "Has your psychology department stopped teaching that ineffective approach to therapy yet?" (The question assumes—and a yes-or-no response to the question affirms—that the approach is ineffective.) Or: "Why must you always take positions that are so unscientific?" (The question assumes that all of the person's positions are unscientific.)

Sometimes this fallacy takes the form of a statement such as "No one can deny that [my theoretical orientation] is the only valid theoretical orientation" or "It must be acknowledged that [whatever psychological test battery I use] is the only legitimate test battery."

Sometimes it takes the form of a logical argument, such as "My new method of conducting meta-analyses is the most valid there is because it is the only one capable of such validity, the only one that has ever approached such validity, and the only one that is so completely valid."

6. Composition Fallacy

This fallacy takes the form of assuming that a group possesses the characteristics of its individual members.

Example: "Several years ago, a group of 10 psychologists started a psychology training program. Each of those psychologists is efficient, effective, and highly regarded. Their training program must be efficient, effective, and highly regarded."

7. Denying the Antecedent

This fallacy takes the form of:
If x, then y.
Not x.
Therefore: not y.

Example: "If this test were based on fraudulent norms, then it would be invalid. But the norms are not fraudulent. Therefore, this test is valid."

8. Disjunctive Fallacy

> This fallacy takes the form of:
> Either x or y.
> x.
> Therefore: not y.

Example: "These test results are clearly wrong, and it must be either because the client was malingering or because I bungled the test administration. Taking another look at the test manual, I see now that I bungled the test administration. Therefore, the client was not malingering."

9. Division Fallacy

The division or decomposition fallacy takes the form of assuming that the members of a group posses the characteristics of the group.

Example: "This clinic sure makes a lot of money. Each of the psychologists who work there must earn a large income."

10. Existential Fallacy

The existential fallacy begins with two universal premises and draws a specific conclusion from them. The two premises may be true, but that does not logically establish the existence of any members in the categories they represent.

Example: "I currently have as patients in my practice all the patients in this town who are willing and able to pay $5,000 per session for long-term twice-weekly therapy." If you buy my practice, all my clients will be included. Therefore, if you buy my practice, you then will have at least some patients willing and able to pay $5,000 per session for long-term twice-weekly therapy.

11. False Analogy

The false or faulty analogy fallacy takes the form of argument by analogy in which the comparison is misleading in at least one important aspect.

Example: "There were wonderful psychologists who passed away several decades ago. If they could be effective in what they did without reading any of the studies or other articles that have been published in the last several decades, there's no need for me to read any of those works in order to be effective."

12. False Dilemma

Also known as the either/or fallacy or the fallacy of false choices, this fallacy takes the form of acknowledging only two (one of which is usually extreme) options from a continuum or other array of possibilities.

Example: "Either we accept the findings of this study demonstrating that this new intervention is the best to be used for this disorder, or we must no longer call ourselves scientists, psychologists, or reasonable people."

13. Genetic Fallacy

In this fallacy, whether a proposition is true or false is deduced or inferred from the proposition's origin.

Example: This theory originally occurred to a scientist in the form of a dream; therefore it cannot be valid.

Example: Since it was a deathbed confession, it must be true.

14. Golden Mean Fallacy

The fallacy of the Golden Mean (or fallacy of compromise, or fallacy of moderation) takes the form of assuming that the most valid conclusion is that which accepts the best compromise between two competing positions.

Example: "In our psychology department, half of the faculty believe that a behavioral approach is the only valid approach; the other half believe that the only valid approach is psychodynamic. Obviously the most valid approach must be one that incorporates both behavioral and psychodynamic elements."

15. Mistaking Deductive Validity for Truth

This fallacy takes the form of assuming that because an argument is a logical syllogism, the conclusion must be true. It ignores the possibility that the premises of the argument may be false.

Example: "I just read a book that proves that that book's author can do much better than any psychological test at finding out if someone is malingering. The book's author reviews the literature showing that no psychological test is perfect at identifying malingering. All have at least some false positives and false negatives. But the author has a new method of identifying malingerers. All he does is listen to the sound of their voice as they say a sentence or two. And he included in the book a chart showing that by using this method, he has never been wrong in hundreds of cases. That proves his method is better than using psychological tests."

16. Naturalistic Fallacy

The naturalistic fallacy takes the form of logically deducing values (e.g., what is good, best, right, ethical, or moral) based only on statements of fact.

Example: "There is no intervention for victims of domestic violence that has more empirical support from controlled studies than this one. It is clear that this is the right way to address this problem and we should all be providing this therapy whenever victims of domestic violence come to us for help."

17. Nominal Fallacy

The nominal fallacy is the mistake of assuming that because we have given a name to something, we have explained it.

Example:

Therapist A: I just don't care about my patients anymore. I don't pay attention to what they say. I show up late for sessions. I don't care if they show up. I ask them if they'd rather we just use the session playing a game of tennis or sharing a cup of coffee. I don't keep records.
Therapist B: You have a classic case of burn-out!
Therapist A: But why am I doing all these things?
Therapist B: Because you're burned out.

18. Post Hoc, Ergo Propter Hoc (*After This, Therefore on Account of This*)

The *post hoc, ergo propter hoc* fallacy takes the form of confusing correlation with causation and concluding that because Y follows X, Y must be a result of X.

Example: "My new sport psychology intervention works! I chose the player with the lowest batting average based on the last game from each of the teams in our amateur baseball league. Then I gave each of them my 5-minute intervention. And almost all of them improved their batting average in the next game!" (Note: This example may also involve the statistical phenomenon of regression to the mean.)

19. Red Herring

This fallacy takes the form of introducing or focusing on irrelevant information to distract from the valid evidence and reasoning. It takes its name from the strategy of dragging a herring or other fish across the path to distract hounds and other tracking dogs and to throw them off the scent of whatever they were searching for.

Example: "Some of you have objected to the new test batteries that were purchased for our program, alleging that they have no demonstrable validity, were not adequately normed for the kind of clients we see, and are unusable for clients who are physically disabled. What you have conveniently failed to mention, however, is that they cost less than a third of the price for the other tests we had been using, are much easier to learn, and can be administered and scored in less than half the time of the tests we used to use."

20. Slippery Slope (also known as the Continuum Fallacy and Camel's Nose Fallacy)

The slippery slope fallacy is a form of the *non causa pro causa* (mistaking a noncause as a cause) and the non sequitur (it does not follow), which claims (without proof) that A inevitably must cause B, and B can have no other outcome than C, and C is sufficient cause for D, and D must lead to E, and E must produce F, and so on, and because the last link in the supposedly causal chain is undesirable, therefore the first step is undesirable.

Examples: "If the government allows psychologists to prescribe medications, there will be no basis to block them from obtaining competence and legal authority to conduct other traditionally medical procedures, such as diagnosing minor skin irritations, treating a sprained ankle, setting a broken bone, and performing neurosurgery." Or: "Never reduce a fee for any patient for any reason or else you'll find yourself constantly reducing fees for everyone, everyone will take advantage of you, your patients will lose respect for you and for therapy, and you'll lose money and go bankrupt."

21. Straw Person

The straw person, or straw man, or straw woman fallacy takes the form mischaracterizing someone else's position in a way that makes it weaker, false, or ridiculous.

Example: "Those who believe in behavior modification obviously want to try to control everyone by subjecting them to rewards and punishments."

22. You Too! (Tu Quoque)

This fallacy takes the form of distracting attention from error or weakness by claiming that an opposing argument, person, or position has the same error or weakness.

Example: "I have been accused of using an *ad hominem* approach in trying to defend my research. But those who attack me and my research are also using *ad hominem*. And they started it!"

LANGUAGE

Language shapes the way we experience the world. What we call things matters.

An executive director hesitates to fire therapists who helped found a clinic and remained loyal through the lean years. Can she push these colleagues out the door and cut off their income just to raise profits by hiring less qualified therapists as independent contractors for lower pay? She finds it easier when she throws a word blanket over what she does and the people she does it to. She can use language to block our view. She never mentions firings or individual colleagues. Office bulletins describe a "multitude of unfortunate but inescapable factors necessitating a substantial but temporary reduction in force in order to maximize competitive preparedness and responsiveness in a volatile and challenging marketplace." Press releases hail an "innovative and state-of-the-art intervention and development strategy of providing maximum direction, safety, and assistance activity during the discrete transitional process steps associated with the temporary downsizing implementation phase and the arrangement of management-directed outplacement services." (This means the company has hired armed guards to escort each therapist out of the building, help carry any belongings, and make sure the therapist does not reenter the building.)

These descriptions hide the firings and the therapists. Language can deceive by design. It conceals, misdirects, and creates the verbal equivalent of optical illusions. But even when used with the best of intentions, careless or bloated language makes it hard to think clearly. Many of us have gone missing in professional articles, last seen slogging our way through a paragraph packed with professional jargon, clichés, and not-quite-right words.

In his classic essay, "Politics and the English Language," George Orwell (1946) rewrote a widely quoted biblical passage in what he called "modern English." Here's the original passage from Ecclesiastes in the King James Bible:

> I returned and saw under the sun, that the race is not to the swift, nor the battle to the strong, neither yet bread to the wise, nor yet riches to men of understanding, nor yet favor to men of skill; but time and chance happeneth to them all.

See if Orwell's translation reminds you of any professional articles, lectures, or discussions: "Objective consideration of contemporary phenomena compels the conclusion that success or failure in competitive activities exhibits no tendency to be commensurate with innate capacity, but that a considerable element of the unpredictable must invariably be taken into account" (p. 163).

Too often we lose sight of ethical issues as they disappear in clouds of clichés, jargon, deceptive words, and careless language. This section looks at common language patterns that hide or confuse ethical issues, responsibilities, or consequences. We present the patterns in extreme form so that they are easy to recognize and remember. If we learn these basic patterns in simplified form, we can spot them more easily when they try to sneak by us in the busy rush of our day-to-day work.

Most of us will find it easy to remember seeing these patterns in the newspaper, on television, and during our professional meetings. What is much harder—but much more useful—is to try to remember when we ourselves have fallen into these patterns.

Orwell emphasized how universal and persistent these word tricks are. He notes that they "are a continuous temptation, a packet of aspirin always at one's elbow. Look back through this essay, and for certain you will find that I have again and again committed the very faults I am protesting against" (1946, p. 168).

We start with Jack, our hypothetical therapist, who did something unethical, was caught and formally disciplined, knows what he did was wrong, is sorry, and wants to make a public statement to take responsibility and apologize. Here is what Jack did: He stole therapy records of the clinic's famous clients, altered them to make it look as if the clients had described lurid sexual activity to their therapists, and then sold the records to tabloids.

In his public statement, Jack says:

> I stole the patient files, added some lies to them, and sold them. I have no excuses or explanations. I am solely responsible. I knew it was wrong and would hurt innocent people who trusted the clinic, and I did it anyway because I wanted the money. I apologize to everyone, especially to those whom I've hurt. I will do whatever I can to try to make things right.

Here are some alternate statements that show common language patterns that can interfere with clear thinking about ethics. As in the prior section on logical fallacies, there is a brief description and example of each pattern.

Substitute the General for the Specific

In this pattern, both the specific individual and the specific act disappear. A description of a general category of acts and a vague reference in the third person replace (and hide) the specifics. Jack might say: "I believe that everyone knows that taking a patient's file without the patient's permission and using it for some purpose for which it was not intended is wrong. Anyone who does something like that is out of line."

Use a Conditional Frame for Consequences

The speaker shifts the focus to the question of whether the acts affected anyone. The apology is made contingent on how others reacted or were affected. Example: "If my actions harmed, or even just offended, anyone—and I can well understand how that could happen—I apologize."

Use Denied Motivation as Misdirection

Instead of honestly stating the motivation, the speaker seeks self-exoneration by talking about what the motivation was not. Denying an irrelevant charge that no one has made can be an effective rhetorical tactic. The denials are often true. For example, the person who repeatedly embezzles pension funds, uses substandard materials to build high-rises, speeds while drunk, and stresses that he or she never meant to hurt anyone was probably not acting with the intention of making other people suffer. Example: "I can honestly say that at no time during these unfortunate events with the clinic records did I ever intend for anyone to be hurt."

Use the Abstract Language of Technicalities

The speaker translates people and events into abstractions, using the jargon of technicalities. Jack could say:

> I know that many of you have heard rumors and you deserve to know what happened. I want to acknowledge publicly, in closing this unfortunate chapter, that I did not fulfill all requirements in the JCAHO [Joint Commission on Accreditation of Healthcare Organizations] manual for the handling of charts. There were instances in which I reviewed and added information without following all the bureaucratic specifications for identifying the source of additional material, and I did not always follow the precise procedures for obtaining informed consent for release of information in transferring these charts to individuals who lacked proper authorization to receive them. I regret my lack of attention to JCAHO and similar regulations, and I assure everyone that I will be reviewing those regulatory specifications and will make every attempt to conform to those guidelines in the future.

Use the Passive Voice

The speaker disappears. Things are done without reference to who does them. Jack would say:

> I know that all of you, like me, want to know the results of the extensive, no-holds-barred investigation that was conducted in the light of recent allegations. I have been authorized to provide you with a complete report of the findings. Regrettably, the investigation confirmed that some files were taken without authorization, were altered, and were provided to those who should not have received them. Both the policies of our own clinic and the regulations of external authorities were violated. We wish to assure everyone that appropriate actions will be taken so that the problems will be addressed. Relevant steps have already been taken toward remedying this situation.

Make Unimportant by Contrasting With What Did Not Occur

The speaker anchors the presentation in scenarios of extreme consequences that did not occur. The contrast makes whatever may have happened seem trivial. Here is Jack's statement:

All of us have been concerned about the effects of recent events. As you know, allegations led to thorough investigations by several agencies. These investigations are now concluded. Let me assure you that regardless of what you may have heard, no patient died or even suffered any physical injury whatsoever, whether chronic or acute, significant or trivial. I believe that some of you have been concerned that some of the patients might, as a result of these events, become distraught and take their own lives. However, I want to assure each and every one of you that no patient has committed suicide or, to the best of our knowledge, threatened or attempted suicide. As a final note, I believe that some of you were distressed that the events may have involved serious criminal behavior of the kind exemplified by what our state terms a Class A felony. However—and I want to emphasize this!—not only were there no charges of Class A felonies for anyone involved in this sequence of events, but no one from the district attorney's office ever mentioned even the remote possibility of such charges. Although I think any of us might acknowledge that perhaps things might have been handled a bit better, it is important—and an issue of fundamental fairness—to keep what happened in perspective, to avoid the witch hunt mentality, and to remember that none of us is perfect. Thank you for your time and attention.

Replace Intentional Unethical Behavior With the Language of Accidents, Misfortune, and Mistakes

The speaker fails to mention making a conscious decision to profit by stealing charts, filling them with lies, and selling them to the highest bidder, which would strike most people as unethical. The description makes the speaker a victim of being an imperfect human, of lacking omniscience and infallibility. The speaker pushes the acts into the category of those random, inevitable mistakes that afflict us all and are beyond our control. At worst, they are a matter of having fumbled a matter of judgment, although, if this construction is examined closely, it seems to assume that almost anyone would have difficulty judging whether stealing charts, inserting bogus material that will hurt patients, and selling them to those who will publish them is ethical. This may not be quite as hard a judgment as the rhetoric implies. Here is how Jack would use that tactic:

> I wanted to address the unfortunate events that have troubled us all lately, so that you would understand what occurred and why. To my great regret, I have realized now in hindsight—hindsight being 20-20—that in handling clinic records, I made some mistakes. I'm sure you all know how I feel about this, and I hope you will be understanding and chalk this unfortunate error in judgment up to youthful indiscretion, my tendency to want to take on a little too much so that this clinic will function as well as possible, and to a momentary lapse of attention in the crush of daily demands that I face as

clinic director. All of us make mistakes in our work here, and I want you to know how sorry I am for this misstep.

Smother the Events in the Language of Attack

Assuming that the best defense is a good offense, the speaker avoids responsibility by attacking others. Whatever the speaker may have done becomes trivial or justifiable in light of the terrible things other people have done. The language of attack stirs up emotional responses. It works against people joining together to examine the facts and their implications and sets people against each other, dividing them into "us" (the good people, unjustly attacked) and "them" (the bad people, who deserve what we can dish out). The speaker's rhetoric serves to draw listeners into his or her camp and to ridicule or intimidate those who are on the other side (i.e., the enemy). The rhetoric encourages listeners to evaluate claims not in terms of whether they are valid and relevant but in terms of whether they support the listener's loyalty to one side.

Jack comes out swinging:

> Thank you for coming today. I will take just a few minutes of your time with the following statement about the recent events in which I have had to endure the most vicious attacks. It is a sad sign of our "take no responsibility" culture that several patients who came to our clinic in need and were not turned away have shown their gratitude for all we have done for them by trying to gain publicity for themselves—their 15 minutes of fame—and to enrich themselves at our expense by filing formal complaints. This is one of the most destructive aspects of the modern mind-set: it's all me-me-me, without thinking of how such complaints might affect the rest of us who have dedicated our lives to healing the sick, comforting those in need, and helping those who turn to us in their hour of crisis. The selfishness of such formal complaints is hard to comprehend. These scurrilous complaints rob us of the time and resources that we would otherwise use to provide services to those who have nowhere else to turn. And it is for those people who have so little and suffer so much that this clinic has resolved to fight these complaints with every resource we can muster. We have hired some of the most skilled and successful attorneys that this nation has yet produced, and they have already filed countercharges in civil court. The support staff aiding these attorneys have discovered, in the course of their extensive background research, some facts about those who filed complaints against us that I believe will surprise the public and place these vicious complaints in their proper perspective. I've been asked by our attorneys not to reveal that material at this time, but I assure you that our attorneys will present it at the proper time—in court—should these complaints go to trial. Again, pursuant to the advice of our attorneys, I will have no more comment on this matter at this time. Thank you for your time and attention.

JUSTIFICATIONS

Justifications turn the search for an ethical response around backward. Instead of searching for an ethical response to a situation until we find it, we begin by thinking of a way we would like to respond and then search for ways to justify it. With enough hard work and creativity, most of us can come up with justifications for almost anything we want to do.

The most common justifications rely on twisted judgment, appealing fallacies, and juggled language. They can spin the most questionable behaviors into ethical ideals. To restate a major theme of this book, we believe that the overwhelming majority of psychologists are conscientious, caring individuals, committed to ethical behavior. We also believe that none of us is infallible and that perhaps all of us, at one time or another, have been vulnerable to at least a few of these ethical justifications and might be able extend the list.

Many of the justifications appeared in previous editions of this book, and some were added when the list appeared in *What Therapists Don't Talk About and Why: Understanding Taboos that Hurt Us and Our Clients* (Pope, Sonne, & Greene, 2006):

1. It's not unethical as long as a managed care administrator or insurance case reviewer required or suggested it.
2. It's not unethical if the professional association you belong to allows it.
3. It's not unethical if an ethics code never mentions the concept, term, or act.
4. It's not unethical as long as no law was broken.
5. It's not unethical if we can use the passive voice and look ahead. If someone discovers that our c.v. is full of degrees we never earned, positions we never held, and awards we never received, all we need do is nondefensively acknowledge that mistakes were made and it's time to move on.
6. It's not unethical as long as we can name others who do the same thing.
7. It's not unethical as long as we didn't mean to hurt anyone.
8. It's not unethical even if our acts have caused harm as long as the person we harmed had it coming, provoked us, deserved it, was really asking for it, or practically forced us to do it—or, failing that, has not behaved perfectly, is in some way unlikable, or is acting unreasonably.
9. It's not unethical as long as there is no body of universally accepted, methodologically perfect (i.e., without any flaws, weaknesses, or limitations) studies showing—without any doubt whatsoever—that exactly what we did was the necessary and sufficient proximate cause of harm to the client and that the client would otherwise be free of all physical and psychological problems, difficulties, or challenges. This view was succinctly stated by a member of the Texas pesticide regulatory board

charged with protecting Texas citizens against undue risks from pesticides. In discussing Chlordane, a chemical used to kill termites, one member said, "Sure, it's going to kill a lot of people, but they may be dying of something else anyway" ("Perspectives," *Newsweek*, April 23, 1990, p. 17).

10. It's not unethical if we could not (or did not) anticipate the unintended consequences of our acts.

11. It's not unethical if we acknowledge the importance of judgment, consistency, and context. For example, it may seem as if a therapist who has submitted hundreds of thousands of dollars' worth of bogus insurance claims for patients he never saw might have behaved "unethically." However, as attorneys and others representing such professionals often point out: It was simply an error in judgment, completely inconsistent with the high ethics manifest in every other part of the person's life, and insignificant in the context of the unbelievable good that this person does.

12. It's not unethical if we can say any of the following about it (feel free to extend the list):
    "What else could I do?"
    "Anyone else would've done the same thing."
    "It came from the heart."
    "I listened to my soul."
    "I went with my gut."
    "It was the smart thing to do."
    "It was just common sense."
    "I just knew that's what the client needed."
    "Look, I was just stuck between a rock and a hard place."
    "I'd do the same thing again if I had it to do over."
    "It worked before."
    "I'm only human, you know!"
    "What's the big deal?"

13. It's not unethical if we have written an article, chapter, or book about it.

14. It's not unethical as long as we were under a lot of stress. No fair-minded person would hold us accountable when it is clear that it was the stress we were under—along with all sorts of other powerful factors—that must be held responsible.

15. It's not unethical as long as no one ever complained about it.

16. It's not unethical as long as we know that the people involved in enforcing standards (e.g., licensing boards or administrative law judges) are dishonest, stupid, destructive, and extremist; are unlike us in some significant way; or are conspiring against us.

17. It's not unethical as long as it results in a higher income or more prestige (i.e., is necessary).

18. It's not unethical if we're victims. Claiming tragic victim status is easy: We can always use one of two traditional scapegoats: (1) our anything-goes society, which lacks clear standards and leaves us ethically adrift; or, conversely, (2) our coercive, intolerant society, which tyrannizes us with "political correctness," dumbs us down, and controls us like children. Imagine, for example, we are arrested for speeding while drunk, and the person whose car we hit presses vengeful charges against us. We show ourselves as the real victim by pointing out that some politically correct, self-serving tyrants have hijacked the legal system and unfairly demonized drunk driving. These powerful people of bad character and evil motivation refuse to acknowledge that most speeding while drunk is not only harmless—actuarial studies show that only a small percentage of the instances of drunk speeding actually result in harm to people or property—but also sometimes unavoidable, profoundly ethical, and a social good, getting drivers to their destinations faster and in better spirits. We stress that any studies seeming to show drunk speeding is harmful are not just unscientific (e.g., none randomly assigns drivers to drunk speeding and nondrunk speeding conditions) but hopelessly biased (e.g., focusing on measures of harm but failing to include measures sensitive to the numerous benefits of drunk speeding).

19. It's not unethical as long as it would be almost impossible to do things another way.

20. It's not unethical as long as there are books, articles, or papers claiming that it is the right thing to do.

21. It's not unethical as long as we can find a consultant who says it's okay. Remaining mindfully aware of the ways that each of us as individuals may be vulnerable—particularly at times of stress or fatigue, of great temptation or temporary weakness—to these cognitive strategies may be an important aspect of our ability to respond ethically to difficult, complex, constantly evolving situations, particularly at moments when we are not at our best.

Reminding ourselves of our own unique patterns of vulnerability—particularly when we are tired, stressed, or distressed—to these justifications may help us to keep searching for the most ethical response to our work's complex, constantly changing challenges.

Chapter 4

TRUST, POWER, AND CARING

Psychotherapy is a remarkable venture. It involves three very different phenomena: trust, power, and caring. Understanding, respecting, and handling carefully all three is one of our greatest ethical challenges.

TRUST

States and provinces grant us professional status in acknowledgment of our fiduciary relationship to our clients. Society expects us to be trustworthy, to avoid exploiting the trust that people place in us. Society depends on us to fulfill the trust for the benefit of our clients as well as the social order. (Many ethical dilemmas result from the clash between the client's benefit and society's benefit, or between the client's benefit and the therapist's benefit.) In return for assuming a role in which the safety, welfare, and ultimate benefit of clients is to be held as a sacred trust, therapists are entitled to the roles, privileges, and power due professionals.

This concept of trust is crucial for understanding the context in which clients enter into a working relationship with us. Clients rightfully expect or desperately hope that their trust in us is not misplaced. Many clients fear that their trust might be betrayed. Some clients struggle agonizingly with issues of trust. Some clients come to therapy unaware of how their problems trusting others have made it hard for them to love, work, and enjoy life.

This strange phenomenon shines a light on the trust underlying therapy: Clients may walk into the consulting room of an absolute stranger and begin saying things that they would say to no one else. Therapists may ask questions that would be rude and intrusive if anyone else asked them.

Acknowledging and respecting the power of the private, sensitive, and sometimes secret information that patients tell us, virtually all states and provinces recognize some form of professional confidentiality and therapist-patient privilege. Laws prevent therapists, with some specific exceptions, from disclosing to others what clients tell them during therapy (see Chapter 19).

Therapy is like surgery in replying on trust. Surgery patients allow themselves to be physically opened up in the hope that their condition will improve. They trust surgeons not to take advantage of their vulnerability to harm or exploit them. Therapy patients undergo a process of psychological opening up in the hope that their condition will improve. They trust us not to harm or exploit them.

Freud (1952) noticed this similarity. He wrote that the newly developed "talking therapy" was "comparable to a surgical operation" (p. 467) and emphasized that "the transference especially...is a dangerous instrument....If a knife will not cut, neither will it serve a surgeon" (p. 471).

Recognizing and respecting the potential harm that could result from psychotherapy was, according to Freud (1963), essential:

> It is grossly to undervalue both the origins and the practical significance of the psychoneuroses to suppose that these disorders are to be removed by pottering about with a few harmless remedies.....Psychoanalysis...is not afraid to handle the most dangerous forces in the mind and set them to work for the benefit of the patient. (p. 179)

Our personal responsibility includes respecting our clients' trust that we will do nothing that places them at risk for deep, pervasive, and lasting harm.

When we betray our clients' trust, we can cause pervasive and lasting damage. Mann and Winer (1991), discussing the ways that exploitation of trust can harm patients, quote Adrienne Rich:

> When we discover that someone we trusted can be trusted no longer, it forces us to reexamine the whole instinct and concept of trust. For a while, we are thrust back into some bleak, jutting ledge...in a world before kinship, or naming, or tenderness exist; we are brought close to formlessness. (p. 325)

We all face the challenge of understanding what the careless handling of trust can mean for the person who is the client. Our clients do not live their lives in abstractions like "fiduciary relationships" and "social order." Trusting us is deeply personal.

POWER

The trust that society and individual clients give to therapists is a source of power—for example, the power to handle trust respectfully or to betray and abuse it. The role of therapist holds power ranging from superficial to profound, from fleeting to enduring.

Power Conferred by the State

State and provincial licensing confers power. Licensed professionals can do things that people without a license cannot.

With patients' consent, surgeons can cut human beings wide open and remove internal organs, anesthesiologists can drug them until they are unconscious, and many therapists can administer mind- or mood-altering drugs to them, all with the law's authorization.

People will take off their clothes and willingly (well, somewhat willingly) submit to all sorts of indignities during a medical examination. They allow physicians to do things to them that they would not dream of letting anyone else do.

Similarly, clients will open up and allow us as therapists to explore private aspects of their history, fantasies, hopes, and fears. Clients will tell us their most guarded secrets, material shared with literally no one else. We can ask questions that might get us slapped or worse if anyone else asked.

States and provinces recognize the importance of protecting clients against the misuse of this power to violate privacy. Except in certain instances, we are legally required to keep confidential what we have learned about their clients through the professional relationship. Holding private information about our clients gives us power in relation to their clients (see Chapter 19).

Through licensing, governments also invest us with the power of state-recognized authority to affect our clients' lives. We have the power to make decisions (subject to judicial review) about our clients' civil liberties. In some cases, we have the power to determine whether a person constitutes an immediate danger to the life of someone else and should be held against his or her will for observation or treatment. Alan Stone (1978), professor of law and psychiatry at Harvard University and a former president of the American Psychiatric Association, points out that the United States has incarcerated more of its citizens against their will for mental health purposes than any other country, that this process reached its peak in the 1950s when 1 out of every 300 citizens was held involuntarily in a mental institution, and that the abuse of this power led to extensive reforms and formal safeguards.

Power to Name and Define

We hold the power of naming and defining. To diagnose someone is to exercise power. In one of the most widely cited psychological research studies, "On Being Sane in Insane Places," Rosenhan (1973) wrote, "Such labels, conferred by mental health professionals, are as influential on the patient as they are on his relatives and friends, and it should not surprise anyone that the diagnosis acts on all of them as a self-fulfilling prophesy. Eventually, the patient himself accepts the diagnosis, with all of its surplus meanings and expectations, and behaves accordingly" (p. 254; see also Heingartner, 2009; Langer & Abelson, 1974; Mednick, 1989; Murphy, 1976; Pope, 1996; Pope, Butcher & Seelen, 2006; Reiser & Levenson, 1984; Scribner, 2001; Slater, 2004).

The potential power of diagnosis and other forms of clinical naming to affect how individuals are perceived is illustrated in Caplan's description (1995) of psychiatrist Bruno Bettelheim's analysis of student protesters:

> In the turbulent 1960s, Bettelheim . . . told the United States Congress of his findings: student anti-war protesters who charged the University of Chicago with complicity in the war machine had no serious political agenda; they were acting out an unresolved Oedipal conflict by attacking the university as a surrogate father. (p. 277)

Power of Testimony

We also possess authority to affect lives through our testimony as experts in the civil and criminal courts and through similar judicial or administrative proceedings. Whether someone convicted of murder is executed or paroled may depend on our testimony. Our testimony may affect whether a parent gains or loses custody of a child. It may influence a jury's decision about whether a defendant was capable of committing a crime, was likely to have committed it, was legally sane at the time the crime was committed, or is likely to commit similar crimes in the future. It may lead a jury to believe that a young child was sexually abused or that the child fantasized the event or was coached as part of a custody dispute. Our testimony may lead a jury to believe that the plaintiff is an innocent victim of a needless trauma who is suffering severe and chronic harm or that the same plaintiff is a chronic liar, a gold digger, or a malingerer.

Power of Knowledge

Our role as therapist involves power beyond what a license establishes. There is power that comes from knowledge. We study human behavior and the factors that affect motivation, decision, and action. We learn methods to bring about change. Acknowledging and respecting the power of knowledge and expertise is essential to avoid the subtle ways of manipulating and exploiting clients.

Power of Expectation

The process of psychotherapy itself creates and uses different forms of power. Most therapies recognize the force of the client's expectation that the therapist's interventions will be able to induce beneficial change. One aspect of this expectation is the placebo effect, a factor that must be taken into account when studying the efficacy and effectiveness of interventions. The client's investing the therapist with power to help bring about change can become a significant part of the change process itself.

The therapist often becomes invested with other important meanings as well. Psychodynamic theory, for example, describes a process termed *transference*: Clients transfer feelings, attachments, or styles of relationship associated with figures from their past, such as parents, onto the therapist. Deep feelings, such as love, rejection, shame, guilt, longing for approval, dependence, panic, and neediness—each perhaps representing the unfinished business of development or traumatic experiences needing understanding and healing—originally experienced within an early relationship may emerge in the therapist-client relationship in ways that tend to shock and overwhelm the client.

Our potential to elicit such profound feelings—simply by serving as a therapist—and to "feel" to the client as if the we were a figure from the client's past (with the client frequently functioning as if he or she were at an earlier stage of development) represent the sometimes surprising aspects of our power to affect their clients.

Creating Power

In some approaches, the therapist works to create specific kinds of power. A family therapist may unbalance the equilibrium and alliances among family members. A behavior therapist may create a hospital ward or halfway house in which desirable behaviors bring a rewarding response from the staff (perhaps in the form of tokens that can be exchanged for goods or privileges); the power of the therapist and staff is used to control, or at least influence, the client's behavior.

Psychologist Laura Brown (1994b) describes another domain of the therapist's power:

> The therapist also has the power to engage in certain defining behaviors that are real and concrete. She sets the fee; decides the time, place, and circumstances of the meeting; and determines what she will share about herself and not disclose. Even when she allows some leeway in negotiating these and similar points, this allowance proceeds from the implicit understanding that it is within the therapist's power to give, and to take away, such compromises. (p. 111)

Inherent Power Differential

The power differential is inherent in psychotherapy. Although some approaches emphasized egalitarian ideals in which therapist and client are equal, such goals are viewed only within a narrowly limited context of the relationship. In truly equal relationships, in which there is no appreciable power differential, there is no designation of one member as "therapist" in relation to the other member, there is no fee charged by one member to the other for the relationship, there is no designation of the activity as "professional" (and falling within the scope of a professional liability policy), there is no use by one member of a license to work with the other, and so on. A defining attribute of the professional is the recognition, understanding, and careful handling of the considerable power—and the personal responsibility for that power—inherent in the role.

CARING

Both the individual client and society recognize the diverse powers of the professional role and place their trust in us to use those powers to benefit—never to harm or exploit—those who seek help from the therapist. The trust that society and the individual client give must be matched by our caring. Only within a context of caring—specifically caring about the client's well-being—are our professional status and powers justified.

Historically, charging high fees did not create or define professional status, nor did spending long years in training or reaching a high level of expertise. The professional's defining characteristic was an ethic of placing the client's welfare foremost and not allowing professional judgment or services to be drawn off course by one's own needs.

The touchstone for the approaches discussed in this book is caring for and about the people we work with. This book's concept of caring avoids passive, empty sentimentality. Caring includes responding to a client's legitimate needs and recognizing that the client must never be exploited. It also includes assuming personal responsibility for working to help and to avoid harming or endangering our clients.

Unfortunately, this concept may not receive adequate attention in graduate training programs. As Sarason (1985) wrote:

> On the surface, trainees accept the need for objectivity—it does have the ring of science, and its importance can be illustrated with examples of the baleful consequences of "emotional over-involvement"—but internally there is a struggle, as one of my students put it, "between what your heart says you should say and do and what theory and your supervisor say you should say and do." Many trainees give up the struggle but there are some who continue to feel that in striving to maintain the stance of objectivity they are robbing themselves and their clients of something of therapeutic value. The trainee's struggle, which supervisors gloss over as a normal developmental phase that trainees grow out of, points to an omission in psychological-psychiatric theories. Those theories never concern themselves with caring and compassion. What does it mean to be caring and compassionate? When do caring and compassion arise as feelings? What inhibits or facilitates their expression?

Why do people differ so widely in having such feelings and the ways they express them? It is, of course, implicit in all of these theories that these feelings are crucial in human development, but the reader would be surprised how little attention is given to their phenomenology and consequences (positive and negative). (p. 168; see also Pope, Sonne, & Greene, 2006; Pope, Sonne, & Holroyd, 1993; Pope & Tabachnick, 1993, 1994)

Caring about clients and what happens to them is one of the strongest foundations for the formal rules and regulations that are society's attempt to hold us accountable, but it also encourages us to look beyond those generalities. Caring is a foundation of our personal responsibilities as therapists.

Chapter 5

THERAPY IN THE DIGITAL WORLD: THE ETHICAL CHALLENGES OF THE NEW TECHNOLOGIES

Technology creates new ways for us to connect with our patients. Geographic barriers fall. Relationships take new forms. We may start and end therapy without ever being together in the same room with the patient. Hawn (2009) wrote in "Take Two Aspirin and Tweet Me in the Morning: How Twitter, Facebook, and Other Social Media Are Reshaping Health Care": "across the health-care industry, from large hospital networks to patient support groups, new media tools like weblogs, instant messaging platforms, video chat, and social networks are reengineering the way doctors and patients interact" (p. 361). The new technologies can change not only ways we interact with our patients but also the treatments we provide. Mohr (2009) noted: "Existing and emerging telecommunications technologies not only allow us to extend access to mental health care, but they also provide opportunities to develop fundamentally new treatment paradigms" (p. 343).

CONSIDER THESE VIGNETTES

Roberto lives in a small Florida town and uses a wheelchair to get around. He does not own a car. Feeling lonely and trapped in a job he hates, he is ready to begin therapy again. Ten years ago a cognitive behavioral therapist had helped him after he had been in a serious car wreck. Wanting to work with a cognitive behavior therapist again, he discovers that the closest CBT office is over

2 hours away. The distance is impractical: He could not take that much time off work even if he could find someone to drive him there and back once or twice a week. He decides to search the Web, examining professional sites, consulting referral databases, and following leads. Within days he has found Dr. Spillane, a psychologist specializing in CBT who will provide therapy online. During a 45-minute session each week, they each sit at their computers, using Web cams and their computers' audio systems to communicate with each other.

■ ■ ■

Dr. Mosley's third patient of the day is Edgar, a young man with an impulse control disorder and a history of violence and alcohol abuse. It is Edgar's sixth session and he seems starkly different. He is flushed, agitated, and clearly not sober. He begins speaking loudly and is soon screaming. His company downsized and fired him four days ago. The bank won't give him a loan he needs to tide him over. It seems everyone is against him. This morning he found evidence that his best friend, a man he had often mentioned in therapy—their families shared a vacation each year and often went on weekend hiking and camping trips together—had been sleeping with Edgar's wife. Edgar got up and began pacing as he talked about how a man just could not put up with something like this, that he would put a stop to it and make his friend pay. He seemed to get more and more worked up. He stopped pacing and turned to face Dr. Mosely: "I'm going to get a gun and kill him and all his family right now." Edgar was out the door before Dr. Mosely had any chance of stopping him. She ran to her phone, called 911, and told the police her patient's name, intentions, and home address, though he had been clear that he was going straight to a gun shop and then to murder his friend and the friend's family. She did not know the name of the friend. She then called Edgar's home phone, hoping someone there would be able to identify the friend, but there was no answer. She sat down at her computer and Googled her patient's full name. She found his Facebook page, which included vacation photos and the name of Edgar's friend. She used that name to find the friend's phone number, which she gave to the police, who were able to contact the family and protect them until they found Edgar and placed him on a 72-hour hold in a locked facility for a psychological evaluation.

■ ■ ■

Dr. Christie is the only therapist in a very remote rural setting. A man who just moved there from Rwanda contacts him because his 13-year-old daughter is distraught and depressed. She refuses to tell her family why she is upset but tells her father that she needs to see a therapist. The problem is that although the father can speak a little English, his daughter speaks only Swahili. The daughter will say nothing to the therapist if her father is to serve as translator. No one else in the area speaks both Swahili and English. Dr. Christie begins searching the Web and soon finds someone fluent in both Swahili and English who has been trained to serve as a translator in mental health settings. She is aware of the sensitive issues and intense emotional reactions that can arise, the need for rapport and precise translation, potential problems due to cultural differences and regional dialect, and confidentiality requirements. During each of Dr. Christie's sessions with the daughter, the translator will join them in videoconference.

■ ■ ■

Jean is a born-again Christian who tries to live her life in accordance with the Bible. Profoundly depressed, she talks with her pastor, who prays with her, provides spiritual guidance, and suggests that meeting with a therapist might be helpful. There are three therapists in her town. She schedules an initial session with each but never feels comfortable talking with them and does not feel that they understand, appreciate, or perhaps even respect her beliefs. She asks her pastor for help in finding a therapist who shares her religious beliefs. Her pastor asks the church hierarchy and his fellow pastors for help, and a week later he provides Jean with the name of a therapist, Dr. Salter, who is a member of another church in the same denomination who will meet with her weekly via videophone. Though Jean does not have a videophone and does not even own a computer, the pastor will let her use the church's videophone in one of the church offices once a week.

RISKS, COSTS, AND DISASTERS

These vignettes illustrate just a few of the many benefits that digital technologies provide to us and our patients. But the benefits come with costs, risks, and occasional disasters. Digital technologies take confidential information that was once confined to handwriting in a paper chart kept under lock and key and spread it over electronic networks. Freeny (2007) wrote:

> The gravitation to an electronic medical record promises much greater speed and efficiency in using client medical information in critical situations. However, it is a direction that also contains great confidentiality compromises for the client as the world has gone global in distributing confidential information. Unfortunately, mental health clinicians are largely ignorant of the full ramifications of these new initiatives. The HIPAA [Health Insurance Portability and Accountability Act] privacy rules suggested that the bar would be raised for clinical privacy, but, in fact, the standards were significantly lowered. (p. 13; see also Richards, 2009)

On that issue of HIPAA's ineffectiveness, Alonso-Zaldivar (2008) concurred, noting that in 2008, "despite 34,000 complaints of violations in the last five years, the federal act has resulted in only a few prosecutions, and no civil fines have been levied."

Sometimes patient information has been kept in databases without informed consent. Those who maintain the databases may react strongly against those who object. The *British Medical Journal*, for example, reported that a "junior doctor . . . was excluded from work for five years after she objected to the inclusion of patients' medical records, including her own, on research databases without consent" (Dyer, 2008).

As we house confidential patient information in distant servers, send it over many networks, and carry it around in our laptops and personal digital assistants, it becomes ever more vulnerable to theft and other forms of loss. Here are just a few examples:

- Elder (2010) reported that the "University of Texas Medical Branch has mailed letters notifying 1,200 patients that sensitive information about them had been available to a woman charged with identity theft."
- Krebs (2007) described the loss of a backup tape containing information on 83,000 patients at Johns Hopkins Hospital.
- Krebs (2007) also noted that "two different Kaiser Permanente hospitals had lost laptops over the past nine months that endangered patient data."
- Channel WTVF in Nashville, Tennessee, reported: "Blue Cross will be contacting customers . . . whose personal information was exposed when hard drives were stolen. Someone stole 57 hard drives from a storage closet at one of their training centers" ("Major Insurance Company Announces Security Breach," 2010).
- Campisi (2009) reported how medical records containing Social Security numbers, date of birth, name and occupation of University of Pennsylvania Health System were taken and used to create bogus credit cards in the patients' names.
- Allday wrote of the information on about 600 UCSF patients was breached "when a faculty physician in the UCSF School of Medicine provided a user name and password in response to a scam e-mail message."
- Zavis (2009) reported on the theft of over 1,000 patient records from Cedars-Sinai Hospital in Los Angeles.
- Sturdevant (2009) wrote that "a hard drive with seven years of personal and medical information on about 1.5 million Health Net customers . . . was lost six months ago and was first reported Wednesday, state and company officials said."
- Sturdevant also noted that "Earlier this month, Anthem Blue Cross and Blue Shield of Connecticut reported that a laptop was stolen this

summer in the Chicago area, compromising personal information of nearly 850,000 doctors, therapists and other health-care providers in 50 states. . . ." (see also Lazar, 2009)

- Naughton (2008) described the sale of UCLA Medical Center patient files for public figures to the *National Enquirer*, and how "a total of 1,041 patients had their records inappropriately accessed at UCLA medical facilities."

Technology presents other potential problems. Clinicians may discover that their informal tweets and their entries in Facebook and other social networking technologies affect their careers. Jain (2009) wrote:

> In an e-mail to students and faculty of Harvard Medical School, Dean for Medical Education Jules Dienstag wrote: "Caution is recommended...in using social networking sites such as Facebook or MySpace. Items that represent unprofessional behavior that are posted by you on such networking sites reflect poorly on you and the medical profession. Such items may become public and could subject you to unintended exposure and consequences." At the Drexel University College of Medicine, medical students are warned about the possibility that information placed on social-networking sites might influence the fate of their applications for postgraduate training: "Programs/employers are increasingly gaining access to social networking sites such as Facebook and MySpace to see what they can learn about candidates." Although legal questions surrounding the relationship between clinical medicine and social networking are as yet undefined, there are obvious concerns for individuals and institutions, since their Internet presence makes clinicians' attitudes and activities increasingly visible. (p. 650; see also Dolan, 2009; McCoy, 2009)

Rubenstein (2008) described another kind of problem that occurred with a social networking site: "Two workers at University of New Mexico Hospital were fired for using their cellphone cameras to take shots of patients in treatment, then posting the pics on MySpace."

The *Journal of the American Medical Association* reported a survey of medical students' unprofessional online postings:

> The majority of medical school representatives reported incidents involving students posting unprofessional content online. Some of the incidents involved violation of patient confidentiality. While most incidents resulted in informal warnings, some were serious enough to lead to dismissal. However, few respondents reported having professionalism policies that could apply to student online postings and very few of these explicitly mentioned Internet use.
> (Chretien, Greysen, Chretien, & Kind, 2009, p. 1313)

One of the most fascinating accounts of a clinician undone through his use of technology involved an Ivy League–educated physician on trial for malpractice. During cross-examination, he was suddenly asked if he was "Flea." As the *Boston Globe* (2007) reported:

> Flea, jurors in the case didn't know, was the screen name for a blogger who had written often and at length about a trial remarkably similar to the one that was going on in the courtroom that day.
>
> In his blog, Flea had ridiculed the plaintiff's case and the plaintiff's lawyer. He had revealed the defense strategy. He had accused members of the jury of dozing.
>
> With the jury looking on in puzzlement, Lindeman admitted that he was, in fact, Flea.
>
> The next morning, on May 15, he agreed to pay what members of Boston's tight-knit legal community describe as a substantial settlement—case closed.

Digital technologies also provide the opportunity to make information about psychological tests—including the test items themselves and scoring guides—widely available to anyone who can access the Internet. A controversial instance involved the Wikipedia. Cohen (2009) reported that "the online encyclopedia Wikipedia has been engulfed in a furious debate involving psychologists who are angry that the 10 original Rorschach plates are reproduced online, along with common responses for each." Lobello and Zachar (2007) found that

> psychological test materials are available on eBay. Overall, about half of the test items listed for sale did not specify any restrictions on purchases. The sale of test manuals containing the administration procedures and responses to items represents the greatest potential breach of test security. However, even when test manuals were offered for sale, almost 40% of these items were listed without purchase restrictions. (p. 69)

The tests they found for sale on the Internet included the Wechsler Adult Intelligence Scale—Revised, Wechsler-Bellevue Intelligence Scale, Wechsler Individual Achievement Test, Wechsler Preschool and Primary Scale of Intelligence—Revised, Wechsler Memory Scale-Revised, Rorschach, Thematic Apperception Test, Minnesota Multiphasic Personality Inventory, Minnesota Multiphasic Personality Inventory—Adolescent, and Behavior Assessment System for Children—Second Edition. For examples involving other tests, see Bauer and McCaffrey (2006).

FIVE SPECIAL PITFALLS

The research, news reports, case examples, and other material reviewed to this point—along with the six potential disasters described in Chapter 2's section "Computer Coincidences"—identify areas that warrant special awareness as we make use of the benefits of rapidly evolving technologies. What follows are five pitfalls, each illustrated by a vignette, and a set of questions that may be helpful in navigating the digital world.

Pitfall 1

Skeptical at first about trying to conduct therapy sessions over the Internet—he used his simple computer only for e-mail—Dr. Chandler had finally decided to develop a niche practice of working with patients using Web cams. Not trusting his limited computer skills, he hired his neighbor's daughter, a Massachusetts Institute of Technology graduate student home for a two-week break, to select a comprehensive system, install it for him, and teach him how to use it. She spent the first week buying and installing the components. She spent the second week teaching him the system's wonders: How to use the Web cam to talk with another person, how to record the sessions, how to keep his patient information and treatment files in digital form, how to use the system's scheduling software, and how to back up all his data using an independent hard drive. When Dr. Chandler felt confident he knew how to operate the comprehensive system she'd created, she uploaded a Web site announcing his services and allowing people to request appointments and pay in advance using credit cards or PayPal.

Within months he had six clients, one of whom was Philip, a fragile, shy, anxious ballet dancer. Phillip felt that no one really listened to him but was also afraid to talk honestly with others about himself. He would refer indirectly to his "secrets," suggesting that if anyone knew what he was really like, they'd hate him and never speak to him again. It took Philip months to work up the courage and trust to tell Dr. Chandler what he had never told another soul. He had barely gotten his secret out before he began sobbing, unable to continue. It was at this moment that Dr. Chandler's system crashed.

It was only later that afternoon, after he'd finally found a computer specialist in the yellow pages who made emergency office visits, that he learned that the data kept on his computer was gone. A new computer worm had systematically erased and repeatedly overwritten his schedule, his billing records, his patient contact information and files, his recorded sessions, and the award acceptance address he'd written for the convention next week when he was to receive Niche Practitioner of the Year honor from his state psychological association.

This, however, was not the worst of it. The worst of it was when the computer specialist pointed out that because he'd left the independent hard drive on which he made his backups plugged into the main system "for convenience," the worm had been able to access it, erase it, and overwrite the disk repeatedly, making any attempt to rescue the original data hopeless. All of his data, including his backup copies, were gone.

Dr. Chandler wanted to contact Philip right away, to tell him what had happened and to find out how he was, but because he no longer had any contact information, it was some time before he was able to track him down.

Dr. Chandler's adventures in Internet therapy illustrate an important reality: It is not just therapists who are both fallible and vulnerable; so are our computers. An important part of using computers in a therapy practice is evaluating carefully when and how they can fail and preparing for those failures.

Pitfall 2

Dr. Doyle was tired of it all. In solo practice, she sat in the same chair in the same room most of the day, getting very little exercise. She was exhausted by the end of the day and didn't feel like doing much of anything excerpt going home, eating dinner, and going to bed.

On impulse, she signed up for a noon beginner's class in belly dancing. It changed her life. She loved it. She looked forward to it every day, and every afternoon she felt energized. She knew she was becoming more fit, building stamina, and toning her muscles. But mainly belly dancing brought joy to her life.

A woman in her class told her about a belly dancing Web site. You could sign up and become part of a discussion list. Members shared their love of belly dancing and traded information about dances, costumes, courses, and festivals. Dr. Doyle visited the Web site and signed up.

It was only later that Dr. Doyle learned that by signing up, she had agreed to allow the organization to access her computer's address book. It used the names to send invitations to join the belly dancing list to everyone in her address book. The invitations mentioned her name and were written ambiguously so that recipients might assume they came from her. Her address book contained the names of her current and former therapy patients, attorneys she'd been in contact with for cases in which they'd be deposing and cross-examining her as an expert witness, a former boyfriend, various colleagues including members of the state licensing board, her rabbi, and her bank's loan officer to whom she'd applied for some funds to tide her over.

Dr. Doyle's misfortune shows the hazards of not understanding the implications of participating in cyberactivities such as joining lists or providing information on Web sites. Many of us become used to reflexively clicking "agree" without reading all the dull boilerplate and legalese of policy statements when we install new software. That the reflex takes over when we journey around the Web. And even if we read every statement before agreeing, many of them may not cover material that is crucial to us in making informed decisions and avoiding disasters.

Pitfall 3

Dr. Hammett had been working via video with a girl in her mid-teens for close to three months. Her parents lived in a remote area, were desperate to find some way to help her, but were unable to travel on a regular basis to a therapist's office. The girl was home schooled and highly intelligent. Dr. Hammett was sure that one of her problems was loneliness: She spent most of her time in her room, painstakingly creating stop-action videos, which she refused to share with Dr. Hammett, saying only that she always put them on the Web and that he could find them if he was really interested.

Attempts to engage her in conversation, to encourage her to talk, or to ask any kind of questions were met with sullen evasions or passive-aggressive comments. It took time to gain her trust.

The session she finally started talking, she began telling Dr. Hammett how much she hated him. He was like almost everyone else in her life. He did not listen. He didn't care about her. He just wanted to control her. He said stupid things. She hated him.

It wasn't the most comfortable session for Dr. Hammett, but he felt very good about the breakthrough. She was expressing what was going on inside her in a very honest and direct way. The real work had begun.

It was only several days later that Dr. Hammett's friends and colleagues alerted him to how he was becoming an international sensation. When he typed his name into Google and followed the links, he discovered what his patient had done.

She had been recording their sessions, and had posted a clever short video, "My Experience of Therapy with Dr. Hammett," on YouTube. Her video had gone viral.

The video showed segment after segment of her saying something she'd never said during the session but had recorded later for her video. After each segment, she'd inserted a clip of something Dr. Hammett had said during their sessions, taken completely out of context but chosen because it made him look like a fool.

One segment showed her saying "Dr. Hammett, I feel like no one listens to me, no one hears what I really say," followed by a clip of something he'd said when the audio feed had been temporarily interrupted: "I can see you but I can't hear anything you're saying."

Another segment showed her saying "My parents are only interested in my always-perfect brother, he's all they want to talk about, it's like no one is interested in me, I don't even exist," followed by Dr. Hammett saying "I wonder if we could talk about your brother."

Another showed her yelling "I can't take it anymore! I'm going to hang myself with this noose!" followed by him smiling and saying "What a wonderful idea! I was hoping you would! I think this is a good time to end our session."

Dr. Hammett discovered a growing number of alternate versions of his patient's video gaining popularity on the Web. Kids had downloaded the video, making copies, and replaced his actual patient with themselves as the patient, making up new lines for him to respond to, each boy or girl trying to create a funnier or more outrageous version.

Stunned and enraged at what his patient was doing to his dignity, image, and reputation, Dr. Hammett grabbed the phone and called the city's most powerful law firm, making an appointment that afternoon with the firm's most feared and successful litigator.

Quickly taking a seat in the litigator's office that afternoon, Dr. Hammett explained the decision and his intention not only to take legal action to have the videos taken down but also to sue his patient for every penny her family had.

Accustomed to listening to outraged people consumed with a molten determination to sue, the attorney listened with the patience of someone who charged $500 an hour for consultation. He explained the difficulties of legal action against something that was clearly satire and likely protected by the First Amendment, the significant expenses—expenses that Dr. Hammett would have to pay out of his own pocket—involved in preparing for and conducting a trial, the fact that filing suit would make the videos more popular than ever, the problems of dealing with the many jurisdictions—some outside the United States—from which different kids had uploaded their versions of the video, and what would happen to his reputation if the media began portraying him as someone suing parents for not stopping his child patient from making fun of him.

Dr. Hammett had been unaware of how the technology he used had changed the nature of his practice, affected the privacy of what he said and did as a therapist in his own office, and given tools to his patients that could be used in ways he had not imagined.

Pitfall 4

Dr. MacDonald had worked as hard as anyone else in his graduate training program, and his transcripts were as good as anyone else's who graduated that year. He'd worked with some of the program's best professors, and they seemed to like him. He'd gotten into a good internship and done well. His supervisors had praised his skills and invited him to stay on an extra year so that he could be licensed by the time he was ready to look for a position as a clinician in the student counseling center of one of the universities.

He found entry-level openings for a counselor at 10 centers and submitted applications, making sure all the transcripts, letters of recommendation, and other materials arrived before the deadline. What surprised him was that not one of the schools called him for an initial interview.

He had a very rough year after leaving his internship setting, able to find a clinical job—but not in a university counseling center—only after 10 months of searching.

It was only after he'd been licensed for almost three years that a friend who'd been working at a university counseling center explained why he'd had such a hard time finding work.

Dr. MacDonald had become well known among psychologists on the Internet, and not in a particularly good way. He posted frequently on psychology lists, pointing out mistakes in his colleagues' messages, ridiculing questions as stupid or naive, and insulting anyone who disagreed with him. He was especially hard on students and on colleagues who did not belong to the particular list on which he was posting.

Dr. MacDonald was unaware of how his posts, which he thought were so effective in shaping opinions about other people, actually shaped how people viewed him. He did not realize that the reputation he created in cyberspace might play a role in how future employers and members of hiring committees viewed him as a job candidate.

Pitfall 5

Dr. James had a thriving videoconferencing therapy practice. She had set up her Web site so that applicants, who created a user name and password, filled out applications. When she found an appropriate candidate for therapy, the patient scheduled an appointment and paid (using a credit card or PayPal) via the Web site. At the scheduled time, she and the patient met via Web cam for each therapy session.

One of her most interesting patients was a young software engineer who had become independently wealthy when he sold his company to a large corporation. His problems were mainly indecision about what he now wanted to do with his life and his travel schedule (he had to fly to other countries to troubleshoot their implementation of the software products his company made—he was obligated to travel as one of the contractual stipulations to the corporation that had bought his company).

Three months into the treatment, Dr. James received an unpleasant letter, sent registered mail, return receipt requested, from an attorney in a distant state. She discovered that the patient was actually a minor whose parents were involved in a bitter divorce. The lawyer, representing one of the parents, wanted to know why Dr. James was providing treatment to a minor without the informed consent of the boy's parent. He also wanted to know why Dr. James was providing services that required a license when a check with the state licensing board showed that Dr. James was not licensed to practice in the state where the boy lived and was receiving treatment. He asked Dr. James to send the boy's assessment and treatment records to him within the next five business days. Soon after, Dr. James learned that the boy was not a software engineer and had never owned his own business. He was in high school and worked part time at a fast food outlet. The boy apparently believed his fantasies and suffered from a serious psychological disorder. However, Dr. James had not recognized the disorder, conducted an adequate assessment, or provided the appropriate treatment.

Dr. James's focus on the wonders of Web site and videoconferencing technologies led her to overlook the responsibilities they bring with them. She failed to notice that the Web cam's power to let her to work with patients in distant states and provinces meant that she needed to be familiar with and comply with the relevant laws and regulations. Working within the framework of videoconferencing seemed to distract her from doing the kind of careful assessment she no doubt would have conducted had she been working with the client in person.

QUESTIONS TO ASSESS USES OF DIGITAL MEDIA

These questions may be helpful in avoiding pitfalls when clinicians use computers, Web sites, videocams, and other digital media in their work.

Where Is the Computer?

Some readers may have visited clinics and seen confidential information about patients on a computer screen. One of the first questions to ask is: When this computer is on, who can see the screen? Can anyone who is not authorized see patient names or other sensitive information on the screen? This can be a problem for those who work with confidential information on portable computers during long flights or in terminals, waiting rooms, and other public spaces.

When the computer is unattended—whether for only a few minutes or overnight—is there a secure barrier between it and anyone who might want to access it or steal it? If you were to offer someone a considerable sum of money to access the computer without authorization or to steal it, how confident are you that you would not lose your money?

Is the Computer Protected From Hackers?

If the computer is hooked up to the Internet, a software or hardware firewall can help protect against unauthorized entry. Note the word *help*. No method of protection is foolproof. All have strengths but also vulnerabilities. The more layers of protection you use, the more secure your confidential data will be. If one or two layers fail to block unauthorized entry, others may work. Like a house with many locks and forms of security, a well-protected computer may discourage all but the most determined and skilled hackers.

Is the Computer Protected From Malicious Code That Can Access Confidential Information?

When computers connect to the Internet, they are vulnerable. Security hardware and software can lower but not remove the vulnerability. Viruses, Trojans, worms, and other malware continue to find more devious paths to fool a computer's defenses. E-mails formatted in HTML can mask malicious code. E-mail attachments can infect a computer before they are opened. A visit to a Web site may result in a malicious program downloading into the computer without the user's knowledge. These programs can look for a computer's most sensitive files (e.g., those that fit the patterns of social security numbers, credit card numbers, passwords, financial statements; those that contain words like *private, confidential, clinical,* or *medical*). They can transmit those files to a temporary throwaway address in another country, post them on an anonymous Web site, or send them to every e-mail address in your computer's memory.

One approach to protecting confidential information on a computer is a two-step process: (1) keep several layers of protection on the computer and (2) keep the information encrypted on a removable medium (such as a portable external hard drive, CD, or DVD). The removable medium would always be kept secure and would be hooked up to the computer only when the therapist is using it.

An approach that offers more protection is to use one computer for connecting with the Internet and storing nonconfidential data and a separate computer that is never hooked up to the Internet or other networks to store confidential information. Because the confidential information is stored on a completely isolated, stand-alone computer, there is no wired or wireless link from it to any network and it cannot transmit data to unauthorized recipients.

Is Your Computer Protected From Viruses and Other Malware?

Do you have a good antivirus program? Do you maintain it by installing the company's new virus definitions?

Is the Computer Password-Protected?

If someone finds a computer unattended or steals it, a system of passwords can make it difficult to access confidential information. Loading the operating system when turning on the computer, gaining access to a set of files, and opening a particular file can be made contingent on passwords.

Words do not make the most secure passwords. Dictionary programs are readily available to hackers, who use them to enter a password-protected computer. A password is likely to block password-breaking software if it has a combination of lowercase letters, uppercase letters, and symbols and if it runs at least 12 characters long.

Any password is useless if someone who is determined to access your computer sees it written down somewhere. Someone sitting at your computer and attempting to gain unauthorized access is likely to look through the papers on and in your desk (including under the keyboard and on the monitor) to see if the password has been jotted down.

Is Confidential Information Encrypted?

Even if someone defeats your password protection, he or she will still face a formidable layer of protection if your computer's files are encrypted. Apple, Microsoft, and other makers of the major computer operating systems as well as other companies (e.g., PGP at www.pgp.com) provide software programs that will encrypt files.

How Are Confidential Files Deleted?

On most computers, using the Delete key to get rid of a file leaves virtually all of the file on the hard disk, where it can be retrieved easily by an inexpensive data recovery program. To dispose confidential files, it is useful to use some form of secure deleting, such as one that involves repeatedly overwriting the old file with random characters.

How Are Computer Disks Discarded?

From time to time, the news media report what has become a standard story: Someone sells or discards a computer on which confidential information is discovered. A few examples were cited earlier in this chapter. If a computer disk or other electronic storage medium stored confidential information, it should be completely degaussed or physically destroyed.

How Do You Guard Against Human Error in Handling Confidential Information?

Most people who have been online for a while are familiar with the sudden surprise that comes with the realization: I just sent that message to the wrong person! When we communicate over the Internet about confidential patient information, the price of human error can be steep. What procedures do you have in place to make sure that confidential information is not misaddressed?

How Do You Make Sure That Only the Intended Recipient Receives Your Confidential Information?

Even when we have made sure that an e-mail containing confidential information is addressed to the right person, the right person's e-mail address may be used by more than one person. Sometimes partners or family members share an e-mail address. Even if the sharing is not routine, a friend or family member may monitor someone's e-mails while the person is temporarily disabled, ill, or on vacation.

Do Your Clients Clearly Understand the Ways in Which They Can or Can't Communicate with You via E-Mail, Text Message, or Other Digital Means?

Each of us has our own way of approaching—or staying away from—digital technology in our work with patients. As the examples at the beginning of the chapter illustrated, e-mail, videoconferencing, and other digital formats are wonderful resources. But they also have risks. What is important is that patients understand how a specific clinician uses e-mail or other methods of digital communication. Clear understanding can prevent problems like:

- A therapist gives a patient her e-mail address for anything important that the patient needs to communicate before the next session, which is two weeks later, and the patient begins sending 30 to 50 messages each day.
- A patient searching the Web to find an e-mail address for the therapist, finding it, and sending messages to that address, when in fact it is the address of another person with the same name.
- A patient finding an e-mail address for the therapist and using it to send messages between therapy sessions about material that is too difficult for the patient to say face-to-face, when the e-mail address is an old one that the therapist does not use anymore.
- A patient finding a therapist's e-mail address and using it to tell the therapist that the patient will be taking an overdose of sleeping pills to commit suicide later that night but that the therapist should respond only if the therapist thinks the patient is worth saving, and the e-mail account is one that the therapist checks only once a week.

Is Your Professional Web Site or the Web Site of the Clinic, Hospital, or Group Practice at Which You Work Accessible to People With Disabilities?

For additional resources in this area, please see "Seven Easy Steps Toward Web Site Accessibility" at http://kpope.com/seven/index.php; "Web Accessibility Verifiers" at http://kpope.com/verify/index.php; and the section titled "Accessibility for People with Disabilities" in Chapter 13.

If Your Web Site Includes a Function That Enables Patients to Communicate With You (e.g., by Signing on With a User Name and Password), Has It Been Adequately Secured?

Many of the security measures you take will be versions of the steps you take to secure your personal computer and network, guarding against hackers, hijackers, malware, unintentional viewing of confidential material, and so on.

If You Use Social Networking Media, Such as Facebook, Twitter, and So On, Does the Medium Form a Link Between You and Any of Your Patients or Your Patients' Family Members? If So, How, if at All, Does It Affect the Therapy or Your Relationships With Your Patients?

Introducing new forms of relationships with patients should be done with thoughtfulness and care. Countless problems—and sometimes catastrophes—can be avoided if we ourselves avoid entering new domains in a thoughtless and careless way. Thinking through new forms of relationships in terms of our own theoretical orientation and approach, the individual patient, the available research, the practicalities involved, informed consent issues, documentation, and so on, can help us meet the highest ethical and clinical standards.

Are You Competent to Provide Services Through Digital Media?

If, for example, you provide services in which you do not meet the patient face-to-face but provide therapy and communicate with the patient solely via e-mail, through a Web site, or using a Web camera and microphone, have you received adequate training in this kind of therapy?

Are You Aware of the Relevant Laws and Regulations Governing the Use of Digital Media in Providing Clinical Services?

This area can be particularly complicated if you are in one state or province and the patient is in another state or province. Cross-jurisdictional provision of services may be limited to a certain period of time or may not be allowed at all. One good step to take is to check with the licensing boards in both jurisdictions. The provider of your professional liability policy may also provide helpful information and guidance. The company insuring your work has an obvious interest in helping you avoid problems.

Are You Aware of Emerging Research on Clinical Services Offered Through Digital Media?

Research in these areas continues to evolve, using increasingly sophisticated methodologies. Recent articles presenting or reviewing research into teletherapy and clinical uses of videoconferencing include Antonacci, Bloch, and Saeed (2008); De Las Cuevas, Arredondo, Cabrera, Sulzenbacher, and Meise (2006); Germain, Marchand, Bouchard, Drouin, and Guay (2009); Hailey,

Roine, and Ohinmaa (2008); King et al. (2009); Mitchell et al. (2008); Nieves, Godleski, Stack, and Zinann (2009); Richardson, Frueh, Grubaugh, Egede, and Elhai (2009); and Simpson (2009).

Are You Aware of the Professional Guidelines for Teletherapy, Internet Therapy, and Other Clinical Services Provided Through Digital Media?

These documents made available by professional organizations may be useful in deciding whether and how to use different kinds of digital technology to provide clinical services. Links to each of them are available at http://kspope .com/ethcodes/index.php.

American Academy of Child and Adolescent Psychiatry Staff. (2008). Practice parameter for telepsychiatry with children and adolescents.

American Medical Informatics Association. (1998). Guidelines for the clinical use of electronic mail with patients.

American Mental Health Counselors Association. (2010). Principles for AMHCA code of ethics, Section IB(6), technology assisted counseling.

American Telemedicine Association. (2009). Evidence-based practice for telemental health.

American Telemedicine Association. (2009). Practice guidelines for videoconferencing-based telemental health.

Canadian Psychological Association. (2006). Draft Ethical guidelines for psychologists providing psychological services via electronic media.

National Board for Certified Counselors, Inc. (2007). The practice of Internet counseling.

Ohio Psychological Association. (2010). Telepsychology guidelines, revised.

Chapter 6

COMPETENCE AND THE HUMAN THERAPIST

When patients come to us for help, they trust us to be competent. Ethical practice hinges on competence. Society holds us accountable for competence through courts and licensing boards.

Cynthia Belar (2009; see also Fouad et al., 2009; Kaslow et al., 2009) discusses our ethical responsibility to train competent psychologists and to maintain our own competence as our "social contract." She emphasizes that a central question for our training programs

> is whether we are producing what we say we are producing—a psychologist competent for entry to practice. This question comes from prospective students, prospective employers, and the public. Indeed our social contract with the public as an independent profession requires that we self-regulate in these matters. (p. S63)

Of course, patients may hold unrealistic, almost magical expectations. Some hope that we can always act without error, guarantee results, and meet all needs. Unfortunately, some clinicians suffer from such delusions and seem to encourage these beliefs in their clients.

This chapter is intended to serve as a simple reminder that as therapists, we are all human and imperfect. We all have weaknesses and blind spots along with our strengths and insights. In fact, failures of competence often spring from human vulnerabilities.

The opening chapters of this book rejected views of ethics as rigid rule following and presented an approach in which professional codes, administrative directives, legislative requirements, and other givens mark the beginning of a process of creative questioning and critical thinking. Therapists strive to find what they believe is the most ethical and positive way to respond to a unique patient with unique needs and resources in a unique context.

We carry on this creative questioning and critical thinking as fallible human beings, vulnerable to fatigue, discouragement, frustration, anger, fear, and feeling overwhelmed. Our work depends on not just intellectual competence (knowing about and knowing how) but also what might be called *emotional competence for therapy* (Pope & Brown, 1996).

COMPETENCE AS AN ETHICAL AND LEGAL RESPONSIBILITY

Competence is hard to define. Licensing boards and civil courts sometimes specify defining criteria for areas of practice. More often, however, they require only that in whatever area of therapy and counseling the clinician is practicing, he or she should possess demonstrable competence. Demonstrable competence requires clinicians to produce evidence of the competence. Generally this evidence comes from formal education, professional training, and carefully supervised experience, followed by continuing education.

A competence requirement often appears in ethical, legal, and professional standards. Here are some examples:

- Article 8 (Rules of Professional Conduct), Section 1396, of California Title 16 declares: "The psychologist shall not function outside his or her particular field or fields of competence as established by his or her education, training and experience."
- Section 1.6 of the *Specialty Guidelines for the Delivery of Services by Clinical Psychologists* (American Psychological Association [APA], 1981, p. 7) states: "Clinical psychologists limit their practice to their demonstrated areas of professional competence."
- Ethical Standard 2.01a of the APA's "Ethical Principles of Psychologists and Code of Conduct" (2010) states: "Psychologists provide services, teach, and conduct research with populations and only within the boundaries of their competence, based on their education, training, supervised experience, or appropriate professional experience."
- The "Canadian Code of Ethics for Psychologists" (Canadian Psychological Association [CPA], 2000, p. 16) Standard II.6 states that in adhering to the Principle of Responsible Caring, psychologists would "offer or carry out (without supervision) only those activities for which they have established their competence to carry them out to the benefit of others."

The ethical requirement of competence recognizes that the therapist's power and influence (see Chapter 4) should not be handled in a careless, ignorant, thoughtless manner. The complex, hard-to-define nature of therapy tends to obscure why this requirement makes sense. It becomes more vivid by analogy to other fields. A physician who is an internist or general practitioner may do excellent work, but would any of us want that physician to perform coronary surgery or neurosurgery on us if he or she does not have adequate education, training, and supervised experience in these forms of surgery? A skilled professor of linguistics may have a solid grasp of a variety of Indo-European languages and dialects but be completely unable to translate a Swahili text.

COMPETENCE AND CONFLICT

Pulled by patients holding exaggerated beliefs about our abilities and pushed by our own impulse to step in and help, sometimes we can find it hard to admit that we lack the competence needed in a particular situation. And it can get harder if we fear disappointing or alienating a valued referral source or if we desperately need new clients to cover office overhead. Managed care can make it hard to turn away a client assigned to us. Nevertheless, extensive education, training, and supervised experience in working with adults do not qualify us to work with children, solid competence in providing individual therapy does not qualify us to lead a therapy group, and expertise in working with people who are profoundly depressed does not qualify us to work with people who have developmental disabilities.

At times, complex situations require great care to determine how to respond most effectively and ethically to a client's needs while staying within our areas of competence.

For example, a counselor begins working with a client on issues related to depression, an area in which the counselor has had considerable education, training, and supervised experience. Much later the therapeutic journey leads into a problem area—bulimia—for which the counselor has no competence.

As another example, a client starts counseling to deal with what seem like moderately severe difficulties concentrating at work. Soon it becomes apparent that the client suffers from agoraphobia. Can the counselor ethically assume that the course on anxieties and phobias that she took 10 years ago in graduate school makes her competent? The counselor must decide whether she has the time, energy, and commitment to gain competence through continuing education, study, or consultation (APA, 2010) to provide the most up-to-date treatment for agoraphobia or whether she needs to refer the client to someone who is a specialist or at least competent to work with someone suffering from agoraphobia.

Clinicians who work in isolated or small communities often face this dilemma when they encounter unfamiliar problems. These practitioners face special challenges in fulfilling the ethical requirement of competence. They often take workshops and consult long distance with experts to make sure that their clients receive competent care.

Despite the clear ethical and legal mandates to practice only with competence, some of us suffer lapses. A national survey of psychologists, for example, found that almost one-fourth of the respondents indicated that they had practiced outside their area of competence either rarely or occasionally (Pope, Tabachnick, & Keith-Spiegel, 1987).

INTELLECTUAL COMPETENCE: KNOWING ABOUT AND KNOWING HOW

Intellectual competence involves "knowing about." In our graduate training, internships, supervised experience, continuing education, and other contexts, we learn about the empirical research, theories, interventions, and other topics that we need to do our work. We learn to question the information and evaluate its validity and relevance for different situations and populations. We learn to create and test hypotheses about assessment and interventions. We find ways to stay abreast of the latest therapy effectiveness research.

Part of intellectual competence is learning which clinical approaches, strategies, or techniques show evidence or promise of effectiveness. If clinical methods are to avoid charlatanism, hucksterism, and well-meaning ineffectiveness, they must work (at least some of the time). The practitioner's supposed competence means little if his or her methods lack competence. In his provocative article "The Scientific Basis of Psychotherapeutic Practice: A Question of Values and Ethics," Jerry Singer (1980) emphasized the importance of clinicians remaining knowledgeable concerning the emerging research basis of the methods they use.

Intellectual competence also means learning what approaches have been shown to be invalid or perhaps even harmful. George Stricker (1992) wrote:

> Although it may not be unethical to practice in the absence of knowledge, it is unethical to practice in the face of knowledge. We all must labor with the absence of affirmative data, but there is no excuse for ignoring contradictory data. (p. 544)

Intellectual competence is not frozen in time. David Barlow has shown how quickly well-designed research can change our views of which interventions are effective, worthless, or even detrimental. "Stunning developments in health care have occurred during the last several years. Widely accepted health-care strategies have been brought into question by research evidence as not only lacking benefit but also, perhaps, as inducing harm" (Barlow, 2004, p. 869; see also 2005a, 2005b, & 2010; Huppert, Fabbro, & Barlow, 2006; McHugh, Murray, & Barlow, 2009).

Intellectual competence also means recognizing what we do not know. We may know about depression in adults but not about depression in kids. We may be familiar with the culture of one Asian population but not others. We may understand the degree to which the Minnesota Multiphasic Personality Inventory—2 is useful in assessing malingering but not whether it is useful in assessing leadership abilities.

Intellectual competence also involves knowing how to do certain clinical tasks. We achieve this aspect of competence through carefully supervised experience. Knowing how to do therapy is not something we can learn solely from reading a book or sitting in a classroom. The APA Ethics Code Standard 2.01c (APA, 2010) encourages properly trained psychologists planning to provide services new to them to achieve competence in those new services through relevant education, training, supervised experience, consultation, or study. Both the APA Ethics Code (Standard 2.03) and the CPA's Ethics Code (Standards IV.3 and IV.4) recognize that knowledge becomes obsolete and that psychologists don't stop developing and maintaining competence when they become licensed.

EMOTIONAL COMPETENCE FOR THERAPY: KNOWING YOURSELF

Emotional competence for therapy, as described by Pope and Brown (1996), reflects our awareness and respect for ourselves as unique, fallible human beings. It includes self-knowledge, self-acceptance, and self-monitoring. We must know our own emotional strengths and weaknesses, our needs and resources, our abilities and limits for doing clinical work.

Therapy often provides the occasion for strong emotional reactions for both therapist and client. Some kinds of work may place exceptional emotional demands. For example, Pope and Garcia-Peltoniemi (1991) discussed the various emotional responses of many therapists who work with people who survive torture.

To the degree that we are unprepared or unable to experience the emotional stresses and strains of therapy, our well-intentioned efforts may prove unhelpful and perhaps even harmful.

Table 6.1 presents research findings about intense emotions experienced in therapy. The numbers indicate the percentage of therapists in each study who reported at least one instance of each behavior. Readers who have had experience as therapists or patients may wish to compare their own experience to these findings.

Therapists, of course, bring something to the work they do. Each of us has a unique personal history. Table 6.2 presents national survey results showing therapists' self-reports of their experiences of various kinds of abuse during childhood, adolescence, and adulthood (Pope & Feldman-Summers, 1992). These results suggest that almost one-third of male therapists and over two-thirds of female therapists experience at least one of these forms of abuse over their lifetimes.

Table 6.1. Intense Emotion and Other Reactions in Therapy (in percentages).

Behavior	Study 1[a]	Study 2[b]	Study 3[c]
Crying in the presence of a client	56.5		
Telling a client that you are angry at him or her	89.7	77.9	
Raising your voice at a client because you are angry at him or her			57.2
Having fantasies that reflect your anger at a client			63.4
Feeling hatred toward a client			31.2
Telling clients of your disappointment in them	51.9		
Feeling afraid that a client may commit suicide			97.2
Feeling afraid that a client may need clinical resources that are unavailable			86.0
Feeling afraid because a client's condition gets suddenly or seriously worse			90.9
Feeling afraid that your colleagues may be critical of your work with a client			88.1
Feeling afraid that a client may file a formal complaint against you			66.0
Using self-disclosure as a therapy technique	93.3		
Lying on top of or underneath a client			0.4
Cradling or otherwise holding a client in your lap		8.8	
Telling a sexual fantasy to a client			6.0
Engaging in sexual fantasy about a client	71.8		
Feeling sexually attracted to a client	89.5		87.3
A client tells you that he or she is sexually attracted to you			73.3
Feeling sexually aroused while in the presence of a client			57.9
A client seems to become sexually aroused in your presence		48.4	
A client seems to have an orgasm in your presence			3.2

[a]A national survey of 1,000 psychologists with a 46% return rate.
[b]A national survey of 4,800 psychologists, psychiatrists, and social workers with a 49% return rate.
[c]A national survey of 600 psychologists with a 48% return rate.

Source: Study 1 adapted from "Ethics of Practice: The Beliefs and Behaviors of Psychologists as Therapists," by K. S. Pope, B. G. Tabachnick, and P. Keith-Spiegel, 1987, *American Psychologist, 42,* pp. 993–1006. Study 2 adapted from "Dual Relationships between Therapist and Client: A National Study of Psychologists, Psychiatrists, and Social Workers," by D. S. Borys and K. S. Pope, 1989, *Professional Psychology: Research and Practice, 20,* pp. 283–293. Study 3 is adapted from. "Therapists' Anger, Hate, Fear, and Sexual Feelings: National Survey of Therapists' Responses, Client Characteristics, Critical Events, Formal Complaints, and Training," by K. S. Pope and G. B. Tabachnick, 1993, *Professional Psychology: Research and Practice, 24,* pp.142–152. Copyright 1987, 1993, by the American Psychological Association. Adapted with permission.

Table 6.2. Percentages of Male and Female Therapists Reporting Having Been Abused.

Type of Abuse	Men	Women
Abuse during childhood or adolescence		
Sexual abuse by relative	5.84	21.05
Sexual abuse by teacher	0.73	1.96
Sexual abuse by physician	0.0	1.96
Sexual abuse by therapist	0.0	0.0
Sexual abuse by nonrelative (other than those previously listed)	9.49	16.34
Nonsexual physical abuse	13.14	9.15
At least one of the above	26.28	39.22
Abuse during adulthood		
Sexual harassment	1.46	37.91
Attempted rape	0.73	13.07
Acquaintance rape	0.0	6.54
Stranger rape	0.73	1.31
Nonsexual physical abuse by a spouse or partner	6.57	12.42
Nonsexual physical abuse by an acquaintance	0.0	2.61
Nonsexual physical abuse by a stranger	4.38	7.19
Sexual involvement with a therapist	2.19	4.58
Sexual involvement with a physician	0.0	1.96
At least one of the above	13.87	56.86
Abuse during childhood, adolescence, or adulthood	32.85	69.93

Source: From "National Survey of Psychologists' Sexual and Physical Abuse History and Their Evaluation of Training and Competence in These Areas," by K. S. Pope and S. Feldman-Summers, 1992, *Professional Psychology: Research and Practice, 23*, pp. 353–361. Copyright 1992 by the American Psychological Association. Adapted with permission.

Such experiences can affect emotional competence. It is important not to assume a one-size-fits-all theory about how any particular form of abuse (or any other experience) may affect an individual therapist. No research supports the notion that all those who have a history of abuse are more competent or less competent as therapists, or that those who have no history of abuse are more or less competent as therapists. Each instance must be evaluated on an individual basis, with the full range of available information and without stereotypes. What is important is for us to be aware of how such events affect us and whether they affect our emotional competence.

Ethical responsibility requires continuous awareness to prevent compromised performance, especially during difficult or challenging periods. Chapter 7 discusses common consequences when the therapist is distressed, drained, or demoralized. These common consequences include disrespecting clients; disrespecting work; making more mistakes; lacking energy; using work to block out unhappiness, pain, and discontent; and losing interest.

Emotional competence includes the process of constant questioning of the self: Do the demands of the work or other factors suggest that the therapist needs therapy in order to maintain or restore emotional competence? For many of us, creating self-care strategies that fit us as unique individuals and that sustain, replenish, and give meaning are an essential part of our work to maintain competence (see Chapter 7), particularly to maintain "emotional competence for therapy" (Pope & Brown, 1996; Pope, Sonne, & Greene, 2006).

The psychology profession now acknowledges the ethical aspects of self-care. General Principle A, Beneficence and Nonmaleficence, and Standard 2.06 of the APA Ethics Code (APA, 2010) encourage psychologists to be aware of the possible effects of their own physical and mental health on their ability to help those with whom they work. The Canadian Code of Ethics for Psychologists, Standard II.11 (CPA, 2000), states that psychologists "seek appropriate help and/or discontinue scientific or professional activity for an appropriate period of time, if a physical or psychological condition reduces their ability to benefit and not harm others." Standard II.12 states that psychologists "engage in self-care activities that help to avoid conditions (e.g., burnout, addictions) that could result in impaired judgment and interfere with their ability to benefit and not harm others."

The National Association of Social Workers (2008) and the American Counseling Association (2005) are among the other major mental health professions that emphasize the importance of self-care to prevent impairment and ensure competence in their ethics codes.

Table 6.3 presents the results of a national study of therapists as therapy patients (Pope & Tabachnick, 1994). Eighty-four percent of the therapists in this study reported that they had been in personal therapy. Only 2 respondents indicated that the therapy was not helpful, but 22% reported that their own therapy included what they believed to be harmful aspects (regardless of whether it also included positive aspects).

This research suggests that most therapists experience, at least once, intense emotional distress. For example, 61% reported experiencing clinical depression, 29% reported suicidal feelings, and 3.5% reported attempting suicide. About 4% reported having been hospitalized. Readers may wish to consider their own experiences in the light of these findings.

Emotional competence in therapy is no less important than intellectual competence, and it is for that reason that we have included, beginning with

Table 6.3. Therapists' Experiences as Therapy Patients.

Item	Never	Once	Rarely	Sometimes	Often
In your own personal therapy, how often (if at all) did your therapist (N = 400):					
Cradle or hold you in a nonsexual way	73.2	2.7	8.0	8.8	6.0
Touch you in a sexual way	93.7	2.5	1.8	0.3	1.0
Talk about sexual issues in a way that you believe to be inappropriate	91.2	2.7	3.2	0.5	1.3
Seem to be sexually attracted to you	84.5	6.2	3.5	3.0	1.5
Disclose that he or she was sexually attracted to you	92.2	3.7	1.0	1.3	0.8
Seem to be sexually aroused in your presence	91.2	3.7	2.2	0.8	1.3
Express anger at you	60.7	14.3	16.8	5.7	1.8
Express disappointment in you	67.0	11.3	14.8	4.7	1.3
Give you encouragement and support	2.5	0.8	6.2	21.8	67.5
Tell you that he or she cared about you	33.7	6.7	19.5	21.8	16.3
Make what you consider to be a clinical or therapeutic error	19.8	18.0	36.2	19.0	5.5
Pressure you to talk about something you didn't want to talk about	57.5	7.5	21.3	8.8	4.0
Use humor in an appropriate way	76.7	8.8	10.0	2.2	1.5
Use humor in an inappropriate way	5.2	2.5	12.5	35.0	43.5
Act in a rude or insensitive manner toward you	68.7	13.0	12.0	4.0	1.5
Violate your rights to confidentiality	89.7	4.5	2.7	1.3	1.8
Violate your rights to informed consent	93.2	3.2	1.3	0.3	0.3
Use hospitalization as part of your treatment	96.2	1.8	0.5	0.5	1.0

Table 6.3.   (continued)

Item	Never	Once	Rarely	Sometimes	Often
In your own personal therapy, how often (if at all) did your therapist (N = 400):					
Feel sexually attracted to your therapist	63.0	8.0	14.0	7.5	6.5
Tell your therapist that you were sexually attracted to him or her	81.5	6.2	5.5	3.0	2.7
Have sexual fantasies about your therapist	65.5	8.0	12.8	7.0	5.2
Feel angry at your therapist	13.3	9.5	32.7	28.5	15.0
Feel that your therapist did not care about you	49.5	13.0	19.0	12.3	5.5
Feel suicidal	70.0	8.5	9.5	8.3	3.0
Make a suicide attempt	95.5	2.5	1.0	0.0	0.0
Feel what you would characterize as clinical depression	38.5	15.8	16.0	16.5	12.5

Note: Rarely = two to four times; sometimes = five to ten times; often = over ten times.

Source: From "Therapists as Patients: A National Survey of Psychologists' Experiences, Problems, and Beliefs," by K. S. Pope and B. G. Tabachnik, 1994, *Professional Psychology: Research and Practice, 25,* pp. 247–258.

Chapter 13, specific clinical scenarios at the end of each chapter. These scenarios describe hypothetical situations that this book's readers might encounter. Each is followed by a handful of questions designed to provide practice in the processes of the critical thinking explored in detail in Chapter 3. The first question in each sequence is a variant of "What do you feel?" An honest recognition of the emotional response to clinical situations is an important aspect of emotional competence.

To the extent that these scenarios and questions form the basis of class or group discussion in graduate school courses, internships, in-service training, continuing education workshops, or other group settings, their value may be in direct proportion to the class's or group's ability to establish a genuinely safe environment in which participants are free to disclose responses that may be politically incorrect or "psychologically incorrect" (Pope et al., 2006) or otherwise at odds with group norms or with what some might consider the "right" response. Only if participants are able to speak honestly with each other about responses that they might be reluctant to speak aloud in other settings and to discuss these responses with mutual respect will the task of confronting these questions likely prove helpful in developing emotional competence (Pope et al., 2006).

Learning to discuss these sensitive topics and our personal responses with others is important not only in developing our own emotional competence but also in developing resources for maintaining our competence throughout our careers (see Pope et al., 2006, for a more thorough discussion of understanding taboos that hurt therapists and clients). Our colleagues constitute a tremendous resource for helping us to avoid or correct mistakes, identify stress or personal dilemmas that threaten to become overwhelming, and provide fresh ideas, new perspectives, and second and third opinions. A national survey of psychologists, in fact, found that therapists rated informal networks of colleagues as the most effective resource for prompting effective, appropriate, and ethical practice (Pope, Tabachnick, & Keith-Spiegel, 1987). Informal networks were seen as more valuable in promoting ethical practice than laws, ethics committees, research, continuing education programs, or formal ethical principles. Our colleagues can help sustain us, replenish us, enrich our lives, and play an important role in our self-care, the focus of the next chapter.

Chapter 7

CREATING STRATEGIES FOR SELF-CARE

The theme of personal responsibility runs through this book. We cannot escape responsibility for what we choose to say and do or for those times we choose to remain silent and do nothing. We cannot hand over responsibility for our actions or failure to act to an ethics code, our colleagues, our government, our employer, an insurance company, a managed care organization, a professional association, or any other source outside ourselves. Ethical decision making is an active process that involves increasing awareness and constant questioning. Few of us can engage in this process effectively if we are personally drained, overwhelmed, or demoralized. Self-care is crucial.

We recommend creating strategies for self-care as early as possible in your education, training, and practice. Neglecting self-care early on can drain the enthusiasm, joy, resilience, and meaning out of a career. It can hurt our ability to practice ethically. It can sink us in discouragement, compassion fatigue, and burnout.

PAYING ATTENTION TO THE SELF

Psychotherapy is demanding work. It can leave us physically and emotionally drained. Even what we have to do when we are not doing psychotherapy—writing chart notes, requesting authorizations from managed care companies, billing insurance companies, returning phone calls between sessions, sending a second bill to insurance companies after receiving notification that they never received the first bill we sent, filling out disability claim forms, sitting on hold while waiting to ask the insurance company why it is now saying that we used the wrong code on the second bill we sent when that is exactly the code it told us to use when we called before sending in the first bill, and trying to find time in our schedule to consult about a suicidal patient who does not seem to be responding to therapy—can run us ragged.

In the midst of these demands, paying attention to the self is crucial. An occupational hazard that trips up too many of us is failing to stop and pay attention when we become too exhausted, too discouraged, too frustrated, too sad, too angry, too disillusioned, or too cynical. We try to plow ahead, pushing aside the awareness that we are hurting. Instead of taking steps to acknowledge the problem and do something about it, we try to ignore it. Or explain it away. Or assume there is nothing we can do.

Good strategies for self-care include reminders to stop and ask ourselves if we are hurting and, if we are, to ask ourselves why and what we can do about it. Actively looking for red flags—common signs that we may not be taking good care of ourselves—can be helpful. The next section discusses a few of these red flags.

WHAT HAPPENS WHEN SELF-CARE IS NEGLECTED

Neglecting self-care can have corrosive consequences for the therapist and the work. Every psychologist is unique in important ways, does work that is unique in important ways, and experiences the effects of neglecting self-care in a personal way. Yet some themes appear often. Each of the following may be a consequence of, intensified by, or a reflection of neglecting self-care, though each, of course, can have other causes.

Disrespecting Clients

When work is overwhelming, therapists may start disrespecting their clients, talking about them in ways that are demeaning and lack fundamental respect. They may complain about how unmotivated, ungrateful, selfish, insensitive, dishonest, lazy, and generally undesirable their clients are. They may grow harsh, judgmental, and rejecting. They may lose empathy, kindness, and connection. They may distance and dehumanize their clients, referring to them only by labels (e.g., "that schizo"). They may tell jokes about their clients and ridicule them in other ways.

Disrespecting Work

Depleted and discouraged through lack of self-care, therapists may trivialize or ridicule their work. They may speak of therapy as a charade, a fraud, or a joke. They may view their work as empty, ineffective, and meaningless. They may repeatedly show up late for sessions, decide to skip some scheduled sessions altogether, or fail to return clients' telephone calls.

Making More Mistakes

Despite our best efforts, we all make mistakes. Acknowledging, accepting responsibility for, and attempting to address the consequences of our mistakes is one of our fundamental responsibilities as therapists. But self-neglect can hurt our ability to attend to work. We may begin making more and more mistakes. We find ourselves scheduling two clients at the same time, forgetting to show up for an appointment, calling a client by the wrong name, misplacing a client's chart, or locking ourselves out of our own office.

Lacking Energy

If we do not take care of ourselves, we can run out of energy and find ourselves without sources of rest and renewal. We wake up tired, barely find the will to drag ourselves out of bed and to work, fight to stay awake during a session, wonder how we will ever make it through the rest of the day, leave work—*finally!*—too exhausted to socialize or do anything fun, and face the prospect of going to bed only to start the grueling routine all over again.

Becoming Anxious and Afraid

If we fail to care for ourselves, we may fall victim to exaggerated fear and anxiety. We begin to feel that we are no longer up to dealing with the uncertainties, challenges, demands, and stresses of practice. What if our referral sources all dry up and our current clients terminate? Did we bungle that last assessment, wind up with the wrong diagnosis, and miss crucial aspects? Did we say the wrong thing when responding to a suicidal crisis, and will that person commit suicide before the next session? What if that agitated client becomes violent during a session? What if someone files a malpractice suit?

Using Work to Block Out Unhappiness, Pain, and Discontent

If our self-care has been neglected and work no longer brings meaning or satisfaction to our lives, one self-defeating response is to try to lose ourselves and our uncomfortable feelings in work—wall-to-wall work. More and more clients, projects, and responsibilities crowd our lives until we lack free time to reflect on our lives, spend time alone apart from work, or face how lost, empty, or miserable we are. Some therapists work long hours and revel in it, finding great joy and fulfillment, but the pattern here is different: Filling the time with work brings little to nourish the self—it only distracts us from an unfulfilling life. Work is only one of the destructive coping strategies (others are food, alcohol, and drugs) that we use to block out what happens when self-care is neglected.

Losing Interest

Neglecting self-care can lead to an empty professional life that no longer brings excitement, joy, growth, meaning, and fulfillment; as a result, we may lose interest in it. We no longer feel committed to the work or connected to our clients. We go numb and try to get by on automatic pilot. We go through the motions, forcing ourselves to do as good a job as we can. Our heart is no longer in it.

MAKING SURE THE STRATEGIES FIT

Goodness of fit is as important in self-care strategies as it is in clothes. Making or buying clothes that fit our friends, or that fit the "average" person, or that match the most popular sizes won't help most of us find clothes that fit well. Using self-care strategies that are lifesavers for our colleagues may make us miserable. What sustains, replenishes, and gives meaning may flow far from the mainstream. Few of us would tell someone who has found happiness, significance, and contentment in choosing a solitary monastic life with vows of silence and poverty, "You know, you really ought to get out and socialize more and find ways to earn some money so that you'll have a nest egg you could rely on. I know you'd feel better about yourself and have a better life! It's worked for me and so many others!"

Listening to ourselves, experimenting, being honest with ourselves about what does and does not work are part of creating self-care strategies that fit us as individuals. Although there is no one-size-fits-all to any self-care strategy, here are a few of the challenging areas that many therapists contend with in making sure that they are taking good care of themselves.

Isolation

Solo practice can isolate us by its very nature. We spend our days in our office, seeing client after client. Especially if we work long hours, we can lose touch with our friends, colleagues, and the world beyond our office. Even during "free" time when no patient is scheduled, there are always charts to update, bills to prepare, work-related telephone calls to make, and so on. Some therapists find it helpful to place strict limits on the time they spend in the office and schedule activities that bring them out of isolation. Creating ways to stay connected to others seems a basic self-care strategy for many therapists.

Monotony

Even when we limit our time with clients to, say, 30 to 35 hours a week, spending so much time seeing clients can be too much for some therapists. Some find work to break up their days and provide variety: teaching a course;

consulting; leading a supervision group; getting active in local, state, regional, or national professional organizations.

Fatigue

How much time do you need between clients: 5, 10, or 15 minutes? How many clients can you see in a row without needing a longer break of at least an hour or more? How many clients can you see in the course of a day without feeling so tired that the quality of your work falls toward the end of the day? Therapists differ greatly in these areas. Some work four consecutive 50-minute sessions with a 10-minute break between each, take an hour off for lunch, and return for another four consecutive sessions without any lapse in enthusiasm or competence. Others can do their best work with no more than five clients each day. Knowing and respecting our personal limits is a key aspect of self-care. Some consider 25 to 30 client-hours a week to be full time because of the additional hours needed to keep clinical records, return telephone calls, and so on.

Part of self-care in this area is learning what workload we can handle well and creating a schedule that matches that workload. The focus must remain on the amount of work that we can do well, not the amount that we feel we should do, or used to be able to do, or that some of our colleagues do. Sometimes the number of hours we can do good work with clients conflicts with the number of hours we believe we must spend with clients in order to pay the bills, develop our practice, or please our employer.

Effective self-care strategies not only influence our patterns of breaks—everything from the breaks we take between sessions to our vacations—but also emphasize activities, attitudes, and approaches that help us recover from fatigue, that replenish and renew us.

The Sedentary Life

Psychological assessment and therapy are usually—not always—done while the client is sitting (or lying down) and the psychologist is sitting, neither of them moving around much. For many therapists, self-care includes creating opportunities during the day for moving, stretching, and physical exercise. Physical exercise is a major self-care strategy for many therapists, not only for its physical benefits and the break it provides from work, but also for its psychological benefits (see, e.g., Hays, 2002).

The Dispirited Life

If a psychology practice does not provide enough physical movement and exercise for many therapists, it may also fail for many to nurture the life of the spirit adequately. Setting aside time and opportunity for meditation, prayer, and other spiritual or religious practices can be an important aspect of self-care for some therapists. Some find that such diverse activities as reading or writing poetry, hiking through the woods, playing or listening to music, sitting on a riverbank, acting in or viewing a play, or watching a sunset helps nourish their spiritual lives.

The Unsupported Life

Graduate schools and internships place us in a network of professors, supervisors, administrators, and other students. Facing a challenge, we can talk it over with teachers and classmates. Our clinical work is closely monitored, and we receive positive and negative feedback, ideas, suggestions, and guidance. When we start an independent practice or begin work in an agency that tends to be unsupportive and isolating, the responsibility to create that network of support falls to us. What are some important components of a support network?

Supervision, Consultation, and Additional Training

Identify or create resources for talking over your work, expanding your knowledge and skills, and continuing to grow as a psychologist. Is there someone you would like to hire to provide you with supervision or consultation? (Understanding how *supervision* and *consultation* are defined under state laws and regulations is crucial. They tend to differ in such areas as who is primarily responsible for clinical care and decision making.) Would you like to create a peer-consultation group that meets on a regular basis? What continuing education courses, workshops, and other activities would you find helpful in updating your knowledge, improving your skills, and expanding your areas of competence? Consider what other sources of support you'll need to practice effectively.

Accountant

We recommend that you find and work with an accountant you trust, reviewing your business plans, looking at your current financial resources, and advising you on tax matters. The accountant will be able to discuss issues such as the pros and cons of incorporation, what expenses will be deductible, procedures for keeping records and receipts for tax purposes, and comparing the relative financial merits of a home office compared to a separate office.

Billing/Bookkeeper

Many practitioners do their own billing and bookkeeping. If you choose this route, you might look into software programs that can help with these tasks. Other clinicians prefer not to take on this additional administrative task. Instead, they hire an individual or company to do their bookkeeping and billing. Some communities have services that specialize in this area for psychotherapists or for health-care providers more generally. Check with colleagues in your community for recommendations.

Psychopharmacology Resources
Unless you are able to prescribe medications, find someone skilled in psychopharmacology who will work collaboratively with you and your patients. Some patients, of course, do not need psychotropic medications, and others may come to you already taking medications prescribed by someone else. You may wish to refer some patients to a psychopharmacologist with prescription authority for an evaluation to see if medications might be helpful.

Emergency and Hospitalization Resources
What are the emergency, inpatient, day treatment, and similar mental health services available in your community? How much do they cost, and what are their admission criteria? Visit them, and introduce yourself to the staff and administration. Find out about their policies and procedures and whether you are eligible for staff privileges. If one of your clients needs hospitalization or other crisis services, you will be familiar with available options and the necessary steps for each. Some clinicians include a telephone number for emergency services on their answering machine's outgoing message; others include it on their informed consent form.

Mandatory and Discretionary Reporting Resources
Find the contact information for the agencies to which you would file mandatory or discretionary reports of such matters as suspected child abuse or elder abuse. There may be times when you are unsure of whether you are obligated to file a report. One source of consultation you can draw on at such times is the agency to which you would file the report. You can call and, without disclosing any identifying information about the actual people involved, provide the agency with a hypothetical situation and ask if such a fact pattern falls under the duty to report. Be sure to document that consultation as one of the steps you took to decide whether to report. You may also call your attorney or your professional liability carrier for guidance.

Attorney
We recommend finding an attorney experienced in mental health issues in your jurisdiction as early as possible in your career. He or she can review your forms, policies, and procedures; answer your questions about legal requirements and pitfalls; and be a telephone call away if you are in the midst of responding to an urgent situation and need legal advice.

Personal Relationships

Good relationships can be key to our sense of well-being. An absence of good friends (and the time to spend with them) or spending too much time in toxic relationships can lead to burnout. Feminist Jean Baker Miller (1988, 1991) described the qualities and dynamics of relationships that make us feel understood, valued, and more alive. Judy Jordon (1997) emphasized the importance of a sense of connection. "Ruptures" in our important personal or work relationships can be devastating. Seymour Sarason (1974) looked at the social environment that we find or create for ourselves and emphasized the "psychological sense of community," that feeling that one is part of a larger dependable and stable structure" (p. 157; see also Clark, Murdock, & Koetting, 2009; Love, 2007; Obst & White, 2007).

Neglected Health

Moving from a graduate school environment that often includes a student health service and health coverage to suddenly being out on our own in independent practice or into organizational employment that offers little or no health coverage makes it easy to neglect our health and medical needs. It becomes our responsibility to find affordable health-care coverage well matched to our individual needs and a competent physician whom we trust. Medical insurance can be obtained from a variety of sources, including professional organizations; self-employment associations, such as the National Association for the Self-Employed; and some local associations, such as the local chamber of commerce. Colleagues and local insurance brokers may be good sources of information.

The Stressed or Distressed Life

Therapists may experience periods of extreme unhappiness and distress. Some of the themes in Chapter 5 are worth reviewing here. In one national study of therapists' accounts of their own experiences as therapy patients (Pope & Tabachnick, 1994), of the 84% of the therapists who had been in therapy, 61% reported experiencing at least one episode of what they termed clinical depression, 29% reported having felt suicidal, and 4% reported having attempted suicide.

Practice itself may be stressful. In another national study of practicing therapists (Pope & Tabachnick, 1993), 97% reported fearing that a client would commit suicide, 91% reported fearing that a client would get worse, 89% reported fearing that client would attack a third party, 88% reported fearing that colleagues would be critical of their work with a patient, 86% reported fearing that a client would need clinical resources that are unavailable, 83% reported fearing being attacked by a patient, and 18% reported having been attacked by a patient. Over half reported having been so afraid about a client that it affected their eating, sleeping, or concentration. About 12% reported that a client had filed a formal complaint (e.g., about malpractice or licensing) against them. Over 3% had obtained a weapon to protect themselves from a patient.

Anger was another major theme of the study. For example, 83% reported anger at a client because of unpaid bills, 81% reported anger at a client who was verbally abusive at them, and 46% reported having become so angry at a patient that they did something that they later regretted.

Effective self-care strategies take realistic account of both how stressful doing therapy can be and how distressed we can become. What resources can we develop for coping with the stresses of our work? How can we address our own distress, seek professional help if we need it, and become aware if we reach a point of being too distressed or impaired to work effectively?

THE NEED FOR CHANGE

Self-care strategies that support, strengthen, deepen, replenish, and enliven may, less than a year later, become a senseless obligation, distraction, and waste of time. Therapists who focus on the subtle, sweeping, and profound changes in their clients' lives can overlook changes in their own lives and how these changes can affect self-care needs and strategies. Effective self-care includes paying attention to the ways in which our needs for self-care can change over time, calling us to create new strategies.

Chapter 8

CREATING A PROFESSIONAL WILL

Only therapists who are invulnerable and immortal don't need to bother preparing a professional will.

The theme of therapists as vulnerable human beings runs throughout this book. We all share many vulnerabilities. We can't wall ourselves off from the unexpected. At any time a drunk driver, stroke, mugger, heart attack, fire, plane crash, and countless other unwelcome surprises can strike us down. It is an ethic of both personal and professional responsibility to take our mortality and vulnerability into account in our planning.

A professional will is a plan for what happens if we die suddenly or become incapacitated without warning. It helps those whom we designate to respond promptly and effectively to our clients' needs and to the unfinished business of our practice. It gives others the basic information and guidance that can be so hard to come by at a time of shock and mourning.

We recommend preparing a professional will as early as possible. We cannot schedule our personal misfortunes or postpone accidents so that they happen only late in our careers. We must prepare for the possibility that something can happen to us—robbing us of our ability to function—at any time, without warning.

No standardized professional will works well with every therapist or situation. The next sections provide a set of steps to help you create your own professional will so that it fits your needs, resources, setting, and practice.

WHO TAKES CHARGE?

Who would respond effectively in the event that you suddenly die or are incapacitated? Who can make necessary arrangements in a time of great stress; take care of matters sensitively, efficiently, and effectively; and make sure nothing important is overlooked? Who is the best person to talk to your clients?

A good professional will clearly designates a qualified person to serve as the executor and authorizes that individual to carry out the will's tasks.

How can the designee be contacted in the event of your sudden death or incapacitation? What are the person's telephone, fax, and pager numbers? What are the person's office and e-mail addresses? Are others likely to know where the person is if he or she proves hard to reach?

WHO SERVES AS BACKUP?

Life tends to be full of surprises and sometimes hesitates to cooperate with our plans. At the time he or she needs to step in and take charge, the person you designated to serve as executor may be overseas at a conference or on vacation, may be attending to a family emergency, or may be seriously ill or otherwise unavailable. It is important to have a second and third designee, each ready to step in if necessary.

COORDINATED PLANNING

Coordinated planning can make for a much more useful professional will and make it easier for the executor to carry it out. You can meet with your primary designee and both backups to outline what you want done, what needs to be done, and what information the designee will need. One person may think of something that the others have overlooked, and what may seem to the therapist writing the will to "go without saying" ("You all know that bookshelf where I keep my appointment book, don't you?") may need to be explained.

If designees don't understand where something essential is, you can show them. You can introduce them to the people they will need to work with (e.g., your secretary, the executor of your personal will, your accountant, your attorney, your office landlord). They can exchange contact information with each other. When the time comes for the designee to take charge, he or she will have detailed instructions and information in your professional will and will also know the rationale for each step (having been involved in the planning process), will know the key people to work with, and will know where the records and other materials are.

YOUR OFFICE, ITS KEY, AND ITS SECURITY

In addition to providing your office address, it is helpful to be as specific as possible about where each key to your office can be found—for example, "There are four copies of the key to my office. One is on the key ring that I always carry with me. It is the key with the blue plastic on it. My partner, whose contact information is …, also has a key to the office. My secretary, whose contact information is … has a key. The building manager, who can be contacted in an emergency at … has a key."

There may be separate keys for each of the consulting room doors, the storage room, the filing cabinets, the desks, the computer, and the door to the building itself. It is easy to overlook a key that someone will find essential to carry out the responsibilities of your professional will.

Some office security systems require a code. Be sure to specify the necessary codes and instructions and where the system is located.

YOUR SCHEDULE

Where is your schedule kept: in a daily planner you keep with you, an appointment book at the office, on your computer or personal digital assistant? Once the record of your scheduled appointments is located, is additional information needed to access it? For example, if you keep your schedule on your computer, what passwords are used to log on and access the schedule, where on the drive is the schedule kept, what are the names of the relevant files, and is there a backup somewhere if the copy on your computer has become corrupted or if the computer itself is unavailable (e.g., destroyed in an office fire or earthquake or stolen)?

CLIENT RECORDS AND CONTACT INFORMATION

The executor may need to contact your clients. A professional will must include clear instructions about how to locate and access client records and contact information. The ability to locate treatment records promptly may become exceptionally important because the sudden death of a therapist may trigger a crisis for some clients. The professional will should also designate whether the executor or someone else will maintain the client records of the incapacitated or deceased therapist. This information can be announced in the local newspapers and/or filed with the state psychology licensing board and state psychological association, or both.

AVENUES OF COMMUNICATION FOR CLIENTS AND COLLEAGUES

How do clients and colleagues contact you: answering machine, e-mail, other methods? Clearly describe each and how the person carrying out your professional will can access the messages. What codes are used to retrieve messages from your answering machine? What are the names of any relevant e-mail accounts along with the user name, password, server address for receiving and sending mail, and so on?

INFORMED CONSENT

Clients have a right to give or withhold informed consent for release of information. Documentation of consent for providing the executor with client contact information and access to client charts can be kept with the client charts and a note of it made in the professional will. One option is to include the name(s) of the executor in the original description of services that patients read and sign as part of informed consent.

CLIENT NOTIFICATION

Therapists may choose one or more methods to notify clients of a therapist's incapacitation or death, such as calling each client, placing a notice in the local newspaper, changing the outgoing message on the answering machine to include the announcement, changing the answering machine message to ask clients to call the clinician who is implementing the deceased therapist's professional will, and sending letters. It is worth spending some time considering the potential impact of each method and considering it in terms of the Golden Rule—Would any of us want to learn of our own therapist's or clinical supervisor's death by reading about it in the newspaper or hearing a recorded announcement on an answering machine?—and of how each of our current and former clients might respond. Are there resources that clients might find helpful in these circumstances (e.g., designated colleagues who will make appointments available to your clients to help them deal with the immediate consequences and, if the clients choose, to locate subsequent therapists)? You will have a good sense of which approaches will work best for your individual practice and the relationship you have with your clients. Some long-term patients may require special consideration.

The notification method must respect each client's right to privacy. Letters and phone messages that are not carefully handled can lead unintentionally to the disclosure to third parties that a person is seeing a therapist. Family members and others may not always respect the privacy of someone's mail and may, perhaps "accidentally," open and read mail that is not addressed to them. A telephone message left on an answering machine sometimes can be heard by those for whom it was not intended. In some cases, such unintentional disclosures can place a client at great risk. The abusive partner, for example, of a client who sought therapy because she is a battered woman may become enraged at finding out, through an intercepted letter or telephone message, that the client has sought help and may react violently, perhaps lethally.

COLLEAGUE NOTIFICATION

What colleagues should be notified immediately? Are you a member of a group practice, or do you share a suite of offices? Are there clinicians who provide consultation or supervision to you on a regular basis or who receive those services from you? Do you co-lead a therapy group or family sessions with anyone? Are there conferences or workshops where you are regularly present? It can be helpful to check the listings in your scheduling book for a few months to make sure that you do not overlook any colleagues who should be listed (along with contact information) in your professional will for immediate notification.

PROFESSIONAL LIABILITY COVERAGE

It is useful to include the name of the company providing professional liability coverage, contact information, the policy number, and instructions for the company to be notified immediately on the therapist's death or incapacitation.

ATTORNEY FOR PROFESSIONAL ISSUES

Many therapists have consulted an attorney for professional issues. The attorney might have reviewed the therapist's office forms (informed consent, release of information, etc.) to ensure that they conform to state legislation and case law requirements. The attorney might have discussed the therapist's policies and procedures, format for keeping records, or particularly troublesome cases that raised puzzling legal questions. The therapist might have sought legal consultation about how to respond to a subpoena or legal representation in a malpractice suit. It is useful to provide contact information for an attorney whom the therapist consults for practice issues.

BILLING RECORDS, PROCEDURES, AND INSTRUCTIONS

The person whom the professional will designates to take charge will need to know where the billing records are, how to access them (e.g., if they are maintained by computer software), who prepares and processes the bills (e.g., a billing service, accountant, or office clerical worker), and how pending charges are to be handled.

Some therapists may wish to forgive part or all of any remaining unpaid bills that were to be paid out of their clients' own pockets. Some may wish to provide a session—at the deceased therapist's expense—for each client, during which the clinician serving as executor of the professional will would work with the client to discuss the situation, assess current needs, and explore options for future therapy. The professional will should include explicit instructions about any such wishes.

EXPENSES

How have the therapist preparing the professional will and the person designated to serve as professional executor decided that the executor will be compensated? Perhaps the easiest arrangement is at the executor's customary hourly rate, but other approaches can be used—for example, a flat fee, a token payment, the executor declining any compensation for rendering this service to a friend, or a contribution to a charity chosen by the executor.

A professional will needs to include clear instructions about how all business-related expenses are to be paid.

YOUR PERSONAL WILL

To avoid unintended problems and conflicts, it is helpful to review both your professional will and your personal will side by side to ensure that they are consistent. If a personal will, for example, directs all assets to be disbursed in a certain way but makes no mention of funds to be used to pay the executor of your professional will, problems can arise. It is useful if each will makes explicit reference to the other.

LEGAL REVIEW

Review of the professional will by an attorney skilled and experienced in mental health law can prevent numerous problems. The executor of the professional will can consult with the attorney about any legal questions arising in the days, weeks, and months after the therapist's death.

The attorney can advise on whether, in the light of state legislation and case law, the professional will is best authenticated simply by the signatures of disinterested witnesses, the seal of a notary, or other means.

COPIES OF THE PROFESSIONAL WILL

Copies of your professional will can be given to those designated as potential executors and to your attorney. Some therapists may consider making special arrangements to ensure the executor gains access to information such as their passwords for retrieving e-mail and answering machine messages only after their death. These arrangements avoid having confidential information in multiple copies of the will distributed to others

REVIEW AND UPDATE

People, practices, situations, and times change. A professional will that is perfectly suited to us when we draw it up may have out-of-date contact information and aspects that do not fit us well at all just a year or two later. It is helpful to review a professional will on a regular basis—say, once a year—and make an immediate update whenever there is a significant change in our circumstances.

Chapter 9

CODES AND COMPLAINTS IN CONTEXT: HISTORICAL, EMPIRICAL, AND ACTUARIAL FOUNDATIONS

A s therapists, we are members of the mental health profession. Exactly what we profess has been subject to debate from the beginning. We have a hard time defining what we do.

The 1949 Boulder Conference tried to define psychotherapy so it could be taught to clinical and counseling psychologists. Carl Rogers, president of the American Psychological Association (APA) in 1947, appointed David Shakow to chair a committee on defining and teaching psychotherapy. The Shakow report, adopted at the 1947 APA convention, resulted in the Boulder Conference two years later.

On August 28, 1949, the recorder for the Boulder task force for defining psychotherapy and setting forth criteria for adequate training provided this

We greatly appreciate the extraordinary help we received from these people, who provided the actuarial data that are key to this chapter and who reviewed early drafts: the APA Ethics Office staff, including Stephen Behnke, executive director, Sonja Wiggins, APA Membership Office; Steve DeMers, executive director, and Janet Pippin, staff, Association of State and Provincial Psychology Boards; Bruce Bennett, CEO, APA Insurance Trust; John Service, executive director, Canadian Psychological Association; and Carole Sinclair, CPA Ethics Committee Chair.

summary: "We have left therapy as an undefined technique which is applied to unspecified problems with a nonpredictable outcome. For this technique we recommend rigorous training" (Lehner, 1952, p. 547).

Since the Boulder Conference, other conferences and various groups have tried to define psychotherapy and the practice of psychology. The "2002 Competencies Conference: Future Directions in Education and Credentialing in Professional Psychology" (Kaslow et al., 2004), for example, identified competencies in professional psychology and discussed effective strategies for teaching and assessing these competencies (Kaslow, 2004; see also Belar, 2009; Fouad et al., 2009; Kaslow et al., 2009). Chapter 6 presents a more detailed discussion of competence.

Forces outside the profession also influence practice. For example, managed care companies can require a diagnosis from a specific manual, can limit or deny assessment and therapy sessions, can require therapists to document that therapy is a matter of medical necessity, can require specific interventions for particular disorders, and can require that outcome be measured using a limited number of criteria defined by the company.

Not surprisingly, these measures—often described as cost cutting—can create conflict between company administrators and therapists (Reed & Eisman, 2006). The requirement that only certain interventions be used for a particular diagnosis highlights a controversy within the profession: Should the definition and practice of psychotherapy be limited to interventions supported by research and, if so, what kind of research? Must the research use random assignment in a double-blind model, be published in peer-reviewed journals, be independently replicated by other researchers, and meet other standards?

The answer to this question will profoundly affect what therapies are seen as legitimate and reimbursable by third parties. Kazdin (2008b; see also Kazdin, 2008a; Duncan, Miller, Wampold, & Hubble, 2010) points out that there are over 550 psychological interventions designed for children and adolescents but that only a relatively small percentage have been researched.

Littell (2010) describes the tensions between the work of therapists and researchers:

> Clinicians and social scientists have distinct imperatives and sensibilities. Therapy requites action and faith in the process, whereas science demands observation and skepticism. Most scientific knowledge is tentative and nomothetic, not directly applicable to individual cases. Experts have stepped into this breach by packaging empirical evidence for use in practice. Sometimes this is little more than a ruse to promote favorite theories and therapies. Yet, wrapped in scientific rhetoric, some authoritative pronouncements have become orthodoxy. (pp. 167–168)

Westen and Bradley (2005) note that

> evidence-based practice is a construct (i.e., an idea, abstraction, or theoretical entity) and thus must be operationalized (i.e., turned into some concrete form that comes to define it). The way it is operationalized is not incidental to whether its net effects turn out to be positive, negative, or mixed. (p. 226; see also Westen, Novotny, & Thompson-Brenner, 2004)

Psychotherapy researchers Crits-Christoph, Wilson, and Hollon (2005) believe that "randomized controlled trials remain the most powerful way to test notions of causal agency" (p. 412). Yet Kazdin (2006), previous editor of the Association for Psychological Science's journal *Current Directions in Psychological Science*, wrote: "Psychotherapy outcome research has been dominated by randomized controlled trials. . . . However, pivotal features of these trials make them not very relevant for clinical practice" (p. 170; see also Goodheart, 2006; Sternberg, 2006).

The APA's (2006) Presidential Task Force on Evidence-Based Practice noted both the limits of clinical hypothesis testing and need for clinical expertise:

> Yet clinical hypothesis testing has its limits, hence the need to integrate clinical expertise with the best available research. Perhaps the central message of this task force report—and one of the most heartening aspects of the process that led to it—is the consensus achieved among a diverse group of scientists, clinicians, and scientist-clinicians from multiple perspectives that EBPP [evidence-based psychology practice] requires an appreciation of the value of multiple sources of scientific evidence. In a given clinical circumstance, psychologists of good faith and good judgment may disagree about how best to weigh different forms of evidence; over time, we presume that systematic and broad empirical inquiry—in the laboratory and in the clinic—will point the way toward best practice in integrating best evidence. What this document [*Report of the APA Presidential Task Force on Evidence-Based Practice*] reflects, however, is a reassertion of what psychologists have known for a century: The scientific method is a way of thinking and observing systematically, and it is the best tool we have for learning about what works for whom. (p. 282)

MECHANISMS OF ACCOUNTABILITY

Difficulties in defining psychotherapy and psychological practice with precision do not free the profession from the basic responsibility of setting forth its ethics. The hallmark of a profession is the recognition that the work its members carry out affects the lives of their clients, sometimes in direct, profound, and immediate ways. The powerful nature of this influence makes the customary rules of the marketplace (often resting on variations of the principle "Let the buyer beware") inadequate (see Chapter 4).

Society asks that the profession set forth a code to which the members of the profession agree to be held accountable. At its heart, this code calls for the professional to protect and promote the welfare of clients and avoid letting the professional's self-interests place the client at risk for harm. In addition to the fundamental code of ethics, there may be codes or statements of the rights of patients (see, e.g., APA, 1997) or of the ethics as applicable in a specific setting, such as managed care organizations (see, e.g., National Academies of Practice, 1997).

Perhaps because society never completely trusts professions to enforce their own standards and perhaps because the professions have demonstrated that they, at least occasionally, are less than effective in governing their own behavior, society has established its own means for making sure that professions meet minimal standards in their work and that those whom professionals serve are protected from incompetent, negligent, and dishonest practitioners.

Four major mechanisms hold therapists and counselors accountable to explicit standards: professional ethics committees, state licensing boards, civil (e.g., malpractice) courts, and criminal courts. Each of these four mechanisms uses different standards, though they may overlap. Behavior may be clearly unethical and yet not form the basis for criminal charges.

In some cases, therapists and counselors may feel that these different standards clash. They may, for example, feel that the law compels them to act in a way that violates the welfare of the client and the clinician's own sense of what is ethical. A national survey of psychologists found that a majority (57%) of the respondents had intentionally violated the law or a similar formal standard because, in their opinion, not to do so would have injured the client or violated some deeper value (Pope & Bajt, 1988). The actions reported by two or more respondents included refusing to report child abuse (21%), illegally divulging confidential information (21%), engaging in sex with a patient (9%), engaging in nonsexual dual relationships (6%), and refusing to make legally required warnings regarding dangerous patients (6%).

That almost 1 out of 10 of the respondents reported engaging in sex with a client (see Chapter 16) using the rationale of patient welfare or deeper moral value highlights the risks, ambiguities, and difficulties of evaluating the degree to which our own individual behavior is ethical.

Pope and Bajt (1988) reviewed the attempts of philosophers and the courts to judge those times when a person decides to go against the law (e.g., engage in civil disobedience). On one hand, for example, the U.S. Supreme Court emphasized that in the United States, no one could be considered higher than the law: "In the fair administration of justice no man can be judge in his own case, however exalted his station, however righteous his motives, and irrespective of his race, color, politics, or religion" (*Walker* v. *City of Birmingham*, 1967, pp. 1219–1220).

On the other hand, courts endorsed Henry David Thoreau's (1849/1960) injunction that if a law "requires you to be the agent of injustice to another, then ... break the law" (p. 242). The California Supreme Court, for example, tacitly condoned violation of the law only when the principles of civil disobedience are followed

> If we were to deny to every person who has engaged in ... nonviolent civil disobedience ... the right to enter a licensed profession, we would deprive the community of the services of many highly qualified persons of the highest moral courage
>   (*Hallinan v. Committee of Bar Examiners of State Bar*, 1966, p. 239)

As Pope and Bajt note, civil disobedience (Gandhi, 1948; King, 1958, 1964; Plato, 1956a,b; Thoreau, 1849/1960; Tolstoy, 1894/1951) is useful in many contexts for resolving this dilemma. The individual breaks a law considered to be unjust and harmful but does so openly, inviting the legal penalty both to demonstrate respect for the system of law and to call society's attention to the supposedly unjust law. Counselors and therapists, however, often find this avenue of openness unavailable because of confidentiality requirements (see Chapter 19).

If we as individuals and a profession are to address the possible conflicts between the law and the welfare of our clients, one of the initial steps is to engage in frequent, open, and honest discussion of the issue. The topic needs open and active discussion in graduate courses, internship programs, case conferences, professional conventions, and informal meetings with colleagues.

Clients may understandably wind up confused about how therapists are held accountable for their actions. They may mistakenly believe that a professional ethics committee can revoke a license or that a licensing board can expel a practitioner from a professional organization like the APA. The next sections describe the four major mechanisms of accountability.

ETHICS COMMITTEES, CODES, AND COMPLAINTS

Professional associations of therapists and counselors are voluntary organizations; membership is not a state or federal requirement for the practice of the profession. A psychologist can, for example, be licensed (by the state) and practice as a psychologist without being a member of the APA or any other association. An association, through its ethics committee, holds its members accountable to the ethical principles it sets forth in the code it has developed. To illustrate how such a code is developed, we will describe how two organizations approached the challenge.

The American Psychological Association, at the end of 2009, had 152,223 members, including 91,588 full members (2,771 fellows; 68,507 members; 7,737 associates; 1,234 Canadians; and 11,339 life status members) and 60,635 affiliates (52,583 students, 4,007 international; 2,528 high school teachers, and 1,517 community college teachers) (S. Wiggins, personal correspondence, January 20, 2010).

The 2009 Annual Report of the Canadian Psychological Association (CPA) cites 6,524 members (4,316 members and fellows, 1,812 students, 236 honorary life member/fellows, and 160 affiliates and retired fellows and members).

American Psychological Association Approach to an Ethics Code

Founded in 1892 and incorporated in 1925, the APA first formed the Committee on Scientific and Professional Ethics in 1938. As complaints were brought to its attention, this committee improvised solutions on a private, informal basis. There was no formal or explicit set of ethical standards, so all of the committee's work was, of necessity, done on the basis of consensus and persuasion.

A year later, the committee was charged with determining whether a formal code of ethics would be useful for the organization. In 1947, it decided that a formal code of ethics would indeed be useful, stating "The present unwritten code is tenuous, elusive, and unsatisfactory" ("A Little Recent History," 1952, p. 425). The board of directors established the Committee on Ethical Standards for Psychology to determine what methods to use in drafting the code. Chaired by Edward Tolman, the committee members were John Flanagan, Edwin Ghiselli, Nicholas Hobbs, Helen Sargent, and Lloyd Yepsen (Hobbs, 1948).

Some members strongly opposed the development of an explicit set of ethical standards, and many of their arguments appeared in *American Psychologist*. Calvin Hall (1952), for example, wrote that any code, no matter how well formulated,

> plays into the hands of crooks. . . . The crooked operator reads the code to see how much he can get away with, and since any code is bound to be filled with ambiguities and omissions, he can rationalize his unethical conduct by pointing to the code and saying, "See, it doesn't tell me I can't do this," or "I can interpret this to mean what I want it to mean." (p. 430)

Hall endorsed accountability, but he believed that it could be enforced without an elaborate code. He recommended that the application form for APA membership contain this statement:

> As a psychologist, I agree to conduct myself professionally according to the common rules of decency, with the understanding that if a jury of my peers decides that I have violated these rules, I may be expelled from the association. (pp. 430–431)

Hall placed most of the responsibility on graduate schools. He recommended that "graduate departments of psychology, who have the power to decide who shall become psychologists, should exercise this power in such a manner as to preclude the necessity for a code of ethics" (p. 431).

The APA Committee on Ethical Standards (APA Committee) determined that because empirical research was a primary method of psychology, the code itself should be based on such research and should draw on the experience of APA members. As Hobbs (1948, p. 84) wrote, the method would produce "a code of ethics truly indigenous to psychology, a code that could be lived." The board of directors accepted this recommendation, and a new committee was appointed to conduct the research and draft the code. Chaired by Nicholas Hobbs, the new committee members were Stuart Cook, Harold Edgerton, Leonard Ferguson, Morris Krugman, Helen Sargent, Donald Super, and Lloyd Yepsen (APA Committee, 1949).

In 1948, all 7,500 members of the APA were sent a letter asking each member "to share his experiences in solving ethical problems by describing the specific circumstances in which someone made a decision that was ethically critical" (APA Committee, 1949, p. 17). The committee received reports of over 1,000 critical incidents. During the next years, the incidents, with their accompanying comments, were carefully analyzed, categorized, and developed into a draft code.

The emerging standards, along with the illustrative critical incidents, were published in *American Psychologist* (APA Committee, 1951a,b,c). The standards were grouped into six major sections:

1. Ethical standards and public responsibility
2. Ethical standards in professional relationships
3. Ethical standards in client relationships
4. Ethical standards in research
5. Ethical standards in writing and publishing
6. Ethical standards in teaching

The draft generated considerable discussion and was revised several times. Finally, in 1952, it was formally adopted as the Ethical Standards of Psychologists, and it was published in 1953.

In 1954, information on the complaints that the committee had handled for the past 12 years (during most of which there had been no formal code of ethics) was published in *American Psychologist* ("Cases and Inquiries," 1954). During this period, the ethical principles most frequently violated were

- Invalid presentation of professional qualifications (cited 44 times).
- Immature and inconsiderate professional relations (23).
- Unprofessional advertisement or announcement (22).
- Unwarranted claims for tests or service offered usually by mail (22).
- Irresponsible public communication (6).

The most recent version of the ethical principles (APA, 2010), the *Ethical Principles of Psychologists and Code of Conduct With the 2010 Amendments*, is the eleventh version. (It is reprinted in Appendix A.) APA published versions of the code in these years: 1953, 1959, 1963, 1968, 1977, 1979, 1981, 1990, and 1992, 2002, and 2010. The 2010 version consists of an introduction, a preamble, five general principles, and specific ethical standards. The preamble and general principles, which include beneficence and nonmaleficence, fidelity and responsibility, integrity, justice, and respect for people's rights and dignity, are aspirational goals to guide psychologists toward the highest ideals of psychology. The specific ethical standards are enforceable rules for conduct.

Canadian Psychological Association's Approach to an Ethics Code

The CPA was organized in 1939 and incorporated under the Canada Corporations Act, Part II, in May 1950. In the mid-twentieth century, Canada was a large country with relatively few psychologists. Because it would have been hard to bring these psychologists together to create an ethics code, "the Canadian Psychological Association ... decided to adopt the 1959 ... APA code for a three-year trial. This was followed by adoptions (with minor wording changes) of the 1963 and 1977 APA revised codes" (Sinclair & Pettifor, 2001, p. i).

Discontent with the APA code and the perception that it was not a good fit for Canadian psychologists led the CPA to create its own code:

> Prior to developing its own code, there was evidence of periodic discontent by CPA members with the APA code. For example, in a 1976 document titled "Alternative Strategies for Revising CPA's Code of Ethics," the statement was made that the 10 APA ethical principles were "clearly designed for the current American social and moral climate and geared to American traditions and law." However, it was not until the 1977 revision of the APA code that the discontent became serious. Of particular concern was the fact that, in response to U.S. court applications of antitrust law to professional activities, the APA had removed some of its restrictions on advertising. Many Canadian psychologists believed such application of antitrust laws ran the risk of changing the nature of the professional relationship from a primarily fiduciary contract to a commercial one.
> *(Sinclair, Simon, & Pettifor, 1996, p. 7)*

To create an ethics code, CPA began by sending out 37 ethical dilemmas (Truscott & Crook, 2004). Psychologists were asked how they would act in these situations and, equally important, to describe their reasoning. The responses yielded four basic ethical principles (CPA, 1986):

1. Respect for the Dignity of Persons
2. Responsible Caring

3. Integrity in Relationships
4. Responsibility to Society

The original CPA ethics code provided not only ethical principles but also a model of ethical decision making (see Chapter 9; see also Sinclair, 1998; Sinclair, Poizner, Gilmour-Barrett, & Randall, 1987). The third edition of the Canadian Code of Ethics for Psychologists was approved by the CPA board of directors at its meeting in June 2000 (CPA, 2000). It comprises a preamble and four ethical principles to be considered and balanced in ethical decision making. Each principle is followed by statements of values that give definition to each principle, and those are followed by a list of standards that illustrate the application of the principles and values to the activities of psychologists (CPA, 2000; the document is reproduced in Appendix B).

Patterns of Ethics Complaints

The CPA Ethics Committee did not take action against members between 2001 and 2005. Since 2006, the CPA Ethics Committee received nine complaints, and only one received full adjudication (inadequate assessment of a child). This represents a substantial change from the 1980s and 1990s, when CPA fully adjudicated one or two complaints a year.

CPA entered into a formal agreement to wait for regulatory bodies to adjudicate complaints. Consequently, complaints rarely get sent to the CPA Ethics Committee (J. Service, personal communication, May 26, 2006; C. Sinclair, personal communication, January 26, 2010). Other possible reasons for this change include the fact that more formal problem-resolution structures in society address issues (e.g., Research Ethics Boards [REBs], Institutional Review Boards [IRBs]), there is wider acceptance of sexual harassment complaints by various employers, and there is a willingness of regulatory bodies to accept complaints from students. In addition, CPA has increased its consultation services to psychologists. CPA does accept complaints about CPA members who are not registered with a regulatory body.

Processing complaints continues to be an important focus of the APA Ethics Committee (APA Ethics Committee, 1997–2008, 2009b), although recently it has placed more emphasis on education (including presentations to state psychological associations, state licensing boards, at APA conventions, international programs), monthly *Monitor on Psychology* publications, consultation, diversity initiatives, and policy statement development. APA bylaws require that the Ethics Committee reports how many and what kinds of complaints it investigates each year.

Table 9.1 provides data from *American Psychologist*'s "Report of the Ethics Committee" for 2005, 2006, 2007, 2008.

Table 9.1 Primary and Multiple Categories of Cases Opened in 2005, 2006, 2007, and 2008

	Year								Totals	
	2005		2006		2007		2008			
Category	P	M	P	M	P	M	P	M	P	M
Cases adjudicated in other jurisdictions										
Felony conviction	4	4	7	7	4	4	2	2	17	17
Loss of licensure	25	26	15	16	20	21	8	8	68	71
Expulsion from state association										
Malpractice										
Other	2	2	3	3	3	4	2	2	10	11
Dual relationship										
Sexual misconduct, adult	0	12	0	6	1	9	0	4	1	32
Sexual misconduct, minor	0	4	0	1	1	5			1	10
Sexual harassment							1	1	1	1
Nonsexual dual relationship	0	4	0	4	1	5	1	2	2	15
Inappropriate professional practice										
Child custody	1	1	3	5	1	2	1	2	6	10
Hospitalizaton										
Hypnosis										
Outside competence	0	1	0	2	1	5			1	8
Controlling client							1	0	1	0
Inappropriate response to crisis	0	1	0	3	0	1			0	5
Confidentiality			1	2					1	2
Inappropriate follow-up/ termination	0	1					0	1	0	2
Test misuse			0	2					0	2
Insurance/fee problems	0	6	0	8	0	3	0	2	0	19
Inappropriate professional relations			0	1					0	1
Other	0	2			0	1	0	2	0	5

Table 9.1   (*continued*)

Category	Year 2005 P	2005 M	2006 P	2006 M	2007 P	2007 M	2008 P	2008 M	Totals P	M
Inappropriate research, teaching, or administrative practice										
Authorship contro-versies/credits										
Improper research techniques										
Plagiarism										
Biasing data										
Grading/violation of student rights										
Termination/supervision										
Absence of timely evaluations										
Discrimination										
Animal research subjects' welfare										
Other										
Inappropriate public statements										
Misuse of media										
False, fraudulent, or misleading							0	1	0	1
Did not correct misrepresentation										
Public allegation about colleague										
Other										
Failure to uphold standards of the profession										
Response to APA Ethics Committee										
Adherence to standards										

(*continued*)

Table 9.1 (continued)

Category	2005		2006		2007		2008		Totals	
	P	M	P	M	P	M	P	M	P	M
Other	0	1	0	1	0	1	0	1	0	4
TOTAL CASES	32	32	29	29	32	32	16	16	109	109

Note: P = number of cases with category as primary factor. M = number of cases with category as multiple factor. We thank the staff of the APA Ethics Office who offered guidance with this table, including Stephen Behnke, executive director.

Sources: Adapted from "Report of the Ethics Committee, 2005," by American Psychological Association Ethics Committee, 2006, *American Psychologist, 61*, pp. 522–529. "Report of the Ethics Committee, 2006," by American Psychological Association Ethics Committee, 2007, *American Psychologist, 62*, pp. 504–511. "Report of the Ethics Committee, 2007," by American Psychological Association Ethics Committee, 2008, *American Psychologist, 63*, pp. 452–459. "Report of the Ethics Committee, 2008," by American Psychological Association Ethics Committee, 2009, *American Psychologist, 64*, pp. 464–473.

Table 9.2 provides totals from "Reports of the Ethics Committee" from 2000 to 2004 and for 2005 to 2008, along with totals for the nine years 2000 to 2008.

These figures show a declining caseload resulting from adjudicative reforms made after an extensive review of the ethics program and a discussion of the program at the February 2001 Council of Representatives meeting (Behnke, 2005). The reforms included:

- All respondents under ethics investigation are offered an opportunity to resign. A psychologist who is the subject of an ethics matter and wants to resign from APA is not required to begin the adjudication process.
- Respondents in show-cause matters (matters in which an official, non-APA entity has already taken serious action against the psychologist) are expelled from APA automatically unless they request that APA review their case. The committee and board do not need to follow the entire adjudication process for psychologists who do not provide a substantive response to APA notification following a significant adjudication by an organization other than APA.
- The annual dues notice sent to all members lists the names of psychologists who resign under ethics investigation or are automatically expelled.

The Ethics Committee handles many cases secondary to actions taken by state licensure boards (APA Ethics Committee, 2009). Loss of licensure continues to be the most common reason for complaints processed. Over nine

Table 9.2　Summaries for Primary and Multiple Categories for Cases Opened 2000–2004 and 2005–2008

| | Period of Time | | | | | | %P | %M |
| | 2000–2004 | | 2005–2008 | | Totals | | | |
Category	P	M	P	M	P	M		
Cases adjudicated in other jurisdictions								
Felony conviction	8	8	17	17	25	25	9	9
Loss of licensure	92	92	68	71	160	163	59	60
Expulsion from state association								
Malpractice								
Other	13	14	10	11	23	25	8	9
Dual relationship								
Sexual misconduct, adult	10	59	1	32	11	91	4	33
Sexual misconduct, minor	0	3	1	10	1	13	.3	5
Sexual harassment	1	2	1	1	2	3	.7	1
Nonsexual dual relationship	5	24	2	15	7	39	3	14
Inappropriate professional practice								
Child custody	16	25	6	10	22	35	8	13
Hospitalizaton	0	2	0	0	0	2	0	.7
Hypnosis								
Outside competence	1	7	1	8	2	15	.7	5
Controlling client	0	1	1	0	1	1	.3	.3
Inappropriate response to crisis	2	3	0	5	2	8	.7	3
Confidentiality	3	10	1	2	4	12	1	4
Inappropriate follow-up/termination	1	4	0	2	1	6	.3	2
Test misuse	1	3	0	2	1	5	.3	2
Insurance/fee problems	0	18	0	19	0	37	0	13

(continued)

Table 9.2 *(continued)*

	Period of Time						%P	%M
	2000–2004		2005–2008		Totals			
Category	P	M	P	M	P	M		
Inappropriate professional relations	1	2	0	1	1	3	.3	1
Other	2	11	0	5	2	16	.7	6
Inappropriate research, teaching, or administrative practice								
Authorship contro-versies/credits	0	1	0	0	0	1	0	.3
Improper research techniques	0	1	0	0	0	1	0	.3
Plagiarism	2	2	0	0	2	2	.7	.7
Biasing data								
Grading/violation of student rights								
Termination/ supervision	0	3	0	0	0	3	0	1
Absence of timely evaluations	1	1	0	0	1	1	.3	.3
Discrimination								
Animal research subjects' welfare								
Other	0	1	0	0	0	1	0	.3
Inappropriate public statements								
Misuse of media								
False, fraudulent,	0	2	0	1	0	3	0	1
Did not correct misrepresentation								
Public allegation about colleague	1	1	0	0	1	1	.3	.3
Other								
Failure to uphold standards of the profession								
Response to APA Ethics Committee	4	7	0	0	4	7	2	2

Table 9.2   *(continued)*

Category	Period of Time						%P	%M
	2000–2004		2005–2008		Totals			
	P	M	P	M	P	M		
Adherence to standards								
Other	0	1	0	4	0	5	0	2
Total cases	164	164	109	109	273	273	*99	—

Note: P = number of cases with category as primary factor. M = number of cases with category as multiple factor. We thank the staff of the APA Ethics Office who offered guidance with this table, including Steve Behnke, executive director.

*Rounded Percentages

The dash indicates that a percentage is not applicable here because each case may be counted in multiple categories.

Sources: Summaries 2000–2004 adapted from "Report of the Ethics Committee, 2000," by the American Psychological Association Ethics Committee, 2001, *American Psychologist, 56,* pp. 680–688. "Report of the Ethics Committee, 2001," by American Psychological Association Ethics Committee, 2002, *American Psychologist, 57,* pp. 646–653. "Report of the Ethics Committee, 2002," by American Psychological Association Ethics Committee, 2003, *American Psychologist, 58,* pp. 650–657. "Report of the Ethics Committee, 2003," by American Psychological Association Ethics Committee, 2004, *American Psychologist, 59,* pp. 434–441. "Report of the Ethics Committee, 2004," by American Psychological Association Ethics Committee, 2005, *American Psychologist, 60,* pp. 523–528. Copyright American Psychological Association 2001, 2002, 2003, 2004, 2005. Adapted with permission.

From *Ethics in Psychotherapy and Counseling: A Practical Guide* (3rd ed., pp. 85-87), by K. S. Pope and J. T. Vasquez, 2007, San Francisco: Jossey-Bass.

Summaries 2005–2008 adapted from "Report of the Ethics Committee, 2005," by American Psychological Association Ethics Committee, 2006, *American Psychologist, 61,* pp. 522–529. "Report of the Ethics Committee, 2006," by American Psychological Association Ethics Committee, 2007, *American Psychologist, 62,* pp. 504–511. "Report of the Ethics Committee, 2007," by American Psychological Association Ethics Committee, 2008, *American Psychologist, 63,* pp. 452–459. "Report of the Ethics Committee, 2008," by American Psychological Association Ethics Committee, 2009, *American Psychologist, 64,* pp. 464–473.

years, there were 160 cases (59%) with loss of licensure as primary factor and 163 cases (60%) with loss of licensure as one of multiple factors.

Multiple issues per allegations reported are important because the primary category states the basis on which APA is processing the case rather than the underlying behavior, and a secondary category is always assigned. Over the nine-year period (2000–2008) sexual misconduct (see Chapter 16), for example, was the primary underlying behavior in cases in the category "loss of licensure." Over that period, sexual misconduct involving adults (11 cases as primary factor and 91 as a multiple factor) accounted for the higher number of cases. Nonsexual dual relationships (7 cases as primary factor and 39 cases as multiple factor) and child custody (22 cases as primary factors and 35 cases as multiple factors) are categories with a higher numbers of cases. Confidentiality (4 cases as primary factors and 12 as multiple factors) also had a moderately high number of cases. Insurance/fee problems, although not listed as a primary factor for those nine years, are often listed as one of the multiple factors (no cases as primary factors, 37 as multiple factors).

The report of cases opened and closed from 2000 to 2008 reflects a significant decline in total active cases each year (APA Ethics Committee, 2009). Interestingly, only a very small percentage of the APA membership have complaints filed against them through the APA Ethics Committee.

Empirical Approach Half a Century Later

Many of the early APA pioneers provided reasons that an empirical approach would be useful in constructing an ethics code. But a critical incident survey of APA members could also serve another purpose. While the actuarial data of ethics committees, licensing boards, and civil and criminal courts can reveal trends in ethical or legal violations as they are established by review agencies, empirical critical incident studies can reveal ethical dilemmas and concerns as they are encountered in day-to-day practice by the broad range of psychologists (i.e., not just those who are subject to formal complaint).

The APA critical incident study undertaken in the 1940s was replicated in the 1990s and published in the *American Psychologist* (Pope & Vetter, 1992). In this study, 1,319 randomly sampled APA members were asked to describe incidents that they found ethically challenging or troubling: 679 psychologists described 703 incidents in 23 categories, as shown in Table 9.3.

Here is a sample of the ethical concerns that the psychologists described in this anonymous survey:

Confidentiality

- "The executive director of the mental health clinic with which I'm employed used his position to obtain and review clinical patient files of clients who were members of his church. He was [clerical title] in a...church and indicated his knowledge of this clinical (confidential) information would be of help to him in his role as [clerical title]."
- "Having a psychologist as a client who tells me she has committed an ethical violation and because of confidentiality I can't report it."
- "One of my clients claimed she was raped; the police did not believe her and refused to follow up (because of her mental history). Another of my clients described how he raped a woman (the same woman)."

Table 9.3   Ethical Problems Reported by a National Sample of APA Members

Category	Number	Percentage
Confidentiality	128	18
Blurred, dual, or conflictual relationships	116	17
Payment sources, plans, settings, and methods	97	14
Academic settings, teaching dilemmas, and concerns about training	57	8
Forensic psychology	35	5
Research	29	4
Conduct of colleagues	29	4
Sexual issues	28	4
Assessment	25	4
Questionable or harmful interventions	20	3
Competence	20	3
Ethics and related codes and committees	17	2
School psychology	15	2
Publishing	14	2
Helping the financially stricken	13	2
Supervision	13	2
Advertising and (mis)representation	13	2
Industrial-organizational psychology	9	1
Medical issues	5	1
Termination	5	1
Ethnicity	4	1
Treatment records	4	1
Miscellaneous	7	1

Source: Adapted with permission from "Ethical Dilemmas Encountered by Members of the American Psychological Association: A National Survey," by K. S. Pope and V. A. Vetter, 1992, *American Psychologist, 47,* 397–411, p. 399. Available at http://kspope.com. Copyright 1992 by the American Psychological Association.

Blurred, Dual, or Conflictual Relationships

- "I live and maintain a . . . private practice in a rural area. I am also a member of a spiritual community based here. There are very few other therapists in the immediate vicinity who work with transformational, holistic, and feminist principles in the context of good clinical training that 'conventional' people can also feel confidence in.

Clients often come to me because they know me already, because they are not satisfied with the other services available, or because they want to work with someone who understands their spiritual practice and can incorporate its principles and practices into the process of transformation, healing, and change. The stricture against dual relationships helps me to maintain a high degree of sensitivity to the ethics (and potentials for abuse or confusion) of such situations, but doesn't give me any help in working with the actual circumstances of my practice. I hope revised principles will address these concerns!"

- "Six months ago, a patient I had been working with for three years became romantically involved with my best and longest friend. I could write no less than a book on the complications of this fact! I have been getting legal and therapeutic consultations all along and continue to do so. Currently they are living together, and I referred the patient (who was furious that I did this and felt abandoned). I worked with the other psychologist for several months to provide a bridge for the patient. I told my friend soon after I found out that I would have to suspend our contact. I'm currently trying to figure out if we can ever resume our friendship and under what conditions." [This latter example is one of many that demonstrate the extreme lengths to which most psychologists are willing to go to ensure the welfare of their patients.]

Payment Sources, Plans, Settings, and Methods

- "A 7-year-old boy was severely sexually abused and severely depressed. I evaluated the case and recommended six months treatment. My recommendation was evaluated by a managed health care agency and approved for 10 sessions by a nonprofessional in spite of the fact that there is no known treatment program that can be performed in 10 sessions on a 7-year-old that has demonstrated efficacy."
- "Much of my practice is in a private hospital that is in general very good clinically. However, its profit motivation is so very intense that decisions are often made for $ reasons that actively hurt the patients. When patients complain, this is often interpreted as being part of their psychopathology, thus reenacting the dysfunctional families they came from. I don't do this myself and don't permit others to do so in my presence — I try to mitigate the problem — but I can't speak perfectly frankly to my patients and I'm constantly colluding with something that feels marginally unethical."
- "A managed care company discontinued a benefit and told my patient to stop seeing me, then referred her to a therapist they had a lower fee contract with."

Academic Settings, Teaching Dilemmas, and Concerns about Training

- "I employ over 600 psychologists. I am disturbed by the fact that those psychologists with marginal ethics and competence were so identified in graduate school and no one did anything about it."

Forensic Psychology

- "A psychologist in my area is widely known to clients, psychologists, and the legal community to give whatever testimony is requested in court. He has a very commanding presence, and it works. He will say anything, adamantly, for pay. Clients/lawyers continue to use him because if the other side uses him, that side will probably win the case (because he's so persuasive, though lying)."
- "Another psychologist's report or testimony in a court case goes way beyond what psychology knows or his own data supports. How or whether I should respond."
- "I find it difficult to have to testify in court or by way of deposition and to provide sensitive information about a client. Although the client has given permission to provide this information, there are times when there is much discomfort in so doing."

Research

- "I am co-investigator on a grant. While walking past the secretary's desk, I saw an interim report completed by the PI [principal investigator] to the funding source. The interim report claimed double the number of subjects who had actually entered the protocol."
- "I have consulted to research projects at a major university medical school where 'random selection' of subjects for drug studies was flagrantly disregarded. I resigned after the first phase."
- "Deception that was not disclosed, use of a data videotape in a public presentation without the subject's consent (the subject was in the audience), using a class homework assignment as an experimental manipulation without informing students."

Conduct of Colleagues

- "As a faculty member, it was difficult dealing with a colleague about whom I received numerous complaints from students."
- "At what point does 'direct knowledge' of purportedly unethical practices become direct knowledge which I must report—is reporting through a client 'direct' knowledge?"
- "I referred a child to be hospitalized at a nearby facility. The mother wanted to use a particular psychiatrist.... When I called the psychiatrist to discuss the case, he advised me that, since he was the admitting

professional, he'd assume full responsibility for the case. . . . He advised how he had a psychologist affiliated with his office whom he preferred to use."

- "I see foster children who have little control over their lives and case workers who have little time/interest in case management. How can I maintain good professional relationships with those who don't function up to their duties?"

- "A director of the mental health center where I worked was obviously emotionally disturbed, and it impacted on the whole center—quality of service to clients, staff morale, etc. He would not get professional help or staff development assistance."

- "The toughest situations I and my colleague seem to keep running into (in our small town) are ones involving obvious (to us) ethical infractions by other psychologists or professionals in the area. On three or more occasions he and I have personally confronted and taken to local boards ... issues which others would rather avoid, deal with lightly, ignore, deny, etc., because of peer pressure in a small community. This has had the combined effect of making me doubt my reality (or experience), making me wonder why I have such moral compunctions, making me feel isolated and untrusting of professional peers, etc."

Sexual Issues

- "A student after seeing a client for therapy for a semester terminated the therapy as was planned at the end of the semester, then began a sexual relationship with the client. . . . I think APA should take a stronger stance on this issue."

- "I currently have in treatment a psychiatrist who is still in the midst of a six-year affair with a patient. He wishes to end the affair but is afraid to face the consequences."

- "My psychological assistant was sexually exploited by her former supervisor and threatened her with not validating her hours for licensure if she didn't service his needs."

LICENSING BOARDS

Each of the United States and Canadian jurisdictions (e.g., states, provinces) has its own requirements and standards for practicing as (or, in some states and jurisdictions to identify oneself as) a therapist or counselor. Some, but not all, administrative standards embody ethical principles. (e.g., some may set forth the relatively mundane obligation to pay an annual licensing fee.) Formal licensing actions are how therapists and counselors are held accountable to these standards of practice. Violation of these standards can lead to the suspension or revocation of the practitioner's license or certification.

Table 9.4 Reported Disciplinary Actions for Psychologists in the United States and Canada, August 1983–December 2009

Reason for Disciplinary Action	Number Disciplined
Sexual Misconduct	795
Unprofessional Conduct	791
Nonsexual Dual Relationship or Boundary Violation	494
Negligence	473
Conviction of Crime	400
Failure to Maintain Adequate or Accurate Records	335
Improper or Inadequate Supervision or Delegation	247
Substandard or Inadequate Care	242
Incompetence	235
Breach of confidentiality	221
TOTAL OF REPORTED DISCIPLINARY RECORDS	4,397*

*The difference in the total number of reported disciplinary actions and this total is that some jurisdictions do not report reasons or the reason reported does not fall into one of the categories in this table.

Source: Compiled by the Association of State and Provincial Psychology Boards from actions reported to the ASPPB Disciplinary Data System by member boards. Obtained through personal communication with ASPPB staff member Janet Pippin, January 22, 2010.

The data reviewed in Table 9.4 concerning licensing disciplinary actions of psychologists were collected by the Association of State and Provincial Psychology Boards (ASPPB) from actions reported to the ASPPB disciplinary data system by member boards in the United States and Canada (J. Pippin, Association of State and Provincial Psychology Boards, personal communication, January 22, 2010). The data are abstracted from the ASPPB Disciplinary Data Reports from August 1983 to December 2009. Since our last edition in 2007, ASPPB has made many changes to the disciplinary data system. It combined many reason codes in order to better match the Healthcare Integrity and Protection Data Bank (HIPDB) coding system, the national reporting data bank.

Sexual misconduct, unprofessional conduct, nonsexual dual relationship or boundary violation, negligence, and conviction of crime stand out as the top five causes of disciplinary actions by AASPB member boards. Because of changes in reporting, categories that no longer remain in the top 10 reported reasons include: continuing education (failure to complete); fraudulent acts, now split according to what type of act; impairment, now split into what type of impairment; fraud in application, now part of a new category, fraud, deceit, or material omission in obtaining a license or renewal, but is no longer in the top 10 (J. Pippin, personal communication, January 27, 2010).

Van Horne (2004) reviewed data about licensing complaints against psychologists. She found that "few complaints are filed, many of those complaints are not investigated, informal actions taken that are not reported to the ASPPB Disciplinary Data System are few, and even fewer formal actions are taken against psychologists' licenses" (p. 157). She noted:

> The perception of disciplinary actions taken by licensing boards is dependent on the vantage point of the observer. If one is the subject of a licensing board action, there is no doubt the board is vigilant, if not downright victimizing, in the pursuit of discipline. If one is the consumer/complainant seeking action by the licensing board, there is no doubt the board is cautious, if not downright distrustful of the complainant, in the investigative process. If one is a board member, there is no doubt the board is fair, if not downright obsessive, in its efforts to consider the rights of all concerned. If one is a journalist, there is no doubt the licensing board is protective of the psychologist, if not downright negligent in its failure to hold colleagues accountable. There is little doubt that one can find evidence for each of these perspectives. However, the larger picture of psychology licensing board complaints and both informal and formal disciplinary actions reflects a much more balanced outcome of the board mandate to protect consumers of psychological services. It is no surprise that fears abound in light of the high stakes involved for both complainants and licensees, but the facts should ease those fears. (p. 170)

Stephen T. DeMers, executive officer of ASPPB, described several projects that ASPPB has developed. The Certificate of Professional Qualification allows psychologists to avoid mobility problems and facilitates obtaining a license in a new jurisdiction. In addition, an interjurisdictional practice credential has been designed to help industrial organizational and forensic psychologists to engage in short-term practice in a jurisdiction in a sanctioned and regulated way (S. T. DeMers, personal communication, November 11, 2005; J. Pippin, personal communication, February 16, 2010).

CIVIL STATUTES AND CASE LAW

Each state and province has its own legislation and accumulated case law that can serve as the basis of malpractice suits against therapists and counselors. Because the states and provinces differ in their legal standards, an act that one jurisdiction may require can violate the legal standards in another jurisdiction.

The United States and Canada provide a stark contrast in lawsuits against psychologists. Unlike their colleagues south of the border, Canadian

Table 9.5 Major Areas of Professional Liability Claims Against Psychologists

Source of Loss	% of Overall Losses
Ineffective treatment/failure to consult/failure to refer	29%
Failure to diagnose/improper diagnosis	16%
Custody dispute	10%
Sexual intimacy/sexual harassment and/or sexual misconduct	9%
Breach of confidentiality	8%
Suicide	4%
Supervisory issues, conflict of interest or improper multiple relationships, all other losses less than 1 percent	3%
Libel/slander, conflicts in reporting sexual abuse, licensing dispute, no coverage applies	2%
Abandonment, premises liability, repressed memory, failure to monitor, countersuits resulting from fee disputes, client harmed others including homicide, business disputes, miscellaneous liability claims, discrimination/harassment	1%

psychologists apparently get sued very rarely (J. Service, personal communication, May 26, 2006).

What are the primary reasons clinicians are sued in the United States? The data reviewed in Table 9.5, provided by the American Psychological Association Insurance Trust, are the most recent incidence statistics available. The data present a snapshot of the relative sources of loss for the major areas of claims in the trust-sponsored professional liability program for a decade. (B. Bennett, personal communication, December 19, 2005, June 13, 2006, January 19, 2010).

Bruce Bennett, chief executive of the trust (personal correspondence, December 19, 2005), placed these data in context:

- The data were collected and assigned to the respective categories by staff at the insurance company following a cursory review of the initial claim filed against the defendant.
- It is assumed that assignment of claims to a specific category is based on the primary allegation listed in the lawsuit; however, this is only an assumption.
- Most lawsuits contain a number of counts against the defendant. As a malpractice suit proceeds through the judicial system, the lawsuit is frequently amended to add new counts or remove certain counts. These data do not reflect any such amendments, subsequent filings, or final dispositions.

- Many lawsuits against psychologists are based on the shotgun approach, where the defendant is accused of multiple misdeeds, even though some of the allegations of wrongdoing may be dropped during the settlement discussions or prior to or during trial. Regardless of the underlying alleged misconduct, it is highly likely that the lawsuit will assert ineffective treatment, failure to consult, failure to refer, failure to diagnose, and/or improper diagnosis. Thus, the first two categories account for 45% of the claims regardless of other allegations. This would be especially true when the underlying primary issue may be something like improper financial transactions or sexual misconduct.
- Psychologists tend to place heavy reliance on data such as provided here. In many cases, numbers tend to garner more significance than is appropriate.

With these caveats in mind, Bennett pointed out some interesting trends:

- The percentage of claims for custody disputes has increased from 3% to 10 %.
- The percentage of claims for sexual misconduct has decreased from 20% to 9%.
- The percentage of claims involving suicide has dropped from 5% to 4%.
- Supervision should be a major area of concern for the practitioner (2% to 3%).
- Forensic work (custody evaluations and evaluations affecting hiring, promotion, or retention in the workplace, etc.) represent an emerging high-risk area of practice.
- Suits filed in retaliation for fee collection appear to have decreased from 4% to 1%, probably because psychologists, knowing the dangers associated with fee collection actions, are less likely to bring such suits against current or former patients.
- One area has become apparent: The number of licensing board complaints has increased dramatically. In fact, of all the claims filed against psychologists, 60% (up from 30% in 2005) or more are for licensing board complaints, many related to forensic work or custody and family issues (B. Bennett, personal correspondence, January 19, 2010).

CRIMINAL STATUTES

Each state and province has its own set of criminal laws, generally set forth in the penal code. Although we were unable to find reliable actuarial data concerning therapists convicted of crimes, one of the most frequently mentioned areas involves fraud, particularly related to third-party billings. Donald Bersoff, then attorney representing the APA, emphasized the importance of conforming to all rules and regulations regarding billing practices for third-party coverage, both public and private, and noted that therapists currently serving time in prison could attest to the significance of violating those rules and regulations (see APA Ethics Committee, 1988).

Another of the areas in which therapists may face criminal prosecution is sexual involvement with patients (see Chapter 16). While many of the laws are civil reporting laws and injunctive relief statutes, as of October 2005, at least 25 states had enacted criminal statues regarding therapist-patient sexual contact (see Pope, 1994; Pope, Sonne, & Greene, 2006).

CONCLUSION

Exceptional caution is appropriate in attempts to generalize, compare, or interpret this chapter's actuarial data from ethics committees, licensing boards, and malpractice courts. Various types of actual violations, as the research indicates, may lead only rarely to a formal complaint with a criminal court, civil court, licensing board, or ethics committee. Certain types of violation can be hard to prove. Formal complaints may be informally resolved and not appear in archival data. And, as noted, there are significantly different ways of classifying complaints.

Nevertheless, the general trends in the archival data and critical incident studies can be useful to us. They call attention to aspects of our own practice where there is room for improvement. They suggest possible topics for which we might want to take continuing education courses. They provide a resource for us as individuals and as a helping profession seeking to maintain the high standards and integrity of our work and to minimize possible harm to those we serve.

These mechanisms of accountability and their relationship to ethical behavior warrant caution. It is so easy to confuse ethical behavior with what keeps us out of trouble with these review agencies (see Chapter 3). Our sense of what is ethical runs through a reductionistic mill and becomes, in the worst-case scenarios, "avoiding detection," "eliminating risk," or "escaping accountability." Much that we may do that is unethical may never come to the light and may never trigger inquiry by one of these mechanisms of accountability.

As noted in Chapter 1, the principles articulated by our profession, the licensing boards, and the civil and criminal courts should never serve to inhibit careful ethical deliberation or function as a substitute for thoughtful decision making and personal responsibility. They provide a framework that broadens our awareness and informs our thinking. They support us in the process of ethical struggle and constant questioning that are an inescapable part of what we do as therapists and counselors.

Chapter 10

RESPONDING TO ETHICS, LICENSING, OR MALPRACTICE COMPLAINTS

Malpractice suits can hit like earthquakes. Confidence, reputation, self-image, and the most taken-for-granted areas of personal and professional life come tumbling down. Interrogatories, depositions, planning, meetings with attorneys, worry, and what-ifs steal the time we once spent with patients, friends, and family. Complaints to a licensing board or ethics committee can cause the same havoc.

Stunned, the unprepared therapist can respond impulsively, making a bad situation terrible. Preparation helps us take informed, thoughtful, effective steps.

Preparation also helps us to view the possibility of a formal complaint realistically. Some therapists let anxiety about being sued grow into terror or obsession. Striving to avoid a lawsuit blots out their practice's original focus: helping clients; earning money to support themselves and their loved ones; doing meaningful, fulfilling work that they enjoy and are good at. They change their primary occupation from therapist to risk manager.

Intelligent risk management is part of a good practice, but that is all it is. Once therapists start living and working in fear of a complaint and allow that fear to dominate all decisions, something vital is lost.

We recommend preparing for these possibilities early, as part of thinking through an approach to ethics and therapy, which is why we do not tack this chapter at the end of the book.

Here are some considerations you may find helpful in responding to a formal complaint.

DON'T PANIC

Okay, panic just a little if you can't help it or it feels like the right thing to do. Then take deep breaths, pull yourself together, and do whatever you need to do to think clearly. Avoid letting panic drive your decisions.

CONSULT YOUR ATTORNEY FIRST—AND MAKE SURE YOU HAVE A GOOD ONE!

It is amazing how many therapists forget this step or try to save time and money by ignoring it. Opening an envelope to discover a licensing complaint, a psychologist figures that this simple misunderstanding can be resolved quickly by sending an explanation along with supporting documents. Receiving notice of a malpractice suit, the therapist hopes that asking the client to come in for a free session to discuss it "without all these lawyers" is the best way to reach a positive resolution and convince the client that a suit should never have been filed in the first place.

Responding to a formal complaint before consulting an attorney can lead to disasters. The psychologist is moving into a different realm. An attorney can help guide us through the minefields of formal complaints. Good attorneys are knowledgeable about the complex legislation, case law, and court customs governing malpractice actions. Attorneys experienced in licensing and ethics hearings know the norms and customs. They can interpret the rules and procedures.

Good attorneys bring not only specialized knowledge and experience. They also bring another perspective: The attorney is not the object of the complaint. As the old aphorism has it, the person who represents him- or herself has a fool for a client.

Attorneys point out the pitfalls of strategies that otherwise seem to make perfect sense. A psychologist who has not consulted an attorney may talk to colleagues about the case, talk to the opposing attorney, write letters to various people mentioning the case, or blow off steam about the case within earshot of others and discover only later that these spoken and written statements and outpourings, which are not privileged, become key evidence.

The attorney may give strong advice—sometimes a more authoritative list of dos and don'ts. But a good part of what an attorney does is to lay out options. For example, the attorney can tell us whether we can discuss the case with a supervisor, a consultant, a colleague, a friend, a family member, or anyone else and have what we say remain confidential and privileged. As another example, the attorney can explain the consequences of our turning down a settlement offer from the plaintiff in a malpractice suit.

Since so much can depend on your attorney's knowledge, skill, experience, trustworthiness, and dedication, make sure you have a good one. It is amazing how many therapists spend much more time researching a new computer, car, or refrigerator than a new attorney. They may talk with several carpenters or contractors before hiring one to do work on their home but hire an attorney without considering alternatives. Ask colleagues about their experiences and recommendations. How many cases like yours has the attorney handled? What were the outcomes? How available is he or she? Will the attorney you are researching be handling the case, or will it be handled by a junior associate?

NOTIFY YOUR PROFESSIONAL LIABILITY CARRIER

A professional liability policy may include a requirement to notify the company immediately not only if you are sued but also if you have reason to believe that you will or may be sued. But regardless of the fine print of such requirements, it makes sense to let the carrier know if you become aware of a possible or actual formal complaint. The carrier may give you helpful guidance and provide you with an attorney. Some liability insurance companies offer financial coverage of legal representation for licensing complaints

WHO IS YOUR ATTORNEY'S CLIENT?

The answer seems obvious: *You* are your attorney's client. But if the insurance company is paying the attorney, are the insurance carrier's interests and your interests the same? For example, what if the insurance company approves only a very limited discovery, hoping to hold down expenses? What if the carrier believes it makes sense financially (i.e., it is in the *carrier's* financial interests) to settle a case that you believe is bogus and would be decided in your favor were it vigorously defended? Settling the case, which would likely become a matter of public record, could devastate your career, particularly if you often testify as an expert witness.

In some rare circumstances, if you (or you and the attorney) are unable to persuade the carrier to litigate rather than settle the case or to provide an adequate discovery and vigorous defense, you might consider hiring a separate attorney with your own funds to press your claims with the carrier.

IS THE COMPLAINT VALID?

When someone takes the step of filing a formal complaint against us, it is natural to feel hurt and attacked. Malpractice trials can fan the fires of anger. Before that process goes too far, ask yourself: Did you actually do what someone has accused you of doing? Setting aside defensiveness, rationalization, counterattacks, and the fact that the charges may be overstated and wrong in the details, is there any truth to the claim that you did something you should not have done or that you failed to do something that you should have done?

Being relentlessly honest under these circumstances is anything but easy. Acknowledging that you may have done something wrong may seem self-destructive, indulging a tendency to beat yourself up when you need all your survival skills to rescue your reputation and career. But holding tight to the reality of what happened—avoiding memory's revisionism—can help us to respond effectively to the complaint and survive the ordeal in a way that is the very opposite of self-destructive.

DID YOU MAKE A FORMAL COMPLAINT MORE LIKELY?

It is worth asking: Regardless of whether you did or did not do what you are accused of doing, did you somehow make the complaint more likely? Did you, for example, make a normal, run-of-the-mill human error—not something illegal or unethical but just a mistake—and, when confronted by the client, refuse to acknowledge it or say you were sorry? Was there a misunderstanding—perhaps a client mistakenly thought you had done something wrong—that you refused to clarify? In other words, as you think through what happened with the benefit of hindsight, did your attitude or behavior increase the chances that this complaint would be filed?

In our experience, many (but by no means all) formal complaints seem to have less to do with a therapist doing something unethical than with the therapist-client relationship. The therapist has come across to the client as lacking respect, caring, and a reasonable ability to listen. Therapists who communicate these qualities to clients often seem to make all sorts of mistakes, misjudgments, and violations of standards without triggering a complaint, while therapists who fail to communicate these qualities must endure complaints even when they have otherwise seemed to adhere to the highest standards. (This, of course, does not imply that it is somehow okay to bumble our way into careless mistakes, misjudgments, and violations or that we can use what we communicate to the client to justify, discount, trivialize, or rationalize what we've done wrong and the consequences of our behavior, a process described in the section "Justifications" in Chapter 3.) Formal complaints sometimes seem to represent a client's last desperate attempt to catch the attention of an unresponsive therapist.

APOLOGIZE AND ACCEPT RESPONSIBILITY?

If the complaint is valid, we must choose whether to acknowledge what we did, accept responsibility, and apologize. It seems to be part of the human condition that it is difficult for many of us to admit mistakes, especially when those mistakes have hurt someone, and to apologize. It can be much harder when it will go on the record, may be influential in sustaining the validity of the complaint, and is given to someone who is angry—perhaps enraged—at us. There may also be friends and colleagues who advise us to despise the person who filed the complaint and to fight the complaint no matter what the circumstances.

When facing a valid complaint, therapists may carefully consider, in consultation with their attorney, apologizing, accepting responsibility, and—if possible and appropriate—trying to make things right. Discussion with an attorney is an important part of this consideration. Attorneys may advise that a therapist should not speak to a complainant once a formal complaint has been filed. The attorney can explain the legal consequences (e.g., possible effects on the resolution of the complaint) and possible formats (e.g., in some situations it may be prohibited for the therapist to contact the complainant directly).

There can be strong reasons favoring and opposing a direct apology at this stage, depending on the circumstances, and it is impossible to foresee all the consequences and implications of taking or not taking this path. Each psychologist must choose what is right for his or her own values and situation.

WHAT ARE YOU WILLING TO HAVE DONE?

If you contest the charges, consider—*before* the adversarial process heats up—what you are and are not willing to allow in defending your case. To examine an extreme hypothetical, imagine that you are sued for malpractice by an extremely fragile single mother. You believe her to be a basically good and competent person who has mistakenly but in good faith filed suit against you. Whatever your view of her, the claim she has filed threatens your reputation and career. If the verdict goes against you, referral sources for new patients may dry up, the licensing board may launch an investigation, and your work as an expert witness on the standard of care may be in jeopardy.

With all that at stake, would you be willing for your attorney to depose her and cross-examine her at trial in a way that misleadingly raises questions about her honesty? Would you be willing for the attorney to use your chart notes to create through innuendo the false impression that she is not an adequate mother and that perhaps she even neglected or abused her child? Would you be willing to testify (falsely) that she suffers from borderline personality disorder and threatened to sue you and ruin your reputation if you did go along with her attempts at seducing you?

Or would you be tempted to "clarify" your chart notes, a euphemism for changing your notes after the fact but submitting them as if they were contemporaneous? The potential self-serving justifications for submitting fraudulent records—a practice that is never ethical—are endless. Those notes may have been done hurriedly, may not have mentioned everything that was done, and may be misleading because of the way they were written. Wouldn't it be better to copy over those notes so that they include the material that you had neglected to put in the first time around on what are, really, if you come to think of it, your draft notes? Wouldn't it actually be a service to the court to remove the unintentional ambiguities along with the parts that are relatively unimportant, that clutter up your account of the treatment? In other words, stripped of its rationalization, would you be willing to hide your actual notes and submit a bogus chart more favorable to your defense?

Feeling under attack and struggling to save our reputation and career can bring out our most primitive instincts to fight, to do virtually anything to survive. We may be tempted toward unethical extremes, such as perjury while testifying or committing a fraud on the court by submitting bogus chart notes that we've secretly doctored after the fact. We may feel drawn toward pretending our hands are clean by letting unethical or unfair tactics be done on our behalf by others (e.g., our attorney). A question worth asking before the process builds up too much steam is: Am I willing to win at any cost? If not, where do I draw the line? What, if anything, am I unwilling to do—or to have done by others in my defense—to "win"?

RECOGNIZE HOW THE COMPLAINT IS AFFECTING YOU

A formal complaint can devastate us. A malpractice suit or other formal complaint can hit a therapist with all of these feelings and more:

- Numbing shock that suddenly reputation and career may be at stake.
- A sense of betrayal that someone we tried to help has turned against us.
- Fear of uncertainty and the unknown horrors in store for us.
- Reflexive self-blame, assuming that we must have done something terrible or else we would not be in this fix.
- Embarrassment, imagining that our colleagues now think the worst about us.
- Self-doubt; if we did so poorly with this patient that we wound up in court, what if our other patients sue us?
- Depression.
- Suspicion of our other patients (are they going to sue us?) and colleagues (whom can we trust to talk this over with?).
- Anxiety about what lies ahead—being deposed and cross-examined, who will be in the courtroom during the trial (the media?), and on and on and on.
- Obsessive and intrusive thoughts, finding it hard to think about anything else.
- Insomnia, tossing and turning, thinking endlessly about what has happened and what may happen.

- Catastrophizing.
- Loss of appetite, eating or drinking too much, or abusing prescription or illegal drugs as a response to the stress.

We believe that for some therapists, being sued can bring on reactions akin to posttraumatic stress disorder. If we can be honest about our reactions, we are in a better position to respond to those reactions constructively.

GET THE HELP AND SUPPORT YOU NEED

What help, if any, do you need in dealing with these reactions? Some clinicians return to therapy or start therapy for the first time. Some reach out to friends, colleagues, and family. An attorney's guidance can be invaluable in keeping what you say to others from becoming part of the case against you. Ethics experts in your state may be able to provide you and your attorney with additional consultation.

WHAT CAN THE ORDEAL TEACH?

For understatement it is hard to beat: No one ever wishes a formal complaint. But this unwelcome process brings opportunity.

We may discover flaws and weaknesses in our policies, procedures, and approach to clinical work. We may learn to spot to red flags in our practice *and* to do something about them. We may learn about our colleagues—who can be counted on for support and who abandons and avoids us. We may learn how our own work and the complaints against us are evaluated during adversarial procedures. And in our reactions and decisions, we may learn about ourselves.

Chapter 11

STEPS IN ETHICAL DECISION MAKING

This chapter provides steps helpful in thinking through how to respond to ethical dilemmas. The steps help identify key aspects of a situation, consider benefits and drawbacks of our options, and discover better approaches.

The Canadian Psychological Association (CPA) emphasized the importance of such steps by including 7 in its original ethics code (1986) and increasing the number to 10 in subsequent editions (1991, 2000). The asterisks in the following list mark steps that are versions of those that appear in the CPA code.

Seventeen steps appear here, but not every step fits every situation, and some steps may need to be adapted.

STEP 1: STATE THE QUESTION, DILEMMA, OR CONCERN AS CLEARLY AS POSSIBLE

Does the statement do the situation justice? Does it make clear what the problem is and why it is a problem? Does it miss anything important to thinking through possible courses of action? Does any part of it get lost in the mists of vagueness, ambiguity, or professional jargon? Are some of the words misleading or not quite right? Is there anything questionable about the statement's scope, perspective, or assumptions? Are there other valid ways to define the problem?

Tight schedules, urgent situations, and an eagerness to "solve the problem" can rush us past this step, but coming up with the best approach depends on clearly understanding the ethical challenge.

STEP 2: *ANTICIPATE WHO WILL BE AFFECTED BY THE DECISION

No one lives in a vacuum. How often do our ethical decisions affect only a single person and no one else? A client shows up for a session drunk. Whether the client drives home drunk and kills a pedestrian can depend on how we define our responsibility. A colleague begins to show signs of Alzheimer's. Our choices can affect the safety and well-being of the colleague and his or her patients. A therapy client tells us about embezzling pension funds. Confidentiality laws may direct us to tell no one else, and the client may refuse to discuss the issue. How we respond can affect whether hundreds of families retain the pensions they earned or are thrown into poverty. An insurance claims manager refuses to authorize additional sessions for a client we believe is at risk for killing his wife and children and then committing suicide. Our supervisor may agree with the manager that no more sessions are needed. Whether the family lives or dies can depend on what we do.

STEP 3: FIGURE OUT WHO, IF ANYONE, IS THE CLIENT

Is there any ambiguity, confusion, or conflict about who the client is (if it is a situation that involves a psychotherapist-client relationship)? If one person is the client and someone else is paying our fee, is there any divided loyalty, any conflict that would influence our judgment?

STEP 4: ASSESS WHETHER OUR AREAS OF COMPETENCE— AND OF MISSING KNOWLEDGE, SKILLS, EXPERIENCE, OR EXPERTISE— ARE A GOOD FIT FOR THIS SITUATION

Are we well prepared to handle this situation? What steps, if any, could we take to make ourselves more effective? In the light of all relevant factors, is there anyone else who is available that we believe could step in and do a better job?

STEP 5: REVIEW RELEVANT FORMAL ETHICAL STANDARDS

Do the ethical standards speak directly or indirectly to this situation? Are the ethical standards ambiguous when applied to this situation? Does this situation involve conflicts within the ethical standards or between the ethical standards and other (e.g., legal) requirements or values? In what ways, if at all, do the ethical standards seem helpful, irrelevant, confusing, or misdirected when applied to this situation? Would it be helpful to talk with an ethicist or a member of a national, state, or provincial ethics committee?

STEP 6: REVIEW RELEVANT LEGAL STANDARDS

Do legislation and case law speak to this situation? Are the legal standards clear? Does a legal standard conflict with other standards, requirements, or values? Do the relevant laws seem to support—or at least allow—the most ethical response to the situation, or do they seem to work against or even block the most ethical response? Would it be helpful to consult an attorney and obtain legal guidance?

STEP 7: REVIEW THE RELEVANT RESEARCH AND THEORY

Is there new research or theory that helps us think through the situation? An occupational hazard of a field with such diverse approaches—cognitive, psychodynamic, pharmacological, behavioral, feminist, psychobiosocial, family, multicultural, and existential, to name but a few—is that we often lose touch with the research and theory emerging outside our own theoretical orientation.

STEP 8: *CONSIDER WHETHER PERSONAL FEELINGS, BIASES, OR SELF-INTEREST MIGHT AFFECT OUR ETHICAL JUDGMENT

Does the situation make us angry, sad, or afraid? Do we want to please someone? Do we desperately want to avoid conflict? Do we fear that doing what seems most ethical will get us into trouble, make someone mad at us, be second-guessed by colleagues, or be hard to square with the law or the ethics code? Will doing what seems right cost us time, money, friends, referrals, prestige, a promotion, our job, or our license?

STEP 9: CONSIDER WHETHER SOCIAL, CULTURAL, RELIGIOUS, OR SIMILAR FACTORS AFFECT THE SITUATION AND THE SEARCH FOR THE BEST RESPONSE

The same act can take on sharply different meanings in different societies, cultures, or religions. What seems ethical in one context can violate fundamental values in another society, culture, or spiritual tradition. What contexts—or conflicts between contexts—may have escaped our notice? Does our own social identity in relation to the client's social identity enter into the process? Could any potential issues of stereotyping or bias be relevant?

STEP 10: CONSIDER CONSULTATION

Is there anyone who could provide useful consultation for this specific situation? Is there an acknowledged expert in the relevant areas? Is there someone who has faced a similar situation and handled it well—or who might tell us what does not work and what pitfalls to avoid? Is there a colleague whose perspective might be helpful? Is there someone whose judgment we trust? When drawing a blank in the face of these questions, sometimes it is useful when a question takes this form: If what we decide to do were to end in disaster, is there some particular person we wish we had consulted?

STEP 11: *DEVELOP ALTERNATIVE COURSES OF ACTION

What possible ways of responding to this situation can you imagine? What alternative approaches can you create? At first we may come up with possibilities that seem "not bad" or "good enough." The challenge is not to quit too soon but to keep searching for our best possible response.

STEP 12: *THINK THROUGH THE ALTERNATIVE COURSES OF ACTION

What impact is each action likely to have—and what impact could each have under the best possible and worst possible outcome that you can imagine—for each person who will be affected by your decision? What are the immediate and longer-term consequences and implications for each individual, including yourself, and for any relevant organization, discipline, or society? What are the risks and benefits? Almost any significant action has unintended consequences—what could they be for each possible course of action?

STEP 13: TRY TO ADOPT THE PERSPECTIVE OF EACH PERSON WHO WILL BE AFFECTED

Putting ourselves in the shoes of those who will be affected by our decisions can change our understanding. What would each person consider the most ethical response? This approach can compensate for the distortion that often comes from seeing things only from our own perspective. One example is what Jones (1979; see also Blanchard-Fields, Chen, Horhota, & Wang, 2007; Gawronski, 2003; Gilbert & Malone, 1995; Weary, Vaughn, Stewart, & Edwards, 2006) called "correspondence bias." Although we often explain our own behavior in specific situations as due to external factors, we tend to attribute the behavior of others to their dispositions. Another example is what Meehl (1977) called a "double-standard of morals" (p. 232): We tend to hold explanations provided by other people to much more scientifically and logically rigorous standards than we use for our own explanations.

STEP 14: *DECIDE WHAT TO DO, REVIEW OR RECONSIDER IT, AND TAKE ACTION

Once we have decided on a course of action, we can—if time permits—rethink it. Sometimes simply making a decision to choose one option and exclude all others makes us suddenly aware of flaws in that option that had gone unnoticed up to that point. Rethinking gives us one last chance to make sure we have come up with the best possible response to a challenging situation.

STEP 15: *DOCUMENT THE PROCESS AND ASSESS THE RESULTS

Keeping track of the process through documentation can help us remain clear about what went into our decision: the elements of the problem; the options and potential consequences; the guidance provided by others; the perspective of the client, including the relevant rights, responsibilities, risks, and possible unintended consequences. Careful record keeping involves not only tracking what led up to our decision but also what happened afterward. What happened when we acted? Did we accomplish what we'd hoped and intended? Were their unforeseen consequences? Knowing what we know now, would we have taken the same path or tried a different response?

STEP 16: *ASSUME PERSONAL RESPONSIBILITY FOR THE CONSEQUENCES

If our response to the situation seems in hindsight to have been wrong or has caused unnecessary trouble, pain, loss, or problems, do we need to address the consequences of what we have done or failed to do?

STEP 17: *CONSIDER IMPLICATIONS FOR PREPARATION, PLANNING, AND PREVENTION

Did this situation and the effects of our response to it suggest any useful possibilities in the areas of preparation, planning, and prevention? Are there practical steps that would head off future problems or enable us to address them more effectively? Would changes in policies, procedures, or practices help?

Chapter 12

DIFFERENT CONCLUSIONS: EXAMPLE FROM THE INTERROGATION CONTROVERSY

L ife would be so much easier—and so much duller—if we all agreed on everything. But universal agreement on virtually any topic is pretty hard to find.

It is not hard to find disagreements among psychologists when ethics are at issue. The steps for ethical decision making outlined in Chapter 11 can help us to think through ethical issues carefully and thoughtfully, considering possibilities, perspectives, and different sources of information and guidance. But those steps do not necessarily lead all knowledgeable, open-minded professionals of good faith to reach the same conclusions.

Thoughtful psychologists who have read extensively ethical writings as well as theory and research and considered the full range of differing views may follow the steps of ethical decision making and nonetheless fundamentally disagree on such important issues as these:

- Is it right for a therapist to help a client obtain an abortion?
- Is it ever ethical for a therapist to provide treatment to a minor without the prior informed consent of the custodial parent or guardian?
- Would a therapist ever be justified in supporting a client's decision to commit suicide?

- If a client tells a therapist that several years ago he testified falsely in some trials and as a result some innocent people are currently serving jail terms, is it okay for the therapist to break confidentiality even if it would be breaking the law?
- Is it ethical for an individual therapist or a clinic to see only clients who are from one religion, one race, one ethnic group, or one gender?
- Would it ever be ethical for a therapist to break confidentiality if a client told the therapist that the client: had submitted false information to obtain disability status and payments, was driving while drunk, had plagiarized his dissertation, had published articles in influential journals reporting the results of research she had never conducted, or was embezzling and gambling away the pension funds on which hundreds of employees were counting for their retirement?

Similarly, as members of professional associations, those same thoughtful and informed psychologists may find themselves in honest disagreement as the association addresses through policies, reports, or public statements such complex and controversial issues as

- Is abortion detrimental to mental health?
- Are sexual orientation change therapies ethical?
- Is it appropriate to pursue steps to become more diverse and, if so, how?
- Is it appropriate to pursue prescription privileges for psychologists?
- Should the association take a public stance on the use of restraints or aversive therapies with children, adolescents, or adults in mental hospitals or similar settings; if so, what should the stance be?

In this chapter, we present examples of two different conclusions about a set of ethical issues in psychology that are representative of such an organizational ethical dilemma. We chose a recent controversy for our example: the disagreements among psychologists regarding psychologists' participation in detainee interrogations and related concerns about the 2002 *Ethical Principles of Psychologists and Code of Conduct* of the American Psychological Association (APA's) (APA, 2002; hereinafter referred to as the Ethics Code) Standards 1.02 and 1.03. One of us presents the reasoning and evidence leading to one conclusion. The other presents the reasoning and evidence leading to a different conclusion.

The aim of this chapter is *not* to determine which of the two conclusions is "right"—indeed, there is no "right" answer—but rather to illustrate how people of good faith can reach different conclusions and respectfully disagree about important ethical issues and to explore your reactions.

Each of the nine chapters that follow this one ends with a set of questions. In this chapter we reverse the order, revealing the questions before the chapter's two main sections so that you can keep them in mind as you read the material.

Here are the questions:

- How did you feel reading this chapter? Did your feelings differ in kind or intensity depending on whether you were reading Section 1 or Section 2?
- Did you find your mind wandering or racing through one of the sections or any part(s) of either section? Why do you think this happened? Do you believe that this interfered with your ability to consider the information, reasoning, or conclusions in those parts?
- Did any part of this chapter cause you to rethink your beliefs in this area? Did the rethinking lead you to different beliefs?
- Did you find it easier or a more positive experience to read the parts that you agreed with?
- To what degree do you seek out readings that present material contrary to your beliefs, that you know you disagree with? What readings have challenged your beliefs to the extent that you changed your mind in each of these areas: theoretical orientation, assessment, psychotherapy, and training?
- In your experience, what are the major ways in which psychologists respond to controversial topics or to writings that challenge their own beliefs? How could this be improved?

SECTION 1: PSYCHOLOGISTS' PRESENCE IN CHALLENGING SETTINGS: "DO NO HARM"

by Melba J. T. Vasquez

Introduction: Interrogation and APA Ethics Code Standards 1.02 and 1.03

From 2004 to the present (2010), APA (also referred to as the "Association") has been engaged in two challenging dialogues that are related but distinct. One dialogue addressed the involvement of psychologists in military interrogations. The second dialogue has involved how the APA Ethics Code addresses conflicts between ethics and law and conflicts between ethics and organizational demands. This section discusses the dialogue and debate within the Association about these two issues and the ethical principles and processes that guided decision making.

Psychologists Involvement in Military Interrogations

The principle of "Do no harm" provides the foundation for the Association's policies and resolutions regarding psychologists' involvement in military interrogations. The question arises, though: What does "Do no harm" mean in this context? As a general principle, our Association members can agree with and strongly support the principle of do no harm—indeed, it is the first of the five principles in the Ethics Code. What this principle means in application, however, is not always obvious and was the subject of passionate, at times contentious, and even painful discussions within APA over the past five years.

As APA examined psychologists' involvement in military interrogation, two issues emerged: the issue of what behaviors were permissible for psychologists and the issue of in what settings psychologists can act as consultants to military interrogations. Regarding the first issue, that of behaviors, there was unanimous consensus in the Association that torture and abuse are unethical and always to be prohibited. On the second issue, that of settings in which psychologists can consult to interrogations, reasonable, ethically minded psychologists passionately differed.

Behaviors Permissible for Psychologists

For many years, APA articulated and expanded its policy (APA, 1985, 1986) against torture to underscore its absolute prohibition against all forms of torture and abusive treatment. APA reiterated its stance against torture and abuse in a series of policies and resolutions beginning in 2005.

In late 2004, reports in the media began to emerge about the abuse of detainees. In response to these reports, concerns among APA members and governance led to the appointment of an APA Presidential Task Force, which issued the Report of the Presidential Task Force on Psychological Ethics and National Security (PENS). The first sentence of the PENS report states: "Psychologists do not engage in, direct, support, facilitate, or offer training in torture or other cruel, inhuman or degrading treatment." The second statement imposes an obligation on psychologists to report torture and abusive acts: "Psychologists are alert to acts of torture and other cruel, inhuman or degrading treatment, and have a responsibility to report these acts to the proper authorities" (APA, PENS, 2005, p. 4). APA repeated this absolute prohibition against torture and abuse as well as the obligation to report in 2006 and again in 2007.

In 2006, the APA Council of Representatives, the policymaking body of the Association (hereinafter referred to as "APA Council"), reiterated its condemnation of torture and abuse with the "Resolution Against Torture and Other Cruel, Inhuman, and Degrading Treatment or Punishment." This resolution included the statement:

> BE IT RESOLVED that the APA reaffirms its 1986 condemnation of torture and other cruel, inhuman, or degrading treatment or cruel, inhuman, or degrading punishment wherever it occurs. (para. 13)

In its 2006 resolution, the APA Council invoked the United Nations Convention Against Torture in order to emphasize that there could never be a justification of torture:

> BE IT RESOLVED that the APA reaffirms its support for the United Nations Declaration and Convention Against Torture and Other Cruel, Inhuman, or Degrading Treatment or Punishment and its adoption of Article 2.2, which states "[T]here are no exceptional circumstances whatsoever, whether induced by a state of war or a threat of war, internal political instability or any other public emergency, that may be invoked as a justification of torture." (para. 14)

Thus, by its 2006 resolution, the APA Council explicitly and emphatically rejected that there could be any post–September 11, 2001, justification for torture or abuse. In this manner, Council rejected the notion that there would be a post–September 11 ethic in psychology for any justification for torture or abuse.

In its 2006 resolution, the APA Council of Representatives also reiterated that psychologists have an ethical responsibility to report torture or abuse.

> BE IT RESOLVED that psychologists shall be alert to acts of torture and other cruel, inhuman, or degrading treatment or cruel, inhuman, or degrading punishment and have an ethical responsibility to report these acts to the appropriate authorities. (para. 23)

APA's work on prohibited behaviors was not yet complete. Much to the horror of APA members and a large segment of the public, legal memos from the Bush administration that had been made public argued that abusive interrogation techniques did not constitute torture and were therefore legal. APA members and the APA Council concluded that it was essential for APA to add specificity to APA's prohibitions against torture and cruel, inhuman, and degrading treatment or punishment to make absolutely clear that techniques such as waterboarding were included in APA's prohibition.

In 2007, the APA Council adopted the "Reaffirmation of the American Psychological Association Position Against Torture and Other Cruel, Inhuman, or Degrading Treatment or Punishment and Its Application to Individuals Defined in the United States Code as 'Enemy Combatants' " (APA, 2007). In its 2007 resolution, APA prohibited specific techniques the Bush administration Department of Justice memos had argued were legal. In 2008, the APA Council slightly edited this prohibition so that in its final form, the prohibition read

> BE IT RESOLVED that this unequivocal condemnation includes all techniques considered torture or cruel, inhuman or degrading treatment or

punishment under the United Nations Convention Against Torture and Other Cruel, Inhuman, or Degrading Treatment or Punishment; the Geneva Conventions; the Principles of Medical Ethics Relevant to the Role of Health Personnel, Particularly Physicians, in the Protection of Prisoners and Detainees against Torture and Other Cruel, Inhuman, or Degrading Treatment or Punishment; the Basic Principles for the Treatment of Prisoners: or the World Medical Association Declaration of Tokyo. An absolute prohibition against the following techniques therefore arises from, is understood in the context of, and is interpreted according to these texts: mock executions; water-boarding or any other form of simulated drowning or suffocation; sexual humiliation; rape; cultural or religious humiliation; exploitation of fears, phobias or psychopathology; induced hypothermia; the use of psychotropic drugs or mind-altering substances; hooding; forced nakedness; stress positions; the use of dogs to threaten or intimidate; physical assault including slapping or shaking; exposure to extreme heat or cold; threats of harm or death; isolation; sensory deprivation and over-stimulation; sleep deprivation; or the threatened use of any of the above techniques to an individual or to members of an individual's family. Psychologists are absolutely prohibited from knowingly planning, designing, participating in or assisting in the use of all condemned techniques at any time and may not enlist others to employ these techniques in order to circumvent this resolution's prohibition.

(APA, 2008, amended, para. 11)

This prohibition against specific techniques of interrogation illustrates the evolving nature of APA's position. Initially, APA had set forth an absolute prohibition against torture and cruel, inhuman, or degrading treatment or punishment. In response to events in the public domain, APA elaborated its absolute prohibition by specifying how that absolute prohibition was to be applied in the interrogation context. The *Washington Post* called APA's prohibition against specific techniques of interrogation a "rebuke" of Bush administration interrogation policies (Vedantam, 2007). It is important to note that APA's evolving position received strong support from all segments of the Council of Representatives, including psychoanalysis, military, forensic, and the peace psychology divisions.

These strongly worded APA Council resolutions against torture and abuse were communicated in various advocacy efforts directed to the Bush administration and other government officials. APA strongly condemned the abuse of detainees in letters to President Bush, Attorney General Mukasey, CIA Director Hayden, and members of Congress and in articles in the media. In addition, APA urged the establishment of policies and procedures that fully protect the human rights of detainees, including judicial review of the detainees' confinement (see APA's Web site, www.apa.org, for a detailed list of these letters and related APA correspondence and policy statements).

APA's 2007 resolution made five other important statements.

1. The 2007 resolution reiterated language from the United Nations Convention Against Torture that there can never be a justification for torture. Thus, for a second time, APA explicitly rejected any post–September 11 justification for torture.
2. The 2007 resolution reiterated that psychologists have a responsibility to report acts of torture or abuse.
3. The resolution called on U.S. judicial systems to reject testimony that results from torture and abuse.
4. The resolution stated that psychologists have an ethical responsibility to cooperate fully with investigations into the torture or abuse of detainees.
5. The resolution affirmed the prerogative or psychologists under the Ethics Code to disobey laws, regulations, or orders when they conflict with the Ethics Code and thus to engage in civil disobedience.

All of these statements by APA were guided by the principle of do no harm. It is important that all of these statements—the absolute prohibition of torture and abuse, the explicit rejection of a 9/11 justification for torture, the prohibition against specific techniques of interrogation—met with universal support within the Association. Psychologists from a wide range of interests and areas of expertise all strongly and unequivocally supported these positions. Indeed, the APA Council resolutions were the product of a strong collaborative effort by representatives of the APA divisions of Psychoanalysis; Society for the Study of Peace, Conflict, and Violence: Peace Psychology; American Psychology-Law Society; and Society for Military Psychology, among many others. On the issue of what behaviors were appropriate for psychology, there was unanimity within APA.

Settings in Which Psychologists Could Act as Consultants to Military Interrogations

An issue that did generate considerable debate within APA is the issue of the settings in which psychologists can ethically consult to interrogations. This issue proved enormously contentious because psychologists spoke with great passion on both sides of this issue. Some psychologists believed that psychology had an ethical obligation to be present wherever interrogations were taking place, as a voice against abusive interrogation tactics. Other psychologists believed that even to be present in certain settings was unethical because the possibility of ethical behavior was precluded by the very nature of the setting.

Psychologists on either side of this debate invoked data to support their position. Psychologists advocating for a presence wherever interrogations were taking place pointed to the actions of a psychologist who reported abusive techniques to his superior at the Pentagon. On the basis of this psychologist's report, the secretary of defense rescinded a number of abusive interrogation techniques. In addition, reports disclosed following a Freedom of Information Act request by the American Civil Liberties Union depicted a psychologist stopping an interrogation and calling for medical attention when it appeared that a detainee might have been abused. This example illustrates the advantage of a psychologist's presence to protect detainees.

Psychologists arguing against a presence of psychologists in certain international settings pointed to documented cases of abuse and to statements by the United Nations saying that the very conditions of confinement in certain settings constituted torture. These psychologists believed that there was no possibility of an ethical presence in these settings. Unlike the debate over behaviors, the debate over settings had two sides on which ethically minded and informed psychologists could debate honestly and passionately.

Delivering his presidential address in San Francisco at the 2007 annual convention, the president of Division 41, the Psychology-Law Society, commented on the challenge of knowing when to engage and disengage from settings that violate constitutional rights.

> In my travels across the country, my work as a consultant or expert witness has often led me into conditions that were not only unconstitutional, but horrifying. And yet, in those same systems, I have seen seemingly decent and hard-working psychologists, working tirelessly to provide solace and hope to people in very difficult straits.
>
> Some ethicists argue that participating in unacceptable systems is wrong. They argue that the participation of credentialed professionals legitimizes and thus perpetuates these systems. They admonish such professionals to simply walk away, to refuse to play in such a filthy sandbox. And these arguments seem reasonable.
>
> But when I meet the people who have stayed, I do not find them less ethical or less moral for it. To the contrary, many of these psychologists, nurses, psychiatrists, social workers, correctional officers, and psychiatric technicians have become heroes to me. To maintain one's standards of decency and professionalism in the face of an apparently uncaring political system takes courage and tenacity and goodness of heart.
>
> These observations lead to several important questions. How then does one make sense of this dilemma? How bad can the system be before it is time to walk away? And how does one walk away from people in such dire need?

I have learned over the years that I am not a perfectionist. (I mean, I am really, really, really not a perfectionist.) It's way too depressing to me; perfectionists of course never succeed at anything. Their lives are spent climbing a ladder that has no top rung. (No offense to those of you who are; in fact, my heart goes out to you.) And since I actually enjoy making creative mistakes, for me, perfectionism is especially uninviting.

No, my friends, I am, to the core of my being, an incrementalist. I believe in trying to leave everything just a little better than I found it. I believe in the hokey "star fish" story with all of my heart. I believe that if everyone who visited a park would just take one extra piece of trash out with them when they leave, the park would be spotless in less than a week.

Granted, to many of you, it will not seem like much of an assignment. But it is my assignment, and I have accepted it.

But what about perpetuating evil? Nonsense. Watch what happens when a psychologist quits in moral indignation. See if the place closes down. It won't, and no matter how good the quitter feels about themselves, if they were any good, it will be their clients who have been hurt, not the system.

To me, the moral thing, the ethical thing, is not to quit in moral indignation. It is to maintain one's dignity and professionalism in the face of bad circumstances. It is to understand the difference between reasonable flexibility and selling out. It is speaking with honor and humility (even in court) about how it ought to be, and resisting the understandable temptation to sink into self righteous and angry denunciations. It is protecting your own hope against all assaults, because hope is the most precious gift you share with your clients.

So, to those of you who do good work in bad settings, I have something to say. Not only are you behaving in a morally and ethically acceptable manner; to me you are heroes. Your jail or prison or hospital or free clinic is a little better each day because you are there. You leave each of your clients a little better than you find them, and occasionally foster hope in people for whom hope is but a distant memory.

The time to quit? That's an easy one. Quit when you run out of gas. Quit when it hurts you more than it helps them. Quit when the system won't let you help, even a little bit. Quit when you become an instrument of harm. Until then, Godspeed to you, and thanks.

(*Dvoskin*, 2007, *pp.* 20–23)

This eloquent passage brilliantly captures the dilemma. The passage exhorts psychologists to stay engaged but to disengage when the system will not let them help or when they become instruments of harm. Here the debate was intense and growing among psychologists.

In 2008, the issue of setting became the subject of a petition resolution under the APA bylaws. Article XX of the Bylaws of the American Psychological Association allows that amendments may be proposed by a petition signed by 4% or more of the members of the Association (APA, 2008d, pp. 32–33). In 2008, this resolution was placed before the membership:

> Be it resolved that psychologists may not work in settings where persons are held outside of, or in violation of, either International Law (e.g., the UN Convention Against Torture and the Geneva Conventions) or the US Constitution (where appropriate), unless they are working directly for the persons being detained or for an independent third party working to protect human rights.
>
> (APA, 2008g, para. 11)

The membership passed the petition resolution by 8,792 to 6,152 votes, a tally that reflected how the association was of two minds on this issue. Immediately following passage of the resolution, APA began informing officials in the government of the adoption of this position. At the same time, APA members began to ask how the petition resolution would be implemented. The 2008 APA president, Alan Kazdin, appointed a task force and charged it with developing recommendations for the implementation of the petition resolution.

Kazdin believed it was enormously important that the sponsors of the petition resolution have a strong voice in this process. He therefore appointed all three of the petition resolution sponsors to be on the APA Presidential Advisory Group on the Implementation of the Petition Resolution. This advisory group met and set forth a series of specific recommendations for APA governance to implement the petition resolution. The advisory group issued its report in December 2008 (APA, 2008h). As of this writing, APA has implemented or otherwise addressed each of the advisory group's recommendations, including amending the Ethics Code, and APA staff members continue to implement the agenda set forth in the advisory group report.

In February 2009, the APA Council took action on the petition resolution and on the advisory group report and approved these motions related to the petition resolution:

> That the Council of Representatives votes to suspend Association Rule 30-3.1 to stipulate that the petition resolution is "complete" as of the February 2009 meeting and is now APA policy.
>
> That the Council of Representatives adopts the following title for the petition resolution to clarify that it is not intended to be applied broadly to

jails, detention centers, and psychiatric hospitals: "Psychologists and Unlawful Detention Settings with a Focus on National Security" and requests that the title be incorporated into the minutes, along with the resolution, and that the petition resolution ballot be included as an attachment.

That the Council of Representatives receives the "Report of the APA Presidential Advisory Group on the Implementation of the Petition Resolution" and forwards the report to APA Central Office and relevant Boards and Committees for their review and appropriate action. The APA Central Office will include in its regular reports to the Council and Board of Directors steps taken to implement the petition resolution as proposed by the advisory group in the report section entitled "Options for Council to Consider Related to the Implementation of the Petition Resolution."

(APA, 2009a)

Thus, by 2009, APA had adopted policies regarding both behaviors and settings related to psychologists consulting to military interrogations. Along the way, APA members had voiced passionate feelings about the Association's first principle: Do no harm. The debates had been productive yet at times painful. Importantly, APA had shown a vote of confidence in a member-driven association and in honoring the varied voices and perspectives. Perhaps this was best on display at the 2007 annual convention where APA put on a program "Ethics and Interrogation: Confronting the Challenge," at which 44 speakers presented their views in a series of nine 2-hour sessions. The APA Board of Directors strongly supported this series of programs—the Board funded the planning group—and the final program was the result of collaboration among a wide range of APA divisions. The Board was adamant that every voice in the Association would be represented at the convention program and that it wanted the membership to hear from the most ardent critics of APA's position.

As author of this section and as APA president elect at the time of this writing, I hope that this process, long and arduous as it has been, will be seen as evidence of APA's strength. Rather than shy away from a difficult dialogue, APA embraced an enormously challenging issue that confronted not only APA but society as a whole. Along the way, APA was subject to much criticism, and many commentators and the media compared APA unfavorably to other associations on this issue. Nonetheless, certain commentators felt that APA had adopted the correct position and that other associations had fallen short in explaining how their members could contribute to preventing acts of violence in an ethical and responsible manner. In May 2009 an editorial in the highly prestigious journal *Nature* remarked that in the debate over interrogations, "there are few easy answers" (Responsible Interrogation, 2009, p. 300). The editorial went on to favorably contrast

APA's position with the positions of the American Medical and American Psychiatric associations:

> But such restrictions [imposed on member involvement in interrogations by the American Medical and American Psychiatric Associations] fly in the face of the reality that interrogation is a necessity in preventing loss of life from terrorism, and that some professionals feel it is their duty to ensure that the activity is conducted responsibly. The risks of abuse are ever present, and having a professional present should serve as protection for detainees, provided the professional adheres to, and is held accountable to, the most fundamental medical ethic of all: "do no harm."

APA's position evolved over time. The evolution in APA's position was fueled by our members' passion and interest in examining what do no harm means for psychologists.

APA Ethics Code Standards 1.02 and 1.03

Concurrent with the issue of psychologist involvement in military interrogations, APA was addressing a related but distinct issue: how the Ethics Code addresses conflicts between ethics and law and between ethics and organizational demands. The 1992 Ethics Code (APA, 1992) had this ethical standard:

Standard 1.02 Relationship of Ethics and Law

If psychologists' ethical responsibilities conflict with law, psychologists make known their commitment to the Ethics Code and take steps to resolve the conflict in a responsible manner.

The 1992 standard imposed on psychologists an obligation to engage in a process when a conflict between ethics and law arose. The process involved making known the commitment to the Ethics Code and taking steps to resolve the conflict in a responsible manner. The 1992 code was silent regarding what should happen if the psychologist was not able to resolve the conflict.

In 1996, four years after the 1992 Ethics Code was adopted, APA appointed a task force to begin the process of revising the 1992 Code. I was a member of this task force the entire time that it met. Part of the revision process involved multiple calls for member and public comment throughout. The revision process lasted for five years until the 2002 Ethics Code (the 1992 code's successor) was adopted in August 2002.

Although the Ethics Code Task Force received only a handful of comments regarding Standard 1.02—about 10 out of the over 1,400 submitted during the 5-year revision process—a significant concern had arisen in the practice and forensic communities. Judges who were not always familiar with psychology ethics sometimes ordered that raw test data and psychotherapy notes be submitted into legal proceedings. Such an order was inconsistent with the 1992 Ethics Code prohibition against releasing test data to unqualified persons. At times, judges ordered psychologists to make custody, visitation, or supervision recommendations in the absence of an appropriate evaluation, which was inconsistent with the Ethics Code requirement that psychologists have an appropriate foundation for their recommendations and opinions. Psychologists in these and related areas of practice became increasingly concerned that they could be placed in an irreconcilable conflict between ethics and law. As a consequence, these psychologists felt they would have to choose between violating the law and violating their ethics, that is, between answering to a court, an ethics committee, or a psychology licensing board.

At its fall 2000 meeting, the Ethics Code Task Force responded to such concerns by revising the language of Standard 1.02 to say that if a conflict between ethics and law arose, psychologists would engage in a process of making known their commitment to the Ethics Code and taking steps to resolve the conflict. If that process was not successful, the task force felt that it would be appropriate for a psychologist to have the option of following the "law, regulations, or other governing legal authority." This language seemed reasonable insofar as it created a process for resolving a conflict between ethics and law but did not require a psychologist to violate a court order and thus risk being jailed or fined. Under the revised language, the psychologist could, nonetheless, engage in civil disobedience if he or she chose. This language, adopted by the Ethics Code Task Force in the fall of 2000, was eventually adopted by the APA Council in August 2002 as part of the 2002 Ethics Code.

Neither the APA Council nor the Ethics Code Task Force had any idea of the context in which the language revised in the fall of 2000 would be read. Over the next years, as the Bush administration responded to the events of September 11, 2001, deeply disturbing news emerged that seemed to many almost as unpredictable as the attacks themselves.

Techniques of interrogation tantamount to torture were being used. Lawyers in the Bush administration Department of Justice had authored legal opinions that concluded such techniques were consistent with the law. APA members began to ask what would happen if a psychologist was ordered to engage in torture or cruel, inhuman, or degrading treatment or punishment. What would the psychologist's ethical obligations be? Could the Ethics Code itself now be used as a defense by virtue of how Ethical Standard 1.02 had been revised? A growing number of the Council of Representatives and APA members began to call for amending Ethical Standards 1.02 and 1.03, the latter of which addressed conflicts between ethics and organizational demands. The APA Council directed the Ethics Committee to work on drafting language to make clear that the Ethics Code could never be used as a defense to violating human rights.

The Ethics Committee began its work by calling for member and public comment. The committee received an overwhelming response, and engaged in a dialogue with the APA Council to find the right words. Over time, language emerged that garnered considerable consensus from all quarters of APA. Central to the proposed amendments were three elements: a process for resolving conflicts between ethics and law, deletion of blanket language permitting psychologists to follow the law without regard to what the law required, and addition of language stating that the Ethics Code could never be used as a defense to violating human rights.

Here again is an example of APA's position evolving as events unfolded in the public domain. Actions by the Bush administration placed language in the revised Ethics Code in a context that had never been considered or even imagined by the people who had drafted and adopted APA's 2002 Ethics Code. When the new context became clear to APA, it began examining how to respond appropriately to this change in circumstances.

There were two aspects to this response. In June 2009, the APA Ethics Committee adopted a statement and policy titled "No Defense to Torture under the APA Ethics Code."

> There is no defense to torture under the Ethical Principles of Psychologists and Code of Conduct (2002).
>
> The APA Ethics Committee will not accept any defense to torture in its adjudication of ethics complaints.
>
> Torture in any form, at any time, in any place, and for any reason, is unethical for psychologists and wholly inconsistent with membership in the American Psychological Association.
>
> No exceptional circumstances whatsoever, whether a state of war or a threat of war, internal political instability or any other public emergency, legal compulsion or organizational demand, may be invoked as a justification for torture.
>
> *(APA, Ethics Committee, 2009a, p. 1)*

In an addendum to its statement "No Defense to Torture under the APA Ethics Code," the Ethics Committee also stated that it considered the prohibition against torture to encompass the specific techniques prohibited by the Council of Representatives 2008 "Amendment to the Reaffirmation of the American Psychological Association Position Against Torture and Other Cruel, Inhuman, or Degrading Treatment or Punishment and Its Application to

Individuals Defined in the United States Code as 'Enemy Combatants' " (APA, Ethics Committee, 2009a, p. 2).

The Ethics Committee thus made clear that it would not accept any defense to torture under the Ethics Code; Standards 1.02 and 1.03 could not be used as a defense to torture. In addition to adopting this policy statement, the Ethics Committee continued to follow the Council's directive on drafting language to emphasize and remove any possible doubt among the membership and the public that the Ethics Code did not offer a defense to violating human rights.

In response to member and public comments offering amendment language, the Ethics Committee proposed and in February 2010 the Council overwhelmingly approved these amendments to the 2002 Ethics Code (note that strike-through indicates text was deleted; underline indicates text was added).

From the Introduction and Applicability Section

If psychologists' ethical responsibilities conflict with law, regulations, or other governing legal authority, psychologists make known their commitment to this Ethics Code and take steps to resolve the conflict in a responsible manner. ~~If the conflict is unresolvable via such means, psychologists may adhere to the requirements of the law, regulations, or other governing authority~~ in keeping with basic principles of human rights. (APA, 2009c, p. 1)

From Ethical Standard 1.02

1.02 Conflicts Between Ethics and Law, Regulations, or Other Governing Legal Authority

If psychologists' ethical responsibilities conflict with law, regulations, or other governing legal authority, psychologists <u>clarify the nature of the conduct</u>, make known their commitment to the Ethics Code and take <u>reasonable</u> steps to resolve the conflict <u>consistent with the General Principles and Ethical Standards of the Ethics Code.</u> ~~If the conflict is unresolvable via such means, psychologists may adhere to the requirements of the law, regulations, or other governing legal authority.~~ <u>Under no circumstances may this standard be used to justify or defend violating human rights.</u> (APA, 2009c, p. 1)

From Ethical Standard 1.03

1.03 Conflicts Between Ethics and Organizational Demands

If the demands of an organization with which psychologists are affiliated or for whom they are working are in conflict with this Ethics Code, psychologists clarify the nature of the conflict, make known their commitment to the Ethics Code, and ~~to the extent feasible, resolve the conflict in a way that permits adherence to the Ethics Code.~~ take reasonable steps to resolve the conflict consistent with the General Principles and Ethical Standards of the Ethics Code. Under no circumstances may this standard be used to justify or defend violating human rights. (APA, 2009c, p. 2)

Following adoption of the Ethics Committee policy statement "No Defense to Torture" and the amendments to the Ethics Code Standards 1.02 and 1.03, APA has emphatically clarified that there is no defense to torture or human rights violations under the APA Ethics Code.

Difficult Dialogues

These years have been very challenging to APA, as they have been to our entire society. Part of the challenge has been the very difficult dialogues that have occurred within the association as members have expressed their passionate feelings about the issues discussed in this chapter. At times, these dialogues have been open, transparent, collegial, and productive. At other times, they have been less so.

One of the challenges has been in the form of various statements that have cast APA's work in a light that, in my opinion and the opinion of others in the association, has been unfair. As an example, several prominent psychologists have linked changes in the Ethics Code during the 1996 to 2002 revision process regarding conflicts between ethics and law to the events of September 11, 2001. The implication has been that changes were made in 2002 for the purpose of allowing psychologists to engage in inappropriate behavior, even torture. This linkage is demonstrably false. The record makes clear that there is no association between changes made to the Ethics Code during the 1996 to 2002 revision process and the events of September 11. The language that became the subject of controversy—that faced with an irreconcilable conflict between ethics and law psychologists "may adhere to the requirements of the law, regulations, or other governing legal authority"—was drafted in the fall of 2000, nearly a year before the events of September 11, 2001, and before the Bush administration came into office. Moreover, the data refuting any connection between the 2002 revisions and the events of September 11 have been available on the APA Web site for anyone wishing to trace the evolution of language in the Ethics Code. Continued writings that link these two, despite the available data, have made an already challenging dialogue even more difficult.

Equally unfortunate has been the innuendo that APA included the Nuremberg Defense in its Ethics Code as a response to the events of September 11. Nuremberg, or "I was just following orders," is about the abdication of moral agency. According to the Nuremberg Defense, one need not engage in a moral struggle because the law simply dictates what one must do. This has never been APA's position. APA has imposed on psychologists an obligation to make known their commitment to the Ethics Code and to engage in a process of resolving conflicts between ethics and law. The APA Ethics Committee has taken these obligations very seriously. Even the suggestion that APA included such a defense in the Ethics Code as a reaction to the events of September 11 is seriously misguided. The linking of changes in the Ethics Code to September 11, the failure to include the full history of the revision process in discussions about changes in the Ethics Code, and the invocation of the highly provocative imagery of Nuremberg have neither displayed a respectful attitude to the gravity of the issues involved nor facilitated a productive dialogue.

It is noteworthy that few if any of the individuals who have expressed such strong feelings about Ethical Standards 1.02 and 1.03 during the interrogation debate actually submitted comments during the 1996 to 2002 Ethics Code revision process, even after the fall 2000 language was drafted. Perhaps these individuals failed, like so many of us, to realize the implications of the revised language for the coming societal context. If such a conjecture is correct, that means the entire membership has learned an important lesson about unforeseen and unintended consequences in writing language for our Ethics Code.

Honest-minded and informed people had different views on the issues. Members were earnest and passionate as they voiced their concerns. The very hard work of representatives from the APA Divisions of Social Justice, of various members of governance, and of APA staff involved in all of these endeavors were such that this writer will be forever grateful for the integrity reflected in the care all took in the deliberations.

In Chapter 11 of this book, we discussed steps in the ethical decision-making processes. During the controversial organizational dilemma discussed here, I observed members of the association truly engaged in ethical decision making including:

- The identification of the dilemma
- Attempts to determine who would be affected by various decisions
- Deliberate review of the ethical principles, standards, laws, and relevant research

- Multiple consultations
- Consideration of alternatives
- Consideration of impact of decisions

This section of this chapter has been an attempt to document the decision-making process from my perspective.

SECTION 2: ARE APA'S DETAINEE INTERROGATION POLICIES ETHICAL AND EFFECTIVE?[1]

by Kenneth S. Pope

My dear friend Melba Vasquez and I reached different views about APA's approach to detainee interrogations. My part of this chapter[1] serves as a companion to Melba's thoughtful essay.

The events of 9/11 cast all of us into a tangle of complex issues, dangerous realities, and hard choices. I respectfully disagree with APA's post–9/11 policies and public statements. I believe those choices wrenched APA away from its ethical foundation and defining values. APA moved beyond what I could in good conscience support with my membership.

My choice to resign from APA reflects my effort to judge what was right for me. I respect those who saw things differently, held other beliefs, took other paths.

APA has presented its reasoning in support of its policies in its press releases, its journals, its Web site, its Internet lists, its conventions, the *APA Monitor on Psychology*, and other venues. This chapter section touches on a few of the points raised by those who disagree with APA's policies in this area. Not all of these played a role in my personal decision, but I believe openly considering them—even if the result is to reject their validity—is part of a comprehensive approach to these issues based on critical thinking and weighing material from all points of view.

In reviewing material from different points of view, I have chosen in many instances to quote directly the words of those whom APA selected to serve as members of its task force on ethics and national security, and also those who have been some of the most prominent critics of APA's policies in this area. Some of the rhetoric on both sides may seem intense, confrontational, or divisive. It is important to not let the rhetoric on either side become a focus or distraction but to understand and consider carefully the substance of what each person is saying.

The issues are many and complex, but in this short space I'll review a few key APA decisions and outline four main points.

[1] I am indebted to Harvard Medical School professor Thomas G. Gutheil, with whom I coauthored articles discussing these issues (Pope & Gutheil, 2009a, b). Parts of this chapter are based on my discussions with Tom and our articles.

Key APA Policies and Public Statements

To shape its interrogation policy, APA formed what was called a "blue ribbon" panel (James, 2008, p. 246): the Presidential Task Force on Psychological Ethics and National Security (PENS Task Force). The task force report became APA's policy, although there seems to have been some confusion about the process of its adoption.

Typically the APA Council of Representatives carefully reviews and discusses task force reports prior to voting on whether to approve the report. Council members are elected by APA's 54 diverse divisions and by the state and provincial psychological associations. The Council's deliberative processes subject proposed policies to intense scrutiny, critical evaluation, and vigorous debate from multiple points of view. Concerns from APA members who are not a part of governance can be voiced through their Council representatives. This rigorous review process can uncover a policy proposal's fallacies, bias, unfounded conclusions, significant weaknesses, overlooked information, unexamined alternatives, and possible unintended consequences prior to Council voting on whether to accept, endorse, and approve the proposal as APA policy.

The APA president during whose term the APA Presidential Task Force was appointed and submitted its report mistakenly announced in *American Psychologist*, APA's journal of record, that "the APA Council of Representatives approved the PENS Task Force Report at its August 2005 meeting" (Levant, 2006a, p. 385). APA issued a press release emphasizing that: "The American Psychological Association (APA) Council of Representatives, the Association's governing body, has endorsed a Task Force Report on Psychological Ethics and National Security today. . . ." (APA, 2005). APA's *Monitor on Psychology*, which is sent to all APA members and made available to the public on the APA Web site, noted that the PENS report "was accepted by APA's Council of Representatives" (Mumford, 2006, p. 68). Over a year after the PENS report had become policy, APA submitted a statement that was published in Salon: "The reality is that APA's Council of Representatives endorsed the current policy . . ." (Benjamin, 2006).

Unfortunately, the announcements that APA's Council of Representatives had accepted, endorsed, and approved the PENS report were incorrect. Before the Council had an opportunity to review, debate, and vote on the PENS report at its regularly scheduled meeting the following month, the APA Board of Directors had invoked Article VII, Section 4, of the APA Bylaws to declare an emergency and voted by e-mail on July 1 to approve the report as APA ethics policy. In some instances, the incorrect announcements that it was the Council that had approved the report as APA policy were followed by some form of an erratum. For example, a statement appeared in *Monitor on Psychology* that "it was incorrect to state that the Council accepted the report" ("Correction," 2006). Similarly, *Salon* published an e-mail that the APA spokesperson had circulated to Council acknowledging that "Council took no official action on the report" (Benjamin, 2006). APA Council member Bernice Lott, reviewing the history of these announcements, wrote: "APA's policy ... presented in the report of the Presidential Task Force on Psychological Ethics and National Security (Report, 2005), was never adopted or approved by the Council Representatives. Nor was the Council ever asked to do so. Public statements that have implied or said otherwise have been inaccurate, and some have been publicly corrected" (2007, pp. 35–36).

Incorrect information in an organization's initial news release often finds its way into newspaper articles and other coverage of the announcement. When the incorrect statement is also disseminated over the course of more than a year to such venues as the organization's journal of record, its magazine, its web site, and the popular media, there occurs the risk that, however unintentionally, a widespread misunderstanding and misleading historical record will be created. In those instances in which a correction was attempted, an erratum appearing months after the original incorrect statement may not be seen by all or even most of the readers of the original article or be reflected in the secondary literature. APA's official statements in its news releases, on its web site, in its journal of record, and elsewhere should be reliable, trustworthy, and valid.

Before taking a look at the PENS policy, it is worth noting that although the PENS Task Force originally included 10 members, one member sent a message to the chair and other members after the report was written. The message included this passage:

> Out of ethical concerns, I have decided to step down from the PENS Task Force because continuing work with the Task Force tacitly legitimates the wider silence and inaction of the APA on the crucial issues at hand. . . . The . . . approach the APA has taken on these issues is inappropriate to the situation, inconsistent with the Association's mission, and damaging to our profession. It has been encouraging to see a more robust statement recently from the President of the American Psychiatric Association. This is the kind of leadership warranted in the situation we face.
>
> (Wessells, 2006)

Another PENS Task Force member also took a critical stance. She wrote that "the platitudinous PENS report, as I see it, largely represents political damage control" (Arrigo, 2006; see also "APA Interrogation Task Force Member Dr. Jean Maria Arrigo Exposes Group's Ties to Military," 2007).

The PENS report affirmed psychologists' national security work of obtaining information: "Psychologists have a valuable and ethical role to assist in protecting our nation, other nations, and innocent civilians from harm, which will at times entail gathering information that can be used in our nation's and other nations' defense" (APA, 2005).

With the PENS report, APA moved toward making psychologists central to the interrogation process. APA's statement on psychology and interrogations submitted to the U.S. Senate Select Committee on Intelligence explained that "conducting an interrogation is inherently a psychological endeavor" and that "psychology is central to this process.... Psychologists have valuable contributions to make toward ... protecting our nation's security through interrogation processes" (APA, 2007b).

According to APA, psychiatrists and other physicians lacked various competencies that made psychologists uniquely qualified to play an important role in the interrogation process. The director of APA's Ethics Office wrote: "This difference, which stems from psychologists' unique competencies, represents an important distinction between what role psychologists and physicians may take in interrogations" (Behnke, 2006a, p. 67).

Other groups disagreed that competence was the issue. American Psychiatric Association president Steven Sharfstein (2006), for example, focused on "core values" when he wrote:

> I told the generals that psychiatrists will not participate in the interrogation of persons held in custody. Psychologists, by contrast, had issued a position statement allowing consultations in interrogations. If you were ever wondering what makes us different from psychologists, here it is. This is a paramount challenge to our ethics and our Hippocratic training.... Our profession is lost if we play any role in inflicting these wounds. (p. 1713)

The military acted on the contrast between APA's policies and those of the American Psychiatric Association and American Medical Association:

> Pentagon officials said ... they would try to use only psychologists, not psychiatrists, to help interrogators devise strategies to get information from detainees at places like Guantánamo Bay, Cuba. The new policy follows by little more than two weeks an overwhelming vote by the American Psychiatric Association discouraging its members from participating in those efforts.
> *(Lewis, 2006)*

According to APA, psychologists' "unique competencies" meant that they were "in a unique position to assist in ensuring that processes are safe, legal, ethical, and effective for all participants" (Behnke, 2006b, p. 154; see also APA, 2005). APA repeatedly assured the public that psychologists would not be involved in harming detainees. The director of the APA Ethics Office emphasized that "psychologists knew not to participate in activities that harmed detainees" (Lewis, 2006).

APA claimed that not only would psychologists avoid any role in harming detainees, their unique competencies and work had been helping keep the detainee interrogations safe and ethical. The 2007 APA president, for example, wrote to the *Washington Monthly* that psychologists' consultation in interrogations "makes an important contribution toward keeping interrogations safe and ethical" (Brehm, 2007).

Different Perspectives

The next four sections present some different perspectives on APA's policies and public statements, and include views of diverse critics.

Keeping Interrogations Safe and Avoiding Activities That Harmed Detainees

Does the record support the assurance that psychologists knew "not to participate in activities that harmed detainees," that they were devoted to "keeping interrogations safe"?

The *Boston Globe* (2008; see also Goodman, 2007) summarized a series of investigative news reports in an editorial that began: "From the moment US military and civilian officials began detaining and interrogating Guantanamo Bay prisoners with methods that the Red Cross has called tantamount to torture, they have had the assistance of psychologists." Eban (2007) reported that "psychologists weren't merely complicit in America's aggressive new interrogation regime. Psychologists . . . had actually designed the tactics and trained interrogators in them while on contract to the C.I.A." A Senate investigation found that "[m]ilitary psychologists were enlisted to help develop more aggressive interrogation methods, including snarling dogs, forced nudity and long periods of standing, against terrorism suspects" (Flaherty, 2008).

Mayer broadened the focus from psychologists designing tactics and training investigators in the "aggressive new interrogation" to include psychologists' other roles. She reported that "[General] Dunlavey soon drafted military psychologists to play direct roles in breaking detainees down. The psychologists were both treating the detainees clinically and advising interrogators on how to manipulate them and exploit their phobias . . ."(Mayer, 2008a, p.196). She wrote that "psychologists were heavily involved in drawing up and monitoring interrogation plans, which were designed individually for each detainee. . . . Sleep deprivation was such a common technique . . . pornography [was used] to manipulate detainees. . . . Detainees were routinely shackled in painful 'stress positions'" (Mayer, 2008b).

The CIA special review of counterterrorism, detention, and interrogation activities, marked "Top Secret" but later declassified, documented yet another area of psychologists' involvement (U.S. Central Intelligence Agency, Inspector General, 2004). In addition to psychologists designing the aggressive interrogation techniques and their "direct roles in breaking detainees down," still other psychologists (i.e., "outside psychologists") played key roles in providing assurances that use of aggressive techniques, such as waterboarding, were safe and would not cause lasting mental harm.

The special review's appendix C, a communication from the U.S. Department of Justice to the CIA Acting General Counsel, noted that the CIA "consulted with outside psychologists, completed a psychological assessment and reviewed the relevant literature on this topic. Based on this inquiry, you believe that the use of the procedures, including the waterboard, and as a course of conduct would not result in prolonged mental harm." The input from outside psychologists fit with the reports of the various on-site psychologists: "Your on-site psychologists have also indicated that JPRA [Joint Personnel Recovery Agency] has likewise not reported any significant long-term mental health consequences from the use of the waterboard."[2]

It is worth noting that some documents and critics suggest that psychologists also engaged in activities relevant to APA's reassurances about keeping interrogations legal. The American Civil Liberties Union (ACLU) made government documents obtained under the Freedom of Information Act publicly available. The ACLU (2008) pointed out that the government's own documents confirmed that "psychologists supported illegal interrogations in Iraq and Afghanistan." For additional concerns about legal issues relevant to interrogations, please see "Guantanamo Bay: Overview of ICRC's work for internees" (International Committee of the Red Cross, 2004).

Scholars like Robert Jay Lifton (2008) critiqued APA's policies and assurances that "psychologists knew not to participate in activities that harmed detainees" and should be engaged in "keeping interrogations safe." He stated: "The idea that psychologists should be kept around during interrogation in order to protect the person being interrogated or avoid or advise against extreme harmful measures, that idea seems quite absurd to me. . . . Some of the greatest roles in bringing that [i.e., "some of the worst abuses . . . to break down our prisoners"] about have been played by psychologists."

Amnesty International, Physicians for Human Rights, and 11 other organizations sent an open letter to APA ("Open letter," 2009) about what it termed APA's "grievous mismanagement of this issue"; APA's "providing ethical cover

---

[2] The Joint Personnel Recovery Agency is in charge of the Survival, Evasion, Resistance, and Escape (SERE) schools. The agency is "responsible for missions to include the training for SERE and Prisoner of War and Missing In Action operational affairs including repatriation" (U.S. Central Intelligence Agency, Inspector General, 2004). The SERE program trains soldiers (and civilians working for the Defense Department or private contractors working with the military) to survive, evade capture, resist torture and interrogation, escape, and maintain the military code of conduct.

for psychologists' participation in detainee abuse"; and APA's handling of the detainee interrogation issue creating "the greatest ethical crisis" in the profession's history and making a "terrible stain on the reputation of American psychology."

Professor of Medicine and Bioethics Steven Miles, author of *Oath Betrayed: America's Torture Doctors*, wrote: "The American Psychological Association was unique among U.S. health professional associations in providing policy cover for abusive interrogations" (2009).

Keeping Interrogations Ethical

Did sound ethical reasoning support APA's stance that the Nuremberg Ethic should be dropped from the ethics code and replaced by the doctrine that psychologists should be able to set aside their "ethical responsibilities" if those responsibilities inherently conflict with military orders, governmental regulations, national and local laws, and any other form of governing legal authority?

On August 21, 2002, for the first time in its history, APA took a stand counter to a basic ethic that seized the world's attention at the Nuremberg trials. In what became known as the Nuremberg Defense, the Nazi defendants said they were just "following the law" or "just following orders." The Nuremberg Court and world opinion rejected that attempt to avoid responsibility. The resulting Nuremberg Ethic was clear: People who chose to violate fundamental ethical responsibilities could not blame laws, orders, or regulations.

APA's post–9/11 ethics code rejected the historic Nuremberg Ethic, stating that when facing an irreconcilable conflict between their "ethical responsibilities" and the state's authority, "psychologists may adhere to the requirements of the law, regulations, or other governing legal authority" (Section 1.02). One draft had added "in keeping with basic principles of human rights." APA decided to allow that specific limitation in the code's introduction but to drop it from the code's *enforceable* section. This enforceable Standard 1.02 letting psychologists violate fundamental ethical responsibilities in favor of following a regulation, a law, or a governing legal authority clashed with APA's ethical foundation and what had been its defining values.

It is important to note that this doctrine of "giving psychologists the option to violate their ethical responsibilities in order to follow the law, regulations, or other forms of legal authority had been discussed before September 11" (Pope & Gutheil, 2008). Not only had the doctrine been included in various ethics code drafts over the years, but the controversy over conflicts between ethical and legal responsibilities has a long history in psychology. For example, "When Laws and Values Conflict: A Dilemma for Psychologists" (Pope & Bajt, 1988), appearing in *American Psychologist* over two decades ago, reported a survey of psychologists' beliefs and experiences in this area. However, it was only after 9/11 that APA took a step unprecedented in its over 100-year history: The APA

Council of Representatives voted to let psychologists set aside basic ethical responsibilities if they conflicted irreconcilably with laws, regulations, and other forms of governing legal authority, which included military orders. APA's vote to reject the Nuremberg Ethic, occurring less than a year after and in the context of both the 9/11 attack on the United States and the U.S. military's launch of Operation Enduring Freedom in Afghanistan in response to that attack, clearly communicated to the profession, policy makers, and the public its shift in values.

The U.S. military emphasized APA's new enforceable ethical standard in its formal policy for psychologists involved in "detention operations, intelligence interrogations, and detainee debriefings" (U.S. Department of the Army, 2006, p. 152). Citing APA's changed ethical standard, the army policy stated: "A process for maintaining adherence to the Code when it conflicts with applicable law, regulation, and policy is outlined below" (p. 154). The policy states that after addressing and attempting to resolve the issue, and after appropriate consultation, "If the issue continues to elude resolution, adhere to law, regulations, and policy in a responsible manner."

By adopting an enforceable standard letting psychologists set aside their "ethical responsibilities" whenever they were in irreconcilable conflict with military orders, governmental regulations, national and local laws, and any other form of governing legal authority, APA created a paradoxical context not only for public statements about psychologists' commitment to their ethical responsibilities but also for APA's repeated assurances about psychologists' unique competencies to help keep interrogations ethical.

APA's change in its ethics code drew widespread criticism. The editor of the *British Medical Journal* placed a photograph from Abu Ghraib prison on the cover of one issue and wrote:

> Just obeying the rules has long been insufficient for doctors. The judges at Nuremberg made clear that obeying commands from superiors didn't remove personal accountability. Doctors couldn't deviate from their ethical obligations even if a country's laws allowed or demanded otherwise.... So deeply ingrained is this ethic in health care that it's surprising, even shocking, to find that the same code isn't shared by psychologists, at least in the United States.
>
> (*Godlee*, 2009)

A British psychologist responded to the editor's critique with a letter to the editor titled "Fortunately UK psychologists Don't Use the APA Code of Ethics" (Triskel, 2009). Similarly, Burton and Kagan (2007), writing in the British Psychological Society's *Psychologist*, wrote:

> Most concerning of all, the APA allows its members the "Nuremberg defence" that "I was only following orders." ... The implication is that

psychologists are permitted to assist in torture and abuse if they can claim that they first tried to resolve the conflict between their ethical responsibility and the law, regulations or government legal authority. Otherwise they can invoke the Nuremberg defence. (p. 485)

After adopting this enforceable standard in 2002, APA continued to hold it as its official policy for eight years, including the period that some of the most controversial state policies regarding interrogations were in still in place. Other groups spoke out against the notion that state authority can serve as an acceptable reason to abandon basic ethical responsibilities. Less than a year after APA discarded the Nuremberg Ethic from its code, for example, the World Medical Association's president issued a public reminder:

At Nuremberg in 1947, accused physicians tried to defend themselves with the excuse that they were only following the law and commands from their superiors . . . the court announced that a physician could not deviate from his ethical obligations even if legislation demands otherwise.

APA did not reverse its opposition to the Nuremberg Ethic until 2010, when it amended enforceable Standard 1.02.[3]

Humane Treatment of Detainees

In the context of APA's claim that psychologists should play a central role in the interrogation process, does the record support their stance against adding any enforceable standard focusing on "humane treatment" of detainees to the Ethics Code?

In shaping an ethics code that differed from the Nuremberg Ethic, APA carefully distinguished between those parts of its Ethics Code, policies, guidelines, and public statements that were *aspirational* versus the code's 89 *enforceable* standards. APA allowed the constraining phrase "in keeping with basic principles of human rights" to appear in the code's aspirational introduction but decisively removed that constraint from the enforceable section. Similarly APA refused to add to the enforceable sections of the Ethics Code protections that explicitly addressed detainees.

Historically, when concerns arose about the impact of psychologists' behavior on groups at risk, APA moved decisively to create specific requirements and limitations in the ethics code's enforceable standards. These groups included persons "for whom testing is mandated by law or governmental regulations," "persons with a questionable capacity to consent," research participants, "subordinates," clients, students, supervisees, and employees. Facing concerns about the impact of psychologists' behavior on research animals, for example, APA created

[3] For a more detailed history of APA's decision to adopt an enforceable ethical standard contrary to the Nuremberg Ethic, please see Pope and Gutheil (2009b).

an enforceable standard supporting the "humane treatment" of laboratory animals. But APA decided that its code should not recognize detainees as a group that might be vulnerable or at risk during interrogations.

By making an exception and declining to include detainees as a vulnerable or at-risk group in the ethics code, any formal ethical principle, standard, or guideline about avoiding harmful activities, taking care to do no harm, protecting clients and others from harm, became subject to varying interpretations when it came to detainees. As a member of the APA PENS Task Force explained in a recorded radio interview:

> And psychologists were supposed to be do-gooders. You know, the idea that they would be involved in producing some pain just seems to be, you know, at first blush, something that would be wrong because we do no harm. But the real ethical consideration would say, well, by producing pain or questioning of somebody, if it does the most good for the most people, it's entirely ethical, and to do otherwise would be unethical. ("Military Psychologist Says Harsh Tactics Justified," 2009)

According to this analysis, the ethical focus shifts from detainees to American citizens:

> The ethical consideration is always to do the most good for the most people. And America happens to be my client. Americans are who I care about. I have no fondness for the enemy, and I don't feel like I need to take care of their mental health needs" ("Military Psychologist Says Harsh Tactics Justified," 2009)

APA's decision to adopt an enforceable standard focusing on "humane treatment" of animals but not to adopt an enforceable standard focusing on "humane treatment" of detainees moved APA further away from its ethical foundations and what had been its defining values, which should have endured even in the midst of post–9/11 risks and realities.

APA's Statements on Torture

Does the record support APA's preference for nonenforceable policies in this area?

APA took the same stance on its various statements, clarifications, and modifications of its stance on torture. These included, for example, the 2006 "Resolution Against Torture" (APA, 2006); the 2007 "Reaffirmation of the APA Position against Torture" (APA, 2007a); and the 2008 "Amendment to the Reaffirmation of the APA Position Against Torture" (APA, 2008b). In each case, APA decided against adding the resolution on torture, the reaffirmation, the amendment to the reaffirmation, or any other statements about torture to the 89 enforceable standards in the Ethics Code.

On September 17, 2008, APA issued a press release about a new policy:

> The petition resolution stating that psychologists may not work in settings where 'persons are held outside of, or in violation of, either International Law (e.g., the UN Convention Against Torture and the Geneva Conventions) or the US Constitution (where appropriate), unless they are working directly for the persons being detained or for an independent third party working to protect human rights' was approved by a vote of the APA membership.
>
> (*APA, 2008c*)

APA's press release did not note that this policy was not enforceable. However, the APA Office of Public Affairs issued clarifications about the ballot initiative under the title "Petition on Psychologists' Work Settings: Questions and Answers." The response to the question "If adopted would the petition be enforceable by APA?" includes this statement: "As explained above, the petition would not become part of the APA Ethics Code nor be enforceable as are prohibitions set forth in the Ethics Code" (APA, 2008d).

Similarly the ballot sent to members for a vote on this policy was accompanied by a statement that the policy would not be enforceable. APA (2008a) wrote: "A ballot mailing dated August 1, 2008 included the full text of the petition statement and the following con statement." This con statement, written by a former APA president, emphasized that "APA is clear that the petition, if adopted, is not enforceable" (Resnick, 2008).

Responses to Criticisms

The four points just discussed provide examples of the kinds of material and perspectives that have led some critics to disagree with APA's policies and public statements in this area. In weighing these points critically, it is important to consider not only the points themselves but also criticism of them. This process of considering not only points of disagreement with APA's policy and public statements but also responses to those points echoes a central theme of this book: the need to question ourselves, our beliefs, positions, assumptions, and conclusions.

Those who believe that some or all of the four points are a valid basis of disagreement with APA may or may not continue to believe in the points after carefully considering responses to them. However, respectfully considering the responses can lead to greater understanding of how the assumptions, beliefs, reasoning, and perspectives of those in support of APA's policies and public statements may differ from the assumptions, beliefs, reasoning, and perspectives of those who respectfully disagree. If critics can appreciate how they themselves and their criticisms are viewed by others, it may lead them to reevaluate the validity and importance of their criticisms and to find new opportunities for dialogue.

This section provides a few examples of the criticism of the four points. As with all of the material cited in this chapter, readers are strongly encouraged to read the original works in their entirety rather than rely on the brief quotes excerpted here.

Two of the points, for example, cite the International Committee of the Red Cross (ICRC), which received Nobel Prizes in 1917, 1944, and 1963, as a source of data. But some believe that the ICRC's motives were anti-American. As a member of the PENS Task Force explained:

> Like most other soldiers, I saw the ICRC representatives as a bunch of radical do-gooders, mostly from Europe, who were as interested in giving America a black eye as they were in truly helping the innocent. . . . The ICRC claimed, very wrongly and without any evidence, that psychologists were stealing detainee medical information and helping investigators craft torture.
>
> *(James, 2008, pp. 180–181)*

According to this view, the story of health-care professionals participating in torture was a fabrication: "It was the ICRC who concocted the story of medical torture" (James, 2008, p. 181).

Similarly, material from the U.S. Defense Department reporting that a psychologist "conspired to teach psychologists and interrogators from Cuba how to reverse engineer SERE school to torture detainees" (James, 2008, p. 248) was viewed as completely off base. The PENS member wrote that the "DOD inspector had gotten the story about the SERE psychology training at Fort Bragg all wrong. . . . It was either one hell of a lie, flat-out bullshit, or a factual error—it didn't happen the way the August 2006 DOD inspector said it happened" (p. 249).

Disagreements with APA's PENS Report that came from human rights organizations, physician groups, and APA members were considered in light of the unreasonableness of disagreeing with an APA report that was clearly right. The PENS report's conclusions were characterized as "no brainers. What decent, moral psychologist could disagree?" (James, 2008, p. 247). Critics were suspect because of their alleged political leanings and tendencies to invent facts. "But this was not enough for many of the radical left-wing members of the American Psychological Association and other human rights and physician societies around the country. . . . They disregarded the facts and created their own" (James, 2008, p. 248).

Those who disagree with APA's PENS policies can also be seen not as offering alternative approaches to this complex area but instead as seeking to cut and run. Another PENS member, in a coauthored article in an APA journal, wrote that "to run away from an area where we can help both the country and the individuals in detention is simply wrong" (Greene & Banks, 2009, p. 30).

A third PENS member emphasized the tendency of critics who have not been in these situations (detainee interrogations) to lack the necessary knowledge to speak on the topic:

> Anyone who wants to throw stones in this situation really needs to step back and figure out what they would do themselves in these situations, and not just kind of be ivory tower critics, but get down and either get in a situation or really keep their mouths shut. Most of the time, they have no idea what they're talking about. ("Military Psychologist Says Harsh Tactics Justified," 2009)

A passage from a PENS member's book also raised the issue of critics speaking without knowing what they were talking about:

> At a meeting of the American Psychological Association in 2006, I confronted one of my critics and threatened to shut his mouth for him if he didn't do it himself. I'm told it was the most excitement at an APA meeting in about 20 years.
> (James, 2008, p. 251)

APA's Tradition of Openness and Transparency

This chapter outlined a few ways in which, in my opinion, APA moved away from its historic ethical foundations and what had been its defining values. I believe it is possible that APA also, however unintentionally, may not have followed its traditions in an area separate from ethics: openness and transparency.

For example, traditionally when APA appointed a task force, the names of the task force members were published along with the task force report (see, e.g., "APA Presidential Task Force on Enhancing Diversity" [APA, 2005]; "APA Presidential Task Force on Evidence-Based Practice" [APA, 2006]; "APA Presidential Task Force on the Future of Psychology" [APA, 2009]; "APA Presidential Task Force on the Implementation of the Multicultural Guidelines" [APA, 2008]; "APA Presidential Task Force on Integrated Health Care for an Aging Population" [APA, 2008]; "APA Presidential Task Force on Posttraumatic Stress and Trauma in Children and Adolescents" [APA, 2008]; and "Report of the APA Task Force on Advertising and Children" [APA 2004]).

APA departed from this tradition of transparency when publishing the *Report of the American Psychological Association Presidential Task Force on Psychological Ethics and National Security* (APA Presidential Task Force on Psychological Ethics and National Security, 2005): The names of the task force members were not disclosed.

Even later, after the board of directors invoked emergency action to approve the PENS report as APA policy, there still seemed to be reluctance to mention the names of the task force members. After a subsequent APA annual convention where the PENS report was discussed, a member of the PENS task force posted a message to the PENS listserv, noting that the PENS member "was once again impressed" with how the person who had chaired the APA convention panel had "eloquently represented our work and insured the confidentiality of the panel, despite pressure to reveal the identities of the task force members" (Gelles, 2005).

When APA convenes a task force to shape ethical policy in an important area, it would seem reasonable for the report to include the names of its authors, as is APA's tradition for presidential task force reports. Similarly, it would seem reasonable to adopt a policy of transparency in other areas as well rather than keep the task force members' identities secret under a cloak of confidentiality at a subsequent APA convention.

CONCLUSION

APA is the largest organization of psychologists in the world, with over 148,000 members and a distinguished history reaching back over 100 years. No one can know how persuasive APA's many reassurances were and what impact they may have had on the public's beliefs about whether the interrogations at Guantanamo, Abu Ghraib, and other sites were safe, legal, ethical, and effective.

It is possible, however, to ask basic questions about APA's policies and public statements. This would mean setting aside the views put forth by various members of APA's Presidential Task Force on Psychological Ethics and National Security that the ethics policies they wrote were the only viable option (e.g., "no brainers. What decent, moral psychologist could disagree?") and that those who have not been in interrogation situations lack the necessary knowledge to take a critical position.

The questions I suggest next can be useful no matter what our current beliefs. Constantly rethinking our response to them—always asking "What if I'm wrong about this?"; "What information, insight, or perspective could I be missing?"; "Is there another way to understand this that might be more valid or useful?"—can be an important part of the discipline and science of psychology, leading us to new realizations.

A few of the key questions, whose themes are found in this chapter, include:

- However well intended, were APA's interrogation policies ethically sound?
- Were they valid, realistic, and able to achieve their purpose?
- Did APA subject them to adequate critical scrutiny from sufficiently diverse perspectives to identify fallacies, unfounded conclusions, significant weaknesses, overlooked information, unexamined alternatives, and possible unintended consequences prior to adopting the policies and making the public assertions?
- Was it reasonable, productive, and effective to depart from tradition by keeping the task force members' names off the report that they wrote and taking other steps affecting transparency?

- Does the record support APA's assurances that psychologists knew "not to participate in activities that harmed detainees," that they were devoted to "keeping interrogations safe"?
- Did sound ethical reasoning support APA's stance that the Nuremberg Ethic should be dropped from its ethics code and replaced by the doctrine that psychologists should be able to set aside their "ethical responsibilities" if those responsibilities were in inherent conflict with military orders, governmental regulations, national and local laws, and any other form of governing legal authority?
- In the context of APA's claim that psychologists should play a central role in the interrogation process, does the record support their stance against adding any enforceable standard focusing on "humane treatment" of detainees to the ethics code?
- Were the PENS policies APA's only viable option, or were other approaches available that would address interrogation issues more directly, comprehensively, and actively, that were more ethically and scientifically based, and that would have had a greater likelihood of success?
- Should APA continue to endorse the PENS policies, which were never revoked, as its formal ethical policies?

Chapter 13

BEGINNINGS AND ENDINGS, ABSENCE AND ACCESS

A man calls to schedule an appointment to begin therapy. He has been moderately anxious and distressed about the possibility of losing his job and not being able to support his family. You talk with him about 10 or 15 minutes getting basic information, including his insurance, and set up an appointment 10 days later, your first opening. Four days later you receive a call from the man's public defender. Having been laid off from work, the man returned with a gun and shot his supervisor. The public defender is calling you to ask if you would send him your records and talk with him a little about your assessment of the man, who has identified you as his therapist. Had the initial discussion with the man made you his therapist? Did you assume any professional responsibilities by talking with him, taking the basic information, and scheduling a session with him?

A client stops coming to therapy. You do not know why. She does not return the phone messages you leave for her or respond to the letter you sent her. Five weeks have passed. Has the therapy been terminated?

A fragile client has been making gradual progress in therapy when her partner dies unexpectedly and she becomes suicidal. The same week the managed care company sends you notice that no additional sessions are approved for this patient.

Being clear with our clients about the boundaries of our relationship with them is a fundamental ethical responsibility. Two of the most important boundaries are beginning and ending. Information about the beginning and ending of therapy, as well as about availability of services during therapy, is important if the client's decisions about whether to consent to treatment are to be truly informed. (Chapter 14 provides a more detailed discussion of informed consent.) People who come to us for help have a right to know when they become our client as well as when the professional relationship ends. They need to know how accessible we are, including when and how can they get in touch with us. This chapter discusses some of those issues of beginnings, access, absences, and endings.

ACCESSIBILITY FOR PEOPLE WITH DISABILITIES

Our decisions about how accessible we make our structures and services to people with disabilities reflect our ethical values (Pope, 2005). They also affect many people. Psychologist Martha Banks (2003) wrote:

> Approximately one-fifth of U.S. citizens have disabilities. The percentage is slightly higher among woman and girls (21.3%) than among men and boys (19.8%). Among women, Native American women and African American women have the highest percentages of disabilities....As a result of limited access to funds, more than one-third of women with work disabilities and more than 40% of those with severe work disabilities are living in poverty. (p. xxiii)

What barriers, if any, do people who use wheelchairs encounter when they come to the building in which you do therapy and enter your office (Pope & Vasquez, 2005)? Would a person who is deaf face any needless difficulties contacting you for an initial session? Would a person who is blind have any unnecessary problems in navigating your building? If you have a professional Web site, is it accessible to those who are disabled and use assistive technologies? (For articles and other resources to address these issues, go to *Accessibility and Disability Information and Resources in Psychology Training and Practice* at http://kpope.com.)

CLARIFICATION

Therapists must be alert to possible complications and confusions. An individual may call for an initial appointment. The therapist may assume that the session is one of initial evaluation regarding possible courses of action (e.g., if therapy makes sense for the individual, or what modality of therapy under what conditions implemented by what clinician seems most promising). The individual, however, may assume that the clinician, by virtue of accepting that request for an initial appointment, has become his or her therapist. Similarly, several months into treatment, a client may become enraged at the therapist but be unable to express that anger directly. The client may leave suddenly halfway through a session and miss the regular appointment time for the next five weeks, during which time the client fails to return any of the therapist's telephone calls. Is that client still a client, or has a de facto termination occurred?

Acting to prevent unnecessary misunderstandings about the beginning and ending of therapy is part of a clinician's more general ethical responsibility to clarify the availability of and access to therapeutic resources. One of the more immediate aspects of this responsibility is for both therapist and client to understand clearly when and under what circumstances the therapist will be available for sessions or for telephone communication and what resources will be available for the client when the therapist is not available.

Clarification is important for at least five reasons.

1. It forces the therapist to consider carefully this client's needs for telephone access during the course of therapy. For example, is this an impulsive, depressed client with few friends who might need telephone contact with the therapist or some other professional in the middle of the night to avert a suicide? Clarification enables the therapist to plan for such contingencies.

2. By leading the therapist to specify backup availability—for example, what clients can do if they are unable to reach the therapist by telephone in an emergency—the efforts to clarify availability enable the therapist to prepare for therapeutic needs that are difficult or impossible to anticipate. For example, a client with moderate coping resources may attend appointments regularly over the course of a year or two, never contacting the therapist between sessions. However, during a period when the therapist is seriously ill and unavailable, the client may receive numerous shocks, such as the loss of a job or the death of a child. The client may become acutely suicidal and need prompt access to therapeutic resources. Careful planning by the therapist may meet such needs that are virtually impossible to anticipate with a specific client.

3. Explicit clarification of client access to the therapist or to other therapeutic resources encourages the therapist to think carefully about the effects that availability and unavailability are likely to have on clients and the course of treatment. For example, some clients are likely to experience overwhelming feelings of sadness, anger, or abandonment when the therapist goes on vacation. Other clients may find the clear boundaries that the therapist has established so uncomfortable and infuriating that they are constantly testing both the therapist and the boundaries. Such clients may frequently show up at the therapist's office at the wrong time for their appointment, may leave urgently cryptic messages ("Am quitting therapy; no hope; life too painful; can't go on") on the

therapist's answering machine without leaving a number where they can be reached, and may persistently try to discover the therapist's home address and home telephone number (if the therapist customarily keeps these private).

4. When therapist and client work together to develop a plan for emergencies during which the therapist might not be immediately available, the process can help the patient to assess realistically his or her dependence and needs for help and to assume—to the extent that he or she is able—realistic responsibility for self-care during crises. For example, the therapist may ask the client to locate the nearest hospital providing 24-hour services and develop ways of reaching the hospital in an emergency. As the client assumes responsibility for this phase of crisis planning, he or she increases the sense of self-efficacy and self-reliance (within a realistic context), becomes less inclined to view therapy as a passive process (in which the therapist does all the "work"), and may feel less panicky and helpless when facing an impending crisis or the therapist's future absences. In this sense, planning becomes an empowering process for the client.

5. The process of clarification encourages the therapist to consider carefully his or her own needs for time off, away from the immediate responsibilities of work. Such planning helps ensure that the therapist does not become overwhelmed by the demands of work and does not experience burnout. The drawing of such boundaries also encourages the therapist to attend explicitly to other sources of meaning, joy, fulfillment, and support so that he or she does not begin looking to clients to fill personal needs (see Chapter 7). This is a crucial aspect of the therapist's maintaining emotional competence (see Chapter 6).

All therapists need to clarify major areas of accessibility in a manner consistent with their own needs and style of practice and with the clinical needs of each client. Some clinicians hold to exact time boundaries. With virtually no exceptions, they begin and end the session on the dot. Even if the client has just experienced a painful breakthrough and is in obvious distress, they do not extend the therapy session. In some situations, ending promptly is a practical necessity: The therapist may have another client scheduled to begin a session immediately. In other situations, observing strict time boundaries is required by the theoretical orientation: Running over the time boundary might be considered by the therapist to constitute a breaking of the frame of therapy or represent the therapist and client colluding in acting out.

Therapists must consider carefully the approach to time boundaries of the session that best fits their own theoretical orientation and personal needs. The effects of the policy on individual clients need to be considered, and clients should understand the policy.

THERAPIST AVAILABILITY BETWEEN SESSIONS

When and under what conditions can the client normally speak with the therapist between sessions? Some therapists receive nonemergency calls from clients during reasonable hours (e.g., 9:00 A.M. to 6:00 P.M.) of weekdays when they are not otherwise engaged. A very few therapists take nonemergency calls when they are conducting therapy. We recommend against this practice, which seems disrespectful of the client who is in session and seems to have numerous potentially harmful effects on the course of therapy of the client whose session is interrupted (or is aware that any session might be interrupted at any time by nonemergency calls to the therapist).

The therapist needs to be clear about the times between sessions when he or she can be contacted on a nonemergency basis. For example, are weekend calls or calls on holidays such as Labor Day, Memorial Day, or Martin Luther King Day acceptable?

An extremely important point to clarify is whether the therapist will speak with the client more than briefly by telephone when there is no emergency. Some clients may wish to use telephone calls to address unresolved issues from the previous therapy session, share a dream while it is still fresh in their mind, or talk over how to handle a situation at work. Some therapists may see such telephone sessions as therapeutically useful for some clients. The telephone sessions may, for example, help particularly fragile and needy clients, who might otherwise require day treatment or periodic hospitalizations, to function under the constraints of once- or twice-weekly outpatient therapy. They may help some clients learn how to use and generalize the adaptive skills they are acquiring in office sessions; the telephone sessions serve as a bridge between office therapy sessions and independent functioning by the client.

Other therapists may prefer to keep the work in the frame of the therapy session. They believe that telephone sessions during which therapy is conducted are—except under rare emergency conditions—countertherapeutic. For example, they might view extended telephone contacts between sessions as similar in nature and effect to going beyond the temporal boundary at the end of a session. Other therapists may, as part of their own self-care (see Chapter 7), limit out-of-office telephone contacts to emergencies.

Again, whether the therapist uses an approach that includes therapy sessions conducted by telephone on an ad hoc basis or prohibits them is less important than that (a) the therapist thinks through the issues carefully in terms of consistency with his or her theoretical orientation and personal approach, (b) the therapist considers carefully the implications of the policy for the individual client, and (c) both therapist and client clearly understand the ground rules.

It can also be important to clarify under what circumstances, if any, the therapist will be available for e-mail communication and how privacy issues will be addressed; for example, do any third parties have access to the therapist's or the client's e-mail accounts? Some therapists have been surprised to receive unexpected e-mail from a client who has searched the Internet and discovered the therapist's supposedly "personal" e-mail address. Both therapist and client must clearly understand whether e-mail can be used to schedule and cancel sessions, check in between regularly scheduled office sessions, or provide therapy or counseling over the Internet.

Many standards, guidelines, and codes listed in the appendixes include sections addressing communication with clients using telephone, e-mail, or other electronic means. A few (e.g., the National Board for Certified Counselors' "The Practice of Internet Counseling" and the American Psychological Association's "Statement on Services by Telephone, Teleconferencing, & Internet") focus exclusively on electronic communications. Chapter 5 of this book provides a discussion of the benefits and pitfalls of the electronic communication technologies.

An excellent resource is a survey of ethical dilemmas that psychologists encountered in telephone counseling (Dalen, 2006). Dilemmas involving "confidentiality and professional secrecy" were the most frequently reported (p. 240). Dilemmas involving integrity were also frequently reported, although dilemmas involving competence were rarely mentioned.

VACATIONS AND OTHER ANTICIPATED ABSENCES

Extended and sometimes even brief interruptions in the schedule of appointments can evoke deep and sometimes puzzling or even overwhelming reactions in a client. What is important is that therapists give the client adequate notice of the anticipated absence. If therapists take a two-week vacation at the same time each year or travel frequently for various reasons, there may be no reason to omit this information from the customary orientation provided to a new client. Therapists who find that they will be taking a six-week sea cruise during the coming year should consider carefully if there is any compelling clinical or practical reason to withhold this information from a client as soon as reservations are made. Prompt notification of anticipated therapist absences minimizes the likelihood that a client will experience a psychologically paralyzing traumatic shock, gives the client maximal time to mobilize the resources to cope with a therapist's absence in a way that promotes independence and growth, and enables the client to become aware of reactions and work with them during the sessions before and after the absence.

SERIOUS ILLNESS AND OTHER UNANTICIPATED ABSENCES

Both therapists and clients tend to find comforting the myth that the therapist is immortal and invulnerable (Pope, Sonne, & Greene, 2006). Therapists may enjoy the feeling of strength and of being a perfect caregiver that such a fantasy, which sometimes occurs on an unconscious level, provides. Clients may soothe themselves (and avoid confronting some personal issues) with the fantasy that they are being cared for by an omnipotent, immortal parental figure.

Although we have not completed our careful study of every therapist who has ever lived, our preliminary results suggests that there has yet to appear a therapist who is immortal and invulnerable. For all of us who are mortal and vulnerable, it is important to prepare for those unexpected times when we are suddenly unavailable to our clients (see Chapter 8).

STEPS FOR MAKING HELP AVAILABLE IN A CRISIS

Once clients clearly understand how to contact the therapist by telephone between regularly scheduled appointments, therapist and clients can discuss appropriate arrangements for situations in which this system is inadequate. A client, for example, may experience an unanticipated crisis and be unable to reach the therapist promptly by telephone because the therapist's line is busy for an extended time, the therapist's answering service mishandles the client's call, the therapist is in session with another client who is in crisis, or any number of other typical or once-in-a-lifetime delays, glitches, or human errors. For the reasons cited at the beginning of this chapter, planning for such "unanticipated" breakdowns in communication can enable access to prompt clinical services in time of crisis and can foster more careful therapeutic planning.

If the client's need for help is urgent and the therapist is unavailable, is there a colleague who is providing coverage for the therapist? Some organization settings, such as health maintenance organizations and community mental health centers, as a matter of policy and procedure assign clinicians to serve on-call rotations so that there is always someone available to provide coverage in a crisis when a client's therapist is unavailable. However, many therapists, particularly those in solo independent practice, may need to create and implement their own plans to ensure coverage in an emergency, should they be unavailable.

The decision of whether to arrange for coverage for a specific client is complex. Perhaps the first question is what sort of information the covering clinician will be provided about the client. Will the covering therapist receive a complete review and periodic update of the client's clinical status, treatment plan, and therapeutic progress? Will the covering therapist have access to the client's chart? Will the covering therapist keep a separate set of notes regarding information supplied by the primary therapist? To what extent will the covering therapist need to secure independent informed consent for treatment by the client? The more foreseeable or the greater the risk is that the client will experience a serious crisis demanding prompt intervention, the more compelling the reason is for the primary therapist to brief the covering therapist in a careful, thorough manner.

Once the therapist has determined what degree of coverage seems appropriate for a specific client, a second question is how to introduce the possibility of or actually implement such coverage affecting the client's status or treatment. Some clients might feel greatly reassured to know that the therapist is taking his or her responsibilities seriously and is carefully thinking through possible, even if unlikely, treatment needs. Other clients may become alarmed and feel as if the therapist is predicting that a crisis will occur. Still other clients may stall in their progress; the strict privacy and confidentiality of therapy is essential for them, and the knowledge that the therapist will be sharing the contents of sessions with the covering therapist inhibit their ability to explore certain issues or feelings. In many cases, discussion between the therapist and client of the question of whether specific coverage will be provided is useful therapeutically.

If it is decided that specific coverage will be provided, a third question for the therapist is what will best ensure the client's right to adequate informed consent for sharing information with the covering therapist and otherwise making arrangements for the coverage.

A fourth question addresses the selection of a clinician to provide the coverage. The primary therapist may incur legal (i.e., malpractice) liability for negligence in selecting the coverage. If, for example, the clinician providing the coverage mishandles a crisis situation or otherwise harms the client through inappropriate acts or failures to act, the primary therapist may be held accountable for failure to screen and select an appropriate clinician. However, the ethical and clinical issues are much more subtle. It is important to select a clinician who is well trained to provide the type of care that the client may need. The primary therapist may be tempted to select a clinician solely (and perhaps inappropriately) on grounds of expedience. The primary therapist may know that the clinician is not a very good one and is perhaps less than scrupulous in professional attitudes and actions. Furthermore, the primary therapist may be aware that the clinician does not tend to work effectively with the general client population that the therapist treats. Nevertheless, the therapist may push such uncomfortable knowledge out of awareness because this particular clinician is handy, and it might take considerable effort to locate an appropriate and trustworthy covering therapist. As in so many other situations discussed in this book, the Golden Rule seems salient. If we were the client, or if it were our parent, spouse, or child who desperately needed help in a crisis when the primary therapist is unavailable, if the careful handling of the crisis were potentially a matter of life and death, what level of care would we believe adequate in selecting a clinician to provide the coverage? If, for example, our parent became suddenly despondent, received a totally inadequate response from the clinician providing the coverage, and committed suicide, would convenience seem sufficient rationale for the primary therapist's selection of that clinician to provide the coverage?

If no clinician has been identified to provide coverage or if the identified clinician is for some reason unavailable, to whom does the client in crisis turn when the primary therapist is unavailable? It may be useful for the client to locate a psychiatric hospital, a general hospital with psychiatric services, or other facility providing emergency psychiatric services. There are at least five crucial questions:

1. Is the facility nearby?
2. Are the services available on a 24-hour basis? (If the crisis occurs in the middle of the night, on a weekend, or on a holiday, will the client find help available?)
3. Can the client afford to use the facility? Some facilities charge exceptionally high prices and may offer services only to those who can provide proof of ability to pay—for example, an insurance policy currently in effect.
4. Does the client know where the facility is located and what its telephone number is? Especially during a crisis, even basic information (such as the name of a hospital) may be hard to remember. In some instances—for example, both the therapist and client believe that there is a high risk for a crisis—it may be useful for the client to write down the name of the hospital, the address, and the telephone number to carry with him or her and to leave by the telephone at home. Sometimes close friends or family play a vital role in supporting a client in times of crisis. If the circumstances are appropriate, the client may also wish to give this information to a close friend or relative.
5. Do both therapist and client have justifiable confidence that the facility provides adequate care? Substandard care may make a crisis worse. Sometimes no care from certain facilities may be better than an inappropriate response.

If the primary therapist, secondary therapist, and designated facility are all unavailable—for whatever reason—in time of crisis, is there an appropriate hot line or other 24-hour telephone service that can provide at least an immediate first-aid response to the crisis and attempt to help the client locate a currently available source of professional help? Some locales have 24-hour suicide hot lines. There may be a 24-hour crisis line providing help for individuals with certain kinds of problems. At a minimum, such a telephone service may help a client survive a crisis. For some clients (e.g., those who cannot afford a telephone at their residence), identifying locations of telephones that will be accessible in times of crisis will be an important part of the planning.

If all of the resources noted are inaccessible to the client, the client may nevertheless be able to dial 911, the operator, or a similar general call for emergency response. The client may then be guided to sources of help, or, if appropriate, an ambulance or other emergency response may be dispatched.

Whenever a therapist is assessing a client's resources for coping with a crisis that threatens to endanger or overwhelm the client, it is important to assess not only the professional resources but also the client's social resources. Individual friends and family members may play key roles in helping a client to avert or survive a crisis (although a friend or family member can also initiate, intensify, or prolong a crisis). In some instances, nonprofessional groups, such as Alcoholics Anonymous, may provide access to support. The presence of such social supports gains in relative importance when the client's access to professional help is difficult. For example, some clients (especially those who cannot afford a telephone) cannot access a telephone, particularly if they are experiencing a crisis in the middle of the night. For many clients, the awareness of such social supports helps them to feel less isolated and thus less vulnerable to becoming overwhelmed by a crisis.

It is worth noting that sometimes therapy begins with the client in crisis and that the client's access to a team of clinicians or caregivers may be useful. *American Psychologist* presented the next case study illustrating a situation in which the immediate creation of crisis team proved helpful when a person without funds or coverage needed help:

> In an instance in which a woman required daily sessions during a critical time in her life, colleagues accepted [the therapist's] request that they serve pro bono as an interdisciplinary team, offering detailed daily consultation to him and providing periodic psychological assessment and clinical interviews for the woman. Her meetings with diverse professionals let her know that many people cared about her. These colleagues mobilized to help a battered woman, a victim of multiple sexual assault, now penniless and homeless, living in her car and hiding from a stalker. She and [the therapist] began meeting daily (later gradually reduced to weekly) for crisis intervention. They agreed that the first priority was her safety. [The therapist] gave her the number of an old college friend in another state. The friend immediately wired her $500 for food and housing and an airline ticket with an open date for use any time she felt in danger from the stalker. The friend asked her not to repay this loan directly to him but rather to give the money to someone else for whom it would make a difference as it did for her now. Within a year, the woman had taken legal action against the stalker and recovered enough to support herself. ("Biography," 1995, p. 242)

ENDINGS

An easily overlooked responsibility in regard to ending the therapeutic relationship is the therapist's responsibility to terminate the relationship under certain conditions. The APA Ethics Code (APA, 2010) Standard 10.10a clarifies responsibilities to end the therapeutic relationship when appropriate by indicating that "psychologists terminate therapy when it becomes reasonably clear that the client no longer needs the service, is not likely to benefit, or is being harmed by continued service." The Canadian Psychological Association Code of Ethics (CPA, 2000) Standard II.37 requires that psychologists "terminate an activity when it is clear that the activity carries more than minimal risk of harm and is found to be more harmful than beneficial, or when the activity is no longer needed" (p. 24).

Therapy termination may be conceptualized as an intentional process that happens over time when a client has achieved most of the goals of treatment or when therapy must end for other reasons. The process of termination typically allows clients an opportunity to review their goals, describe the changes they have incorporated, and work through feelings in bringing the therapy process to an end (Vasquez, Bingham, & Barnett, 2008).

Ideally, therapists provide continuing service as long as it is needed and beneficial. Some insurance coverage or managed care plans can create stark challenges. For example, an insurance company may refuse to approve continuing services for a client, despite the therapist's professional judgment that terminating services would be harmful for the client, leading to the client's suicide. A managed care company may provide only four to six sessions annually for any client, with exceptions provided only for "medical necessity," which might be defined as imminent risk of suicide or homicide. Some clients who do not meet the relevant criteria of medical necessity may suffer from conditions or crises that cannot be adequately addressed in four to six sessions. For some such patients, interruption of their treatment, even though in accordance with a managed care company's policies and procedures, may constitute abandonment.

How do therapists and clients know when to terminate therapy? A key psychotherapeutic strategy is to review the presenting concerns, goals, and progress from time to time. Doing this helps clarify how much has been accomplished, as well as what still needs to be addressed, and whether the client and therapist collaboratively wish to continue. Some clients are able to easily announce that they are ready to stop coming or that their employer has switched insurance therapists and that they would like your help to choose their next therapist from their new therapist list. Others may be panicked at the notion of stopping without appropriate preparation.

The issue becomes complex if the therapist perceives that the treatment is progressing well, and the client or patient either is not clear about how long to continue or no longer wishes to continue but has difficulty raising the issue. Often these clients just stop coming. They either indicate that they will call to schedule the next appointment or cancel and do not reschedule. In addition, many people use therapy in short installments and drop out for a while, later returning to the same clinician or starting with a new therapist. When clients who seemed successfully engaged in therapy stop coming, a note or call to provide them with options can be helpful and provide useful information. Examples of options may include to come in for a review and termination session, terminate by telephone or note, or return to therapy.

When approaching termination, therapists must—if they are able— adequately address the questions that tend to be an inherent part of termination. The American Psychological Association's Ethical Principles and Code of Conduct (2010) Standard 10.10c states the responsibilities of a therapist to engage in a termination process: "Except where precluded by the actions of clients or third-party payors, prior to termination psychologists provide pretermination counseling and suggest alternative service therapists as appropriate." The Ethics Code notes that we have the right to terminate therapy when we are threatened by the client or patient or another person with whom the client or patient has a relationship (Standard 10.10b). This is an attempt to balance the importance of therapist self-care with the responsibilities to the client. It is probably not appropriate to terminate when a client is in crisis.

Vasquez, Bingham, and Barnett (2008, pp. 661–662) provide 12 recommendations for helping to make sure that termination goes as well as possible, meeting the highest ethical and clinical standards:

1. Provide patients with a complete description of the therapeutic process, including termination; obtain informed consent for this process at the beginning of treatment, and provide reminders throughout treatment.
2. Ensure that the therapist and client collaboratively agree on the goals for therapy and the ending of therapy.
3. Provide periodic progress updates that include discussions of termination and, toward the end of therapy, provide pretermination counseling.
4. Offer a contract that provides patients with a plan in case the therapist is suddenly unavailable (including death, or financial, employment, or insurance complications).
5. Help clients develop health and referral plans for posttermination life.
6. Make sure you understand termination, abandonment, and their potential effects on patients.
7. Consider developing (and updating) your professional will to proactively address unexpected termination and abandonment, including the name(s) of colleagues who will contact current patients in the case of your sudden disability or death.
8. Contact clients who prematurely terminate via telephone or letters to express your concern and offer to assist them.
9. Use the APA Ethics Code (2002), your state practice regulations, and consultation with knowledgeable colleagues to help guide your understanding and behavior in regard to therapy termination.
10. Review other ethics codes for discussions of abandonment. The American Counseling Association...and the American Mental Health Counselors Association...contain prohibitions against abandonment.

11. Make the topic of termination a part of your regular continuing education or professional development.
12. Be vigilant in monitoring your clinical effectiveness and personal distress (e.g., Baker, 2003; Norcross & Guy, 2007). Therapists who self-monitor and practice effective self-care are less likely to have inappropriate terminations or clients who feel abandoned.

For those looking for a more detailed discussion of the practical issues of termination and how they can be addressed in ethically and clinically sound ways, we highly recommend Denise Davis's (2008) book, *Terminating Therapy: A Professional Guide to Ending on a Positive Note*.

CONCLUSION

Constant awareness—particularly a careful, imaginative awareness—and a sense of personal responsibility play a fundamental role in ensuring that clients have adequate access to the help they need, particularly in times of crisis when the therapist is not immediately available. In hospital and similar organizational settings, the apparent abundance of staff may lead to a diffusion of responsibility in which no one is available to help a patient in crisis. Levenson and Pope (1981), for example, present a case study in which a psychology intern was assigned responsibility to promptly contact a suicidal individual who had been referred to the outpatient unit by the crisis service and arrange for conducting an intake assessment. The intern, however, was absent from the staff meeting at which the assignment was made. His supervisor, also absent from the meeting, had sent him to attend a two-day training session at another institution. During the next few days, the individual committed suicide.

> The hospital's thanatology committee concluded that the crisis service had handled the situation appropriately in referring to the outpatient unit. The outpatient unit itself was not involved in the postmortem investigation because, according to the hospital's procedures, outpatient cases are not opened until the potential patient is contacted by the outpatient unit for an intake screening. The intern himself struggled with his reactions to these events. Among his conclusions was that he had "at some level internalized the organizational view that no one is really responsible." (p. 485)

Imagination is useful in creating an awareness of the types of crises a client might experience and what difficulties he or she might experience in trying to gain timely access to needed resources. The scenarios for discussion presented at the end of this chapter provide examples.

Thinking things through on a worst-possible-case basis can help the therapist to anticipate the ways in which Murphy's law can make itself felt in human endeavors. If we look back from that imaginative perspective, we can ask our-selves: If any of the worst possible case outcomes had happened, what, if any-thing, do we wish we would have done to prevent them, lessen their impact, or prepare for addressing these events?

No therapist is infallible. The most careful and confident assessment of a client's potential for crisis can go awry for any number of reasons. But the therapist should take into account his or her own fallibility and plan for the unexpected.

Similarly, imaginative approaches can create accessibility to needed resources. For example, a therapist was treating an extremely isolated, anxious, and troubled young woman pro bono because of the client's lack of money. From time to time, the client became overwhelmed by anxiety and was acutely suicidal. However, she had no practical access to hospitalization because of her financial status and the absence in the community of sufficient beds for those who lacked adequate funds or insurance coverage. In similar cases, the therapist had encouraged clients to make arrangements to have a trusted friend come by to stay with them during periods of extreme dysfunction and suicidal risk. However, this client was so socially isolated that she had no friends, and the therapist was unable to locate an individual—from local church and syna-gogue groups or from hospital volunteer organizations—who could stay with her in times of crisis. Determined to come up with some arrangement that would help ensure the client's safety and welfare should she experience a cri-sis and the therapist be unavailable, the therapist and client finally hit on the possibility of her going to the local hospital's waiting room. (The waiting room adjacent to the emergency room was open around the clock.) The therapist contacted hospital personnel to make sure that they would have no objection to the client showing up at odd hours to sit for indefinite periods of time in the waiting room.

The arrangement worked well during the remaining course of therapy. According to the client, simply knowing that there was someplace for her to go helped her to avoid becoming completely overwhelmed by external events or by her own feelings. On those occasions when she did feel that she was in crisis and at risk for taking her own life, she found that going to the hospital waiting room seemed helpful; it made her feel more active and aware that she was doing something for herself. Being out of her rather depressing and claustrophobic apartment, sitting in a "clean, well-lighted place," and being around other people (who, because they were strangers, would be unlikely to make, in her words, "demands" on her) were all factors that helped her feel better. Knowing that there were health-care profession-als nearby (even though she had no contact with them) who could intervene should her impulses to take her own life become too much for her, and aware that she was carrying out a "treatment plan" that she and her therapist had developed together, helped her to feel calmer, less isolated, and comforted in crisis. The waiting room strategy enabled this highly suicidal client to be treated safely, although hospitalization was not feasible, during the initial period of therapy when outpatient treatment alone seemed, in the judgment of both the therapist and an independent consultant, inadequate and when the client could not afford additional resources. It made imaginative use of resources that were readily available in the community and were accessible to the client.

Understanding the degree to which individual clinicians and mental health organizations will be accessible and will make help available is a crucial aspect of the client's informed consent, the focus of Chapter 14.

SCENARIOS FOR DISCUSSION

Chapters 13 through 21 in this book end with scenarios, each accompanied with a set of questions for discussion. This approach had been used in *Sexual Feelings in Therapy: Explorations for Therapists and Therapists-in-Training* (Pope, Sonne, & Holroyd, 1993). Although we have created original vignettes for the other chapters in this book, the following scenarios and questions come from *Sexual Feelings in Therapy* and *What Therapists Don't Talk About and Why: Understanding Taboos That Hurt Us and Our Clients* (Pope, Sonne, & Greene, 2006).

You notice that it is exactly 2:00 P.M., the time you are scheduled to meet a new client, and no one is in the waiting room. The telephone rings. It is your new client. She asks if you would mind coming out to the front steps. You're puzzled but say "I'll be right there." When you go to the front steps, you see your new client in her wheelchair at the bottom of the steps.

- How do you feel?
- What thoughts go through you mind?
- What do you think is the first thing you would say?
- What would you like to do?
- What do you think you would do?

■ ■ ■

You are late getting to the airport, in danger of missing your plane (during a holiday season, so it would be very hard to get space on a later flight), when you receive an emergency call from a local hospital. One of your therapy patients has tried to commit suicide and has been hospitalized. The client is desperate to talk with you in person—refusing to talk over the telephone— immediately about having just discovered a horrifying secret. You have no idea what the "secret" is.

- How do you feel?
- Are there any feelings about the patient, the emergency room staff person who called you, or the situation that are particularly difficult to acknowledge?
- What are your immediate options?
- What do you think you would do?
- To what extent, if at all, do any concerns about a malpractice suit influence your judgment?

■ ■ ■

A new client begins the first session by saying "I need therapy because I lost my job, and my partner, whom I lived with for three years, left me for someone else. I don't know whether to kill myself, kill my boss, kill everyone else, or just try to hang on since now I'm all my little baby has left."

- How do you feel?
- Assuming that you cannot rule out that the person's threats are serious, what steps do you take in clarifying access to you and others before the client leaves this first appointment?
- What concerns, if any, do you have about this person's adequate access to prompt and adequate help?
- Is there anything you wish you would have told the person about your availability or anything else before the person made these statements?

■ ■ ■

You work for a large managed care company, providing individual and family therapy full time. You meet with your manager late Friday afternoon and are told that the company has been taken over by a new owner, who is merging several companies. There are now too many therapists, and it is with the greatest regret that your manager tells you that reorganization has led to your no longer being retained by the company. This is your last day. Your clients are being reassigned. You will be allowed to

(continued)

(*continued*)

return to your office only with a security guard, you will be able to stay only 30 minutes to clean out your desk, and you will not be allowed to copy any telephone numbers or other information or to take any charts with you.

- How do you feel?
- What are your options?
- What steps do you think you would take?
- Would you make any effort to contact the clients you had been seeing? If so, how and what would you tell them?

■ ■ ■

A former client, whom you had seen in therapy for three years, called in crisis. She said that she had started therapy with someone else, given a change of jobs and a new insurance plan. You were not listed on the managed care therapist list. However, she cannot reach that new therapist during her crisis. Besides, she feels more comfortable with you.

- What do you feel?
- Do you have any legal or ethical obligations to this former client, and, if so, what are they?
- If you agree to talk with this client on the telephone for a while or meet with her for one or more crisis sessions, what legal, ethical, or clinical responsibilities, if any, do you have in regard to coordinating your work with her current managed care therapist?
- Do you chart this telephone call?
- Do you have a clear policy regarding contacts with former clients? If so, are clients made aware of this policy prior to termination?

Chapter 14

INFORMED CONSENT AND INFORMED REFUSAL

The right to informed consent reflects respect for individual freedom, autonomy, and dignity. It is fundamental to the ethics of therapy and counseling. The APA ethics code (see Appendix A) sets forth specific standards for informed consent (Sections 3.10, 10.01, 10.02, 10.03, and 10.04). Truscott and Crook (2004) note that "informed consent is the most represented value in the Canadian Code of Ethics for Psychologists" (p. 55; see Appendix B). Informed consent is a cornerstone of the trust inherent in the professional relationship (Campbell, Vasquez, Behnke, & Kinscherff, 2010).

This fundamental concept can trip us up if we are not careful. Nothing blocks a patient's access to help with such cruel efficiency as a bungled attempt at informed consent. We may have struggled successfully with the challenges outlined in Chapter 13. The doors to our offices and clinics are open wide. Resources are all in place. But not even the most hardy, persistent patients can make their way past intimidating forms (which clerks may shove at them when they first arrive), our set speeches full of noninformative information, and our nervous attempts to meet externally imposed legalistic requirements such as the Health Insurance Portability and Accountability Act (HIPAA).

One trap we can fall into is resenting consent as a formality to be gotten out of the way. Daniel Sokol (2009) wrote:

> [W]hat is the most redoubtable obstacle to valid consent? It is the still prevalent attitude that obtaining consent is a necessary chore, a...hurdle to jump over. Too often "consenting" a patient is reduced to the mechanistic imparting of information from clinician to patient or, worse still, the mere signing of a consent form, rather than the two way, meaningful conversation between clinician and patient it should be. If we can change this mindset [sic] and

view obtaining consent as an ethical duty first and foremost, one that is central to respecting the autonomy and dignity of patients, then we will have taken a major step towards first class consent and uninterrupted lunches. (p. 3224)

Viewing consent as an obligation and burden makes it hard to meet the needs of patients. Discussing their questionnaire study of patients' perceptions of written consent, Andrea Akkad and her colleagues (2006) wrote:

> Our findings add to evidence showing that even when the consent process satisfies administrative and legal requirements, patients' needs may not be met....Though patients did identify several important advantages of the consent process, there was substantial uncertainty about the implications of signing or not signing the consent form....Many patients did not see written consent as functioning primarily in their interests nor as a way of making their wishes known....Although there is no straightforward relation between knowledge of rights and ability to exercise those rights, a lack of awareness of the limits and scope of consent is clearly undesirable, potentially causing patients to feel disempowered and lacking in control. (p. 529)

A first step in remedying the situation is to recognize that informed consent is not a static ritual but a *useful* process.

PROCESS OF INFORMED CONSENT

The Canadian Psychological Association (CPA) Ethics Code notes that psychologists "recognize that informed consent is the result of a process of reaching an agreement to work collaboratively, rather than of simply having a consent form signed" (see Appendix B). The process of informed consent provides both the patient and therapist an opportunity to make sure that they adequately understand their shared venture. It is a process of communication and clarification. Does the therapist possess at least a sufficient initial understanding of why the patient is seeking help? Does the therapist know what the patient expects, or hopes, or fears from the assessment and therapy? Does the patient adequately understand the approach the clinician will be using to assess and address the problem? Does the patient know the common effects of using such an approach and alternative approaches to his or her problem?

Culture can affect this process of communication and clarification. For example, the therapist might be from the majority culture while the patient might be a recent immigrant who is currently in the process of adapting to the majority culture. Chong Wang (2009) points out that the level of acculturation can influence the desire for independent decision making; ways of relating within cultural contexts; and the ways in which psychological disorders, authority, and so on are perceived.

Wang suggests 11 steps as helpful in assessing the level of acculturation:

1. In general, what language(s) do you read and speak?
2. What was the language(s) you used as a child?
3. What language(s) do you usually speak at home?
4. In which language(s) do you usually think or dream?
5. What language(s) do you usually speak with your friends?
6. In what language(s) are your preferred TV/radio programs?
7. In general, what language(s) are the movies, TV, and radio programs you prefer to watch and listen to?
8. Your close friends are...?
9. You prefer going to social gatherings/parties at which people are...?
10. The persons you visit or who visit you are...?
11. If you could choose your children's friends you would want them to be...?

Informed consent also involves making decisions. The patient must decide whether to undertake this course of assessment and treatment, whether to start now or delay, and whether to try an alternative approach or an alternative therapist.

The therapist must decide whether the patient is competent to exercise informed consent. For example, very young children, adults who have been declared legally incompetent, and those who have significant intellectual impairment may not be capable of providing fully informed consent.

The presence of a severe psychological disorder requiring hospitalization does not by itself mean that the patient lacks the ability to give or refuse meaningful consent to therapy. Debra Pinals (2009) wrote:

> Adult patients with psychotic disorders are not automatically or always incompetent. Research has shown that most inpatients with mental illness have capacities to make treatment decisions similar to persons with medical illness. Patients with schizophrenia, however, have deficits relevant to capacity to make treatment decisions more often than patients with medical illnesses and depressive disorders. Patients with depressive disorders also are more likely to have some decision-making impairment compared with persons with medical illnesses. (p. 35)

If informed consent is not possible, the therapist must decide whether the situation justifies an intervention in the absence of fully informed consent. The therapist must also consider whether a fully competent patient has the information to make an informed decision, adequately understands that information, is providing consent voluntarily.

Patrick O'Neill, a former president of the CPA, suggests that the process of informed consent take the form of negotiation:

> While most therapists recognize that negotiation can clear up clients' misconceptions, fewer recognize that negotiation is also a vehicle for clearing up

the *therapist's* misconceptions. An open dialogue can make the therapist aware of features of the case that depart from both the therapist's model and his or her previous experience, and thus it serves as a corrective to the representativeness and availability biases. (1998, p. 176)

Finally, informed consent tends to be a continuing or recurrent process. Williams (2008) wrote: "Obtaining consent is not a discrete event; rather, it is a process that should occur throughout the relationship between clinician and patient" (p. 11). The patient may consent to an initial psychological, neuropsychological, and medical assessment as well as to a course of individual therapy based on an initial, very provisional treatment plan. Later the assessment results, the patient's response to treatment, and changing circumstances may lead to a radical revision in the treatment plan. The patient needs to understand these revisions and agree to them.

BASIS OF INFORMED CONSENT

Informed consent is one way we try to make sure that the patient's trust is justified, we do not abuse our power, and we express our caring in ways that the patient understands and agrees to. The appellate courts have described the basic requirements. Many of these decisions involve medical practice, but much of the reasoning applies to assessment and therapy.

Traditionally, the health-care professions took an arrogant, authoritarian approach: The physician alone decided what treatment the patient received. The Hippocratic Oath lacked the principle of informed consent. During the centuries leading up to the modern era, physicians tended to share the belief that doctors' decisions should not be questioned and that patients obviously lacked the training, knowledge, and objectivity to know what was good for them. This approach failed to recognize and respect the patient's autonomy (Campbell et al., 2010).

One landmark in the shift away from this authoritarian approach appeared in a New York case. In 1914, Judge Benjamin Cardozo, who later became a justice of the U.S. Supreme Court, wrote that "every human being of adult years and sound mind has a right to determine what shall be done with his own body" (*Schloendorf* v. *Society of New York Hospital*, 1914, p. 93).

It was not so much that this case changed the customary procedures by which doctors went about their work; it was more that Judge Cardozo articulated clearly the principle that it was the patient, rather than the doctor, who had the right to decide whether to undertake a specific treatment approach. The implications of this principle lay dormant for decades.

The Nuremberg trials and subsequent Nuremberg Code on Medical Intervention and Experimentation focused attention on the importance of informed consent. The trials revealed the horrific and inhumane practices of many health-care professionals during World War II under the guise of "treatment" and "research" (Adam, 2007; Cocks, 1985; Gallagher, 1990; Geuter, 1992; Koenig, 2000; Lifton, 1986; Lopez-Munoz et al., 2007; Muller-Hill, 1988; Pope, 1991; Proctor, 1988; Spitz, 2005; Thiren & Mauron, 2007). The Nuremberg trials and code emphasized the individual's fundamental right to informed consent to or informed refusal of participation in treatment or research. O'Neill (1998) wrote:

> The two main ways of protecting the public from the healer are oversight and consent. Throughout most of the history of healing, the emphasis was on oversight: monitoring of professional activity by professional associations, regulatory bodies, or the courts. The Nuremberg Declaration gave a new, privileged position to consent, putting control into the hands of the client. (pp. 13–14)

Shuster (1998) noted how easy it could be, when the right to consent or refusal is ignored, to allow purportedly good ends to justify inflicting terrible — sometimes fatal — "treatments" on human beings without their knowledge or consent:

> This was the case of ionising radiation research motivated by the cold war and sponsored by the US government for national security. Patients in hospital, children, mentally ill and impaired persons, pregnant women, workers, soldiers, and others were used as experimental subjects often without their knowledge, or that of their families; many believed they were being treated for their medical conditions. (p. 976; see also Advisory Committee on Human Radiation Experiments, 1995)

Another landmark appeared in 1960, in the Kansas case of *Natanson* v. *Kline*. The court reaffirmed the Cardozo principle: "Anglo-American law starts with the premise of thorough-going self-determination. It follows that each man is considered to be master of his own body" (p. 1104). The court stated that to make this determination, the patient obviously needed the relevant information. But what information was relevant was left entirely to the community of doctors to decide:

> The duty…to disclose…is limited to those disclosures which a reasonable …practitioner would make under the same or similar circumstances…. So long as the disclosure is sufficient to assure an informed consent, the physician's choice of plausible courses should not be called into question if it appears, all circumstances considered, that the physician was motivated only by the patient's best therapeutic interests and he proceeded as competent medical men would have done in a similar situation. (p. 1106)

This case exemplifies the "community standard" rule: Informed consent procedures must adhere only to what the general community of doctors customarily do. It also reflects the strong value of autonomy and self-determination that underlies western law, policy, and ethical decision making.

In 1972, with decisions handed down by the Federal District Court in Washington, D.C., and the California Supreme Court, the full implications of Judge Cardozo's principle were realized. The reasoning began with the reaffirmation of *Schloendorf* v. *Society of New York Hospital* and an emphasis that the patient must have relevant information that only the doctor can provide:

> The root premise is the concept, fundamental in American jurisprudence, that "every human being of adult years and sound mind has a right to determine what shall be done with his own body. . . ." True consent to what happens to one's self is the informed exercise of a choice, and that entails an opportunity to evaluate knowledgeably the options available and the risks attendant upon each. The average patient has little or no understanding of the medical arts, and ordinarily has only his physician to whom he can look for enlightenment with which to reach an intelligent decision. From these almost axiomatic considerations springs the need, and in turn the requirement, of a reasonable divulgence by physician to patient to make such a decision possible.
>
> (*Canterbury* v. *Spence*, 1972, p. 780)

It is the patient, and not the doctor, who must make the final decision, and this decision, to be meaningful, must be based on an adequate range of information provided by the doctor:

> It is the prerogative of the patient, not the physician, to determine for himself the direction in which he believes his interests lie. To enable the patient to chart his course knowledgeably, reasonable familiarity with the therapeutic alternatives and their hazards becomes essential.
>
> (*Cobbs* v. *Grant*, 1972, p. 514)

This line of reasoning emphasized the exceptional trust and dependence inherent in health care, differentiating them from the milder versions of trust and dependence, often dealt with using a caveat emptor principle, characteristic of less intense, less intimate transactions in the marketplace:

> A reasonable revelation in these aspects is not only a necessity but, as we see it, is as much a matter of the physician's duty. It is a duty to warn of the dangers lurking in the proposed treatment, and that is surely a facet of due care. It is, too, a duty to impart information which the patient has every right to expect. The patient's reliance upon the physician is a trust of the kind which

traditionally has exacted obligations beyond those associated with arms-length transactions. His dependence upon the physician for information affecting his well-being, in terms of contemplated treatment, is well-nigh abject.

(*Canterbury* v. *Spence*, 1972, p. 782)

This landmark case law specifically rejected the idea that doctors, through their "community standards," could determine what degree of information the patient should or should not have. It was not up to doctors, individually or collectively, to decide what rights a patient should have with regard to informed consent or to determine those rights indirectly by establishing customary standards regarding what information was and was not to be provided. Patients were held to have a right to make an informed decision, and the courts were to guarantee that they had the relevant information for making the decision. The court observed in *Canterbury* v. *Spence*:

> We do not agree that the patient's cause of action is dependent upon the existence and nonperformance of a relevant professional tradition.... Respect for the patient's right of self-determination on particular therapy demands a standard set by law for physicians rather than one which physicians may or may not impose upon themselves. (1972, pp. 783–784)

The case law clearly states the need for doctors to provide adequate relevant information regardless of whether the patient actively asked the "right" questions in each area. Thus, doctors were prevented from withholding or neglecting to provide relevant information because a patient did not inquire. The doctors were seen as having an affirmative duty to make an adequately full disclosure:

> We discard the thought that the patient should ask for information before the physician is required to disclose. Caveat emptor is not the norm for the consumer of medical services. Duty to disclose is more than a call to speak merely on the patient's request, or merely to answer the patient's questions: it is a duty to volunteer, if necessary, the information the patient needs for intelligent decision. The patient may be ignorant, confused, overawed by the physician or frightened by the hospital, or even ashamed to inquire.... Perhaps relatively few patients could in any event identify the relevant questions in the absence of prior explanation by the physician. Physicians and hospitals have patients of widely divergent socio-economic backgrounds, and a rule which presumes a degree of sophistication which many members of society lack is likely to breed gross inequalities.
>
> (*Canterbury* v. *Spence*, 1972, p. 783)

Realizing that some patients would certainly choose not to undertake specific assessment or treatment procedures, the courts emphasized that understanding what might happen as a result of not getting adequate assessment or treatment was as relevant to making an informed decision as understanding the assessment and treatment procedures themselves. Thus, the California Supreme Court in 1980 not only reaffirmed the principles previously set forth in *Canterbury* v. *Spence* and *Cobbs* v. *Grant* but also affirmed that patients have a right to informed refusal of treatment as well as a right to informed consent to treatment:

> The rule applies whether the procedure involves treatment or a diagnostic test.... If a patient indicates that he or she is going to *decline* a risk-free test or treatment, then the doctor has the additional duty of advising of all the material risks of which a reasonable person would want to be informed before deciding not to undergo the procedure. On the other hand, if the recommended test or treatment is itself risky, then the physician should always explain the potential consequences of declining to follow the recommended course of action.
>
> (*Truman* v. *Thomas*, 1980, p. 312)

Recognizing that some doctors might be intimidated by the daunting thought of presenting to patients essentially all they had learned during their training and that patients might be ill-suited recipients of jargon-filled lectures, the court emphasized that the patient needed only the relevant information to make an informed decision but needed it in clear, straightforward language: "The patient's interest in information does not extend to a lengthy polysyllabic discourse on all possible complications. A mini-course in medical science is not required" (*Cobbs* v. *Grant*, 1972, p. 515).

In summary, the courts in the 1970s tended to shift the locus of decision making clearly to the patient and the responsibility for ensuring that the decision was based on adequate, relevant information clearly to the doctor. The California Supreme Court attempted to articulate the basis of this concept of informed consent:

> We employ several postulates. The first is that patients are generally persons unlearned in the medical sciences and therefore, except in rare cases, courts may safely assume the knowledge of patient and physician are not in parity. The second is that a person of adult years and in sound mind has the right, in the exercise of control over his own body, to determine whether or not to submit to lawful medical treatment. The third is that the patient's consent to treatment, to be effective, must be an informed consent. And the fourth is that the patient, being unlearned in medical sciences, has an abject dependence upon and trust in his physician for the information upon which he relies during the decisional process, thus raising an obligation in the physician that transcends arm-length transactions. From the foregoing axiomatic ingredients emerges a necessity, and a resultant requirement, for divulgence by the physician to his patient of all information relevant to a meaningful decisional process.
>
> (*Cobbs* v. *Grant*, 1972, p. 513)

These principles began to pass from case law into legislation. Section F of Indiana's House Enrolled Act of 1984, for example, stated:

> All patients or clients are entitled to be informed of the nature of treatment or habilitation program proposed, the known effects of receiving and of not receiving such treatment or habilitation, and alternative treatment or habilitation programs, if any. An adult voluntary patient or client, if not adjudicated incompetent, is entitled to refuse to submit to treatment or to a habilitation program and is entitled to be informed of this right.

The American Psychological Association's Ethics Code reflects the increasing emphasis on the importance of informed consent. Celia Fisher, director of the Fordham University Center for Ethics Education and Marie Doty University Chair in Psychology, wrote:

> Informed consent is seen by many as the primary means of protecting the self-governing and privacy rights of those with whom psychologists work. In the 1992 Ethics Code, the obligation to obtain informed consent was limited to research and therapy. In the 2002 Ethics Code, the broader informed consent requirement for most psychological activities reflects the societal sea change from a paternalistic to an autonomy based view of professional and scientific ethics. (2003, p. 77)

ADEQUATE INFORMATION

The information provided during the consent process will differ according to the professional service (e.g., assessment, therapy) and other factors. However, any consent process can be evaluated in terms of whether it adequately addresses the next questions. This list may be useful in planning and in concurrent review of consent procedures in any setting:

- Does the patient understand who is providing the service and the clinician's qualifications (e.g., license status)? If more than one person is involved (e.g., a therapist and clinical supervisor; see Chapter 21), does the patient understand the nature and implications of this arrangement?
- Does the patient understand the reason for the initial session? Although in many instances patients will have scheduled an initial appointment on their own initiative and for relatively clear reasons, in other instances they may have been referred by others (perhaps an internist or a court) and not clearly understand the reason for the session.
- Does the patient understand the nature, extent, and possible consequences of the services the clinician is offering? Does the patient understand the degree to which there may be alternatives to the services provided by the clinician?

- Does the patient understand actual or potential limitations to the services (e.g., a managed care plan's limitation of 8 therapy sessions; an insurance policy's limitation of coverage to a specific dollar amount) or to the clinician (e.g., the therapist is an intern whose rotation will conclude in 3 months, after which he or she will no longer be available to the patient)? Does the patient understand the ways in which the services may be terminated?
- Does the patient understand fee policies and procedures, including information about missed or canceled appointments?
- Does the patient understand policies and procedures concerning access to the clinician, to those providing coverage for the clinician, or to emergency services? For example, under what conditions, if any, will a therapist (or someone else providing coverage) be available by telephone between sessions during business hours, at night, or on weekends? (Chapter 13 discusses these issues.)
- Does the patient understand exceptions to confidentiality, privilege, or privacy? For example, does the patient understand the conditions, if any, under which the clinician might disclose information about the patient to an insurance company, the police, or the courts? Does the person understand under what conditions other people in the setting (such as clerical workers, clinical supervisors or consultants, administrative supervisors or other administrative staff, quality control personnel, utilization review committees, auditors, researchers) may learn about the patient and the services provided to him or her, whether through discussion (case conferences, supervision, consultation) or writings (clinical chart notes, treatment summaries, administrative records)? Chapter 19 provides a discussion of these issues and exceptions.

CONSIDERATIONS IN PROVIDING INFORMED CONSENT

No unvarying and inflexible method exists for legitimately ensuring a patient's informed consent. No method can relieve us of a thoughtful response to the particulars before us. All of us have developed unique and personal styles as therapists or counselors. Each of our patients is unique.

Informed consent is a recurring process, not a static set of pro forma gestures, that develops out of the relationship between clinician and patient. It must fit the situation and the setting. It must respond not only to the explicit standards of the clinician's professional associations, such as the APA or the CPA, but also to the relevant state and federal laws and evolving case law. It must be sensitive to the client's ability to understand the relevant information (Is the client a young child, developmentally disabled, suffering from severe thought disorder?) and the patient's situation (Is the patient in the midst of a crisis, referred for mandatory treatment by the courts, being held against his or her will in a mental hospital?). Human sensitivity and professional judgment are required.

As we attempt to create and sustain the process of informed consent, several considerations, noted in the remainder of this chapter, are useful.

Failing to Provide Informed Consent

In considering how to ensure the patient's right to informed consent, we must remain aware that the right is violated, perhaps often. We can take those instances to justify our own decisions not to accord patients informed consent, or we can use those instances as an opportunity to consider the matter from the patient's perspective. How would we feel if we were the patients who had been kept in the dark and had not been given the chance to make a decision on an informed basis?

An example of the withholding of informed consent involved the provision of free medical care to hundreds of U.S. citizens (J. H. Jones, 1981; see also Rivers, Schuman, Simpson, & Olansky, 1953; U.S. Public Health Service, 1973). The program began in 1932 and continued to 1972. If all we were told was that the government, through what eventually became the U.S. Public Health Service, was giving us comprehensive medical care, how would we likely feel? Grateful? Relieved that we would be spared financial burdens? Excited that we would have access to state-of-the-science medical interventions provided by the federal government? Who among us would turn down this rare opportunity?

What the participants were not told is that they were being used to research the effects of syphilis when it goes untreated. Treatment for syphilis was in fact withheld from all the individuals. Research procedures were presented as treatment; for example, painful spinal taps were described to the subjects as a special medical treatment. Although Public Health Service officials denied that there were any racist aspects to this research, admission to the program was limited to male African Americans. The 40-year Tuskegee syphilis experiment is one of the most infamous in United States history and stands as one of the worst violations of ethical standards of biomedical research. It led to the institution of federal Institutional Review Boards for protection of human subjects (U.S. Center for Disease Control and Prevention, retrieved February 28, 2010).

More recent examples are numerous. Hospitals, for example, perform AIDS tests on virtually all patients without patients' knowledge or permission, sometimes in direct violation of state law (Pope & Morin, 1990). As another example, Stevens (1990) described a testing center that administered the Stanford-Binet Intelligence Scale so that students could be placed in the appropriate classes at school. The information schools received contradicted that given to the child's parents. In one case, for example, the report sent to the school "recommended that David be placed in a class for average students"; the report sent to the parents recommended that "David should be placed in a class for superior students" (p. 15). Here is how the testing center explained the policy: "The [report] we send to the school is accurate. The report for the parents is more soothing and positive" (p. 15).

How would we feel if we relied on the government and health-care professions to provide us with free medical care when in fact they were observing the untreated consequences of a painful, virulent, usually fatal disease? How would we feel if we went to a hospital for help and were given an AIDS test without our knowledge or permission? How would we feel if we were given completely inaccurate information about the results of an intelligence assessment because someone else thought it would be "more soothing"?

Benefits of Informed Consent

Approaching the issue of informed consent, we may, as clinicians, fear that providing adequate information to patients and explicitly obtaining their consent will somehow derail therapy and may in fact have detrimental consequences for our patients. The research has not supported these fears. The process of informed consent tends to be beneficial. A variety of studies have indicated that the use of informed consent procedures makes it more likely that patients will become less anxious, follow the treatment plan, recover more quickly, and be more alert to unintended negative consequences of the treatment (Handler, 1990). Debra Pinals (2009) wrote that "informed consent can enhance the therapeutic alliance and help improve treatment adherence" (p. 33).

Limits of Consent

Informed consent is not a strategy to insulate a clinician from responsibility when performing unethical or illegal acts:

> At least one case has suggested that there are limits to what a patient can validly consent to. In that case, several adults were treated with a form of therapy that involved physically beating them. The defendants argued they could not be sued because the plaintiffs had consented to the treatment; however, the Court of Appeals refused to accept the consents as a defense. This decision implies that a patient's consent will not be deemed valid if acts consented to would otherwise be illegal or contrary to public policy (such as a sexual relationship between therapist and patient). An earlier case held that whether touching is therapeutic or nontherapeutic goes to the essence of the act and may vitiate a consent.
>
> (*Caudill & Pope*, 1995, pp. 553–554)

Consent for Families and Other Multiple Clients

Individual therapy is only one model for providing services. Sometimes clinicians provide therapy to couples, families, or groups. Therapists must ensure that adequate informed consent and informed refusal is provided for each person and that the consent addresses issues specific to therapy when more than one client is involved. For example, what are the limits of confidentiality and privilege for material disclosed by one of the patients involved in couples, family or group services? Will the therapist hold confidential from one family member material disclosed by another family member? What effect would that have on the trust of the other family member if that other family member discovers the secret and that you kept it from him or her? If one client receiving couple therapy waives privilege, does the privilege still apply to the other member of the couple? APA Ethics Code (APA, 2010) standards 10.02 (a) and (b), Therapy Involving Couples or Families, describes the importance of clarifying who the patient is and the relationship the psychologist will have with each person involved. The standard also provides guidance in addressing conflicting roles, should they arise.

These issues are best clarified at the outset of the treatment, and on a continuing basis to clarify conflicts or potential conflicts that might arise during the therapy process. The 2002 APA Ethics Code included a new standard10.03, Group Therapy, that requires that "when psychologists provide services to several persons in a group setting, they describe at the outset the roles and responsibilities of all parties and the limits of confidentiality" (p. 1073). Thus, psychologists must describe at the outset of group therapy the unique roles and responsibilities of both therapist and patients in the group therapy, including the fact that while group members are advised to maintain confidentiality about other group members, they are not held to legal liability or ethical codes of conduct. It may be helpful, although not required, to have group members sign an informed consent document, including the group rules and guidelines.

Unequal Opportunity for Informed Consent

It is crucial that we do not accord unequal opportunities to our clients for informed consent based on prejudice and stereotypes (see Chapter 18). Research suggests that this unfortunately happens, at least occasionally, thus depriving some clients of their right to informed consent. For example, in an examination of informed consent practices, Benson (1984) found that whether important information was disclosed by a sample of physicians was systematically related to such factors as the patient's race and socioeconomic status.

Cognitive Processes

Clinicians must maintain up-to-date knowledge of the evolving research and theory regarding the cognitive processes by which people arrive at decisions (see, e.g., Arbuthnott, Arbuthnott, & Thompson, 2006; Bell, Raiffa, & Tversky, 1989; Bursztyajn, Feinbloom, Hamm, & Brodsky, 2000; Evans, 1989; Goleman, 1985; Janis, 1982; Janis & Mann, 1977; Kahneman, Slovic, & Tversky, 1982; Kahneman & Tversky, 2000; Kramer, 2010; Langer, 1989; Plous, 1993; Pope, Butcher, & Seelen, 2006; Rachlin, 1989; Wemer, Duschek, & Schandry, 2009). This research and theory can help clinicians understand the factors that influence clients who are choosing whether to participate in assessment or treatment procedures.

At a Harvard University hospital, McNeil, Pauker, Sox, and Tversky (1982) presented individuals with two options based on actuarial data concerning patients suffering from lung cancer. The data indicated whether patients had chosen a surgical or a radiological treatment for their cancer and what the outcome had been. Of those who chose surgery, 10% died during the operation itself, an additional 22% died within the first year after the surgery, and another 34% died within five years. Of those who chose radiation therapy, none died during the radiation treatments, 23% died within the first year, and an additional 55% died by the end of five years.

If you were given those actuarial data, which intervention would you choose? When these data were presented, 42% of the participants in the study indicated that they would choose radiation. Note that the data were presented in terms of mortality—the percentages of patients who died. When the same actuarial information was presented in terms of percentages of patients who survived at each stage—for radiation, 100% survived the treatment, 73% survived the first year, and 22% survived five years—only 25% chose radiation. The change from a mortality to a survivability presentation caused a change in the way individuals cognitively processed the information and arrived at a decision.

Because our interventions may have profound effects for our patients and the decisions they may make regarding whether to begin therapy and what sort of therapeutic approaches to try are significant, we have an important ethical responsibility to attend carefully to the form in which we present information relevant to those decisions.

Problems With Forms

Many of us may be so eager to start doing therapy that we try to avoid talking with our clients about consent issues. We try to push all the responsibility off onto a set form and let the form do the work. Those of us who work in clinics or hospitals may not even handle such forms. The client who shows up for an initial appointment may be handed an imposing-looking form by the receptionist, asked to read it, sign it, and return it before seeing the therapist. The form itself may have been crafted by the clinic's or hospital's attorney and may not even have been reviewed by a clinician. The wording may be in intimidating legalese and bureaucratic jargon. Such forms may be intended more to protect the organization against successful lawsuits than to help the client understand the options and make reasonable decisions.

Providing information in written form can be vital in ensuring that clients have the information they need. But the form cannot serve as a substitute for an adequate process of informed consent. At a minimum, the clinician must discuss the information with the client and arrive at a professional judgment that the client has adequate understanding of the relevant information.

Clinicians using consent forms must ensure that their clients have the requisite reading skills. Illiteracy is a major problem in the United States; clinicians cannot simply assume that all of their clients can read. Moreover, some clients may not be well versed in English, perhaps having only rudimentary skills in spoken English as a second or third language.

Not only must the client be able to read, but the form itself must be readable. Grundner (1980) noted that great effort has been made to ensure that "consent forms have valid content, but little effort has been made to ensure that the average person can read and understand them" (p. 900). He analyzed five forms with two standardized readability tests and found that "the readability of all five was approximately equivalent to that of material intended for upper division undergraduates or graduate students. Four of the five forms were written at the level of a scientific journal, and the fifth at the level of a specialized academic magazine."

Reading a form does not ensure that the client understands the material or can remember it even a short time later. Robinson and Merav (1976) reinterviewed 20 patients four to six months after they had read and signed a form for informed consent and had undergone treatment. They found that all patients showed poor recall regarding all aspects of the information covered by the form, including the diagnosis, potential complications, and alternate methods of management. Cassileth, Zupkis, Sutton-Smith, and March (1980) found that only one day after reading and signing a form for informed consent, only 60% of the patients understood the purpose and nature of the procedures. A perfunctory indication from clients that they understand can be unreliable (Irwin et al., 1985). The clinician bears the responsibility for ensuring that the client understands the information

It would be comforting to believe that the identification of problems in these early studies led to effective solutions. Unfortunately, the problems continue to emerge in contemporary research. For example, research by Akkad et al., (2006; see also Commons et al., 2006; Dixon-Woods et al., 2006; Walfish & Ducey, 2007; Wallace et al., 2008) found that:

As suggested in previous work, . . . many thought the primary function of the form was to protect the hospital. . . . These findings are disconcerting for healthcare professionals and patients alike and raise questions about how far current consent processes genuinely fulfil their aim of safeguarding autonomy and protecting patients' rights. (p. 529)

Additional Resources

A Web page (*Informed Consent in Therapy & Counseling: Forms, Standards & Guidelines, & References*) at http://kspope.com/consent/index.php provides resources that may be helpful in thinking through the process of informed consent. The Web page's resources fall into three categories:

1. Links to a variety of forms for informed consent from the APA Insurance Trust; the University of Rochester Counseling Center; Laura Brown, Ph.D., ABPP; and the Center for Ethical Practice
2. Excerpts addressing informed consent from the standards and guidelines of professional associations (with links to the original documents) including: American Association for Marriage & Family Therapy; American Association of Christian Counselors; American Association of Spinal Cord Injury Psychologists & Social Workers; American Group Therapy Association; American Mental Health Counselors Association; American Psychoanalytic Association; American Psychological Association; Association for Specialists in Group Work; British Association for Counselling & Therapy; British Columbia Association of Clinical Counsellors; California Board of Behavioral Sciences; Canadian Counselling Association; Canadian Psychiatric Association; Canadian Psychological Association; European Federation of Psychologists' Associations; Irish Association for Counseling & Therapy; National Association of Social Workers; National Board for Certified Counselors; and Psychological Society of Ireland.
3. Quotes and information about informed consent from articles, books, and studies.

SCENARIOS FOR DISCUSSION

> You work full time for a health maintenance organization (HMO) that requires the clinician to obtain written informed consent from all patients before providing therapy. One of the HMO physicians refers a patient to you for therapy. When the patient shows up for the initial session, you discover that the patient has recently been permanently blinded by an explosion

and wants help in making the transition to living without reliance on this particular sense.

- How do you feel?
- What are the initial consent issues that you consider?
- In what ways, if at all, should the consent process explicitly address therapeutic approaches specifically developed for those without sight?
- If you were not fluent in Braille, the HMO provided no consent forms in Braille, and no HMO employee could write in Braille, how would you approach the HMO's requirement that written consent be obtained before clinical services were provided?
- If the patient asked if any of the interventions you planned to use had been validated as effective for those without sight, how would you respond?
- If the patient asked if your graduate training and supervised experience included adequate work with sightless patients so that you were competent to provide services to this population, how would you respond?

■ ■ ■

You work for a managed care facility that allows no more than eight sessions of outpatient therapy in any given year. A new client tells you during the first session that surprising and intrusive memories have started to occur about experiences of incest as a child. The client thinks that the parent who perpetrated the incest may now be sexually abusing several grandchildren.

- How do you feel?
- What are the informed consent and informed refusal issues, if any, that you consider during this initial session regarding a formal assessment of this client?
- What are the informed consent and informed refusal issues, if any, that you consider during this initial session regarding potential clinical interventions for this person?

■ ■ ■

You have just begun working as a counselor at a university counseling center. At your first meeting with the counseling center

(continued)

(*continued*)

director, you ask if the center has consent forms. The director replies, "I'm so glad you brought that up. We've been leaving that up to individual counselors, but we need one that everyone can use. I've been looking at your curriculum vitae, and I think you're the perfect person to design the form. Please have it on my desk by next Thursday."

- How do you feel?
- Assuming that there is no way you can get out of this task, what process would you use for designing the form?
- What issues or elements are you sure the informed consent form should address?

■ ■ ■

You have agreed to provide therapy to an adolescent who had gotten in trouble for drinking. The parents have agreed to allow the sessions to be confidential, given your ethical responsibilities. However, they now request to see the records because they have reason to believe that their adolescent is smoking pot.

- How do you feel?
- What are the legal and ethical factors you consider?
- What do you think you might say to the parents?
- What do you think you might say to your client?
- To what extent does your form for informed consent adequately address the issues that this scenario raises?

■ ■ ■

You are a provider of services for a managed care company. Utilization reviews are required before additional sessions are provided. You realize, during the review, that although you believe sexual orientation is a critical issue and focus for your gay client, you did not inform your client that the information would be revealed to the reviewer.

- How do you feel?
- What consent issues does this situation involve?
- What possible approaches do you consider in deciding how to handle this situation?
- What information concerning utilization review, peer review, and similar review processes should an adequate form for informed consent and informed refusal contain?

Chapter 15

ASSESSMENT, TESTING, AND DIAGNOSIS

Assessment, testing, and diagnosis can change the course of clients' lives. A psychological evaluation can determine whether someone gets a job, custody, security clearance, declaration of disability, or release from involuntary hospitalization. It can impact a jury's verdict or a judge's sentence.

Those of us who practice in institutional settings can face externally imposed limitations on the time and other resources we can devote to assessment. Those of us in solo practice may face challenges in conducting evaluations that are ethical, accurate, useful, and consistent with the latest advances in research and theory. We often lack the ready-made professional support, educational resources, and peer review that many clinics and hospitals provide through in-service training programs, grand rounds, case conferences, and program evaluation. We may need to be more active in updating, improving, and monitoring our evaluation services.

Campbell, Vasquez, Behnke, and Kinscherff (2010) describe how the expanding scope of assessment brings new areas of specialization, each requiring its own set of competencies. The once-popular "general psychological evaluation" has tended to give way to forensic assessment, educational testing, neuropsychological assessment, assessment focusing on diagnosis and psychotherapy, industrial and organizational assessment, and other diverse specialties given to address specific questions.

The considerations discussed in this chapter are useful in identifying ethical pitfalls and making sure that diagnosis, testing, and assessment are as valid and useful as possible.

AWARENESS OF STANDARDS AND GUIDELINES

The American Psychological Association (APA) and the Canadian Psychological Association (CPA) publish several documents relevant to testing, assessment, and diagnosis. Reviewing them periodically helps us make sure that our work meets the highest standards. For example, APA's (2010) Ethical Principles and Code of Conduct includes sections relevant to assessment, including "Evaluation, Diagnosis, and Interventions in Professional Context," "Competence and Appropriate Use of Assessments and Interventions," "Test Construction," "Use of Assessment in General and with Special Populations," "Interpreting Assessment Results," "Unqualified Persons," "Obsolete Tests and Outdated Test Results," "Test Scoring and Interpretation Services," "Explaining Assessment Results," "Maintaining Test Security," "Forensic Assessments," and "Describing the Nature and Results of Psychological Services." The Canadian Code of Ethics for Psychologists (2000) includes relevant statements such as that psychologists "provide suitable information about the results of assessments, evaluations, or research findings to the persons involved, if appropriate and if asked. This information would be communicated in understandable language" (Section III.15) and that psychologists "protect the skills, knowledge, and interpretations of psychology from being misused, used incompetently, or made useless (e.g., loss of security of assessment techniques by others)" (Section IV.11).

APA and CPA publish other documents helpful in this area, including:

- "Guidelines for Psychological Practice with Older Adults" (APA, 2004)
- "Guidelines on Multicultural Education, Training, Research, Practice, and Organizational Change for Psychologists" (APA, 2003b)
- "Guidelines for Child Custody Evaluations in Family Law Proceedings" (APA, 2009)
- "Guidelines for the Evaluation of Dementia and Age-Related Cognitive Decline" (APA, 1998a)
- "Guidelines for Providers of Psychological Services to Ethnic, Linguistic, and Culturally Diverse Populations" (APA, 1993)
- "General Guidelines for Providers of Psychological Services" (APA, 1987b)
- *Practice Guidelines for Providers of Psychological Services* (CPA, 2001a)
- *Rights and Responsibilities of Test Takers: Guidelines and Expectations* (APA, 1998b)
- *Standards for Educational and Psychological Testing* (American Educational and Research Association, APA, and National Council on Measurement in Education, 1999). (There are links to the full text of these documents at http://kspope.com/ethcodes/index.php.).

Many of these are updated every few years or so. For example, a committee of researchers and experts in educational and psychological testing has been appointed to revise the Standards for Educational and Psychological Testing (see APA, 2008).

STAYING WITHIN AREAS OF COMPETENCE

A psychology degree, internship, and license do not by themselves qualify a professional to administer, score, interpret, or otherwise use psychological tests.

Hall and Hare-Mustin (1983) reported an APA ethics case in which

> one psychologist charged another with incompetence, especially in testing....CSPEC (Committee on Scientific and Professional Ethics and Conduct [the former name of the APA Ethics Committee]) reviewed the report of the state committee, which had carried out the investigation, and found that the person had no training or education in principles of psychological testing but was routinely engaged in evaluations of children in child custody battles. The committee found violation of Principle 2a, competence in testing, and stipulated that the member should work under the supervision of a clinical psychologist for one year. (p. 718)

Psychological testing requires competence. This competence cannot merely be asserted but must be demonstrable through formal education, training, and supervised experience. This point applies to diagnosis, evaluation, and assessment more generally, even if testing is not involved. For example, when a diagnosis is based on interview and observation, training and supervised experience in those assessment methods are necessary.

MAKING SURE THAT OUR TESTS AND ASSESSMENT METHODS STAY WITHIN THEIR AREAS OF COMPETENCE

We must make sure that we ourselves are competent to do a particular assessment. We may be competent to assess a child's intellectual strengths and weaknesses but not an adult's neuropsychological functioning. Our competence in one area does not necessarily generalize to another area. The tests and other assessment methods we use face the same limitation. A particular standardized test, for example, might help us determine whether clients are malingering but not whether they will respond better to group than individual therapy.

When we consider a particular psychological test, we must consider whether it is both valid and reliable for the use to which we want to put it and has been normed and validated for the relevant groups (e.g., age) to which our client belongs.

Perlin and McClain (2009) provide an example of important issues of equivalence to consider when taking culture into account:

> Technical equivalence refers to the method of data collection. For example, in some cultures unfamiliar with formal testing, results may not lead to valid outcomes due to reluctance to disclose or confusion regarding test-ing....Metric equivalence refers to analysis of the same concepts across cultures and the notion that the construct can be measured through the same scale after proper translation. Statistical behavior of the items in each culture must be the same. Validity of the measurement itself is the most critical issue in the cross-cultural application of testing. In other words, do the results really represent the issues being measured? Validity for the threshold or cut-off point refers to the point at which results should be considered impaired or psychopathological. Decisions about the criteria for threshold should be determined based upon sociocultural considerations and will likely affect various cultural groups differently. (p. 265)

UNDERSTANDING MEASUREMENT, VALIDATION, AND RESEARCH

Being able to document substantial course work, supervised training, and extensive experience in a given area like neuropsychological assessment of geriatric populations, intelligence testing of young children, or personality testing of adults helps a professional establish competence in that area of test-ing in an ethics committee hearing, licensing hearing, or malpractice suit. But beyond this evidence of competence, whether there is basic understanding of measurement, validation, and research is an important issue.

Sanders and Keith-Spiegel (1980) described an APA ethics case in which a psychologist evaluated a person using a Minnesota Multiphasic Personality Inventory (MMPI), among other resources. The person who was evaluated felt that the test report, particularly the part based on the MMPI results, was not accurate. All materials, including the test report and raw data, were sub-mitted to the APA Ethics Committee, which in turn submitted the materials for evaluation to two independent diplomates with expertise in testing.

The committee concluded that the psychologist did not demonstrate ade-quate understanding of measurement, validation, and inference in his report:

> The only test used by the complainee that has any established validity in identifying personality disorders is the MMPI, and none of the conclusions allegedly based on the MMPI are accurate. We suspect that the complainee's conclusions are based upon knowledge of a previous psychotic episode and information from the psychiatric consultant, whose conclusions seem to have been accepted uncritically. The complainee's report is a thoroughly unprofessional performance, in our opinion. Most graduate students would do much better.
>
> (Sanders & Keith-Spiegel, 1980, p. 1098)

ENSURING THAT PATIENTS UNDERSTAND AND CONSENT TO TESTING

Making sure that a patient understands the nature, purposes, and techniques of a given instrument helps to fulfill the client's right to give or withhold informed consent to assessment or treatment. Determining that the patient understands the testing is different from just presenting the information. Some patients may be anxious, distracted, preoccupied, or so eager to please that they nod their heads as if to acknowledge that they understand an explanation when, in fact, they have understood none of it. Some patients are unfamiliar with technical terms and concepts that we take for granted. Often this lack of communication combines with our own eagerness to get on with the testing and the client's fear of appearing ignorant.

The clinician is responsible for both explaining the assessment process and for forming a professional opinion about whether the patient understands and consents. For a patient to be adequately informed, the consent must be given or withheld in the light of adequate knowledge about who will or may receive the results, which in turn may be affected by the Health Insurance Portability and Accountability Act (HIPAA) and other legislation. Although these issues concern the variety of people who may eventually receive copies of the report and the associated raw data once the assessment has been completed, they must be addressed with the patient *before* starting the assessment, so that the client's decision to give or withhold consent is adequately informed. The next section discusses clarifying these issues.

CLARIFYING ACCESS TO THE TEST REPORT AND RAW DATA

Therapists function within a complex framework of legal and ethical standards regarding the discretionary and mandatory release of test information. The U.S. Privacy Act of 1974, the California truth-in-testing statute, *Detroit Edison* v. *National Labor Relations Board*, the 1996 HIPAA, and the Canadian 2000 Personal Information Protection and Electronic Documents Act (PIPEDA) are examples of legislation and case law that affect access to assessment documents. The APA Ethics Code (APA, 2010) Standard 9.04, Release of Test Data, (a) and (b) provides a definition of *test data* and guidance about the release of test data:

> (a) The term *test data* refers to raw and scaled scores, patient responses to test questions or stimuli, and psychologists' notes and recordings concerning patient statements and behavior during an examination. Those portions of test materials that include patient responses are included in the definition of *test data*. Pursuant to a patient release, psychologists provide test data to the patient or other persons identified in the release. Psychologists may refrain from releasing test data to protect a patient or others from substantial

harm or misuse or misrepresentation of the data or the test, recognizing that in many instances release of confidential information under these circumstances is regulated by law. (See also Standard 9.11, Maintaining Test Security.)

(b) In the absence of a patient release, psychologists provide test data only as required by law or court order.

The next fictional vignette shows the complex judgments therapists must make about withholding or disclosing assessment information:

A 17-year-old boy comes to your office and asks for a comprehensive psychological evaluation. He has been experiencing some headaches, anxiety, and depression. A high school dropout, he has been married for a year and has a 1-year-old baby but has left his wife and child and returned to live with his parents. He works full time as an auto mechanic and has insurance that covers the testing procedures. You complete the testing. During the following year, you receive requests for information about the testing from a number of people:

- The boy's physician, an internist.
- The boy's parents, who are concerned about his depression.
- The boy's employer, in connection with a worker's compensation claim filed by the boy.
- The attorney for the insurance company that is contesting the worker's compensation claim.
- The attorney for the boy's wife, who is suing for divorce and for custody of the baby.
- The attorney for the boy, who is considering suing you for malpractice because he does not like the results of the tests.

Each request asks for the full formal report, the original test data, and copies of each test (e.g., instructions and all items for the MMPI-2).

To which of these people are you ethically or legally obligated to supply all information requested, partial information, a summary of the report, or no information at all? Which requests require the boy's written informed consent for release of information?

There is no set of answers to these complex questions that would be generally applicable for all or even most readers. Each state, province, and other jurisdiction has its own evolving legislation and case law that address, sometimes in an incomplete or confusing manner, clinician responsibilities. Such questions can, however, provide a basis for discussion in ethics courses, clinical supervision and consultation, staff meetings, or workshops. Answers can be sought for a specific jurisdiction.

Practitioners can work through their local professional associations to develop clear guidelines to the current legal requirements. If the legal requirements in this or any other area of practice seem unethical, unreasonable, unclear, or potentially damaging to clients, practitioners can propose and support remedial legislation.

FOLLOWING STANDARD PROCEDURES FOR ADMINISTERING TESTS

When we are reciting the instructions to the Wechsler Intelligence Scale for Children-Revised (WISC-R) or the Halstead Category Test for the 500th time, we may experience the urge to break the monotony, liven things up, and let our originality show through. And particularly when we are in a hurry, we may want to shorten the instructions. After all, the client will catch on as we go along.

The assumption underlying standardized tests is that the test-taking situation and procedures are as similar as possible for everyone. If we change the procedures on which 'the norms are based, the standardized norms lose their direct applicability and the "standard" inferences drawn from those norms fall into question.

Reasonable accommodations for assessing people with disabilities may sometimes include changing the method of test administration. Lee, Reynolds, and Willson (2003) wrote:

> The 1999 Standards for Educational and Psychological Testing adopted by AERA [American Educational Research Association], APA, and NCME [National Council on Measurement in Education] requires examiners to make reasonable accommodations for individuals with disabilities when administering psychological tests to such persons. Changes in test administration may be required, but the Standards also require the examiner to provide evidence associated with the validity of test score interpretation in the face of such changes in administration. Departures from standard procedures during test administration may change the meaning of test scores, because scores based on norms derived from standardized procedures may not be appropriate; error terms and rates may also be affected. (p. 55)

APA's Committee on Professional Standards (1984) published a finding that allowing a client to take home a test such as the MMPI departs from the "standard procedure." The "Casebook for Providers of Psychological Services" (Committee on Professional Standards, 1984) describes a case in which a psychologist permitted his client to take the MMPI home to complete. When the complaint was filed with APA, the Committee on Professional Standards stated that whenever a psychologist

> does not have direct, first-hand information as to the condition under which the test is taken, he or she is forced (in the above instance, unnecessarily) to

assume that the test responses were not distorted by the general situation in which the test was taken (e.g., whether the client consulted others about test responses). Indeed the psychologist could have no assurance that this test was in fact completed by the client. In the instance where the test might be introduced as data in a court proceeding, it would be summarily dismissed as hearsay evidence. (p. 664)

Unless the assessment is carefully monitored, there is no way to know the conditions under which the person filled out response sheets and completed other aspects of the testing. Psychologist Jack Graham, an expert in the MMPI, described an interesting test administration in an inpatient setting (Pope, Butcher, & Seelen, 2006). He observed a large gathering of patients. Several times a minute, some of the patients would raise their hands. Graham became intrigued and asked one of the patients to tell him what was going on. The patient explained that a psychologist had given an MMPI to one of the patients, asking him to complete it and then return it to the psychologist's office. The patient had asked for help from the other patients. The patient was reading each MMPI item aloud, and the patients raised their hands to vote on whether that item should be answered true or false.

Psychologist Jim Butcher, another expert in the MMPI, observed a patient sitting with his spouse outside a psychologist's office while filling out an MMPI. From time to time as the patient marked an answer, his wife, reading along, would tell him he was wrong and should change his answer, which the patient dutifully did (Pope et al., 2006).

KNOWING THE LITERATURE ON RECORDINGS AND THIRD-PARTY OBSERVERS

If we audiotape or videotape an assessment, or allow a third party to be present, we need to know how this can affect the assessment. For example, Constantinou, Ashendorf, and McCaffrey (2002) found that "in the presence of an audio-recorder the performance of the participants on memory tests declined. Performance on motor tests, on the other hand, was not affected by the presence of an audio-recorder" (p. 407). Gavett, Lynch, and McCaffrey (2005) found that "third party observers have been found to significantly impair neuropsychological test performance on measures of attention, verbal memory, verbal fluency, and cognitive symptom validity" (p. 49; see also Constantinou et al., 2005; Lynch, 2005; Yantz & McCaffrey, 2005).

We also need to be aware of the policy statements and similar articles in this area. For example, the documents that address third-party presence in neuropsychological assessments include:

- American Academy of Clinical Neuropsychology's "Policy Statement on the Presence of Third Party Observers in Neuropsychological Assessment" (2001)

- Axelrod and colleagues' "Presence of Third Party Observers During Neuropsychological Testing: Official Statement of the National Academy of Neuropsychology" (2000)
- Duff and Fisher's "Ethical Dilemmas with Third Party Observers" (2005)
- Lynch and McCaffrey's "Neuropsychological Assessments in the Presence of Third Parties: Ethical Issues and Literature Review" (2004)
- McSweeny and colleagues' "Ethical Issues Related to the Presence of Third Party Observers in Clinical Neuropsychological Evaluations" (1998)

The APA's Committee on Psychological Tests and Assessment (2007) summarizes the complex issues involving third parties:

> Inclusion of a third party in the assessment and testing process may affect validity of an evaluation or threaten test security and copyright. However, a third party may facilitate validity and fairness of the evaluation or be required by law. Options to address the request for external observation include, but are not limited to (1) conducting the evaluation in the presence of an observer, (2) minimizing the intrusion afforded by observation, (3) utilizing assessment measures that are less affected by observation, (4) recommending that the request for a third party be withdrawn, and (5) declining to perform the assessment under observation. (p. 5)

AWARENESS OF BASIC ASSUMPTIONS

Fundamental assumptions and theoretical frameworks often affect our assessments. Langer and Abelson's classic study (1974), "A Patient by Any Other Name," for example, shows one way in which behavior therapists and psychoanalytically oriented therapists can differ when viewing the same individual:

Clinicians representing two different schools of thought, behavioral and analytic, viewed a single videotaped interview between a man who had recently applied for a new job and one of the authors. Half of each group was told that the interviewee was a "job applicant" while the remaining half was told that he was a "patient." At the end of the videotape, all clinicians were asked to complete a questionnaire evaluating the interviewee.

The interviewee was described as fairly well adjusted by the behavioral therapists regardless of the label supplied. This was not the case, however, for the more traditional analytic therapists. When the interviewee was labeled "patient," he was described as significantly more disturbed than he was when he was labeled "job applicant" (p. 4).

The point here is not whether either of these two orientations is more valid, reliable, respectable, empirically based, or useful but rather to underscore the obvious: Different theoretical orientations can lead to different assessments. Clinicians conducting assessments and assigning diagnoses need to be continually aware of their own theoretical orientation and how that orientation will affect the evaluation. Langer and Abelson (1974) wrote:

> Despite the questionable light in which the analytic therapist group was cast in the present study, one strongly suspects that conditions might be arranged wherein the behavior therapists would fall into some kind of error, as much as the traditionalists. No single type of orientation toward clinical training is likely to avoid all types of biases or blind spots. (p. 9)

Woodward, Taft, Gordon, and Meis (2009) conducted a similar study and wrote:

> The finding that psychodynamic therapists were more likely to diagnose BPD [borderline personality disorder] than PTSD [posttraumatic stress disorder] is consistent with previous research which has found that psychodynamic clinicians tend to apply the BPD diagnosis when BPD criteria are not met more frequently than clinicians of other orientations. ... It is also of note that in the current study, CBT [cognitive behavioral therapy] clinicians were more likely to diagnose PTSD than BPD. That theoretical orientation significantly affects a clinician's diagnosis raises concerns because it suggests that clinicians may be applying their own theories to the atheoretical diagnostic criteria of DSM-IV [*Diagnostic and Statistical Manual of Mental Disorders*, 4th ed.]. How clinicians conceptualize their clients' distress will impact those clients' treatment plans and possibly the effectiveness of the intervention. We encourage clinicians to reflect upon their own theoretical biases when assessing new clients and to form comprehensive treatment plans to address those difficulties most relevant for each patient. (p. 287)

AWARENESS OF PERSONAL FACTORS LEADING TO MISUSING DIAGNOSIS

In addition to a lack of awareness of our basic assumptions and our assumptions in specific areas, insufficient attention to our own personal reactions and dynamics makes us vulnerable to faulty evaluations. Reiser and Levenson's excellent article, "Abuses of the Borderline Diagnosis" (1984), focuses on six ways in which the diagnosis of borderline personality disorder is commonly abused "to express countertransference hate, mask imprecise thinking, excuse treatment failures, justify the therapist's acting out, defend against sexual clinical material, and avoid pharmacologic and medical treatment interventions" (p. 1528). Openness to such issues within ourselves and frequent consultations with colleagues can help prevent abuses of this kind and help our assessments meet the highest ethical standards.

AWARENESS OF FINANCIAL FACTORS LEADING TO MISUSING DIAGNOSIS

Therapists who depend on third-party coverage learn quickly which diagnostic categories are "covered" and which are not. Insurance companies, health maintenance organizations (HMOs), and managed care companies may authorize services for only a very restricted range of diagnoses. For example, the personality or character disorders are rarely covered. Unfortunately, the temptation to substitute a fraudulent but covered diagnosis for an honest but unreimbursable one can influence even senior and well-respected practitioners, as shown in a national study (Pope & Bajt, 1988). Kovacs (1987), in his strongly worded article on insurance billing, issues a stern warning that those

> who are naive about insurance billing or who play a little fast and loose with carriers are beginning to play Russian Roulette. The carriers are now prepared to spend the necessary funds for investigators and for lawyers which will be required to sue in civil court and/or to bring criminal charges against colleagues who do not understand their ethical and legal responsibility in completing claim forms on behalf of their patients. (p. 24)

"Advice on Ethics of Billing Clients" (1987), an article in the *APA Monitor*, lists among "billing practices that should be avoided": "Changing the diagnosis to fit reimbursement criteria" (p. 42).

The APA's Ethical Principles of Psychologists and Code of Conduct (2010), Standard 6.06, Accuracy in Reports to Payors and Funding Sources, states:

> In their reports to payors for services or sources of research funding, psychologists take reasonable steps to ensure the accurate reporting of the nature of the service provided or research conducted, the fees, charges, or payments, and where applicable, the identity of the provider, the findings, and the diagnosis. (See also Standards 4.01, Maintaining Confidentiality; 4.04, minimizing Intrusions on Privacy; and 4.05, Disclosures.)

Unfortunately, many managed care companies and other third-party payers limit reimbursement for assessment to one hour. Often a full evaluation to determine accurate diagnoses requires several hours of testing and report preparation. Either the provider of services must provide rationale for further reimbursement or provide services pro bono. (Note: Finn [2007] describes an assessment process that has therapeutic impact and also describes how to bill third-party payers for therapeutic assessment sessions.)

The problem of financial factors leading to false diagnosis appears to be significant. Gross (2004) wrote that

> the abuse of insurance is one of the most common ethical and legal violations committed by practicing therapists, resulting in imposed sanctions by licensing

agencies and criminal convictions.…Unfortunately for the profession, abuse of insurance has become so commonplace that many practitioners have deceived themselves into believing it is normal or acceptable behavior. (p. 36)

ACKNOWLEDGING LOW BASE RATES

Source: "Fallacies and Pitfalls in Psychological Assessment." Copyright © 2003 by K. S. Pope. Used with permission. Retrieved from http:// kspope.com/fallacies/ index.php

If an assessment involves something—for example, a condition, ability, aptitude, or quality—rarely found in the population, overlooking the low base rate causes problems. Even when psychological tests are accurate, low base rates can cause big mistakes.

Imagine you have been commissioned to develop an assessment procedure that will identify crooked judges so that candidates for judicial appointment can be screened. It is a difficult challenge, in part because only 1 out of 500 judges is (hypothetically speaking) dishonest.

You pull together all the actuarial data you can find and develop a screening test for crookedness based on personality characteristics, personal history, and test results. Your method is 90% accurate.

When your method is used to screen the next 5,000 judicial candidates, there might be 10 candidates who are crooked (because about 1 out of 500 is crooked). A 90% accurate screening method will identify 9 of these 10 crooked candidates as crooked and 1 as honest.

So far, so good.

The problem is the 4,990 honest candidates. Because the screening is wrong 10% of the time and the only way for the screening to be wrong about honest candidates is to identify them as crooked, it will falsely classify 10% of the honest candidates as crooked. The test will incorrectly classify 499 of these 4,990 honest candidates as crooked.

So out of the 5,000 candidates who were screened, the 90% accurate test classified 508 of them as crooked: Nine who actually were crooked and 499 who were honest. Every 508 times the screening method indicates crookedness, it tends to be right only nine times. And it has falsely branded 499 honest people as crooked.

ACKNOWLEDGING DUAL HIGH BASE RATES

Source: "Fallacies and Pitfalls in Psychological Assessment." Copyright © 2003 by K. S. Pope. Used with permission. Retrieved from http:// kspope.com/fallacies/ index.php

The next example shows why it is crucial to recognize dual high base rates:

As part of a disaster response team, you are flown in to work at a community mental health center in a city that has experienced a severe earthquake. Taking a quick look at the records the center has compiled, you note that of the 200 people who have come for services since the earthquake, there are 162 who are of a particular religious faith and are diagnosed with posttraumatic stress disorder (PTSD) related to the earthquake and 18 of that faith who came for services unrelated to the earthquake. Of those who are not of that faith, 18 have been diagnosed with PTSD related to the earthquake, and 2 have come for services unrelated to the earthquake.

It looks like there is a strong link between that particular religious faith and developing PTSD related to the earthquake: 81% of the people who came for services were of that religious faith and had developed PTSD. Perhaps this faith makes people vulnerable to PTSD. Or perhaps it is a more subtle association: This faith might make it easier for people with PTSD to seek mental heath services.

But the inference of an association is a fallacy: Religious faith and the development of PTSD in this community are independent factors. Ninety percent of all people who seek services at this center happen to be of that specific religious faith (90% of those who had developed PTSD and 90% who had come for other reasons) and 90% of all people who seek services after the earthquake (90% of those with that particular religious faith and 90% of those who are not of that faith) have developed PTSD. The two factors appear to be linked because both have high base rates, but they are statistically unrelated.

AVOIDING CONFUSION BETWEEN RETROSPECTIVE AND PREDICTIVE ACCURACY

The *predictive accuracy* of an assessment instrument focuses first on the test results and asks: What are the chances, expressed as a conditional probability, that a person with these results has a particular condition, ability, aptitude, or quality? The *retrospective accuracy* of an assessment instrument focuses first on the particular condition, ability, aptitude, or quality and asks: What are the chances, expressed as a conditional probability, that a person who has this particular condition or ability will show these test results? Many problems spring from this common mistake of confusing the directionality of the inference.

This mistake of confusing retrospective with predictive accuracy often resembles the *affirming the consequent* logical fallacy (see Chapter 3):

> People with condition X are overwhelmingly likely to have these specific test results.
> Person Y has these specific test results.
> Therefore, Person Y is overwhelmingly likely to have condition X.

AWARENESS OF FORENSIC ISSUES

As our society becomes more litigious, we find ourselves as therapists (fact witnesses) or expert witnesses appearing in court more frequently and preparing documents that will become part of legal proceedings. Forensic settings set forth specific demands, and practitioners need to become aware of them. For example, financial factors can, under certain circumstances, create a bias—or at least the appearance of bias—in carrying out and reporting assessments. For this reason, forensic texts have long mandated that no psychologist accept a contingency fee. Blau (1984) wrote: "The psychologist should never accept a fee contingent upon the outcome of a case" (p. 336). Shapiro (1990) stated: "The expert witness should never, under any circumstances, accept a referral on a contingent fee basis" (p. 230). Only about 15% of the respondents in a national survey reported engaging in this practice (Pope, Tabachnick, & Keith-Spiegel, 1987), and about the same percentage (14%) believe it to be good practice or good under most circumstances (Pope, Tabachnick, & Keith-Spiegel, 1988). Kesselhelm and Studdert (2007) note that "many codes . . . reject witness fees that are contingent on the litigation outcome" (p. 2907). The Committee on Medical Liability and Risk Management of the American Academy of Pediatrics (2009) emphasizes that "the medical profession has deemed it unethical for expert witnesses to base their fees for testifying contingent on the outcome of the case" (p. 433).

Another potentially troublesome area in forensic practice involves conducting child custody assessments. Shapiro (1990), for example, states that "under no circumstances should a report on child custody be rendered to the court, based on the evaluation of only one party to the conflict" (p. 99). The "Guidelines for Child Custody Evaluations in Family Law Practice" (APA, 2009) provides guidance for psychologists in this area. According to this document, the best interest of the child is the primary purpose of the evaluation and is considered paramount. Other useful sources of information on potential problems in this area include: Ackerman (2006); Acklin and Cho-Stutler (2006); Bow (2006); Bow, Gould, Fiens, & Greenhut (2006); Frieldhandler (2008); Gutheil (2009); Martindale et al. (2007); O'Donohue, Beitz, and Tolle (2009); and Otto and Martindale (2007).

ATTENTION TO POTENTIAL MEDICAL CAUSES

Whenever the patient's symptoms hit all of the diagnostic criteria for a psychological disorder, it is tempting to ignore possible medical causes for a distress or disability (such as pain, weight loss, or bleeding from bodily orifices). A comprehensive evaluation, however, needs to rule out (or identify) possible medical causes.

Rick Imbert, when he was president of the American Professional Agency, a company that provides professional liability coverage, stressed that "if there is any indication of a physical problem, then have a full medical screening; for example, symptoms which appear to be part of a schizophrenic process can actually be caused by a brain tumor" (personal communication, April 18, 1988). The case of Mr. Alvarez in Chapter 2 is a vivid reminder of what can happen when we reflexively dismiss possible physical causes for symptoms that appear to have psychological causes.

AWARENESS OF PRIOR RECORDS AND HISTORY

Prior records of assessment and treatment can be an invaluable resource as part of a comprehensive psychological evaluation. The courts have held that neglecting to make any effort to recognize, obtain, and use this resource violates, in some instances, the standard of care. In the federal case of *Jablonski* v. *United States* (1983), for example, the U.S. Ninth Circuit Court of Appeals upheld a "district court judge's findings of malpractice...for failure to obtain the past medical records."

Regardless of whether prior records exist or are obtainable, obtaining an adequate history can be crucial to an adequate assessment. Psychologist Laura Brown (1994b), for instance, discussed the pioneering work of independent practitioner Lynne Rosewater and George Washington University professor Mary Anne Dutton in demonstrating how overlooked history could lead to misdiagnosis when relying on standardized tests:

> Their work has involved collecting data on large numbers of battered women and identifying common patterns of response on the testing. In effect, they have noted that the standard mainstream texts and computerized scoring systems for the MMPI do not take into account the possibility that the person taking the test is a woman who currently is, or recently has been, beaten by her spouse or partner....
>
> As Rosewater first pointed out, without the context, specifically the identification of the presence of violence, battered women look like schizophrenics or borderline personalities on the MMPI. With the context of violence explicitly framing the interpretation of the test findings, however, it is possible to note that the sort of distress indicated on the testing is a reasonable response to events in the test-taker's life. That is to say, when a woman's partner is beating her, it makes sense that she is depressed, confused, scattered, and feeling overwhelmed. It is not necessarily the case that this state of response to life-threatening violence is either usual for the woman in question or a sign of psychopathology. (p. 187)

INDICATING ALL RESERVATIONS ABOUT RELIABILITY AND VALIDITY

If any circumstances might have affected the results of psychological testing, such as dim lighting, frequent interruptions, a noisy environment, or medication, or if there is doubt that the person being tested shares all relevant characteristics with the reference groups on which the norms are based, these factors must be taken into account when interpreting test data and must be included in the formal report.

One implication of this responsibility is that psychologists must remain alert to the diverse array of factors that may affect validity and reliability. For example, psychologists who test individuals whose first language is not English face a challenge to determine whether the testing in English is appropriate. Often, referral of the client to a mental health professional who is competent in the client's language may be important. If translation is necessary, psychologists do not retain the services of translators or paraprofessionals who may have a dual role with the client (e.g., a family member) to avoid jeopardizing the validity of evaluation or the effectiveness of intervention.

PROVIDING ADEQUATE FEEDBACK

Feedback is a dynamic, interactive process in which the results and implications of testing or other forms of assessment are shared with the person who is being assessed (Pope, 1992). APA (2010) Ethics Code Standard 9.10, Explaining Assessment Results, states:

> Regardless of whether the scoring and interpretation are done by psychologists, by employees or assistants, or by automated or other outside services, psychologists take reasonable steps to ensure that explanations of results are given to the individual or designated representative unless the nature of the relationship precludes provision of an explanation of results (such as in some organizational consulting, preemployment or security screenings, and forensic evaluations), and this fact has been clearly explained to the person being assessed in advance.

Three major factors can block this process.

1. HMOs and other managed care organizations can inflict harsh, sometimes unrealistic, demands on clinicians' time. The rationing of time may allow too little opportunity to sit with a client to discuss an assessment and attend carefully to the client's questions and concerns. Similarly, federal, state, and private mental health insurance may disallow coverage for all but the most minimal feedback session. For example, there may be a standard fixed payment for administrating a specific psychological test; the payment may barely (sometimes inadequately) cover

the time necessary to administer the test and prepare a brief write-up of the results. The clinician may have to donate pro bono the time required to provide adequate feedback.

2. Advertisements and marketing literature may promote individual tests, versions of tests, or test batteries by stressing how little time they take. One continually reads of quick, brief, short, and abbreviated tests. Such promotion may unintentionally nurture the notion that a complex assessment can be carried out in just a few minutes with no real demands on the clinician's time, skills, judgment, or even attention. This rush to judgment may encourage clinicians to match their quick, brief, short, and abbreviated testing with quick, brief, short, and abbreviated feedback.

3. On a personal level, therapists and counselors may be uncomfortable discussing assessment results with a client. Some may be reluctant to be the bearer of what they fear the client will receive as bad news. Others may be uncomfortable trying to translate for the client the technical jargon that clogs so many test interpretation texts, computer interpretation printouts, volumes on diagnosis, and so forth. Still others may be uneasy facing a client's expectations of clear results with test results that may necessarily leave many important questions unanswered.

These and other factors may encourage clinicians to forget that feedback is a dynamic, interactive process that is an aspect of the larger process of assessment and that the assessment often continues during what is called the feedback session or phase. Consequently, feedback may come to be viewed as simply a pro forma, static method of closure or an obligatory technicality in which the "results" are dumped in the client's lap (or referral source or someone else). This view of feedback seems so aversive and unproductive that some clinicians may decide—wrongly—to withhold feedback altogether. No rote, by-the-numbers approach to feedback can replace a thoughtful discussion with the client of what the results are, what they mean, and what they do not mean.

SCENARIOS FOR DISCUSSION

> You are attending your first rounds at the community mental health center where you began working last week. Your supervisor discusses a recent intake who will be assigned to you for therapy. The supervisor, who assessed the new client using the MMPI-2 and a clinical interview, says that the assessment shows that the client's claims about being raped are clearly false. The
>
> *(continued)*

(*continued*)

treatment plan, which you will be implementing, will be to help the new client realize that this confabulation is not real.

- How do you feel?
- What options do you have?
- What would you like to say to the supervisor?
- What do you think that you would say to the supervisor?

■ ■ ■

You work for an HMO. A new patient shows up at your office for an initial session. The person says: "I have felt so incredibly edgy all week. I don't know what's wrong with me. But I feel like I want to smash someone in the mouth, like I want to get my gun and blow someone's brains out. I don't even know who, but it's like something's building up and it just won't be stopped."

- How do you feel?
- When the person stopped talking, what would be the first things you would say?
- How do you go about creating an assessment plan in this situation? What phases of the assessment would you make sure to complete before the person left your office, and how would you go about completing them? What phases of the assessment would you schedule for later? Who else, if anyone, would you involve in the assessment?

■ ■ ■

You are responsible for all intakes on Mondays, Wednesdays, and Fridays. After discussing recent intakes with you, your supervisor tells you: "From now on, I want to obtain standardized testing data on all intakes. I want you to administer the [names a test] to all intakes. I think we need to base our decisions on test data." You believe that this test lacks adequate validity and reliability for clinical work and is therefore not useful. You diplomatically say that you are not sure about giving the test, but your supervisor says, "I can understand that. No method is endorsed by everyone. But I'm responsible for intakes, and I'll take responsibility for this. All you need to do is administer, score, and interpret them."

- How do you feel?
- What would you like to say to the supervisor?

- What do you think you'd end up saying to the supervisor?
- What are your options?
- What would you do?

■ ■ ■

A parent schedules an appointment with you. The parent shows up with a child and says, "The people at school say that my Jesse here cheats at school. Can you talk with Jesse and give some tests to find out if that's true?"

- How do you feel?
- What are your options?
- What ethical concerns do you have? How would you address them?

■ ■ ■

A former client, whom you liked very much, calls and reports that she and her spouse are getting divorced. The client asks to return for an evaluation, as requested by her attorney, regarding a child custody dispute. She expresses her assumption that you will testify in court on her behalf.

- How do you feel?
- What are your options?
- What issues do you consider?
- How do you think you would respond?

■ ■ ■

An attorney calls to ask you to provide a basic evaluation for a patient who will be deported unless proof can be provided that the attorney's client is under severe duress as a refugee. The hearing is in 1 week, and the attorney says that no other resources for obtaining an evaluation are available and that there are waiting lists at the clinics providing such evaluations. The hearing judge has refused to grant an extension. The client does not speak English but has a family member who can interpret. You do not speak the client's language. You have attended multicultural diversity workshops and classes.

- How do you feel?

(*continued*)

(continued)

- What issues do you consider in deciding whether to schedule the assessment?
- What assessment approaches, including any standardized tests, would you consider in planning such an evaluation?
- Assume you agreed to conduct the assessment and when, you began, you found that the family member had minimal skills in speaking English. What would you do?

Chapter 16

SEXUAL RELATIONSHIPS WITH CLIENTS

Andrea Calenza (2007) wrote: "The fantasy that one might desire another person profoundly enough to risk one's entire professional career is at once horrifying and intriguing" (p. 27). The horror and intrigue of attraction to patients—a very common experience among therapists—and the temptation or fear of acting on that attraction have been difficult for the profession to face honestly and realistically.

Therapists who fantasize about beginning a sexual relationship with a client are daydreaming about violating one of the oldest ethical mandates in the health-care professions. Annette Brodsky (1989) noted that this rule is even older than the 2,500-year-old Hippocratic Oath. The ancient code of the Nigerian healing arts included the prohibition. The prohibition against therapist-patient sexual involvement is one of the most widely accepted and respected ethical mandates. Tom Gutheil and Archie Brodsky (2008) wrote that "there is a unanimity of reputable opinion that having sexual relationships with a patient is incompatible with any form of professional mental health treatment" (p. 175).

Even fantasizing about becoming sexually involved with a client *after termination* is a fantasy about an act that can involve considerable risk. Gorman (2009) pointed out that in "nearly two dozen states, a psychologist risks losing his license to practice if he has sex with a former client within one, two, or even five years of the end of treatment" (p. 983; see also Feeny, 2009; Sarkar, 2009). Some ethics codes prohibit sexual relationships between therapists and their former patients in perpetuity. Principle 2.6 of the Code of Ethics of the Royal Australian and New Zealand College of Psychiatrists (2004), for example, states: "Sexual relationships between psychiatrists and their former patients are always unethical" (p. 6).

PROHIBITION AND MODERN ETHICS CODES

Modern ethics codes contained no explicit mention of this topic until research began revealing that many therapists were violating the prohibition. Although the codes had not highlighted this particular form of patient exploitation by name, therapist-patient sex violated ethics codes sections prior to the 1970s. Rachel Hare-Mustin (1974), former chair of the American Psychological Association's Ethics Committee, noted that the 1963 *Ethical Standards of Psychologists* of the APA contained standards that would prohibit therapist-patient sexual involvement. She wrote that in the light of "a review of principles relating to competency, community standards and the client relationship that genital contact with patients is ethically unacceptable" (p. 310).

Jean Holroyd, professor at the University of California–Los Angeles and senior author of the first national study of therapist-patient sex, explained that the 1977 code did not represent a change in the standards regarding sexual activities with patients:

> Administrative law judge: Was it [the 1977 ethics code] a codification of what was already the standard of practice?
>
> Holroyd: Yes, it was making it very explicit in the ethics code.
>
> Administrative law judge: What I am asking is whether or not the standard of practice prior to the inclusion of that specific section in the [1977] ethics code, whether or not that changed the standard of practice.
>
> Holroyd: No, it did not change the standard of practice. The standard of practice always precluded a sexual relationship between therapist and patient.
>
> Administrative law judge: Even though it was not expressed in the ethics codes?
>
> Holroyd: From the beginning of the term psychotherapy with Sigmund Freud, he was very clear to prohibit it in his early publications.
> (*In the Matter of the Accusation Against: Myron E. Howland*, 1980, pp. 49–50)

The courts recognized the long history of prohibition against therapist-patient sexual involvement. In the mid-1970s, New York Supreme Court Presiding Justice Markowitz noted the long history of professional agreement that therapist-patient sex harms patients: "Thus from [Freud] to the modern practitioner we have common agreement of the harmful effects of sensual intimacies between patient and therapist" (*Roy v. Hartogs*, 1976, p. 590).

That this prohibition has remained constant over so long a time and throughout so many diverse cultures reflects to some extent the recognition that sex involvement places the patient at risk for serious harm.

Until relatively recently, our understanding of therapist-client sexual involvement was based mainly on theory, common sense, and individual case studies. Only in the past quarter century has a considerable body of diverse systematic investigations informed our understanding with empirical data. This chapter summarizes some of the findings. (For more detailed presentations of this research, see Gabbard, 1989; and Pope, 1993, 1994, 2001.)

HOW CLIENTS CAN BE INJURED

Beginning with Masters and Johnson (1966, 1970, 1975), investigators examined how therapist-client sexual involvement affects clients (Bouhoutsos, Holroyd, Lerman, Forer, & Greenberg, 1983; Brown, 1988; Butler & Zelen, 1977; Feldman-Summers & Jones, 1984; Herman, Gartrell, Olarte, Feldstein, & Localio, 1987; Nachmani & Somer, 2007; Pope & Vetter, 1991; Sonne, Meyer, Borys, & Marshall, 1985; Vinson, 1987). Approaches to learning about effects included studies of clients who have returned to therapy with a subsequent therapist as well as those who undertook no further therapy after their sexual involvement with a therapist.

The consequences for clients who have been sexually involved with a therapist have been compared to those for matched groups of therapy clients who have not been sexually involved with a therapist and of patients who have been sexually involved with a (nontherapist) physician. Subsequent treating therapists (of those clients who undertook a subsequent therapy), independent clinicians, and the clients themselves have evaluated the effects. Standardized psychological assessment instruments supplemented clinical interview and behavioral observation. These diverse approaches to systematic study have supplemented individual patients' firsthand accounts (Bates & Brodsky, 1989; Freeman & Roy, 1976; Noel & Waterson, 1992; Plaisil, 1985; Walker & Young, 1986).

The consequences for the clients tend to cluster into 10 very general categories:

1. Ambivalence
2. Guilt
3. Emptiness and isolation
4. Sexual confusion
5. Impaired ability to trust
6. Confused roles and boundaries
7. Emotional lability
8. Suppressed rage

9. Increased suicide risk
10. Cognitive dysfunction, frequently in the areas of concentration and memory and often involving flashbacks, intrusive thoughts, unbidden images, and nightmares (Pope, 1988b, 1994, 2001).

GENDER AND OTHER PATTERNS OF PERPETRATORS AND VICTIMS

Despite the prohibition and the harm that can occur to sexually abused clients, a significant number of therapists have reported on anonymous surveys that they have become sexually involved with at least one client. When the data from the first eight national self-report surveys published in peer-reviewed journals are pooled, 5,148 participants provided anonymous self-reports (Akamatsu, 1988; Bernsen, Tabachnick, & Pope, 1994; Borys & Pope, 1989; Holroyd & Brodsky, 1977; Pope, Keith-Spiegel, & Tabachnick, 1986; Pope, Levenson, & Schover, 1979; Pope, Tabachnick, & Keith-Spiegel, 1987). Each of the three professions—psychiatry, psychology, and social work—is represented by at least two studies conducted in different years.

According to these pooled data, about 4.4% of the therapists reported becoming sexually involved with a client. The gender differences are significant: 6.8% of the male therapists and 1.6% of the female therapists reported engaging in sex with a client.

Data from these studies as well as others (e.g., reports by therapists working with patients who have been sexually involved with a prior therapist) suggest that therapist-patient sex resembles other forms of abuse such as rape and incest in that the perpetrators are overwhelmingly (though not exclusively) male and the victims are overwhelmingly (thought not exclusively) female (Pope, 1989b). For example, Bouhoutsos et al. (1983) reported a study in which 92% of the cases of therapist-patient sex involved a male therapist and female patient. Gartell, Herman, Olarte, Feldstein, and Localio (1986), who reported the first national self-report study of sexual involvement between psychiatrists and their patients, found that 88% of the "contacts for which both the psychiatrist's and the patient's gender were specified occurred between male psychiatrists and female patients" (p. 1128).

Data based on therapists' reports of engaging in sex with patients or on therapists' work with patients who have been sexually exploited by a prior therapist have been supplemented with national survey data from patients who have been sexually involved with a therapist. In one study, about 2.19% of the men and about 4.58% of the women reported having become sexually involved with their own therapists (Pope & Feldman-Summers, 1992).

Yet another source of data (supplementing those provided through reports by subsequent therapists, therapists' anonymous self-reports, and patients' anonymous self-reports) is consistent with the significant gender differences.

Data obtained from licensing disciplinary actions suggested that about 86% the therapist-patient cases are those in which the therapist is male and the patient is female (Pope, 1993).

This significant gender difference has long been a focus of scholarship in the area of therapist-patient sex but is still not well understood. Holroyd and Brodsky's report (1977) of the first national study of therapist-patient sex concluded with a statement of major issues that had yet to be resolved: "Three professional issues remain to be addressed: (a) that male therapists are most often involved, (b) that female patients are most often the objects, and (c) that therapists who disregard the sexual boundary once are likely to repeat" (p. 849). Holroyd (1983) suggested that the significant gender differences reflected sex role stereotyping and bias: "Sexual contact between therapist and patient is perhaps the quintessence of sex-biased therapeutic practice" (p. 285).

Holroyd and Brodsky's landmark research (1977) was followed by a second national study focusing on not only therapist-patient but also professor-student sexual relationships (Pope et al., 1979):

When sexual contact occurs in the context of psychology training or psychotherapy, the predominant pattern is quite clear and simple: An older, higher-status man becomes sexually active with a younger, subordinate woman. In each of the higher-status professional roles (teacher, supervisor, administrator, therapist), a much higher percentage of men than women engage in sex with those students or clients for whom they have assumed professional responsibility. In the lower-status role of student, a far greater proportion of women than men are sexually active with their teachers, administrators, and clinical supervisors (p. 687; see also Pope, 1989a, 1994).

Although statistical analyses of the first eight national self-report studies published in peer-reviewed journals reveal significant gender effects and also significant effects related to the year of the study (the pooled data suggest that each year, there are about 10% fewer self-reports of therapist-patient sex than the year before), there is no significant effect due to profession. According to these data, psychologists, psychiatrists, and social workers report engaging in sex with their patients at about the same rates. Apparent differences are actually due to differing years in which the studies were conducted (there was a confounding correlation between the professions and the years they were studied). The statistical analysis tested the predictive power of each variable (profession and year) once the variance accounted for by the other variable had been subtracted. Year had significantly more predictive power once effects due to profession had been accounted for than the predictive power of profession once effects due to year had been accounted for. Once year of study is taken into account, significant differences between professions disappear.

Bates and Brodsky (1989) examined the various risk factors that have been hypothesized at one time or another to make certain clients more vulnerable to sexual exploitation by a therapist. Their analysis led them not to the personal history or characteristics of the client but rather to prior behavior of the therapist: The most effective predictor of whether a client will become sexually involved with a therapist is whether that therapist has previously engaged in sex with a client.

With access to a considerable set of historical and actuarial data, the APA Insurance Trust (1990) revealed that "the recidivism rate for sexual misconduct is substantial" (p. 3). Holroyd and Brodsky's landmark survey (1977) found that 80% of the therapists who reported engaging in therapist-patient sexual intimacies indicated that they became involved with more than 1 patient. The California Department of Consumer Affairs (1997) published its findings in a document that was sent to all licensed therapists and counselors in California and that must, according to California law, be provided by a therapist to any patient who reports having been sexually involved with a prior therapist. This document notes that "80% of the sexually exploiting therapists have exploited more than one client. In other words, if a therapist is sexually exploiting a client, chances are he or she has done so before" (p. 14).

Table 16.1 presents additional information, based on a national survey, of 958 patients who had been sexually involved with a therapist. In this study,

Table 16.1.   Characteristics of 958 Patients Who Had Been Sexually Involved with a Therapist.

Characteristics	Number	Percentage
Patient was a minor at the time of the involvement	47	5
Patient married the therapist	37	3
Patient had experienced incest or other child sex abuse	309	32
Patient had experienced rape prior to sexual involvement with therapist	92	10
Patient required hospitalization considered to be at least partially a result of the sexual involvement	105	11
Patient attempted suicide	134	14
Patient committed suicide	7	1
Patient achieved complete recovery from any harmful effects of sexual involvement	143	17[a]
Patient seen pro bono or for reduced fee	187	20
Patient filed formal (for example, licensing, malpractice) complaint	112	12

[a]Refers to 17% of the 866 patients who experienced harm.

Source: Adapted from "Prior Therapist-Patient Sexual Involvement among Patients Seen by Psychologists," by K. S. Pope and V. A. Vetter, 1991, *Psychotherapy, 28,* pp. 429–438. Available at http://kspope.com. Copyright 1991 Division of Psychotherapy (22) of the American Psychological Association. Reprinted with permission.

80% of the patients who had become sexually involved with a therapist only after termination of the therapy were found to have been harmed.

Five percent of the patients described in Table 16.1 were minors at the time that they were sexually involved with a therapist. This finding underscores an important aspect of therapist-patient sex: Although much of the literature on this topic seems to assume that the patient is an adult, this is not always the case. In a national study focusing exclusively on minor patients who were sexually involved with a therapist, most (56%) were female (Bajt & Pope, 1989). The average age of these girls who were sexually involved with a therapist was 13, and the range was from age 17 down to age 3. The average age of the male minor patients was 12, ranging from 16 down to 7.

COMMON SCENARIOS

It is useful for therapists to be aware of the common scenarios in which therapists sexually exploit their patients. Pope and Bouhoutsos (1986, p. 4) presented 10 of the most common scenarios:

1. *Role Trading.* Therapist becomes the "patient" and the wants and needs of the therapist become the focus.
2. *Sex Therapy.* Therapist fraudulently presents therapist-patient sex as valid treatment for sexual or related difficulties.
3. *As If. . . .* Therapist treats positive transference as if it were not the result of the therapeutic situation.
4. *Svengali.* Therapist creates and exploits an exaggerated dependence on the part of the patient.
5. *Drugs.* Therapist uses cocaine, alcohol, or other drugs as part of the seduction.
6. *Rape.* Therapist uses physical force, threats, and/or intimidation.
7. *True Love.* Therapist uses rationalizations that attempt to discount the clinical/professional nature of the professional relationship and its duties.
8. *It Just Got Out of Hand.* Therapist fails to treat the emotional closeness that develops in therapy with sufficient attention, care, and respect.
9. *Time Out:* Therapist fails to acknowledge and take account of the fact that the therapeutic relationship does not cease to exist between scheduled sessions or outside the therapist's office.
10. *Hold Me.* Therapist exploits patient's desire for nonerotic physical contact and possible confusion between erotic and nonerotic contact.

It is important to emphasize, however, that these are only general descriptions of some of the most common patterns, and many instances of therapist-patient sexual involvement will not fall into these categories.

WHY DO THERAPISTS REFRAIN WHEN THEY ARE TEMPTED?

Although our apparent insights into our own motives as therapists may be questionable at best, it is worth asking: Why do the overwhelming majority of therapists avoid sexually exploiting patients? Table 16.2 presents the answers to this question as provided by therapists in two national studies: one of psychologists and the other of social workers.

CONFRONTING DAILY ISSUES

The issue of therapist-client sexual involvement reflects some major themes of this book. The great vulnerability of the client highlights the power of the therapist and the trust that must characterize the client's relationship with the therapist (see Chapter 4). The therapist's caring may be crucial in protecting against the temptation to exploit the client.

Table 16.2. Reasons Therapists Offer for Refraining from Sexual Involvement with Clients.

Reasons	Social Workers	Psychologists
Unethical	210	289
Countertherapeutic/exploitative	130	251
Unprofessional practice	80	134
Against therapist's personal values	119	133
Therapist already in a committed relationship	33	67
Feared censure/loss of reputation	7	48
Damaging to therapist	39	43
Disrupts handling transference/countertransference	10	28
Fear of retaliation by client	2	19
Attraction too weak/short-lived	16	18
Illegal	14	13
Self-control	8	8
Common sense	7	8
Miscellaneous	13	3

Sources: Adapted from "Prior Therapist-Patient Sexual Involvement among Patients Seen by Psychologists," by K. S. Pope and V. A. Vetter, 1991, *Psychotherapy, 28,* pp. 429–438. Available at http://kspope.com. Copyright 1991 Division of Psychotherapy (22) of the American Psychological Association. Reprinted with permission.

The issue of therapist-client sexual involvement illustrates another fundamental theme of this book: Ethics is not mindlessly following a list of dos and don'ts but always involves active awareness, thinking, and questioning. There is, of course, a clear prohibition: Avoid any sexual involvement with clients. No cause, situation, or condition could ever legitimize such intimacies with any client (see, e.g., Gabbard & Pope, 1989). "Context is important for understanding the transgression of sexual boundaries in therapy, but this behavior is unethical in any context" (Gutheil & Brodsky, 2008, p. 175). The prohibition stands as a fundamental ethical mandate no matter what the rationalizations. Taking this prohibition seriously, however, marks the initial rather than the final steps in meeting our ethical responsibilities in this area. Several associated issues that we must confront and struggle with follow.

Physical Contact With Clients

The very topic of therapist-client sexual involvement as well as concern that we may be subject to an ethics complaint or malpractice suit may make many of us very nervous. We may go to great lengths to ensure that we maintain physical distance from our clients and under no circumstances touch them for fear that this might be misconstrued. A similar phenomenon seems to be occurring in regard to increasing public acknowledgment of child sexual abuse: Adults may be reluctant to hold children and engage in nonsexual touch that is a normal part of life.

Is there any evidence that nonsexual touching of patients is actually associated with therapist-client sexual involvement? Holroyd and Brodsky (1980) examined this question and found no indications that physical contact with patients made sexual contact more likely. They did find evidence that differential touching of male and female clients (i.e., touching clients of one gender significantly more than clients of the other gender) was associated with sexual intimacies:

> Erotic contact not leading to intercourse is associated with older, more experienced therapists who do not otherwise typically touch their patients at a rate different from other therapists (except when mutually initiated). Sexual intercourse with patients is associated with the touching of opposite-sex patients but not same-sex patients. It is the differential application of touching—rather than touching per se—that is related to intercourse. (p. 810)

If the therapist is personally comfortable engaging in physical contact with a client, maintains a theoretical orientation for which therapist-client contact is not antithetical, and has competence (education, training, and supervised experience) in the use of touch, then the decision of whether to make physical contact with a particular client must be based on a careful evaluation of the clinical needs of the client at that moment in the context of any relevant cultural and other contextual factors. When solidly based on clinical needs and a clinical rationale, touch can be exceptionally caring, comforting, reassuring, or healing. When not justified by clinical need and therapeutic rationale, nonsexual touch can also be experienced as intrusive, frightening, or demeaning. The decision must always be made carefully and in full awareness of the power of the therapist and the trust (and vulnerability) of the client. For discussions of various approaches to nonerotic touch in psychotherapy, please see Ashieri (2009); Bonitz (2008); Downey (2001); Kepner (2001); McNeil-Haber (2004); Phelan (2009); Pope, Sonne, and Greene (2006); Stenzel and Rupert (2004); and Young (2007).

Our responsibility to be sensitive to the issues of nonsexual touch and explore them carefully extends to other therapeutic issues conceptually related to the issue of therapist-client sexual involvement. Our unresolved concerns with therapist-client sexual intimacies may prompt us to respond to the prospect of nonsexual touching either phobically—avoiding in an exaggerated manner any contact or even physical closeness with a client—or counterphobically—engaging in apparently nonsexual touching such as handshakes and hugs as if to demonstrate that we are very comfortable with physical intimacy and experience no sexual impulses. These unresolved concerns can also elicit phobic or counterphobic behavior in other areas, such as the clinician's initiating discussion or focusing on sexual issues to an extent that is not based on the client's clinical needs. To respond ethically, authentically, and therapeutically to such issues, we must come to terms with our own unresolved feelings of sexual attraction to our clients.

Sexual Attraction to Clients

Sexual attraction to clients seems to be a prevalent experience that evokes negative reactions. National survey research suggests that over 4 out of 5 psychologists (87%) and social workers (81%) report experiencing sexual attraction to at least 1 client (Bernsen et al., 1994; Pope et al., 1986). As Table 16.3 illustrates, therapists identify many aspects of patients that, according to the therapists, are the source or focus of the attraction. Yet simply experiencing the attraction (without necessarily even feeling tempted to act on it) causes most of the therapists who report such attraction (63% of the psychologists and 51% of the social workers) to feel guilty, anxious, or confused about the attraction.

That sexual attraction causes such discomfort among so many psychologists and social workers and psychologists may be a significant reason that graduate training programs and internships tend to neglect training in this area. Only 9% of psychologists and 10% of social workers surveyed in these national studies reported that their formal training on the topic in graduate school and

Table 16.3.   Characteristics of Clients to Whom Therapists Are Attracted.

Characteristics	Social Workers	Psychologists
Physical attractiveness	175	296
Positive mental/cognitive traits or abilities	84	124
Sexual	40	88
Vulnerabilities	52	85
Positive overall character/personality	58	84
Kindness	6	66
Fills therapist's needs	8	46
Successful	6	33
"Good patient"	21	31
Client's attraction	3	30
Independence	5	23
Other specific personality characteristics	27	14
Resemblance to someone in therapist's life	14	12
Availability (client unattached)	0	9
Pathological characteristics	13	8
Long-term client	7	7
Sociability (sociable, extroverted)	0	6
Miscellaneous	23	15
Same interests/philosophy/background as therapist	10	0

Sources: Social work data are from "National Survey of Social Workers' Sexual Attraction to Their Clients: Results, Implications, and Comparison to Psychologist," by A. Bernsen, B. C. Tabachnick, and K. S. Pope, 1994, *Ethics and Behavior, 4*, pp. 369–388. Available at http://kspope.com. Copyright 1994 Lawrence Erlbaum Associates, Inc. Adapted with permission. Psychology data are from "Sexual Attraction to Patients: The Human Therapist and the (Sometimes) Inhuman Training System," by K. S. Pope, P. Keith-Spiegel, and B. G. Tabachnick, 1986, *American Psychologist, 41*, pp. 147–158. Available at http://kspope.com. Copyright 1986, American Psychological Association. Adapted with permission.

internships had been adequate. A majority of psychologists and social workers reported receiving no training about attraction.

This discomfort may also be a significant reason that scientific and professional books seem to neglect this topic:

> In light of the multitude of books on human sexuality, sexual dynamics, sex therapies, unethical therapist-patient sexual contact, management of the therapist's or patient's sexual behaviors, and so on, it is curious that sexual

attraction to clients per se has not served as the primary focus of a wide range of texts. The professor, supervisor, or librarian seeking books that turn their *primary* attention to exploring the therapist's *feelings* in this regard would be hard pressed to assemble a selection from which to choose an appropriate course text. If someone unfamiliar with psychotherapy were to judge the prevalence and significance of therapists' sexual feelings on the basis of the books that focus exclusively on that topic, he or she might conclude that the phenomenon is neither widespread nor important.

(Pope, Sonne, & Holroyd, 1993, p. 23)

These and similar factors may form a vicious circle: Discomfort with sexual attraction may have fostered an absence of relevant textbooks and graduate training; in turn, an absence of relevant textbooks and programs providing training in this area may sustain or intensify discomfort with the topic (Pope et al., 1993). The avoidance of the topic may produce a real impact. Koocher (1994) wrote, "How can the extant population of therapists be expected to adequately address [these issues] if we pay so little attention to training in these matters?" (p. viii).

These studies reveal significant gender effects in reported rates of experiencing sexual attraction to a patient. About 95% of the male psychologists and 92% of the male social workers compared with 76% of the female psychologists and 70% of the female social workers reported experiencing sexual attraction to a patient. The research suggests that just as male therapists are significantly more likely to become sexually involved with their patients, male therapists are also more likely to experience sexual attraction to their patients.

These national surveys suggest that a sizable minority of therapists carry with them—in the physical absence of the client—sexualized images of the client and that a significantly greater percentage of male than of female therapists experience such cognitions. About 27% of male psychologists and 30% of male social workers, compared with 14% of female psychologists and 13% of female social workers, reported engaging in sexual fantasies about a patient while engaging in sexual activity with another person (not the patient). National survey research has found that 46% of psychologists reported engaging in sexual fantasizing (regardless of the occasion) about a patient on a rare basis and that an additional 26% reported more frequent fantasies of this kind (Pope et al., 1987), and 6% have reported telling sexual fantasies to their patients (Pope & Tabachnick, 1993). Such data may be helpful in understanding not only how therapists experience and respond to sexual feelings but also how therapists and clients represent (e.g., remember, anticipate, think about, fantasize about) each other when they are apart and how this affects the psychotherapeutic process and outcome (see Geller, Cooley, & Hartley, 1981; Orlinsky & Geller, 1993; Pope & Brown, 1996; Pope & Singer, 1978b; Pope, Sonne, & Greene, 2006).

For any of us who experience sexual attraction to a client, it is important to recognize that the research suggests that this is a common experience. To feel attraction to a client is not unethical; to acknowledge and address the attraction promptly, carefully, and adequately is an important ethical responsibility. For some of us, consultation with respected colleagues will be useful. For others, obtaining formal consultation (if licensed; supervision if not) for our work with that client may be necessary. For still others, entering or reentering psychotherapy can be helpful.

WHEN THE THERAPIST IS UNSURE WHAT TO DO

What can the therapist do when he or she does not know what to do? The book *Sexual Feelings in Psychotherapy* (Pope et al., 1993) suggests a 10-step approach to such daunting situations, which are summarized here. A repeated theme of that book is that therapists lack easy, one-size-fits-all answers to what sexual feelings about patients mean or their implications for the therapy. Different theoretical orientations provide different, sometimes opposing ways of approaching such questions. Each person and situation is unique. Therapists must explore and achieve a working understanding of their own unfolding, evolving feelings and the ways in which these feelings may play a helpful role in deciding what to say or do next. Cookbook approaches can block rather than foster this process.

The approach outlined here places fundamental trust in the individual therapist, adequately trained and consulting with others, to draw his or her own conclusions. Almost without exception, therapists learn at the outset the fundamental resources for helping themselves explore problematic situations. Depending on the situation, they may introspect, study the available research and clinical literature, consult, seek supervision, or begin or resume personal therapy. But sometimes, even after the most sustained exploration, the course is not clear. The therapist's best understanding of the situation suggests a course of action that seems productive yet questionable and perhaps potentially harmful. To refrain from a contemplated action may cut the therapist off from legitimately helpful spontaneity, creativity, intuition, and ability to respond effectively to the patient's needs. But engaging in the contemplated action may lead to disaster. When reaching such an impasse, therapists may find it useful to consider the potential intervention in the light of these 10 considerations.

Fundamental Prohibition

Is the contemplated action consistent with the fundamental prohibition against therapist-client sexual intimacy? Therapists must never violate this special trust. If the considered course of action includes any form of sexual involvement with a patient, it must be rejected.

Slippery Slope

The second consideration may demand deeper self-knowledge and self-exploration. Is the contemplated course of action likely to lead to or create a risk for sexual involvement with the patient? The contemplated action may seem unrelated to any question of sexual exploitation of a patient. Yet depending on the personality, strengths, and weaknesses of the therapist, the considered action may constitute a subtle first step on a slippery slope. In most cases, the therapist alone can honestly address this consideration.

Consistency of Communication

The third consideration invites the clinician to review the course of therapy from the start to the present: Has the therapist consistently and unambiguously communicated to the client that sexual intimacies cannot and will not occur, and is the contemplated action consistent with that communication? Does the contemplated action needlessly cloud the clarity of that communication? The human therapist may be intensely tempted to act in ways that stir the patient's sexual interest or respond in a self-gratifying way to the client's sexuality. Does the contemplated action represent, however subtly, a turning away from the legitimate goals of therapy?

Clarification

The fourth consideration invites therapists to ask if the contemplated action would be better postponed until sexual and related issues have been clarified. Assume, for example, that a therapist's theoretical orientation does not preclude physical contact with clients and that a client has asked that each session conclude with a reassuring hug between therapist and client. Such ritualized hugs could raise complex questions about their meaning for the client, their impact on the relationship, and how they might influence the course and effectiveness of therapy. It may be important to clarify such issues with the client before making a decision to conclude each session with a hug.

Client's Welfare

The fifth consideration is one of the most fundamental touchstones of all therapy: Is the contemplated action consistent with the client's welfare? The therapist's feelings may become so intensely powerful that they may create a context in which the client's clinical needs may blur or fade out altogether. The client may express wants or feelings with great force. The legal context—with the litigiousness that seems so prevalent in current society—may threaten the therapist in a way that makes it difficult to keep a clear focus on the client's welfare. Despite such competing factors and complexities, it is crucial to assess the degree to which any contemplated action supports, is consistent with, is irrelevant to, or is contrary to the patient's welfare.

Consent

The sixth consideration is yet another fundamental touchstone of therapy: Is the contemplated action consistent with the basic informed consent of the client?

Adopting the Client's View

The seventh consideration urges the therapist to empathize imaginatively with the client: How is the client likely to understand and respond to the contemplated action?

Therapy is one of many endeavors in which exclusive attention to theory, intention, and technique may distract from other sources of information, ideas, and guidance. Therapists in training may cling to theory, intention, and technique as a way of coping with the anxieties and overwhelming responsibilities of the therapeutic venture. Seasoned therapists may rely almost exclusively on theory, intention, and technique out of learned reflex, habit, and the sheer weariness that approaches burnout. There is always risk that the therapist will fall back on repetitive and reflexive responses that verge on stereotype. Without much thought or feeling, the anxious or tired therapist may, if analytically minded, answer a client's question by asking why the client asked the question; if holding a client-centered orientation, may simply reflect or restate what the client has just said; if gestalt-trained, may ask the client to say something to an empty chair; and so on.

One way to help avoid responses that are driven more by anxiety, fatigue, or other similar factors is to consider carefully how the therapist would think, feel, and react if he or she were the client. Regardless of the theoretical soundness, intended outcome, or technical sophistication of a contemplated intervention, how will it likely be experienced and understood by the client? Can the therapist anticipate at all what the client might feel and think? The therapist's attempts to try out, in his or her imagination, the contemplated action and to view it from the perspective of the client may help prevent, correct, or at least identify possible sources of misunderstanding, miscommunication, and failures of empathy (Pope et al., 1993, pp. 185–186).

Competence

The eighth consideration is one of competence: Is the therapist competent to carry out the contemplated intervention? Ensuring that a therapist's education, training, and supervised experiences are adequate and appropriate for his or her work is a fundamental responsibility.

Uncharacteristic Behaviors

The ninth consideration involves becoming alert to unusual actions: Does the contemplated action fall substantially outside the range of the therapist's usual behaviors? That an action is unusual does not, of course, mean that something is necessarily wrong with it. Creative therapists occasionally try creative interventions, and it is unlikely that even the most conservative and tradition-bound therapist conducts therapy the same way all the time. However, possible actions that are considerably outside the therapist's general approaches likely warrant special consideration.

Consultation

The tenth consideration concerns secrecy: Is there a compelling reason for not discussing the contemplated action with a colleague, consultant, or supervisor? Therapists' reluctance to disclose an action to others is a red flag to possibly inappropriate action. Therapists may consider any possible action in the light of this question: If they took this action, would they have any reluctance for all of their professional colleagues to know that they had taken it? If the response is yes, the reasons for the reluctance warrant examination. If the response is no, it is worth considering if one has adequately taken advantage of the opportunities to discuss the matter with a trusted colleague. If discussion with a colleague has not helped to clarify the issues, consultation with additional professionals, each of whom may provide different perspectives and suggestions, may be useful.

WORKING WITH CLIENTS WHO HAVE BEEN SEXUALLY INVOLVED WITH A THERAPIST

It is likely that any therapist, counselor, or trainee reading this book will encounter clients who have been sexually victimized by a prior therapist. A national study of 1,320 psychologists found that 50% reported working with at least 1 client who, in the therapist's professional opinion, had been a victim of therapist-client sexual intimacies (Pope & Vetter, 1991). About 4% reported working with at least 1 client who, in the therapist's opinion, had made false allegations about sex with a prior therapist.

It is crucial that clinicians working with such clients be genuinely knowledgeable about this area. Clients who have been sexually exploited tend to be exceptionally vulnerable to revictimization when their clinical needs are not recognized. Special methods and considerations for providing therapeutic services to victims of therapist-patient sexual intimacies have been developed and continue to evolve (Pope, 1994). One of the first steps toward gaining competence in this area is recognition of the diverse and sometimes extremely intense reactions that encountering a client who reports sexual involvement with a former therapist can evoke in the subsequent therapist. Table 16.4 identifies some of the most common reactions.

Table 16. 4.   Common Therapists' Reactions to Victims of Therapist-Patient Sexual Involvement.

1. **Disbelief and denial:** The tendency to reject reflexively—without adequate data gathering—allegations about therapist-patient sex (because, for example, the activities described seem outlandish and improbable)
2. **Minimization of harm:** The tendency to assume reflexively—without adequate data gathering—that harm did not occur or that, if it did, the consequences were minimally, if at all, harmful
3. **Making the patient fit the textbook:** The tendency to assume reflexively—without adequate data gathering and examination—that the patient must inevitably fit a particular schema
4. **Blaming the victim:** The tendency to attempt to make the patient responsible for enforcing the therapist's professional responsibility to refrain from engaging in sex with a patient and holding the patient responsible for the therapist's offense
5. **Sexual reaction to the victim:** The clinician's sexual attraction to or feelings about the patient; such feelings are normal but must not become a source of distortion in the assessment process
6. **Discomfort at the lack of privacy:** The clinician's (and sometimes patient's) emotional response to the possibility that under certain conditions (for example, malpractice, licensing, or similar formal actions against the offending therapist; a formal review of assessment and other services by the insurance company providing coverage for the services) the raw data and the results of the assessment may not remain private
7. **Difficulty "keeping the secret":** The clinician's possible discomfort (and other emotional reactions) when he or she has knowledge that an offender continues to practice and to victimize other patients but cannot, in the light of confidentiality or other constraints, take steps to intervene
8. **Intrusive advocacy:** The tendency to want to guide, direct, or determine a patient's decisions about what steps to take or what steps not to take in regard to a perpetrator
9. **Vicarious helplessness:** The clinician's discomfort when a patient who has filed a formal complaint seems to encounter unjustifiable obstacles, indifference, lack of a fair hearing, and other responses that seem to ignore or trivialize the complaint and fail to protect the public from offenders
10. **Discomfort with strong feelings:** The clinician's discomfort when experiencing strong feelings (for example, rage, neediness, or ambivalence) expressed by the patient and focused on the clinician

Awareness of these reactions can prevent them from blocking the therapist from rendering effective services to the patient. The therapist can be alert for such reactions and sort through them should they occur. In some instances, the therapist may seek consultation to help gain perspective and understanding.

ETHICAL ASPECTS OF REHABILITATION

Unfortunately, therapists and counselors may act in ways that discount the harm done by perpetrators of therapist-patient sex, obscure the responsibilities of perpetrators, and enable perpetrators to continue—sometimes after a period of suspension—victimizing clients (Bates & Brodsky, 1989; Gabbard, 1989). The rehabilitation methods by which perpetrators are returned to practice focus many of this book's themes and pose difficult ethical dilemmas. Pope (1990c,d, 1994) reviewed some of the crucial but difficult ethical questions facing therapists and counselors considering rehabilitation efforts; they are summarized next.

Competence

Does the clinician who is implementing the rehabilitation plan possess demonstrable competence in the areas of rehabilitation and therapist-patient sexual intimacies?

Has the rehabilitation method the clinician uses been adequately validated through independent studies? Obviously, a clinician who was claiming an effective "cure" for pedophilia, kleptomania, dyslexia, panic attacks, or a related disorder would need to present the scientific evidence for the intervention's effectiveness. Ethical standards for claims based on evidence in this area—particularly given the risks for abuse to which future patients may be exposed—should not be waived. Such evidence must meet the customary requirement of publication in peer-reviewed scientific or professional journals. As Pope (1990d) noted:

> Research results that survive and benefit from this painstaking process of systematic review created to help ensure the scientific integrity, merit, and trustworthiness of new findings may be less likely (than data communicated *solely* through press conferences, popular lectures, books, workshops, and television appearances) to contribute to... "social-science fiction." (p. 482)

We have been unable to locate any independently conducted, replicated research published in peer-reviewed scientific or professional journals that supports the effectiveness of rehabilitation efforts in this area.

Informed Consent

Whether the rehabilitation technique is viewed as an intervention of proven effectiveness (through independently conducted research trials) or an experimental research trial for a promising approach, have those who are put at risk for harm been adequately informed and been given the option of not assuming the risk, should the rehabilitation fail to be 100% effective?

Assessment

Do the research trials investigating the potential effectiveness of the rehabilitation method meet at least minimal professional standards? For example, is the research conducted independently? (We are rarely disinterested judges of the profundity, effectiveness, and near perfection of our own work.)

A more complex requirement concerns whether the base rate of discovery of abuse is adequately taken into account in conducting and reporting the results of experimental trials of rehabilitation efforts. Perpetrators may continue to engage in sexual intimacies with clients during (or after) rehabilitation efforts, even when they are supervised (see, e.g., Bates & Brodsky, 1989). The abuse may come to the light only if the client reports it. Yet the base rate of such reports by clients is quite low. Surveys of victims suggest that only about 5% report the behavior to a licensing board (see Pope & Vetter, 1991). The percentage appears to be significantly lower when the number of instances of abuse estimated from anonymous surveys of clinicians (who report instances in which they have engaged in abuse) is compared with complaints filed with licensing boards, ethics committees, and the civil and criminal courts. Using the higher 5% reporting estimate, assume that you conduct research in which a licensing board refers 10 offenders to you for rehabilitation. You work with the offenders for several years and are convinced that you have completely rehabilitated all 10. You assure the licensing board of your complete confidence that none of the 10 will pose any risk to future clients. But also assume that your rehabilitation effort fails miserably: All 10 offenders will engage in sex with a future client. What are the probabilities that any of the 10 future abuse victims will file a complaint? If each client has only a 5% probability of reporting the abuse, there is a 59.9% probability that none of the 10 will file a complaint. Thus, there is close to a 60% chance that these research trials, even if independently evaluated, will appear to validate your approach as 100% effective when in fact it was 100% ineffective. If ignored in conducting and reporting research, the low base rate can make a worthless intervention appear completely reliable.

Power and Trust

The ethics of psychotherapy and counseling are inherently related to power and trust. How are these factors relevant to the dilemmas of rehabilitation?

If a judge were convicted of abusing the power and trust inherent in the position of judgeship by allowing bribes to determine the outcome of cases, numerous sanctions, both criminal and civil, might follow. However, even after the judge paid the debt due to society by the abuse of power and trust, the judge would not be allowed to resume the bench, regardless of any "rehabilitation."

Similarly, if a preschool director were discovered to have sexually abused students, he or she would likely face both civil and criminal penalties. The director might undergo extensive rehabilitation efforts to help reduce the risk that he or she would engage in further abuse of children. However, regardless of the effectiveness of the rehabilitation efforts, the state would not issue the individual a new license to found and direct another preschool.

Neither of these two offenders would necessarily be precluded from practicing their professions. The former judge and preschool director, once rehabilitated, might conduct research, consult, publish, lecture, or pursue other careers within the legal and educational fields. However, serving as judge or as preschool director are positions that involve such trust by both society and the individuals subject to their immediate power that the violation of such an important and clearly understood prohibition against abuse of trust (and power) precludes the opportunity to hold such special positions within the fields of law and education.

The helping professions must consider the ethical, practical, and policy implications of allowing and enabling offenders to resume the positions of special trust that they abused. Do psychotherapy and counseling involve or require a comparable degree of inviolable trust, from individual clients and from the society more generally, and ethical integrity as the positions of judge and preschool director within the legal and educational fields?

Hiring, Screening, and Supervising

Those who work within health maintenance organizations, hospitals, and other structures hiring clinicians have a responsibility to attend carefully to the risks that staff may sexually exploit clients. Carefully structured and adequately comprehensive forms and procedures (verifying education, supervision, licensure, employment, history of licensing or ethics complaints, etc.) for screening potential personnel, establishing and monitoring policies prohibiting sex with clients, and so on have long been advocated as important in minimizing the risk that organizational personnel will sexually exploit clients (see Pope, 1994; Pope & Bouhoutsos, 1986). More recently, however, the usefulness of such forms and procedures that operationally define screening procedures and policy implementation has been recognized as an important component of malpractice risk management not only in hospitals but also in clinics, group practices, and similar settings. As defense attorney Brandt Caudill (1993) stated:

> Given the current state of the law, it seems clear that psychologists must assume that they may be sued if a partner, employee, or supervisee engages in a sexual relationship with a patient, because it appears that the courts are moving to the position that a sexual relationship between a therapist and a patient is a recognizable risk of employment which would be within the scope of the employer-employee relationship. (pp. 4–5)

It may be very difficult for employers and those with administrative or clinical supervisory responsibilities to argue successfully that the sexual relationship involving a supervisee or employee was not within the scope of employment. As one court held:

> We believe that the nature of the work performed by a therapist is substantially different than that of a day-care teacher as in *Randi F.* or a security guard as in *Webb* or a medical doctor as in *Hoover* so that a therapist who engages in sexual relations with a patient could not be said, as a matter of law, to have acted outside the scope of his employment.
> (*St. Paul Fire & Marine Insurance Company v. Downs*, 1993, *p. 344*)

Illinois is an example of a state that enacted legislation making an employer liable when it knows or should reasonably know that a therapist-employee engaged in sexual contact with a patient (Ill. Rev. Stat. 1991, chap. 70, para. 803).

Here are some steps that have been suggested previously as useful in addressing these issues when screening job applicants (Pope, 1994; Pope & Bouhoutsos, 1986):

- Discuss with the applicant any formal or informal training experiences in such areas as identifying and addressing both the clinician's and the client's sexual feelings. Are there classroom teachers, practicum supervisors, or previous employers who have provided such training and could be contacted to obtain information?
- Use an employment application form that traces back in sufficient detail from the present to college graduation. Ensure that there are no gaps in education or employment that are not clearly explained in writing.
- Provide a form for release of information that will enable the prospective employer to check with each setting of previous training, employment, or experience.
- Check with supervisors at any institutions at which the applicant obtained graduate training.

- Verify that the applicant was awarded all degrees claimed on the application form.
- Verify that any internships, practica, or postdocs were successfully completed. Check with a supervisor at each site.
- Check for information with each state that has issued the applicant a clinical license. Verify that no license has been revoked or subject to disciplinary procedures in which the applicant was found to have engaged in prohibited activities.
- Obtain a copy of all significant certifications.
- Obtain a copy of the applicant's resume or curriculum vitae. Ensure that it is consistent with the responses to the application form described in the second bullet point.
- Ensure that the applicant fully understands the explicit policies of the organization in regard to prohibited activities with clients and that he or she signs an agreement to that effect.

If entering into a sexual relationship with a client must be avoided, what about entering into a nonsexual relationship? The next chapter focuses on these nonsexual dual and multiple relationships.

SCENARIOS FOR DISCUSSION

It has been an extremely demanding week, and you are looking forward to going to the new movie with your life partner. The theater is packed, but you find two seats on the aisle not too close to the screen. You feel great to have left work behind you at the office and to be with your lover for an evening on the town. As the lights go down, you lean over to give your partner a passionate kiss. For some reason, while kissing, you open your eyes and notice that, sitting in the seat on the other side of your partner and watching you, is a therapy client who just that afternoon had revealed an intense sexual attraction to you.

- What feelings does this scenario evoke in you?
- If you were the therapist, what, if anything, would you say to the client at the time of this event? What would you say during the next therapy session?
- How would the client's presence affect your subsequent behavior at the theater?
- How might this event affect the therapy and your relationship with the client?
- What, if anything, would you say to your partner—either at the theater or later—about what had happened? Are there any circumstances under which you would call the

client before the next scheduled appointment to discuss the matter?

- Imagine that during a subsequent therapy session, the client begins asking about whom you were with at the theater. How would you feel? What would you say?
- What if the client were a business client of your partner (or knew your partner in another context) and they begin talking before the movie? What feelings would this discovery evoke in you? What would you consider in deciding how to handle this matter?
- To what extent do you believe that therapists should be free to be themselves? To what extent should they behave in public as if a client might be observing them?

■ ■ ■

During your first session with a new client, he tells you that he has always been concerned that his penis was too small. Suddenly he pulls down his pants and asks you if you think it is too small. [Consider the same scenario with a new patient who is concerned about the size of her breasts.]

- What are you feelings?
- What are you thinking?
- What are your fantasies about this scenario?
- What would you, as therapist, want to say first? Why?
- What do you think you would say first? Why?
- What difference would it make if this were a client you had been treating for a year rather than a new client?
- How, if at all, would your feelings and actions be different according to whether treatment was conducted on an inpatient or an outpatient basis?
- How, if at all, would your feelings and actions differ according to the gender of the client?
- Imagine that the client in the scenario is 15 years old. What feelings does the scenario evoke in you? What do you do? What fantasies occur to you about what might happen after the event described in the scenario?

■ ■ ■

Your client describes to you her troubled marriage. Her husband used to get mad and hit her—"not too hard," she says—but he has pretty much gotten over that. Their sex life is not good. Her

(continued)

(*continued*)

husband enjoys anal intercourse, but she finds it frightening and painful. She tells you that she would like to explore her resistance to this form of sexual behavior in her therapy. Her goal is to become comfortable engaging in the behavior so that she can please her husband, enjoy sex with him, and have a happy marriage.

- What are you feeling when the client says that her husband used to "get mad and hit her"?
- What are you thinking?
- What are you feeling when she says that she finds anal intercourse frightening and painful?
- What are you thinking?
- What do you feel when she describes her goals in therapy?
- What are you thinking?
- In what ways do you believe that your feelings may influence how you proceed with this client?

■ ■ ■

The therapy group you are leading is into its eighth month of weekly meetings. One of the members of the group begins sobbing, describes terrible feelings of depression, and ends by pleading "I need someone to hold me!"

Bob, another member of the group, spontaneously jumps up and goes over to the other member, who stands up. As they embrace, it becomes obvious that Bob is getting an erection. He continues the hugging, which the other group member seems to find comforting, and seems to be stimulating himself by rubbing up against the other person.

- When you imagine this scenario, what do you feel?
- Would you, as therapist, call attention to what is happening? If so, how?
- If you were the therapist, could you imagine that such an event might make you feel aroused? frightened? upset? angry? confused?
- Do any of the following considerations change the feelings that this scenario evokes in you:
    ◦ Whether your supervisor is watching this scene through a one-way mirror
    ◦ Whether Bob and the client are the same gender
    ◦ Whether Bob is suffering from schizophrenia
    ◦ Whether Bob is a pedophile

- ° Whether the client receiving the hug seems to be aroused
- ° Whether Bob had been sexually abused during childhood
- ° Whether this is an inpatient group
- ° Whether all members of this group are suffering from terminal illnesses
- ° Whether the client receiving the hug had been sexually abused during childhood
- ° Whether the client receiving the hug has sued a prior therapist for malpractice in regard to sexual issues

■ ■ ■

You are working in a busy mental health center in which the doors to the consulting rooms, while offering some privacy, are not completely soundproof. As long as therapist and client are talking at a normal level, nothing can be heard from outside the door. But words spoken loudly can be heard and understood in the reception area.

A client, Sal, sits in silence during the first 5 minutes of the session, finally saying "It's been hard to concentrate today. I keep hearing these sounds, like they're ringing in my ear, and they're frightening to me. I want to tell you what they're like, but I'm afraid to."

After offering considerable reassurance that describing the sounds would be okay and that you and Sal can work together to try to understand what is causing the sounds, what they mean, and what you might do about them, you notice that Sal seems to be gathering the courage to reveal them to you.

Finally, Sal leans back in the chair and imitates the sounds. They build quickly to a very high pitch and loud volume. They sound exactly like someone becoming more and more sexually aroused and then experiencing an intense orgasm.

You are reasonably certain that these sounds have been heard by the receptionist, some of your colleagues, the patients sitting in the waiting room, and a site visitor from the Joint Commission for the Accreditation of Hospitals who is deciding whether the hospital in which your clinic is based should have its accreditation renewed.

- What feelings does this scenario evoke in you?
- As you imagined the scene, was the client male (Salvador) or female (Sally)? Does the client's gender make any difference in the way you feel?

(continued)

(continued)

- If Sal began to make the sounds again, would you make any effort to interrupt or ask the client to be a little quieter? Why?
- If none of the people who might have heard the sounds mentioned this event to you, would you make any effort to explain what had happened?
- Imagine that just as Sal finishes making these sounds, someone knocks loudly on the door and asks, "What's going on in there?" What do you say or do?
- Would your feelings or behavior be any different if the sounds were of a person being beaten rather than having an orgasm?
- How would you describe this session in your chart notes?
- If you were being supervised, would you feel at all apprehensive about discussing this session with your supervisor?
- What approach do you usually take toward your clients' making loud noises that might be heard outside the consulting room?

Chapter 17

NONSEXUAL MULTIPLE RELATIONSHIPS AND OTHER BOUNDARY ISSUES

Crossing a boundary can be a powerfully therapeutic act. It can transform the patient's view of the therapist. It can strengthen the therapist's and patient's working relationship. It can help the patient rethink a certainty, grow emotionally, and reach a treatment goal. It can unlock possibilities when the therapy seems stuck. It can make a patient feel less alone, less hopeless, less like committing suicide.

In some cases, a refusal to cross a boundary be more than a lost opportunity, it can be harmful. For example, one of this book's authors (Pope), as one of the descriptions over the decades of his own nonsexual boundary crossings with patients and how they turned out, described in *American Psychologist* in 1995 ("Biography") his daily therapy sessions with a patient that included such boundary crossings as having a friend to send $500 and an open airline ticket to the patient. He believed that not to cross these boundaries would have been harmful to this patient in these circumstances.[1] Vasquez (2009) describes how failure to cross boundaries with multicultural clients can sometimes risk damage to the basic working alliance (Vasquez, 2009), which in turn can lead clients to abandon therapy.

Like many powerful resources, crossing a boundary involves risk. Done in the wrong situation, or at the wrong time, or with the wrong person, it can knock the therapy off track, sabotage the treatment plan, and offend, exploit, or even harm the patient.

---

[1] Martin Williams's discussion of this case appears later in this chapter.

The question "Do I cross this particular boundary with this particular patient now?" confronts us every day.

- My client has just told me that his mother died unexpectedly and he's asked me to attend the funeral. What should I tell him?
- My favorite musician who never tours in this part of the country has scheduled a one-night-only concert here. It was sold out before I could buy a ticket but now a client has brought me a ticket and backstage pass as a gift. Is there any reason I should turn her down?
- Every month the eight of us in my reading group meet to discuss a new novel and how it relates to our lives. On the way to our cars at the end of the meeting, one member asked to make an appointment with me. He wants to begin therapy. It really caught me off guard—I didn't know what to say.
- My client just asked me if I believe in God. I'm not sure how I should handle that question. She has been talking about how her synagogue views her sexuality and I believe she will also ask me my sexual orientation. I wish I knew how to handle those kinds of personal questions.
- My client is in so much pain right now and has just started sobbing— Should I end the session on time—which is now—or extend it another 5-10-15 minutes? If I decide to extend it, do I charge for the extra time?
- Just as I was ending the last session of the day, a sudden thunderstorm started. My client usually walks home—it's about a quarter of a mile. Is there any reason I shouldn't offer a ride?
- My client will lose her home if she can't come up with a payment by tomorrow. She starts her new job in two weeks. If she has nowhere else to turn, should I lend her the money to tide her over until she starts receiving her salary?

The way that the profession approached these questions changed radically in the period that began in 1980 and ran into the mid-1990s. During this tumultuous period of intense questioning and healthy controversy, thoughtful articles, books, and chapters explored boundaries from virtually every possible point of view. Virtually all the old ideas about dual relationships and other boundary issues were challenged. New ideas were argued. New perspectives were tried on for size. Authors explored key factors that had been relatively neglected. Every suggested standard, guideline, and approach was examined carefully for possible benefits, drawbacks, and unintended consequences.

In 1981 Samuel Roll and Leverett Millen, for example, presented "A Guide to Violating an Injunction in Psychotherapy: On Seeing Acquaintances as Patients." Patricia Keith-Spiegel and Gerald Koocher's 1985 edition of their widely used textbook, *Ethics in Psychology: Professional Standards and Cases*, examined ways in which boundary crossings in ethical therapy and counseling may be unavoidable. They provided an approach to examining the ethical aspects of various dual relationships and other boundary issues. Karen

Kitchener's influential 1988 article, "Dual Role Relationships," helped readers sort out "counselor-client relationships that are likely to lead to harm and those that are not likely to be harmful" (p. 217). Kitchener suggested that dual relationships are more likely to cause problems if they involve "(1) incompatibility of expectations between roles; (2) diverging obligations associated with different roles, which increases the potential for loss of objectivity; and (3) increased power and prestige between professionals and consumers, which increases the potential for exploitation" (p. 217).

Robert Ryder and Jeri Hepworth (1990) argued thoughtfully that the AAMFT should not prohibit dual relationships in its ethics code. Janet Sonne (1994) examined the ways in which the then-current APA ethics code addressed multiple relationships and argued that some segments represented "steps backward" (p. 343). Vincent Rinella and Alvin Gerstein wrote that "the underlying moral and ethical rationale for prohibiting dual relationships (DRs) is no longer tenable" (1994, p. 225). Tom Gutheil and Glen Gabbard (1993) maintained that "boundary crossings may be benign or harmful" (p. 195) and explored factors that influence the impact.

Elisabeth Horst (1989), Amy Stockman (1990), and Floyd Jennings (1992) helped foster awareness and appreciation of the special challenges that rural settings present for dual relationships and other boundary issues. Laura Brown (1989; see also 1994b) was among those who thoughtfully argued against a simple prohibition when considering dual relationships and other boundary issues in the lesbian therapy community in "Beyond Thou Shalt Not: Thinking About Ethics in the Lesbian Therapy Community." Melanie Geyer (1994) proposed adopting some of the special guidelines for considering multiple relationships and other boundary issues in rural settings and adapting them for difficult dilemmas faced by Christian counselors (and counselors for whom other religious faiths are a primary foundation and concern of practice). Bruce Sharkin and Ian Birky (1992) focused attention on the unplanned, unexpected encounters between therapists and clients and on the difficulties of maintaining boundaries during incidental encounters.

Jeanne Adleman and Susan Barrett (1990) were among those who pioneered considering multiple relationships and other boundary issues afresh using feminist principles. Patruska Clarkson's "In Recognition of Dual Relationships" explored the implications of believing in a "mythical, single relationship" and cautioned therapists and counselors against "an unrealistic attempt to avoid all dual relationships" (1994, p. 32). Ellen Bader (1994) maintained that we should stop focusing on whether there are dual roles and consider instead whether each instance represents exploitation.

In 1994, the journal *Ethics and Behavior* invited some of the major voices in the area to debate the topic of boundaries in therapy (Borys, 1994; Bennett, Bricklin, & VandeCreek, 1994; Brown, 1994a; Gabbard, 1994; Gottlieb, 1994; Gutheil, 1994; Lazarus, 1994a, 1994b).

The care with which this and other work from the 1980s and 1990s called attention to the many factors (for example, setting, culture, expectations, theoretical orientation) to be taken into account when considering whether a specific multiple relationship or other boundary crossing with a specific client in a specific situation is likely to be helpful or hurtful has encouraged therapists and counselors to appreciate the complexity of these decisions and engage in careful questioning rather than unthinking rule following. It is a process that also often involves the therapist's or counselor's feelings, as Jeffrey Kottler's frank exploration discloses:

> Sorting out dual relationships has become the most prevalent ethical issue of our time.... Our family members and friends constantly ask us for advice. Although we may do our best to beg off, the truth of the matter is that we may well enjoy being needed. I love it when people ask me what to do.... I feel so self-important that someone else thinks I know something that they do not. I pretend I am a little annoyed by those who ask me how to handle their children, confront their bosses, or straighten out their lives, but I appreciate the fact that they thought enough of me to ask. (2003, p. 4)

WHAT MAKES THIS AREA SO HARD FOR US?

Sabine Wingenfeld-Hammond (2010) notes that "one of the most challenging ethical issues for professional psychologists involves maintaining and managing professional boundaries" (p.135). Why is this area so challenging for almost all of us as individuals and as a profession? Here are five potential causes that may be at work.

First, major boundary dilemmas often catch us off-guard and unprepared. They can sweep us into unfamiliar, unexpected territory where we must make a quick decision of great importance, perhaps influencing the therapy in a decisive way. In Chapter 20 on responding to suicidal risk, we provide an example of how a sudden decision about a boundary crossing can have a profoundly transformative and healing effect. In this example, Stone (1982) describes a young woman, hospitalized during a psychotic episode, who continuously vilified her therapist for not caring about her. Without warning, she escaped from the hospital:

> The therapist, upon hearing the news, got into her car and canvassed all the bars and social clubs in Greenwich Village which her patient was known to frequent. At about midnight, she found her patient and drove her back to the hospital. From that day forward, the patient grew calmer, less impulsive, and made great progress in treatment. Later, after making substantial recovery, she told her therapist that all the interpretations during the first few weeks in the hospital meant very little to her. But after the "midnight rescue mission" it was clear, even to her, how concerned and sincere her therapist had been from the beginning. (p. 271)

Interestingly, from the time that this example and related accounts of the positive and healing potential of what are now called boundary crossings appeared in the first edition of this book over 15 years ago, they have been one of the most frequent topics of reader comments.

Second, opportunities to cross boundaries can—as Jeffrey Kottler's courageously honest statement acknowledges—tap into some of our most basic needs and strongest desires. It is possible to fall vulnerable to fallacies in reasoning and judgment (see Chapter 2) and mistake our own self-interest as if it were the client's needs. Our own needs and desires prompt us to see crossing the boundaries that we want to cross in the way that we want to cross them as the only meaningful clinical intervention, the only humane approach, the only prospect for helping the client. We become convinced that what we want to do is an ethical imperative. Glen Gabbard wrote:

> Harry Stack Sullivan (1954) once observed that psychotherapy is a unique profession in that it requires therapists to set aside their own needs in the service of addressing the patient's needs. He further noted that this demand is an extraordinary challenge for most people, and he concluded that few persons are really suited for the psychotherapeutic role. Because the needs of the psychotherapist often get in the way of the therapy, the mental health professions have established guidelines, often referred to as boundaries, that are designed to minimize the opportunity for therapists to use their patients for their own gratification. (1994, p. 283)

Third, the need for clarity about boundaries can be misunderstood as the need for inflexible boundaries reflexively applied. Clarity in thinking through boundary issues for each client/patient is essential. Reflexively applying a rigid set of rules about inflexible boundaries can never be an acceptable substitute for thinking through boundary issues for an individual client as clearly and carefully as possible. Decisions about boundaries must be made with the greatest possible clarity about the potential benefits and harm, the patient's needs and well-being, informed consent and informed refusal, the psychotherapist's motives, and the psychotherapist's knowledge and competence. A subsequent section in this chapter lists resources that can help psychotherapists as they make clear and thoughtful decisions in this area.

Fourth, boundary decisions can evoke anxiety and even fear. For example, clinical and forensic psychologist Martin Williams points out that some may try to avoid the area entirely to minimize the risk of being sued. He describes how the fear of lawsuits and ethics complaints can lead clinicians to avoid even justifiable boundary crossings. He uses the work of one of this book's authors as an example. This example, originally published in *American Psychologist* ("Biography," 1996), was mentioned at the opening of this chapter. The example involved providing psychological services to a homeless woman who had survived an assault, who was being stalked, and whose life was at risk.

Williams noted how the author's work with the client included instances of what Gutheil and Gabbard (1993) might term boundary crossings (although not boundary violations)

> ....[This] treatment carried out by Pope had included daily meetings without fee and his arranging for a personal friend of his to lend the patient money and to provide her with an airline ticket and a place to stay. In the context of the particular case, these boundary excursions appeared to be both humane and sensible. However, some practitioners might, in the interest of risk management, avoid making similar modifications. (1997, p. 248)

Fifth, we find relatively little guidance in making real-world decisions about boundary crossings in our classrooms and treatment guides. Moreover, many boundary crossings are subject to misinterpretation. American Psychological Association president Gerry Koocher's account of his own boundary crossings frequently, as he writes, makes some of his students gasp:

> On occasion I tell my students and professional audiences that I once spent an entire psychotherapy session holding hands with a 26-year-old woman together in a quiet darkened room. That disclosure usually elicits more than a few gasps and grimaces. When I add that I could not bring myself to end the session after 50 minutes and stayed with the young woman holding hands for another half hour, and when I add the fact that I never billed for the extra time, eyes roll.

> Then, I explain that the young woman had cystic fibrosis with severe pulmonary disease and panic-inducing air hunger. She had to struggle through three breaths on an oxygen line before she could speak a sentence. I had come into her room, sat down by her bedside, and I asked how I might help her. She grabbed my hand and said, "Don't let go." When the time came for another appointment, I called a nurse to take my place. By this point in my story most listeners, who had felt critical of or offended by the "hand holding," have moved from an assumption of sexualized impropriety to one of empathy and compassion. The real message of the anecdote, however, lies in the fact that I never learned this behavior in a classroom. No description of such an intervention exists in any treatment manual or tome on empirically-based psychotherapy. (2006, p. xxii)

RESEARCH LEADING TO A CALL FOR A CHANGE IN THE ETHICS CODE

Chapter 9 noted that the original APA ethics code was empirically based, the result of a survey of the membership, asking them what ethical dilemmas they encountered. It also described a replication of that critical incident study a half-century later. This 1992 replication, published in *American Psychologist*, found that the second most often reported ethical dilemmas were in the area of "blurred, dual, or conflictual relationships" (Pope & Vetter, 1992).

On the basis of their findings, Pope and Vetter called for changes to the APA ethical principles in the areas of dual relationships, multiple relationships, and boundary issues so that the ethics code would, for example:

> Define dual relationships more carefully and specify clearly conditions under which they might be therapeutically indicated or acceptable

> Address clearly and realistically the situations of those who practice in small towns, rural communities, remote locales, and similar contexts (emphasizing that neither the current code in place at the time nor the draft revision under consideration at that time fully acknowledged or adequately addressed such contexts)

> Distinguish between dual relationships and accidental or incidental extratherapeutic contacts (for example, running into a patient at the grocery market or unexpectedly seeing a client at a party) and to address realistically the awkward entanglements into which even the most careful therapist can fall

The following excerpt from that article ("Ethical Dilemmas Encountered by Members of the American Psychological Association: A National Survey") presents those findings and recommendations in detail, including examples provided by the survey participants:

BLURRED, DUAL, OR CONFLICTUAL RELATIONSHIPS

The second most frequently described incidents involved maintaining clear, reasonable, and therapeutic boundaries around the professional relationship with a client. In some cases, respondents were troubled by such instances as serving as both "therapist and supervisor for hours for [patient/supervisee's] MFCC [marriage, family, and child counselor] license" or when "an agency hires one of its own clients." In other cases, respondents found dual relationships to be useful "to provide role modeling, nurturing and a giving quality to therapy"; one respondent, for example, believed that providing therapy to couples with whom he has social relationships and who are members of his small church makes sense because he is "able to see how these people interact in group context." In still other cases, respondents reported that it was sometimes difficult to know what constitutes a dual relationship or

(continued)

(continued)

conflict of interest; for example, "I have employees/supervisees who were former clients and wonder if this is a dual relationship." Similarly, another respondent felt a conflict between his own romantic attraction to a patient's mother and responsibilities to the child who had developed a positive relationship with him:

> I was conducting therapy with a child and soon became aware that there was a mutual attraction between myself and the child's mother. The strategies I had used and my rapport with the child had been positive. Nonetheless, I felt it necessary to refer to avoid a dual relationship (at the cost of the gains that had been made).

Taken as a whole, the incidents suggest, first, that the ethical principles need to define dual relationships more carefully and to note with clarity if and when they are ever therapeutically indicated or acceptable. For example, a statement such as "Minimal or remote relationships are unlikely to violate this standard" ("Draft," 1991, p. 32) may be too vague and ambiguous. A psychologist's relationship to a very casual acquaintance whom she or he meets for lunch a few times a year, to an accountant who only does very routine work in filling out her or his tax forms once a year (all such business being conducted by mail), to her or his employer's husband (who has no involvement in the business and with whom the psychologist never socializes), and to a travel agent (who books perhaps one or two flights a year for the psychologist) may constitute relatively minimal or remote relationships. However, will a formal code's assurance that minimal or remote relationships are unlikely to violate the standard provide a clear, practical, valid, and useful basis for ethical deliberation to the psychologist who is serves as therapist to all four individuals? Research and the professional literature focusing on nonsexual dual relationships underscores the importance and implications of decisions to enter into or refrain from such activities (e.g., Borys & Pope, 1989; Ethics Committee, 1988; Keith-Spiegel & Koocher, 1985; Pope & Vasquez, 1991; Stromberg et al., 1988).

Second, the principles must address clearly and realistically the situations of those who practice in small towns, rural communities, and other remote locales. Neither the current code nor the current draft revision explicitly acknowledges and adequately addresses such geographic contexts. Forty-one of the dual relationship incidents involved such locales. Many respondents implicitly or explicitly complained that the principles seem to ignore the special conditions in small, self-contained communities. For example,

> I live and maintain a … private practice in a rural area. I am also a member of a spiritual community based here. There are very few other therapists in the immediate vicinity who work with transformational, holistic, and feminist principles in the context of good clinical training that "conventional" people can also feel confidence in. Clients often come to me because they know me already, because they are not satisfied with the other services available, or because they want to work with someone who understands their spiritual practice and can incorporate its principles and practices into the process of transformation, healing, and change. The stricture against dual relationships helps me to maintain a high degree of sensitivity to the ethics (and potentials for abuse or confusion) of such situations, but doesn't give me any help in working with the actual circumstances of my practice. I hope revised principles will address these concerns!

Third, the principles need to distinguish between dual relationships and accidental or incidental extratherapeutic contacts (e.g., running into a patient at the grocery market or unexpectedly seeing a client at a party) and to address realistically the awkward entanglements into which even the most careful therapist can fall. For example, a therapist sought to file a formal complaint against some very noisy tenants of a neighboring house. When he did so, he was surprised to discover "that his patient was the owner-landlord." As another example, a respondent reported,

> Six months ago a patient I had been working with for three years became romantically involved with my best and longest friend. I could write no less than a book on the complications of this fact! I have been getting legal and therapeutic consultations all along, and continue to do so. Currently they are living together and I referred the patient (who was furious that I did this and felt abandoned). I worked with the other psychologist for several months to provide a bridge for the patient. I told my friend soon after I found out that I would have to suspend our contact. I'm currently trying to figure out if we can ever resume our friendship and under what conditions.

The latter example is one of many that demonstrate the extreme lengths to which most psychologists are willing to go to

(continued)

> (*continued*)
> ensure the welfare of their patients. Although it is impossible to
> anticipate every pattern of multiple relationship or to account for
> all the vicissitudes and complexities of life, psychologists need and
> deserve formal principles that provide lucid, useful, and practical
> guidance as an aid to professional judgment (Pope & Vetter, 1992,
> pp. 400–401).

MULTIPLE RELATIONSHIPS AS DEFINED BY THE APA AND CPA ETHICS CODES

Janet Sonne has noted how concerns about multiple relationships may not be founded on an accurate understanding of multiple relationships or the ethical standards:

> You may have heard in workshops or read in books or journals that hugging a client, giving a gift to a client, or meeting a client outside of the office constitutes a multiple relationship and is prohibited by our ethics code or by the standard of care sustained by professional licensing boards.
>
> Not accurate.
>
> You may also have heard or read that telling a client something personal about yourself or unexpectedly encountering a client at a social event are examples of unprofessional multiple relationships.
>
> Again, not accurate.
>
> The inaccuracies, or errors, in our thinking about nonsexual multiple relationships, mire us in confusion and controversy. (2005)

It is worth taking a look at the APA and CPA codes to see how they define this concept. The APA Ethics Code defined multiple relationships for the first time in the 2002 revision (APA, 2002). According to Standard 3.05a,

> A multiple relationship occurs when a psychologist is in a professional role with a person and (1) at the same time is in another role with the same person, (2) at the same time is in a relationship with a person closely associated with or related to the person with whom the psychologist has the professional relationship, or (3) promises to enter into another relationship in the future with the person or a person closely associated with or related to the person. (p. 1065)

Most commonly, the second role is social, financial, business, or professional.

Standard 3.05a notes that *not all* (emphasis added) multiple relationships are problematic and provides guidance as to when to avoid inappropriate multiple relationships:

> A psychologist refrains from entering into a multiple relationship if the multiple relationship could reasonably be expected to impair the psychologist's objectivity, competence, or effectiveness in performing his or her functions as a psychologist, or otherwise risks exploitation or harm to the person with whom the professional relationship exists. (p. 1065)

Thus, psychologists avoid dual or multiple roles with clients unless there is no reasonable likelihood that a secondary role would interfere with one's objectivity, competence, or effectiveness in therapy.

The Canadian Ethics Code (CPA, 2000) provides a similar caution. Section III.33 states, "Avoid dual or multiple relationships (e.g., with clients, research participants, employees, supervisees, students, or trainees) and other situations that might present a conflict of interest or that might reduce their ability to be objective and unbiased in their determinations of what might be in the best interests of others" (p. 31).

Standard III.34 also acknowledges that some multiple relationships are unavoidable and suggests ways to avoid risk of harm:

> Manage dual or multiple relationships that are unavoidable due to cultural norms or other circumstances in such a manner that bias, lack of objectivity, and risk of exploitation are minimized. This might include obtaining ongoing supervision or consultation for the duration of the dual or multiple relationship, or involving a third party in obtaining consent (e.g., approaching a client or employee about becoming a research participant). (p. 27)

THREE EXAMPLES OF MULTIPLE RELATIONSHIPS

In part it may be the relative simplicity and abstraction of the definition that lulls many of us into ignoring the diverse, subtle ways that therapists can enter into multiple relationships with their clients. Specific examples, more than abstract definitions, may provide us with a useful awareness of how these entanglements occur. The following three fictional scenarios illustrate nonsexual multiple relationships.

Opportunity

Bill has just opened a private practice office and has exactly two patients. One of them, Mr. Lightfoot, is an extremely successful investment analyst who is grateful to Bill for all the benefits he is getting from psychotherapy. The worst of Mr. Lightfoot's depression seems to be in remission, and he is now focusing on his relationships with those whose financial matters he handles. Bill, who genuinely likes Mr. Lightfoot, finds himself especially attentive when his patient talks about new investment opportunities. Unexpectedly, Mr. Lightfoot says that Bill might make a great deal of money if he invests in a certain project that is now being planned. The more Bill thinks about it, the more this seems like a terrific opportunity. It will help Mr. Lightfoot's sense of self-esteem because he will be in the position of helping Bill rather than always receiving help from him. It will not cost Mr. Lightfoot anything. Finally, it may allow Bill to survive in private practice and thus enable him to continue to help others. (Bill's overhead was greater than expected, the anticipated referrals were not materializing, and he was down to his last ten thousand dollars in savings, which would not last long given his office rent and other expenses.) He decides to give his savings to Mr. Lightfoot to invest for him.

Employee Benefits

Dr. Ali is a successful psychotherapist who now owns and manages his own mental health clinic. Lately he has noticed that his normally outstanding secretary, Mr. Miller, has been making numerous mistakes, some of them resulting in considerable financial losses for the clinic. Dr. Ali's customary toleration, encouragement, and nonjudgmental pointing out of the errors have not improved his secretary's performance. He decides that a serious and frank discussion of the situation is necessary. When he begins talking with his secretary about the deteriorating performance, Mr. Miller reveals some personal and financial stresses that he has been encountering that make it difficult for him to attend to his work. Dr. Ali is aware that his secretary cannot afford therapy and that the chances of hiring a new secretary with anywhere near Mr. Miller's previous level of skills is at best a long shot. Even if a good secretary could be found in what is a cutthroat job market, there would be a long period of orientation and training during which Dr. Ali anticipates he would continue to lose revenue. He decides that the only course of action that makes sense, that creatively solves all problems, is to take on Mr. Miller as a patient for two or three hours each week until Mr. Miller has a chance to work through his problems. Mr. Miller could continue to work as secretary and would not be charged for the therapy sessions. Dr. Ali would provide them without charge as part of a creative and generous "employee benefit."

Helping as a Friend

Rosa, an attorney, is going through one of the worst times in her life. For several weeks, she had been experiencing mild abdominal discomfort and had dismissed it as a muscle strained while jogging or nervousness about the case she was preparing to argue in her first appearance before the state supreme court. The pains become worse, and she manages to drive herself to the emergency room. A rather brusk medical resident informs her that he has located a large lump on her ovary. He advises her to make an appointment to undergo extensive tests to determine the nature of the lump, which may be cancerous.

Rosa is terrified. The tests are scheduled for two days from now. She has to cope not only with the pain but also with the uncertainty of what the physicians will discover. She goes immediately to the house of her best friend, June, a psychotherapist. June suggests showing Rosa some self-hypnotic and imagery techniques that might help her cope with her pain and anxiety. As June leads her through the exercises, Rosa begins to feel relieved and comforted. However, when she tries to use the techniques by herself, she experiences no effects at all. June agrees to lead her through the hypnotic and imagery exercises two or three times a day until the medical crisis is resolved. During the fourth meeting, spontaneous images that are quite troubling begin occurring. Rosa starts talking about them and feels they are related to things that happened to her as a small child. She discusses them in detail with June, and by the end of the sixth session, June recognizes that an intense transference has developed. She encourages Rosa to consult another therapist but Rosa refuses, saying that there is no one else she could trust with these matters and that terminating the sessions would make her feel so betrayed and abandoned that she fears she would take her own life.

REVIEW OF RESEARCH

There has been considerable research regarding sexual multiple relationships (see Chapter 16). Research concerning the prevalence of nonsexual multiple relationships, however, has been rarer. Tallman (1981) conducted perhaps the earliest study on nonsexual multiple relationships. Of the 38 psychotherapists participating, about 33% indicated that they had formed social relationships with at least some of their patients. An intriguing aspect of the findings was that although only half of the participants were male, all of the therapists who developed these social relationships with patients were male. This significant gender difference is remarkably consistent not only in terms of both sexual and nonsexual multiple relationships in psychotherapy but also in terms of multiple relationships involving teaching and supervision.

Borys and Pope summarized the research that had accumulated over the past dozen or so years:

> First, the significant difference (i.e., a greater proportion of male than of female psychologists) that characterizes sexualized multiple relationships conducted by both therapists and educators (teachers, clinical supervisors, and administrators) also characterizes nonsexual multiple relationships conducted by therapists in the areas of social/financial involvements and multiple

professional roles. Male respondents tended to rate social/financial involvements and multiple professional roles as more ethical and reported engaging in these involvements with more clients than did female respondents. Second, the data suggest that male therapists tend to engage in nonsexual multiple relationships more with female clients than with male clients....Third, these trends hold for psychologists, psychiatrists, and clinical social workers. Note that these statistical analyses take into account the fact that most therapists are male and most patients are female. (1989, p. 290)

Pope, Tabachnick, and Keith-Spiegel (1987) included several items regarding nonsexual multiple relationships—"accepting services from a client in lieu of fee," "providing therapy to one of your friends," "going into business with a former client"—in their survey of the ethical beliefs and practices of a thousand clinical psychologists (the return rate was 46%). Their findings were consistent with a larger-scale multidisciplinary study focusing on multiple relationships.

This survey of 1600 psychiatrists, 1600 psychologists, and 1600 social workers (with a 49% return rate) examined beliefs and behaviors regarding a range of multiple relationships (Borys & Pope, 1989). The survey's findings included these three points:

1. There was no significant difference among the professions in terms of sexual intimacies with clients before or after termination (see Chapter 13) or in terms of nonsexual multiple professional roles, social involvements, or financial involvements with patients.
2. The percentage of therapists who rated each multiple relationship behavior as ethical under most or all conditions was invariably less than the percentage of therapists viewing it as never ethical or ethical under only some or rare conditions.
3. Psychiatrists tend, as a whole, to view such relationships as less ethical than do psychologists or social workers.

The study found that various beliefs and behaviors in regard to these boundary issues tended to be significantly related to

- Therapist's gender
- Profession (psychiatrist, psychologist, social worker)
- Therapist's age
- Therapist's experience
- Therapist's marital status
- Therapist's region of residence
- Client gender
- Practice setting (such as solo or group private practice and outpatient clinics)
- Practice locale (size of the community)
- Therapist's theoretical orientation

In a separate analysis of these data, Borys (1988, p. 181) found "a clear relationship between sexual and nonsexual multiple role behaviors" (see also American Psychological Association Ethics Committee, 1988). She used a systems perspective to explore this association between nonsexual and sexual multiple relationships:

> As with familial incest, sexual involvement between therapist and client may be the culmination of a more general breakdown in roles and relationship boundaries which begin on a nonsexual level. This link was predicted by the systems perspective, which views disparate roles and behaviors within a relational system as interrelated. Changes in one arena are expected to affect those in other realms of behavior. The results of the current study suggest that the role boundaries and norms in the therapeutic relationship, just as those in the family, serve a protective function that serves to prevent exploitation. (p. 182)

Baer and Murdock (1995) conducted a national survey using a slightly modified version of the Therapeutic Practices Survey reported by Borys and Pope (1989). Their findings suggested

> that overall, therapists thought that nonerotic dual-relationship behaviors were ethical in only limited circumstances at best....Therapists judged social and/or financial involvements with their clients as the least ethical of the three classes of nonerotic dual relationships....That psychologists appear clear about the importance of meeting their own social and financial needs (other than payment for therapy) through people who are not their clients is important and can be viewed as promising. (p. 143)

Lamb and Catanzaro (1998) interviewed therapists, supervisors and instructors in an academic setting and found that those who admitted to engaging in sexual relationships with clients, supervisees, or students also reported being more likely to engage in nonsexual multiple relationships. They also rated nonsexual multiple relationships as less negative than participants who did not engage in sexual boundary violations. The authors provided helpful guidelines cited later in this chapter.

Lamb, Catanzaro, and Moorman (2004) found that

> a new relationship involving social interactions and events appears to be the type of new relationship that psychologists face most often and about which the greatest clarification may be needed, but psychologists need to be aware of other new relationships as well (e.g., new collegial or professional relationships). Discussing new relationships was reported as occurring most frequently with former (as opposed to current) clients, supervisees, or students, particularly former supervisees. (p. 252)

These studies of nonsexual multiple relationships in psychotherapy provide some initial empirical data on which to develop an understanding of the phenomenon and provide some intriguing hypotheses. What is striking, however, is the scarcity of such studies. We need critical self-study, including the systematic collection of data, regarding the occurrence and effects of multiple relationships.

In contrast to multiple relationships, therapist self-disclosure is one of the most extensively researched boundary issues. Jourard's pioneering book, *The Transparent Self*, sparked widespread interest in the topic when it was published in 1964. His subsequent book, *Self Disclosure: Experimental Analysis of the Transparent Self* (1971) fostered diverse studies. In 1978, Weiner's landmark *Therapist Disclosure: The Use of Self in Psychotherapy*, followed by an updated second edition in 1983, reviewed theory, research, and practice in this area. Recent works that review this area include those by Denney, Aten, and Gingrich (2008); Farber (2006); Farber, Khurgin-Bott, and Feldman; Gutheil and Brodsky (2008); Henretty and Levitt (2010), Kuchuck (2009), and Tsai, Plummer, Kanter, Newring, and Kohlenberg (2010).

Gutheil and Brodksy (2008) suggest four ideas for therapists to consider when making self-disclosure decisions:

1. Some degree of self-disclosure by a therapist is inevitable, but such disclosures can become boundary violations when they are not made for the benefit of the patient.
2. Different schools of therapy involve different levels of disclosure, which in turn serve the needs of different patients.
3. Self-disclosures of a personal nature that do not have a clinical purpose...may [not be helpful and may violate boundaries].
4. Decisions about the therapeutic use of self-disclosure need to be made on a case-by-case basis in the context of the type of therapy offered. (p. 128)

BARTERING

Hill (1999) noted that although bartering carried risks, "it is one way of increasing the availability of therapy, respecting class differences, and avoiding the problems associated with using insurance for payment" (p. 81).

APA allows bartering under some conditions and states that "barter is the acceptance of goods, services, or other nonmonetary remuneration from clients/patients in return for psychological services. Psychologists may barter only if (1) it is not clinically contraindicated, and (2) the resulting arrangement is not exploitative (see also Standards 3.05, Multiple Relationships, and 6.04, Fees and Financial Arrangements)" (APA, 2010; see also Sonne, 1994).

Different disciplines have tended to take different views of boundary issues—for example, a national survey found that psychiatrists viewed a variety of boundary-crossing behaviors as less ethical than did psychologists or social workers (Borys & Pope, 1989)—and this is true for bartering as well. A national survey of the beliefs and behaviors of psychologists who were therapists found that most participants viewed bartering with a client as either unethical or unethical under most circumstances (Pope, Tabachnick, & Keith-Spiegel, 1987; see also Baer & Murdock, 1995). A similar survey of certified counselors, however, found that 63% viewed bartering for a client's goods and 53% viewed bartering for a client's services as ethical (Gibson & Pope, 1993).

The *APA Ethics Code Commentary and Case Illustrations* (Campbell, Vasquez, Behnke, & Kinscherff, 2010) describes why the APA Ethics Code allows bartering as a means of payment. Psychologists may consider bartering primarily in the light of the client's financial limitations or the values of the community or culture in which the therapist works. Pro bono services, although sometimes a good option, may not always be possible because of therapeutic issues, the discomfort or unwillingness of the patient to accept free services, or financial pressures on the therapist. However, the therapeutic impact of financial agreements may affect the quality of the relationship.

A number of factors can affect decision making about bartering:

- The client's strengths, weaknesses, needs, and expectations
- The cultural and other relevant context and history
- The nature, duration, and intensity of the psychological services
- Possible benefits and possible harm
- Informed consent and informed refusal
- The therapist's theoretical approach, competence, and motives
- The nature of possible bartering arrangements

The Canadian Ethics Code (CPA, 2000) does not directly address bartering, but many of the standards would apply in decision making; for example, Standard I.15 requires that fees be fair, and Standard IV.12 encourages psychologists to contribute to the welfare of society by providing work for little or no financial return.

A number of therapists oppose bartering. Robert Woody (1998), for example, provides a thoughtful review of the ethical and legal issues and wrote that his "foremost conclusion is that bartering is a bad idea and should be avoided" (p. 177). However, for those who choose to barter with a client, Woody suggests the following guidelines:

1. Unique financial arrangements should be minimized; that is, terms and conditions for any compensation, including the use of bartering, should be as close to established practices as possible and be consonant with the prevailing standards of the profession.
2. The rationale for any compensation decision, including the use of bartering, should be documented in the case records.
3. Discussions about any financial matters should be detailed in writing, giving equal emphasis to what is said by the psychologist and the client.

4. If bartering is used, there should be a preference for goods instead of services; this will minimize (but not eliminate) the possibility of inappropriate personal interactions.

5. The value of the goods (or services) should be verified by an objective source; this may, however, involve additional cost.

6. To guard against any semblance of undue influence, both parties should reach a written agreement for the compensation by bartering.

7. Any new, potentially relevant observations or comments about compensation by bartering should be entered into the client's records, even though a previous agreement exists.

8. The agreement should contain a provision for how valuations were determined and how any subsequent conflicts will be resolved (e.g., a mediator); this may, however, involve additional cost (and a concern about confidentiality), which will have to be accommodated by the psychologist (i.e., the added expense should not elevate the cost to the client beyond the established service fee).

9. If a misunderstanding or disagreement begins to develop, the matter should be dealt with by the designated conflict resolution source (e.g., a mediator), not the psychologist and client; again, recall the issues of added cost and concern for confidentiality stated in the preceding guideline.

10. If monitoring by the individualized treatment plan reveals a possible negative effect potentially attributable to the compensation arrangement, it should be remedied or appropriate termination of the treatment relationship should occur (p. 177).

MULTIPLE RELATIONSHIPS AND BOUNDARY ISSUES IN SMALL COMMUNITIES

A community's size and nature provide important context for boundary issues. A varied and helpful literature explores boundary questions for therapists working in closely knit communities. Examples include some lesbian, gay, bisexual, and transgender communities (Brown, 1984, 1989, 1996; Dworkin, 1992; Gartrell, 1992; Greene, 1997a, 1997b; Greene & Croom, 1999; Kessler & Waehler, 2005; Smith, 1990), some ethnic minority communities (Comas-Diaz & Greene, 1994; Landrine, 1995; Pack-Brown & Williams, 2003; Ridley, Liddle, Hill, and Li, 2001; D. W. Sue & Sue, 2003; Vasquez, 2005; Velasquez, Arellano, & McNeill, 2004), and some rural communities (Barnett & Yutrzenka, 1995; Brownlee, 1996; Campbell & Gordon, 2003; K. K. Faulkner & Faulkner, 1997; Gripton & Valentich, 2004; Harowski, Turner, LeVine, Schank, & Leichter, 2006; Horst, 1989; Jennings, 1992; Pugh, 2007; Schank & Skovholt, 1997, 2006; Simon & Williams, 1999).

A central theme of this book is that we cannot shift responsibility to a set of rules, reflexively applied. Every client is unique in some ways, as is every therapist. Each situation is unique in some ways, and situations continue to change. Nothing can spare us the personal responsibility of making the best effort we can to assess the potential effects of boundary crossings, which tend to occur more often in small communities, and to act in the most ethical, informed, aware, and creative way possible.

The Feminist Therapy Institute's feminist code of ethics (1987) and the APA Multicultural Guidelines (APA, 2003b) encourage advocacy efforts, community involvement, and activism (see also Arredondo et al., 1996; Constantine & Sue, 2005; Harper & McFadden, 2003; Moodley & Palmer, 2006; Pack-Brown & Williams, 2003; Roysircar, Sandu, & Bibbins, 2003; Sue, 1995). These activities may create overlapping relationships among therapists and clients, which require careful attention to informed consent, privacy and confidentiality issues, power differentials, and potential pitfalls.

Vasquez (2005) described how small communities and other contexts brought awareness that it is often useful to think of boundaries as continuous rather than dichotomous features of our work. In some small communities, for example, therapists encounter clients and clients' families and friends almost any time they set foot outside. Vasquez addresses decision making in areas like self-disclosure, nonsexual touch (see also the section on nonsexual touch in Chapter 16), giving and receiving gifts, attending an important event for a client (for example, a wedding or funeral), and others. Culture can be critical (see Chapter 18). For example, refusing to accept a gift can create a shaming experience for clients from some cultures.

COGNITIVE ERRORS AND MENDING FENCES

The article "A Practical Approach to Boundaries in Psychotherapy: Making Decisions, Bypassing Blunders, and Mending Fences" (Pope & Keith-Spiegel, 2008) discusses common cognitive errors when making boundary decisions. The errors fall into the following 7 categories:

> Error #1: What happens outside the psychotherapy session has nothing to do with the therapy.
> Error #2: Crossing a boundary with a therapy client has the same meaning as doing the same thing with someone who is not a client.
> Error #3: Our understanding of a boundary crossing is also the client's understanding of the boundary crossing.
> Error #4: A boundary crossing that is therapeutic for one client will also be therapeutic for another client.
> Error #5: A boundary crossing is a static, isolated event.
> Error #6: If we ourselves don't see any self-interest, problems, conflicts of interest, unintended consequences, major risks, or potential downsides to crossing a particular boundary, then there aren't any.

Error #7: Self-disclosure is, per se, always therapeutic because it shows authenticity, transparency, and trust.

The article also suggests 9 steps that may be helpful when boundary crossings cause or seem headed toward serious problems.

SOURCES OF GUIDANCE

Although Chapter 11 provides steps useful in thinking through ethical issues and making ethical decisions, there are decision-making guides that focus specifically on multiple relationships. Here are seven decision-making guides that readers may find helpful when considering multiple relationships and other boundary issues:

- Gottlieb's "Avoiding Exploitive Dual Relationships: A Decision-Making Model" (1993, available at http://kspope.com/dual/ index.php)
- Faulkner and Faulkner's guide for practice in rural settings: "Managing Multiple Relationships in Rural Communities: Neutrality and Boundary Violations" (1997)
- Lamb and Catanzaro's model in "Sexual and Nonsexual Boundary Violations Involving Psychologists, Clients, Supervisees, and Students: Implications for Professional Practice" (1998)
- Younggren's model in "Ethical Decision-Making and Dual Relationships" (2002, available at http://kspope.com/dual/index.php)
- Campbell and Gordon's five-step approach for considering multiple relationships in rural communities: "Acknowledging the Inevitable: Understanding Multiple Relationships in Rural Practice" (2003)
- Sonne's "Nonsexual Multiple Relationships: A Practical Decision-Making Model for Clinicians" (2005, available at http://kspope.com)
- Pope and Keith-Spiegel's "A Practical Approach to Boundaries in Psychotherapy: Making Decisions, Bypassing Blunders, and Mending Fences" (2008, available at http://kspope.com)

In addition, Pope, Sonne, and Greene (2006) provide a decision-making model for when we are stuck and have no idea what to do. It was created for those times when "our best understanding of the situation may suggest a course of action that seems productive yet questionable and potentially harmful. To refrain from a contemplated action may shut the door to our spontaneity, creativity, intuition, and ability to help; to refrain may stunt the patient's progress or impede recovery. To engage in the contemplated action, however, may lead to disaster." They suggest eight steps that can help therapists and counselors find their ways through such impasses.

For internship settings, Burian and Slimp provide a thoughtful approach to making decisions in "Social Dual-Role Relationships During Internship: A Decision-Making Model" (2000; see also Slimp & Burian, 1994).

ADDITIONAL RESOURCES

A Web page ("Dual Relationships, Multiple Relationships, & Boundary Decisions") at http://kspope.com/dual/index.php provides resources that may be helpful in thinking through possible dual relationships, multiple relationships, and other boundary issues. The Web page's resources fall into four categories:

1. **Widely-used decision-making guides** (Sonne's "Nonsexual Multiple Relationships: A Practical Decision-Making Model For Clinicians"; Younggren's "Ethical Decision-making and Dual Relationships"; and Gottlieb's "Avoiding Exploitive Dual Relationships: A Decision-making Model")

2. **Excerpts addressing dual relationships and multiple relationships from the standards and guidelines of professional associations** (with links to the original documents) including American Association for Marriage and Family Therapy (AAMFT); American Association of Christian Counselors; American Association of Pastoral Counselors; American Association of Sex Educators, Counselors and Therapists; American Board of Examiners in Clinical Social Work; American Counseling Association; American Mental Health Counselors Association; American Music Therapy Association; American Psychoanalytic Association; American Psychological Association; American School Counselor Association; Association of State and Provincial Psychology Boards; Australian Association of Social Workers; Australian Psychological Society; British Association for Counselling and Psychotherapy; British Association of Social Workers; British Columbia Association of Clinical Counsellors; California Association for Counseling and Development; California Association of Marriage and Family Therapists; Canadian Counselling Association; Canadian Psychological Association; Canadian Traumatic Stress Network [Reseau Canadien du Stress Traumatique]; European Association for Body-Psychotherapy; European Federation of Psychologists' Associations; Feminist Therapy Institute; Irish Association for Counseling and Therapy; National Association of Social Workers; National Council for Hypnotherapy; and Psychological Society of Ireland;

3. **Quotes and Information about boundaries in therapy and counseling from articles, books, and studies**

4. **Articles on dual relationships, multiple relationships, and other boundary topics from** *American Psychologist, Professional Psychology, American Journal of Psychiatry,* **etc.** ("A Practical Approach to Boundaries in Psychotherapy: Making Decisions, Bypassing Blunders, and Mending Fences"; "Misuses and Misunderstandings of Boundary Theory in Clinical and Regulatory Settings"; "The Concept of Boundaries in Clinical Practice: Theoretical and Risk-Management Dimensions"; "A Study Calling for Changes in the APA Ethics Code regarding

Dual Relationships, Multiple Relationships, and Boundary Decisions";
"Dual Relationships Between Therapist and Client: A National Study
of Psychologists, Psychiatrists, and Social Workers"; "Dual Relationships: Trends, Stats, Guides, and Resources"; "Nonsexual Multiple
Relationships & Boundaries in Psychotherapy

SCENARIOS FOR DISCUSSION

You decide to teach a course in basic psychopathology as part of
the local community college's associate of arts degree program.
You show up on the first day of class and see that there are ten
students who have signed up. Two of them are current psychotherapy clients in your practice.

- How do you feel?
- Does their presence change how you teach your first class
  session?
- What options do you have for addressing this issue?
- What do you think you would do?
- How, if at all, would you address this issue in the chart
  notes for these two clients?

■ ■ ■

You live in a very small community. You are the only psychotherapist providing services through the local managed care plan.
One day one of your closest friends, someone you have known
for several decades, shows up at your office, seeking therapy.

- How do you feel?
- Do you share any of your feelings or concerns with the client during this session? If so, what do you say?
- Assume that you do not believe that you can serve as therapist in the light of your close friendship with this person.
  However, the client points out that not only are you the
  only one designated to provide therapy under the managed care plan, but that since you are also virtually the
  only one anywhere near this small community who
  matches the client in terms of characteristics that the client feels are important (this person believes that only
  someone who matches the patient's gender, race, and sexual orientation will understand the issues and be able to

help), the client cannot really get help from anyone but you. How do you address this? What are your options? What steps would you take?

■ ■ ■

You have been suffering some financial losses and are close to bankruptcy. You will likely lose everything if you are unable to sell your house. You have been trying to sell your house for close to two years and have not received a serious offer. You hold yet another open house. The only person to show up is one of your psychotherapy clients/patients who says, "This is a great house! I'd love to buy it. And although I'd be buying it anyway, it's nice that it'll end up helping you."

- How do you feel?
- What do you think you would say?
- What options do you consider?
- What do you think you'd end up doing?

■ ■ ■

A couple, who are your close friends, are aware that you will likely be spending Thanksgiving alone. They invite you to share Thanksgiving day with them, preparing the meal during the morning, feasting at lunch, going for a leisurely walk in the woods during the afternoon, then returning for a light dinner. You show up to discover that they have, without letting you know, invited another unattached person who is presumably your blind date for the day. That person is currently a client/patient to whom you have been providing psychotherapy for two years.

- How do you feel?
- What are your options?
- What do you think you would do?
- How, if at all, would your feelings, options, or probable course change were the person a former client?
- What if the other guest were your therapy supervisor rather than your client?
- What if the other guest were your own therapist?

(continued)

(continued)

■ ■ ■

During a session, a patient mentions that because of her job, she receives many free tickets to concerts, plays, and other events. She loves giving them to her various doctors because she greatly appreciates their hard work and because it costs her nothing. She tells you that the day before, she mailed you a pair of tickets to an upcoming concert because you had happened to mention that you are a fan of the performer, who has never held a concert in your part of the country before. You have tried to find tickets to take your daughter, who very much wants to attend, but tickets were immediately sold out and no source seems to have them available at any price.

- What do you feel?
- What issues do you consider?
- Is there any more information that you would want before deciding what to do? If so, what information would you seek?
- Under what conditions, if any, would you accept the tickets?
- After the session is over, how, if at all, would you describe this situation in your chart notes?

■ ■ ■

You are very involved in your community, and you have been appointed to a new board that is engaged in the kind of activism that you value. When you attend your first board meeting, you discover that one of your new clients is also on the board. Your client comes over at a break to tell you how pleased she is that you share similar values and will be working together.

- How do you feel?
- What feelings do you imagine that your client might be experiencing?
- What issues do you consider?
- What do you think you would say to your client?
- Would you remain on the board? What reasoning leads you to this decision?
- How, if at all, would you chart this interaction?

Chapter 18

CULTURE, CONTEXT, AND INDIVIDUAL DIFFERENCES

We live and work in countries of rich diversity. Different groups develop in different contexts, often revealing striking patterns. For example, Jeanne Miranda (2006) wrote that

> Rates of depression and substance abuse disorders are low among Mexican Americans born in Mexico (Vega et al., 1998), and immigrant Mexican American women have a lifetime rate of depression of 8%, similar to the rates of nonimmigrant Mexicans (Vega et al., 1998). However, after 13 years in the United States, rates of depression for those women who immigrated to the U.S. rise precipitously. U.S.-born women of Mexican heritage experience lifetime rates of depression similar to those of the White population in the United States, nearly twice the rate of immigrants. These findings are mirrored in other indicators of health.... Despite high rates of poverty, Mexican American immigrant women have low rates of physical and mental health problems (Vega et al., 1998), Chinese American immigrant women have a lifetime rate of major depression near 7%, approximately half that of White women (Takeuchi et al., 1998). These results suggest that some aspects of culture may protect against culture. (pp. 115–116)

Catharine Costigan, Tina Su, and Josephine Hua (2009) provide another example, focusing on how a country's policies may support and encourage diversity:

> Canada has an official policy of multiculturalism, which promotes the maintenance of one's cultural heritage alongside full participation and acceptance

259

in the larger society (Berry, 2003; Noels & Berry, 2006). Consistently, Canadians, on average, support the bicultural integration of new immigrants into Canadian society over assimilation or separation modes of integration (Berry & Kalin, 1995). Therefore, immigrant and ethnic minority youth in Canada live in a national context that encourages and values the retention of a strong sense of ethnic identity. (pp. 261–262)

Jennifer Glick, Littisha Bates, and Scott Yabiku (2009) provide a third example. They explored patterns of relationship between the cognitive development young children from diverse cultures and their mother's age when their mother arrives in the United States. They found that "parenting practices and home environment are associated with cognitive development and act as partial mediators between cognitive scores and mother's age at arrival" (p. 367).

We also live amid diversity of languages. Glenn Flores (2006; see also Pew Hispanic Center, 2009; Snowden, Masland, & Guerrero, 2007; U.S. Bureau of the Census, 2003) wrote:

Some 49.6 million Americans (18.7% of U.S. residents) speak a language other than English at home; 22.3 million (8.4%) have limited English proficiency, speaking English less than "very well," according to self-ratings. Between 1990 and 2000, the number of Americans who spoke a language other than English at home grew by 15.1 million (a 47% increase), and the number with limited English proficiency grew by 7.3 million (a 53% increase . . .). The numbers are particularly high in some places: in 2000, 40% of Californians and 75% of Miami residents spoke a language other than English at home, and 20% of Californians and 47% of Miami residents had limited English proficiency." (p. 229)

Similarly, Statistics Canada (2006) reports that about one in four children under 18 living in Toronto and Vancouver were recent immigrants or born in Canada to parents who were recent immigrants. Most of these children lived in homes where the main language spoken by the parents was neither English nor French.

We live also in the midst of an amazing religious diversity. Melton's (2009) *Encyclopedia of American Religions* describes over 2,800 religious groups in the U.S. and Canada. Just a few of the many religions represented by those living in these two countries include Baptist, Buddhist, Catholic, Christian Science, Church of Jesus Christ of Latter-day Saints (Mormon), Eastern Orthodox, Episcopal, First Nations, Greek Orthodox, Hindu, Islam, Jehovah's Witnesses, Judaism, Methodist, Muslim, Native American, Pentecostalism, Russian Orthodox, Sikhism, and Unitarian Universalist. An important aspect of the religious diversity, of course, is that there are many who are atheist or agnostic. We are also home to diverse spiritual traditions not based on religion (see, e.g., Comas-Diaz, 2008).

This diversity of cultures, languages, religion, and other factors has ethical implications for therapists and counselors. Both the American Psychological Association (2010) and the Canadian Psychological Association (2000) offer helpful guidance in their ethics codes for situations in which there are significant social class, cultural, or other group differences. Therapists can also find useful resources in CPA's (2001c) *Guidelines for Nondiscriminatory Practice*; APA's *Guidelines on Multicultural Education, Training, Research, Practice, and Organizational Change for Psychologists* (2003b); APA's *Guidelines for Psychological Practice with Older Adults* (2004); APA's *Guidelines for Psychotherapy with Lesbian, Gay, and Bisexual Clients* (2003a); and APA's *Guidelines for Providers of Psychological Services to Ethnic, Linguistic, and Culturally Diverse Populations* (1990b).

Our cultural diversity also provides a rich context for becoming more aware of how culture can influence our own ethical views and reasoning. Ronald Francis (2009) wrote:

> One of the singular merits of ethical considerations in a cross-cultural context is the way in which it forces us to confront our own values, to develop them, and to defend them. Cross-cultural comparisons afford a marvelous opportunity to examine the bases of our ethical codes in a manner which does not invite the heat more commonly attending intercultural value debates.
>
> Ethics is essentially about human values. Since not all values are shared we are compelled to consider the issues we have in common; and those on which we divide. For instance, what may seem self-evident in one culture may be ethically repugnant to another. Ethics affords an opportunity to discuss and resolve these human values in a non-threatening frame of reference. (pp. 182–193)

CONTEXT, COMPETENCE, AND PERSONAL RESPONSIBILITY

Our personal responsibility in this area begins with an honest appraisal of our own competence in a specific situation. The CPA Code of Ethics Standard II.10, in the section on competence and self-knowledge, encourages psychologists to "evaluate how their own experiences, attitudes, culture, beliefs, values, social context, individual differences, specific training, and stresses influence their interactions with others, and integrate this awareness into all efforts to benefit and not harm others" (2010, p. 22). Standard IV.15 requires that psychologists "acquire an adequate knowledge of the culture, social structure, and customs of a community before beginning any major work there" (p. 35).

APA Ethics Code Standard 2.01b, Boundaries of Competence, states:

> Where scientific or professional knowledge in the discipline of psychology establishes that an understanding of factors associated with age, gender, gender identity, race, ethnicity, culture, national origin, religion, sexual orientation, disability, language, or socioeconomic status is essential for effective implementation of their services or research, psychologists have or obtain the training, experience, consultation, or supervision necessary to ensure the competence of their services, or they make appropriate referrals, except as provided in Standard 2.02, Providing Services in Emergencies. (2010, pp. 1063–1064)

Competence includes adequate awareness of both individual and group differences. On the one hand, the clinician must become adequately knowledgeable and respectful of the client's relevant cultural or socioeconomic contexts. Therapists who ignore cultural values, attitudes, and behaviors different from their own deprive themselves of crucial information and may tend to impose their own worldview and assumptions on clients in a misguided and harmful approach. On the other hand, the clinician must avoid making simplistic, unfounded assumptions on the basis of cultural or socioeconomic contexts. Knowledge of cultural and socioeconomic contexts becomes the basis for informed inquiry rather than the illusion of uniform group characteristics with which to stereotype the client. Neither variation between groups nor within groups can be discounted or ignored.

Some readers may object to the apparent restriction of this twofold ethical responsibility to clinical situations in which the clinician and client are of different cultural or socioeconomic backgrounds. They might argue that the need to understand any client's background or context and avoid assuming that the individual can somehow be summarized by certain group characteristics are essential ethical responsibilities in any clinical endeavor. We agree with that view. As Pedersen, Draguns, Lonner, and Trimble (1989, p. 1) emphasize in *Counseling Across Cultures*, "Multicultural counseling is not an exotic topic that applies to remote regions, but is the heart and core of good counseling with any client."

Our training, however, sometimes fails to teach us how to apply the basic principles of therapy and counseling beyond the values and views of the majority culture. Greene (1997a), for example, notes that sometimes the empirical literature does not take account of cultural and other differences:

> A preponderance of the empirical research on or with lesbians and gay men has been conducted with overwhelmingly white, middle-class respondents (Chan, 1989, 1992; Gamets & Kimmel, 1991; Gock, 1985; Greene, 1994, 1996; Greene & Boyd-Franklin, 1996; Mays & Cochran, 1988; Morales, 1992). Similarly, research on members of ethnic minority groups rarely acknowledges differences in sexual orientation among group members.

Hence there has been little exploration of the complex interaction between sexual orientation and ethnic identity development, nor have the realistic social tasks and stressors that are a component of gay and lesbian identity formation in conjunction with ethnic identity formation been taken into account. Discussion of the vicissitudes of racism and ethnic identity in intra- and interracial couples of the same gender and their effects on these couples' relationships has also been neglected in the narrow focus on heterosexual relationships found in the literature on ethnic minority clients. There has been an equally narrow focus on predominantly white couples in the gay and lesbian literature. (pp. 216–217)

Yet even within such a complex framework of cultural and other forms of difference, it may be deceptively tempting to view each person as a fixed set of characteristics or descriptors:

Although identity is a fluid concept in psychological and sociological terms, we tend to speak of identities in fixed terms. In particular, those aspects of identity that characterize observable physical characteristics, such as race or gender, are perceived as unchanging ascribed identities. Examples of these would include identifications such as *Chinese woman*, or *Korean American woman*, or even broader terms such as *woman of color*, which are ways of grouping together individuals who are not of the hegemonic "white" race in the United States. We base these constructions of identity upon physical appearance and an individual's declaration of identity. However, even these seemingly clear distinctions are not definitive. For example, I, as a woman of Asian racial background, may declare myself a woman of color because I see myself as belonging to a group of ethnic/racial minorities. However, my (biological) sister could insist that she is not a woman of color because she does not feel an affiliation with our group goals, even though she is a person of Chinese ancestry. Does her nonaffiliation take her out of the group of people of color? Or does she remain in regardless of her own self-identification because of her obvious physical characteristics? Generally, in the context of identities based upon racial and physical characteristics, ascribed identities will, rightly or wrongly, continue to be attributed to individuals by others. It is left up to individuals themselves to assert their identities and demonstrate to others that they are or are not what they might appear to be upon first notice.
(*Chan, 1997, pp. 240–241; see also Wyatt, 1997*)

These aspects of what we know about cultural and other contexts and how we think about them can be influenced by how we feel about them. For any of us, various cultural, racial, ethnic, political, religious, and other groups—or topics related to these groups—may evoke ·an emotional response. The response may be subtle or powerful. We may be ashamed of it or embrace it as important. We may be reluctant to mention it to certain people. We may view it as not politically correct or—a more forbidding barrier for many of us—as not emotionally correct (Pope, Sonne, & Greene, 2006). These psychological reactions may block or diminish our competence to work with certain issues or certain groups. It is important to assess not only our intellectual competence but also what Pope and Brown (1996) termed *emotional competence for therapy.*

Our awareness of the client's culture or context must be balanced with an awareness of our own culture or context. Easy to recognize in theory, the influence of our own culture and context can sometimes be hard to appreciate in practice. A remarkable book, *The Spirit Catches You and You Fall Down: A Hmong Child, Her American Doctors, and the Collision of Two Cultures* (Fadiman, 1997), illustrates the potential costs of overlooking the influence of culture and context on everyone involved. The book describes the efforts of a California hospital staff and a Laotian refugee family to help a Hmong child whose American doctors had diagnosed her with epilepsy. Everyone involved had the best of intentions and worked hard to help the girl, but a lack of awareness of cultural differences had tragic effects. The book quotes medical anthropologist Arthur Kleinman:

> As powerful an influence as the culture of the Hmong patient and her family is on this case, the culture of biomedicine is equally powerful. If you can't see that your own culture has its own set of interests, emotions, and biases, how can you expect to deal successfully with someone else's culture? (p. 261)

In "Do We Practice What We Preach? An Exploratory Survey of Multicultural Psychotherapy Competencies," Nancy Hansen and her colleagues presented the results of a study that found that "overall and for 86% of the individual items, participants did not practice what they preached" (2006, p. 66) in terms of what they endorsed as the need for multicultural competencies. They concluded that

> psychotherapists need to recognize their vulnerability to not following through with what they know to be competent practice, and they need, in advance, to problem solve creative solutions. It would be helpful to identify your personal barriers in this regard: Are you anxious about raising certain issues with racially/ethnically different clients? Are you uncertain about how best to intervene? Do you fear you will 'get in over your head' exploring these issues? What will it take to work through (or around) these barriers to become more racially/ethnically responsive in your psychotherapy work? (p. 72)

The next section focuses on recognizing those barriers and overcoming them.

OVERCOMING BARRIERS TO ETHICAL SERVICES

The following steps exemplify approaches that can be helpful in recognizing and overcoming barriers to ethical services.

One good place to start is to look at how our graduate training programs are experienced by some students. To what degree is diversity respected, valued, welcomed, its potential approached in positive, creative ways? To what extent is it approached in ways that divide, isolate, set people against each other? Franklin (2009), for example, wrote:

> Ethnic minority students often felt trapped between, if not victimized by, the roles of cultural educator and student. However, students as cultural brokers in class are often educators without a portfolio in the eyes of professors and fellow classmates. Challenging psychological information being presented that did not accurately represent our experiences could bring...a label as an impudent student. Parenthetically, it was not uncommon to have our personal insights as members of the community also challenged or dismissed by professors or researchers who had no experience with our communities other than their readings in psychology. This was infuriating to many colleagues and students, given their lived experiences....These in class and work experiences were frustrating, intimidating, humiliating, and discouraging to students and subsequently early career professionals in particular. This circumstance continues to contribute to the attrition of students of color in training programs and later becomes a deterrent to participation in organized psychology. (p. 419; see also Kaduvettoor, O'Shaughnessy, Mori, et al., 2009)

Acknowledging Socioeconomic Differences

Another initial step in an ethical approach to the issue of difference is maintaining active awareness of the socioeconomic differences that exist in our society. It is exceptionally easy for us to create a cognitive map of the world in which over 90% of the area is represented by our own immediate environment. We lose active awareness that many people live in significantly different contexts. We minimize the differences and forget the contrasts and their implications.

An epidemiological study of New York City published in the *New England Journal of Medicine* (McCord & Freeman, 1990) provides an example of the extreme conditions for some U.S. citizens. The analysis showed that 54 of the 353 health areas in New York City had at least double the anticipated mortality rate for people under 65 years old.

With only one exception, all of these 54 areas were predominantly African American or Hispanic. "Survival analysis showed that black men in Harlem were less likely to reach the age of 65 than men in Bangladesh" (p. 173). The authors pointed out that their findings were similar to those for natural disaster areas.

What does it mean to us as psychotherapists and counselors that our fellow citizens live in such conditions? At a minimum, it requires that we acknowledge the reality of such conditions and inform ourselves adequately when we provide services to those from such lethal conditions or from other distinct contexts that differ from our own.

Providing services also entails awareness of how the conditions themselves may affect treatment choices in ways that may be questionable. Research suggests, for example, poor children are four times more likely than children who are not poor to receive anti-psychotic medications, and also to receive them for less severe conditions (Wilson, 2009).

Research also suggests that people of low socioeconomic status are more likely to become depressed and experience persistent depressive symptoms (Lorant et al., 2003). Lack of access to critical economic and social resources is stressful and depression often develops in the context of psychosocial stress. Stress arises not only from material deprivation but also from perceptions and experiences of relative inequality. Stress-based theories of health suggest that lack of access to economic and social resources and other sources of stress exposure due to social disadvantage, such as racism and discrimination, may increase risk for poor physical and mental health.

But such conditions also confront us with inescapable ethical questions regarding the degree to which we as individuals and as a profession view ourselves as responsible in some part for addressing these conditions, regardless of whether circumstances bring clients from those conditions to our offices. There is an extensive literature exploring these questions from diverse perspectives (APA, 2003b; Arredondo et al., 1996; Brown, 1994b, 2008; Casas & Vasquez, 1989; Constantine & Sue, 2005; Feminist Therapy Institute, 1987; Goodyear & Sinnett, 1984; Harper & McFadden, 2003; Lott & Bullock, 2001, 2007; Moodley & Palmer, 2006; Pack-Brown & Williams, 2003; Pope, 1990b; Roysircar, Sandhu, & Bibbins, 2003; Sue, 1995).

Potential Problems With Assessment Instruments

A third useful step in addressing the issue of difference is to remain alert to the possibility that standardized tests and other assessment instruments may manifest bias. APA Ethics Code Standard 9.06, Interpreting Assessment Results, speaks to competency in assessment in reminding psychologists that when interpreting assessment results, they take into account various factors, including situational, personal, linguistic, and cultural differences that might affect psychologists' judgments or reduce the accuracy of their interpretations (APA, 2010).

LaFromboise and Foster (1989), for example, discuss the case of *Larry P. v. Riles* in which the intelligence testing that led to the placement of an African American student into a special education class was unlawful because of the bias of the tests used. They describe two instruments that were specifically developed to avoid racial or cultural bias in assessment of abilities: the Adaptive Behavior Scale (American Association on Mental Deficiency, 1974) and the System of Multicultural Pluralistic Assessment (Mercer, 1979).

An example of a standardized personality test that has been called into question in regard to potential bias is the original Minnesota Multiphasic Personality Inventory (MMPI; not the revised MMPI-2). African Americans, Native Americans, Hispanics, and Asian Americans were among the groups omitted from the sample from which the original MMPI norms were developed. What implications does this exclusion have for the ethical use of the test? Faschingbauer (1979) vividly described his reservations:

> The original Minnesota group seems to be an inappropriate reference group for the 1980s. The median individual in that group had an eighth-grade education, was married, lived in a small town or on a farm, and was employed as a lower level clerk or skilled tradesman. None was under 16 or over 65 years of age, and all were white. As a clinician I find it difficult to justify comparing anyone to such a dated group. When the person is 14 years old, Chicano, and lives in Houston's poor fifth ward, use of original norms seems sinful. (p. 385)

A former president of the APA Division of the Society for Personality Assessment, Phil Erdberg (1988), reported that in one research study, a single item from the original MMPI discriminated perfectly on the basis of race, that is, it differentiated all African American test takers from all Caucasian test takers in this rural community. These problems were carefully considered in the revision process leading to the MMPI-2 and MMPI-A (Pope, Butcher, & Seelen, 2006).

Fallacies of Difference

Another useful step in addressing issues of difference effectively is to remain mindfully aware of common fallacies in the interpretation of group and individual differences. Pat O'Neill (2005), a former president of the Canadian Psychological Association, discusses the common fallacy of misinterpreting correlation between a particular difference and a problem as the difference causing the problem:

> In those days (the early 1970s), we early community psychology graduate students were reading William Ryan's (1971) *Blaming the Victim*. Ryan presented example after example of social problems being reduced to individual differences. The strategy, Ryan said, was to find out how the afflicted person differed from others, then treat that difference as the cause of the problem. He called this "the art of savage discovery." (p. 13)

Potential Problems in the Clinical Relationship

Maintaining active awareness of the subtle ways that issues of difference affect our relationship with clients can be an essential step to avoiding pitfalls. Whether we are conducting an assessment or conducting therapy or counseling, our interaction with the client is of great significance. J. M. Jones (1990b) reviewed a variety of research studies demonstrating the degree to which such factors as race could, if not addressed carefully, undermine the process. For example, failing to take such factors into account can contribute to a high premature dropout rate for minorities seeking mental health services.

One set of studies conducted by Word, Zanna, and Cooper (1974) demonstrates the degree to which subtle, unintentional discrimination by the individual conducting the assessment can lead to impaired performance by the person being assessed. In the first part of the study, white interviewers asked questions of both white and African American individuals. There were significant differences in interviewer behavior. Those conducting the assessment spent more time with the white interviewees, looked directly at white interviewees a greater portion of the time, maintained less physical distance from white interviewees, and made fewer speech errors with white interviewees.

For the second part of the study, white interviewers were trained to become aware of and use both styles of interview. They were then asked to interview a number of white people. With half of the white interviewees, the interviewer conducted the interview in a style consistent for white interviewees (for example, a longer interview at less distance). With the other half of the white interviewees, the interviewer followed a style consistent for black interviewees (shorter interview, more distance). The latter interviewees performed much less well on a series of objective measures during the assessment interview. Thus, even if the tests or assessment instruments themselves are relatively free of bias, the behavior of the interviewer can influence those who are being assessed in a discriminatory way that impairs performance.

In "Why Can't We Just Get Along? Interpersonal Biases and Interracial Distrust," Dovidio, Gaertner, Kawakami, and Hodson (2002) reviewed a series of studies showing that contemporary racism can be subtle, unintentional, and below the level of awareness. The ways that racial bias—operating outside awareness—can influence interactions between two people (for example, a therapist and client) may create or nurture race-based self-fulfilling processes. Taking into consideration research findings by Dovidio and his colleagues and others who study this area may help enable us to acknowledge and address these issues more directly.

Perhaps one of the greatest challenges is how to reconcile the trend toward using interventions that have been supported by research—a trend that in practice has led toward uniform therapies provided to broad ranges of clients— with the exceptional diversity of clients. In "Cultural Adaptation of Treatments: A Resource for Considering Culture in Evidence-Based Practice," Bernal, Jiménez-Chafey, and Rodríguez (2009) wrote that

> with the increased focus on empirical information regarding treatment development, efficacy, or effectiveness, the past two decades have been marked by efforts to achieve uniformity in providing care to a broad base of clients.

> Promoting a systematic approach to treatment is a double-edged sword; on one hand, greater structure for researchers and practitioners and a call for accountability for treatment and research procedures are attractive features for those who espouse a scientist–practitioner model to psychological practice or training. On the other hand, such systematization can potentially increase the risk of adopting a one-size-fits-all approach to interventions and intervention research that is contrary in practice to what the movement intended to promote in spirit (i.e., competent practice). (p. 361)

Creative methods being developed to meet this challenge are provided or reviewed by Bernal, Jiménez-Chafey, and Rodríguez (2009); Hays (2008, 2009); Horell (2008); Hwang (2009); Kendall and Beidas (2007); Kim, Yang, and Hwang (2006); Matos, Torres, and Santiago (2006); Nicolas, Arntz, and, Hirsch (2009); Pederson, Draguns, Lonner, et al. (2008); D. W. Sue and Sue (2008); Vasquez (2007); and Whaley and Davis (2007).

Understanding the Context

Addressing the issue of difference involves more than acknowledging important differences and avoiding prejudice and stereotyping; it involves an active appreciation of the context in which clients live and understand their lives. Westermeyer (1987, pp. 471–472) provides an example of this appreciation:

> A 48-year-old ethnic Chinese woman had been receiving antipsychotic and antidepressant medication for psychotic depression. On this regimen, the patient had lost even more weight and more hope and had become more immobilized. A critical element in this diagnosis of psychosis was the woman's belief that her deceased mother, who had been appearing in her dreams, had traveled from the place of the dead to induce the patient's own death and to bring her to the next world. We interpreted this symptom not as a delusional belief but as a culturally consistent belief in a depressed woman who had recently begun to see her deceased mother in her dreams (a common harbinger of death in the dreams of some Asian patients). This patient responded well after the antipsychotic medication was discontinued, the antidepressant medication was reduced in dosage, and weekly psychotherapy was instituted.

Similarly, the research of Amaro, Russo, and Johnson (1987) demonstrates the importance of an attentive and informed appreciation of different contexts. In comparing sources of strength and stress for Hispanic and Anglo female professionals, they found similar family and work characteristics to be associated with positive mental health. Income was the most consistently related demographic factor across all measures of psychological well-being. In addition, Hispanic women's psychological well-being was related to the experience of discrimination, which was reported by more than 82% of the sample.

Those of us who are not subject to discrimination in our day-to-day lives may find it easy to misinterpret and mistreat the distress and dysfunction that can result from prejudice.

In some cases, cultural and other forms of difference are relevant to therapists and counselors in assessing their fundamental competence to render services:

> When approached by people in need, therapists need to evaluate whether the anticipated issues fall within their realm of competence or expertise. To use an extreme example, an Anglo therapist who speaks only English and has never learned about or conducted clinical work with abuse victims should evaluate carefully whether he or she is the best person to work with a Hispanic patient who speaks very little English and who has recently recovered memories of childhood sexual abuse. Even when therapist and client speak the same basic language, it can be important to attend carefully to possible regional cultural or language differences that could lead to potentially problematic confusions of meaning. In one instance, a woman born in Puerto Rico walked into her office and found someone rifling through her purse. The potential thief ran off in the midst of an emotional confrontation, although no one was touched. Later, the woman described this event in Spanish to a social worker who had been born in Cuba. She used the word *asalto* to mean a "confrontation." The social worker, however, understood this term to refer to a physical assault…because the term was used differently in Cuban Spanish than in Puerto Rican Spanish.
>
> (*Pope & Brown, 1996, pp. 179–180*)

Perlin and McClain (2009) describe another example of the problems that can occur when cultural factors are not considered in translations:

> Semantic or translation equivalence refers specifically to whether concepts can be appropriately conveyed from one culture to another when translated. Discrepancies can lead to nonequivalence. For example, a Chinese man living in the United States was charged with [the] homicide of his work supervisor. At the trial, interpreters were used by both prosecution and defense. However, the (female) defense interpreter modified the words to avoid using disrespectful curse words…spoken by the victim instead of his actual words.…Similarly, the prosecution interpreter used the word "killed" the boss more than ten times with a knife instead of "stabbed." Thus, instead of interpreting the defendant's words to say he used a knife to try to defend himself when his boss pulled a knife, his words were interpreted to say that he "killed" the boss.…(p. 265)

H. R. Searight and Searight (2009) provide recommendations for clinicians working with foreign language interpreters. Centeno (2009) discusses practical issues in providing clinical services to minority bilingual patients whose ability to communicate has been impaired by strokes and other medical causes.

Creativity

Yet another step involves a creative and thorough approach to human diversity. In a careful series of studies at Harvard University, Langer, Bashner, and Chanowitz (1985) asked children to consider individuals who were different from the mainstream in that they were physically disabled. In one study, the experimental group of children were asked to think of as many ways as possible that a disabled person might meet a particular challenge, and the control group children were simply asked if the disabled person could meet the challenge. For example, children were shown a picture of a woman in a wheelchair and were asked either *how* the woman could drive a car or *whether* the woman could drive a car. In another study, children in the experimental group were asked to give numerous reasons not only that a disabled individual—a blind person, for example—might be bad at a particular profession but also why he or she might be good at it.

In these and other studies, Langer (1989) found that creativity in responding to forms of human difference can indeed be taught and that it can lead to more realistic, less prejudiced reactions to individuals who differ in some way from the mainstream. The research showed

> that children can be taught that handicaps are function-specific and not person-specific. Those given training in making mindful distinctions learned to be discriminating without prejudice. This group was also less likely than the control group to avoid a handicapped person. In essence, the children were taught that attributes are relative and not absolute, that whether or not something is a disability depends on context. (pp. 169–170)

Whether we practice in private offices, HMOs, hospitals, clinics, community mental health centers, university settings, or elsewhere, we must remain alert and creative in regard to the contexts in which we work and the characteristics of those who need our help. Is our setting responsive to the needs of those who use wheelchairs, those for whom English is a new language, those who use American Sign Language to communicate, or those who are blind? For whom is our setting open, inviting, accessible, and genuinely helpful? Who is shut out or discouraged from approaching? To what degree do we acknowledge or assume responsibility for the nature of the settings in which we practice?

Beware Barnum

In 1949, Bert Forer published a landmark experiment. He gave his students the results of a personality test they had taken. The students tended to be surprised at how well the test had captured their own unique personality. He then revealed that each student had received the same description: a list of statements that tended to apply to almost everyone. Paul Meehl (1956) named Forer's finding the "Barnum Effect" in honor of P. T. Barnum's idea that the circus should have something for everybody.

Research continues to find the "Barnum Effect" popping up in diverse environments. Alison, Smith, and Morgan (2003), Claridge, Clark, Powney, and Hassan (2008), Liliendfeld and Landfield (2008), Russo (2008), and Wyman and Vyse (2008) provide a few recent examples.

Levy (2010) discusses how easy such fits-almost-everyone statements can play into stereotypes. Here are a few of his "Sociocultural Barnum Statements" (p. 255):

- Caucasians favor members of their own group.
- Latinos can be very passionate.
- Italians enjoy food.
- African Americans are sensitive to certain words.
- Christians try to forgive.
- Jewish people yearn to survive.
- Europeans have had their share of troubles.
- Americans are a diverse group of individuals.
- Minorities just want their rights.
- Senior citizens don't want to be ignored.
- Infants seek pleasure.
- Teenagers want to be seen for who they are.
- Men care about success.
- Women resent being taken for granted.
- The physically disabled resent being seen as inferior.
- Artists want the freedom to express themselves.
- Schizophrenics view the world in a unique way.

Speaking Openly, Honestly, and Directly

Racial, cultural, and other group differences can make us uncomfortable. Pope, Sonne, and Greene (2006) discussed the ways in which certain topics have become taboo, the myths that flourish in the absence of frank discussion, and the harm that often follows. It is important that relevant issues be addressed openly and frankly. This process obviously does not mean replacing silence and avoidance with politically correct (or psychologically correct) clichés but rather approaching the issues honestly. Discussing how race, religion, and culture influenced clinical work with older people, Hinrichsen (2006) wrote:

> How are ethnic or minority service providers perceived by White older clients? An African American psychology intern in her mid-20s whom I supervised began to conduct psychotherapy with a man in his 70s for the treatment of depression triggered by an increasing number of health problems. The

intern mentioned that the older client persisted with telling stories about "Negro fellas" in the army during World War II. The emphasis of the stories was usually on how much he liked his Black comrades and the contributions that they made to the army. When asked how she handled this issue, the intern reported she said to the older client, "I guess you noticed I'm Black." This statement led to a productive discussion of a variety of concerns that included worry that he might say something racially related that would offend the intern and concern about whether a Black service provider could understand his experience. At times, during intakes into our geriatric clinic, a prospective client will frankly state, "I'd like a White doctor" or "I want a Jewish doctor." Clinical geropsychologists sometimes have noted that some older adults will make disparaging racial or ethnic remarks rarely made by younger adults. In part, open expression of these remarks reflects the reality that the current generation of older adults grew into adulthood during a time when racial and ethnic segregation were government and institution sanctioned and that it was socially acceptable in some circles to publicly and unfavorably caricature racial or ethnic minorities. (p. 32)

SCENARIOS FOR DISCUSSION

You are conducting an intake examination at an HMO. The client's first words to you are, "I'm having some problems with my sexual identity, but I think I can only work with someone who understands where I'm coming from, who has faced these same issues, and who knows what its like. What's your sexual orientation?"

- How do you feel?
- What goals would you have in mind in responding to the client?
- Under what conditions, if any, would you disclose your sexualidentity to the client?
- To what extent has your training included research and theory relevant to sexual identity?

■ ■ ■

You share a suite of offices with several other therapists. The name of each therapist is on the door to that therapist's office. One morning you find that the door to one of the offices has been broken in and the office vandalized. The name on the door

(continued)

(continued)

was Jewish. Swastikas along with epithets have been spray-painted on the walls, desk, floor, and bookshelves. You have no evidence but believe the vandal may have been one of your patients—someone who has expressed strong anti-Semitic views during therapy sessions, embraces the view that the Holocaust is fiction, and has described fantasies of vandalizing synagogues. But if you were to ask him during the next therapy session whether he had anything to do with vandalizing your colleague's office, he would deny it.

- How do you feel?
- What would you like to do?
- What do you would actually do?
- Would you mention your suspicion that your client may have vandalized your colleague's office to the colleague, the police, or anyone else? If so, how do you address issues of client privacy and confidentiality?
- Would you mention your suspicion to your client? If so, how?
- How, if at all, would you address your client's anti-Semitism in therapy?

■ ■ ■

You are a Latino psychotherapist who speaks Spanish only moderately well. Your policy is to try to refer all those who speak only Spanish to fluent Spanish speakers, but you will see Spanish speakers who also speak English if they wish. A South American client who speaks fluent English and Spanish sees you because you are the only Latino available on her HMO list. At the first session, she insists that you should be ashamed for not speaking better Spanish and that you therefore have no culture.

- How do you feel?
- What are your thoughts and feelings about this client?
- How would you respond to this client?
- Under what conditions would you continue to see or decline to see this client?

■ ■ ■

You have been leading a therapy group at a large mental health facility. As one of the session begins, a group member interrupts you and says, "I want to ask you about something. Have you noticed how none of the doctors here are black, Latino, or Latina but almost all the cleaning crew are? Why do you work in a system like that? Don't you think that has any effects on us patients?"

- How do you feel?
- What are the possible replies you consider?
- What do you think you would say?
- What effects, if any, such a system might have on clients?

■ ■ ■

You work in a large office building. As your therapy client, a Sikh, is getting ready to leave your office, the police show up at the door, handcuff him, and say they are taking him to the station for questioning. When they leave, the accountant across the hall comes over and says that someone saw your client in the lobby, thought he was acting suspiciously, and called the police to report someone who seemed to be an Arab terrorist.

- How do you feel?
- What do you consider doing?
- What would you like to do?
- What do you think you would do?
- How, if at all, might this affect the therapy?
- How, if at all, would you chart this?

■ ■ ■

You are working with a client who is of a different race and sexual orientation from you and your supervisor. One day the client is 15 minutes late for a session, and you spend some of the session discussing the reasons for the client not being on time. When you bring up the topic to your supervisor, the response is, "Oh, that lateness doesn't mean anything psychological. That's just the way those people are."

- How do you feel?
- What possible responses to your supervisor's comments do you consider?
- What do you think that you'd actually say to your supervisor?

(continued)

(*continued*)

- When you imagined this scenario, what race and sexual orientation did you imagine the client was? Why?

■ ■ ■

A married couple come to you for counseling. Both believe that men are the natural leaders in a marriage and that a woman's rightful place is to be obedient to her husband. However, they often have what they describe as "slips," when he seems to look to her for guidance or when she finds it hard to accept his decisions. They are seeking marital counseling to help them eliminate these "slips."

- How do you feel?
- What are your thoughts and feelings about the wife?
- What are your thoughts and feelings about the husband?
- What are your thoughts and feelings about the marital relationship that they value and have chosen for themselves?
- How do you think you would respond?

■ ■ ■

You are a therapist at an agency with a policy that says that if a client misses two appointments without calling, the therapy automatically terminates. A client who is a single mother, uses public transportation, has no telephone, and is often distressed by a babysitter who does not show up, misses her appointment for the second time. Your supervisor insists that you terminate by letter, given the long waiting list of potential clients.

- What feelings do you experience?
- What are your assumptions about the client's not showing up? In what way, if any, might her diagnosis be relevant?
- What do you think and feel about the relevance of the policy for clients such as this one?
- What are your options in responding to your supervisor? To the agency policy? To the client?

Chapter 19

CONFIDENTIALITY

Confidentiality is key to many therapist-patient relationships, but it trips up many of us. The problems often spring from understandable lapses in ethical awareness. The first of this book's seven basic assumptions described ethical awareness as a continuous, active process. The hard work of psychotherapy makes maintaining this awareness a challenge for even the most dedicated clinicians. Fatigue, stress, and routine dull our awareness, lull us into ethical sleep, put us on automatic when we need to wake up to what we are missing. Irritating distractions, unjustified assumptions, overwhelming demands, unrealistic expectations, and conflicting agendas can muddle our awareness.

Note to Readers

Confidentiality has emerged as a major, persistent ethical challenge for psychologists. Over half (62%) of the therapists in one national study reported unintentionally violating their patients' confidences (Pope, Tabachnick, & Keith-Spiegel, 1987). Another national study found that the most frequently reported intentional violation of the law or ethical standards by senior, prominent psychologists involved confidentiality (Pope & Bajt, 1988). In 21% of the cases, therapists violated confidentiality in transgression of law. In another 21% of the cases, therapists refused to breach confidentiality to make legally required reports of child abuse. Therapists may have experienced violations of confidentiality when they themselves were patients. In one national survey, about 10% of the therapists who had been in therapy reported that their own therapist had violated their rights to confidentiality (Pope & Tabachnick, 1994).

A lapse in active awareness can be brief but undo excellent work. We do the hard work of sorting through the legislation and case law that govern confidentiality and privilege in our local jurisdiction, study the relevant ethics codes and professional guidelines, consult with an attorney, and keep up with the evolving standards of care. But somehow our mind wanders when it should be focused, and we stumble into a pitfall we could have avoided.

Allen (2009) discusses additional layers of complexity and potential confusion—resulting in additional pitfalls—that variations in the nature of confidential material and the number of people entitled to receive it can cause. She emphasizes that confidential material includes more than facts alone. "Facts, impressions, events, and data of all sorts can be deemed confidential" (p. 127). Similarly, she notes the great range of people to whom the therapist may—or may not—be allowed or obligated to disclose confidential information. "[T]he community authorized to receive confidential information can be smaller than a family or as large as a workforce" (p. 127; see also Jan & Roberts, 2009).

This chapter highlights some of those easy-to-overlook pitfalls that can lead to violations of confidentiality.

REFERRAL SOURCES

We appreciate referrals. But should we tell the referral source whether a specific individual has scheduled an appointment with us, whether the individual kept the initial appointment, or what might have been discussed or decided if the patient has not authorized the disclosure? Unfortunately, therapists may unintentionally violate confidentiality by sending referral sources a thank-you note mentioning a specific patient and providing a detail or two about what happened without the patient's knowledge or content.

PUBLIC CONSULTATION

Consultation can be an invaluable resource for meeting the highest ethical, legal, and clinical standards. It gives us easy access to new information, support, informal peer review, and a different perspective. Psychologists in a national study rated "consultation with colleagues" as the most effective source of guidance for practice (Pope, Tabachnick, & Keith-Spiegel, 1987). They judged such consultation to be more effective than fourteen other possible sources, such as graduate programs, internships, state licensing boards, and continuing education programs.

Consultation about patients deserves the same confidentiality as the psychotherapy it focuses on. We lead busy lives and want to make the most of our time. Often the most convenient way to catch a colleague for a quick consult is while we are walking through the halls of a clinic, or sitting together at a large table while waiting for the last arrivals so that a meeting can begin, or at a restaurant during a lunch break, or in other public places. The problem with such on-the-run consultations is that confidential information is often discussed within earshot of people who are not authorized to receive the information. Many of us have probably overheard such consultations in clinic hallways or elevators. Perhaps we heard the patient's name, someone we recognized as a friend, neighbor, or colleague. In one case, a therapist consulted a colleague on a crowded elevator about a particularly "difficult" patient, unaware that the patient was standing only a few feet behind her, listening carefully.

Making sure that we keep private consultations private is an important ethical responsibility.

GOSSIP

Few would argue that therapy is easy work. Sometimes it involves considerable stress, and we need to blow off steam. Talking about our work with others—at lunch, in the staff lounge, on the racquetball court, at parties—may make us feel better. Those settings make it easy to let slip the identity of one of our patients or betray what a patient has told us in confidence.

Some patients may be in the news or tell us fascinating information. The urge to tell others that we know them can be almost overwhelming. Many of us may know through the grapevine who is in treatment with whom and even what led them to seek therapy. To the extent that the information nourishing the grapevine is provided by counselors or therapists rather than by the patients, it is a clear ethical breach.

CASE NOTES AND PATIENT FILES

Have you ever seen a patient's chart you were not authorized to see? It is likely that at least some—if not most—of this book's readers have happened to see unsecured documents containing patient names and other confidential information. Some clinics and individuals may have difficulty meeting their responsibility to keep confidential records confidential. During a visit to a prestigious university-affiliated teaching hospital, one of the authors noticed, while walking down a public hallway, that the mental health clinic's patient charts were stacked along the walls. The hallway was unattended. The names of the patients were clearly visible, and had the author opened any of the charts, he could have read a wealth of confidential information. When he asked later about charts being left in the hall, he was assured that this was temporary: due to insufficient funds, additional storage space was not yet available, and this manner of "filing" was most convenient for the business office personnel.

Some of us may have visited colleagues who leave charts and other patient information lying on top of their desks. Not only patients' names but also other information may be in full view.

There are at least two important issues here. One is keeping information about patients out of sight of people who are not authorized to see that information. Making sure that documents are inside the chart (or some other protective covering), the chart folder is closed, and the patient's/ name does not appear on the outside of the chart (a coding system can provide for convenient filing and retrieval) are useful steps to take when charts are visible in a well-attended area open to the public or other patients. The protection of even the patient's name may seem excessive to some, yet the fact that a person is consulting a therapist is a fact worth treating confidentially.

The second issue concerns the security of charts left in an unattended area. There should be a lock between the charts and anyone not authorized to see them. Regarding the security of charts, as in so many other aspects of maintaining appropriate confidentiality, the Golden Rule can be a useful guide. What steps would we want a therapist to take if it were our chart, containing our deepest secrets, our personal and family history, our conflicts, our diagnosis, the medications we were taking, and our prognosis? What steps would we want our therapist to take to make sure that no part of this confidential information was carelessly left visible or available to whomever—other patients, our employer or employees, neighbors, relatives, colleagues—might, for any reason, pass by? How much care would we want our own therapist to use in handling these documents?

PHONES, FAXES, AND MESSAGES

Some of this book's readers may have visited clinics in which telephone messages mentioning a patient's name, telephone number, and reason for calling were left out where they could be seen by those without legitimate access to that information. Some may have visited a colleague's office just as a fax about a patient was coming in and . . . well, just could not help seeing who it was from and what it was about. Some readers may have overheard a therapist take a phone call from a patient and heard both sides of the conversation (and may have been surprised to recognize the patient's voice).

Answering machines create special pitfalls for confidentiality. It is tempting, if our time for lunch is limited, to play back accumulated messages—some from patients—while a colleague or friend is waiting to accompany us to the nearest restaurant. If our answering machine is at home, it may take special measures to make certain that family members, friends, and others do not overhear messages as they are recorded or played back. Again, the Golden Rule can provide a useful guide to anticipating potential problems and recognizing the need to remain constantly mindful, aware, and alerts.

HOME OFFICE

As discussed in prior editions of this book and in *How to Survive and Thrive as a Therapist* (Pope & Vasquez, 2005), home offices pose special challenges to confidentiality and privacy if there are others living in the home. Is it likely that patients—some of whom may not want anyone else to know that they are in psychotherapy—will encounter family members when arriving, waiting for the appointment, or leaving? Any chance that young children will interrupt therapy sessions? Will files, appointment books, message slips, and other documents be secure and out of sight when family members enter the office? Will family members be able to overhear telephone calls or other discussions with patients? Is confidential information about patients stored on a computer that other family members use? If so, how is it secured against accidental discovery? Is the telephone answering machine that receives calls from or about patients shared with other family members? If so, how can those calls be protected against accidental playback for other family members? Are answering machine messages from or about clients ever played back in the presence of family members?

SHARING WITH LOVED ONES

Some therapists may hold back no secrets from a spouse, partner, or other loved ones. For some, sharing what happened during the day with a loved one may be a crucial act of intimacy. The ethical challenge is to do this without violating patient confidentiality.

COMMUNICATIONS IN GROUP OR FAMILY THERAPY

When therapy includes more than one individual, as in group and family therapy, patients have a right to know in advance, as part of the informed consent process, any limitations of privacy, confidentiality, or privilege affected by the presence of more than one patient. For example, if a clinician is providing family therapy, will he or she keep confidential from other family members information conveyed in a telephone call from a minor son that he is using drugs, from a minor daughter that she is pregnant, from the father that he is engaging in an extramarital affair and plans to leave his wife, or from the mother that she has secretly withdrawn the family's savings and is using it to gamble? What does a psychotherapists need to tell prospective patients about how "secrets" will be handled so that the clients' consent can be informed (see, e.g., Kuo, 2009)?

Psychotherapy involving more than one patient emphasizes a major theme of this book: trust. The therapist and members of a therapy group may assume that everyone involved is trustworthy. But what if that is wrong? What if a group member is a newspaper or magazine reporter gathering information for an exposé of what the reporter considers bogus therapy groups, or of the therapist, or of what the reporter considers a "culture of dependency"? Or what if a group member later decides to write a memoir to be published in a magazine or book about what the experience of group therapy was like? Or what if some of the group members simply pass along what they learn about other group members to their family and friends and that information ripples outward to those who recognize and know members of the group? Group and family therapists must struggle with these issues in a way that respects the patients' legitimate rights to privacy, confidentiality, and privilege and their right to know the limits—both legal and practical—of their privacy, confidentiality, and privilege.

Therapy involving more than one person also presents challenges to documentation. If, for example, the therapist keeps one set of therapy records for "the family" or "the group," what happens if one member of the family or group requests or subpoenas a copy of those records? How can a therapy record that mentions more than one patient by name be turned over without the informed consent or legal waiver of each patient? One approach that some therapists use is to keep a separate chart for each patient in a family or group.

WRITTEN CONSENT

A common cause of needless problems is failing to obtain written informed consent to release confidential information.

As discussed in Chapter 14, both the APA Ethics Code and the CPA Ethics Code address documenting a patient's consent with either a signed consent form or a note in the record about obtaining consent orally.

Obtaining written consent can help promote clarity of communication between therapist and patient in situations when misunderstandings can be disastrous. Both need to understand exactly what information the therapist will release. Is the therapist free to discuss any aspect of the client's history, situation, and treatment? Is the therapist authorized to provide a written summary or all clinical files? When exactly does the client's authorization end? If the person who is to receive the confidential information contacts the therapist with additional questions next month, next year, or several years from now, does the written consent need to be renewed, or does it explicitly cover such future requests?

Patients may not understand the type of information that insurance companies require to authorize coverage and the degree to which information will or will not be sufficiently safeguarded by the insurance company. Keith-Spiegel and Koocher (1985) describe a hypothetical example of a therapist's routine statement to patients regarding insurance coverage: "If you choose to use your coverage, I shall have to file a form with the company telling them when our appointments were and what services I performed (i.e., psycho-therapy, consultation, or evaluation). I will also have to formulate a diagnosis and advise the company of that. The company claims to keep this informa-tion confidential, although I have no control over the information once it leaves this office. If you have questions about this you may wish to check with the company providing the coverage. You may certainly choose to pay for my services out-of-pocket and avoid the use of insurance altogether, if you wish" (p. 76).

MANAGED CARE ORGANIZATIONS

An easily overlooked aspect of confidentiality is how confidential information can circulate within health maintenance organizations and other managed care facilities. Many patients feel betrayed when records of their psychother-apy sessions become part of their general medical or health record in an HMO and may in turn find their way into other hands. One women was shocked to find her treatment mentioned on the employee relations bulletin board where she worked. Management and the union, eager to cut both sick leave and the costs for their health-care plan, had decided to post all utilizations of the health-care plan by employees. Under the terms of the contract that had been negotiated by labor and management, the date and reason for each utilization was provided by the health-care organization to officials for both union and management.

Confidentiality issues continue to become more complex as managed care organizations require more and more information traditionally regarded as pri-vate in order to monitor the allocation of resources and compliance with eligibility criteria:

> Managed care companies generally ask for much more information than third parties have traditionally requested from clinicians. The ethical expla-nations given for such requests generally have fallen into two categories. One is based on the known history of some clinicians to distort information on forms. . . . Then managed care companies began to discover that some clini-cians charged for sessions not provided or approved. A more general reason applicable to all clinicians is to make sure that the intended treatment meets criteria of medical necessity as designated in the third-party benefits. In addi-tion to treatment plans, managed care companies will often ask for copies of any notes kept on patients; they sometimes do on-site reviews of charts in hospitals, and on occasion they even talk directly to the patient to try to verify information.
>
> (*Moffic, 1997, p. 97*)

The Council of the National Academies of Practice (including dentistry, medicine, nursing, optometry, osteopathic medicine, podiatric medicine, psychology, social work and veterinary medicine) adopted *Ethical Guidelines for Professional Care in a Managed Care Environment* (1997). Confidentiality is one of five guidelines listed as a primary concern. While the National Academies of Practice acknowledges that utilization and quality assurance reviews are appropriate functions in a health-care system, they emphasize the importance of safeguards to protect the privacy and confidentiality of patient data and the practitioner's clinical materials. They state,

> The rationale for this position is founded on the patient's autonomous right to control sensitive personal information. It is further based upon an historical recognition in the oath of Hippocrates and corroborated throughout the centuries, of the enduring value of preserving confidentiality in order to enhance mutual trust and respect in the patient-provider relationship. (p. 5)

Anne Slowther and Irwin Kleinman (2008) observed:

> The increasing capacity to generate and disseminate information in health care, together with the increasing complexity of healthcare provision, has implications for our understanding of the nature and limits of confidentiality. Development of multidisciplinary healthcare teams raises questions of how much information can be shared within the team, and who is recognized as a team member for this purpose. (p. 43)

Health-care organizations may not always monitor who attends case conferences, and discussions of a patient's condition may be overheard inadvertently by an inappropriate audience.

Similarly, Anne Ward (2010) discusses "how difficult it can be for teams to keep the psychotherapeutic aspects of confidentiality in mind and how, in the current electronic age, fears can arise that patient records may be circulated more widely than is appropriate" (p. 113).

Electronic medical records (EMRs) post difficult challenges to confidentiality. In "Electronic Medical Records: Confidentiality Issues in the Time of HIPAA," Margaret Richards (2010) wrote:

> For a psychologist in a major academic or medical institution, the EMR provides unique ethical conflicts of which the psychologist may be unaware. By documenting within the EMR, the psychologist is potentially informing all members of that patient's medical team that this patient is involved in psychological care. While most informed consents discuss the limits of confidentiality, patients may not always realize the information that is being shared and with whom. At a minimum, the psychologist using an EMR is providing information regarding the patient's participation in therapy, dates of appointments, types of services offered, and diagnoses, even if the content of the

session is not revealed. Typically, this is the same information that is being provided to insurance companies as a natural part of the billing process since the advent of HIPAA (Freeny, 2007). Yet, this may not be information that a client wants his primary care physician to have. (p. 553)

Who participates in treatment planning, implementation, and review can be a challenging issue in small towns. In one instance, the chief health-care administrator proposed a periodic case review of current patients to be conducted by staff psychologists. In this town of fewer than 10,000 people, the psychologists would have known many of the patients in a variety of social and business roles. The patients had not given informed consent for this review. This confidentiality issue is not easily addressed. One solution would be for the administrator to agree to hire a psychologist from another community who did not know the population served by the hospital to visit the hospital once a month to review the cases and make sure that patients understood the review process.

DISCLOSING CONFIDENTIAL INFORMATION FOR MANDATED REPORTS ONLY TO THE EXTENT REQUIRED BY LAW

Evolving legislation and case law in each jurisdiction define the limits of information to reveal in making legally mandated reports. For example, a psychologist was contacted by a mother who wished to arrange appointments for her daughter and her daughter's stepfather to see the therapist regarding allegations that the stepfather engaged in sexual intimacies with his stepdaughter. The psychologist agreed to meet with him and immediately filed a formal report of suspected child abuse.

The next day, a deputy sheriff contacted the psychologist for information. The psychologist furnished information about his meeting with the daughter. He would meet with the stepfather later in the day. The deputy called later and asked for information concerning the session with the stepfather and, reading from the Child Abuse Reporting Law, emphasized that the psychologist was obligated to supply additional information, which the psychologist reluctantly provided.

The stepfather claimed in court that the psychologist, after making the initial formal report, should not have disclosed any additional information. The Supreme Court of California agreed with the stepfather:

The psychologist was under no statutory obligation to make a second report concerning the same activity. . . . We have recognized the contemporary value of the psychiatric [sic] profession, and its potential for the relief of emotional disturbances and of the inevitable tensions produced in our modern, complex society. . . . That value is bottomed on a confidential relationship; but the doctor can be of assistance only if the patient may freely relate his thoughts and actions, his fears and fantasies, his strengths and weaknesses, in a completely uninhibited manner.

(*People* v. *Stritzinger*, 1983, p. 437)

Psychotherapists who disclose confidential information even in court settings may be subject to suit by the client. California, for example, has general legislation protecting individuals from lawsuits for any statements made as part of court proceedings. Nevertheless, a district court of appeal ruled that a psychologist "can be sued for disclosing privileged information in a court proceeding when it violates the patient's constitutional right of privacy" (Chiang, 1986, p. 1).

PUBLISHING CASE STUDIES

Publishing case studies or other confidential information about patients requires exceptional care. Merely changing the patient's name and a few other details may not be sufficient. Pope, Simpson, and Weiner (1978), for example, discussed a case in New York in which a therapist was successfully sued for publishing a book in which he described his treatment of a patient. The patient asserted that the therapist had not obtained her consent to write about her treatment and had not adequately disguised the presentation of her history.

APA's *Casebook on Ethical Principles of Psychologists* (1987a, p. 72) presents a situation in which a psychologist wished to write a book about an assessment:

> Psychologist G conducted a professional evaluation of the accused murderer in a sensational and well-publicized case in which six teenage girls, who vanished over a period of 18 months, were later found stabbed to death in an abandoned waterfront area of the city. The lurid nature of the crimes attracted nationwide publicity, which only increased as allegations of negligence were pressed against the city administration and the police force. In order to construct a psychological diagnostic profile, Psychologist G spent several days with the accused, conducting interviews and psychometric tests. He presented his findings in court with the full consent of the accused.

> Six months later, following the sentencing of the now convicted murderer, Psychologist G determined that he would like to write a book about the murderer and the psychology behind the crimes, which he anticipated would be a lucrative undertaking.

> Psychologist G wrote to the Ethics Committee to inquire whether it would be ethical for him to do so. The convicted murderer had refused permission

to publish in a book the results of the psychological evaluation, despite the fact that the information was now considered part of the public domain because it had been admitted in court as evidence.

Opinion: The Ethics Committee responded to Psychologist G that to write the proposed book would be a legal but unethical undertaking. The fact that material has entered the public domain or that there may have been an implied waiver of consent does not free the psychologist from the obligation under Principle 5.b of the Ethical Principles to obtain prior consent before presenting in a public forum personal information acquired through the course of professional work. In this case, the ethics code sets a higher standard than the law would require. Psychologist G thanked the Committee for its advice and dropped the idea of writing the book.

DISTRACTION

This chapter opened with a fundamental theme of this book: the importance of active, continuous alertness and awareness. A momentary distraction can cause problems. No matter how senior our status, how extensive our training, or how naturally skilled any of us may be, none of us is perfect. All of us have moments when we are tired, overwhelmed, rushing, or careless. James F. Masterson, a prominent therapist who has written extensively concerning borderline personality disorders, showed courage in writing about an instance in which he betrayed a patient's confidence because of something that had happened in his own life:

> One morning I was late and dented my car as I parked in the office garage. A bit frazzled from the experience, I rushed into my office and admitted my first patient who asked me how another patient of mine was doing, calling her by name. I was startled because their appointments were at very different times. I wondered if they had met socially, or if he was dating her. Then I realized what had happened. Worried about my dented fender, I had inadvertently picked her file out of the drawer instead of his, and he had read her name on the folder. My distraction represented a countertransferential failure to pay proper attention to my patient. I apologized for taking out the wrong chart and told him I was distracted by the accident.
>
> (*Masterson*, 1989, p. 26)

FOCUSING ON LEGAL RESPONSIBILITIES TO THE EXCLUSION OF ETHICAL RESPONSIBILITIES

Mary Alice Fisher (2008) discussed ways in which confidentiality workshops often focus on laws and risk management while spending relatively little time on ethical responsibilities. Noting that HIPAA brought forth the growth of attorney-led HIPAA-compliance training that further overshadowed ethics training in confidentiality, Fisher wrote:

> Such legally based training creates several ethical problems for psychologists. First, it fosters the impression that attorneys—not clinicians—have become the only "real" experts about this aspect of practice. Second, it creates a legal language about confidentiality that threatens to usurp psychologists' own clinical or ethical language about it: Laws take center stage, when what is needed is a language for placing them into ethical context. Third, it exacerbates the figure–ground confusion (by substituting legal rules for ethical rules) and often takes a risk-management perspective that raises anxiety: It encourages psychologists to focus on obeying laws in order to avoid risks to *themselves*, when what they need is a clearer focus on their ethical obligations and the potential risks to *clients*. Finally, the legal emphasis obscures an important fact about risk management: Understanding and following the relevant ethical principles is an essential ingredient in avoiding a malpractice suit. . . . (p. 6)

SCENARIOS FOR DISCUSSION

You have been working for two years with a patient who has multiple problems and has disclosed extremely sensitive information to you. The insurance company sends you a letter requesting the entire file, including all of your chart notes and all raw data from the psychological assessment, in order to determine whether further therapy is warranted and, if so, in what form. When you call the insurance company to discuss the matter, the head of claims review (not a mental health professional and whose previous job was quality control officer in a paper clip company) tells you that they must have all these materials within five business days or else therapy will be discontinued.

- How do you feel?
- What options do you consider?
- If the patient refuses to provide consent for you to send the materials, even though it means there are no longer resources to pay for the therapy, and decides to terminate therapy rather than allow the information to go to third parties, what do you do?

■ ■ ■

You have been working with a 14-year-old patient for several months. During one session, the patient suddenly discloses having sex with a parent for the past four years. The patient, who has been chronically depressed, threatens, "If you tell anyone about this, I will find a way to kill myself." You believe that this is not an idle threat.

- How do you feel?
- Under what circumstances, if any, do you believe you might disclose information about the client's claim of having been sexually involved with a parent to any of the following: (a) child protective services or other governmental agency authorized to receive reports of suspected child abuse, (b) your clinical supervisor, (c) any family member, or (d) anyone else?
- What objectives or priorities would shape your interventions?
- To what extent, if at all, would your own potential legal liability affect your emotional responses to this situation and your course of action?

■ ■ ■

You are working with a patient who engages in unprotected sex with a variety of partners. Two months ago, the client became infected with HIV. Recent sessions have focused on many topics, one of which is the patient's decision not to begin using protection during sex and not to disclose the HIV status to any partners. The client shows no likelihood of changing this decision.

- How do you feel?
- Does the patient's decision affect your ability to empathize in any way?

Under what conditions, if any, would you act against the patient's wishes and communicate information about the client's HIV status and sexual activity to third parties? What information would you disclose, to whom would you disclose it, and what are the likely or possible outcomes?

■ ■ ■

You work for an HMO, spending 4 hours a day, three days a week, providing outpatient therapy at its facility. Four other

(continued)

(continued)

clinicians provide therapy in the same office. According to HMO policy, all patient charts of all clinicians using that room must remain locked in a single filing cabinet in the corner of the room. Each clinician has a key to the filing cabinet. You become aware that several of your patients have social relationships with the other therapists. You are also aware that their charts contain extremely sensitive information about them. You also notice the names of two of your friends on the charts of the other clinicians. The HMO refuses to change this policy.

- How do you feel?
- What courses of action do you consider?
- Are the clients entitled to know about this arrangement? If so, at what point should they be made aware of it?
- If you were the client in such a situation, do you believe that you would be entitled to know about this arrangement?

■ ■ ■

You have reached a therapeutic impasse with a patient. For weeks, the therapy has seemed stalled, but you have not understood what is wrong. During the past few supervision sessions, you discovered that this client has stirred up some intense emotions in you. You've mentioned to your supervisor some painful events in your own history about which you have felt ashamed and confused. You have yet to discuss these events with anyone else, even your own therapist. One afternoon you head to the staff lounge but pause just before entering the room. Through the door, you hear your supervisor talking with others about the painful events you had discussed in supervision.

- How do you feel?
- Which of the following do you think you'd do and why: (a) leave immediately, hoping no one saw you; (b) linger at the door, hoping to hear more; (c) enter the room, pretending that you hadn't heard anything; (d) enter the room and indicate that you had heard what they had said; or (e) something else?
- Under what circumstances, if any, do you believe that clinical supervisors should discuss what their supervisees tell them? In your experience, have these boundaries of confidentiality been explicit and well understood by

supervisees and supervisors? In your experience, have supervisors respected these boundaries?

- Have the clinical supervisors you have known or known of kept notes or otherwise documented the supervision sessions? What ethical, legal, or other considerations affect the privacy and confidentiality of supervision notes (for example, are they legally privileged communications)?

Chapter 20

RECOGNIZING, ASSESSING, AND RESPONDING TO SUICIDAL RISK

Responding to suicidal risk can be intimidating. The need for careful assessment is great. Suicide remains among the top dozen causes of death in the United States, as high as number two for some groups. Homicide rates seize popular attention, but far more people kill themselves than kill others. Experts almost unanimously voice the view that the reported figures vastly understate the problem because reporting procedures are flawed.

Assessing and responding to suicidal risk is a source of extraordinary stress for many therapists. This part of our work focuses all the troublesome issues that run through this book: questions of the therapist's influence, competence, efficacy, fallibility, over- or under-involvement, responsibility, and ability to make life-or-death decisions. Litman's study (1965) of over 200 clinicians soon after their clients/patients had committed suicide found the experience to have had an almost nightmarish quality. They felt intense grief, loss, and sometimes depression as anyone—professional or nonprofessional—might at the death of someone they cared about. But as therapist they also felt guilt, inadequacy, self-blame, and fears that they would be sued, investigated, or vilified in the media. A study of short-term and permanent effects of patient's suicide on the therapist led Goldstein and Buongiorno (1984) to recommend providing support groups for surviving therapists. Mangurian and her colleagues (2009) wrote that the "suicide of a patient is arguably the most traumatic event that can occur during a psychiatrist's professional life" (p. 278).

Solo practitioners may be even more vulnerable than their colleagues who practice in groups and clinics with their natural support systems. Trainees may be among the most vulnerable. Kleespies, Smith, and Becker (1990) found that "trainees with patient suicides reported stress levels equivalent to that found in patient samples with bereavement and higher than that found with professional clinicians who had patient suicides" (p. 257). They recommend that all training programs create a plan to help trainees with client suicide:

> There is a need for an immediate, supportive response to the student to prevent traumatization and minimize isolation ... and ... for a safe forum that will allow the student to express his or her feelings, will ensure positive learning from the experience, and will help the student to integrate it constructively into future work with high-risk patients. (pp. 262–263; see also Mangurian et al., 2009)

If the challenges of helping the suicidal patient evoke extraordinary feelings of discomfort from many therapists, they also show the extraordinary efforts that some therapists take to help their clients stay alive. Davison and Neale (1982), for instance, described the ways in which "the clinician treating a suicidal person must be prepared to devote more energy and time than he or she usually does even to psychotic patients. Late-night phone calls and visits to the patient's home may be frequent."

Bruce Danto, a former director of the Detroit Suicide Prevention Center and former president of the American Association of Suicidology, stated:

> With these problems, you can't simply sit back in your chair, stroke your beard and say, "All the work is done right here in my office with my magical ears and tongue." There has to be a time when you shift gears and become an activist. Support may involve helping a patient get a job, attending a graduation or play, visiting a hospital, even making house calls. I would never send somebody to a therapist who has an unlisted phone number. If therapists feel that being available for phone contact is an imposition, then they're in the wrong field or they're treating the wrong patient. They should treat only well people. Once you decide to help somebody, you have to take responsibility down the line.
>
> (Colt, 1983, p. 50)

Norman Farberow, a preeminent pioneer in helping suicidal clients, described instances in which the therapist provided very frequent and very long sessions (some lasting all day) to a severely suicidal client as

> examples of the extraordinary measures which are sometimes required to enable someone to live. Providing this degree of availability to the client gives the client evidence of caring when that caring is absolutely necessary to convince that client that life is both livable and worth living, and nothing less extreme would be effective in communicating the caring. In such

circumstances, all other considerations—dependence, transference, countertransference, and so on—become secondary. The overwhelming priority is to help the client stay alive. The secondary issues—put "on hold" during the crisis—can be directly and effectively addressed once the client is in less danger.

(*Farberow, 1985, p. C9*)

Stone (1982) describes a vivid example of the lengths to which a therapist can go to communicate caring in an effective and therapeutic manner to a patient in crisis. Suffering from schizophrenia, a young woman who had been hospitalized during a psychotic episode continuously vilified her therapist for "not caring" about her. Without warning, she escaped from the hospital:

The therapist, upon hearing the news, got into her car and canvassed all the bars and social clubs in Greenwich Village which her patient was known to frequent. At about midnight, she found her patient and drove her back to the hospital. From that day forward, the patient grew calmer, less impulsive, and made great progress in treatment. Later, after making substantial recovery, she told her therapist that all the interpretations during the first few weeks in the hospital meant very little to her. But after the "midnight rescue mission" it was clear, even to her, how concerned and sincere her therapist had been from the beginning. (p. 271)

ASSESSING SUICIDAL RISK

Clinicians may find the following 22 factors useful in assessing suicidal risk. Four qualifications are important. First, the comments concerning each factor are extremely general, and exceptions are frequent. In many instances, two or more factors may interact. For example, being married and being younger, taken as individual factors, tend to be associated with lower risk for suicide. However, married teenagers have historically shown an extremely high suicide rate (Peck & Seiden, 1975). Second, the figures are not static. New research alters our understanding of the data as well as reflects apparent changes. The suicide rate for women, for example, has been increasing, bringing it closer to that for men. Third, the list is far from comprehensive. Fourth, these factors may be useful as general guidelines but cannot be applied in an unthinking, mechanical, conclusive manner. A given individual may rank in the lowest-risk category of each of these factors and still commit suicide. These factors serve as aids to and not substitutes for a comprehensive, humane, and personal evaluation of a unique person's suicidal risk. Again it is worth emphasizing a central theme of this book's approach to ethics: perhaps the most frequent threat to ethical behavior is the therapist's inattention. Making certain that we consider such factors with each patient can help us prevent the ethical lapses that come from neglect.

1. *Direct verbal warning.* A direct statement of intention to commit suicide is one of the most useful single predictors. Take any such statement seriously. Resist the temptation to reflexively dismiss such warnings as "a hysterical bid for attention," "a borderline manipulation," "a clear expression of negative transference," "an attempt to provoke the therapist," or "yet another grab for power in the interpersonal struggle with the therapist." It may be any or all of those and yet still foreshadow suicide.

2. *Plan.* The presence of a plan increases the risk. The more specific, detailed, lethal, and feasible the plan is, the greater the risk posed.

3. *Past attempts.* Most, and perhaps 80% of, completed suicides were preceded by a prior attempt. Schneidman (1975; see also Wong, Stewart, & Claassen, 2008) found that the client group with the greatest suicidal rate were those who had entered into treatment with a history of at least one attempt.

4. *Indirect statements and behavioral signs.* People planning to end their lives may communicate their intent indirectly through their words and actions—for example, talking about "going away," speculating on what death would be like, giving away their most valued possessions, or acquiring lethal instruments.

5. *Depression.* The suicide rate for those with clinical depression is about 20 times greater than for the general population. Guze and Robins (1970; see also Vuorilehto, Melartin, & Isometsa, 2006), in a review of seventeen studies concerning death in primary affective disorder, found that 15% of the individuals suffering from this disorder killed themselves. Effectively treating depression may lower the risk of suicide (Gibbons, Hur, Bhaumik, & Mann, 2005; Mann, 2005).

6. *Hopelessness.* The sense of hopelessness appears to be more closely associated with suicidal intent than any other aspect of depression (Beck, 1990; Beck, Kovaks, & Weissman, 1975; Maris, 2002; Petrie & Chamberlain, 1983; Wetzel, 1976; however, see also Nimeus, Traskman-Bendz, & Alsen, 1997).

7. *Intoxication.* Between one-fourth and one-third of all suicides are linked to alcohol as a contributing factor; a much higher percentage may be associated with the presence of alcohol (without clear indication of its contribution to the suicidal process and lethal outcome). Moscicki (2001; see also Buri, Von Bonin, Strik, et al., 2009; Crosby et al., 2009; Kõlves, Värnik, Tooding, & Wasserman, 2006; Sher, 2006; Sher et al., 2009) notes that perhaps as many as half of those who kill themselves are intoxicated at the time. Darke, Duflou, and Torok (2009) found that

> [a]lcohol was more common where a suicide note was left and where relationship problems were involved. Pharmaceuticals were more common where a previous attempt was noted. Licit and illicit substances are

strongly associated with suicide, even when the method does not involve drug overdose. (p. 490)

Hendin, Haas, Maltsberger, Koestner, and Szanto's study, "Problems in Psychotherapy with Suicidal Patients" (2006), emphasized that "addressing and treating suicidal patients' substance abuse, particularly alcohol abuse, is critical in effective treatment of other problems, including lack of response to antidepressant medication" (p. 71; see also Zhang, Conner, & Phillips, 2010).

8. *Marital separation (distinct from divorce).* Wyder, Ward, and De Leo (2009) found that "[f]or both males and females separation created a risk of suicide at least four times higher than any other marital status. The risk was particularly high for males aged 15 to 24 . . ." (p. 208).

9. *Clinical syndromes.* People suffering from depression or alcoholism are at much higher risk for suicide. Other clinical syndromes may also be associated with an increased risk. Perhaps as many as 90% of those who take their own lives have a diagnosis from the *Diagnostic and Statistical Manual of Mental Disorders* (American Psychiatric Association, 1994; Moscicki, 2001). Kramer, Pollack, Redick, and Locke (1972) found that the highest suicide rates exist among clients diagnosed as having primary mood disorders and psychoneuroses, with high rates also among those having organic brain syndrome and schizophrenia (see also Draper, Peisah, Snowdon, & Brokaty, 2010; Novick, Schwartz, & Frank, 2010). Palmer, Pankratz, and Bostwick (2005; see also Brenner, Homaifar, Adler, et al., 2009; Loas et al., 2009; Pretti, Meneghelli, & Cocchi, 2009) found that the lifetime risk for suicide among people with schizophrenia was around 5%. Drake, Gates, Cotton, and Whitaker (1984) discovered that those suffering from schizophrenia who had very high internalized standards were at particularly high risk. In a long-term study, Tsuang (1983) found that the suicide rate among the first-degree relatives of schizophrenic and manic-depressive clients was significantly higher than that for a control group of relatives of surgery patients; furthermore, relatives of clients who had committed suicide showed a higher rate than relatives of clients who did not take their lives. Using meta-analytic techniques, Harris and Barraclough (1997) obtained results suggesting that "virtually all mental disorders have an increased risk of suicide excepting mental retardation and dementia. The suicide risk is highest for functional and lowest for organic disorders" (p. 205; see also Chan et al., 2009).

10. *Sex.* The suicide rate for men is more than three times that for women (CDC, 2010; see also Joiner, 2005, 2010). For youths, the rate is closer to five to one (see Safer, 1997). The rate of suicide attempts for women is about three times that for men.

11. *Age.* A significant change occurred relatively recently in this category. The prior three editions of this book had noted that the risk for suicide tended to increase over the adult life cycle. However, more recently suicide has peaked in middle age: "The highest rates of suicide by age group occurred among persons aged 45–54 years, 75–84 years, and 35–44 years (17.6, 16.4, and 16.3 per 100,000 population, respectively" (CDC, 2010, p. 9). Suicide risk assessment differs also according to whether the client is an adult or a minor. The assessment of suicidal risk among minors presents special challenges. Safer's review of the literature indicated that the "frequent practice of combining adult and adolescent suicide and suicide behavior findings can result in misleading conclusions" (1997, p. 61). Zametkin, Alter, and Yemini (2001) note that the

> rate of suicide among adolescents has significantly increased in the past 30 years. In 1998, 4153 young people aged 15 to 24 years committed suicide in the United States, an average of 11.3 deaths per day. Suicide is the third leading cause of death in this age group and accounts for 13.5% of all deaths.... Children younger than 10 years are less likely to complete suicide, and the risk appears to increase gradually in children between 10 and 12 years of age. However, on average, 170 children 10 years or younger commit suicide each year. (p. 3122)

12. *Race.* Generally in the United States, Caucasians tend to have one of the highest suicide rates (CDC, 2010). Gibbs (1997) discusses the apparent cultural paradox: "African-American suicide rates have traditionally been lower than White rates despite a legacy of racial discrimination, persistent poverty, social isolation, and lack of community resources" (p. 68). EchoHawk (1997) notes that the suicide rate for Native Americans is "greater than that of any other ethnic group in the U.S., especially in the age range of 15–24 years" (p. 60).

13. *Religion.* The suicide rates among Protestants tend to be higher than those among Jews and Catholics.

14. *Living alone.* The risk of suicide tends to be reduced if someone is not living alone, reduced even more if he or she is living with a spouse, and reduced even further if there are children.

15. *Bereavement.* Brunch, Barraclough, Nelson, and Sainsbury (1971) found that 50% of those in their sample who had committed suicide had lost their mothers within the past three years (compared with a 20% rate among controls matched for age, sex, marital status, and geographical location). Furthermore, 22% of the suicides, compared with only 9% of the controls, had experienced the loss of their father within the past five years. Krupnick's review of studies (1984) revealed "a link between childhood bereavement and suicide attempts in adult life," perhaps doubling the risk for depressives who had lost a parent compared to

depressives who had not experienced the death of a parent. Klerman and Clayton (1984; see also Beutler, 1985) found that suicide rates are higher among the widowed than the married (especially among elderly men) and that among women, the suicide rate is not as high for widows as for the divorced or separated.

16. *Unemployment.* Unemployment tends to increase the risk for suicide.

17. *Health status.* Illness and somatic complaints are associated with increased suicidal risk, as are disturbances in patterns of sleeping and eating. Clinicians who are helping people with AIDS, for example, need to be sensitive to this risk (Pope & Morin, 1990).

18. *Impulsivity.* Those with poor impulse control are at increased risk for taking their own lives (Patsiokas, Clum, & Luscumb, 1979; see also Maloney et al., 2009; Wu et al., 2009).

19. *Rigid thinking.* Suicidal individuals often display a rigid, all-or-none way of thinking (Maris, 2002; Neuringer, 1964). A typical statement might be, "If I can't find a job by the end of the month, the only real alternative is suicide."

20. *Stressful events.* Excessive numbers of undesirable events with negative outcomes have been associated with increased suicidal risk (Cohen-Sandler, Berman, & King, 1982; Isherwood, Adam, & Homblow, 1982). Bagley, Bolitho, and Bertrand (1997), in a study of 1,025 adolescent women in grades 7 to 12, found that "15% of 38 women who experienced frequent, unwanted sexual touching had 'often' made suicidal gestures or attempts in the previous 6 months, compared with 2% of 824 women with no experience of sexual assault" (p. 341; see also McCauley et al., 1997). Some types of recent events may place clients at extremely high risk. For example, Ellis, Atkeson, and Calhoun (1982) found that 52% of their sample of multiple-incident victims of sexual assault had attempted suicide.

21. *Release from hospitalization.* Beck (1967, p. 57) has noted that "the available figures clearly indicate that the suicidal risk is greatest during weekend leaves from the hospital and shortly after discharge." Hunt and colleagues' study of "Suicide in Recently Discharged Psychiatric Patients: A Case-control Study" found that the

> weeks after discharge ... represent a critical period for suicide risk. Measures that could reduce risk include intensive and early community follow-up. Assessment of risk should include established risk factors as well as current mental state and there should be clear follow-up procedures for those who have self-discharged. (p. 443)

Francis (2009) points out the relationship between suicidal risk and release from hospitalization may be complex when borderline personality disorder is at issue:

People with borderline personality disorder (BPD) are sometimes admitted to inpatient wards due to risk to themselves. However, recent research indicates inpatient settings are detrimental to BPD and can worsen symptoms (unless they are planned short stays). Staff are often too fearful ... to release them if they are still expressing suicidal thoughts. If the presentation is not different (no major crises have occurred, no major losses made) then clinically indicated risk-taking is the recommended course of action. (p. 253)

22. Lack of a sense of belonging. Joiner's review of the research and his own studies led him to conclude that

an unmet need to belong is a contributor to suicidal desire: suicidal individuals may experience interactions that do not satisfy their need to belong (e.g., relationships that are unpleasant, unstable, infrequent, or without proximity) or may not feel connected to others and cared about. (2005, p. 97)

Appelbaum and Gutheil (2007) focus on the risk factor of

personal isolation, which can derive from a number of sources (for example, immigrants who have not found a local community, those who are retired or unemployed, those living alone, even those living in transient or disorganized areas such as resort towns whose populations fluctuate wildly on a seasonal basis). (p. 52)

SPECIAL CONSIDERATIONS

The risk of client suicide creates a special set of responsibilities. The themes stressed throughout this book gain exceptional importance: failure of the therapist to take necessary steps can literally be fatal for the patient. The following steps, which extend or supplement this book's themes, may be helpful in identifying and coping with the chance that a patient may be at risk for suicide:

- *Screen all clients/patients for suicidal risk during initial contact, and remain alert to this issue throughout the therapy.* Even clients/patients who are seriously thinking of taking their own life may not present the classic picture of agitated depression or openly grim determination that is stereotypically (and sometimes falsely) portrayed as characteristic of the suicidal individual. Some suicidal clients/patients seem, during initial sessions, calm, composed, and concerned with a seemingly minor presenting problem. Clients/patients who are not suicidal during initial sessions and who started therapy for a minor problem may become suicidal. The rise in suicidal risk may be caused by external events, such as the loss of a job or a loved one, or to internal events, such as setting aside psychological defenses or the start of Alzheimer's disease. What is crucial is an assessment of the patient's suicidal potential at adequate intervals. In some cases, comprehensive psycho-logical testing or the use of standardized scales developed to evaluate suicidal risk may be useful (see, for example, Beck, Resnick, & Lettieri, 1974; Butcher, Graham, Williams, & Ben-Porath, 1990; Lettieri, 1982; Neuringer, 1974; Nugent, 2006; Schulyer, 1974; Weisman & Worden, 1972). Range and Knott (1997) evaluated 20 suicide assessment instruments for validity and reliability. On the basis of their analysis, they recommended three most highly: Beck's Scale for Suicide Ide-ation series, Linehan's Reasons for Living Inventory, and Cole's self-administered adaptation of Linehan's structured interview called the Suicidal Behaviors Questionnaire.

- *Work with the client to arrange an environment that will not offer easy access to whatever the patient might use to commit suicide.* Suicidal cli-ents who have purchased a gun may agree to place it where they will not have access to it until the crisis is over. Suicidal clients who are cur-rently taking psychotropic or other medication may be planning an overdose. The use of materials prescribed by and associated with men-tal health professionals may have great symbolic meaning for the patient. Arrange that the patient does not have access to enough medi-cation at one time to carry out a suicidal plan. In a study of the relation-ship between diagnosis and means in completed suicide, Huisman, van Houwelingen, and Kerkhof (2009) found:

> Possible means of suicide prevention suggested by this study include limit-ing access to tall buildings or structures to patients with psychotic disorders; careful prescription of medication to female patients and particularly to patients with substance-related disorders; and limiting easy access to rail-ways near clinical settings to patients with bipolar and psychotic disorders. Limiting access to means of suicide may be less effective for suicidal patients with depressive disorders who may switch to other available methods.

- *Work with the patient to create an actively supportive environment.* To what extent can family, friends, and other resources such as community agencies and group or family therapy help a suicidal person through a crisis?
- *While not denying or minimizing the patient's problems and desire to die, also recognize and work with the patient's strengths and desire to live.* Patients' awareness of their strengths, resilience, and reasons to live can often help them regain perspective, often lost during despair.
- *Make every effort to communicate realistic hope.* Discuss practical approaches to the patient's problems.
- *Explore any fantasies the client may have regarding suicide.* Reevaluating unrealistic beliefs about what suicide will and will not accomplish can be an important step for clients attempting to remain alive.

- *Make sure communications are clear, and assess the probable impact of any interventions.* Ambiguous or confusing messages are unlikely to be helpful and can cause considerable harm. The literature documents the hazards of using such techniques as paradoxical intention with suicidal clients. Even well-meant and apparently clear messages may go awry in the stress of crisis. Beck (1967, p. 53) provides an example:

  > One woman, who was convinced by her therapist that her children needed her even though she believed herself worthless, decided to kill them as well as herself to 'spare them the agony of growing up without a mother.' She subsequently followed through with her plan.

- *When considering hospitalization as an option, explore the drawbacks as fully as the benefits, the probable long-term and the immediate effects of this intervention.* Norman Farberow (see Colt, 1983, p. 58), cofounder and former codirector and chief of research at the Los Angeles Suicide Prevention Center, warns: "We tend to think we've solved the problem by getting the person into the hospital, but psychiatric hospitals have a suicide rate more than 35 percent greater than in the community."

- *Be sensitive to negative reactions to the patient's behavior.* James Chu (quoted by Colt, 1983, p. 56), a psychiatrist in charge of Codman House at McLean Hospital, a psychiatric hospital near Boston, comments:

  > When you deal with suicidal people day after day after day, you just get plain tired. You get to the point of feeling, "All right, get it over with." The potential for fatigue, boredom, and negative transference is so great that we must remain constantly alert for signs that we are beginning to experience them. Maltsberger and Buie discuss therapists' repression of such feelings. A therapist may glance often at his watch, feel drowsy, or daydream—or rationalize referral, premature termination, or hospitalization just to be rid of the patient. (Many studies have detailed the unintentional abandonment of suicidal patients; in a 1967 review of 32 suicides ... Bloom found "each ... was preceded by rejecting behavior by the therapist.") Sometimes, in frustration, a therapist will issue an ultimatum. Maltsberger recalls one who, treating a chronic wrist-cutter, just couldn't stand it, and finally she said, "If you don't stop that I'll stop treatment." The patient did it again. She stopped treatment and the patient killed herself.
  >
  > (*Colt, 1983, p.57*)

- *Perhaps most important, communicate caring.* Therapists differ in how they attempt to express this caring. A therapist (cited by Colt, 1983, p. 60) recounts an influential event early in her career:

  > I had a slasher my first year in the hospital. She kept cutting herself to rib-bons—with glass, wire, anything she could get her hands on. Nobody

could stop her. The nurses were getting very angry.... I didn't know what to do, but I was getting very upset. So I went to the director, and in my best Harvard Medical School manner began in a very intellectual way to describe the case. To my horror, I couldn't go on, and I began to weep. I couldn't stop. He said, "I think if you showed the patient what you showed me, I think she'd know you cared." So I did. I told her that I cared, and that it was distressing to me. She stopped. It was an important lesson.

Relatively unusual and rare interventions such as home visits, long and frequent sessions, therapist's late-night search for a runaway patient, and other special measures already noted are ways some therapists have found useful to communicate this caring, although such approaches obviously do not fit all therapists, all patients, all theoretical orientations, or all situations. Some ethics committee and licensing board members may be concerned about these strategies. However, these strategies may be options on occasion. One of the most basic aspects of this communication of caring is the therapist's willingness to listen, to take seriously what the patient has to say. Farberow (1985, p. C9) puts it well:

If the person is really trying to communicate how unhappy he is, or his particular problems, then you can recognize that one of the most important things is to be able to hear his message. You'd want to say, "Yes, I hear you. Yes, I recognize that this is a really tough situation. I'll be glad to listen. If I can't do anything, then we'll find someone who can."

AVOIDABLE PITFALLS: ADVICE FROM EXPERTS

A central theme of this book is that inattention or a lack of awareness is a frequent cause violating clinical responsibilities and patient trust. We asked prominent therapists with expertise in identifying and responding to suicidal risk to discuss factors that contribute to therapists' inattention or lack of awareness when working with potentially suicidal patients. Careful attention to these factors can help therapists to practice more responsively and responsibly.

Norman Farberow, PhD, cofounder and former codirector and chief of research at the Los Angeles Suicide Prevention Center, believes that there are four main problem areas. First, therapists tend to feel uncomfortable with the subject; they find it difficult to explore and investigate suicidal risk: "We don't want to hear about it. We discount it. But any indication of risk or intention must be addressed." Second, we must appreciate that each client is a unique person: "Each person becomes suicidal in his or her own framework. The person's point of view is crucial." Third, we tend to forget the preventive factors: "Clinicians run scared at the thought of suicide. They fail to recognize the true resources." Fourth, we fail to consult: "Outside opinion is invaluable."

Marsha Linehan, PhD, ABPP, is a professor of psychology, adjunct professor of psychiatry and behavioral sciences at the University of Washington and director of the Behavioral Research and Therapy Clinic. Her primary research is the development of effective treatments for suicidal behaviors, drug abuse, and borderline personality disorder. She believes that

> the single biggest problem in treating suicidal clients is that most therapists have inadequate training and experience in the assessment and treatment of suicidal behaviors. More distressing than that is that there does not appear to be a hue and cry from practicing therapists demanding such training. Deciding to limit one's practice to non-suicidal clients is not a solution because individuals can and do become suicidal after entering treatment. Secondary problems are as follows. (1) Therapists treating clients with disorders that make them high risk for suicide (e.g., depression, borderline personality disorder, bipolar disorder) do not ask about suicide ideation and planning in a routine, frequent way: depending on clients who have decided to kill themselves to first communicate risk directly or indirectly can be a fatal mistake. (2) Fears of legal liability often cloud therapists' abilities to focus on the welfare of the client: fear interferes with good clinical judgment. Many outpatient therapists simply "dump" their suicidal clients onto emergency and inpatient facilities believing that this will absolve them of risk. There is no empirical data that emergency department and/or inpatient treatment reduces suicide risk in the slightest and the available literature could support a hypothesis that it may instead increase suicide risk. (3) Therapists often do not realize that when treating a highly suicidal client they must be available by phone and otherwise after hours: treating a highly suicidal client requires personally involved clinical care.

Nadine J. Kaslow, PhD, ABPP, professor and chief psychologist at Emory School of Medicine, a well-funded researcher on the assessment and treatment of abused and suicidal African American women and the recipient of the American Psychological Association's 2004 award for Distinguished Contributions to Education and Training, told us that

> assessment and intervention of suicidal persons need to be culturally competent, gender sensitive, and developmentally informed. Our approach to suicidal individuals needs to consider both the relevant evidence base and sensitive attention to the person's unique struggles, strengths, and sociocultural context. We need to interact with suicidal people with compassion and a desire to understand why their pain feels so intolerable that they believe that suicide will offer the only form of relief. It is always important to take suicidal concerns seriously, convey an appreciation for the person's plight, and engage in a collaborative process. Since suicidal people often feel socially isolated and social support is a buffer against suicidal behavior, it is imperative that we assist suicidal men and women in mobilizing their social support networks. We must build on people's strengths, help them find meaning and

hope, and empower them to overcome the trials and tribulations that lead them to feel and think that life is not worth living. As therapists, we will find our own countertransference reactions to be a very useful guide with regard to risk assessment, disposition planning, and the implementation of therapeutic strategies. Our own histories with suicide, whether that be our own suicidality, the loss of a loved one to suicide, or the death of a former patient to suicide, will greatly impact how we approach and respond to people who think actively about suicide, take steps to end their own life, or actually kill themselves. Our histories and reactions can also be instrumental in our efforts to help suicidal people heal from their pain so that they find life worth living. This in turn, enriches our own lives.

Ricardo F. Muñoz, PhD, is professor of psychology at the University of California, San Francisco, and principal investigator on the Depression Prevention Research Project involving English-, Spanish-, and Chinese-speaking populations, funded by the National Institute of Mental Health. Here are his thoughts:

> First, clinicians often fail to identify what suicidal clients have that they care about, that they are responsible for, that they can live for. Include animals, campaigns, projects, religious values. Second, inexperienced liberal therapists in particular may fall into the trap of attempting to work out their philosophy regarding the right to die and the rationality or reasonableness of suicide while they are working with a client who is at critical risk. These issues demand careful consideration, but postponing them until the heat of crisis benefits no one. In the same way that we try to convince clients that the darkest hour of a severe depressive episode is not a good time to decide whether to live or die, clinicians must accept that while attempting to keep a seriously suicidal person alive is not a good time to decide complex philosophical questions. Third, don't overestimate your ability to speak someone else's language. Recently, a Spanish-speaking woman, suicidal, came to the emergency room talking of pills. The physician, who spoke limited Spanish, obtained what he thought was her promise not to attempt suicide and sent her back to her halfway house. It was later discovered that she'd been saying that she'd already taken a lethal dose of pills and was trying to get help.

Jessica Henderson Daniel, PhD, ABPP, director of training in psychology in the Department of Psychiatry and associate director of the Leadership Education in Adolescent Health Training Program in the Division of Adolescent Medicine at Boston's Children's Hospital, told us:

> As some adolescents can be prone to be dramatic, that is, saying things that they do not mean, there can be a reluctance to take comments about suicide seriously. The adolescent may make several statements before actually engaging in suicidal behavior. The adolescent needs to know that such comments are in fact taken seriously and that action may be taken: follow-up by their therapist, evaluation in the emergency room, and/or in-patient

hospitalization. Also, adolescents can become very upset about matters that may seem trivial to adults. Providers are reminded that the perspective of the patient trumps their views. When adolescents are in the midst of despair, minimizing the worry, hurt, and hopelessness can be problematic. Some providers may feel that life really cannot be that bad. Then, parents matter. With adolescents, state regulations can determine the legal role of parents. It is important to know this information. Should parents be legally responsible for their adolescent, providers may be reluctant to override the decision of parents who cannot bear to think that their child may be suicidal and who insist on taking them home. When the patient is a child or an adolescent, the parents are a critical part of the management of the case and may need their own providers as well. Finally, consultation is critical in thinking through how to best provide under the particular circumstances.

Danny Brom, PhD, is Director of the Israel Center for the Treatment of Psychotrauma of Herzog Hospital in Jerusalem (www.traumweb.org) and Professor at the Paul Baerwald School of Social Work and Social Welfare of Hebrew University. The mission of his community based trauma center is to develop and test new methods of intervention for mitigating the effects of trauma on children and adults. His latest book, with Pat-Horenczyk and Ford, is *Treating Traumatized Children: Risk, Resilience and Recovery* (Routledge, 2009). He told us:

> The client that taught me this lesson had been abused in ways that I had not heard about before and have rarely heard about after. Tortured, abused, made totally dependent and helpless. She suffered from DID. During the course of a long therapy she would become suicidal. When we discussed suicidality, I wanted to have a clear understanding with her that she would call me first if she would feel that she was going commit suicide. She then made it very clear to me that suicide for her had been and still was her only access to real freedom. If I would take that away from her or block that way by insisting on a contract, she felt that then she really would have to commit suicide. The freedom to commit suicide gave her the freedom to live.

M. David Rudd, PhD, ABPP, is Dean of the College of Social and Behavioral Science at the University of Utah; past president of the American Association of Suicidology; and president elect of APA, Division 12, Section VII (Behavioral Emergencies), and current board member of Division 12, Society of Clinical Psychology. He told us:

> One of the all-too-frequently neglected areas in suicide risk assessment is recognizing, discussing, and implementing a distinction between acute and chronic risk. Assessment of acute risk alone is how the overwhelming majority of clinicians approach the task. Over the past decade, converging scientific evidence suggests it is important to address enduring or "chronic" suicidality in patients. More specifically, those who have made two or more suicide attempts likely

have a "chronic" aspect to their presentation. Although acute risk may well resolve, it is important for the clinician to make a note about the individual's enduring vulnerabilities and continuing suicide risk. It's as straightforward as making a note such as: "Although acute risk has resolved, the patient has made three previous suicide attempts and there are aspects of the clinical scenario that suggest chronic risk for suicide. More specifically, the patient's history of previous sexual abuse, episodic alcohol and cannabis abuse, along with two previous major depressive episodes, all indicate the need for longer-term and continuing care in order to more effectively treat these chronic markers of risk."

David H. Barlow, PhD, is a diplomate in clinical psychology and director of the Center for Anxiety and Related Disorders at Boston University. He is former president of the Society of Clinical Psychology of APA and maintains a private practice. He believes that there are two common problems often encountered in working with young or inexperienced therapists confronting a possible suicidal patient:

> First, after forming an alliance with a new patient, some therapists begin to spin away from a professional, objective clinical stance and treat seemingly offhand comments about not wanting to live as casual conversation that might be occurring after work over a drink with a friend or in a college dormitory. Thus, they may respond sympathetically but not professionally by downplaying the report: "Sometimes I feel that way too—I can understand how you'd get to that place." Of course, one must always step back if this comes up and conduct the proper exam for intent, means, etc., and take appropriate action. Second, some therapists undervalue the power of a contract, since patients sometimes say something like, "Well … I'll say that if you want me to, but I don't know if my word is worth anything." The fact is, in the context of a good therapeutic relationship, the contract is very powerful, the occasional report to the contrary notwithstanding.

Rosa E. Garcia-Peltoniemi, **PhD**, is Staff Clinical Psychologist and Senior Consulting Clinician at the Center for Victims of Torture. For the past 22 years she has been at the forefront of developing clinical services for refugees and asylum seekers who have suffered torture at the hands of foreign government both in the U.S. and internationally. Here is what she states regarding specific issues in treating survivors of torture in this country:

> For torture survivor clients trying to obtain asylum in the U.S., adverse decisions carrying the risk of deportation to the very countries in which they were tortured are frequently times of increased suicidal risk. The prospect of being sent back becomes not only very frightening but also an intolerable repetition of a past that was already extremely costly to escape. It is not unusual for torture survivors in these situations to say that they would rather die by their own means than return to their countries and be tortured again. Even less drastic

immigration outcomes such as being put on an ankle brace electronic monitor, a practice that has become increasingly common, can carry an increased risk of suicide for torture survivors. Diagnoses of illnesses perceived as terminal or to bring shame (e.g. HIV/AIDS) are also triggers for suicidal ideation in torture survivors; chronic, debilitating illnesses preventing the survivor from taking care of important obligations such as providing or caring for family members often lead to suicidal thinking based on the belief that loved ones would not be burdened, would be better off, happy, etc., following their deaths. Interpersonal losses, particularly the death of parents and children left behind in the country of origin, but also through divorce or abandonment, also tend to be triggers for suicidal risk amongst torture survivors. Many survivors from various different cultures have stated that they don't talk about problems unless they are asked; to talk about suicide carries an even higher burden due to cultural proscriptions for some or simply because of the belief that the rest of the community is also suffering in various different ways. Finding ways to give survivors permission to say how they are feeling then becomes extremely important for clinicians and includes knowing culturally sensitive ways to ask about suicidal ideation. Consultation with knowledgeable cultural providers is a must. Finally, it is important to keep in mind that many torture survivors have suffered traumatic brain injury which may lead to less predictable responses to psychiatric medications, increased risk for adverse outcomes, and an overall requirement of close collaboration across disciplines.

The late **Erika Fromm**, PhD, a diplomate in both clinical psychology and clinical hypnosis, was professor emeritus of psychology at the University of Chicago, clinical editor of the *Journal of Clinical and Experimental Hypnosis*, and recipient of the American Psychological Association Division 39 (Psychoanalysis) 1985 Award for Distinguished Contributions to the Field. She stated:

> Perhaps it's the countertransference or the highly stressful nature of this work, but some clinicians seem reluctant to provide suicidal patients anything more than minimal reassurance. We need to realize that the people who are about to take their own lives are crying out, are communicating their feelings that no one really cares about them. They are crying, in the only way they know how: "Show me that you really care!" It is so important for us to communicate that we care about them. When my patients are suicidal, I tell them that I care deeply about them and am fond of them. I do everything I can to let them know this.

Gary Schoener, clinical psychologist and executive director of the Walk-In Counseling Center in Minneapolis for more than 33 years, consults, trains, and testifies around North America concerning professional boundaries and clinical supervision. He states:

> Four most common deadly failures are (1) the failure to screen for the possession of firearms (it's not enough to ask about "weapons") with all distressed

clients; (2) when acute suicidality becomes chronic, failure to appropriately refer to a DBT [dialectic behavior therapy] program or qualified provider for cases of chronic suicidality; (3) reliance on the QPR [question, persuade, refer] method with refugees and others, especially Muslims, for whom suicide is a serious sin and who should not be asked directly about suicidal thinking; and (4) overreliance on "no-suicide agreements" despite the fact that they do not work. (No problem in using them clinically, but don't count on them.)

Marla C. Craig, PhD, is psychologist and clinical director at the University of Texas Counseling and Mental Health Center in Austin, Texas, She has previously worked as instructor and coordinator of a campus-wide suicide prevention program at St. Edward's University. She reported:

> Most clinicians may not know that suicide is the second leading cause of death among college students. This information is important since there may be a tendency for clinicians not to take college students' presenting concerns seriously enough. Presenting concerns such as academic and relationship difficulties may mask the underlying condition of depression. Also, stereotypes of college students' being overly dramatic and emotional with fluctuating moods and situations can interfere with a clinician's judgment to thoroughly assess for suicide. It also may be easy for clinicians to forget that traditional college students are still adolescents transitioning into young adulthood, and they may or may not be able to verbally identify what is going on internally/ emotionally. Hence, it is important to assess for suicide even if the college student does not present as depressed. Finally, due to confidentiality and college students being eighteen years of age and older, clinicians may be reluctant to get parents involved. If the parents are a source of support, do not hesitate to work with the college student to get them involved.

Jesse Geller, PhD, formerly director of the Yale University Psychological Services Clinic and director of the Psychotherapy Division of the Connecticut Mental Health Center, currently maintains an independent practice. He told us:

> One of the two main problems in treating suicidal patients is our own anger and defensiveness when confronted by someone who does not respond positively—and perhaps appreciatively—to our therapeutic efforts. It can stir up very primitive and childish feelings in us—we can start to feel vengeful, withholding, and spiteful. The key is to become aware of these potential reactions and not to act them out in our relationship with the patient. The other main problem seems to be more prevalent among beginning therapists. When we are inexperienced, we may be very cowardly regarding the mention of suicide in our initial interviews. We passively wait for the patient to raise the subject and we may unconsciously communicate that the subject is "taboo." If the subject does come up, we avoid using "hot" language such as "murder yourself "or "blow your brains out." Our avoidance of clear and

direct communication, our clinging to euphemisms implies to the patient that we are unable to cope with his or her destructive impulses.

Danny Wedding, PhD, MPH, is a Professor of Psychology and Associate Dean for Management and International Programs at the California School of Professional Psychology at Alliant International University. Danny has completed Fulbright Fellowships in Thailand and Korea, and he has lectured widely on suicide prevention. He is especially concerned about the growing problem of adolescent suicide in Asian countries. He notes

> Suicide is a serious public health problem, and about a million people die by suicide each year—more than are lost to either homicide or war. Prevalence, methods, and risk factors vary widely across cultures and ethnic groups, and clinicians need to be sensitive to these cultural differences. For example, suicide by pesticide poisoning is common in China and Sri Lanka but rare in Thailand, and suicide rates among American Indian/Alaskan Native adolescents and young adults in the United States are about twice the national average. However, there are also commonalities across cultures—e.g., we know that glamorized media portrayal of suicide can lead to a contagion effect in almost every country. The growing access to the internet found in almost all developing countries poses special challenges (especially cyber bullying) for those of us interested in suicide prevention. Some of the techniques that have been shown to be effective in preventing youth suicide in other countries include screening, gatekeeper training, crisis hotlines, media education and skills training.

Don Hiroto, PhD, maintains a private practice, is chief of the Depression Research Laboratory at the Brentwood Veterans Administration Medical Center, and is a former president of the Los Angeles Society of Clinical Psychologists. He believes that a major area of difficulty involves alcohol use:

> Alcoholics may constitute the highest-risk group for violent death. The potential for suicide among alcoholics is extraordinarily high. At least 85 percent of completed suicides show the presence of at least some level of alcohol in their blood. There are two aspects to the problem for the clinician. First, there is the tendency for us to deny or minimize alcohol consumption as an issue when we assess all of our clients. Second, we are not sufficiently alert to the suicidal risk factors that are especially associated with alcoholics: episodic drinking, impulsivity, increased stress in relationships (especially separation), alienation, and the sense of helplessness.

The late **Helen Block Lewis**, PhD, was a diplomate in clinical psychology who maintained a private practice in New York and Connecticut; she also was professor emeritus at Yale University, president of the American Psychological Association Division of Psychoanalysis, and editor of *Psychoanalytic*

Psychology. She believed that therapists tend to pay insufficient attention to the shame and guilt their clients experience. For example, clients may experience a sense of shame for needing psychotherapy and for being "needy" in regard to the therapist. The shame often leads to rage, which in turn leads to guilt because the client is not sure if the rage is justified. According to Lewis, the resultant "shame/rage" or "humiliated fury" can be a major factor in client suicides:

> Clients may experience this progression of shame-rage-guilt in many aspects of their lives. It is important for the therapist to help the client understand the sequence not only as it might be related to a current incident "out there" but also as it occurs in the session. Furthermore, it is helpful for clients who are in a frenzied suicidal state to understand that the experience of shame and guilt may represent their attempt to maintain attachments to important people in their lives. Understanding these sequences is important not only for the client but also for the therapist. It is essential that we maintain good feelings for our clients. Sometimes this is difficult when the client is furious, suicidal, and acting out. Our understanding that such feelings and behaviors by a client represent desperate attempts to maintain a connection can help us as therapists to function effectively and remain in touch with our genuine caring for the client.

Michael Peck, PhD, a diplomate in clinical psychology, maintains a private practice and was a consultant to the Los Angeles Suicide Prevention Center. He observes,

> Many therapists fail to consult. Call an experienced clinician or an organization like the L.A. Suicide Prevention Center. Review the situation and get an outside opinion. Therapists may also let a client's improvement (for example, returning to school or work) lull them to sleep. Don't assume that if the mood is brighter, then the suicidal risk is gone.

He stresses the importance of keeping adequate notes, including at least the symptoms, the clinician's response, and consultations and inquiries.

> There are special issues in treating adolescents," Peck adds. "When they're under sixteen, keep the parents informed. If they are seventeen (when the client, rather than the parents, possesses the privilege) or older but still living with the parents, tell the client that you will breach confidentiality only to save his or her life. In almost every case, the family's cooperation in treatment is of great importance.

The late **Hans Strupp**, PhD, a diplomate in clinical psychology, is distinguished professor of psychology and director of clinical training at Vanderbilt University. He believed that one of the greatest pitfalls is the failure to assess suicidal potential comprehensively during initial sessions. Another frequent error, he said, is that there too often is a failure to have in place a network of services appropriate for suicidal clients in crisis:

> Whether it is an individual private practitioner, a training program run by a university, a small clinic, or [therapists] associated in group practice—there needs to be close and effective collaboration with other mental health professions ... and with facilities equipped to deal with suicidal emergencies. I'm not talking about pro forma arrangements but a genuine and effective working relationship. In all cases involving suicidal risk, there should be frequent consultation and ready access to appropriate hospitals.

SCENARIOS FOR DISCUSSION

You have been working with a moderately depressed client for four months. You feel that you have a good rapport, but the treatment plan does not seem to be doing much good. Between sessions, you check your answering machine and find this message from the patient: "I want to thank you for trying to help me, but now I realize that nothing will do me any good. I won't be seeing you or anyone else ever again. I've left home and won't be returning. I didn't leave any notes because there really isn't anything to say. Thank you again for trying to help. Good-bye." Your next patient is scheduled to see you in two minutes, and you have patients scheduled for the next four hours.

- What feelings do you experience?
- What do you want to do?
- What are your options?
- What do you think you would do?
- If there are things that you want to do but don't do, why do you reject these options?
- What do you believe that your ethical and legal obligations are? Are there any contradictions between your legal responsibilities and constraints and what you believe is ethical?
- To what extent do you believe that your education and training have prepared you to deal with this situation?

■ ■ ■

(continued)

(continued)

You have been working with a patient within a managed care framework. You believe that the patient is at considerable risk for suicide. The case reviewer disagrees and, noting that the approved number of sessions have been provided, declines, despite your persistent protests, to approve any additional sessions.

- How do you feel?
- What are your options?
- What do you believe your legal obligations to client are?
- What do you believe your ethical responsibilities to the client are?
- What would you do?

■ ■ ■

You have been providing family therapy to a mother and father and their three adolescents for four sessions. After the fourth session, you find that one of the adolescents has left a note on your desk. Here is what the note says: "My father has molested me for the past two years. He has threatened to kill my mother and me if anyone else finds out. I could not take it if you told anyone else. If you do, I will find a way to kill myself." Your clinical judgment, based on what you have learned during the course of the four sessions, is that the adolescent is extremely likely to commit suicide under those circumstances.

- How do you feel?
- More specifically, what are your feelings about the patient who left you the note? What are your feelings about the father? What are your feelings about the mother? What are your feelings about the other two adolescents?
- What do you believe that your legal obligations are?
- What do you believe that your ethical responsibilities are?
- What, if any, conflicts do you experience? How do you go about considering and deciding what to do about these conflicts?
- What do you believe that you would do?

■ ■ ■

A patient you have been seeing in outpatient psychotherapy for two years does not show up for an appointment. The patient has been depressed and has recently experienced some personal and occupational disappointments, but the risk of suicide as you have assessed it has remained at a very low level. You call the patient at home to see if this person has forgotten the appointment or if there has been a mix-up in scheduling. You reach a family member, who tells you that the patient has committed suicide.

- What do you feel?
- Are there any feelings that are difficult to identify or put into words?
- What options do you consider?
- Do you tell the family member that you were the person's therapist? Why or why not? What, if anything, do you volunteer to tell the family?
- Do you send flowers? Why or why not? Do you attend the funeral? Why or why not?
- If a family member says that the suicide must have been your fault, what do you feel? What would you do?
- Do you tell any of your friends or colleagues? Why? What concerns, if any, do you have?
- Do your case notes and documentation show your failure to assess accurately the patient's suicidal risk? Why or why not? Do you have any concerns about your documentation?

■ ■ ■

You have been discussing a new HMO patient, whom you have seen for three outpatient sessions, with your clinical supervisor and the chief of outpatient services. The chief of services strongly believes that the patient is at substantial risk for suicide, but the clinical supervisor believes just as strongly that there is no real risk. You are caught in the middle, trying to create a treatment plan that makes sense in the light of the conflicting views of the two people to whom you report. One morning you arrive at work and are informed that your clinical supervisor has committed suicide.

- What do you feel?
- Are there any feelings that are particularly difficult to identify, acknowledge, or articulate?

(continued)

(continued)

- How, if at all, do you believe that this might influence your work with any of your clients/patients?
- Assume that at the first session, you obtained the patient's written informed consent for the work to be discussed with this particular clinical supervisor who has been countersigning the patient's chart notes. What, if anything, do you tell the patient about the supervisor's suicide or the fact that the clinical work will now be discussed with a new supervisor?
- To what extent has your graduate training and internship addressed issues of clinicians' own suicidal ideation, impulses, or behaviors?

Chapter 21

SUPERVISION

S upervision draws together many themes running through this book. All of us began our clinical careers as supervisees. It is not hard to think of ways, some of them perhaps unintentional, in which our supervisors shaped our development. Supervision involves considerable power, trust, and caring, although they take different forms than in therapy.

CLEAR TASKS, ROLES, AND RESPONSIBILITIES

Supervision involves at least three people: client, supervisee, and supervisor. Relationships and agendas can easily become confused. A basic ethical responsibility for supervisors is to clarify the tasks, roles, and responsibilities. For example, they avoid drifting into the role of the supervisee's therapist. Some forms of supervision may share common aspects with some forms of therapy. If supervisees become aware of psychological problems and decides to seek therapy, they should consult a separate therapist.

Although the supervisor has responsibilities for the client's care and the supervisee's professional growth, the client's welfare must be primary. The supervisor must make sure that no aspect of training puts the client at undue risk. Supervision often takes place in a hospital or clinic, and the therapist-trainees may have predetermined internships or rotations (for example, six months or an academic calendar year). Such time sequences and boundaries must be taken into account when considering the client's welfare. Frequent terminations and transfers can cause significant problems for some clients. The informed consent process should include letting the client know if a therapist will be available for only a few months.

When a therapist-trainee becomes licensed and leaves a setting, do the clients remain at the setting or follow the newly licensed therapist? Who decides? Who keeps the therapy records? These issues are best addressed *before* training begins and should be clarified in a written agreement. Otherwise disagreements can grow into formal complaints and lawsuits (Pope, 1990a).

The supervisor is ultimately responsible, ethically and legally, for the clinical services that the supervisee provides. Supervisor and supervisee must address any conflicts about treatment approaches when they first arise. Both may avoid addressing—or even acknowledging—conflicts that make them uncomfortable (Pope, Sonne, & Greene, 2006).

Unaddressed conflicts between supervisor and supervisee almost always interfere with therapy and supervision. These conflicts are often acted out or mirrored in the supervisee-client relationship. Similarly, the dynamics of the relationship between supervisee and client are often recreated or echoed in the supervisor-supervisee relationship. The ways that unaddressed conflicts affect the therapy and supervision are a normal part of training. They are not a sign that the therapy is terribly misguided, the supervisee needs to withdraw from graduate training and seek a line of work that does not involve being around other people, or the supervisor is a monster suffering from delusions of adequacy. What they do signal is that important dynamics of the supervisor-supervisee-client triad need to be addressed

Nonsexual dual relationships can complicate the supervisor's ethical responsibility to clarify roles. Should a supervisor enter into various social relationships with a supervisee? The answer, as it so often is in our work, is: It depends. A fundamental theme running through this book is that codes, laws, and standards are the beginning—not the end—of our ethical considerations. Nothing can spare us the struggle with complex questions involving unique people in unique situations. The codes, laws, and standards inform—but do not replace—our efforts to think through issues. Burian and Slimp (2000; see also Slimp & Burian, 1994) provide a thoughtful model for thinking through social dual-role relationships during internships that can be adapted to many supervision settings. Their decision-making model helps supervisors to consider a variety of useful issues like the reasons for the relationship, the power difference between supervisor or supervisee, the nature of the social activities, and the effects on other supervisees.

Kitchener (2000) also addresses multiple-role relationships in supervision and uses social role theory to reveal the ambiguity inherent in role conflicts. Supervision involves many responsibilities, such as helping trainees develop, evaluating supervisees, protecting the public from incompetent or inept therapists, and making sure that clients receive a decent standard of care. Kitchener (2000) points out that the supervisee may be involved with the supervisor in a variety of other roles, including consulting, coauthoring papers or presentations, and attending social functions together. These multiple roles are complicated because supervisees may be much more personally vulnerable than those who are in a teacher-student relationship, given the revelation of personal secrets that may be blocking work with clients. Yet supervision differs from therapy, partly because of the evaluative component in supervision and partly because confidentiality and privilege do not have the same status in supervision as they do in therapy.

COMPETENCE

Like therapy, supervision requires demonstrable competence. "It is vital that the supervisor be well trained, knowledgeable, and skilled in the practice of clinical supervision" (Stoltenberg & Delworth, 1987, p. 175). It would be no more ethical to improvise supervision if one lacked education, training, and supervised experience than if one were to improvise hypnotherapy, systematic desensitization, or a neuropsychological assessment without adequate preparation. Carol Falender and Edward Shafranske (2004; see also 2008, 2010; Falender, Shafranske, & Falicov, 2010) emphasize supervision as a distinct professional activity when they define the term:

> Supervision is a distinct professional activity in which education and training aimed at developing science-informed practice are facilitated through a collaborative interpersonal process. It involves observation, evaluation, feedback, the facilitation of supervisee self-assessment, and the acquisition of knowledge and skills by instruction, modeling, and mutual problem solving. In addition, by building on the recognition of the strengths and talents of the supervisee, supervision encourages self-efficacy. Supervision ensures that clinical consultation is conducted in a competent manner in which ethical standards, legal prescriptions, and professional practices are used to promote and protect the welfare of the client, the profession, and society at large. (p. 3)

Despite the importance of supervision and its key role in professional development, training *in* supervision was often overlooked. Kathleen Malloy (2010) and her colleagues pointed out that supervision has not "been well represented in graduate education or in the accreditation process" and that "supervision has only recently received attention as a core domain for clinical training" (p. 161).

The field still struggles with how competence in supervision can best be achieved. There is some evidence that—not surprisingly—how we as individuals were trained to supervise shapes what we view as the best training. Jeffrey Rings and his colleagues (2009) surveyed predoctoral internship training directors about their views of competence in supervision. The survey revealed

> patterns of disagreement on the importance of both supervision coursework and supervision of supervision. On the surface, the degree of importance placed in one's completing supervision coursework seemed to reflect the amount of supervision training one might have had, as indicated by the

type of supervision training received. Those who completed supervision coursework were significantly more likely to agree with its importance than were those who attended a supervision workshop, who in turn agreed with its importance significantly more so than those who had no supervision training whatsoever. (p. 145)

The state of the art and science of supervision does not stand still any more than other areas of our work. Only if we keep up with the literature can we make sure that the evolving research and theory informs our work as supervisors. The supervision literature itself is of course diverse, spanning diverse theoretical orientations (see, e.g., Boswell, Nelson, Nordberg, McAleavey, & Castonguay, 2010; Celano, Smith, & Kaslow, 2010; Farber, 2010; Farber & Kaslow, 2010; Newman, 2010; and Samat, 2010).

Beyond maintaining competence in supervision, supervisors must also maintain competence in the approaches used to assess and treat the client and make sure that supervisees are at least minimally competent to provide services to the client. A temptation for some supervisors is to form a relationship with a promising supervisee who has had course work in clinical techniques for which the supervisor may have only superficial or outdated knowledge. These supervisors may, if they are not scrupulously careful, find themselves supervising interventions for which they have no demonstrable competence. For example, supervisors whose practice is exclusively psychoanalytical and who have no training in cognitive-behavioral techniques may find themselves supervising students who are using covert conditioning; supervisors who have worked only with adults may find themselves supervising child therapy; supervisors who take an existential-humanistic approach and do not use standardized tests may find themselves trying to help a supervisee interpret an MMPI-2.

Constant questioning has been a theme throughout this book. Supervisors can ask themselves, "Even though I have solid competence in supervision and the approaches used to assess and help the client, are there other relevant issues for which I lack competence? For example, are there any issues of background, culture, language, religion, or values among the client, the supervisee, and me that make it hard for us to understand each other and work together? If so, is that issue related to competence and how is it best addressed?" Some resources that may be helpful include the Canadian Psychological Association's "Guidelines for Ethical Practice with Diverse Populations" (part of the Canadian Psychological Association's *Guidelines for Non-Discriminatory Practice*, 2001b) and the American Psychological Association's "Guidelines for Providers of Psychological Services to Ethnic, Linguistic, and Culturally Diverse Populations" (1993) and "Guidelines on Multicultural Education, Training, Research, Practice and Organizational Change for Psychologists" (2003b).

ASSESSMENT AND EVALUATION

The supervisor must assess continually both the clinical services provided to the client and the supervisee's professional development. This responsibility can make many of us supervisors uncomfortable.

The evaluation component of supervision may make supervisees uncomfortable. In graduate training programs, internships, arrangements in which supervised hours are accumulated as a prerequisite to licensure, and many institutional settings, the supervisor must report to third parties an assessment of the supervisee's strengths, weaknesses, and progress. These reports may profoundly influence the supervisee's opportunities for continuing in the training program or for future employment.

Supervisors must clearly, frankly, and promptly communicate *to* supervisees their assessment of strengths, weaknesses, and development. In some cases, supervisors may determine that the supervisee is unable, either temporarily or more permanently, to do clinical work. Those supervisors must try to determine *why* the supervisee is unable to work. Some supervisees suffer from the strain of the work load, a personal loss, financial problems, aging and infirm parents, or marital conflicts. Others find that doing therapy brings up personal conflicts or unresolved issues from the past. Others experience thought disorders, depression, or anxiety so severe that it blocks their ability to function effectively. And still others may suffer from developmental or personality disorders.

The supervisor's responsibility is clear and unavoidable in such circumstances. The APA's policy for training programs more generally is also relevant for individual supervisors. The Committee on Accreditation for the American Psychological Association (1989) stated that all programs "have special responsibility to assess continually the progress of each student" and that "students who exhibit continued serious difficulties and do not function effectively in academic and/or interpersonal situations should be counseled early, made aware of career alternatives, and, if necessary, dropped from the program" (p. B-10).

The Americans With Disabilities Act sets forth special responsibilities in this area. Carol Fallender, Christopher Collins, and Edward Shafranske (2009) provide a helpful discussion of these issues in their article "'Impairment' and performance issues in clinical supervision: After the 2008 ADA Amendments Act." They emphasize:

> After ensuring client care (their first responsibility), supervisors enter into processes in which they must articulate specific areas of problematic professional behavior and develop with their supervisees plans to enhance clinical competence. When evaluating, communicating, and documenting performance problems, supervisors must be mindful to avoid the misuse of

the term *impairment* as well as to understand their legal obligations, when impairment contributes to performance difficulties. (p. 247)

While supervisors must, when circumstances warrant, ensure that unsuitable and unqualified individuals do not become therapists or counselors—a responsibility we owe to future clients who might be harmed by incompetent or unscrupulous practice—we must do so in a way that spares the supervisee any unnecessary pain and that is scrupulously fair. Koocher and Keith-Spiegel (2008) wrote: "Only when sensitive attempts to resolve the problems have failed, when no biases or unfair discrimination exists, and when institutional policies regarding termination from the program have been scrupulously followed should the trainee be dismissed" (p. 361).

INFORMED CONSENT

Supervisors have an ethical responsibility to provide appropriate informed consent to both supervisee and client. Supervisees have a right to know how they will be evaluated—what sorts of information the supervisor will use for forming an opinion and what criteria will be used for evaluating that information. They must understand clearly what is expected of them and what resources are available to them. They need to know to what degree or under what conditions what they reveal to the supervisor will be kept confidential. For example, supervisees may disclose in supervision that they are in therapy, are members of a 12-step program, or were abused as children. They must understand clearly whether such information will be shared with others, and for what purposes.

Clients whose therapists are being supervised also have an ethical right to informed consent to the supervisory arrangements. The first step, of course, is simply to make sure that they know that the clinical services they are receiving are being formally supervised. On January 30, 1984, the APA's Committee on Scientific and Professional Ethics and Conduct (currently termed the Ethics Committee) issued a formal statement about supervision:

> During the onset of a professional relationship with a client, a client should be informed of the psychologist's intended use of supervisors/consultants, and the general nature of the information regarding the case which will be disclosed to the supervisor/consultant. This permits the client to make an informed decision regarding the psychological services with an understanding of the limits of confidentiality attendant to the relationship. Failure to inform the client of such limits violates the patient's confidentiality when the psychologist, without the patient's awareness, discusses the patient/client and his/her diagnosis and treatment or consultation with a supervisor/consultant. The Committee feels that during the onset of a professional relationship with a client, the client should be clearly informed of the limits of confidentiality in that relationship.

The 2010 Ethical Principles of Psychologists and Code of Conduct (APA) Standard 10.01c states:

> When the therapist is a trainee and the legal responsibility for the treatment provided resides with the supervisor, the client, as part of the informed consent procedure, is informed that the therapist is in training and is being supervised and is given the name of the supervisor.

The Canadian Code of Ethics for Psychologists (CPA, 2000), Standard II.22, requires that psychologists "make no attempt to conceal the status of a trainee, and if a trainee is providing direct client service, ensure that the client is informed of that fact" (p. 25).

In some cases, state laws or regulations may specify the obligation of supervisees to disclose their status. Section 1396.4 of California's Rules of Professional Conduct (Title 16) states,

> A psychological assistant shall at all times and under all circumstances identify himself or herself to patients or clients as a psychological assistant to his or her employer or responsible supervisor when engaged in any psychological activity in connection with that employment.

Both supervisor and supervisee have an ethical responsibility to make sure that the client understands the supervisee's qualifications and credentials (Pope, 1990a). Clinicians may engage in extensive rationalizations regarding fraudulently presenting supervisees as possessing a level of training that they have not achieved. For example, in many hospital settings, psychological interns may be presented to patients as "Dr." even though they have not yet received the doctorate. clients have a fundamental right to know whether their therapist possesses the doctorate and a license to practice independently.

SEXUAL ISSUES

Sexual attraction to clients is a common occurrence for therapists. Supervisors have an important ethical responsibility to ensure that the supervisory relationship provides a safe and supportive opportunity to learn to recognize and handle appropriately such feelings.

Supervisors also have an ethical responsibility to ensure that a sexual relationship between supervisor and supervisee does not occur. The ethics code of the American Psychological Association (2010), for example, states in Section 7.07 ("Sexual Relationships with Students and Supervisees"), "Psychologists do not engage in sexual relationships with students or supervisees who are in their department, agency, or training center or over whom psychologists have or are likely to have evaluative authority. (See also Standard 3.05, Multiple Relationships.)" The ethics code of the Canadian Psychological Association (2000) states in Section 11.28 that psychologists should "not encourage or engage in sexual intimacy with students or trainees with whom the psychologist has an evaluative or other relationship of direct authority. (Also see Standard III.31.)"

Anonymous surveys have gathered information about sexual involvements between psychologists and their trainees (Glaser & Thorpe, 1986; Harding, Shearn, & Kitchener, 1989; Pope, Levenson, & Schover, 1979; Robinson & Reid, 1985). The evidence strongly suggests that female trainees, much more than male trainees, are involved in such sexual relationships, even when data are adjusted for the relative numbers of male and female supervisors and of male and female supervisees. One study found that one of every four women who had received her doctorate in psychology within the past six years had engaged in sexual intimacies with at least one of her psychology educators (Pope et al., 1979; see also Pope, 1989b). Glaser and Thorpe (1986) found that in most cases (62%), the intimacy occurred either before or during the student's working relationship with the educator.

Supervisors bear the responsibility not only of seeing that such involvements do not occur but also of making sure that sexual issues arising in the therapy are addressed frankly, sensitively, and respectfully:

> Students need to feel that discussion of their sexual feelings will not be taken as seductive or provocative or as inviting or legitimizing a sexualized relationship with their educators. ... Educators must display the same frankness, honesty, and integrity regarding sexual attraction that they expect their students to emulate. Psychologists need to acknowledge that they may feel sexual attraction to their students as well as their clients. They need to establish with clarity and maintain with consistency unambiguous ethical and professional standards and boundaries regarding appropriate and inappropriate handling of these feelings.
> (Pope, Keith-Spiegel, & Tabachnick, 1986, p. 157; see also Pope, Sonne, & Greene, 2006)

SUPERVISEE PERCEPTIONS OF SUPERVISOR'S UNETHICAL BEHAVIOR

Supervisors serve as ethics mentors and models for supervisees. In some unfortunate cases, they model unethical behavior. Susan Neufeldt (2003) reviewed research suggesting that most supervisees believe that their supervisors have committed at least one ethical violation. She wrote:

> As a supervisor, you should particularly watch the most frequently violated guidelines noted by supervisees: adequate performance evaluation, confidentiality of supervision sessions, and ability to work with and at least respect alternative perspectives. You cannot count on your supervisees' letting you know about their dissatisfactions. If you can create a safe environment where your supervisees can comfortably reveal their feelings and ideas, and especially their negative feelings about you as the supervisor, you will likely have a successful supervisory relationship. (p. 215)

BEGINNINGS AND ENDINGS, ABSENCE AND AVAILABILITY

At the start of supervision, supervisees must clearly understand when the supervisor will and will not be available. If the client has an emergency, does the supervisee know how to reach the supervisor quickly? Will the supervisor be available for telephone supervision between scheduled sessions? Can the supervisor be reached during late-night hours, on weekends, or on holidays? Are there adequate preparations for supervisor absences, both planned and unanticipated? If the supervisor is unavailable during a crisis, does the supervisee have several back-up options for getting help?

Issues regarding the beginning and ending of the supervision process must be adequately addressed. The termination is likely to elicit a variety of feelings. Both supervisor and supervisee may feel tempted to collude in avoiding issues related to the termination of clients. They may also find it easy to avoid issues related to the termination of supervision. If the process has not gone as well as expected, both supervisor and supervisee may feel frustration, regret, anger, and relief at the prospect that it is all—*finally*—over. Open and honest discussion of how the problems arose and why they were not resolved more effectively may be hard. If the process has gone well, both may feel joy, pride, and exhilaration, but they may also experience a sense of loss and sorrow that the time spent together and the shared, intense, productive work are ending.

Such responses should not be denied or neglected. An important part of supervision involves supervisor and supervisee honestly confronting their reactions to each other and to their collaborative work together. What has each gained from the other? In what ways has each surprised, disappointed, angered, or hurt the other? In what ways has the relationship been characterized by interest, attentiveness, support, and creativity? In what ways has it been characterized by dishonesty, betrayal, avoidance, and stubbornness? How has the setting influenced the relationship? How have power, trust, and caring manifested themselves in the relationship between supervisor and supervisee and during supervision?

The integrity of the supervision depends on the degree to which we acknowledge and confront such issues. We begin our clinical work as supervisees, and unless we are exceptionally afraid or uncaring, our growth and development as therapists and counselors continue during our career. As we complete our supervision requirements, we must find alternate ways to nurture this process through consultation, study groups, continuing education, and other means.

We have chosen work that involves intense and intimate relationships with other people. It is work with great influence and great vulnerability. Whether our relationships with our clients and supervisees are helpful or hurtful depends to a great extent on fulfilling our ethical responsibilities in regard to power, trust, and caring.

SCENARIOS FOR DISCUSSION

After receiving your doctorate in psychology, you decide you want to live in an area of the country you have never visited before. After a long search, you secure a job at the only clinic in a small town. You'll be able to secure the year's worth of postdoc supervised hours required for licensing. You pack up and move and find you love the new town and your job at the clinic. Ten months into the year, your supervisor says, "I have some bad news. The clinic has decided to get rid of us psychologists, so we're both losing our jobs as of the end of this week. I've decided to retire and travel for the next year or so. I know that there's no other job for you here in town, and that leaves you without the supervised hours you need for licensure. But you've been a great supervisee and I'm willing to give you credit for the last two months. I'll just put down on the form that you worked under my supervision for a year."

- How do you feel?
- How do you weigh the possibilities?
- What would you like to say to your supervisor?
- What do you think you would say to your supervisor?

■ ■ ■

You are conducting family therapy with a family of five. The mother, age 31, is Caucasian. The mother's partner, age 54, is Hispanic. The three children are preteens. You discuss with your supervisor the tensions that the family members are experiencing and your beliefs about the causes of those tensions. Your supervisor says: "I think maybe you're seeing it that way because you are [your own race or ethnicity]."

- How do you feel?
- What do you think you might say to your supervisor?
- What would you like to say to your supervisor?
- Would your supervisor's race or ethnicity make any difference in how you feel or how you react to this situation? If so, what difference would it make, and why?
- Did you imagine the mother's partner as male or female? What do you believe influenced whether you imagined the person as a man or a woman?

■ ■ ■

You have just completed an intake session with a person who is extremely fearful, hears voices, and seems to have a thought disorder. Your provisional diagnosis is some form of schizophrenia, although there are other possibilities you plan to explore during the next session. You meet with your supervisor, review your notes for the intake, state your opinion that the difficulty likely involves a schizophrenic process, and list the questions that you plan to address in your next session. Your supervisor's first comment is, "Boy, those schizos really are interesting, aren't they!"

- How do you feel?
- What responses do you consider giving to this comment?
- How do you think you actually would respond to this comment?
- If this supervisor had a reputation as extremely thin-skinned and averse to criticism and if this supervisor were also someone with considerable power over your training, how, if at all, might this affect your decision about responding?

■ ■ ■

You are a supervisor who has had a very challenging supervisee. The supervisee has, for example, made demeaning and passive-aggressive comments to clients and often jokes about them in a cruel and disrespectful way. You have attempted to provide feedback throughout supervision, documenting these attempts and their (lack of) effect. The supervisee schedules an additional session with you and says, "I've been looking at my evaluation forms, and I think you've been very unfair with me. I've talked to some other people, and they agree with me. It is important that you change some of these ratings so that they reflect a fair and unbiased evaluation. If you don't, it will continue to hurt my career. My attorney believes that I have a legal right to a fair evaluation that does not defame me."

- How do you feel?
- How, if at all, would your feelings differ depending on the supervisee's gender, race, age, or other demographics?
- What are your options for responding?

(continued)

(continued)

- How would you like to respond? How do you think you would respond? If there is any difference between your answers to these two questions, what causes the difference?
- How, if at all, would the way you responded be affected by the supervisee's gender, race, age, or other demographics?

■ ■ ■

You have been working with a client who is in desperate need of treatment for multiple serious problems. Without treatment, the client, a single parent, is likely to decompensate and perhaps place the children at risk. Suicide is a possibility. Unfortunately, the client does not qualify for therapy in the light of the current symptoms and the terms of insurance coverage. Your supervisor and you discuss all the alternatives, none of which seems acceptable. Finally, your supervisor says, "Look, the only way to get this client the help that is absolutely necessary is to come up with a diagnosis that will meet the terms of the insurance coverage." The supervisor then suggests a diagnosis that will ensure coverage but clearly does not fit the client in any way.

- How do you feel? Are there any feelings that are difficult to acknowledge, disclose, or consider? Aside from your feelings, what thoughts do you have about your supervisor's suggestion? What courses of action do you consider in the light of your supervisor's suggestion? What are your feelings in regard to each one?
- What do you think you would end up doing?
- How, if at all, would your chart notes be affected by your supervisor's suggestion?

■ ■ ■

You are working with a client who describes graphic sexual fantasies that make you somewhat uncomfortable. At your next supervision session, you tell the supervisor about the counseling session and also about your discomfort with the fantasies. Your supervisor says, "So you are uncomfortable with that kind of sexual fantasizing. What kind of sexual fantasies are you comfortable with?"

- How do you feel?
- What would you like to say to your supervisor?

- What do you think you would end up saying to your supervisor?
- If there is any difference between your answers to questions 2 and 3, why is there a difference?
- Does the gender, sexual orientation, age, or race of your supervisor make any difference in terms of the feelings you experience or the responses you would make or would like to make?

■ ■ ■

You and your supervisor have had substantial disagreements about clients'/patients' diagnoses and treatment planning. You discuss your differences extensively, but neither convinces the other. During one supervision session, your supervisor says, "I've been concerned about the difficulties you seem to have in conceptualizing these cases and in formulating effective treatment plans. I believe that there are some personal factors interfering with your clinical judgment. I've discussed these issues with the director of clinical training and senior staff, and we think that you need to enter therapy to address these problems."

- How do you feel? Are there any feelings that are particularly hard to acknowledge, disclose, or discuss?
- What are the possible ways you might respond to the supervisor's comments?
- How would you like to respond to the comments?
- How do you think you would end up responding to the comments?
- If there is any difference between your response to questions 3 and 4, what is the difference, and what is the reason for the difference?
- If you were the supervisor and you believed that the supervisee was experiencing personal problems that interfered with clinical judgment, how would you address it? What feelings would you experience as you addressed this situation? How, if at all, would your feelings affect your ability to address this situation effectively and humanely?
- If you ever experienced problems that interfered with your clinical judgment or competence and you were unaware of the situation, how would you like others to respond? What would you find helpful and what would you find hurtful?

AMERICAN PSYCHOLOGICAL ASSOCIATION ETHICAL PRINCIPLES OF PSYCHOLOGISTS AND CODE OF CONDUCT WITH THE 2010 AMENDMENTS[1]

INTRODUCTION AND APPLICABILITY

The American Psychological Association's (APA) Ethical Principles of Psychologists and Code of Conduct (hereinafter referred to as the Ethics Code) consists of an Introduction, a Preamble, five General Principles, and specific Ethical Standards. The Introduction discusses the intent, organization, procedural considerations, and scope of application of the Ethics Code. The Preamble and General Principles are aspirational goals to guide psychologists toward the highest ideals of psychology. Although the Preamble and General Principles are not themselves enforceable rules, they should be considered by psychologists in arriving at an ethical course of action. The Ethical Standards set forth enforceable rules for conduct as psychologists.

---

[1] Copyright © 2010 by the American Psychological Association.

Most of the Ethical Standards are written broadly, in order to apply to psychologists in varied roles, although the application of an Ethical Standard may vary depending on the context. The Ethical Standards are not exhaustive. The fact that a given conduct is not specifically addressed by an Ethical Standard does not mean that it is necessarily either ethical or unethical.

This Ethics Code applies only to psychologists' activities that are part of their scientific, educational, or professional roles as psychologists. Areas covered include but are not limited to the clinical, counseling, and school practice of psychology; research; teaching; supervision of trainees; public service; policy development; social intervention; development of assessment instruments; conducting assessments; educational counseling; organizational consulting; forensic activities; program design and evaluation; and administration. This Ethics Code applies to these activities across a variety of contexts, such as in person, postal, telephone, internet, and other electronic transmissions. These activities shall be distinguished from the purely private conduct of psychologists, which is not within the purview of the Ethics Code.

Membership in the APA commits members and student affiliates to comply with the standards of the APA Ethics Code and to the rules and procedures used to enforce them. Lack of awareness or misunderstanding of an Ethical Standard is not itself a defense to a charge of unethical conduct.

The procedures for filing, investigating, and resolving complaints of unethical conduct are described in the current Rules and Procedures of the APA Ethics Committee. APA may impose sanctions on its members for violations of the standards of the Ethics Code, including termination of APA membership, and may notify other bodies and individuals of its actions. Actions that violate the standards of the Ethics Code may also lead to the imposition of sanctions on psychologists or students whether or not they are APA members by bodies other than APA, including state psychological associations, other professional groups, psychology boards, other state or federal agencies, and payors for health services. In addition, APA may take action against a member after his or her conviction of a felony, expulsion or suspension from an affiliated state psychological association, or suspension or loss of licensure. When the sanction to be imposed by APA is less than expulsion, the 2001 Rules and Procedures do not guarantee an opportunity for an in-person hearing, but generally provide that complaints will be resolved only on the basis of a submitted record.

The Ethics Code is intended to provide guidance for psychologists and standards of professional conduct that can be applied by the APA and by other bodies that choose to adopt them. The Ethics Code is not intended to be a basis of civil liability. Whether a psychologist has violated the Ethics Code standards does not by itself determine whether the psychologist is legally liable in a court action, whether a contract is enforceable, or whether other legal consequences occur.

The modifiers used in some of the standards of this Ethics Code (e.g., reasonably, appropriate, potentially) are included in the standards when they would (1) allow professional judgment on the part of psychologists, (2) eliminate injustice or inequality that would occur without the modifier, (3) ensure applicability across the broad range of activities conducted by psychologists, or (4) guard against a set of rigid rules that might be quickly outdated. As used in this Ethics Code, the term reasonable means the prevailing professional judgment of psychologists engaged in similar activities in similar circumstances, given the knowledge the psychologist had or should have had at the time.

In the process of making decisions regarding their professional behavior, psychologists must consider this Ethics Code in addition to applicable laws and psychology board regulations. In applying the Ethics Code to their professional work, psychologists may consider other materials and guidelines that have been adopted or endorsed by scientific and professional psychological organizations and the dictates of their own conscience, as well as consult with others within the field. If this Ethics Code establishes a higher standard of conduct than is required by law, psychologists must meet the higher ethical standard. If psychologists' ethical responsibilities conflict with law, regulations, or other governing legal authority, psychologists make known their commitment to this Ethics Code and take steps to resolve the conflict in a responsible manner in keeping with basic principles of human rights.

PREAMBLE

Psychologists are committed to increasing scientific and professional knowledge of behavior and people's understanding of themselves and others and to the use of such knowledge to improve the condition of individuals, organizations, and society. Psychologists respect and protect civil and human rights and the central importance of freedom of inquiry and expression in research, teaching, and publication. They strive to help the public in developing informed judgments and choices concerning human behavior. In doing so, they perform many roles, such as researcher, educator, diagnostician, therapist, supervisor, consultant, administrator, social interventionist, and expert witness. This Ethics Code provides a common set of principles and standards upon which psychologists build their professional and scientific work.

This Ethics Code is intended to provide specific standards to cover most situations encountered by psychologists. It has as its goals the welfare and protection of the individuals and groups with whom psychologists work and the education of members, students, and the public regarding ethical standards of the discipline.

The development of a dynamic set of ethical standards for psychologists' work-related conduct requires a personal, commitment and lifelong effort to act ethically; to encourage ethical behavior by students, supervisees, employees, and colleagues; and to consult with others concerning ethical problems.

GENERAL PRINCIPLES

This section consists of General Principles. General Principles, as opposed to Ethical Standards, are aspirational in nature. Their intent is to guide and inspire psychologists toward the very highest ethical ideals of the profession. General Principles, in contrast to Ethical Standards, do not represent obligations and should not form the basis for imposing sanctions. Relying upon General Principles for either of these reasons distorts both their meaning and purpose.

Principle A: Beneficence and Nonmaleficence

Psychologists strive to benefit those with whom they work and take care to do no harm. In their professional actions, psychologists seek to safeguard the welfare and rights of those with whom they interact professionally and other affected persons, and the welfare of animal subjects of research. When conflicts occur among psychologists' obligations or concerns, they attempt to resolve these conflicts in a responsible fashion that avoids or minimizes harm. Because psychologists' scientific and professional judgments and actions may affect the lives of others, they are alert to and guard against personal, financial, social, organizational, or political factors that might lead to misuse of their influence. Psychologists strive to be aware of the possible effect of their own physical and mental health on their ability to help those with whom they work.

Principle B: Fidelity and Responsibility

Psychologists establish relationships of trust with those with whom they work. They are aware of their professional and scientific responsibilities to society and to the specific communities in which they work. Psychologists uphold professional standards of conduct, clarify their professional roles and obligations, accept appropriate responsibility for their behavior, and seek to manage conflicts of interest that could lead to exploitation or harm. Psychologists consult with, refer to, or cooperate with other professionals and institutions to the extent needed to serve the best interests of those with whom they work. They are concerned about the ethical compliance of their colleagues' scientific and professional conduct. Psychologists strive to contribute a portion of their professional time for little or no compensation or personal advantage.

Principle C: Integrity

Psychologists seek to promote accuracy, honesty, and truthfulness in the science, teaching, and practice of psychology, in these activities psychologists do not steal, cheat, or engage in fraud, subterfuge, or intentional misrepresentation of fact. Psychologists strive to keep their promises and to avoid unwise or unclear commitments. In situations in which deception may be ethically justifiable to maximize benefits and minimize harm, psychologists have a serious obligation to consider the need for, the possible consequences of, and their responsibility to correct any resulting mistrust or other harmful effects that arise from the use of such techniques.

Principle D: Justice

Psychologists recognize that fairness and justice entitle all persons to access to and benefit from the contributions of psychology and to equal quality in the processes, procedures, and services being conducted by psychologists. Psychologists exercise reasonable judgment and take precautions to ensure that their potential biases, the boundaries of their competence, and the limitations of their expertise do not lead to or condone unjust practices.

Principle E: Respect for People's Rights and Dignity

Psychologists respect the dignity and worth of all people, and the rights of individuals to privacy, confidentiality, and self-determination. Psychologists are aware that special safeguards may be necessary to protect the rights and welfare of persons or communities whose vulnerabilities impair autonomous decision making. Psychologists are aware of and respect cultural, individual, and role differences, including those based on age, gender, gender identity, race, ethnicity, culture, national origin, religion, sexual orientation, disability, language, and socioeconomic status and consider these factors when working with members of such groups. Psychologists try to eliminate the effect on their work of biases based on those factors, and they do not knowingly participate in or condone activities of others based upon such prejudices.

STANDARD 1: RESOLVING ETHICAL ISSUES

1.01 Misuse of Psychologists' Work

If psychologists learn of misuse or misrepresentation of their work, they take reasonable steps to correct or minimize the misuse or misrepresentation.

1.02 Conflicts Between Ethics and Law, Regulations, or Other Governing Legal Authority

If psychologists' ethical responsibilities conflict with law, regulations, or other governing legal authority, psychologists clarify the nature of the conflict, make known their commitment to the Ethics Code, and take reasonable steps to resolve the conflict consistent with the General Principles and Ethical

Standards of the Ethics Code. Under no circumstances may this standard be used to justify or defend violating human rights.

1.03 Conflicts Between Ethics and Organizational Demands

If the demands of an organization with which psychologists are affiliated or for whom they are working are in conflict with this Ethics Code, psychologists clarify the nature of the conflict, make known their commitment to the Ethics Code, and take reasonable steps to resolve the conflict consistent with the General Principles and Ethical Standards of the Ethics Code. Under no circumstances may this standard be used to justify or defend violating human rights.

1.04 Informal Resolution of Ethical Violations

When psychologists believe that there may have been an ethical violation by another psychologist, they attempt to resolve the issue by bringing it to the attention of that individual, if an informal resolution appears appropriate and the intervention does not violate any confidentiality rights that may be involved. (See also Standards 1.02, Conflicts Between Ethics and Law, Regulations, or Other Governing Legal Authority, and 1.03, Conflicts Between Ethics and Organizational Demands.)

1.05 Reporting Ethical Violations

If an apparent ethical violation has substantially harmed or is likely to substantially harm a person or organization and is not appropriate for informal resolution under Standard 1.04, Informal Resolution of Ethical Violations, or is not resolved properly in that fashion, psychologists take further action appropriate to the situation. Such action might include referral to state or national committees on professional ethics, to state licensing boards, or to the appropriate institutional authorities. This standard does not apply when an intervention would violate confidentiality rights or when psychologists have been retained to review the work of another psychologist whose professional conduct is in question. (See also Standard 1.02, Conflicts Between Ethics and Law, Regulations, or Other Governing Legal Authority.)

1.06 Cooperating with Ethics Committees

Psychologists cooperate in ethics investigations, proceedings, and resulting requirements of the APA or any affiliated state psychological association to which they belong, in doing so, they address any confidentiality issues. Failure to cooperate is itself an ethics violation. However, making a request for deferment of adjudication of an ethics complaint pending the outcome of litigation does not alone constitute noncooperation.

1.07 Improper Complaints

Psychologists do not file or encourage the filing of ethics complaints that are made with reckless disregard for or willful ignorance of facts that would disprove the allegation.

1.08 Unfair Discrimination Against Complainants and Respondents

Psychologists do not deny persons employment, advancement, admissions to academic or other programs, tenure, or promotion, based solely upon their having made or their being the subject of an ethics complaint. This does not-preclude taking action based upon the outcome of such proceedings or considering other appropriate information.

STANDARD 2: COMPETENCE

2.01 Boundaries of Competence

(a) Psychologists provide services, teach, and conduct research with populations and in areas only within the boundaries of their competence, based on their education, training, supervised experience, consultation, study, or professional experience.

(b) Where scientific or professional knowledge *in* the discipline of psychology establishes that an understanding of factors associated with age, gender, gender identity, race, ethnicity, culture, national origin, religion, sexual orientation, disability, language, or socioeconomic status is essential for effective implementation of their services or research, psychologists have or obtain the training, experience, consultation, or supervision necessary to ensure the competence of their services, or they make appropriate referrals, except as provided in Standard 2.02, Providing Services in Emergencies.

(c) Psychologists planning to provide services, teach, or conduct research involving populations, areas, techniques, or technologies new to them undertake relevant education, training, supervised experience, consultation, or study.

(d) When psychologists are asked to provide services to individuals for whom appropriate mental health services are not available and for which psychologists have not obtained the competence necessary, psychologists with closely related prior training or experience may provide such services in order to ensure that services are not denied if they make a reasonable effort to obtain the competence required by using relevant research, training, consultation, or study.

(e) In those emerging areas in which generally recognized standards for preparatory training do not yet exist, psychologists nevertheless take reasonable steps to ensure the competence of their work and to protect clients/patients, students, supervisees, research participants, organizational clients, and others from harm.

(f) When assuming forensic roles, psychologists are or become reasonably familiar with the judicial or administrative rules governing their roles.

2.02 Providing Services in Emergencies

In emergencies, when psychologists provide services to individuals for whom other mental health services are not available and for which psychologists have not obtained the necessary training, psychologists may provide such services in order to ensure that services are not denied. The services are discontinued as soon as the emergency has ended or appropriate services are available.

2.03 Maintaining Competence

Psychologists undertake ongoing efforts to develop and maintain their competence.

2.04 Bases for Scientific and Professional Judgments

Psychologists' work is based upon established scientific and professional knowledge of the discipline. (See also Standards 2.01e, Boundaries of Competence, and 10.01b, Informed Consent to Therapy.)

2.05 Delegation of Work to Others

Psychologists who delegate work to employees, supervisees, or research or teaching assistants or who use the services of others, such as interpreters, take reasonable steps to (1) avoid delegating such work to persons who have a multiple relationship with those being served that would likely lead to exploitation or loss of objectivity; (2) authorize only those responsibilities that such persons can be expected to perform competently on the basis of their education, training, or experience, either independently or with the level of supervision being provided; and (3) see that such persons perform these services competently. (See also Standards 2.02, Providing Services in Emergencies; 3.05, Multiple Relationships; 4.01, Maintaining Confidentiality; 9.01, Bases for Assessments; 9.02, Use of Assessments; 9.03, Informed Consent in Assessments; and 9.07, Assessment by Unqualified Persons.)

2.06 Personal Problems and Conflicts

(a) Psychologists refrain from initiating an activity when they know or should know that there is a substantial likelihood that their personal problems will prevent them from performing their work-related activities in a competent manner.

(b) When psychologists become aware of personal problems that may interfere with their performing work-related duties adequately, they take appropriate measures, such as obtaining professional consultation or assistance, and determine whether they should limit, suspend, or terminate their work-related duties. (See also Standard 10.10, Terminating Therapy.)

STANDARD 3: HUMAN RELATIONS

3.01 Unfair Discrimination

In their work-related activities, psychologists do not engage in unfair discrimination based on age, gender, gender identity, race, ethnicity, culture, national origin, religion, sexual orientation, disability, socioeconomic status, or any basis proscribed by law.

3.02 Sexual Harassment

Psychologists do not engage in sexual harassment. Sexual harassment is sexual solicitation, physical advances, or verbal or nonverbal conduct that is sexual in nature, that occurs in connection with the psychologist's activities or roles as a psychologist, and that either (1) is unwelcome, is offensive, or creates a hostile workplace or educational environment, and the psychologist knows or is told this or (2) is sufficiently severe or intense to be abusive to a reasonable person in the context. Sexual harassment can consist of a single intense or severe act or of multiple persistent or pervasive acts. (See also Standard 1.08, Unfair Discrimination Against Complainants and Respondents.)

3.03 Other Harassment

Psychologists do not knowingly engage in behavior that is harassing or demeaning to persons with whom they interact in their work based on factors such as those persons' age, gender, gender identity, race, ethnicity, culture, national origin, religion, sexual orientation, disability, language, or socioeconomic status.

3.04 Avoiding Harm

Psychologists take reasonable steps to avoid harming their clients/patients, students, supervisees, research participants, organizational clients, and others with whom they work, and to minimize harm where it is foreseeable and unavoidable.

3.05 Multiple Relationships

(a) A multiple relationship occurs when a psychologist is in a professional role with a person and (1) at the same time is in another role with the same person, (2) at the same time is in a relationship with a person closely associated with or related to the person with whom the psychologist has the professional relationship, or (3) promises to enter into another relationship in the future with the person or a person closely associated with or related to the person.

   A psychologist refrains from entering into a multiple relationship if the multiple relationship could reasonably be expected to impair the psychologist's objectivity, competence, or effectiveness in performing his or her functions as a psychologist, or otherwise risks exploitation or harm to the person with whom the professional relationship exists.

   Multiple relationships that would not reasonably be expected to cause impairment or risk exploitation or harm are not unethical.

(b) If a psychologist finds that, due to unforeseen factors, a potentially harmful multiple relationship has arisen, the psychologist takes reasonable steps to resolve it with due regard for the best interests of the affected person and maximal compliance with the Ethics Code.

(c) When psychologists are required by law, institutional policy, or extraordinary circumstances to serve in more than one role in judicial or administrative proceedings, at the outset they clarify role expectations and the extent of confidentiality and thereafter as changes occur. (See also Standards 3.04, Avoiding Harm, and 3.07, Third-Party Requests for Services.)

3.06 Conflict of Interest

Psychologists refrain from taking on a professional role when personal, scientific, professional, legal, financial, or other interests or relationships could reasonably be expected to (1) impair their objectivity, competence, or effectiveness in performing their functions as psychologists or (2) expose the person or organization with whom the professional relationship exists to harm or exploitation.

3.07 Third-Party Requests for Services

When psychologists agree to provide services to a person or entity at the request of a third party, psychologists attempt to clarify at the outset of the service the nature of the relationship with all individuals or organizations involved. This clarification includes the role of the psychologist (e.g., therapist, consultant, diagnostician, or expert witness), an identification of who is the client, the probable uses of the services provided or the information obtained, and the fact that there may be limits to confidentiality. (See also Standards 3.05, Multiple relationships, and 4.02, Discussing the Limits of Confidentiality.)

3.08 Exploitative Relationships

Psychologists do not exploit persons over whom they have supervisory, evaluative, or other authority such as clients/patients, students, supervisees, research participants, and employees. (See also Standards 3.05, Multiple Relationships; 6.04, Fees and Financial Arrangements; 6.05, Barter with Clients/Patients; 7.07, Sexual Relationships with Students and Supervisees; 10.05, Sexual Intimacies with Current Therapy Clients/Patients; 10.06, Sexual Intimacies with Relatives or Significant Others of Current Therapy Clients/Patients; 10.07, Therapy with Former Sexual Partners; and 10.08, Sexual Intimacies with Former Therapy Clients/Patients.)

3.09 Cooperation with Other Professionals

When indicated and professionally appropriate, psychologists cooperate with other professionals in order to serve their clients/patients effectively and appropriately. (See also Standard 4.05, Disclosures.)

3.10 Informed Consent

(a) When psychologists conduct research or provide assessment, therapy, counseling, or consulting services in person or via electronic transmission or other forms of communication, they obtain the informed consent of the individual or individuals using language that is reasonably understandable to that person or persons except when conducting such activities without consent is mandated by law or governmental regulation or as otherwise provided in this Ethics Code. (See also Standards 8.02, Informed Consent to Research; 9.03, Informed Consent in Assessments; and 10.01, Informed Consent to Therapy.)

(b) For persons who are legally incapable of giving informed consent, psychologists nevertheless (1) provide an appropriate explanation, (2) seek the individual's assent, (3) consider such persons' preferences and best interests, and (4) obtain appropriate permission from a legally authorized person, if such substitute consent is permitted or required by law. When consent by a legally authorized person is not permitted or required by law, psychologists take reasonable steps to protect the individual's rights and welfare.

(c) When psychological services are court ordered or otherwise mandated, psychologists inform the individual of the nature of the anticipated services, including whether the services are court ordered or mandated and any limits of confidentiality, before proceeding.

(d) Psychologists appropriately document written or oral consent, permission, and assent. (See also Standards 8.02, Informed Consent to Research; 9.03, informed Consent in Assessments; and 10.01, Informed Consent to Therapy.)

3.11 Psychological Services Delivered to or Through Organizations

(a) Psychologists delivering services to or through organizations provide information beforehand to clients and when appropriate those directly affected by the services about (1) the nature and objectives of the services, (2) the intended recipients, (3) which of the individuals are clients, (4) the relationship the psychologist will have with each person and the organization, (5) the probable uses of services provided and information obtained, (6) who will have access to the information, and (7) limits of confidentiality. As soon as feasible, they provide information about the results and conclusions of such services to appropriate persons.

(b) If psychologists will be precluded by law or by organizational roles from providing such information to particular individuals or groups, they so inform those individuals or groups at the outset of the service.

3.12 Interruption of Psychological Services

Unless otherwise covered by contract, psychologists make reasonable efforts to plan for facilitating services in the event that psychological services are interrupted by factors such as the psychologist's illness, death, unavailability, relocation, or retirement or by the client's/patient's relocation or financial limitations. (See also Standard 8.02c, Maintenance, Dissemination, and Disposal of Confidential Records of Professional and Scientific Work.)

STANDARD 4: PRIVACY AND CONFIDENTIALITY

4.01 Maintaining Confidentiality

Psychologists have a primary obligation and take reasonable precautions to protect confidential information obtained through or stored in any medium, recognizing that the extent and limits of confidentiality may be regulated by law or established by institutional ruies or professional or scientific relationship. (See also Standard 2.05, Delegation of Work to Others.)

4.02 Discussing the Limits of Confidentiality

(a) Psychologists discuss with persons (including, to the extent feasible, persons who are legally incapable of giving informed consent and their legal representatives) and organizations with whom they establish a scientific or professional relationship (1) the relevant limits of confidentiality and (2) the foreseeable uses of the information generated through their psychological activities. (See also Standard 3.10, Informed Consent.)

(b) Unless it is not feasible or is contraindicated, the discussion of confidentiality occurs at the outset of the relationship and thereafter as new circumstances may warrant.

(c) Psychologists who offer services, products, or information via electronic transmission inform clients/patients of the risks to privacy and limits of confidentiality.

4.03 Recording

Before recording the voices or images of individuals to whom they provide services, psychologists obtain permission from all such persons or their legal representatives. (See also Standards 8.03, Informed Consent for Recording Voices and Images in Research; 8.05, Dispensing with Informed Consent for Research; and 8.07, Deception in Research.)

4.04 Minimizing Intrusions on Privacy

(a) Psychologists include in written and oral reports and consultations, only information germane to the purpose for which the communication is made.

(b) Psychologists discuss confidential information obtained in their work only for appropriate scientific or professional purposes and only with persons clearly concerned with such matters.

4.05 Disclosures

(a) Psychologists may disclose confidential information with the appropriate consent of the organizational client, the individual client/patient, or another legally authorized person on behalf of the client/patient unless prohibited by law.

(b) Psychologists disclose confidential information without the consent of the individual only as mandated by law, or where permitted by law for a valid purpose such as to (1) provide needed professional services; (2) obtain appropriate professional consultations; (3) protect the client/patient, psychologist, or others from harm; or (4) obtain payment for services from a client/patient, in which instance disclosure is limited to the minimum that is necessary to achieve the purpose. (See also Standard 6.04e, Fees and Financial Arrangements.)

4.06 Consultations

When consulting with colleagues, (1) psychologists do not disclose confidential information that reasonably could lead to the identification of a client/patient, research participant, or other person or organization with whom they have a confidential relationship unless they have obtained the prior consent of the person or organization or the disclosure cannot be avoided, and (2) they disclose information only to the extent necessary to achieve the purposes of the consultation. (See also Standard 4.01, Maintaining Confidentiality.)

4.07 Use of Confidential Information for Didactic or Other Purposes

Psychologists do not disclose in their writings, lectures, or other public media, confidential, personally identifiable information concerning their clients/patients, students, research participants, organizational clients, or other recipients of their services that they obtained during the course of their work, unless (1) they take reasonable steps to disguise the person or organization, (2) the person or organization has consented in writing, or (3) there is legal authorization for doing so.

STANDARD 5: ADVERTISING AND OTHER PUBLIC STATEMENTS

5.01 Avoidance of False or Deceptive Statements

(a) Public statements include but are not limited to paid or unpaid advertising, product endorsements, grant applications, licensing applications, other credentialing applications, brochures, printed matter, directory listings, personal resumes or curricula vitae, or comments for use in media such as print or electronic transmission, statements in legal proceedings, lectures and public oral presentations, and published materials. Psychologists do not knowingly make public statements that are false, deceptive, or fraudulent concerning their research, practice, or other work activities or those of persons or organizations with which they are affiliated.

(b) Psychologists do not make false, deceptive, or fraudulent statements concerning (1) their training, experience, or competence; (2) their academic degrees; (3) their credentials; (4) their institutional or association affiliations; (5) their services; (6) the scientific or clinical basis for, or results or degree of success of, their services; (7) their fees; or (8) their publications or research findings.

(c) Psychologists claim degrees as credentials for their health services only if those degrees (1) were earned from a regionally accredited educational institution or (2) were the basis for psychology licensure by the state in which they practice.

5.02 Statements by Others

(a) Psychologists who engage others to create or place public statements that promote their professional practice, products, or activities retain professional responsibility for such statements.

(b) Psychologists do not compensate employees of press, radio, television, or other communication media in return for publicity in a news item. (See aiso Standard 1.01, Misuse of Psychologists' Work.)

(c) A paid advertisement relating to psychologists' activities must be identified or clearly recognizable as such.

5.03 Descriptions of Workshops and Non-Degree-Granting Educational Programs

To the degree to which they exercise control, psychologists responsible for announcements, catalogs, brochures, or advertisements describing workshops, seminars, or other non-degree-granting educational programs ensure that they accurately describe the audience for which the program is intended, the educational objectives, the presenters, and the fees involved.

5.04 Media Presentations

When psychologists provide public advice or comment via print, Internet, or other electronic transmission, they take precautions to ensure that statements (1) are based on their professional knowledge, training, or experience in accord with appropriate psychological literature and practice; (2) are otherwise consistent with this Ethics Code; and (3) do not indicate that a professional relationship has been established with the recipient. (See also Standard 2.04, Bases for Scientific and Professional Judgments.)

5.05 Testimonials

Psychologists do not solicit testimonials from current therapy clients/patients or other persons who because of their particular circumstances are vulnerable to undue influence.

5.06 In-Person Solicitation

Psychologists do not engage, directly or through agents, in uninvited in-person solicitation of business from actual or potential therapy clients/patients or other persons who because of their particular circumstances are vulnerable to undue influence. However, this prohibition does not preclude (1) attempting to implement appropriate coliateral contacts for the purpose of benefiting an already engaged therapy client/patient or (2) providing disaster or community outreach services.

STANDARD 6: RECORD KEEPING AND FEES

6.01 Documentation of Professional and Scientific Work and Maintenance of Records

Psychologists create, and to the extent the records are under their control, maintain, disseminate, store, retain, and dispose of records and data relating to their professional and scientific work in order to (1) facilitate provision of services later by them or by other professionals, (2) allow for replication of research design and analyses, (3) meet institutional requirements, (4) ensure accuracy of billing and payments, and (5) ensure compliance with law. (See also Standard 4.01, Maintaining Confidentiality.)

6.02 Maintenance, Dissemination, and Disposal of Confidential Records of Professional and Scientific Work

(a) Psychologists maintain confidentiality in creating, storing, accessing, transferring, and disposing of records under their control, whether these are written, automated, or in any other medium. (See also Standards 4.01, Maintaining Confidentiality, and 6.01, Documentation of Professional and Scientific Work and Maintenance of Records.)

(b) If confidential information concerning recipients of psychological services is entered into databases or systems of records available to persons whose access has not been consented to by the recipient, psychologists use coding or other techniques to avoid the inclusion of personal identifiers.

(c) Psychologists make plans in advance to facilitate the appropriate transfer and to protect the confidentiality of records and data in the event of psychologists' withdrawal from positions or practice. (See also Standards 3.12, Interruption of Psychological Services, and 10.09, Interruption of Therapy.)

6.03 Withholding Records for Nonpayment

Psychologists may not withhold records under their control that are requested and needed for a client's/patient's emergency treatment solely because payment has not been received.

6.04 Fees and Financial Arrangements

(a) As early as is feasible in a professional *or* scientific relationship, psychologists and recipients of psychological services reach an agreement specifying compensation and billing arrangements.

(b) Psychologists' fee practices are consistent with law.

(c) Psychologists do not misrepresent their fees.

(d) If limitations to services can be anticipated because of limitations in financing, this is discussed with the recipient of services as early as is feasible. (See also Standards 10.09, Interruption of Therapy, and 10.10, Terminating Therapy.)

(e) If the recipient of services does not pay for services as agreed, and if psychologists intend to use collection agencies or legal measures to collect the fees, psychologists first inform the person that such measures will be taken and provide that person an opportunity to make prompt payment. (See also Standards 4.05, Disclosures; 6.03, Withholding Records for Nonpayment; and 10.01, Informed Consent to Therapy.)

6.05 Barter With Clients/Patients

Barter is the acceptance of goods, services, or other nonmonetary remuneration from clients/patients in return for psychological services. Psychologists may barter only if (1) it is not clinically contraindicated, and (2) the resulting arrangement is not exploitative. (See also Standards 3.05, Multiple Relationships, and 6.04, Fees and Financial Arrangements.)

6.06 Accuracy in Reports to Payors and Funding Sources

In their reports to payors for services or sources of research funding, psychologists take reasonable steps to ensure the accurate reporting of the nature of the service provided or research conducted, the fees, charges, or payments, and where applicable, the identity of the provider, the findings, and the diagnosis. (See also Standards 4.01, Maintaining Confidentiality; 4,04, Minimizing Intrusions on Privacy; and 4.05, Disclosures.)

6.07 Referrals and Fees

When psychologists pay, receive payment from, or divide fees with another professional, other than in an employer-employee relationship, the payment to each is based on the services provided (clinical, consultative, administrative, or other) and is not based on the referral itself. (See also Standard 3.09, Cooperation with Other Professionals.)

STANDARD 7: EDUCATION AND TRAINING

7.01 Design of Education and Training Programs

Psychologists responsible for education and training programs take reasonable steps to ensure that the programs are designed to provide the appropriate knowledge and proper experiences, and to meet the requirements for licensure, certification, or other goals for which claims are made by the program. (See also Standard 5.03, Descriptions of Workshops and Non-Degree-Granting Educational Programs.)

7.02 Descriptions of Education and Training Programs

Psychologists responsible for education and training programs take reasonable steps to ensure that there is a current and accurate description of the program content (including participation in required course- or program-related counseling, psychotherapy, experiential groups, consulting projects, or community service), training goats and objectives, stipends and benefits, and requirements that must be met for satisfactory completion of the program. This information must be made readily available to all interested parties.

7.03 Accuracy in Teaching

(a) Psychologists take reasonable steps to ensure that course syllabi are accurate regarding the subject matter to be covered, bases for evaluating progress, and the nature of course experiences. This standard does not preclude an instructor from modifying course content or requirements when the instructor considers it pedagogicaily necessary or desirable, so long as students are made aware of these modifications in a manner that enables them to fulfill course requirements. (See also Standard 5.01, Avoidance of False or Deceptive Statements.)

(b) When engaged in teaching or training, psychologists present psychological information accurately. (See also Standard 2.03, Maintaining Competence.)

7.04 Student Disclosure of Personal Information

Psychologists do not require students or supervisees to disclose personal information in course- or program-related activities, either orally or in writing, regarding sexual history, history of abuse and neglect, psychological treatment, and relationships with parents, peers, and spouses or significant others except if (1) the program or training facility has clearly identified this requirement in its admissions and program materials or (2) the information is necessary to evaluate or obtain assistance for students whose personal problems could reasonably be judged to be preventing them from performing their training- or professionally related activities in a competent manner or posing a threat to the students or others.

7.05 Mandatory Individual or Group Therapy

(a) When individual or group therapy is a program or course requirement, psychologists responsible for that program allow students in undergraduate and graduate programs the option of selecting such therapy from practitioners unaffiliated with the program. (See also Standard 7.02, Descriptions of Education and Training Programs.)

(b) Faculty who are or are likely to be responsible for evaluating students' academic performance do not themselves provide that therapy. (See also Standard 3.05, Multiple Relationships.)

7.06 Assessing Student and Supervisee Performance

(a) In academic and supervisory relationships, psychologists establish a timely and specific process for providing feedback to students and supervisees. Information regarding the process is provided to the student at the beginning of supervision.

(b) Psychologists evaluate students and supervisees on the basis of their actual performance on relevant and established program requirements.

7.07 Sexual Relationships With Students and Supervisees

Psychologists do not engage in sexual relationships with students or supervisees who are in their department, agency, or training center or over whom psychologists have or are likely to have evaluative authority, (See also Standard 3.05, Multiple Relationships.)

STANDARD 8: RESEARCH AND PUBLICATION

8.01 Institutional Approval

When institutional approval is required, psychologists provide accurate information about their research proposals and obtain approval prior to conducting the research. They conduct the research in accordance with the approved research protocol.

8.02 Informed Consent to Research

(a) When obtaining informed consent as required in Standard 3.10, Informed Consent, psychologists inform participants about (1) the purpose of the research, expected duration, and procedures; (2) their right to decline to participate and to withdraw from the research once participation has begun; (3) the foreseeable consequences of declining or withdrawing; (4) reasonably foreseeable factors that may be expected to influence their willingness to participate such as potential risks, discomfort, or adverse effects; (5) any prospective research benefits; (6) limits of confidentiality; (7) incentives for participation; and (8) whom to contact for questions about the research and research participants' rights. They provide opportunity for the prospective participants to ask questions and receive answers. (See also Standards 8.03, Informed Consent for Recording Voices and Images in Research; 8.05, Dispensing with Informed Consent for Research; and 8.07, Deception in Research.)

(b) Psychologists conducting intervention research involving the use of experimental treatments clarify to participants at the outset of the research (1) the experimental nature of the treatment; (2) the services that will or will not be available to the control group(s) if appropriate; (3) the means by which assignment to treatment and control groups will be made; (4) available treatment alternatives if an individual does not wish to participate in the research or wishes to withdraw once a study has begun; and (5) compensation for or monetary costs of participating including, if appropriate, whether reimbursement from the participant or a third-party payor will be sought. (See also Standard 8,02a, Informed Consent to Research.)

8.03 Informed Consent for Recording Voices and Images in Research

Psychologists obtain informed consent from research participants prior to recording their voices or images for data collection unless (1) the research consists solely of naturalistic observations in public places, and it is not anticipated that the recording will be used in a manner that could cause personal identification or harm, or (2) the research design includes deception, and consent for the use of the recording is obtained during debriefing. (See also Standard 8.07, Deception in Research.)

8.04 Client/Patient, Student, and Subordinate Research Participants

(a) When psychologists conduct research with clients/patients, students, or subordinates as participants, psychologists take steps to protect the prospective participants from adverse consequences of declining or withdrawing from participation.

(b) When research participation is a course requirement or an opportunity for extra credit, the prospective participant is given the choice of equitable alternative activities.

8.05 Dispensing with Informed Consent for Research

Psychologists may dispense with informed consent only (1) where research would not reasonably be assumed to create distress or harm and involves (a) the study of normal educational practices, curricula, or classroom management methods conducted in educational settings; (b) only anonymous questionnaires, naturalistic observations, or archival research for which disclosure of responses would not place participants at risk of criminal or civil liability or damage their financial standing, employability, or reputation, and confidentiality is protected; or (c) the study of factors related to job or organization effectiveness conducted in organizational settings for which there is no risk to participants' employability, and confidentiality is protected or (2) where otherwise permitted by law or federal or institutional regulations.

8.06 Offering Inducements for Research Participation

(a) Psychologists make reasonable efforts to avoid offering excessive or inappropriate financial or other inducements for research participation when such inducements are likely to coerce participation.

(b) When offering professional services as an inducement for research participation, psychologists clarify the nature of the services, as well as the risks, obligations, and limitations. (See also Standard 6.05, Barter with Clients/Patients.)

8.07 Deception in Research

(a) Psychologists do not conduct a study involving deception unless they have determined that the use of deceptive techniques is justified by the study's significant prospective scientific, educational, or applied value and that effective nondeceptive alternative procedures are not feasible.

(b) Psychologists do not deceive prospective participants about research that is reasonably expected to cause physical pain or severe emotional distress.

(c) Psychologists explain any deception that is an integral feature of the design and conduct of an experiment to participants as early as is feasible, preferably at the conclusion of their participation, but no later than at the conclusion of the data collection, and permit participants to withdraw their data. (See also Standard 8.08, Debriefing.)

8.08 Debriefing

(a) Psychologists provide a prompt opportunity for participants to obtain appropriate information about the nature, results, and conclusions of the research, and they take reasonable steps to correct any misconceptions that participants may have of which the psychologists are aware.

(b) If scientific or humane values justify delaying or withholding this information, psychologists take reasonable measures to reduce the risk of harm.

(c) When psychologists become aware that research procedures have harmed a participant, they take reasonable steps to minimize the harm.

8.09 Humane Care and Use of Animals in Research

(a) Psychologists acquire, care for, use, and dispose of animals in compliance with current federal, state, and local laws and regulations, and with professional standards.

(b) Psychologists trained in research methods and experienced in the care of laboratory animals supervise all procedures involving animals and are responsible for ensuring appropriate consideration of their comfort, health, and humane treatment.

(c) Psychologists ensure that all individuals under their supervision who are using animals have received instruction in research methods and in the care, maintenance, and handling of the species being used, to the extent appropriate to their role. (See also Standard 2.05, Delegation of Work to Others.)

(d) Psychologists make reasonable efforts to minimize the discomfort, infection, illness, and pain of animal subjects.

(e) Psychologists use a procedure subjecting animals to pain, stress, or privation only when an alternative procedure is unavailable and the goal is justified by its prospective scientific, educational, or applied value.

(f) Psychologists perform surgical procedures under appropriate anesthesia and follow techniques to avoid infection and minimize pain during and after surgery.

(g) When it is appropriate that an animal's life be terminated, psychologists proceed rapidly, with an effort to minimize pain and in accordance with accepted procedures.

8.10 Reporting Research Results

(a) Psychologists do not fabricate data. (See also Standard 5.01a, Avoidance of False or Deceptive Statements.)

(b) If psychologists discover significant errors in their published data, they take reasonable steps to correct such errors in a correction, retraction, erratum, or other appropriate publication means.

8.11 Plagiarism

Psychologists do not present portions of another's work or data as their own, even if the other work or data source is cited occasionally.

8.12 Publication Credit

(a) Psychologists take responsibility and credit, including authorship credit, only for work they have actually performed or to which they have substantially contributed. (See also Standard 8.12b, Publication Credit.)

(b) Principal authorship and other publication credits accurately reflect the relative scientific or professional contributions of the individuals involved, regardless of their relative status. Mere possession of an institutional position, such as department chair, does not justify authorship credit. Minor contributions to the research or to the writing for publications are acknowledged appropriately, such as in footnotes or in an introductory statement.

(c) Except under exceptional circumstances, a student is listed as principal author on any multiple-authored article that is substantially based on the student's doctoral dissertation. Faculty advisors discuss publication credit with students as early as feasible and throughout the research and publication process as appropriate. (See also Standard 8.12b, Publication Credit.)

8.13 Duplicate Publication of Data

Psychologists do not publish, as original data, data that have been previously published. This does not preclude republishing data when they are accompanied by proper acknowledgment.

8.14 Sharing Research Data for Verification

(a) After research results are published, psychologists do not withhold the data on which their conclusions are based from other competent professionals who seek to verify the substantive claims through reanalysis and who intend to use such data only for that purpose, provided that the confidentiality of the participants can be protected and unless legal rights concerning proprietary data preclude their release. This does not preclude psychologists from requiring that such individuals or groups be responsible for costs associated with the provision of such information.

(b) Psychologists who request data from other psychologists to verify the substantive claims through reanalysis may use shared data only for the declared purpose. Requesting psychologists obtain prior written agreement for all other uses of the data.

8.15 Reviewers

Psychologists who review material submitted for presentation, publication, grant, or research proposal review respect the confidentiality of and the proprietary rights in such information of those who submitted it.

STANDARD 9: ASSESSMENT

9.01 Bases for Assessments

(a) Psychologists base the opinions contained in their recommendations, reports, and diagnostic or evaluative statements, including forensic testimony, on information and techniques sufficient to substantiate their findings. (See also Standard 2.04, Bases for Scientific and Professional Judgments.)

(b) Except as noted in 9.01c, psychologists provide opinions of the psychological characteristics of individuals only after they have conducted an examination of the individuals adequate to support their statements or conclusions. When, despite reasonable efforts, such an examination is not practical, psychologists document the efforts they made and the result of those efforts, clarify the probable impact of their limited information on the reliability and validity of their opinions, and appropriately limit the nature and extent of their conclusions or recommendations. (See also Standards 2.01, Boundaries of Competence, and 9.06, Interpreting Assessment Results.)

(c) When psychologists conduct a record review or provide consultation or supervision and an individual examination is not warranted or necessary for the opinion, psychologists explain this and the sources of information on which they based their conclusions and recommendations.

9.02 Use of Assessments

(a) Psychologists administer, adapt, score, interpret, or use assessment techniques, interviews, tests, or instruments in a manner and for purposes that are appropriate in light of the research on or evidence of the usefulness and proper application of the techniques.

(b) Psychologists use assessment instruments whose validity and reliability have been established for use with members of the population tested. When such validity or reliability has not been established, psychologists describe the strengths and limitations of test results and interpretation.

(c) Psychologists use assessment methods that are appropriate to an individual's language preference and competence, unless the use of an alternative language is relevant to the assessment issues.

9.03 Informed Consent in Assessments

(a) Psychologists obtain informed consent for assessments, evaluations, or diagnostic services, as described in Standard 3.10, Informed Consent, except when (1) testing is mandated by law or governmental regulations; (2) informed consent is implied because testing is conducted as a routine educational, institutional, or organizational activity (e.g., when participants voluntarily agree to assessment when applying for a job); or (3) one purpose of the testing is to evaluate decisional capacity, informed consent includes an explanation of the nature and purpose of the assessment, fees, involvement of third parties, and limits of confidentiality and sufficient opportunity for the client/patient to ask questions and receive answers.

(b) Psychologists inform persons with questionable capacity to consent or for whom testing is mandated by law or governmental regulations about the nature and purpose of the proposed assessment services, using language that is reasonably understandable to the person being assessed.

(c) Psychologists using the services of an interpreter obtain informed consent from the client/patient to use that interpreter, ensure that confidentiality of test results and test security are maintained, and include in their recommendations, reports, and diagnostic or evaluative statements, including forensic testimony, discussion of any limitations on the data obtained. (See also Standards 2.05, Delegation of Work to Others; 4.01, Maintaining Confidentiality; 9.01, Bases for Assessments; 9.06, Interpreting Assessment Results; and 9.07, Assessment by Unqualified Persons.)

9.04 Release of Test Data

(a) The term test data refers to raw and scaled scores, client/patient responses to test questions or stimuli, and psychologists' notes and recordings concerning client/patient statements and behavior during an examination.

Those portions of test materials that include client/patient responses are included in the definition of test data. Pursuant to a client/patient release, psychologists provide test data to the client/patient or other persons identified in the release. Psychologists may refrain from releasing test data to protect a client/patient or others from substantial harm or misuse or misrepresentation of the data or the test, recognizing that in many instances release of confidential information under these circumstances is regulated by law. (See also Standard 9.11, Maintaining Test Security.)

(b) In the absence of a client/patient release, psychologists provide test data only as required by law or court order.

9.05 Test Construction

Psychologists who develop tests and other assessment techniques use appropriate psychometric procedures and current scientific or professional knowledge for test design, standardization, validation, reduction or elimination of bias, and recommendations for use.

9.06 Interpreting Assessment Results

When interpreting assessment results, including automated interpretations, psychologists take into account the purpose of the assessment as well as the various test factors, test-taking abilities, and other characteristics of the person being assessed, such as situational, personal, linguistic, and cultural differences, that might affect psychologists' judgments or reduce the accuracy of their interpretations. They indicate any significant limitations of their interpretations. (See also Standards 2.01b and c, Boundaries of Competence, and 3.01, Unfair Discrimination.)

9.07 Assessment by Unqualified Persons

Psychologists do not promote the use of psychological assessment techniques by unqualified persons, except when such use is conducted for training purposes with appropriate supervision. (See also Standard 2.05, Delegation of Work to Others.)

9.08 Obsolete Tests and Outdated Test Results

(a) Psychologists do not base their assessment or intervention decisions or recommendations on data or test results that are outdated for the current purpose.

(b) Psychologists do not base such decisions or recommendations on tests and measures that are obsolete and not useful for the current purpose.

9.09 Test Scoring and Interpretation Services

(a) Psychologists who offer assessment or scoring services to other professionals accurately describe the purpose, norms, validity, reliability, and applications of the procedures and any special qualifications applicable to their use.

(b) Psychologists select scoring and interpretation services (including automated services) on the basis of evidence of the validity of the program and procedures as well as on other appropriate considerations. (See also Standard 2.01b and c, Boundaries of Competence.)

(c) Psychologists retain responsibility for the appropriate application, interpretation, and use of assessment instruments, whether they score and interpret such tests themselves or use automated or other services.

9.10 Explaining Assessment Results

Regardless of whether the scoring and interpretation are done by psychologists, by employees or assistants, or by automated or other outside services, psychologists take reasonable steps to ensure that explanations of results are given to the individual or designated representative unless the nature of the relationship precludes provision of an explanation of results (such as in some organizational consulting, preemployment or security screenings, and forensic evaluations), and this fact has been clearly explained to the person being assessed in advance.

9.11 Maintaining Test Security

The term test materials refers to manuals, instruments, protocols, and test questions or stimuli and does not include test data as defined in Standard 9.04, Release of Test Data. Psychologists make reasonable efforts to maintain the integrity and security of test materials and other assessment techniques consistent with law and contractual obligations, and in a manner that permits adherence to this Ethics Code.

STANDARD 10: THERAPY

10.01 Informed Consent to Therapy

(a) When obtaining informed consent to therapy as required in Standard 3.10, Informed Consent, psychologists inform clients/patients as early as is feasible in the therapeutic relationship about the nature and anticipated course of therapy, fees, involvement of third parties, and limits of confidentiality and provide sufficient opportunity for the client/patient to ask questions and receive answers. (See also Standards 4.02, Discussing the Limits of Confidentiality, and 6-04, Fees and Financial Arrangements.)

(b) When obtaining informed consent for treatment for which generally recognized techniques and procedures have not been established, psychologists inform their clients/patients of the developing nature of the treatment, the potential risks involved, alternative treatments that may be available, and the voluntary nature of their participation. (See also Standards 2.01e, Boundaries of Competence, and 3.10, Informed Consent.)

(c) When the therapist is a trainee and the legal responsibility for the treatment provided resides with the supervisor, the client/patient, as part of the informed consent procedure, is informed that the therapist is in training and is being supervised and is given the name of the supervisor.

10.02 Therapy Involving Couples or Families

(a) When psychologists agree to provide services to several persons who have a relationship (such as spouses, significant others, or parents and children), they take reasonable steps to clarify at the outset (1) which of the individuals are clients/patients and (2) the relationship the psychologist will have with each person. This clarification includes the psychologist's role and the probable uses of the services provided or the information obtained. (See also Standard 4.02, Discussing the Limits of Confidentiality.)

(b) If it becomes apparent that psychologists may be called on to perform potentially conflicting roles (such as family therapist and then witness for one party in divorce proceedings), psychologists take reasonable steps to clarify and modify, or withdraw from, roles appropriately. (See also Standard 3.05c, Multiple Relationships.)

10.03 Group Therapy

When psychologists provide services to several persons in a group setting, they describe at the outset the roles and responsibilities of all parties and the limits of confidentiality.

10.04 Providing Therapy to Those Served by Others

In deciding whether to offer or provide services to those already receiving mental health services elsewhere, psychologists carefully consider the treatment issues and the potential client's/patient's welfare. Psychologists discuss these issues with the client/patient or another legally authorized person on behalf of the client/patient in order to minimize the risk of confusion and conflict, consult with the other service providers when appropriate, and proceed with caution and sensitivity to the therapeutic issues.

10.05 Sexual Intimacies with Current Therapy Clients/Patients

Psychologists do not engage in sexual intimacies with current therapy clients/patients.

10.06 Sexual Intimacies with Relatives or Significant Others of Current Therapy Clients/Patients

Psychologists do not engage in sexual intimacies with individuals they know to be close relatives, guardians, or significant others of current clients/patients. Psychologists do not terminate therapy to circumvent this standard.

10.07 Therapy with Former Sexual Partners

Psychologists do not accept as therapy clients/patients persons with whom they have engaged in sexual intimacies.

10.08 Sexual Intimacies with Former Therapy Clients/Patients

(a) Psychologists do not engage in sexual intimacies with former clients/patients for at least two years after cessation or termination of therapy.

(b) Psychologists do not engage in sexual intimacies with former clients/patients even after a two-year interval except in the most unusual circumstances. Psychologists who engage in such activity after the two years following cessation or termination of therapy and of having no sexual contact with the former client/patient bear the burden of demonstrating that there has been no exploitation, in light of all relevant factors, including (1) the amount of time that has passed since therapy terminated; (2) the nature, duration, and intensity of the therapy; (3) the circumstances of termination; (4) the client's/patient's personal history; (5) the client's/patient's current mental status; (6) the likelihood of adverse impact on the client/patient; and (7) any statements or actions made by the therapist during the course of therapy suggesting or inviting the possibility of a posttermination sexual or romantic relationship with the client/patient. (See also Standard 3.05, Multiple Relationships.)

10.09 Interruption of Therapy

When entering into employment or contractual relationships, psychologists make reasonable efforts to provide for orderly and appropriate resolution of responsibility for client/patient care in the event that the employment or contractual relationship ends, with paramount consideration given to the welfare of the client/patient. (See also Standard 3.12, Interruption of Psychological Services.)

10.10 Terminating Therapy

(a) Psychologists terminate therapy when it becomes reasonably clear that the client/patient no longer needs the service, is not likely to benefit, or is being harmed by continued service.

(b) Psychologists may terminate therapy when threatened or otherwise endangered by the client/patient or another person with whom the client/patient has a relationship.

(c) Except where precluded by the actions of clients/patients or third-party payors, prior to termination psychologists provide pretermination counseling and suggest alternative service providers as appropriate.

HISTORY AND EFFECTIVE DATE

The American Psychological Association's Council of Representatives adopted this version of the APA Ethics Code during its meeting on August 21, 2002. The Code became effective on June 1, 2003. The Council of Representatives amended this version of the Ethics Code on February 20, 2010. The amendments became effective on June 1, 2010. Inquiries concerning the substance or interpretation of the APA Ethics Code should be addressed to the Director, Office of Ethics, American Psychological Association, 750 First St. NE, Washington, DC 20002-4242. The standards in this Ethics Code will be used to adjudicate complaints brought concerning alleged conduct occurring on or after the effective date. Complaints will be adjudicated on the basis of the version of the Ethics Code that was in effect at the time the conduct occurred.

The APA has previously published its Ethics Code as follows:

American Psychological Association. (1953). *Ethical standards of psychologists*. Washington, DC: Author.

American Psychological Association. (1959). Ethical standards of psychologists. *American Psychologist, 14*, 279–282.

American Psychological Association. (1963). Ethical standards of psychologists. *American Psychologist, 18*, 56–60.

American Psychological Association. (1968). Ethical standards of psychologists. *American Psychologist, 23*, 357–361.

American Psychological Association. (1977, March). Ethical standards of psychologists. APA *Monitor*, 22–23.

American Psychological Association. (1979). *Ethical standards of psychologists*. Washington, DC; Author.

American Psychological Association. (1981). Ethical principles of psychologists. *American Psychologist*, 36, 633–638.

American Psychological Association. (1990). Ethical principles of psychologists (Amended June 2, 1989). *American Psychologist*, 45, 390–395.

American Psychological Association. (1992). Ethical principles of psychologists and code of conduct. *American Psychologist*, 47, 1597–1611.

American Psychological Association. (2002). Ethical principles of psychologists and code of conduct. *American Psychologist*, 57, 1060–1073.

Request copies of the APA's Ethical Principles of Psychologists and Code of Conduct from the APA Order Department, 750 First St. NE, Washington, DC 20002-4242, or phone (202) 336–5510.

LANGUAGE OF THE 2002 ETHICS CODE WITH CHANGES MARKED

Introduction and Applicability

If psychologists' ethical responsibilities conflict with law, regulations, or other governing legal authority, psychologists make known their commitment to this Ethics Code and take steps to resolve the conflict in a responsible manner. ~~If the conflict is unresolvable via such means, psychologists may adhere to the requirements of the law, regulations, or other governing authority~~ in keeping with basic principles of human rights.

1.02 Conflicts Between Ethics and Law, Regulations, or Other Governing Legal Authority

If psychologists' ethical responsibilities conflict with law, regulations, or other governing legal authority, psychologists <u>clarify the nature of the conflict</u>, make known their commitment to the Ethics Code and take <u>reasonable</u> steps to resolve the conflict <u>consistent with the General Principles and Ethical Standards of the Ethics Code</u>. ~~If the conflict is unresolvable via such means, psychologists may adhere to the requirements of the law, regulations, or other governing legal authority.~~ <u>Under no circumstances may this standard be used to justify or defend violating human rights.</u>

1.03 Conflicts Between Ethics and Organizational Demands

If the demands of an organization with which psychologists are affiliated or for whom they are working <u>are in</u> conflict with this Ethics Code, psychologists clarify the nature of the conflict, make known their commitment to the Ethics

Code, and ~~to the extent feasible, resolve the conflict in a way that permits adherence to the Ethics Code~~. <u>take reasonable steps to resolve the conflict consistent with the General Principles and Ethical Standards of the Ethics Code. Under no circumstances may this standard be used to justify or defend violating human rights.</u>

CANADIAN CODE OF ETHICS FOR PSYCHOLOGISTS (3rd Ed.)

TABLE OF CONTENTS

From *Canadian Code of Ethics for Psychologists* (3rd ed.), by Canadian Psychological Association, 2002, Ottowa, Onario: Canadian Psychological Association Société canadienne de psychologie. Copyright 2000 by the Canadian Psychological Association. Reprinted with permission.

Principle I: Respect for the Dignity of Persons

    Values Statement

    Ethical Standards

        General respect

        General rights

        Non-discrimination

        Fair treatment/due process

        Informed consent

        Freedom of consent

        Protections for vulnerable persons

        Privacy

        Confidentiality

        Extended responsibility

Principle II: Responsible Caring

    Values Statement

    Ethical Standards

        General caring

        Competence and self-knowledge

        Risk/benefit analysis

        Maximize benefit

        Minimize harm

        Offset/correct harm

        Care of animals

        Extended responsibility

Principle III: Integrity in Relationships

    Values Statement

    Ethical Standards

        Accuracy/honesty

        Objectivity/lack of bias

        Straightforwardness/openness

        Avoidance of incomplete disclosure

Avoidance of conflict of interest

Reliance on the discipline

Extended responsibility

Principle IV: Responsibility to Society

Values Statement

Ethical Standards

Development of knowledge

Beneficial activities

Respect for society

Development of society

Extended responsibility

PREAMBLE

Introduction

Every discipline that has relatively autonomous control over its entry requirements, training, development of knowledge, standards, methods, and practices does so only within the context of a contract with the society in which it functions. This social contract is based on attitudes of mutual respect and trust, with society granting support for the autonomy of a discipline in exchange for a commitment by the discipline to do everything it can to assure that its members act ethically in conducting the affairs of the discipline within society; in particular, a commitment to try to assure that each member will place the welfare of the society and individual members of that society above the welfare of the discipline and its own members. By virtue of this social contract, psychologists have a higher duty of care to members of society than the general duty of care that all members of society have to each other.

The Canadian Psychological Association recognizes its responsibility to help assure ethical behaviour and attitudes on the part of psychologists. Attempts to assure ethical behaviour and attitudes include articulating ethical principles, values, and standards; promoting those principles, values, and standards through education, peer modelling, and consultation; developing and implementing methods to help psychologists monitor the ethics of their behaviour and attitudes; adjudicating complaints of unethical behaviour; and, taking corrective action when warranted.

This *Code* articulates ethical principles, values, and standards to guide all members of the Canadian Psychological Association, whether scientists, practitioners, or scientist practitioners, or whether acting in a research, direct service, teaching, student, trainee, administrative, management, employer, employee, supervisory, consultative, peer review, editorial, expert witness, social policy, or any other role related to the discipline of psychology.

Structure and Derivation of *Code*

Structure. Four ethical principles, to be considered and balanced in ethical decision making, are presented. Each principle is followed by a statement of those values that are included in and give definition to the principle. Each values statement is followed by a list of ethical standards that illustrate the application of the specific principle and values to the activities of psychologists. The standards range from minimal behavioural expectations (e.g., Standards I.28, II.28, III.33, IV.27) to more idealized, but achievable, attitudinal and behavioural expectations (e.g., Standards I.12, II.12, III.10, IV.6). In the margin, to the left of the standards, key words are placed to guide the reader through the standards and to illustrate the relationship of the specific standards to the values statement.

Derivation. The four principles represent those ethical principles used most consistently by Canadian psychologists to resolve hypothetical ethical dilemmas sent to them by the CPA Committee on Ethics during the initial development of the *Code*. In addition to the responses provided by Canadian psychologists, the values statements and ethical standards have been derived from interdisciplinary and international ethics codes, provincial and specialty codes of conduct, and ethics literature.

When Principles Conflict

All four principles are to be taken into account and balanced in ethical decision making. However, there are circumstances in which ethical principles will conflict and it will not be possible to give each principle equal weight. The complexity of ethical conflicts precludes a firm ordering of the principles. However, the four principles have been ordered according to the weight each generally should be given when they conflict, namely:

> Principle I: Respect for the Dignity of Persons. This principle, with its emphasis on moral rights, generally should be given the highest weight, except in circumstances in which there is a clear and imminent danger to the physical safety of any person.

> Principle II: Responsible Caring. This principle generally should be given the second highest weight. Responsible caring requires competence and should be carried out only in ways that respect the dignity of persons.

Principle III: Integrity in Relationships. This principle generally should be given the third highest weight. Psychologists are expected to demonstrate the highest integrity in all of their relationships. However, in rare circumstances, values such as openness and straightforwardness might need to be subordinated to the values contained in the Principles of Respect for the Dignity of Persons and Responsible Caring.

Principle IV: Responsibility to Society. This principle generally should be given the lowest weight of the four principles when it conflicts with one or more of them. Although it is necessary and important to consider responsibility to society in every ethical decision, adherence to this principle must be subject to and guided by Respect for the Dignity of Persons, Responsible Caring, and Integrity in Relationships. When a person's welfare appears to conflict with benefits to society, it is often possible to find ways of working for the benefit of society that do not violate respect and responsible caring for the person. However, if this is not possible, the dignity and well-being of a person should not be sacrificed to a vision of the greater good of society, and greater weight must be given to respect and responsible caring for the person.

Even with the above ordering of the principles, psychologists will be faced with ethical dilemmas that are difficult to resolve. In these circumstances, psychologists are expected to engage in an ethical decision-making process that is explicit enough to bear public scrutiny. In some cases, resolution might be a matter of personal conscience. However, decisions of personal conscience are also expected to be the result of a decision-making process that is based on a reasonably coherent set of ethical principles and that can bear public scrutiny. If the psychologist can demonstrate that every reasonable effort was made to apply the ethical principles of this *Code* and resolution of the conflict has had to depend on the personal conscience of the psychologist, such a psychologist would be deemed to have followed this *Code*.

The Ethical Decision-Making Process

The ethical decision-making process might occur very rapidly, leading to an easy resolution of an ethical issue. This is particularly true of issues for which clear-cut guidelines or standards exist and for which there is no conflict between principles. On the other hand, some ethical issues (particularly those in which ethical principles conflict) are not easily resolved, might be emotionally distressful, and might require time-consuming deliberation.

The following basic steps typify approaches to ethical decision making:

1. Identification of the individuals and groups potentially affected by the decision.

2. Identification of ethically relevant issues and practices, including the interests, rights, and any relevant characteristics of the individuals and groups involved and of the system or circumstances in which the ethical problem arose.

3. Consideration of how personal biases, stresses, or self-interest might influence the development of or choice between courses of action.

4. Development of alternative courses of action.

5. Analysis of likely short-term, ongoing, and long-term risks and benefits of each course of action on the individual(s)/group(s) involved or likely to be affected (e.g., client, client's family or employees, employing institution, students, research participants, colleagues, the discipline, society, self).

6. Choice of course of action after conscientious application of existing principles, values, and standards.

7. Action, with a commitment to assume responsibility for the consequences of the action.

8. Evaluation of the results of the course of action.

9. Assumption of responsibility for consequences of action, including correction of negative consequences, if any, or re-engaging in the decision-making process if the ethical issue is not resolved.

10. Appropriate action, as warranted and feasible, to prevent future occurrences of the dilemma (e.g., communication and problem solving with colleagues; changes in procedures and practices).

Psychologists engaged in time-consuming deliberation are encouraged and expected to consult with parties affected by the ethical problem, when appropriate, and with colleagues and/or advisory bodies when such persons can add knowledge or objectivity to the decision-making process. Although the decision for action remains with the individual psychologist, the seeking and consideration of such assistance reflects an ethical approach to ethical decision making.

Uses of the *Code*

This *Code* is intended to guide psychologists in their everyday conduct, thinking, and planning, and in the resolution of ethical dilemmas; that is, it advocates the practice of both proactive and reactive ethics.

The *Code* also is intended to serve as an umbrella document for the development of codes of conduct or other more specific codes. For example, the *Code* could be used as an ethical framework for the identification of behaviours that would be considered enforceable in a jurisdiction, the violation of which would constitute misconduct; or, jurisdictions could identify those standards in the *Code* that would be considered of a more serious nature and, therefore, reportable and subject to possible discipline. In addition, the principles and values could be used to help specialty areas develop standards that are specific to those areas. Some work in this direction has already occurred within CPA (e.g., *Guidelines for the Use of Animals in Research and Instruction in Psychology*, *Guidelines for Non-Discriminatory Practice*, *Guidelines for Psychologists in Addressing Recovered Memories*). The principles and values incorporated into this *Code*, insofar as they come to be reflected in other documents guiding the behaviour of psychologists, will reduce inconsistency and conflict between documents.

A third use of the *Code* is to assist in the adjudication of complaints against psychologists. A body charged with this responsibility is required to investigate allegations, judge whether unacceptable behaviour has occurred, and determine what corrective action should be taken. In judging whether unacceptable conduct has occurred, many jurisdictions refer to a code of conduct. Some complaints, however, are about conduct that is not addressed directly in a code of conduct. The *Code* provides an ethical framework for determining whether the complaint is of enough concern, either at the level of the individual psychologist or at the level of the profession as a whole, to warrant corrective action (e.g., discipline of the individual psychologist, general educational activities for members, or incorporation into the code of conduct). In determining corrective action for an individual psychologist, one of the judgments the adjudicating body needs to make is whether an individual conscientiously engaged in an ethical decision-making process and acted in good faith, or whether there was a negligent or willful disregard of ethical principles. The articulation of the ethical decision-making process contained in this *Code* provides guidance for making such judgements.

Responsibility of the Individual Psychologist

The discipline's contract with society commits the discipline and its members to act as a moral community that develops its ethical awareness and sensitivity, educates new members in the ethics of the discipline, manages its affairs and its members in an ethical manner, is as self-correcting as possible, and is accountable both internally and externally.

However, responsibility for ethical action depends foremost on the integrity of each individual psychologist; that is, on each psychologist's commitment to behave as ethically as possible in every situation. Acceptance to membership in the Canadian Psychological Association, a scientific and professional association of psychologists, commits members:

1. To adhere to the Association's *Code* in all current activities as a psychologist.

2. To apply conscientiously the ethical principles and values of the *Code* to new and emerging areas of activity.
3. To assess and discuss ethical issues and practices with colleagues on a regular basis.
4. To bring to the attention of the Association ethical issues that require clarification or the development of new guidelines or standards.
5. To bring concerns about possible unethical actions by a psychologist directly to the psychologist when the action appears to be primarily a lack of sensitivity, knowledge, or experience, and attempt to reach an agreement on the issue and, if needed, on the appropriate action to be taken.
6. To bring concerns about possible unethical actions of a more serious nature (e.g., actions that have caused or could cause serious harm, or actions that are considered misconduct in the jurisdiction) to the person(s) or body(ies) best suited to investigating the situation and to stopping or offsetting the harm.
7. To consider seriously others' concerns about one's own possibly unethical actions and attempt to reach an agreement on the issue and, if needed, take appropriate action.
8. In bringing or in responding to concerns about possible unethical actions, not to be vexatious or malicious.
9. To cooperate with duly constituted committees of the Association that are concerned with ethics and ethical conduct.

Relationship of *Code* to Personal Behaviour

This *Code* is intended to guide and regulate only those activities a psychologist engages in by virtue of being a psychologist. There is no intention to guide or regulate a psychologist's activities outside of this context. Personal behaviour becomes a concern of the discipline only if it is of such a nature that it undermines public trust in the discipline as a whole or if it raises questions about the psychologist's ability to carry out appropriately his/her responsibilities as a psychologist.

Relationship of *Code* to Provincial Regulatory Bodies

In exercising its responsibility to articulate ethical principles, values, and standards for those who wish to become and remain members in good standing, the Canadian Psychological Association recognizes the multiple memberships that some psychologists have (both regulatory and voluntary). The *Code* has attempted to encompass and incorporate those ethical principles most prevalent in the discipline as a whole, thereby minimizing the possibility of variance with provincial/territorial regulations and guidelines. Psychologists are expected to respect the requirements of their provincial/territorial regulatory bodies. Such requirements might define particular behaviours that constitute misconduct, are reportable to the regulatory body, and/or are subject to discipline.

Definition of Terms

For the purposes of this *Code*:

a) *"Psychologist"* means any person who is a Fellow, Member, Student Affiliate or Foreign Affiliate of the Canadian Psychological Association, or a member of any psychology voluntary association or regulatory body adopting this *Code*. (Readers are reminded that provincial/ territorial jurisdictions might restrict the legal use of the term *psychologist* in their jurisdiction and that such restrictions are to be honoured.)

b) *"Client"* means an individual, family, or group (including an organization or community) receiving service from a psychologist.

c) Clients, research participants, students, and any other persons with whom psychologists come in contact in the course of their work, are *"independent"* if they can independently contract or give informed consent. Such persons are *"partially dependent"* if the decision to contract or give informed consent is shared between two or more parties (e.g., parents and school boards, workers and Workers' Compensation Boards, adult members of a family). Such persons are considered to be *"fully dependent"* if they have little or no choice about whether or not to receive service or participate in an activity (e.g., patients who have been involuntarily committed to a psychiatric facility, or very young children involved in a research project).

d) *"Others"* means any persons with whom psychologists come in contact in the course of their work. This may include, but is not limited to: clients seeking help with individual, family, organizational, industrial, or community issues; research participants; employees; students; trainees; supervisees; colleagues; employers; third party payers; and, members of the general public.

e) *"Legal or civil rights"* means those rights protected under laws and statutes recognized by the province or territory in which the psychologist is working.

f) *"Moral rights"* means fundamental and inalienable human rights that might or might not be fully protected by existing laws and statutes. Of particular significance to psychologists, for example, are rights to: distributive justice; fairness and due process; and, developmentally appropriate privacy, self-determination, and personal liberty. Protection of some aspects of these rights might involve practices that are not contained or controlled within current laws and statutes. Moral rights are not limited to those mentioned in this definition.

g) "*Unjust discrimination*" or "*unjustly discriminatory*" means activities that are prejudicial or promote prejudice to persons because of their culture, nationality, ethnicity, colour, race, religion, sex, gender, marital status, sexual orientation, physical or mental abilities, age, socio-economic status, or any other preference or personal characteristic, condition, or status.

h) "*Sexual harassment*" includes either or both of the following: (i) The use of power or authority in an attempt to coerce another person to engage in or tolerate sexual activity. Such uses include explicit or implicit threats of reprisal for noncompliance, or promises of reward for compliance. (ii) Engaging in deliberate and/or repeated unsolicited sexually oriented comments, anecdotes, gestures, or touching, if such behaviours: are offensive and unwelcome; create an offensive, hostile, or intimidating working, learning, or service environment; or, can be expected to be harmful to the recipient.[1]

i) The "*discipline of psychology*" refers to the scientific and applied methods and knowledge of psychology, and to the structures and procedures used by its members for conducting their work in relationship to society, to members of the public, to students or trainees, and to each other.

Review Schedule

To maintain the relevance and responsiveness of this *Code*, it will be reviewed regularly by the CPA Board of Directors, and revised as needed. You are invited to forward comments and suggestions, at any time, to the CPA office. In addition to psychologists, this invitation is extended to all readers, including members of the public and other disciplines.

PRINCIPLE I: RESPECT FOR THE DIGNITY OF PERSONS
Values Statement

In the course of their work as scientists, practitioners, or scientist-practitioners, psychologists come into contact with many different individuals and groups, including: research participants; clients seeking help with individual, family, organizational, industrial, or community issues; students; trainees; supervisees;

employees; business partners; business competitors; colleagues; employers; third party payers; and, the general public.

In these contacts, psychologists accept as fundamental the principle of respect for the dignity of persons; that is, the belief that each person should be treated primarily as a person or an end in him/herself, not as an object or a means to an end. In so doing, psychologists acknowledge that all persons have a right to have their innate worth as human beings appreciated and that this worth is not dependent upon their culture, nationality, ethnicity, colour, race, religion, sex, gender, marital status, sexual orientation, physical or mental abilities, age, socio-economic status, or any other preference or personal characteristic, condition, or status.

Although psychologists have a responsibility to respect the dignity of all persons with whom they come in contact in their role as psychologists, the nature of their contract with society demands that their greatest responsibility be to those persons in the most vulnerable position. Normally, persons directly receiving or involved in the psychologist's activities are in such a position (e.g., research participants, clients, students). This responsibility is almost always greater than their responsibility to those indirectly involved (e.g., employers, third party payers, the general public).

Adherence to the concept of moral rights is an essential component of respect for the dignity of persons. Rights to privacy, self-determination, personal liberty, and natural justice are of particular importance to psychologists, and they have a responsibility to protect and promote these rights in all of their activities. As such, psychologists have a responsibility to develop and follow procedures for informed consent, confidentiality, fair treatment, and due process that are consistent with those rights.

As individual rights exist within the context of the rights of others and of responsible caring (see Principle II), there might be circumstances in which the possibility of serious detrimental consequences to themselves or others, a diminished capacity to be autonomous, or a court order, would disallow some aspects of the rights to privacy, self-determination, and personal liberty. Indeed, such circumstances might be serious enough to create a duty to warn or protect others (see Standards I.45 and II.39). However, psychologists still have a responsibility to respect the rights of the person(s) involved to the greatest extent possible under the circumstances, and to do what is necessary and reasonable to reduce the need for future disallowances.

Psychologists recognize that, although all persons possess moral rights, the manner in which such rights are promoted, protected, and exercised varies across communities and cultures. For instance, definitions of what is considered private vary, as does the role of families and other community members in personal decision making. In their work, psychologists acknowledge and respect such differences, while guarding against clear violations of moral rights.

In addition, psychologists recognize that as individual, family, group, or community vulnerabilities increase, or as the power of persons to control their environment or their lives decreases, psychologists have an increasing responsibility to seek ethical advice and to establish safeguards to protect the rights of the persons involved. For this reason, psychologists consider it their responsibility to increase safeguards to protect and promote the rights of persons involved in their activities proportionate to the degree of dependency and the lack of voluntary initiation. For example, this would mean that there would be more safeguards to protect and promote the rights of fully dependent persons than partially dependent persons, and more safeguards for partially dependent than independent persons.

Respect for the dignity of persons also includes the concept of distributive justice. With respect to psychologists, this concept implies that all persons are entitled to benefit equally from the contributions of psychology and to equal quality in the processes, procedures, and services being conducted by psychologists, regardless of the person's characteristics, condition, or status. Although individual psychologists might specialize and direct their activities to particular populations, or might decline to engage in activities based on the limits of their competence or acknowledgment of problems in some relationships, psychologists must not exclude persons on a capricious or unjustly discriminatory basis.

By virtue of the social contract that the discipline has with society, psychologists have a higher duty of care to members of society than the general duty of care all members of society have to each other. However, psychologists are entitled to protect themselves from serious violations of their own moral rights (e.g., privacy, personal liberty) in carrying out their work as psychologists.

Ethical Standards

In adhering to the Principle of Respect for the Dignity of Persons, psychologists would:

General respect   I.1   Demonstrate appropriate respect for the knowledge, insight, experience, and areas of expertise of others.

    I.2   Not engage publicly (e.g., in public statements, presentations, research reports, or with clients) in degrading comments about others, including demeaning jokes based on such characteristics as culture, nationality, ethnicity, colour, race, religion, sex, gender, or sexual orientation.

    I.3   Strive to use language that conveys respect for the dignity of persons as much as possible in all written or oral communication.

	I.4	Abstain from all forms of harassment, including sexual harassment.
General rights	I.5	Avoid or refuse to participate in practices disrespectful of the legal, civil, or moral rights of others.
	I.6	Refuse to advise, train, or supply information to anyone who, in the psychologist's judgement, will use the knowledge or skills to infringe on human rights.
	I.7	Make every reasonable effort to ensure that psychological knowledge is not misused, intentionally or unintentionally, to infringe on human rights.
	I.8	Respect the right of research participants, clients, employees, supervisees, students, trainees, and others to safeguard their own dignity.
Non-discrimination	I.9	Not practice, condone, facilitate, or collaborate with any form of unjust discrimination.
	I.10	Act to correct practices that are unjustly discriminatory.
	I.11	Seek to design research, teaching, practice, and business activities in such a way that they contribute to the fair distribution of benefits to individuals and groups, and that they do not unfairly exclude those who are vulnerable or might be disadvantaged.
Fair treatment/due process	I.12	Work and act in a spirit of fair treatment to others.
	I.13	Help to establish and abide by due process or other natural justice procedures for employment, evaluation, adjudication, editorial, and peer review activities.
	I.14	Compensate others fairly for the use of their time, energy, and knowledge, unless such compensation is refused in advance.
	I.15	Establish fees that are fair in light of the time, energy, and knowledge of the psychologist and any associates or employees, and in light of the market value of the product or service. (Also see Standard IV.12.)
Informed consent	I.16	Seek as full and active participation as possible from others in decisions that affect them, respecting and integrating as much as possible their opinions and wishes.

I.17 Recognize that informed consent is the result of a process of reaching an agreement to work collaboratively, rather than of simply having a consent form signed.

I.18 Respect the expressed wishes of persons to involve others (e.g., family members, community members) in their decision making regarding informed consent. This would include respect for written and clearly expressed unwritten advance directives.

I.19 Obtain informed consent from all independent and partially dependent persons for any psychological services provided to them except in circumstances of urgent need (e.g., disaster or other crisis). In urgent circumstances, psychologists would proceed with the assent of such persons, but fully informed consent would be obtained as soon as possible. (Also see Standard I.29.)

I.20 Obtain informed consent for all research activities that involve obtrusive measures, invasion of privacy, more than minimal risk of harm, or any attempt to change the behaviour of research participants.

I.21 Establish and use signed consent forms that specify the dimensions of informed consent or that acknowledge that such dimensions have been explained and are understood, if such forms are required by law or if such forms are desired by the psychologist, the person(s) giving consent, or the organization for whom the psychologist works.

I.22 Accept and document oral consent, in situations in which signed consent forms are not acceptable culturally or in which there are other good reasons for not using them.

I.23 Provide, in obtaining informed consent, as much information as reasonable or prudent persons would want to know before making a decision or consenting to the activity. The psychologist would relay this information in language that the persons understand (including providing translation into another language, if necessary) and would take whatever reasonable steps are needed to ensure that the information was, in fact, understood.

I.24 Ensure, in the process of obtaining informed consent, that at least the following points are understood: purpose and nature of the activity; mutual responsibilities; confidentiality protections and limitations; likely benefits and risks; alternatives; the likely consequences of non-action; the option to refuse or withdraw at any time, without prejudice; over what period of time the consent applies; and, how to rescind consent if desired. (Also see Standards III.23–30.)

I.25 Provide new information in a timely manner, whenever such information becomes available and is significant enough that it reasonably could be seen as relevant to the original or ongoing informed consent.

I.26 Clarify the nature of multiple relationships to all concerned parties before obtaining consent, if providing services to or conducting research at the request or for the use of third parties. This would include, but not be limited to: the purpose of the service or research; the reasonably anticipated use that will be made of information collected; and, the limits on confidentiality. Third parties may include schools, courts, government agencies, insurance companies, police, and special funding bodies.

Freedom of consent I.27 Take all reasonable steps to ensure that consent is not given under conditions of coercion, undue pressure, or undue reward. (Also see Standard III.32.)

I.28 Not proceed with any research activity, if consent is given under any condition of coercion, undue pressure, or undue reward. (Also see Standard III.32.)

I.29 Take all reasonable steps to confirm or re-establish freedom of consent, if consent for service is given under conditions of duress or conditions of extreme need.

I.30 Respect the right of persons to discontinue participation or service at any time, and be responsive to non-verbal indications of a desire to discontinue if a person has difficulty with verbally communicating such a desire (e.g., young

		children, verbally disabled persons) or, due to culture, is unlikely to communicate such a desire orally.
Protections for vulnerable persons	I.31	Seek an independent and adequate ethical review of human rights issues and protections for any research involving members of vulnerable groups, including persons of diminished capacity to give informed consent, before making a decision to proceed.
	I.32	Not use persons of diminished capacity to give informed consent in research studies, if the research involved may be carried out equally well with persons who have a fuller capacity to give informed consent.
	I.33	Seek to use methods that maximize the understanding and ability to consent of persons of diminished capacity to give informed consent, and that reduce the need for a substitute decision maker.
	I.34	Carry out informed consent processes with those persons who are legally responsible or appointed to give informed consent on behalf of persons not competent to consent on their own behalf, seeking to ensure respect for any previously expressed preferences of persons not competent to consent.
	I.35	Seek willing and adequately informed participation from any person of diminished capacity to give informed consent, and proceed without this assent only if the service or research activity is considered to be of direct benefit to that person.
	I.36	Be particularly cautious in establishing the freedom of consent of any person who is in a dependent relationship to the psychologist (e.g., student, employee). This may include, but is not limited to, offering that person an alternative activity to fulfill their educational or employment goals, or offering a range of research studies or experience opportunities from which the person can select, none of which is so onerous as to be coercive.
Privacy	I.37	Seek and collect only information that is germane to the purpose(s) for which consent has been obtained.

I.38 Take care not to infringe, in research, teaching, or service activities, on the personally, developmentally, or culturally defined private space of individuals or groups, unless clear permission is granted to do so.

I.39 Record only that private information necessary for the provision of continuous, coordinated service, or for the goals of the particular research study being conducted, or that is required or justified by law. (Also see Standards IV.17 and IV.18.)

I.40 Respect the right of research participants, employees, supervisees, students, and trainees to reasonable personal privacy.

I.41 Collect, store, handle, and transfer all private information, whether written or unwritten (e.g., communication during service provision, written records, e-mail or fax communication, computer files, video-tapes), in a way that attends to the needs for privacy and security. This would include having adequate plans for records in circumstances of one's own serious illness, termination of employment, or death.

I.42 Take all reasonable steps to ensure that records over which they have control remain personally identifiable only as long as necessary in the interests of those to whom they refer and/or to the research project for which they were collected, or as required or justified by law (e.g., the possible need to defend oneself against future allegations), and render anonymous or destroy any records under their control that no longer need to be personally identifiable. (Also see Standards IV.17 and IV.18.)

Confidentiality I.43 Be careful not to relay information about colleagues, colleagues' clients, research participants, employees, supervisees, students, trainees, and members of organizations, gained in the process of their activities as psychologists, that the psychologist has reason to believe is considered confidential by those persons, except as required or justified by law. (Also see Standards IV.17 and IV.18.)

I.44 Clarify what measures will be taken to protect confidentiality, and what responsibilities family, group, and community members have for the protection of each other's confidentiality, when engaged in services to or research with individuals, families, groups, or communities.

I.45 Share confidential information with others only with the informed consent of those involved, or in a manner that the persons involved cannot be identified, except as required or justified by law, or in circumstances of actual or possible serious physical harm or death. (Also see Standards II.39, IV.17, and IV.18.)

Extended responsibility

I.46 Encourage others, in a manner consistent with this *Code*, to respect the dignity of persons and to expect respect for their own dignity.

I.47 Assume overall responsibility for the scientific and professional activities of their assistants, employees, students, supervisees, and trainees with regard to Respect for the Dignity of Persons, all of whom, however, incur similar obligations.

PRINCIPLE II: RESPONSIBLE CARING

Values Statement

A basic ethical expectation of any discipline is that its activities will benefit members of society or, at least, do no harm. Therefore, psychologists demonstrate an active concern for the welfare of any individual, family, group, or community with whom they relate in their role as psychologists. This concern includes both those directly involved and those indirectly involved in their activities. However, as with Principle I, psychologists' greatest responsibility is to protect the welfare of those in the most vulnerable position. Normally, persons directly involved in their activities (e.g., research participants, clients, students) are in such a position. Psychologists' responsibility to those indirectly involved (e.g., employers, third party payers, the general public) normally is secondary.

As persons usually consider their own welfare in their personal decision making, obtaining informed consent (see Principle I) is one of the best methods for ensuring that their welfare will be protected. However, it is only when such consent is combined with the responsible caring of the psychologist that there is considerable ethical protection of the welfare of the person(s) involved.

Responsible caring leads psychologists to take care to discern the potential harm and benefits involved, to predict the likelihood of their occurrence, to proceed only if the potential benefits outweigh the potential harms, to develop and use methods that will minimize harms and maximize benefits, and to take responsibility for correcting clearly harmful effects that have occurred as a direct result of their research, teaching, practice, or business activities.

In order to carry out these steps, psychologists recognize the need for competence and self-knowledge. They consider incompetent action to be unethical per se, as it is unlikely to be of benefit and likely to be harmful. They engage only in those activities in which they have competence or for which they are receiving supervision, and they perform their activities as competently as possible. They acquire, contribute to, and use the existing knowledge most relevant to the best interests of those concerned. They also engage in self-reflection regarding how their own values, attitudes, experiences, and social context (e.g., culture, ethnicity, colour, religion, sex, gender, sexual orientation, physical and mental abilities, age, and socio-economic status) influence their actions, interpretations, choices, and recommendations. This is done with the intent of increasing the probability that their activities will benefit and not harm the individuals, families, groups, and communities to whom they relate in their role as psychologists. Psychologists define harm and benefit in terms of both physical and psychological dimensions. They are concerned about such factors as: social, family, and community relationships; personal and cultural identity; feelings of self-worth, fear, humiliation, interpersonal trust, and cynicism; self-knowledge and general knowledge; and, such factors as physical safety, comfort, pain, and injury. They are concerned about immediate, short-term, and long-term effects.

Responsible caring recognizes and respects (e.g., through obtaining informed consent) the ability of individuals, families, groups, and communities to make decisions for themselves and to care for themselves and each other. It does not replace or undermine such ability, nor does it substitute one person's opinion about what is in the best interests of another person for that other person's competent decision making. However, psychologists recognize that, as vulnerabilities increase or as power to control one's own life decreases, psychologists have an increasing responsibility to protect the well-being of the individual, family, group, or community involved. For this reason, as in Principle I, psychologists consider it their responsibility to increase safeguards proportionate to the degree of dependency and the lack of voluntary initiation on the part of the persons involved. However, for Principle II, the safeguards are for the well-being of persons rather than for the rights of persons.

Psychologists' treatment and use of animals in their research and teaching activities are also a component of responsible caring. Although animals do not have the same moral rights as persons (e.g., privacy), they do have the right to be treated humanely and not to be exposed to unnecessary discomfort, pain, or disruption.

By virtue of the social contract that the discipline has with society, psychologists have a higher duty of care to members of society than the general duty of care all members of society have to each other. However, psychologists are entitled to protect their own basic well-being (e.g., physical safety, family relationships) in their work as psychologists.

Ethical Standards

In adhering to the Principle of Responsible Caring, psychologists would:

General caring	II.1	Protect and promote the welfare of clients, research participants, employees, supervisees, students, trainees, colleagues, and others.
	II.2	Avoid doing harm to clients, research participants, employees, supervisees, students, trainees, colleagues, and others.
	II.3	Accept responsibility for the consequences of their actions.
	II.4	Refuse to advise, train, or supply information to anyone who, in the psychologist's judgment, will use the knowledge or skills to harm others.
	II.5	Make every reasonable effort to ensure that psychological knowledge is not misused, intentionally or unintentionally, to harm others.
Competence and self-knowledge	II.6	Offer or carry out (without supervision) only those activities for which they have established their competence to carry them out to the benefit of others.
	II.7	Not delegate activities to persons not competent to carry them out to the benefit of others.
	II.8	Take immediate steps to obtain consultation or to refer a client to a colleague or other appropriate professional, whichever is more likely to result in providing the client with competent service, if it becomes apparent that a client's problems are beyond their competence.
	II.9	Keep themselves up to date with a broad range of relevant knowledge, research methods, and techniques, and their impact on persons and society, through the reading of relevant literature, peer consultation, and continuing education

activities, in order that their service or research activities and conclusions will benefit and not harm others.

II.10 Evaluate how their own experiences, attitudes, culture, beliefs, values, social context, individual differences, specific training, and stresses influence their interactions with others, and integrate this awareness into all efforts to benefit and not harm others.

II.11 Seek appropriate help and/or discontinue scientific or professional activity for an appropriate period of time, if a physical or psychological condition reduces their ability to benefit and not harm others.

II.12 Engage in self-care activities that help to avoid conditions (e.g., burnout, addictions) that could result in impaired judgment and interfere with their ability to benefit and not harm others.

Risk/benefit analysis
11.13 Assess the individuals, families, groups, and communities involved in their activities adequately enough to ensure that they will be able to discern what will benefit and not harm the persons involved.

II.14 Be sufficiently sensitive to and knowledgeable about individual, group, community, and cultural differences and vulnerabilities to discern what will benefit and not harm persons involved in their activities.

II.15 Carry out pilot studies to determine the effects of all new procedures and techniques that might carry more than minimal risk, before considering their use on a broader scale.

II.16 Seek an independent and adequate ethical review of the balance of risks and potential benefits of all research and new interventions that involve procedures of unknown consequence, or where pain, discomfort, or harm are possible, before making a decision to proceed.

II.17 Not carry out any scientific or professional activity unless the probable benefit is proportionately greater than the risk involved.

Maximize benefit
II.18 Provide services that are coordinated over time and with other service providers, in order to avoid duplication or working at cross purposes.

II.19 Create and maintain records relating to their activities that are sufficient to support continuity and appropriate coordination of their activities with the activities of others.

II.20 Make themselves aware of the knowledge and skills of other disciplines (e.g., law, medicine, business administration) and advise the use of such knowledge and skills, where relevant to the benefit of others.

II.21 Strive to provide and/or obtain the best possible service for those needing and seeking psychological service. This may include, but is not limited to: selecting interventions that are relevant to the needs and characteristics of the client and that have reasonable theoretical or empirically-supported efficacy in light of those needs and characteristics; consulting with, or including in service delivery, persons relevant to the culture or belief systems of those served; advocating on behalf of the client; and, recommending professionals other than psychologists when appropriate.

II.22 Monitor and evaluate the effect of their activities, record their findings, and communicate new knowledge to relevant others.

II.23 Debrief research participants in such a way that the participants' knowledge is enhanced and the participants have a sense of contribution to knowledge. (Also see Standards III.26 and III.27.)

II.24 Perform their teaching duties on the basis of careful preparation, so that their instruction is current and scholarly.

II.25 Facilitate the professional and scientific development of their employees, supervisees, students, and trainees by ensuring that these persons understand the values and ethical prescriptions of the discipline, and by providing or arranging for adequate working conditions, timely evaluations, and constructive consultation and experience opportunities.

II.26 Encourage and assist students in publication of worthy student papers.

Minimize harm   II.27 Be acutely aware of the power relationship in therapy and, therefore, not encourage or engage in sexual intimacy with therapy clients, neither during therapy, nor for that period of time following therapy during which the power relationship reasonably could be expected to influence the client's personal decision making. (Also see Standard III.31.)

II.28   Not encourage or engage in sexual intimacy with students or trainees with whom the psychologist has an evaluative or other relationship of direct authority. (Also see Standard III.31.)

II.29   Be careful not to engage in activities in a way that could place incidentally involved persons at risk.

II.30   Be acutely aware of the need for discretion in the recording and communication of information, in order that the information not be misinterpreted or misused to the detriment of others. This includes, but is not limited to: not recording information that could lead to misinterpretation and misuse; avoiding conjecture; clearly labelling opinion; and, communicating information in language that can be understood clearly by the recipient of the information.

II.31   Give reasonable assistance to secure needed psychological services or activities, if personally unable to meet requests for needed psychological services or activities.

II.32   Provide a client, if appropriate and if desired by the client, with reasonable assistance to find a way to receive needed services in the event that third party payments are exhausted and the client cannot afford the fees involved.

II.33   Maintain appropriate contact, support, and responsibility for caring until a colleague or other professional begins service, if referring a client to a colleague or other professional.

II.34   Give reasonable notice and be reasonably assured that discontinuation will cause no harm to the client, before discontinuing services.

II.35   Screen appropriate research participants and select those least likely to be harmed, if more than minimal risk of harm to some research participants is possible.

II.36   Act to minimize the impact of their research activities on research participants' personalities, or on their physical or mental integrity.

Offset/correct
harm

II.37 Terminate an activity when it is clear that the activity carries more than minimal risk of harm and is found to be more harmful than beneficial, or when the activity is no longer needed.

II.38 Refuse to help individuals, families, groups, or communities to carry out or submit to activities that, according to current knowledge, or legal or professional guidelines, would cause serious physical or psychological harm to themselves or others.

II.39 Do everything reasonably possible to stop or offset the consequences of actions by others when these actions are likely to cause serious physical harm or death. This may include reporting to appropriate authorities (e.g., the police), an intended victim, or a family member or other support person who can intervene, and would be done even when a confidential relationship is involved. (Also see Standard I.45.)

II.40 Act to stop or offset the consequences of seriously harmful activities being carried out by another psychologist or member of another discipline, when there is objective information about the activities and the harm, and when these activities have come to their attention outside of a confidential client relationship between themselves and the psychologist or member of another discipline. This may include reporting to the appropriate regulatory body, authority, or committee for action, depending on the psychologist's judgment about the person(s) or body(ies) best suited to stop or offset the harm, and depending upon regulatory requirements and definitions of misconduct.

II.41 Act also to stop or offset the consequences of harmful activities carried out by another psychologist or member of another discipline, when the harm is not serious or the activities appear to be primarily a lack of sensitivity, knowledge, or experience, and when the activities have come to their attention outside of a confidential client relationship between themselves and the psychologist or member of another discipline. This may include talking informally with the psychologist or member of the other discipline, obtaining objective information and, if possible and relevant, the assurance that the harm will discontinue and be corrected. If in a vulnerable position (e.g., employee, trainee) with respect to the other psychologist or member of the other discipline, it may include asking persons in less vulnerable positions to participate in the meeting(s).

II.42 Be open to the concerns of others about perceptions of harm that they as a psychologist might be causing, stop activities that are causing harm, and not punish or seek punishment for those who raise such concerns in good faith.

II.43 Not place an individual, group, family, or community needing service at a serious disadvantage by offering them no service in order to fulfill the conditions of a research design, when a standard service is available.

II.44 Debrief research participants in such a way that any harm caused can be discerned, and act to correct any resultant harm. (Also see Standards III.26 and III.27.)

Care of animals   II.45 Not use animals in their research unless there is a reasonable expectation that the research will increase understanding of the structures and processes underlying behaviour, or increase understanding of the particular animal species used in the study, or result eventually in benefits to the health and welfare of humans or other animals.

II.46 Use a procedure subjecting animals to pain, stress, or privation only if an alternative procedure is unavailable and the goal is justified by its prospective scientific, educational, or applied value.

II.47 Make every effort to minimize the discomfort, illness, and pain of animals. This would include performing surgical procedures only under appropriate anaesthesia, using techniques to avoid infection and minimize pain during and after surgery and, if disposing of experimental animals is carried out at the termination of the study, doing so in a humane way.

II.48   Use animals in classroom demonstrations only if the instructional objectives cannot be achieved through the use of video-tapes, films, or other methods, and if the type of demonstration is warranted by the anticipated instructional gain.

Extended
responsibility

II.49   Encourage others, in a manner consistent with this *Code*, to care responsibly.

II.50   Assume overall responsibility for the scientific and professional activities of their assistants, employees, supervisees, students, and trainees with regard to the Principle of Responsible Caring, all of whom, however, incur similar obligations.

PRINCIPLE III: INTEGRITY IN RELATIONSHIPS

Values Statement

The relationships formed by psychologists in the course of their work embody explicit and implicit mutual expectations of integrity that are vital to the advancement of scientific knowledge and to the maintenance of public confidence in the discipline of psychology. These expectations include: accuracy and honesty; straightforwardness and openness; the maximization of objectivity and minimization of bias; and, avoidance of conflicts of interest. Psychologists have a responsibility to meet these expectations and to encourage reciprocity.

In addition to accuracy, honesty, and the obvious prohibitions of fraud or misrepresentation, meeting expectations of integrity is enhanced by self-knowledge and the use of critical analysis. Although it can be argued that science is value-free and impartial, scientists are not. Personal values and self-interest can affect the questions psychologists ask, how they ask those questions, what assumptions they make, their selection of methods, what they observe and what they fail to observe, and how they interpret their data.

Psychologists are not expected to be value-free or totally without self-interest in conducting their activities. However, they are expected to understand how their backgrounds, personal needs, and values interact with their activities, to be open and honest about the influence of such factors, and to be as objective and unbiased as possible under the circumstances.

The values of openness and straightforwardness exist within the context of Respect for the Dignity of Persons (Principle I) and Responsible Caring (Principle II). As such, there will be circumstances in which openness and straightforwardness will need to be tempered. Fully open and straightforward disclosure might not be needed or desired by others and, in some circumstances, might be a risk to their dignity or well-being, or considered culturally inappropriate. In such circumstances, however, psychologists have a responsibility to ensure that their decision not to be fully open or straightforward is justified by higher-order values and does not invalidate any informed consent procedures.

Of special concern to psychologists is the provision of incomplete disclosure when obtaining informed consent for research participation, or temporarily leading research participants to believe that a research project has a purpose other than its actual purpose. These actions sometimes occur in research where full disclosure would be likely to influence the responses of the research participants and thus invalidate the results. Although research that uses such techniques can lead to knowledge that is beneficial, such benefits must be weighed against the research participant's right to self-determination and the importance of public and individual trust in psychology. Psychologists have a serious obligation to avoid as much as possible the use of such research procedures. They also have a serious obligation to consider the need for, the possible consequences of, and their responsibility to correct any resulting mistrust or other harmful effects from their use.

As public trust in the discipline of psychology includes trusting that psychologists will act in the best interests of members of the public, situations that present real or potential conflicts of interest are of concern to psychologists. Conflict-of-interest situations are those that can lead to distorted judgment and can motivate psychologists to act in ways that meet their own personal, political, financial, or business interests at the expense of the best interests of members of the public. Although avoidance of all conflicts of interest and potential exploitation of others is not possible, some are of such a high risk to protecting the interests of members of the public and to maintaining the trust of the public, that they are considered never acceptable (see Standard III.31). The risk level of other conflicts of interest (e.g., dual or multiple relationships) might be partially dependent on cultural factors and the specific type of professional relationship (e.g., long-term psychotherapy vs. community development activities). It is the responsibility of psychologists to avoid dual or multiple relationships and other conflicts of interest when appropriate and possible. When such situations cannot be avoided or are inappropriate to avoid, psychologists have a responsibility to declare that they have a conflict of interest, to seek advice, and to establish safeguards to ensure that the best interests of members of the public are protected.

Integrity in relationships implies that psychologists, as a matter of honesty, have a responsibility to maintain competence in any specialty area for which they declare competence, whether or not they are currently practising in that area. It also requires that psychologists, in as much as they present themselves as members and representatives of a specific discipline, have a responsibility to actively rely on and be guided by that discipline and its guidelines and requirements.

Ethical Standards

In adhering to the Principle of Integrity in Relationships, psychologists would:

Accuracy/honesty III.1   Not knowingly participate in, condone, or be associated with dishonesty, fraud, or misrepresentation.

III.2   Accurately represent their own and their colleagues' credentials, qualifications, education, experience, competence, and affiliations, in all spoken, written, or printed communications, being careful not to use descriptions or information that could be misinterpreted (e.g., citing membership in a voluntary association of psychologists as a testament of competence).

III.3   Carefully protect their own and their colleagues' credentials from being misrepresented by others, and act quickly to correct any such misrepresentation.

III.4   Maintain competence in their declared area(s) of psychological competence, as well as in their current area(s) of activity. (Also see Standard II.9.)

III.5   Accurately represent their own and their colleagues' activities, functions, contributions, and likely or actual outcomes of their activities (including research results) in all spoken, written, or printed communication. This includes, but is not limited to: advertisements of services or products; course and workshop descriptions; academic grading requirements; and, research reports.

III.6   Ensure that their own and their colleagues' activities, functions, contributions, and likely or actual outcomes of their activities (including research results) are not misrepresented by others, and act quickly to correct any such misrepresentation.

III.7   Take credit only for the work and ideas that they have actually done or generated, and give credit for work done or ideas contributed by others (including students), in proportion to their contribution.

III.8 Acknowledge the limitations of their own and their colleagues' knowledge, methods, findings, interventions, and views.

III.9 Not suppress disconfirming evidence of their own and their colleagues' findings and views, acknowledging alternative hypotheses and explanations.

Objectivity/lack of bias

III.10 Evaluate how their personal experiences, attitudes, values, social context, individual differences, stresses, and specific training influence their activities and thinking, integrating this awareness into all attempts to be objective and unbiased in their research, service, and other activities.

III.11 Take care to communicate as completely and objectively as possible, and to clearly differentiate facts, opinions, theories, hypotheses, and ideas, when communicating knowledge, findings, and views.

III.12 Present instructional information accurately, avoiding bias in the selection and presentation of information, and publicly acknowledge any personal values or bias that influence the selection and presentation of information.

III.13 Act quickly to clarify any distortion by a sponsor, client, agency (e.g., news media), or other persons, of the findings of their research.

Straightforwardness/ openness

III.14 Be clear and straightforward about all information needed to establish informed consent or any other valid written or unwritten agreement (for example: fees, including any limitations imposed by third-party payers; relevant business policies and practices; mutual concerns; mutual responsibilities; ethical responsibilities of psychologists; purpose and nature of the relationship, including research participation; alternatives; likely experiences; possible conflicts; possible outcomes; and, expectations for processing, using, and sharing any information generated).

III.15 Provide suitable information about the results of assessments, evaluations, or research findings to the persons involved, if appropriate and if asked.

This information would be communicated in understandable language.

III.16 Fully explain reasons for their actions to persons who have been affected by their actions, if appropriate and if asked.

III.17 Honour all promises and commitments included in any written or verbal agreement, unless serious and unexpected circumstances (e.g., illness) intervene. If such circumstances occur, then the psychologist would make a full and honest explanation to other parties involved.

III.18 Make clear whether they are acting as private citizens, as members of specific organizations or groups, or as representatives of the discipline of psychology, when making statements or when involved in public activities.

III.19 Carry out, present, and discuss research in a way that is consistent with a commitment to honest, open inquiry, and to clear communication of any research aims, sponsorship, social context, personal values, or financial interests that might affect or appear to affect the research.

III.20 Submit their research, in some accurate form and within the limits of confidentiality, to persons with expertise in the research area, for their comments and evaluations, prior to publication or the preparation of any final report.

III.21 Encourage and not interfere with the free and open exchange of psychological knowledge and theory between themselves, their students, colleagues, and the public.

III.22 Make no attempt to conceal the status of a trainee and, if a trainee is providing direct client service, ensure that the client is informed of that fact.

Avoidance of incomplete disclosure

III.23 Not engage in incomplete disclosure, or in temporarily leading research participants to believe that a research project or some aspect of it has a different purpose, if there are alternative procedures available or if the negative effects cannot be predicted or offset.

III.24 Not engage in incomplete disclosure, or in temporarily leading research participants to believe that a research project or some aspect of it has a different purpose, if it would interfere with the person's understanding of facts that clearly might influence a decision to give adequately informed consent (e.g., withholding information about the level of risk, discomfort, or inconvenience).

III.25 Use the minimum necessary incomplete disclosure or temporary leading of research participants to believe that a research project or some aspect of it has a different purpose, when such research procedures are used.

III.26 Debrief research participants as soon as possible after the participants' involvement, if there has been incomplete disclosure or temporary leading of research participants to believe that a research project or some aspect of it has a different purpose.

III.27 Provide research participants, during such debriefing, with a clarification of the nature of the study, seek to remove any misconceptions that might have arisen, and seek to re-establish any trust that might have been lost, assuring the participants that the research procedures were neither arbitrary nor capricious, but necessary for scientifically valid findings. (Also see Standards II.23 and II.44.)

III.28 Act to re-establish with research participants any trust that might have been lost due to the use of incomplete disclosure or temporarily leading research participants to believe that the research project or some aspect of it had a different purpose.

III.29 Give a research participant the option of removing his or her data, if the research participant expresses concern during the debriefing about the incomplete disclosure or the temporary leading of the research participant to believe that the research project or some aspect of it had a different purpose, and if removal of the data will not compromise the validity of the research design and hence diminish the ethical value of the participation of the other research participants.

III.30 Seek an independent and adequate ethical review of the risks to public or individual trust and of safeguards to protect such trust for any research that plans to provide incomplete disclosure or temporarily lead research participants to believe that the research project or some aspect of it has a different purpose, before making a decision to proceed.

Avoidance of conflict of interest

III.31 Not exploit any relationship established as a psychologist to further personal, political, or business interests at the expense of the best interests of their clients, research participants, students, employers, or others. This includes, but is not limited to: soliciting clients of one's employing agency for private practice; taking advantage of trust or dependency to encourage or engage in sexual intimacies (e.g., with clients not included in Standard II.27, with clients' partners or relatives, with students or trainees not included in Standard II.28, or with research participants); taking advantage of trust or dependency to frighten clients into receiving services; misappropriating students' ideas, research or work; using the resources of one's employing institution for purposes not agreed to; giving or receiving kickbacks or bonuses for referrals; seeking or accepting loans or investments from clients; and, prejudicing others against a colleague for reasons of personal gain.

III.32 Not offer rewards sufficient to motivate an individual or group to participate in an activity that has possible or known risks to themselves or others. (Also see Standards I.27, I.28, II.2, and II.49.)

III.33 Avoid dual or multiple relationships (e.g. with clients, research participants, employees, supervisees, students, or trainees) and other situations that might present a conflict of interest or that might reduce their ability to be objective and unbiased in their determinations of what might be in the best interests of others.

III.34 Manage dual or multiple relationships that are unavoidable due to cultural norms or other circumstances in such a manner that bias, lack of objectivity, and risk of exploitation are minimized. This might include obtaining ongoing supervision or consultation for the duration of the dual or multiple relationship, or involving a third party in obtaining consent (e.g., approaching a client or employee about becoming a research participant).

III.35 Inform all parties, if a real or potential conflict of interest arises, of the need to resolve the situation in a manner that is consistent with Respect for the Dignity of Persons (Principle I) and Responsible Caring (Principle II), and take all reasonable steps to resolve the issue in such a manner.

Reliance on the discipline

III.36 Familiarize themselves with their discipline's rules and regulations, and abide by them, unless abiding by them would be seriously detrimental to the rights or welfare of others as demonstrated in the Principles of Respect for the Dignity of Persons or Responsible Caring. (See Standards IV.17 and IV.18 for guidelines regarding the resolution of such conflicts.)

III.37 Familiarize themselves with and demonstrate a commitment to maintaining the standards of their discipline.

III.38 Seek consultation from colleagues and/or appropriate groups and committees, and give due regard to their advice in arriving at a responsible decision, if faced with difficult situations.

Extended responsibility

III.39 Encourage others, in a manner consistent with this *Code*, to relate with integrity.

III.40 Assume overall responsibility for the scientific and professional activities of their assistants, employees, supervisees, students, and trainees with regard to the Principle of Integrity in Relationships, all of whom, however, incur similar obligations.

PRINCIPLE IV: RESPONSIBILITY TO SOCIETY

Values Statement

Psychology functions as a discipline within the context of human society.[2] Psychologists, both in their work and as private citizens, have responsibilities to the societies in which they live and work, such as the neighbourhood or city, and to the welfare of all human beings in those societies.

Two of the legitimate expectations of psychology as a science and a profession are that it will increase knowledge and that it will conduct its affairs in such ways that it will promote the welfare of all human beings.

Freedom of enquiry and debate (including scientific and academic freedom) is a foundation of psychological education, science, and practice. In the context of society, the above expectations imply that psychologists will exercise this freedom through the use of activities and methods that are consistent with ethical requirements.

The above expectations also imply that psychologists will do whatever they can to ensure that psychological knowledge, when used in the development of social structures and policies, will be used for beneficial purposes, and that the discipline's own structures and policies will support those beneficial purposes. Within the context of this document, social structures and policies that have beneficial purposes are defined as those that more readily support and reflect respect for the dignity of persons, responsible caring, integrity in relationships, and responsibility to society. If psychological knowledge or structures are used against these purposes, psychologists have an ethical responsibility to try to draw attention to and correct the misuse. Although this is a collective responsibility, those psychologists having direct involvement in the structures of the discipline, in social development, or in the theoretical or research data base that is being used (e.g., through research, expert testimony, or policy advice) have the greatest responsibility to act. Other psychologists must decide for themselves the most appropriate and beneficial use of their time and talents to help meet this collective responsibility.

In carrying out their work, psychologists acknowledge that many social structures have evolved slowly over time in response to human need and are valued by the societies that have developed them. In such circumstances, psychologists convey respect for such social structures and avoid unwarranted or unnecessary disruption. Suggestions for and action toward changes or enhancement of such structures are carried out through processes that seek to achieve a consensus within those societies and/or through democratic means.

On the other hand, if structures or policies seriously ignore or oppose the principles of respect for the dignity of persons, responsible caring, integrity in relationships, or responsibility to society, psychologists involved have a responsibility to speak out in a manner consistent with the principles of this *Code*, and advocate for appropriate change to occur as quickly as possible.

In order to be responsible and accountable to society, and to contribute constructively to its ongoing development, psychologists need to be willing to work in partnership with others, be self-reflective, and be open to external suggestions and criticisms about the place of the discipline of psychology in society. They need to engage in even-tempered observation and interpretation of the effects of societal structures and policies, and their process of change, developing the ability of psychologists to increase the beneficial use of psychological knowledge and structures, and avoid their misuse. The discipline needs to be willing to set high standards for its members, to do what it can to assure that such standards are met, and to support its members in their attempts to maintain the standards. Once again, individual psychologists must decide for themselves the most appropriate and beneficial use of their time and talents in helping to meet these collective responsibilities.

Ethical Standards

In adhering to the Principle of Responsibility to Society, psychologists would:

Development of knowledge	IV.1	Contribute to the discipline of psychology and of society's understanding of itself and human beings generally, through free enquiry and the acquisition, transmission, and expression of knowledge and ideas, unless such activities conflict with other basic ethical requirements.
	IV.2	Not interfere with, or condone interference with, free enquiry and the acquisition, transmission, and expression of knowledge and ideas that do not conflict with other basic ethical requirements.
	IV.3	Keep informed of progress in their area(s) of psychological activity, take this progress into account in their work, and try to make their own contributions to this progress.
Beneficial activities	IV.4	Participate in and contribute to continuing education and the professional and scientific growth of self and colleagues.
	IV.5	Assist in the development of those who enter the discipline of psychology by helping them to acquire a full understanding of their ethical responsibilities, and the needed competencies of their chosen area(s), including an understanding of critical analysis and of the variations, uses, and possible misuses of the scientific paradigm.
	IV.6	Participate in the process of critical self-evaluation of the discipline's place in society, and in the development and implementation of structures and procedures that help the discipline to contribute to beneficial societal functioning and changes.

IV.7   Provide and/or contribute to a work environment that supports the respectful expression of ethical concern or dissent, and the constructive resolution of such concern or dissent.

IV.8   Engage in regular monitoring, assessment, and reporting (e.g., through peer review, and in programme reviews, case management reviews, and reports of one's own research) of their ethical practices and safeguards.

IV.9   Help develop, promote, and participate in accountability processes and procedures related to their work.

IV.10   Uphold the discipline's responsibility to society by promoting and maintaining the highest standards of the discipline.

IV.11   Protect the skills, knowledge, and interpretations of psychology from being misused, used incompetently, or made useless (e.g., loss of security of assessment techniques) by others.

IV.12   Contribute to the general welfare of society (e.g., improving accessibility of services, regardless of ability to pay) and/or to the general welfare of their discipline, by offering a portion of their time to work for which they receive little or no financial return.

IV.13   Uphold the discipline's responsibility to society by bringing incompetent or unethical behaviour, including misuses of psychological knowledge and techniques, to the attention of appropriate authorities, committees, or regulatory bodies, in a manner consistent with the ethical principles of this *Code*, if informal resolution or correction of the situation is not appropriate or possible.

IV.14   Enter only into agreements or contracts that allow them to act in accordance with the ethical principles and standards of this *Code*.

Respect for society IV.15   Acquire an adequate knowledge of the culture, social structure, and customs of a community before beginning any major work there.

IV.16   Convey respect for and abide by prevailing community mores, social customs, and cultural expectations in their scientific and professional activities, provided that this does not contravene any of the ethical principles of this *Code*.

IV.17 Familiarize themselves with the laws and regulations of the societies in which they work, especially those that are related to their activities as psychologists, and abide by them. If those laws or regulations seriously conflict with the ethical principles contained herein, psychologists would do whatever they could to uphold the ethical principles. If upholding the ethical principles could result in serious personal consequences (e.g., jail or physical harm), decision for final action would be considered a matter of personal conscience.

IV.18 Consult with colleagues, if faced with an apparent conflict between abiding by a law or regulation and following an ethical principle, unless in an emergency, and seek consensus as to the most ethical course of action and the most responsible, knowledgeable, effective, and respectful way to carry it out.

Development of society

IV.19 Act to change those aspects of the discipline of psychology that detract from beneficial societal changes, where appropriate and possible.

IV.20 Be sensitive to the needs, current issues, and problems of society, when determining research questions to be asked, services to be developed, content to be taught, information to be collected, or appropriate interpretation of results or findings.

IV.21 Be especially careful to keep well informed of social issues through relevant reading, peer consultation, and continuing education, if their work is related to societal issues.

IV.22 Speak out, in a manner consistent with the four principles of this *Code*, if they possess expert knowledge that bears on important societal issues being studied or discussed.

IV.23 Provide thorough discussion of the limits of their data with respect to social policy, if their work touches on social policy and structure.

IV.24 Consult, if feasible and appropriate, with groups, organizations, or communities being studied, in order to increase the accuracy of interpretation of results and to minimize risk of misinterpretation or misuse.

IV.25 Make themselves aware of the current social and political climate and of previous and possible future societal misuses of psychological knowledge, and exercise due discretion in communicating psychological information (e.g., research results, theoretical knowledge), in order to discourage any further misuse.

IV.26   Exercise particular care when reporting the results of any work regarding vulnerable groups, ensuring that results are not likely to be misinterpreted or misused in the development of social policy, attitudes, and practices (e.g., encouraging manipulation of vulnerable persons or reinforcing discrimination against any specific population).

IV.27   Not contribute to nor engage in research or any other activity that contravenes international humanitarian law, such as the development of methods intended for use in the torture of persons, the development of prohibited weapons, or destruction of the environment.

IV.28   Provide the public with any psychological knowledge relevant to the public's informed participation in the shaping of social policies and structures, if they possess expert knowledge that bears on the social policies and structures.

IV.29   Speak out and/or act, in a manner consistent with the four principles of this *Code*, if the policies, practices, laws, or regulations of the social structure within which they work seriously ignore or contradict any of the principles of this *Code*.

Extended responsibility

IV.30   Encourage others, in a manner consistent with this *Code*, to exercise responsibility to society.

IV.31   Assume overall responsibility for the scientific and professional activities of their assistants, employees, supervisees, students, and trainees with regard to the Principle of Responsibility to Society, all of whom, however, incur similar obligations.

NOTES

1. Adapted from *Guidelines for the Elimination of Sexual Harassment*, Canadian Psychological Association, 1985, Ottawa: Author.

2. *Society* is used here in the broad sense of a group of persons living as members of one or more human communities, rather than in the limited sense of state or government.

ETHICS CODES AND PRACTICE GUIDELINES FOR ASSESSMENT, THERAPY, COUNSELING, AND FORENSIC PRACTICE

The ethics codes and practice guidelines listed here, developed by professional organizations, may be useful in thinking through ethics issues. Links to each of these codes appear at http://kspope.com/ethcodes/index.php. Codes are listed only if they appear online.

American Academy of Clinical Neuropsychology: Policy on the Use of Non-Doctoral-Level Personnel in Conducting Clinical Neuropsychological Evaluations

American Academy of Clinical Neuropsychology: Policy Statement on the Presence of Third-Party Observers in Neuropsychological Assessment

American Academy of Forensic Psychology: Specialty Guidelines

American Academy of Psychiatry and Law: Ethical Guidelines for the Practice of Forensic Psychiatry

American Association for Marriage and Family Therapy: Code of Ethics

American Association of Christian Counselors: Code of Ethics

American Association of Pastoral Counselors: Code of Ethics

American Association of Sex Educators, Counselors, and Therapists: Code of Ethics

American Association of Spinal Cord Injury Psychologists and Social Workers: Standards for Psychologists and Social Workers in SCI Rehabilitation

American Bar Association and American Psychological Association: Assessment of Older Adults with Diminished Capacity: A Handbook for Lawyers

American Bar Association, American Psychological Association, and National College of Probate Judges: Judicial Determination of Capacity of Older Adults in Guardianship Proceedings

American Board of Examiners in Clinical Social Work: Clinical Social Work Standards for Delivery of Care and Guidelines for the Three-Party Model of Clinical Social Work Services

American Board of Examiners in Clinical Social Work: Professional Development and Practice Competencies in Clinical Social Work

American College Personnel Association: Statement of Ethical Principles and Standards

American Counseling Association: Code of Ethics and Standards of Practice

American Counseling Association: Layperson's Guide to Counselor Ethics

American Group Psychotherapy Association: Guidelines for Ethics

American Group Psychotherapy Association: Practice Guidelines for Group Psychotherapy

American Hospital Association: Billing and Collection Practices

American Medical Association: Principles of Medical Ethics

American Medical Informatics Association: Guidelines for the Clinical Use of Electronic Mail with Patients

American Mental Health Counselors Association: Code of Ethics

American Music Therapy Association: Code of Ethics

American Nursing Association: Code of Ethics for Nurses

American Psychiatric Association: 2009 Principles of Medical Ethics with Annotations Especially Applicable to Psychiatry

American Psychiatric Association: Opinions of the Ethics Committee on the Principles of Medical Ethics (2009)

American Psychoanalytic Association: Principles and Standards of Ethics for Psychoanalysts

American Psychological Association: Ethical Principles of Psychologists and Code of Conduct

American Psychological Association: Revised Guidelines for Child Custody Evaluations in Family Law Proceedings

American Psychological Association: Guidelines for Ethical Conduct in the Care and Use of Animals

American Psychological Association: Guidelines for the Evaluation of Dementia and Age-Related Cognitive Decline

American Psychological Association: Guidelines for Psychological Evaluations in Child Protection Matters

American Psychological Association: Guidelines for Psychological Practice with Girls and Women

American Psychological Association: Guidelines for Psychological Practice with Older Adults

American Psychological Association: Guidelines for Psychotherapy with Lesbian, Gay, and Bisexual Clients

American Psychological Association: Guidelines on Multicultural Education, Training, Research, Practice, and Organizational Change for Psychologists

American Psychological Association: Record Keeping Guidelines

American Psychological Association: Report from APA Working Group on Assisted Suicide and End-of-Life Decisions

American Psychological Association: Report of the American Psychological Association Presidential Task Force on Psychological Ethics and National Security

American Psychological Association: Resolution on Appropriate Therapeutic Responses to Sexual Orientation

American Psychological Association: Rights and Responsibilities of Test Takers: Guidelines and Expectations

American School Counselor Association: Ethical Standards for School Counselors

American Society of Clinical Hypnosis: Code of Conduct

American Telemedicine Association: Practice Guidelines for Videoconferencing-Based Telemental Health

Association for Applied Psychophysiology and Biofeedback: Ethical Principles of Applied Psychophysiology and Biofeedback

Association for Comprehensive Energy Psychology: Code of Ethics

Association for Specialists in Group Work: Principles for Diversity-Competent Group Workers

Association for Specialists in Group Work: Professional Standards for the Training of Group Workers

Association for the Treatment of Sexual Abusers: Professional Code of Ethics

Association of Clinical Pastoral Education: Standards and Ethics Manual

Association of Professional Chaplains: Code of Ethics

Association of State and Provincial Psychology Boards: Code of Conduct

Association of State and Provincial Psychology Boards: Guidelines for Prescriptive Authority

Australian Association of Social Workers: Code of Ethics

Australian Psychological Society: Code of Ethics

Australian Psychological Society: Ethical Guidelines

British Columbia Association for Clinical Counsellors: Code of Ethical Conduct

British Association for Counselling and Psychotherapy: Ethical Framework for Good Practice in Counselling and Psychotherapy

British Association of Social Workers: Code of Ethics for Social Work

British Columbia Association of Clinical Counsellors: Code of Ethical Conduct and Standards of Clinical Practice for Registered Clinical Counsellors

British Psychological Society: Ethics, Rules, Charter, Code of Conduct

California Association for Counseling and Development: Code of Ethics and Standards of Practice

California Association of Marriage and Family Therapists: Ethical Standards

California Board of Behavioral Sciences: Notice to California Consumers Regarding Online Psychotherapy

California Society for Clinical Social Work: Ethical Standards of the Clinical Social Work Federation

Canadian Counselling Association: Code of Ethics and Standards of Practice

Canadian Medical Association: Code of Ethics

Canadian Psychiatric Association: The CMA Code of Ethics Annotated for Psychiatrists

Canadian Psychiatric Association: Clinical Practice Guidelines: Management of Anxiety Disorders

Canadian Psychiatric Association: Clinical Practice Guidelines: Treatment of Depressive Disorders

Canadian Psychiatric Association: Clinical Practice Guidelines: Treatment of Schizophrenia

Canadian Psychiatric Association: Confidentiality of Psychiatric Records and the Patient's Right to Privacy

Canadian Psychiatric Association: Duty to Protect

Canadian Psychiatric Association: Implications for Psychiatrists of the Supreme Court of Canada *Starson v. Swayze* Decision

Canadian Psychiatric Association: Media Guidelines for Reporting Suicide

Canadian Psychoanalytic Society: Principles of Ethics for Psychoanalysis

Canadian Psychological Association: Canadian Code of Ethics for Psychologists (3rd edition)

Canadian Psychological Association: Draft Ethical Guidelines for Psychologists Providing Psychological Services via Electronic Media

Canadian Psychological Association: Ethical Guidelines for Supervision in Psychology: Teaching, Research, Practice, and Administration

Canadian Psychological Association: Guidelines for Ethical Psychological Practice with Women

Canadian Psychological Association: Guidelines for Nondiscriminatory Practice

Canadian Psychological Association: Guidelines for Professional Practice for School Psychologists

Canadian Psychological Association: Practice Guidelines for Providers of Psychological Services

Canadian Psychological Association: Working with the Media — Guidelines for Psychologists

Canadian Traumatic Stress Network [Reseau Canadien du Stress Traumatique]: Ethical Principles

Catholic Church: Ethical and Religious Directives for Catholic Health Care Services

Christian Association for Psychological Studies: Ethics Statement

Commission on Rehabilitation Counselor Certification: Code of Professional Ethics

Employee Assistance Professionals Association: EAPA Code of Ethics

Equine Assisted Growth and Learning Association: Code of Ethics for Equine Assisted Psychotherapy

European Association for Body-Psychotherapy: Ethical Guidelines and Code

European Federation of Psychologists' Associations: Charter of Professional Ethics for Psychologists

Federation of State Medical Boards: Addressing Sexual Boundaries — Guidelines for State Medical Boards

Feminist Therapy Institute: Code of Ethics

Health on the Net Foundation: Code of Conduct for Medical and Health Web Sites

International Association of Applied Psychology: Universal Declaration of Ethical Principles for Psychologists

International Association of Chiefs of Police: Psychological Services Section: Guidelines for Consulting Police Psychologists

International Association of Chiefs of Police: Psychological Services Section: Officer-Involved Shooting Guidelines

International Association of Chiefs of Police: Psychological Services Section: Peer Support Guidelines

International Association of Chiefs of Police: Psychological Services Section: Pre-employment Psychological Evaluation Services Guidelines

International Association of Chiefs of Police: Psychological Services Section: Psychological Fitness-for-Duty Evaluation Guidelines

International Federation of Social Workers: Ethics of Social Work—
Statement of Principles

International Society for Mental Health Online: Suggested Principles
for the Online Provision of Mental Health Services

International Society for the Study of Dissociation: Treatment Guidelines: Adults With Dissociative Identity Disorder

International Society for the Study of Dissociation: Treatment Guidelines: Children with Dissociative Symptoms

International Union of Psychological Science: Universal Declaration of
Ethical Principles for Psychologists

Irish Association for Counseling and Therapy: Code of Ethics and Practice

Irish Association for Counseling and Therapy: Code of Ethics for
Supervisors

Joint Committee on Testing Practices: Code of Fair Testing Practices in
Education

Louisiana State Board of Social Work Examiners: Guidelines for Child
Custody Evaluations

Mental Health Patient's Bill of Rights

Multi-Health Systems PIPEDA & HIPAA Test Disclosure Privacy
Guidelines

National Academies of Practice: Ethical Guidelines for Professional
Care and Services in a Managed Health Care Environment

National Association of School Psychologists: Professional Conduct
Manual—Principles for Professional Ethics

National Association of Social Workers: Code of Ethics

National Board for Certified Counselors: Code of Ethics

National Board for Certified Counselors: The Practice of Internet
Counseling

National Career Development Association: Ethical Standards

National Council for Hypnotherapy: Code of Ethics and Conduct

National Registry of Certified Group Psychotherapists: Guidelines for
Ethics

National Student Nurses Association: Code of Professional Conduct

New Zealand Association of Counsellors: Code of Ethics

New Zealand Psychological Society: Code of Ethics

Ohio Psychological Association: Telepsychology Guidelines

Psychological Society of Ireland: Code of Professional Ethics

Royal Australian and New Zealand College of Psychiatrists: Code of Ethics

Society for Personality Assessment: Standards for Education and Training in Psychological Assessment

Society for Research in Child Development: Ethical Standards for
Research with Children

World Medical Association: Ethics Policies

World Professional Association for Transgender Health

REFERENCES

Acevedo-Garcia, D., & Bates, L. M. (2007). Latino health paradoxes: Empirical evidence, explanations, future research, and implications. In H. Rodriguez, R. Saenz, & C. Menjivar (Eds.), *Latinas/os in the United States: Changing the face of America* (pp. 101–113). New York, NY: Springer.

Ackerman, M. J. (2006). *Clinician's guide to child custody evaluations* (3rd ed.). Hoboken, NJ: Wiley.

Acklin, M. W., & Cho-Stutler, L. (2006). The science and art of parent-child observation in child custody evaluation. *Journal of Forensic Psychology Practice, 6,* 51–62. doi: 10.1300/J158v06n01_03

Adam, Y. G. (2007). Justice in Nuremberg: The doctors' trial—60 years later. A reminder. *Israel Medical Association Journal, 9*(3), 194–195.

Adleman, J., & Barrett, S. E. (1990). Overlapping relationships: Importance of the feminist ethical perspective. In H. Lermamn & N. Portman (Eds.), *Feminist ethics in psychotherapy* (pp. 87–91). New York, NY: Springer.

Advice on ethics of billing clients. (1987, November). *APA Monitor,* p. 42.

Advisory Committee on Human Radiation Experiments. (1995). *Final report.* Washington, DC: U.S. Government Printing Office.

Akamatsu, T. J. (1988). Intimate relationships with former clients: National survey of attitudes and behavior among practitioners. *Professional Psychology: Research and Practice, 19,* 454–458.

Akkad, A., Jackson, C., Kenyon, S., Dixon-Woods, M., Taub, N., & Habiba, M. (2006). Patients' perceptions of written consent: Questionnaire study. *British Medical Journal, 333*(7567), 528. doi: bmj.38922.516204.55 [pii]10.1136/bmj.38922.516204.55

Alison, L., Smith, M. D., & Morgan, K. (2003). Interpreting the accuracy of offender profilers. *Psychology, Crime & Law, 9,* 185–195. doi: 10.1080/1068316031000116274

Allday, E. (2009, December 22). Internet security breach found at UCSF. *San Francisco Chronicle.* Retrieved from http://bit.ly/5lLhAV

Allen, A. L. (2009). Confidentiality: An expectation in health care. In V. Ravitsky, A. Fiester, & A. L. Caplan (Eds.), *The Penn Center guide to bioethics.* (pp. 127–135). New York, NY: Springer.

Alonso-Zaldivar, R. (2008, April 9). Effectiveness of medical privacy law is questioned. *Los Angeles* Times. Retrieved from http://8.12.42.31/2008/apr/09/nation/na-privacy9

Amaro, H., Russo, N. F., & Johnson, J. (1987). Family and work predictors of psychological well-being among Hispanic women professionals. *Psychology of Women Quarterly, 11,* 505–522.

American Academy of Child and Adolescent Psychiatry Staff. (2008). Practice parameter for telepsychiatry with children and adolescents. *Journal of the American Academy of Child & Adolescent Psychiatry, 47*(12), 1468–1483.

American Academy of Clinical Neuropsychology. (2001). Policy statement on the presence of third party observers in neuropsychological assessment. *Clinical Neuropsychologist, 15,* 433–439.

American Association on Mental Deficiency. (1974). *The Adaptive Behavior Scale: Manual.* Washington, DC: Author.

American Civil Liberties Union. (2008, April 30). Newly unredacted report confirms psychologists supported illegal interrogations in Iraq and Afghanistan. [News release.] Retrieved from http://www.aclu.org/safefree/torture/35111prs20080430 .html

American Counseling Association. (2005). ACA Code of Ethics. Alexandria, VA: Author.

American Educational and Research Association, American Psychological Association, and National Council on Measurement in Education. (1999). *Standards for educational and psychological testing.* Washington, DC: Author.

American Group Psychotherapy Association. (2007). *Practice guidelines for group psychotherapy.* New York, NY: Author.

American Psychiatric Association. (1987). *Diagnostic and statistical manual of mental disorders* (3rd ed., rev.). Washington, DC: Author.

American Psychiatric Association. (1994). *Diagnostic and statistical manual of mental disorders* (4th ed.). Washington, DC: Author.

American Psychological Association. (1953). *Ethical standards of psychologists.* Washington, DC: Author.

American Psychological Association. (1963). Ethical standards of psychologists. *American Psychologist, 18,* 56–60.

American Psychological Association. (1981). *Specialty guidelines for the delivery of services: Clinical psychologists, counseling psychologists, industrial/organizational psychologists, school psychologists.* Washington, DC: Author.

American Psychological Association. (1982). *Ethical principles in the conduct of research with human participants.* Washington, DC: Author.

American Psychological Association. (1985). *Against torture: Joint resolution of the American Psychiatric Association and the American Psychological Association.* Retrieved from http://www.apa.org/news/press/statements/interrogations.aspx

American Psychological Association. (1986). *APA Council resolution: Opposition to torture.* Retrieved from http://www.apa.org/about/governance/council/policy/ chapter-14.aspx

American Psychological Association. (1987a). *Casebook on ethical principles of psychologists.* Washington, DC: Author.

American Psychological Association. (1987b). General guidelines for providers of psychological services. *American Psychologist, 42,* 712–723.

American Psychological Association. (1987c). *Guidelines for conditions of employment of psychologists.* Washington, DC: Author.

American Psychological Association. (1990a). Ethical principles of psychologists. *American Psychologist, 45,* 390–395.

American Psychological Association. (1990b). *Guidelines for providers of psychological services to ethnic, linguistic, and culturally diverse populations.* Retrieved from http:// www.apa.org/pi/oema/resources/policy/provider-guidelines.aspx

American Psychological Association. (1992). Ethical principles of psychologists and code of conduct. *American Psychologist, 47*, 1597–1611. Also available from http://www.apa.org/ethics/code/code-1992.aspx

American Psychological Association. (1993). Guidelines for providers of psychological services to ethnic, linguistic, and culturally diverse populations. *American Psychologist, 48*(1), 45–48.

American Psychological Association. (1994). Guidelines for child custody evaluations in divorce proceedings. *American Psychologist, 49*(7), 677–680.

American Psychological Association. (1997). *Your mental health rights: A joint initiative of mental health professional organizations.* Washington, DC: Author.

American Psychological Association. (1998a). Guidelines for the evaluation of dementia and age-related cognitive decline. *American Psychologist, 53*(12), 1298–1303.

American Psychological Association. (1998b). *Rights and responsibilities of test takers: Guidelines and expectations.* Washington, DC: Author.

American Psychological Association. (1999). Guidelines for psychological evaluations in child protection matters. *American Psychologist, 54*(8), 586–593.

American Psychological Association. (2002). Ethical principles of psychologists and code of conduct. *American Psychologist, 57*, 1060–1073.

American Psychological Association. (2003a). *Guidelines for psychotherapy with lesbian, gay and bisexual clients.* Retrieved from http://www.apa.org/pi/lgbt/resources/guidelines/aspx

American Psychological Association. (2003b). Guidelines on multicultural education, training, research, practice, and organizational change for psychologists. *American Psychologist, 58*, 377–402.

American Psychological Association. (2004a). Guidelines for psychological practice with older adults. *American Psychologist, 59*(4), 236–260.

American Psychological Association. (2004b). *Report of the APA Task Force on Advertising and Children.* Washington, DC: Author. Retrieved from http://www.apa.org/pi/families/resources/advertising-children.pdf

American Psychological Association. (2006, August 9). Resolution against torture and other cruel, inhuman, and degrading treatment or punishment. Retrieved from http://www.apa.org/about/governance/council/policy/chapter-3.aspx

American Psychological Association. (2007a, August 19). Reaffirmation of the American Psychological Association position against torture and other cruel, inhuman, or degrading treatment or punishment and its application to individuals defined in the United States Code as "enemy combatants." Retrieved from http://www.apa.org/about/governance/council/policy/torture.aspx

American Psychological Association. (2007b, September 21). Statement on psychology and interrogations submitted to the United States Senate Select Committee on Intelligence. Retrieved from http://www.apa.org/ethics/programs/position/legislative/senate-select.aspx

American Psychological Association. (2008a). 2008 APA Petition Resolution Ballot—Con Statement. Retrieved from http://www.apa.org/news/press/statements/work-settings-con.aspx

American Psychological Association. (2008b). Amendment to the reaffirmation of the American Psychological Association position against torture. Retrieved from http://www.apa.org/about/governance/council/policy/chapter-3.aspx

American Psychological Association. (2008c, September 17). APA members approve petition resolution on detainee settings. [APA press release.] Retrieved from http://www.apa.org/news/press/releases/2008/09/detainee-petition.aspx

American Psychological Association. (2008d). Bylaws of the American Psychological Association. Retrieved from http://www.apa.org/about/governance/index.aspx

American Psychological Association. (2008e, September 24). Joint Committee named to revise Standards for Educational and Psychological Testing. Retrieved from http://www.apa.org/news/press/releases/2008/09/testing-standards.aspx

American Psychological Association. (2008f, July 28). Petition on psychologists' work settings: Questions and answers. Retrieved from http://www.apa.org/news/press/statements/qa-work-settings.aspx

American Psychological Association. (2008g, February 22). Reaffirmation of the American Psychological Association position against torture and other cruel, inhuman, or degrading treatment or punishment and its application to individuals defined in the United States Code as "enemy combatants" [amended]. Retrieved from http://www.apa.org/about/governance/council/policy/torture.aspx

American Psychological Association, (2008h). Report of the APA Presidential Advisory Group on the Implementation of the Petition Resolution. Retrieved from http://search.apa.org/search?query=Advisory%20Group%20on%20the%20Implementation %20of%20the%20Petition%20Resolution

American Psychological Association. (2008i). *Report of the Task Force on the implementation of the multicultural guidelines*. Washington, DC: Author. Retrieved from http://www.apa.org/about/governance/council/policy/multicultural-report.pdf

American Psychological Association. (2009a). Brief summary of board and council action taken regarding PENS report and interrogation resolutions. Retrieved from http://www.apa.org/news/press/statements/index.aspx

American Psychological Association. (2009b). *Guidelines for evaluation of child custody in family law proceedings*. Washington, DC: Author.

American Psychological Association (2009c). Text of the proposed amendments in response to Council's 2009 resolution. Retrieved from http://search.apa.org/search?query=Ethics%20Code%20Amendments

American Psychological Association. (2010). Ethical principles of psychologists and code of conduct with the 2010 amendments. Retrieved from http://www.apa.org/ethics/code/index.aspx

American Psychological Association, Committee on Accreditation. (1989). Criteria for accreditation, doctoral training programs and internships in professional psychology (amended version). In *Accreditation handbook* (pp. B-1 to B-18). Washington, DC: Author.

American Psychological Association, Committee on Ethical Standards for Psychology. (1949). Developing a code of ethics for psychologists. *American Psychologist*, 4, 17.

American Psychological Association, Committee on Ethical Standards for Psychology. (1951a). Ethical standards for psychology: Sections 1 and 6. *American Psychologist*, 6, 626–661.

American Psychological Association, Committee on Ethical Standards for Psychology. (1951b). Ethical Standards for Psychology: Sections 2, 4, and 5. *American Psychologist*, 6, 427–452.

American Psychological Association, Committee on Ethical Standards for Psychology. (1951c). Ethical standards for psychology: Section 3. *American Psychologist, 6,* 57–64.

American Psychological Association, Committee on Legal Issues. (1996). Strategies for private practitioners coping with subpoenas or compelled testimony for client records or test data. *Professional Psychology: Research and Practice, 27,* 245–251.

American Psychological Association, Committee on Professional Standards. (1984). Casebook for providers of psychological services. *American Psychologist, 39,* 663–668.

American Psychological Association, Committee on Psychological Tests and Assessment. (2007). Statement on third party observers in psychological testing and Assessment: A framework for decision making. Washington, DC: Author.

American Psychological Association, Ethics Committee. (1988). Trends in ethics cases, common pitfalls, and published resources. *American Psychologist, 43,* 564–572.

American Psychological Association, Ethics Committee. (1997). Report of the Ethics Committee, 1996. *American Psychologist, 52,* 897–905.

American Psychological Association, Ethics Committee. (2001). Report of the Ethics Committee, 2000. *American Psychologist, 56,* 680–688.

American Psychological Association, Ethics Committee. (2002). Report of the Ethics Committee, 2001. *American Psychologist, 57,* 646–653.

American Psychological Association, Ethics Committee. (2003). Report of the Ethics Committee, 2002. *American Psychologist, 58,* 650–657.

American Psychological Association, Ethics Committee. (2004). Report of the Ethics Committee, 2003. *American Psychologist, 59,* 434–441.

American Psychological Association, Ethics Committee. (2005). Report of the Ethics Committee, 2004. *American Psychologist, 60,* 523–528.

American Psychological Association, Ethics Committee. (2006). Report of the Ethics Committee, 2005. *American Psychologist, 61,* 522–529.

American Psychological Association, Ethics Committee. (2007). Report of the Ethics Committee, 2006. *American Psychologist, 62,* 504–511.

American Psychological Association, Ethics Committee. (2008). Report of the Ethics Committee, 2007. *American Psychologist, 63,* 452–459.

American Psychological Association, Ethics Committee. (2009a) No defense to torture under the APA Ethics Code. Retrieved from http://www.apa.org/news/press/statements/interrogations.aspx

American Psychological Association, Ethics Committee. (2009b). Report of the Ethics Committee, 2008. *American Psychologist, 64,* 464–473.

American Psychological Association, Insurance Trust. (1990). *Bulletin: Sexual misconduct and professional liability claims.* Washington, DC: Author.

American Psychological Association, Presidential Advisory Group on the Implementation of the Petition Resolution. (2008). Report of the APA Presidential Advisory Group on the Implementation of the Petition Resolution. Retrieved from http://www.apa.org/news/press/statements/interrogations.aspx

American Psychological Association, Presidential Task Force on Enhancing Diversity. (2005, August 17). Final report. Retrieved from http://www.apa.org/pi/oema/resources/taskforce-report.pdf

American Psychological Association, Presidential Task Force on Evidence-Based Practice. (2006). Evidence-based practice in psychology. *American Psychologist, 61*, 271–285. doi: 10.1037/0003-066X.61.4.271

American Psychological Association, Presidential Task Force on the Future of Psychology. (2009, December). Presidential Task Force on the Future of Psychology Practice Final Report. Retrieved from http://www.apa.org/pubs/info/reports/future-practice.pdf

American Psychological Association, Presidential Task Force on Integrated Health Care for an Aging Population. (2008). Blueprint for change: Achieving integrated health care for an aging population. Washington, DC: Author. Retrieved from http://www.apa.org/pi/aging/programs/integrated/integrated-healthcare-report.pdf

American Psychological Association, Presidential Task Force on Posttraumatic Stress Disorder and Trauma in Children and Adolescents. (2008). Children and trauma. Retrieved from http://psycnet.apa.org/psycextra/539742009-001.pdf

American Psychological Association, Presidential Task Force on Psychological Ethics and National Security. (2005, June). Report of the American Psychological Association Presidential Task Force on psychological ethics and national security. Retrieved from http://www.apa.org/pubs/info/reports/pens.pdf

American Psychological Association, Presidential Task Force on Psychological Ethics and National Security LISTSERV correspondence, Intelligence Ethics Collection, Hoover Institution Archives, Stanford University. Retrieved from http://s3.amazonaws.com/propublica/assets/docs/pens_listserv.pdf

American Psychological Association, Task Force on Violence and the Family. (1996). *Violence and the family: Report of the American Psychological Association Task Force on Violence and the Family.* Washington, DC: Author.

American Telemedicine Association. (2009). Evidence-based practice for telemental health. Retrieved from http://bit.ly/alUrPV.

American Telemedicine Association. (2009). Practice guidelines for video-conferencing-based telemental health. Retrieved from http://bit.ly/bu6W5m.

Antonacci, D. J., Bloch, R. M., Saeed, S. A., Yildirim, Y., & Talley, J. (2008). Empirical evidence on the use and effectiveness of telepsychiatry via videoconferencing: Implications for forensic and correctional psychiatry. *Behavioral Sciences & the Law, 26*, 253–269. doi: 10.1002/bsl.812

"APA interrogation task force member Dr. Jean Maria Arrigo exposes group's ties to military." (2007). *Democracy Now*, August 20. Retrieved from http://bit.ly/9W05NG

Appelbaum, P. S., & Gutheil, T. G. (2007). *Clinical handbook of psychiatry & the law.* Philadelphia, PA: Lippincott Williams & Wilkins.

Arbuthnott, K. D., Arbuthnott, D. W., & Thompson, V. A. (2006). *The mind in therapy: Cognitive science for practice.* Mahwah, NJ: Erlbaum.

Arredondo, P., Toporek, R., Brown, S. P., Jones, J., Locke, D. C., Sanchez, J., & Stadler, H. (1996). Operationalization of the multicultural counseling competencies. *Journal of Multicultural Counseling and Development, 24*(1), 42–78.

Arrigo, J. M. (2006). Psychological Torture–The CIA and the APA. *PsycCRITIQUES, 51*(30). doi: 10.1037/a0003712 Retrieved from http://psycnet.apa.org/critiques/51/30/1.html

Asheri, S. (2009). To touch or not to touch: A relational body psychotherapy perspective. In L. Hartley (Ed.), *Contemporary body psychotherapy: The Chiron approach* (pp. 106–120). New York, NY: Routledge/Taylor & Francis.

Axelrod, B., Barth, J., Faust, D., Fisher, J., Heilbronner, R., Larrabee, G., . . . Silver, C. (2000). Presence of third party observers during neuropsychological testing: Official statement of the National Academy of Neuropsychology. *Archives of Clinical Neuropsychology, 15*(5), 379–380.

Bache, R. M. (1894). Reaction time with reference to race. *Psychological Review, 1,* 475–486.

Bacon, F. (1955). The new organon. In *Selected writings of Francis Bacon* (pp. 455–540). New York, NY: Random House. (*The new organon* originally published 1620).

Bader, E. (1994). Dual relationships: Legal and ethical trends. *Transactional Analysis Journal, 24*(1), 64–66.

Baer, B. E., & Murdock, N. L. (1995). Nonerotic dual relationships between therapists and clients: The effects of sex, theoretical orientation, and interpersonal boundaries. *Ethics and Behavior, 5,* 131–145.

Bagley, C., Bolitho, F., & Bertrand, L. (1997). Sexual assault in school, mental health and suicidal behaviors in adolescent women in Canada. *Adolescence, 32,* 341–366.

Bajt, T. R., & Pope, K. S. (1989). Therapist-patient sexual intimacy involving children and adolescents. *American Psychologist, 44,* 455. Available at http://kspope.com

Banks, M. E. (2003). Preface. In M. E. Banks & E. Kaschak (Eds.), *Women with visible and invisible disabilities: Multiple intersections, multiple issues, multiple therapists* (pp. XXI–XXXIX). New York, NY: Haworth Press.

Barlow, D. H. (2004). Psychological treatments. *American Psychologist, 59*(9), 869–878.

Barlow, D. H. (2005a). Clarification on psychological treatments and psychotherapy. *American Psychologist, 60*(7), 734–735.

Barlow, D. H. (2005b). What's new about evidence-based assessment? *Psychological Assessment, 17*(3), 308–311.

Barlow, D. H. (2010). Negative effects from psychological treatments: A perspective. *American Psychologist, 65,* 13–20.

Barnett, J. E., & Yutrzenka, B. A. (1995). Nonsexual dual relationships in professional practice, with special applications to rural and military communities. *Independent Practitioner, 14,* 243–248.

Bass, L., DeMers, S. T., Ogloff, J. R. P., Peterson, C., Pettifor, J. L., Reaves, R. P., & R. M. Tipton. (1996). *Professional conduct and discipline in psychology* (pp. 1–15). Washington, DC: American Psychological Association.

Bates, C. M., & Brodsky, A. M. (1989). *Sex in the therapy hour: A case of professional incest.* New York, NY: Guilford Press.

Bauer, L., & McCaffrey, R. J. (2006). Coverage of the test of memory malingering, victoria symptom validity test, and word memory test on the internet: Is test security threatened? *Archives of Clinical Neuropsychology, 21,* 121–126. doi: 10.1016/j.acn.2005.06.010

Beck, A. T. (1967). *Depression.* Philadelphia: University of Pennsylvania Press.

Beck, A. T., Kovaks, M., & Weissman, A. (1975). Hopelessness and suicidal behavior: An overview. *Journal of the American Medical Association, 234,* 1146–1149.

Beck, A. T., Resnick, H. L. P., & Lettieri, D. (Eds.). (1974). *The prediction of suicide.* New York, NY: Charles Press.

Behnke, S. H. (2005, December 9–11). *Update on ethics program: Minutes of the APA board of directors.* Retrieved from http://www.apa.org/governance/

Behnke, S. H. (2006a, July–August). Ethics and interrogations: Comparing and contrasting the American Psychological, American Medical and American Psychiatric Association positions. *Monitor on Psychology, 37*(7), 66–67.

Behnke, S. [H.]. (2006b). Psychological ethics and national security: The position of the American Psychological Association. *European Psychologist, 11,* 153–155. doi: 10.1027/1016–9040.11.2.153

Belar, C. D. (2009). Advancing the culture of competence. *Training and Education in Professional Psychology, 3,* S63–S65. doi: 10.1037/a0017541

Bell, B. E., Raiffa, H., & Tversky, A. (Eds.). (1989). *Decision making: Descriptive, normative, and prescriptive interactions.* Cambridge, United Kingdom: Cambridge University Press.

Benjamin M. (2006). Psychologists group still rocked by torture debate; In an angry response to Salon, the American Psychological Association defends its policy on participating in terror suspects' interrogation. *Salon,* August 4. Retrieved from http://www.salon.com/news/feature/2006/08/04/apa

Bennett, B. E., Bricklin, P. M., & VandeCreek, L. (1994). Response to Lazarus's "How certain boundaries and ethics diminish therapeutic effectiveness." *Ethics and Behavior, 4*(3), 263–266.

Benson, P. R. (1984). Informed consent. *Journal of Nervous and Mental Disease, 172,* 642–653.

Bernal, G., Jiménez-Chafey, M. I., & Domenech Rodríguez, M. M. (2009). Cultural adaptation of treatments: A resource for considering culture in evidence-based practice. *Professional Psychology: Research and Practice, 40,* 361–368. doi: 10.1037/a0016401

Bernsen, A., Tabachnick, B. G., & Pope, K. S. (1994). National survey of social workers' sexual attraction to their clients: Results, implications, and comparison to psychologist. *Ethics and Behavior, 4,* 369–388. Available at http://kspope.com

Beutler, L. E. (1985). Loss and anticipated death: Risk factors in depression. In H. H. Goldman & S. E. Goldston (Eds.), *Preventing stress-related psychiatric disorders* (pp. 177–194). Rockville, MD: National Institute of Mental Health.

Beutler, L. E., Malik, M., Alimohamed, S., Harwood, T. M., Talebi, H., & Nobel, S. (2003). Therapist variables. In M. J. Lambert (Ed.), *Handbook of psychotherapy and behavior change* (5th ed., pp. 227–306). Hoboken, NJ: Wiley.

Blanchard-Fields, F., Chen, Y., Horhota, M., & Wang, M. (2007). Cultural differences in the relationship between aging and the correspondence bias. *Journals of Gerontology: Series B: Psychological Sciences and Social Sciences, 62B*(6), P362–P365.

Blau, T. H. (1984). *The psychologist as expert witness.* Hoboken, NJ: Wiley.

Block, N. J., & Dworkin, G. (1976). *The IQ controversy.* New York, NY: Pantheon.

Bluestein, G. (2009, March 2). Assisted suicide presents legal quandary. *Washington Post.* Retrieved from http://www.washingtonpost.com/wp-dyn/content/article/2009/03/01/AR2009030101929.html

Bonitz, V. (2008). Use of physical touch in the "talking cure": A journey to the outskirts of psychotherapy. *Psychotherapy: Theory, Research, Practice, Training, 45*, 391–404. doi: 10.1037/a0013311

Borys, D. S. (1988). *Dual relationships between therapist and client: A national survey of clinicians' attitudes and practices* (Doctoral dissertation, University of California, Los Angeles).

Borys, D. S. (1994). Maintaining therapeutic boundaries: The motive is therapeutic effectiveness, not defensive practice. *Ethics and Behavior, 4*(3), 267–273.

Borys, D. S., & Pope, K. S. (1989). Dual relationships between therapist and client: A national study of psychologists, psychiatrists, and social workers. *Professional Psychology: Research and Practice, 20*, 283–293. Available at http://kspope.com

Boston Globe. (2008, August 30). Boston Globe Editorial: Psychologists and torture. *Boston Globe.* Retrieved from http://tinyurl.com/5qhtf2

Boswell, J. F., Nelson, D. L., Nordberg, S. S., McAleavey, A. A., & Castonguay, L. G. (2010). Competency in integrative psychotherapy: Perspectives on training and supervision. *Psychotherapy: Theory, Research, Practice, Training, 47*, 3–11. doi: 10.1037/a0018848

Bouhoutsos, J. C., Holroyd, J., Lerman, H., Forer, B., & Greenberg, M. (1983). Sexual intimacy between psychotherapists and patients. *Professional Psychology: Research and Practice, 14*, 185–196.

Bow, J. N. (2006). Review of empirical research on child custody practice. *Journal of Child Custody, 3*, 23–50. doi: 10.1300/J190v03n01_02

Bow, J. N., Gould, J. W., Flens, J. R., & Greenhut, D. (2006). Testing in child custody evaluations: Selection, usage, and *Daubert* admissibility: A survey of psychologists. *Journal of Forensic Psychology Practice, 6*, 17–38. doi: 10.1300/J158v06n02_02

Brehm, S. (2007, January 9). APA news release of letter from the APA president to the editor of *Washington Monthly.* Retrieved from www.apa.org/news/press/response/washington-monthly-response.pdf

Brenner, L. A., Homaifar, B. Y., Adler, L. E., Wolfman, J. H., & Kemp, J. (2009). Suicidality and veterans with a history of traumatic brain injury: Precipitating events, protective factors, and prevention strategies. *Rehabilitation Psychology, 54*, 390–397. doi: 10.1037/a0017802

Brodsky, A. M. (1989). Sex between patient and therapist: Psychology's data and response. In G. O. Gabbard (Ed.), *Sexual exploitation in professional relationships* (pp. 15–25). Washington, DC: American Psychiatric Press.

Brown, L. S. (1984). The lesbian feminist therapist in private practice and her community. *Psychotherapy in Private Practice, 2.* 9–16.

Brown, L. S. (1988). Harmful effects of posttermination sexual and romantic relationships between therapists and their former clients. *Psychotherapy, 25*, 249–255.

Brown, L. S. (1989). Beyond thou shalt not: Thinking about ethics in the lesbian therapy community. *Women and Therapy, 8*, 13–25.

Brown, L. S. (1994a). Concrete boundaries and the problem of literalmindedness: A response to Lazarus. *Ethics and Behavior, 4*(3), 275–281.

Brown, L. S. (1994b). *Subversive dialogues.* New York, NY: Basic Books.

Brown, L. S. (1996). Ethical concerns with sexual minority patients. In R. P. Cabaj & T. S. Stein (Eds.), *Textbook of homosexuality and mental health* (pp. 897–916). Washington, DC: American Psychiatric Press.

Brown, L. S. (2008). Feminist therapy as a meaning-making practice: Where there is no power, where is the meaning? In K. J. Schneider (Ed.), *Existential-integrative psychotherapy: Guideposts to the core of practice* (pp. 130–140). New York, NY: Routledge/Taylor & Francis.

Brownlee, K. (1996). The ethics of non-sexual dual relationships: A dilemma for the rural mental health professional. *Community Mental Health Journal, 32,* 497–503.

Brunch, J., Barraclough, B., Nelson, M., & Sainsbury, P. (1971). Suicide following death of parents. *Social Psychiatry, 6,* 193–199.

Buri, C., Von Bonin, B., Strik, W., & Moggi, F. (2009). Predictors of attempted suicide among Swiss patients with alcohol-use disorders. *Journal of Studies on Alcohol and Drugs, 70,* 668–674.

Burian, B. K., & Slimp, A. O. C. (2000). Social dual-role relationships during internship: A decision-making model. *Professional Psychology: Research and Practice, 31*(3), 332–338.

Burke, E. (1961). *Reflections on the revolution in France.* New York, NY: Doubleday. (Original work published 1790.)

Burlingame, G. M., Fuhriman, A., & Mosier, J. (2003). The differential effectiveness of group psychotherapy: A meta-analytic perspective. *Group dynamics: Theory, research & practice, 2,* 101–117.

Bursztyajn, H. J., Feinbloom, R. I., Hamm, R. M., & Brodsky, A. (2000). *Medical choices, medical chance: How patients, families, and physicians can cope with uncertainty.* Lincoln: University of Nebraska Press.

Burt, R. A. (1997). The Supreme Court speaks—Not assisted suicide but a constitutional right to palliative care. *New England Journal of Medicine, 337,* 1234–1236.

Burton, M., & Kagan, C. (2007). Psychologists and torture—More than a question of interrogation. *The Psychologist* (British Psychological Society), 20(8), 484–487.

Butcher, J. M., Graham, J. R., Williams, C. L., & Ben-Porath, Y. S. (1990). *Development and use of the MMPI-2 content scales.* Minneapolis: University of Minnesota Press.

Butler, S. E., & Zelen, S. L. (1977). Sexual intimacies between therapists and patients. *Psychotherapy, 14,* 139–145.

California Department of Consumer Affairs. (1997). *Professional therapy never includes sex* (2nd ed.). (Original edition published 1990.) (Available from Board of Psychology, 1422 Howe Avenue, Suite 22, Sacramento, CA 95825)

Campbell, C., & Gordon, M. (2003). Acknowledging the inevitable: Understanding multiple relationships in rural practice. *Professional Psychology: Research and Practice, 34,* 430–434.

Campbell, L., Vasquez, M., Behnke, & S., Kinscherff, R. (2010). *APA Ethics Code commentary and case illustrations.* Washington, DC American Psychological Association.

Campisi, G. (2009, December 18). Feds enter probe of ID thefts from Penn Health agency. *Philadelphia Daily News.* Retrieved from http://bit.ly/7pjrHZ

Canadian Psychological Association. (1986). *Canadian Code of Ethics for psychologists.* Ottawa, Canada: Author.

Canadian Psychological Association. (1991). *Canadian Code of Ethics for psychologists.* Ottawa, Canada: Author.

Canadian Psychological Association. (2000). *Canadian code of ethics for psychologists.* Ottawa, Canada: Author.

Canadian Psychological Association. (2001a). *Annual report, 2000–2001.* Retrieved from http://www.cpa.ca/aboutcpa/ annualreports/

Canadian Psychological Association. (2001b). *Practice guidelines for providers of psychological services.* Retrieved from http://www.acposb.on.ca/ practice.htm

Canadian Psychological Association. (2001c). *Guidelines for nondiscriminatory practice.* Ottawa, Canada: Author.

Canadian Psychological Association. (2002). *Canadian Code of Ethics for psychologists* (3rd ed.). Ottawa, Canada: Author.

Canadian Psychological Association. (2006). *Annual report, 2005–2006.* Retrieved from http://www.cpa.ca/aboutcpa/annualreports/

Canadian Psychological Association. (2009, June). Annual Report, 2008–2009, pp. 12–13. Retrieved from http://www.cpa.ca/home/

Canter, M. B., Bennett, B. E., Jones, S. E., & Nagy, T. F. (1994). Ethics for psychologists: A commentary on the APA Ethics Code. Washington, DC: American Psychological Association.

Canterbury v. Spence, 464 F.2d 772 (D.C. Cir. 1972).

Caplan, P. J. (1995). *They say you're crazy: The inside story of the DSM.* Reading, MA: Addison-Wesley.

Carr, A. (2009a). The effectiveness of family therapy and systemic interventions for adult-focused problems. *Journal of Family Therapy, 31,* 46–74.

Carr, A. (2009b). The effectiveness of family therapy and systemic interventions for child-focused problems. *Journal of Family Therapy, 31,* 3–45.

Carter, G. T., VandeKieft, G. K., & Barren, D. W. (2005). Whose life is it, anyway? The federal government vs. the state of Oregon on the legality of physician-assisted suicide. *American Journal of Hospice and Palliative Medicine, 22*(4), 249–251.

Casas, J. M., & Vasquez, M. J. T. (1989). Counseling the Hispanic client: A theoretical and applied perspective. In P. B. Pedersen, J. G. Draguns, W. J. Lonner, & J. E. Trimble (Eds.), *Counseling across cultures* (3rd ed.) (pp. 153–175). Honolulu: University of Hawaii Press.

Cases and inquiries before the Committee on Scientific and Professional Ethics and Conduct. (1954). *American Psychologist, 9,* 806–807.

Cassileth, B. R., Zupkis, R. V., Sutton-Smith, K., & March, V. (1980). Informed consent—Why are its goals imperfectly realized? *New England Journal of Medicine, 323,* 896–900.

Caudill, O. B. (1993, Winter). Administrative injustice: Can psychologists be vicariously liable for sexual misconduct? *AAP Advance Plan,* Association for the Advancement of Psychology, 4–5.

Caudill, O. B., & Pope, K. S. (1995). *Law and mental health professionals: California.* Washington, DC: American Psychological Association.

Celano, M. P., Smith, C. O., & Kaslow, N. J. (2010). A competency-based approach to couple and family therapy supervision. *Psychotherapy: Theory, Research, Practice, Training, 47*, 35–44. doi: 10.1037/a0018845

Celenza, A. (2007). *Sexual boundary violations: Therapeutic, supervisory, and academic contexts.* Lanham, MD: Jason Aronson.

Centeno, J. G. (2009). Issues and principles in service delivery to communicatively impaired minority bilingual adults in neurorehabilitation. *Seminars in Speech and Language, 30*, 139–152. doi: 10.1055/s-0029-1225951

Centers for Disease Control and Prevention. U.S. Public Health Service Syphilis Study at Tuskegee. Retrieved from http://www.cdc.gov/tuskegee

Chan, C. S. (1997). Don't ask, don't tell, don't know: The formation of a homosexual identity and sexual expression among Asian American lesbians. In B. Greene (Ed.), *Ethnic and cultural diversity among lesbians and gay men* (pp. 240–248). Thousand Oaks, CA: Sage.

Chan, S. S. M., Chiu, H. F. K., Chen, E. Y. H., Chan, W. S. C., Wong, P. W. C., Chan, C. L. W., . . . Yip, P. S. F. (2009). Population-attributable risk of suicide conferred by Axis I psychiatric diagnosis in a Hong Kong Chinese population. *Psychiatric Services, 60*, 1135–1138. doi: 10.1176/appi.ps.60.8.1135

Chanowitz, B., & Langer, E. J. (1981). Premature cognitive commitment. *Journal of Personality and Social Psychology, 41*, 1051–1063.

Chiang, H. (1986, July 28). Psychotherapist is subject to suit for breaching privilege. *Los Angeles Daily Journal*, p. 1.

Chretien, K. C., Greysen, S. R., Chretien, J. P., & Kind, T. (2009). Online posting of unprofessional content by medical students. *Journal of the American Medical Association, 302*(12), 1309–1315. doi: 302/12/1309 [pii] 10.1001/jama.2009 .1387

Claridge, G., Clark, K., Powney, E., & Hassan, E. (2008). Schizotypy and the Barnum Effect. Personality and Individual Differences, 44, 436–444. doi: 10.1016/j.paid .2007.09.006.

Clark, H. K., Murdock, N. L., & Koetting, K. (2009). Predicting burnout and career choice satisfaction in counseling psychology graduate students. The Counseling Psychologist, 37, 580–606. doi: 10.1177/0011000008319985

Clarkson, P. (1994). In recognition of dual relationships. *Transactional Analysis Journal, 24*(1), 32–38.

Cobbs v. Grant, 8 Cal.3d 229, 502 P.2d 1, 104 Cal. Rptr. 505 (Cal. 1972).

Cocks, G. (1985). *Psychotherapy in the Third Reich: The Göring Institute.* New York, NY: Oxford University Press.

Cohen, N. (2009, July 29). Has Wikipedia Created a Rorschach Cheat Sheet? *New York Times*. Accessed on December 27, 2009, from http://bit.ly/4XgITf

Cohen-Sandler, R., Berman, A. L., & King, R. A. (1982). Life stress and symptomotology: Determinants of suicidal behavior in children. *Journal of the American Academy of Child Psychiatry, 21*, 178–186.

Cole, M., & Bruner, J. S. (1972). Cultural differences and inferences about psychological processes. *American Psychologist, 26*, 867–876.

Colt, G. H. (1983). The enigma of suicide. *Harvard Magazine, 86*, 47–66.

Comas-Díaz, L. (2008). Latino psychospirituality. In Schneider, Kirk J. (Ed), Existential-integrative psychotherapy: Guideposts to the core of practice. (pp. 100–109). New York, NY: Routledge/Taylor & Francis Group.

Comas-Díaz, L., & Greene, B. G. (1994). *Women of color: Integrating ethnic and gender identities in psychotherapy.* New York, NY: Guilford Press.

Committee on Medical Liability and Risk Management of the American Academy of Pediatrics. (2009). Policy statement—Expert witness participation in civil and criminal proceedings. *Pediatrics, 124*(1), 428–438. doi: 124/1/428 [pii]10.1542/peds.2009-1132.

Commons, M. L., Rodriguez, J. A., Adams, K. M., Goodheart, E. A., Gutheil, T. G., & Cyr, E. D. (2006). Informed consent: Do you know it when you see it? Evaluating the adequacy of patient consent and the value of a lawsuit. *Psychiatric Annals, 36*(6), 430–435.

Constantine, M. G., & Sue, D. W. (2005). *Strategies for building multicultural competence in mental health and educational settings.* Hoboken, NJ: Wiley.

Constantinou, M., Ashendorf, L., & McCaffrey, R. J. (2002). When the third party observer of a neuropsychological evaluation is an audiorecorder. *Clinical Neuropsychologist, 16*(3), 407–412.

Constantinou, M., Ashendorf, L., & McCaffrey, R. J. (2005). Effects of a third party observer during neuropsychological assessment: When the observer is a video camera. *Journal of Forensic Neuropsychology, 4*(2), 39–47.

"Correction." (2006). *Monitor on Psychology, 37*(5), 7.

Costigan, C., Su, T. F., & Hua, J. M. (2009). Ethnic identity among Chinese Canadian youth: A review of the Canadian literature. *Canadian Psychology/Psychologie canadienne, 50,* 261–272. doi: 10.1037/a0016880

Crits-Christoph, P., Wilson, G. T., & Hollon, S. D. (2005). Empirically supported psychotherapies: Comment on Westen, Novotny, and Thompson-Brenner (2004). *Psychological Bulletin, 131*(3), 412–417.

Crosby, A. E., Espitia-Hardeman, V., Hill, H. A., Ortega, L., & Clavel-Arcas, C. (2009). Alcohol and suicide among racial/ethnic populations—17 states, 2005–2006. *Journal of the American Medical Association, 302,* 733–734.

Curlin, F. A., Nwodim, C., Vance, J. L., Chin, M. H., & Lantos, J. D. (2008). To die, to sleep: US physicians' religious and other objections to physician-assisted suicide, terminal sedation, and withdrawal of life support. *American Journal of Hospice & Palliative Medicine, 25,* 112–120. doi: 10.1177/1049909107310141

Capuzzi, D. (Ed.). *Suicide across the life span: Implications for counselors* (pp. 163–184). Alexandria, VA: American Counseling Association.

Davidson, R. J., Schwartz, G. E., & Shapiro, D. (Eds.).(1978). *Consciousness and self-regulation: Advances in research and theory* (Vol. 2, pp. 101–137). New York, NY: Plenum Press.

Dalen, K. (2006). To tell or not to tell, that is the question: Ethical dilemmas presented by psychologists in telephone counseling. *European Psychologist, 11*(3), 236–243.

Darke, S., Duflou, J., & Torok, M. (2009). Toxicology and circumstances of completed suicide by means other than overdose. *Journal of Forensic Sciences, 54,* 490–494. doi: 10.1111/j.1556-4029.2008.00967.x

Davis, D. (2008). *Terminating therapy: A professional guide to ending on a positive note.* Hoboken, NJ: Wiley.

Davison, G. C., & Neale, J. M. (1982). *Abnormal psychology: An experimental clinical approach.* Hoboken, NJ: Wiley.

De Las Cuevas, C., Arredondo, M. T., Cabrera, M. F., Sulzenbacher, H., & Meise, U. (2006). Randomized clinical trial of telepsychiatry through videoconference versus face-to-face conventional psychiatric treatment. *Telemedicine and e-Health, 12,* 341–350. doi: 10.1089/tmj.2006.12.341

Denney, R. M., Aten, J. D., & Gingrich, F. C. (2008). Using spiritual self-disclosure in psychotherapy. *Journal of Psychology & Theology, 36,* 294–302.

Dickens, B. M., Boyle Jr., J. M., & Ganzini, L. (2008). Euthanasia and assisted suicide. In P. A. Singer & A. M. Viens (Eds.), *The Cambridge textbook of bioethics* (pp. 72–77). New York, NY: Cambridge University Press.

Dixon-Woods, M., Williams, S. J., Jackson, C. J., Akkad, A., Kenyon, S., & Habiba, M. (2006). Why do women consent to surgery, even when they do not want to? An interactionist and Bourdieusian analysis. *Social Science and Medicine, 62*(11), 2742–2753.

Dolan, P. L. (2009, October 12). Social media behavior could threaten your reputation, job prospects. *American Medical News.* Retrieved at http://www.ama-assn.org/amednews/2009/10/12/bil21012.htm

Dovidio, J. F., Gaertner, S. L., Kawakami, K., & Hodson, G. (2002). Why can't we just get along? Interpersonal biases and interracial distrust. *Cultural Diversity and Ethnic Minority Psychology, 8,* 88–102.

Downey, D. L. (2001). Therapeutic touch in psychotherapy. *Psychotherapy Bulletin, 36,* 1, 35–39.

Downie, J. (2004). *Dying justice: The case for decriminalizing euthanasia and assisted suicide in Canada.* Toronto, Canada: University of Toronto Press.

Draft of the APA ethics code published. (1991, June). *APA Monitor,* pp. 30–35.

Drake, R., Gates, C., Cotton, P., & Whitaker, A. (1984). Suicide among schizophrenics: Who is at risk? *Journal of Nervous and Mental Disease, 172,* 613–617.

Draper, B., Peisah, C., Snowdon, J., & Brodaty, H. (2010). Early dementia diagnosis and the risk of suicide and euthanasia. *Alzheimer's & Dementia, 6,* 75–82. doi: 10.1016/j.jalz.2009.04.1229

Duff, K., & Fisher, J. M. (2005). Ethical dilemmas with third party observers. *Journal of Forensic Neuropsychology, 4*(2), 65–82.

Duncan, B. L., Miller, S. D., Wampold, B. E. , & Hubble, M. A. (Eds.) (2010). *The heart and soul of change: Delivering what works in therapy* (2nd ed.). Washington, DC: American Psychological Association. doi: 10.1037/12075-000

Dvoskin, J. A. (2007, August). Presidential address: A psychologist looks at crime and punishment. Paper presented at the meeting of the American Psychological Association, San Francisco, CA.

Dworkin, S. H. (1992). Some ethical considerations when counseling gay, lesbian, and bisexual clients. In S. H. Dworkin & F. J. Gutierrez (Eds.), *Counseling gay men and lesbians: Journey to the end of the rainbow* (pp. 325–334). Alexandria, VA: American Association for Counseling and Development.

Dyer, C. (2008, January 12). Whistleblower who was excluded from work for five years wins apology. *British Medical Journal, 336*(7635): 63. Retrieved from http://www .bmj.com/cgi/content/extract/336/7635/63-a. doi: 10.1136/bmj.39454.502049.DB

Eban, K. (2007, July 17). Rorschach and awe. *Vanity Fair*. Retrieved from http://tinyurl. com/2zkg9p

EchoHawk, M. (1997). Suicide: The scourge of Native American people. *Suicide and Life-Threatening Behavior, 27*, 60–67.

Elder, L. (2010, February 12). UTMB warns 1,200 of identity theft threat. *Galveston County Daily News*. Retrieved from http://www.galvnews.com/story.lasso?ewcd= 710b7dd80a0d2263

Ellis, E. M., Atkeson, B. M., & Calhoun, K. S. (1982). An examination of differences between multiple- and single-incident victims of multiple sexual assault. *Journal of Abnormal Psychology, 91*, 221–224.

Erdberg, P. (1988, August). How clinicians can achieve competence in testing procedures. Paper presented at the annual meeting of the American Psychological Association, Atlanta, GA.

Evans, J. (1989). *Bias in human reasoning: Causes and consequences*. Mahwah, NJ: Erlbaum.

Fadiman, A. (1997). *The spirit catches you and you fall down: A Hmong child, her American doctors, and the collision of two cultures*. New York, NY: Farrar, Straus and Giroux.

Falender, C. A., Collins, C. J., & Shafranske, E. P. (2009, November). "Impairment" and performance issues in clinical supervision: After the 2008 ADA Amendments Act. *Training and Education in Professional Psychology, 3*(4), 240–249.

Falender, C. A., & Shafranske, E. P. (2004). *Clinical supervision: A competency-based approach*. Washington, DC: American Psychological Association.

Falender, C. A., & Shafranske, E. P. (2008). *Casebook for clinical supervision: A competency-based approach*. Washington, DC: American Psychological Association.

Falender, C. A., & Shafranske, E. P. (2010). *Getting the most out of clinical supervision: A practical guide for interns and trainees*. Washington, DC: American Psychological Association.

Falender, C. A., Shafranske, E. P., & Falicov, C. (2010). *Diversity and multiculturalism in clinical supervision: Foundation and praxis*. Washington, DC: American Psychological Association.

Farber, B. A. (2006). *Self-disclosure in psychotherapy*. New York, NY: Guilford Press.

Farber, B. A., Khurgin-Bott, R., & Feldman, S. (2009). The benefits and risks of patient self-disclosure in the psychotherapy of women with a history of childhood sexual abuse. *Psychotherapy: Theory, Research, Practice, Training, 46*, 52–67. doi: 10.1037/ a0015136

Farber, E. W. (2010). Humanistic–existential psychotherapy competencies and the supervisory process. *Psychotherapy: Theory, Research, Practice, Training, 47*, 28–34. doi: 10.1037/a0018847

Farber, E. W., & Kaslow, N. J. (2010). Introduction to the special section: The role of supervision in ensuring the development of psychotherapy competencies across diverse theoretical perspectives. *Psychotherapy: Theory, Research, Practice, Training, 47*, 1–2. doi: 10.1037/a0018850

Farberow, N. (1985, May 12). How to tell if someone is thinking of suicide. *Los Angeles Herald Examiner*, p. C9.

Faschingbauer, T. R. (1979). The future of the MMPI. In C. S. Newmark (Ed.), *MMPI: Clinical and research trends* (pp. 380–392). New York, NY: Praeger.

Faulkner, K. K., & Faulkner, T. A. (1997). Managing multiple relationships in rural communities: Neutrality and boundary violations. *Clinical Psychology: Science and Practice, 4*(3), 225–234.

Feeny, L. J. (2009). There is more to post-termination boundary violations than sex. *Advances in Psychiatric Treatment, 15*, 318. doi: 10.1192/apt.15.4.318

Feldman-Summers, S., & Jones, G. (1984). Psychological impacts of sexual contact between therapists or other health care professionals and their clients. *Journal of Consulting and Clinical Psychology, 52*, 1054–1061.

Feminist Therapy Institute. (1987). *Feminist therapy code of ethics.* Denver, CO: Author.

Festinger, L. (1964). *Conflict, decision, and dissonance.* Stanford, CA: Stanford University Press.

Finn, S. E. (2007). In our clients' shoes: Theory and techniques of therapeutic assessment. Mahwah, NJ: Erlbaum.

Fischer, S., Huber, C. A., Imhof, L., Imhof, R. M., Furter, M., Ziegler, S. J., & Bosshard, G. (2008). Suicide assisted by two Swiss right-to-die organisations. *Journal of Medical Ethics, 34*, 810–814. doi: 10.1136/jme.2007.023887

Fisher, C. B. (2003). *Decoding the ethics code: A practical guide for psychologists.* Thousand Oaks, CA: Sage.

Fisher, C. B., & Oransky, M. (2008). Informed consent to psychotherapy: Protecting the dignity and respecting the autonomy of patients. *Journal of Clinical Psychology, 64*, 576–588. doi: 10.1002/jclp.20472

Fisher, M. A. (2008). Clarifying confidentiality with the ethical practice model. *American Psychologist, 63*, 624–625. doi: 10.1037/0003-066X.63.7.624

Flaherty, A. (2008, June 17). Probe: Officials warned about harsh interrogations. *USA Today.* Retrieved from http://bit.ly/9N63Rc

Flores, G. (2006). Language barriers to health care in the United States. *New England Journal of Medicine, 355*, 229–231.

Forer, B. R. (1949). The fallacy of personal validation: a classroom demonstration of gullibility. *Journal of Abnormal and Social Psychology, 44*, 118–123. doi: 10.1037/h0059240

Fouad, N. A., Grus, C. L., Hatcher, R. L., Kaslow, N. J., Hutchings, P. S., Madson, M. B., . . . Crossman, R. E. (2009). Competency benchmarks: A model for understanding and measuring competence in professional psychology across training levels. *Training and Education in Professional Psychology, 3*, S5–S26. doi: 10.1037/a0015832

Francis, R. D. (2009) *Ethics for psychologists* (2nd ed. Chichester, United Kingdom: BPS Blackwell/John Wiley.

Franklin, A. J. (2009). Reflections on ethnic minority psychology: Learning from our past so the present informs our future. *Cultural Diversity and Ethnic Minority Psychology, 15*, 416–424. doi: 10.1037/a0017560

Freeman, L., & Roy, J. (1976). *Betrayal.* New York, NY: Stein and Day.

Freeny, M. (2007). Whatever happened to clinical privacy. *Annals of the American Psychotherapy Association, 10*, 13–17.

Freud, S. (1952). *A general introduction to psychoanalysis*. [Authorized English translation of the revised edition by J. Riviere.] New York, NY: Washington Square Press. (Originally published 1924.)

Freud, S. (1963). Further recommendations in the technique of psychoanalysis: Observations on transference-love. In P. Rieff (Ed.), *Freud: Therapy and technique* (pp. 167–179). [Authorized English translation of the revised edition by J. Riviere.] New York, NY: Collier Books. (Originally published 1915.)

Frey, D., & Schulz-Hardt, S. (2001). Confirmation bias in group information seeking and its implications for decision making in administration, business and politics. In F. Butera & G. Mugny (Eds.), *Social influence in social reality: Promoting individual and social change*. (pp. 53–73). Ashland, OH: Hogrefe & Huber.

Fridhandler, B. (2008). Science and child custody evaluations: What qualifies as "scientific"? *Journal of Child Custody, 5*, 256–275. doi: 10.1080/15379410802583767

Gabbard, G. O. (1994). Teetering on the precipice: A commentary on Lazarus's "How certain boundaries and ethics diminish therapeutic effectiveness." *Ethics and Behavior, 4*(3), 283–286.

Gabbard, G. O. (Ed.). (1989). *Sexual exploitation in professional relationships*. Washington, DC: American Psychiatric Press.

Gabbard, G. O., & Pope, K. (1989). Sexual involvements after termination: Clinical, ethical, and legal aspects. In G. O. Gabbard (Ed.), *Sexual exploitation in professional relationships* (pp. 115–127). Washington, DC: American Psychiatric Press.

Gallagher, H. G. (1990). *By trust betrayed: Patients, physicians, and the license to kill in the Third Reich*. New York, NY: Holt.

Gandhi, M. K. (1948). *Non-violence in peace and war*. Ahmedabadi, India: Narajivan Publishing.

Ganzini, L. (2006). Physician-assisted suicide. *American Journal of Psychiatry, 163*(6), 1109–1110.

Garb, H. N. (1997). Racial bias, social class bias, and gender bias in clinical judgment. *Clinical Psychology: Science and Practice, 4*, 99–120.

Gartrell, N. K. (1992). Boundaries in lesbian therapy relationships. *Women & Therapy, 12*, 29–49.

Gartrell, N. K., Herman, J. L., Olarte, S., Feldstein, M., & Localio, R. (1986). Psychiatrist-patient sexual contact: Results of a national survey. I: Prevalence. *American Journal of Psychiatry, 143*, 1126–1131.

Gavett, B. E., Lynch, J. K., & McCaffrey, R. J. (2005). Third party observers: The effect size is greater than you might think. *Journal of Forensic Neuropsychology, 4*(2), 49–64.

Gawronski, B. (2003). Implicational schemata and the correspondence bias: On the diagnostic value of situationally constrained behavior. *Journal of Personality and Social Psychology, 84*(6), 1154–1171.

Geller, J. D. (1988). Racial bias in the evaluation of patients for psychotherapy. In L. Comas-Dias & E. H. Griffith (Eds.), *Clinical guidelines in cross-cultural mental health* (pp. 112–134). New York, NY: Wiley.

Geller, J. D., Cooley, R. S., & Hartley, D. (1981–1982). Images of the psychotherapist: A theoretical and methodological perspective. *Imagination, Cognition, and Personality: Consciousness in Theory, Research, Clinical Practice, 3*, 123–146.

Gelles, M. (2005, August 22). [Online forum comment]. The American Psychological Association Presidential Task Force on Psychological Ethics and National Security

LISTSERV correspondence, Intelligence Ethics Collection, Hoover Institution Archives, Stanford University. Retrieved from http://s3.amazonaws.com/propublica/assets/docs/pens_listserv.pdf

Germain, V., Marchand, A., Bouchard, S., Drouin, M., & Guay, S. (2009). Effectiveness of cognitive behavioural therapy administered by videoconference for posttraumatic stress disorder. *Cognitive Behaviour Therapy*, 38, 42–53. doi: 10.1080/16506070802473494

Geyer, M. C. (1994). Dual role relationships and Christian counseling. *Journal of Psychology and Theology*, 22(3), 187–195.

Gibbons, R. D., Hur, K., Bhaumik, D. K., & Mann, J. J. (2005). The relationship between antidepressant medication use and rate of suicide. *Archives of General Psychiatry*, 62, 165–172.

Gibbs, J. T. (1997). African-American suicide: A cultural paradox. *Suicide and Life-Threatening Behavior*, 27, 68–79.

Gibbs, J. T., & Huang, L. N. (1989). *Children of color: Psychological interventions with minority youth*. San Francisco, CA: Jossey-Bass.

Gibson, W. T., & Pope, K. S. (1993). The ethics of counseling: A national survey of certified counselors. *Journal of Counseling and Development*, 71(3), 330–336.

Gielen, J., van den Branden, S., & Broeckaert, B. (2008). Attitudes of European physicians toward euthanasia and physician-assisted suicide: A review of the recent literature. *Journal of Palliative Care*, 24, 173–184.

Gilbert, D. T., & Malone, P. S. (1995). The correspondence bias. *Psychological Bulletin*, 117(1), 21–38.

Glascock, A. (2009). Is killing necessarily murder? Moral questions surrounding assisted suicide and death. In J. Sokolovsky, *The cultural context of aging: Worldwide perspectives* (3rd ed.) (pp. 77–92). Westport, CT: Praeger Publishers/Greenwood Publishing Group.

Glaser, R. D., & Thorpe, J. S. (1986). Unethical intimacy: A survey of sexual contact and advances between psychology educators and female graduate students. *American Psychologist*, 41, 43–51.

Glick, J. E., Bates, L., & and Yabiku, S. T. (2009). Mother's age at arrival in the United States and early cognitive development. *Early Childhood Research Quarterly*, 24, 4, 367–380.

Godlee, F. (2009, May 16). Rules of conscience. *British Medical Journal*, 338, 7704.

Gold, M. (1999). *The complete social scientist: A Kurt Lewin reader*. Washington, DC: American Psychological Association.

Goldstein, L. S., & Buongiorno, P. A. (1984). Psychotherapists as suicide survivors. *American Journal of Psychotherapy*, 38, 392–398.

Goleman, D. (1985). *Vital lies, simple truths: The psychology of self deception*. New York, NY: Simon & Schuster.

Goodheart, C. D. (2006). Evidence, endeavor, and expertise in psychology practice. In C. D. Goodheart, A. E. Kazdin, & R. J. Sternberg (Eds.), *Evidence-based psychotherapy: Where practice and research meet* (pp. 37–61). Washington, DC: American Psychological Association.

Goodheart, C. D., Kazdin, A. E., & Sternberg, R. J. (Eds.). (2006). *Evidence-based psychotherapy: Where practice and research meet* (pp. 153–177). Washington, DC: American Psychological Association.

Goodman, A. (2007, June 8). Psychologists implicated in torture. *Seattle Post-Intelligencer*. Retrieved from http://seattlepi.nwsource.com/opinion/318745_amy07.html

Goodyear, R. K., & Sinnett, E. R. (1984). Current and emerging ethical issues for counseling psychology. *Counseling Psychologist, 12*, 87–98.

Gorman, S. W. (2009, April) Comment: Sex outside of the therapy hour: Practical and constitutional limits on therapist sexual misconduct regulations, 56 *UCLA Law Review*, 983.

Gossett, T. F. (1963). *Race: The history of an idea in America*. Dallas, TX: Southern Methodist University Press.

Gostin, L. (2006). Physician-assisted suicide: A legitimate medical practice? *Journal of the American Medical Association, 295*(16), 1941–1943.

Gottlieb, M. C. (1993). Avoiding exploitive dual relationships: A decision-making model. *Psychotherapy: Theory, Research, Practice, Training, 30*(1), 41–48. Available at http://kspope.com

Gottlieb, M. C. (1994). Ethical decision making, boundaries, and treatment effectiveness: A reprise. *Ethics and Behavior, 4*(3), 287–293.

Gould, S. J. (1981). *The mismeasure of man*. New York, NY: Norton.

Greene, B. G. (1997a). Ethnic minority lesbians and gay men: Mental health and treatment issues. In B. Greene (Ed.), *Ethnic and cultural diversity among lesbians and gay men* (pp. 216–239). Thousand Oaks, CA: Sage.

Greene, B. G. (Ed.). (1997b). *Ethnic and cultural diversity among lesbians and gay men*. Thousand Oaks, CA: Sage.

Greene, B. G., & Croom, G. L. (1999). *Education, research, and practice in lesbian, gay, bisexual, and transgendered psychology: A resource manual*. Thousand Oaks, CA: Sage.

Greene, C. H., III, & Banks, L. M., III. (2009). Ethical guideline evolution in psychological support to interrogation operations. *Consulting Psychology Journal: Practice and Research, 61*, 25–32. doi: 10.1037/a0015102

Gripton, J., & Valentich, M. (2004). Dealing with non-sexual professional-client dual/multiple relationships in rural communities. *Rural Social Work, 9*(2), 216–225.

Gross, B. (2004). Theft by deception. *Annals of the American Psychotherapy Association, 7*(1), 36–37.

Grundner, T. M. (1980). On the readability of surgical consent forms. *New England Journal of Medicine, 302*, 900–902.

Gutheil, T. G. (1994). Discussion of Lazarus's "How certain boundaries and ethics diminish therapeutic effectiveness." *Ethics and Behavior, 4*(3), 295–298.

Gutheil, T. G. (2009). *The psychiatrist as expert witness* (2nd ed.). Arlington, VA: American Psychiatric Publishing.

Gutheil, T. G., & Brodsky, A. (2008). *Preventing boundary violations in clinical practice*. New York, NY: Guilford Press.

Gutheil, T. G., & Gabbard, G. O. (1993). The concept of boundaries in clinical practice: Theoretical and risk-management dimensions. *American Journal of Psychiatry, 150*, 188–196.

Guze, S. B., & Robins, E. (1970). Suicide and primary affective disorders. *British Journal of Psychiatry, 117*, 437–438.

Hailey, D., Roine, R., & Ohinmaa A. (2008). The effectiveness of telemental health applications: A review. *Canadian Journal of Psychiatry.* 53(11):769–778.

Hall, C. S. (1952). Crooks, codes, and cant. *American Psychologist, 7,* 430–431.

Hall, J. E., & Hare-Mustin, R. T. (1983). Sanctions and the diversity of complaints against psychologists. *American Psychologist, 38,* 714–729.

Hallinan v. Committee of Bar Examiners of State Bar. 55 Cal. Rptr. 228 (1966).

Hamilton, N. G., & Hamilton, C. A. (2005). Competing paradigms of response to assisted suicide requests in Oregon. *American Journal of Psychiatry, 162*(6), 1060–1065.

Handler, J. F. (1990). *Law and the search for community.* Philadelphia: University of Pennsylvania Press.

Hansen, N. D., Randazzo, K. V., Schwartz, A., Marshall, M., Kalis, D., Frazier, R., . . . Norvig, G. (2006). Do we practice what we preach? An exploratory survey of multicultural psychotherapy competencies. *Professional Psychology: Research and Practice, 37*(1), 66–74.

Harding, S. S., Shearn, M. L., & Kitchener, K. S. (1989, August). *Dual role dilemmas: Psychology educators and their students.* Paper presented at the annual meeting of the American Psychological Association, New Orleans.

Hare-Mustin, R. T. (1974). Ethical considerations in the use of sexual contact in psychotherapy. *Psychotherapy: Theory, Research and Practice, 11,* 308–310.

Harowski, K., Turner, A. L., LeVine, E., Schank, J. A., & Leichter, J. (2006). From our community to yours: Rural best perspectives on psychology practice, training, and advocacy. *Professional Psychology: Research and Practice, 37*(2), 158–164.

Harper, F. D., & McFadden, J. (2003). *Culture and counseling: New approaches.* Needham Heights, MA: Allyn & Bacon.

Harris, E. C., & Barraclough, B. (1997). Suicide as an outcome for mental disorders: A meta-analysis. *British Journal of Psychiatry, 170,* 205–228.

Hawn, C. (2009). Take two aspirin and tweet me in the morning: How Twitter, Facebook, and other social media are reshaping health care. *Health Affairs, 28*(2), 361–368.

Hays, K. (2002). *Move your body, tone your mood.* New York, NY: Harbinger.

Hays, P. A. (2008). *Addressing cultural complexities in practice: Assessment, diagnosis, and therapy* (2nd ed.). Washington, DC: American Psychological Association.

Hays, P. A. (2009). Integrating evidence-based practice, cognitive-behavior therapy, and multicultural therapy: Ten steps for culturally competent practice. *Professional Psychology: Research and Practice, 40,* 354–360. doi: 10.1037/a0016250

Heingartner, D. (2009, November 30). The doctors were real, the patients undercover. *New York Times.* Retrieved from http://www.nytimes.com/2009/12/01/health/01dutch.html

Hendin, H., Haas, A. P., Maltsberger, J. T., Koestner, B., & Szanto, K. (2006). Problems in psychotherapy with suicidal patients. *American Journal of Psychiatry, 163*(1), 67–72.

Henretty, J. R., & Levitt, H. M. (2010). The role of therapist self-disclosure in psychotherapy: A qualitative review. *Clinical Psychology Review, 30,* 63–77. doi: 10.1016/j.cpr.2009.09.004

Herlihy, B., & Watson, B. (2004). Ethical issues in assisted suicide. In D. Capuzzi (Ed.), *Suicide across the life span* (pp. 163–184). Alexandria, VA: American Counseling Association.

Herman, J. L., Gartrell, N., Olarte, S., Feldstein, M., & Localio, R. (1987). Psychiatrist-patient sexual contact: Results of a national survey. II: Psychiatrists' attitudes. *American Journal of Psychiatry, 144,* 164–169.

Hill, C., Memon, A., & McGeorge, P. (2008). The role of confirmation bias in suspect interviews: A systematic evaluation. *Legal and Criminological Psychology, 13,* 357–371. doi: 10.1348/135532507X238682

Hill, M. (1999). Barter: Ethical considerations in psychotherapy. *Women & Therapy, 22,* 81–91. doi: 10.1300/J015v22n03_08

Hinrichsen, G. A. (2006). Why multicultural issues matter for practitioners working with older adults. *Professional Psychology: Research and Practice, 37*(1), 29–35.

Hobbs, N. (1948). The development of a code of ethical standards for psychology. *American Psychologist, 3,* 80–84.

Hoilette, L. K., Clark, S. J., Gebremariam, A., & Davis, M. M. (2009). Usual source of care and unmet need among vulnerable children: 1998–2006. *Pediatrics, 123*(2), e214–219. doi: 123/2/e214 [pii]10.1542/peds.2008-2454

Holroyd, J. (1983). Erotic contact as an instance of sex-biased therapy. In J. Murray & P. R. Abramson (Eds.), *Bias in psychotherapy* (pp. 285–308). New York, NY: Praeger.

Holroyd, J., & Brodsky, A. (1977). Psychologists' attitudes and practices regarding erotic and nonerotic physical contact with clients. *American Psychologist, 32,* 843–849.

Holroyd, J. C., & Brodsky, A. M. (1980). Does touching patients lead to sexual intercourse? *Professional Psychology, 11,* 807–811.

Horrell, S. C. V. (2008). Effectiveness of cognitive–behavioral therapy with adult ethnic minority clients: A review. *Professional Psychology: Research and Practice, 2,* 160–168.

Horst, E. A. (1989). Dual relationships between psychologists and clients in rural and urban areas. *Journal of Rural Community Psychology, 10*(2), 15–24.

Huisman, A., van Houwelingen, C. A. J., & Kerkhof, A. J. F. M. (2009). Psychopathology and suicide method in mental health care. *Journal of Affective Disorders.* doi: 10.1016/j.jad.2009.05.024

Hunt, I. M., Kapur, N., Webb, R., Robinson, J., Burns, J., Shaw, J., & Appleby, L. (2009). Suicide in recently discharged psychiatric patients: A case-control study. *Psychological Medicine, 39,* 443–449. doi: 10.1017/S0033291708003644

Huppert, J. D., Fabbro, A., & Barlow, D. H. (2006). Evidence-based practice and psychological treatments. In C. D. Goodheart, A. E. Kazdin, & R. J. Sternberg (Eds.), *Evidence-based psychotherapy: Where practice and research meet* (pp. 131–152). Washington, DC: American Psychological Association.

Hwang, W. (2009). The formative method for adapting psychotherapy (FMAP): A community-based developmental approach to culturally adapting therapy. *Professional Psychology: Research and Practice, 40,* 369–377.

International Committee of the Red Cross. (2004, January 30). Guantanamo Bay: Overview of ICRC's work for internees. Retrieved from http://www.icrc.org/web/eng/siteeng0.nsf/iwpList74/951C74F20D2A2148C1256D8D002CA8DC or http://bit.ly/d72a8U

In the matter of the accusation against: Myron E. Howland. (1980). Before the Psychology Examining Committee, Board of Medical Quality Assurance, State of California, No. D-2212. Reporters' transcript, Vol. 3.

Irwin, M., Lovitz, A., Marder, S. R., Mintz, J., Winslade, W. J., Van Putten, T., & Mills, M. J. (1985). Psychotic patients' understanding of informed consent. *American Journal of Psychiatry, 142,* 1351–1354.

Isherwood, J., Adam, K. S., & Homblow, A. R. (1982). Life event stress, psychosocial factors, suicide attempt and auto-accident proclivity. *Journal of Psychosomatic Research, 26,* 371–383.

Jablonski v. United States, 712 F.2d 391 (1983).

Jain, S. H. (2009). Practicing medicine in the age of Facebook. *New England Journal of Medicine, 361*(7), 649–651. doi: 361/7/649 [pii] 10.1056/NEJMp0901277

Jain, S. [H.], & Roberts, L. (2009). Ethics in psychotherapy: A focus on professional boundaries and confidentiality practices. *Psychiatric Clinics of North America, 32*(2), 299–314.

Janis, I. L. (1972). *Victims of groupthink.* Boston, MA: Houghton Mifflin.

Janis, I. L. (1982). *Stress, attitudes, and decisions.* New York, NY: Praeger.

Janis, I. L., & Mann, L. (1977). *Decision making: A psychological analysis of conflict, choice, and commitment.* New York, NY: Free Press.

Jennings, F. L. (1992). Ethics of rural practice. *Psychotherapy in Private Practice, 10*(3), 85–104.

Joiner, T. (2005). *Why people die by suicide.* Cambridge, MA: Harvard University Press.

Joiner, T. (2010). *Myths about suicide.* Cambridge, MA: Harvard University Press.

Jones, E. E. (1979). The rocky road from acts to dispositions. *American Psychologist, 34*(2), 107–117.

Jones, E. E., & Korchin, S. J. (1982). Minority mental health: Perspectives. In E. E. Jones & S. J. Korchin (Eds.), *Minority mental health* (pp. 3– 36). New York, NY: Praeger.

Jones, J. H. (1981). *Bad blood: The Tuskegee syphilis experiment: A tragedy of race and medicine.* New York, NY: Free Press.

Jones, J. M. (1990a, August). *Psychological approaches to race: What have they been and what should they be?* Paper presented at the annual meeting of the American Psychological Association, Boston.

Jones, J. M. (1990b, September 14). *Promoting diversity in an individualistic society.* Keynote address, Great Lakes College Association conference, Hope College, Holland, MI.

Jones, J. M., & Block, C. B. (1984). Black cultural perspectives. *Clinical Psychologist, 37,* 58–62.

Jordan, J. V. (1997). A relational perspective for understanding women's development. In J. V. Jordan (Ed.). *Women's growth in diversity: More writings from the Stone Center* (pp. 9–24). New York, NY: Guilford Press.

Jourard, S. M. (1964). *The Transparent Self.* Princeton, NJ: Van Nostrand.

Jourard, S. M. (1971) *Self Disclosure: Experimental Analysis of the Transparent Self.* New York, NY: Wiley.

Kaduvettoor, A., O'Shaughnessy, T., Mori, Y., Beverly, C., III, Weatherford, R. D., & Ladany, N. (2009). Helpful and hindering multicultural events in group supervision: Climate and multicultural competence. *Counseling Psychologist, 37,* 786–820. doi: 10.1177/0011000009333984

Kahneman, D., Slovic, P., & Tversky, A. (Eds.). (1982). *Judgment under uncertainty: Heuristics and biases.* Cambridge, United Kingdom: Cambridge University Press.

Kahneman, D., & Tversky, A. (Eds.). (2000). *Choices, values, and frames.* Cambridge, United Kingdom: Cambridge University Press.

Kalichman, S. C. (1993). *Mandated reporting of suspected child abuse: Ethics, law, and policy.* Washington, DC: American Psychological Association.

Kaslow, N. J. (2004). Competencies in professional psychology. *American Psychologist, 59,* 774–781.

Kaslow, N. J., Borden, K. A., Collins, F. L., Forrest, L., Illfelder-Kaye, J., Nelson, P. D., . . . Willmuth, M. W. (2004). Competencies conference: Future directions in education and credentialing in professional psychology. *Journal of Clinical Psychology, 60*(7), 699–712.

Kaslow, N. J., Grus, C. L., Campbell, L. F., Fouad, N. A., Hatcher, R. L., & Rodolfa, E. R. (2009). Competency assessment toolkit for professional psychology. *Training and Education in Professional Psychology, 3,* S27–S45. doi: 10.1037/a0015833

Kazdin, A. E. (2006). Assessment and evaluation in clinical practice. In C. D. Goodheart, A. E. Kazdin & R. J. Sternberg, *Evidence-based psychotherapy: Where practice and research meet* (pp. 153–178). Washington, DC: American Psychological Association.

Kazdin, A. E. (2008a). Evidence-based treatments and delivery of psychological services: Shifting our emphases to increase impact. *Psychological Services, 5*(3), 201–215.

Kazdin, A. E. (2008b). Evidence-based treatment and practice: New opportunities to bridge clinical research and practice, enhance the knowledge base, and improve patient patient care. *American Psychologist, 63*(3), 146–159.

Keith-Spiegel, P., & Koocher, G. P. (1985). *Ethics in psychology: Professional standards and cases.* New York, NY: Random House.

Keith-Spiegel, P., & Koocher, G. P. (1995). *Ethics in psychology: Professional standards and cases* (2nd ed.). Mahwah, NJ: Erlbaum.

Kendall, P. C., & Beidas, R. S. (2007). Smoothing the trail for dissemination of evidence-based practices for youth: Flexibility within fidelity. *Professional Psychology: Research and Practice, 38,* 13–20.

Kepner, J. (2001). Touch in Gestalt body process psychotherapy: Purpose, practice, and ethics. *Gestalt Review, 5,* 97–114.

Kesselheim, A. S., & Studdert D. M. (2007). Role of professional organizations in regulating physician expert witness testimony. *Journal of the American Medical Association, 298*(24), 2907–2909.

Kessler, L. E., & Wachler, C. A. (2005). Addressing multiple relationships between clients and therapists in lesbian, gay, bisexual, and transgender communities. *Professional Psychology: Research and Practice, 36*(1), 66–72.

Kim, U., Yang, K, & Hwang, K. K. (Eds). (2006). *Indigenous and cultural psychology: Understanding people in context.* New York, NY: Springer SBM Publications.

King, M. L., Jr. (1958). *Stride toward freedom.* San Francisco, CA: HarperSanFrancisco.

King, M. L., Jr. (1964). *Why we can't wait.* New York, NY: Signet.

King, V. L., Stoller, K. B., Kidorf, M., Kindbom, K., Hursh, S., Brady, T., & Brooner, R. K. (2009). Assessing the effectiveness of an Internet-based videoconferencing platform for delivering intensified substance abuse counseling. *Journal of Substance Abuse Treatment, 36,* 331–338. doi: 10.1016/j.jsat.2008.06.011

Kitchener, K. S. (1988). Dual role relationships: What makes them so problematic? *Journal of Counseling & Development, 67,* 217–221.

Kitchener, K. S. (2000). *Foundations of ethical practice, research, and teaching in psychology.* Mahwah, NJ: Erlbaum.

Kleespies, P. M. (Ed.). (2004). *Life and death decisions: Psychological and ethical considerations in end-of-life care.* Washington, DC: American Psychological Association.

Kleespies, P. M., Smith, M. R., & Becker, B. R. (1990). Psychology interns as patient suicide survivors: Incidence, impact, and recovery. *Professional Psychology: Research and Practice, 21,* 257–263.

Klerman, G. L., & Clayton, P. (1984). Epidemiologic perspectives on the health consequences of bereavement. In M. Osterweis, F. Solomon, & M. Green (Eds.). *Bereavement: Reactions, consequences and care* (pp. 15–44). Washington, DC: National Academy Press.

Koenig, R. (2000). Reopening the darkest chapter in German science. *Science, 288*(5471), 1576–1577.

Kõlves, K., Värnik, A., Tooding, L., & Wasserman, D. (2006). Role of alcohol in suicide: A case-control psychological autopsy study. *Psychological Medicine, 36*(7), 923–930.

Koocher, G. P. (1994). Foreword. In K. S. Pope (Ed.), *Sexual involvement with therapists: Patient assessment, subsequent therapy, forensics* (pp. vii–ix). Washington, DC: American Psychological Association.

Koocher, G. P. (2006). Foreword to the second edition: Things my teachers never mentioned. In K. S. Pope, J. L. Sonne, & B. Greene, *What therapists don't talk about and why: Understanding taboos that hurt us and our clients.* Washington, DC: American Psychological Association.

Kooyman, L., & Barret, B. (2009). The duty to protect: Mental health practitioners and communicable diseases. In J. L. Werth, Jr., E. R. Welfel & G. A. H. Benjamin (Eds.), *The duty to protect: Ethical, legal and professional considerations for mental health professionals.* Washington, DC: American Psychological Association.

Kosters, M., Burlingame, G. M., Nachtigall, C., & Strauss, B. (2006). A meta-analytic review of the effectiveness of inpatient group psychotherapy. *Group Dynamics: Theory, Research, and Practice. 10,* 146–163.

Kottler, J. A. (2003). *On being a therapist* (3rd ed.). San Francisco, CA: Jossey-Bass.

Kovacs, A. L. (1987, May). Insurance billing: The growing risk of lawsuits against psychologists. *Independent Practitioner, 7,* 21–24.

Kramer, M., Pollack, E. S., Redick, R. W., & Locke, B. Z. (1972). *Mental disorders/suicide.* Cambridge, MA: Harvard University Press.

Kramer, R. M. (2010). Dilemmas and doubts: How decision-makers cope with interdependence and uncertainty. In R. M. Kramer, A. E. Tenbrunsel, & M. H. Bazerman (Eds.), *Social decision making: Social dilemmas, social values, and ethical judgments* (pp. 117–143). New York, NY: Routledge/Taylor & Francis.

Krebs, B. (2007, February 22). Data breach hits close to home. *Washington Post.* Retrieved from http://bit.ly/84Omdb

Krupnick, J. L. (1984). Bereavement during childhood and adolescence. In M. Osterweis, F. Solomon, & M. Green (Eds.), *Bereavement: Reactions, consequences, and care* (pp. 99–141). Washington, DC: National Academy Press.

Kuchuck, S. (2009). Do ask, do tell? Narcissistic need as a determinant of analyst self-disclosure. *Psychoanalytic Review, 96,* 1007–1024. doi: 10.1521/prev.2009.96.6.1007

Kuo, F. (2009). Secrets or no secrets: Confidentiality in couple therapy. *American Journal of Family Therapy, 37,* 351–354. doi: 10.1080/01926180701862970

LaFromboise, T. D., & Foster, S. L. (1989). Ethics and multicultural counseling. In P. D. Pedersen, J. G. Draguns, W. J. Lonner, & E. J. Trimble (Eds.), *Counseling across cultures* (3rd ed., pp. 115–136). Honolulu: University of Hawaii Press.

Lamb, D. H., & Catanzaro, S. J. (1998). Sexual and nonsexual boundary violations involving psychologists, clients, supervisees, and students: Implications for professional practice. *Professional Psychology: Research and Practice, 29,* 498–503.

Lamb, D. H., Catanzaro, S. J., & Moorman, A. S. (2004). A preliminary look at how psychologists identify, evaluate, and proceed when faced with possible multiple relationship dilemmas. *Professional Psychology: Research and Practice, 35*(3), 248–254.

Lambert, J. J., & Ogles, B. M. (2004). The efficacy and effectiveness of psychotherapy. In M. J. Lambert (Ed.), *Bergin and Garfield's handbook of psychotherapy and behavior change* (5th ed., pp. 139–193). Hoboken, NJ: Wiley.

Landrine, H. (Ed.). (1995). *Cultural diversity in feminist psychology: Theory, research, and practice.* Washington, DC: American Psychological Association.

Langer, E. (1989). *Mindfulness.* Reading, MA: Addison-Wesley.

Langer, E. J., & Abelson, R. P. (1974). A patient by any other name . . . : Clinician group differences and labeling bias. *Journal of Consulting and Clinical Psychology, 42,* 4–9.

Langer, E. J., Bashner, R., & Chanowitz, B. (1985). Decreasing prejudice by increasing discrimination. *Journal of Personality and Social Psychology, 49,* 113–120.

Lau, A. S. (2006). Making the case for selective and directed cultural adaptations of evidence-based treatments: Examples from parent training. *Clinical Psychology: Science and Practice, 13,* 295–310.

Lazar, K. (2009, October 3). Blue Cross physicians warned of data breach; stolen laptop had doctors' tax IDs. *Boston Globe.* Retrieved from http://bit.ly/15BzNB

Lazarus, A. A. (1994a). How certain boundaries and ethics diminish therapeutic effectiveness. *Ethics and Behavior, 4*(3), 255–261.

Lazarus, A. A. (1994b). The illusion of the therapist's power and the patient's fragility: My rejoinder. *Ethics and Behavior, 4*(3), 299–306.

Lee, D., Reynolds, C. R., & Willson, V. L. (2003). Standardized test administration: Why bother? *Journal of Forensic Neuropsychology, 3*(3), 55–81.

Lehner, G. F. J. (1952). Defining psychotherapy. *American Psychologist, 7,* 547.

Lettieri, D. J. (1982). Suicidal death prediction scales. In P. A. Keller & L. G. Ritt (Eds.) *Innovations in clinical practice,* Vol. 1 (pp. 265–268). Sarasota, FL: Professional Resource Exchange._

Levant, R. F. (2006). Making psychology a household word. *American Psychologist, 61,* 383–395. doi: 10.1037/0003-066X.61.5.383

Levenson, H., & Pope, K. S. (1981). First encounters: Effects of intake procedures on patients, staff, and the organization. *Hospital and Community Psychiatry, 32,* 482–485.

Levy, D. A. (2010). *Tools of critical thinking: Metathoughts for psychology,* 2nd ed. Long Grove, IL: Waveland Press.

Lewin, K. (1976). *Field theory in social science: Selected theoretical papers.* Chicago, IL: University of Chicago Press.

Lewis, N. A. (2006, June 6). Psychologists preferred for detainees. *New York Times,* June 6, 2006. Retrieved from http://bit.ly/cTFLru

Lifton, R. J. (1986). *The Nazi doctors: Medical killing and the psychology of genocide.* New York, NY: Basic Books.

Lifton, R. J. (2008, August 11). Robert Jay Lifton on the American Psychological Association and torture. [Video]. Producer/Director: Hermine Muskat. Studio: Back Bay Films, LLC. Retrieved from http://bit.ly/LiftonAPA

Lilienfeld, S. O., & Landfield, K. (2008). Science and pseudoscience in law enforcement: A user-friendly primer. *Criminal Justice and Behavior, 35*(10), 1215–1230.

Lindblad, A., Löfmark, R., & Lynöe, N. (2008). Physician-assisted suicide: A survey of attitudes among Swedish physicians. *Scandinavian Journal of Public Health, 36,* 720–727. doi: 10.1177/1403494808090163

Litman, R. E. (1965). When patients commit suicide. *American Journal of Psychotherapy, 19,* 570–583.

Littell, J. H. (2010). Evidence-based practice: Evidence or orthodoxy? In B. L. Duncan, S. D. Miller, B. E. Wampold, & M. A. Hubble (Eds.), *The heart and soul of change: Delivering what works in therapy* (2nd ed.) (pp. 167–198). Washington, DC: American Psychological Association. doi: 10.1037/12075–006

A little recent history. (1952). *American Psychologist, 7,* 425.

Loas, G., Azi, A., Noisette, C., Legrand, A., & Yon, V. (2009). Fourteen-year prospective follow-up study of positive and negative symptoms in chronic schizophrenic patients dying from suicide compared to other causes of death. *Psychopathology, 42,* 185–189. doi: 10.1159/000209331

LoBello, S. G., & Zachar, P. (2007). Psychological test sales and internet auctions: Ethical considerations for dealing with obsolete or unwanted test materials. *Professional Psychology: Research and Practice, 38,* 68–70. doi: 10.1037/0735-7028 .38.1.68

Lonner, W. J., & E. J. Trimble (Eds.), *Counseling across cultures* (3rd ed., pp. 153–176). Honolulu: University of Hawaii Press.

Lopez-Munoz, F., Alamo, C., Dudley, M., Rubio, G., Garcia-Garcia, P., Molina, J. D., & Okasha, A. (2007). Psychiatry and political-institutional abuse from the historical perspective: The ethical lessons of the Nuremberg trial on their 60th anniversary. *Progress in Neuropsychopharmacology and Biological Psychiatry, 31*(4), 791–806. doi: S0278–5846(06)00442–8 [pii]10.1016/j.pnpbp.2006.12.007

Lorant, V., Deliege, D. Eaton, W. Robert, A. Phillppot, P., & Ansseau, M. (2003). Socioeconomic inequalities in depression: A meta-analysis. *American Journal of Epidemiology, 157,* 98–112.

Lott, B. (2007). APA and the participation of psychologists in situations in which human rights are violated: Comment on "Psychologists and the use of torture in interrogations." *Analyses of Social Issues and Public Policy (ASAP), 7*(1), 35–43.

Lott, B., & Bullock, H. E. (2001). Who are the poor? *Journal of Social Issues, 57,* 189–206.

Lott, B., & Bullock, H. E. (2007). *Psychology and economic injustice.* Washington, DC: American Psychological Association.

Love, M. S. (2007). Security in an insecure world: An examination of individualism-collectivism and psychological sense of community at work. *Career Development International, 12,* 304–320. doi: 10.1108/13620430710745917

Lyall, S. (2009). Guidelines in England for assisted suicide. *New York Times,* September 23. Retrieved from http://www.nytimes.com/2009/09/24/world/europe/24britain.html

Lynch, J. K. (2005). Effect of a third party observer on neuropsychological test performance following closed head injury. *Journal of Forensic Neuropsychology, 4*(2), 17–25.

Lynch, J. K., & McCaffrey, R. J. (2004). Neuropsychological assessments in the presence of third parties: Ethical issues and literature review. *New York State Psychologist, 16*(3), 25–29.

"Major Insurance Company Announces Security Breach." (2010, January 10). Channel WTVF (News Channel 5), Nashville, TN. Retrieved from http://www.newschannel5.com/Global/story.asp?S=11799310

Malloy, K. A., Dobbins, J. E., Ducheny, K., & Winfrey, L. L. (2010). The management and supervision competency: Current and future directions. In M. B. Kenkel & R. L. Peterson (Eds.), *Competency-based education for professional psychology* (pp. 161–178). Washington, DC: American Psychological Association.

Maloney, E., Degenhardt, L., Darke, S., & Nelson, E. C. (2009). Impulsivity and borderline personality as risk factors for suicide attempts among opioid-dependent individuals. *Psychiatry Research, 169,* 16–21. doi: 10.1016/j.psychres.2008.06.026

Mangurian, C., Harre, E., Reliford, A., Booty, A., & Cournos, F. (2009). Improving support of residents after a patient suicide: A residency case study. *Academic Psychiatry, 33,* 278–281. doi: 10.1176/appi.ap.33.4.278

Mann, C. K., & Winer, J. D. (1991). Psychotherapist's sexual contact with client. *American Jurisprudence Proof of Facts* (3rd ser., vol. 14, pp. 319–431). Rochester, NY: Lawyers Cooperative.

Mann, J. J. (2005, October 27). Drug therapy: The medical management of depression. *New England Journal of Medicine, 353,* 1819–1834.

Maris, R. W. (2002). Suicide. *Lancet, 360*(9329), 319–326.

Martindale, D. A. (2007). Reporter's foreword to the Association of Family and Conciliation Courts' Model Standards of Practice for Child Custody Evaluation. *Family Court Review, 45,* 61–69. doi: 10.1111/j.1744-1617.2007.129_2.x

Martindale, D. A., Martin, L., Austin, W. G., Gould-Saltman, D., Kuehnle, K., McColley, D., . . . Drozd, L. (2007). Model Standards of Practice for Child Custody Evaluation. *Family Court Review, 45,* 70–91. doi: 10.1111/j.1744-1617.2007.129_3.x

Masters, W. H., & Johnson, V. E. (1966). *Human sexual response.* New York, NY: Bantam.

Masters, W. H., & Johnson, V. E. (1970). *Human sexual inadequacy.* New York, NY: Bantam.

Masters, W. H., & Johnson, V. E. (1975, May). *Principles of the new sex therapy.* Paper presented at the annual meeting of the American Psychiatric Association, Anaheim, CA.

Masterson, J. F. (1989, May). Maintaining objectivity crucial in treating borderline patients. *Psychiatric Times,* pp. 1, 26–27.

Matos, M., Torres, R., Santiago, R., Jurado, M., & Rodríguez, I. (2006). Adaptation of parent-child interaction therapy for Puerto Rican families: A preliminary study. *Family Process, 45,* 205–222.

Mayer, J. (2008a). *The dark side*. New York, NY: Doubleday.

Mayer, J. (2008b, July 11). The experiment. *New Yorker*. Retrieved from http://www .newyorker.com/archive/2005/07/11/050711fa_fact4

McCauley, J., Kern, D. E., Kolodner, K., Dill, L., & Schroeder, A. F. (1997). Clinical characteristics of women with a history of childhood abuse: Unhealed wounds. *Journal of the American Medical Association, 277*(17), 1362–1368.

McCord, C., & Freeman, H. P. (1990). Excess mortality in Harlem. *New England Journal of Medicine, 322*, 173–177.

McCoy, J. (2009, October 5). Outdated web policies expose hospitals to professional and legal trouble. *HealthLeaders Media*. Retrieved from http://bit.ly/Jypie

McHugh, R. K., Murray, H. W., & Barlow, D. H. (2009). Balancing fidelity and adaptation in the dissemination of empirically-supported treatments: The promise of transdiagnostic interventions. *Behaviour Research and Therapy*, n.p. doi: 10.1016/j .brat.2009.07.005

McNeil, B., Pauker, S. G., Sox, H. C., & Tversky, A. (1982). On the elucidation of preferences for alternative therapies. *New England Journal of Medicine, 306*, 1259– 1262.

McNeil-Haber, F. M. (2004). Ethical considerations in the use of nonerotic touch in psychotherapy with children. *Ethics & Behavior, 14*, 123–140. doi: 10.1207/ s15327019eb1402_3

McSweeny, A. J., Becker, B. C., Naugle, R. I., Snow, W. G., Binder, L. M., & Thompson, L. L. (1998). Ethical issues related to the presence of third party observers in clinical neuropsychological evaluations. *Clinical Neuropsychologist, 12*(4), 552– 559.

Mednick, M. T. (1989). On the politics of psychological constructs: Stop the bandwagon, I want to get off. *American Psychologist, 44*, 1118–1123.

Meehl, P. (1977). Why I do not attend case conferences. In P. Meehl (Ed.), *Psychodiagnosis: Selected papers* (pp. 225–302). New York, NY: Norton. (Originally published 1973.)

Meehl,, P. E.(1956). Wanted—A good cookbook. *American Psychologist, 11*, 262–272.

Melton, J. G. (2009). *Encyclopedia of American religions*, 8th ed. Detroit, MI: Gale Cengage Learning.

Mercer, J. R. (1979). *Technical manual: System of multicultural pluralistic assessment*. New York, NY: Psychological Corporation.

Miles, S. H. *Oath betrayed: America's torture doctors*, 2nd ed. Berkeley: University of California Press, 2009.

Miles, S. H. (2009, May 1). Psychologists and torture. [Letter]. *British Medical Journal*. Retrieved from http://bmj.com/cgi/eletters/338/apr30_2/b1653#213065

"Military Psychologist Says Harsh Tactics Justified." (2009, May 4). All Things Considered, National Public Radio. Retrieved from http://n.pr/harshtactics

Miller, J. B. (1988). *Connections, disconnections and violations*. Retrieved from http:// www.wcwonline.org/component/page,shop.product_details/flypage,shop.flypage/ product_id,947/category_id,440

Miller, J. B. (1991). The development of women's sense of self. In J. V. Jordan, A. G. Kaplan, J. B. Miller, I. P. Stiver, & J. L. Surrey (Eds.), *Women's growth in connection: Writings from the Stone Center*. New York, NY: Guilford Press.

Miranda, J. (2006). Improving services and outreach for women with depression. In C. M. Mazure & G. P. Keita (Eds.), *Understanding depression in women: Applying empirical research to practice and policy* (pp. 113–135). Washington, DC: American Psychological Association.

Mitchell, J. E., Crosby, R. D., Wonderlich, S. A., Crow, S., Lancaster, K., Simonich, H., . . . Myers, T. C. (2008). A randomized trial comparing the efficacy of cognitive-behavioral therapy for bulimia nervosa delivered via telemedicine versus face-to-face. *Behaviour Research and Therapy, 46,* 581–592. doi: 10.1016/j.brat.2008.02.004

Moffic, H. S. (1997). *The ethical way.* San Francisco, CA: Jossey-Bass.

Mohr, D. C. (2009). Telemental health: Reflections on how to move the field forward. *Clinical Psychology: Science and Practice, 16,* 343–347. doi: 10.1111/j.1468–2850. 2009.01172.x

Monahan, J. (1993). Limiting therapist exposure to Tarasoff liability: Guidelines for risk containment. *American Psychologist, 48,* 242–250.

Monahan, J. (Ed.). (1980). *Who is the client?* Washington, DC: American Psychological Association.

Montgomery, L. M., Cupit, B. E., & Wimberley, T. K. (1999). Complaints, malpractice, and risk management: Professional issues and personal experiences. *Professional Psychology: Research and Practice, 30,* 402–410.

Moodley, R., & Palmer, S. (2006). *Race, culture and psychotherapy: Critical perspectives in multicultural practice.* Philadelphia, PA: Routledge/Taylor & Francis.

Moscicki, E. (2001). Epidemiology of suicide. In S. Goldsmith (Ed.), *Risk factors for suicide* (pp. 1–4). Washington, DC: National Academy Press.

Muller-Hill, B. (1988). *Murderous science: Elimination by scientific selection of Jews, Gypsies, and others, Germany 1933–1945.* (G. Fraser, Trans). New York, NY: Oxford University Press.

Mumford, G. (2006). When legislative objectives are in conflict. *Monitor on Psychology, 37*(3), 68–69.

Munro, G. D., & Stansbury, J. A. (2009). The dark side of self-affirmation: Confirmation bias and illusory correlation in response to threatening information. *Personality and Social Psychology Bulletin, 35,* 1143–1153. doi: 10.1177/0146167209337163

Murphy, J. M. (1976). Psychiatric labeling in cross-cultural perspective. *Science, 191,* 1019–1028.

Murray, J., & Abramson, P. R. (Eds.). *Bias in psychotherapy* (pp. 285– 308). New York, NY: Praeger.

Nachmani, I., & Somer, E. (2007). Women sexually victimized in psychotherapy speak out: The dynamics and outcome of therapist-client sex. *Women & Therapy, 30,* 1–17. doi: 10.1300/J015v30n01_01

Natanson v. Kline, 186 Kans. 393, 406, 350 P.2d 1093 (1960).

National Academies of Practice. (1997). *Ethical guidelines for professional care in a managed care environment.* Washington, DC: Author.

National Association of Social Workers (2008). Code of Ethics of the National Association of Social Workers. Retrieved from http://www.socialworkers.org/pubs/Code/code.asp

Naughton, P. (2008, December 2). Lawanda Jackson pleads guilty to selling celebrity medical records. London Times. Retrieved from http://bit.ly/6bMFLK

Neufeldt, S. A. (2003). Becoming a clinical supervisor. In M. J. Prinstein & M. D. Patterson (Eds.), *The portable mentor: Expert guide to a successful career in psychology* (pp. 209–218). New York, NY: Kluwer Academic/Plenum.

Neuringer, C. (1964). Rigid thinking in suicidal individuals. *Journal of Consulting Psychology, 28,* 54–58.

Neuringer, C. (1974). *Psychological assessment of suicidal risk.* New York, NY: Charles C. Thomas.

Newman, C. F. (2010). Competency in conducting cognitive-behavioral therapy: Foundational, functional, and supervisory aspects. *Psychotherapy: Theory, Research, Practice, Training, 47,* 12–19. doi: 10.1037/a0018849

Nicolas, G., Arntz, D. L., Hirsch, B., & Schmiedigen, A. (2009). Cultural adaptation of a group treatment for Haitian American adolescents. *Professional Psychology: Research and Practice, 40,* 378–384.

Nieves, J. E., Godleski, L. S., Stack, K. M., & Zinanni, T. (2009). Videophones for intensive case management of psychiatric outpatients. *Journal of Telemedicine and Telecare, 15,* 51–54. doi: 10.1258/jtt.2008.080706

Nimeus, A., Traskman-Bendz, L., & Alsen, M. (1997). Hopelessness and suicidal behavior. *Journal of Affective Disorders, 42,* 137–144.

Noel, B., & Watterson, K. (1992). *You must be dreaming.* New York, NY: Poseidon.

Novick, D. M., Swartz, H. A., & Frank, E. (2010). Suicide attempts in bipolar I and bipolar II disorder: A review and meta-analysis of the evidence. *Bipolar Disorders, 12,* 1–9. doi: 10.1111/j.1399–5618.2009.00786.x

Nugent, W. R. (2006). A psychometric study of the MPSI Suicidal Thoughts subscale. *Stress, Trauma and Crisis: An International Journal, 9*(1), 1–15.

Obst, P. L., & White, K. M. (2007). Choosing to belong: The influence of choice on social identification and psychological sense of community. *Journal of Community Psychology, 35,* 77–90. doi: 10.1002/jcop.20135

O'Donohue, W. T., Beitz, K., & Tolle, L. (2009). Controversies in child custody evaluations. In J. L. Skeem, K. S. Douglas, & S. O. Lilienfeld (Eds.), *Psychological science in the courtroom: Consensus and controversy.* (pp. 284–308). New York, NY: Guilford Press.

Ohio Psychological Association. (2010.) Telepsychology guidelines, revised. Retrieved from http://bit.ly/9jtzlK

Okie, S. (2005). Physician-assisted suicide—Oregon and beyond. *New England Journal of Medicine, 352*(16), 1627–1630.

O'Neill, P. (1998). *Negotiating consent in psychotherapy.* New York: New York University Press.

O'Neill, P. (2005). The ethics of problem definition. *Canadian Psychology, 46*(1), 13–20.

"Open letter in response to the American Psychological Association Board." (2009). Retrieved from http://bit.ly/Y2bFj

Orlinsky, D. E., & Geller, J. D. (1993). Psychotherapy's internal theater of operation: Patients' representations of their therapists and therapy as a new focus of research. In N. E. Miller, J. Docherty, L. Luborsky, & J. Barber (Eds.), *Psychodynamic treatment research* (pp. 423–466). New York, NY: Basic Books.

Orwell, G. (1946). Politics and the English language. In G. Orwell (Ed.), *A collection of essays* (pp. 156–171). Orlando, FL: Harcourt.

Otto, R. K., & Martindale, D. A. (2007). The law, process, and science of child custody evaluation. In M. Costanzo, D. Krauss, & K. Pezdek (Eds.), *Expert psychological testimony for the courts.* (pp. 251–275). Mahwah, NJ: Erlbaum.

Pack-Brown, S. P., & Williams, C. B. (2003). *Ethics in a multicultural context.* Thousand Oaks, CA: Sage.

Palmer, B. A., Pankratz, V. S., & Bostwick, J. M. (2005). The lifetime risk of suicide in schizophrenia: A reexamination. *Archives of General Psychiatry, 62,* 247–253.

Patsiokas, A. T., Clum, G. A., & Luscumb, R. L. (1979). Cognitive characteristics of suicidal attempters. *Journal of Consulting and Clinical Psychology, 47,* 478–484.

Peck, M., & Seiden, R. (1975, May). *Youth suicide. exChange.* Sacramento: California State Department of Health.

Pedersen, P. D., Draguns, J. G., Lonner, W. J., & Trimble, E. J. (1989). Introduction and overview. In P. D. Pedersen, J. G. Draguns, W. J. Lonner, & E. J. Trimble (Eds.), *Counseling across cultures* (3rd ed., pp. 1–2). Honolulu: University of Hawaii Press.

Pedersen, P. B., Draguns, J. G., Lonner, W. J., & Trimble, J. E. (Eds.). (2008). *Counseling across cultures* (6th ed.). Thousand Oaks, CA: Sage.

People v. Stritzinger, 194 Cal. Rptr. 431 (Cal. September 1, 1983).

Perlin, M. L., & McClain, V. (2009). "Where souls are forgotten": Cultural competencies, forensic evaluations, and international human rights. *Psychology, Public Policy, and Law, 15,* 257–277. doi: 10.1037/a0017233

Perspectives. (1990, April 23). *Newsweek,* p. 17.

Petrie, K., & Chamberlain, K. (1983). Hopelessness and social desirability as moderator variables in predicting suicidal behavior. *Journal of Consulting and Clinical Psychology, 51,* 485–487.

Pew Hispanic Center. (2009, December 11). *Between two worlds: How young Latinos come of age in America.* Washington, DC: Pew Research Center.

Phelan, J. E. (2009). Exploring the use of touch in the psychotherapeutic setting: A phenomenological review. *Psychotherapy: Theory, Research, Practice, Training, 46,* 97–111. doi: 10.1037/a0014751

Pinals, D. (2009). Informed consent: Is your patient competent to refuse treatment? *Current Psychiatry, 8,* 4, 33–43.

Plaisil, E. (1985). *Therapist.* New York, NY: St. Martin's Press.

Plant, E. A., & Sachs-Ericsson, N. (2004). Racial and ethnic differences in depression: The roles of social support and meeting basic needs. *Journal of Consulting and Clinical Psychology, 72,* 41–52.

Plato. (1956a). The apology. In E. H. Warmington & P. G. Rouse (Eds.), *Great dialogues of Plato* (W. H. D. Rouse, Trans., pp. 423–446). New York, NY: New American Library.

Plato. (1956b). Crito. In E. H. Warmington & P. G. Rouse (Eds.), *Great dialogues of Plato* (W. H. D. Rouse, Trans., pp. 447–459). New York, NY: New American Library.

Plous, S. (1993). *Psychology of judgment and decision making.* New York, NY: McGraw-Hill.

Pope, K. S. (1988b). How clients are harmed by sexual contact with mental health professionals: The syndrome and its prevalence. *Journal of Counseling and Development, 67,* 222–226.

Pope, K. S. (1989a). Malpractice suits, licensing disciplinary actions, and ethics cases: Frequencies, causes, and costs. *Independent Practitioner, 9*(1), 22–26.

Pope, K. S. (1989b). Student-teacher sexual intimacy. In G. O. Gabbard (Ed.), *Sexual exploitation within professional relationships* (pp. 163–176). Washington, DC: American Psychiatric Press.

Pope, K. S. (1990a). Ethical and malpractice issues in hospital practice. *American Psychologist, 45,* 1066–1070. Available at http://kspope.com

Pope, K. S. (1990b). Identifying and implementing ethical standards for primary prevention. In G. B. Levin, E. J. Trickett, & R. E. Hess (Eds.), *Ethical implications of primary prevention* (pp. 43–64). Binghamton, NY: Haworth Press.

Pope, K. S. (1990c). Therapist-patient sex as sex abuse: Six scientific, professional, and practical dilemmas in addressing victimization and rehabilitation. *Professional Psychology: Research and Practice, 21,* 227–239. Available at http://kspope.com

Pope, K. S. (1990d). Therapist-patient sexual involvement: A review of the research. *Clinical Psychology Review, 10,* 477–490. Available at http://kspope.com

Pope, K. S. (1991). Promoting ethical behaviour: The Canadian Psychological Association model. *Canadian Psychology, 32*(1), 74–76.

Pope, K. S. (1992). Responsibilities in providing psychological test feedback to clients. *Psychological Assessment, 4,* 268–271. Available at http://kspope.com

Pope, K. S. (1993). Licensing disciplinary actions for psychologists who have been sexually involved with a client: Some information about offenders. *Professional Psychology: Research and Practice, 24,* 374–377. Available at http://kspope.com

Pope, K. S. (1994). *Sexual involvement with therapists: Patient assessment, subsequent therapy, forensics.* Washington, DC: American Psychological Association.

Pope, K. S. (1996). Memory, abuse, and science: Questioning claims about the false memory syndrome epidemic. *American Psychologist, 51,* 957–974. Available at http://kspope.com

Pope, K. S. (2001). Sex between therapists and clients. In J. Worell (Ed.), *Encyclopedia of women and gender* (Vol. 2, pp. 955–962). Orlando, FL: Academic Press.

Pope, K. S. (2005). Disability and accessibility in psychology: Three major barriers. *Ethics and Behavior, 15*(2), 103–106. Available at http://kspope.com

K. S. Pope biography. (1995). *American Psychologist, 50*(4), 242.

Pope, K. S., & Bajt, T. R. (1988). When laws and values conflict: A dilemma for psychologists. *American Psychologist, 43,* 828. Retrieved from http://kspope.com

Pope, K. S., & Bouhoutsos, J. C. (1986). *Sexual intimacies between therapists and patients.* Westport, CT: Praeger.

Pope, K. S., & Brown, L. (1996). *Recovered memories of abuse: Assessment, therapy, forensics.* Washington, DC: American Psychological Association.

Pope, K. S., Butcher, J. N., & Seelen, J. (2001). *The MMPI, MMPI-2, and MMPPA in court: A practical guide for expert witnesses and attorneys* (2nd ed.). Washington, DC: American Psychological Association.

Pope, K. S., Butcher, J. N., & Seelen, J. (2006). *The MMPI, MMPI-2 and MMPI-A in court: A practical guide for expert witnesses and attorneys* (3rd ed.). Washington, DC: American Psychological Association.

Pope, K. S., & Feldman-Summers, S. (1992). National survey of psychologists' sexual and physical abuse history and their evaluation of training and competence in these areas. *Professional Psychology: Research and Practice, 23,* 353–361. Available at http://kspope.com

Pope, K. S., & Garcia-Peltoniemi, R. E. (1991). Responding to victims of torture: Clinical issues, professional responsibilities, and useful resources. *Professional Psychology: Research and Practice, 22,* 269–276. Available at http://kspope.com

Pope, K. S., & Gutheil, T. G. (2009). Psychologists abandon the Nuremberg ethic: Concerns for detainee interrogations. *International Journal of Law and Psychiatry, 32,* 161–166. doi: 10.1016/j.ijlp.2009.02.005

Pope, K. S., & Keith-Spiegel, P. (2008). A practical approach to boundaries in psychotherapy: Making decisions, bypassing blunders, and mending fences. *Journal of Clinical Psychology, 64,* 638–652. Available at http://bit.ly/ksp777

Pope, K. S., Keith-Spiegel, P., & Tabachnick, B. G. (1986). Sexual attraction to patients: The human therapist and the (sometimes) inhuman training system. *American Psychologist, 41,* 147–158. Available at http://kspope.com

Pope, K. S., Levenson, H., & Schover, L. R. (1979). Sexual intimacy in psychology training: Results and implications of a national survey. *American Psychologist, 34,* 682–689. Available at http://kspope.com

Pope, K. S., & Morin, S. F. (1990). AIDS and HIV infection update: New research, ethical responsibilities, evolving legal frameworks, and published resources. *Independent Practitioner, 10,* 43–53.

Pope, K. S., Simpson, N. H., & Weiner, M. F. (1978). Malpractice in psychotherapy. *American Journal of Psychotherapy, 32,* 593–602.

Pope, K. S., & Singer, J. L. (1978a). Regulation of the stream of consciousness: Toward a theory of ongoing thought. In G. E. Schwartz & D. Shapiro (Eds.), *Consciousness and self-regulation: Advances in research* (pp.101–135). New York, NY: Plenum Press.

Pope, K. S., & Singer, J. L. (Eds.). (1978b). *The stream of consciousness: Scientific investigations into the flow of human experience.* New York, NY: Plenum Press.

Pope, K. S., & Singer, J. L. (1980). The waking stream of consciousness. In J. M. Davidson & R. J. Davidson (Eds.), *The psychobiology of consciousness* (pp. 169–191). New York, NY: Plenum Press.

Pope, K. S., Sonne, J. L., & Greene, B. (2006). *What therapists don't talk about and why: Understanding taboos that hurt us and our clients.* Washington, DC: American Psychological Association.

Pope, K. S., Sonne, J. L., & Holroyd, J. (1993). *Sexual feelings in psychotherapy: Explorations for therapists and therapists-in-training.* Washington, DC: American Psychological Association.

Pope, K. S., & Tabachnick, B. G. (1993). Therapists' anger, hate, fear and sexual feelings: National survey of therapists' responses, client characteristics, critical events, formal complaints and training. *Professional Psychology: Research and Practice, 24,* 142–152. Available at http://kspope.com

Pope, K. S., & Tabachnick, B. G. (1994). Therapists as patients: A national survey of psychologists' experiences, problems, and beliefs. *Professional Psychology: Research and Practice, 25,* 247–258. Available at http://kspope.com

Pope, K. S., Tabachnick, B. G., & Keith-Spiegel, P. (1987). Ethics of practice: The beliefs and behaviors of psychologists as therapists. *American Psychologist, 42*, 993–1006. Available at http://kspope.com

Pope, K. S., Tabachnick, B. G., & Keith-Spiegel, P. (1988). Good and poor practices in psychotherapy: National survey of beliefs of psychologists. *Professional Psychology: Research and Practice, 19*, 547–552. Available at http://kspope.com

Pope, K. S., & Vasquez, M. J. T. (2005). *How to survive and thrive as a therapist: Information, ideas, and resources for psychologist in practice.* Washington, DC: American Psychological Association.

Pope, K. S., & Vetter, V. A. (1991). Prior therapist-patient sexual involvement among patients seen by psychologists. *Psychotherapy, 28*, 429–438. Available at http://kspope.com

Pope, K. S., & Vetter, V. A. (1992). Ethical dilemmas encountered by members of the American Psychological Association: A national survey. *American Psychologist, 47*, 397–411. Available at http://kspope.com

Preti, A., Meneghelli, A., Pisano, A., Cocchi, A., & the Programma 2000 Team. (2009). Risk of suicide and suicidal ideation in psychosis. *Schizophrenia Research, 113*, 145–150. doi: 10.1016/j.schres.2009.06.007

Proctor, R. N. (1988). *Racial hygiene: Medicine under the Nazis.* Cambridge, MA: Harvard University Press.

Pugh, R. (2007). Dual relationships: Personal and professional boundaries in rural social work. *British Journal of Social Work, 37*, 1406–1423. doi: 10.1093/bjsw/bcl088

Rachlin, H. (1989). *Judgment, decision, and choice: A cognitive/behavioral synthesis.* New York, NY: Freeman.

Radtke, R. (2005). A case against physician-assisted suicide. *Journal of Disability Policy Studies, 16*(1), 58–60.

Range, L. M., & Knott, E. C. (1997). Twenty suicide assessment instruments: Evaluation and recommendations. *Death Studies, 21*, 25–58.

Reed, G. M., & Eisman, E. J. (2006). Uses and misuses of evidence: Managed care, treatment guidelines, and outcomes measurement in professional practice. In C. D. Goodheart, A. E. Kazdin, & R. J. Sternberg (Eds.), *Evidence-based psychotherapy: Where practice and research meet* (pp. 13–35). Washington, DC: American Psychological Association.

Reiser, D. E., & Levenson, H. (1984). Abuses of the borderline diagnosis: A clinical problem with teaching opportunities. *American Journal of Psychiatry, 141*, 1528–1532.

Resnick, R, J. (2008). Con statement. Retrieved from http://www.apa.org/news/press/statements/work-settings-con.aspx

Responsible interrogation: Psychologists have a moral duty to help prevent torture. (2009, May 21). *Nature, 459*, 300.

Richards, M. M. (2009). Electronic medical records: Confidentiality issues in the time of HIPAA. *Professional psychology: Research and practice, 40*, 550–556. doi: 10.1037/a0016853

Richardson, L. K., Frueh, B. C., Grubaugh, A. L., Egede, L., & Elhai, J. D. (2009). Current directions in videoconferencing tele-mental health research. *Clinical Psychology: Science and Practice, 16*, 323–338. doi: 10.1111/j.1468-2850.2009.01170.x

Ridley, C. R. (1989). Racism in counseling as adversive behavioral process. In P. B. Pedersen, J. G. Draguns, W. J. Lonner, & J. E. Trimble (Eds.), *Counseling across cultures* (3rd ed., pp. 55–78). Honolulu: University of Hawaii Press.

Ridley, C. R., Liddle, M. C., Hill, C. L., & Li, L. C. (2001). Ethical decision making in multicultural counseling. In J. G. Ponterotto, J. M. Casas, L. A. Suzuki, & C. M. Alexander (Eds.), *Handbook of multicultural counseling* (2nd ed.) (pp. 165–188). Thousand Oaks, CA: Sage Publications.

Rinella, V. J., & Gerstein, A. I. (1994). The development of dual relationships: Power and professional responsibility. *International Journal of Law and Psychiatry, 17*(3), 225–237.

Rings, J. A., Genuchi, M. C., Hall, M. D., Angelo, M.-A., Cornish, J. A. & Erickson, J. A. (2009). Is there consensus among predoctoral internship training directors regarding clinical supervision competencies? A descriptive analysis. *Training and Education in Professional Psychology, 3*(3), 140–147.

Ritt, L. G. (Eds.), *Innovations in clinical practice* (Vol. 1, pp. 265–268). Sarasota, FL: Professional Resource Exchange.

Rivers, E., Schuman, S. H., Simpson, L., & Olansky, S. (1953). Twenty years of follow-up experience in a long-range medical study. *Public Health Reports, 68*(4), 391–395. Retrieved from http://www.nlm.nih.gov/hmd/manuscripts/ead/tuskegee 264.html

Robinson, G., & Merav, A. (1976). Informed consent: Recall by patients tested postoperatively. *Annals of Thoracic Surgery, 22*, 209–212.

Robinson, W. L., & Reid, P. T. (1985). Sexual intimacies in psychology revisited. *Professional Psychology, 16*, 512–520.

Roll, S., & Millen, L. (1981). A guide to violating an injunction in psychotherapy: On seeing acquaintances as patients. *Psychotherapy: Theory, Research and Practice, 18*(2), 179–187.

Rosenfeld, B. (2004). *Assisted suicide and the right to die: The interface of social science, public policy, and medical ethics.* Washington, DC: American Psychological Association.

Rosenhan, D. L. (1973). On being sane in insane places. *Science, 179*, 250–258.

Roy v. Hartogs, 381 N.Y.S.2d 587, 85 Misc. 2d 891 (1976).

Royal Australian and New Zealand College of Psychiatrists. (2004). Code of ethics. Melbourne, Australia: Author.

Roysircar, G., Sandhu, D. S., & Bibbins, V. E. (2003). *Multicultural competencies: A guidebook of practices.* Alexandria, VA: Association for Multicultural Counseling and Development.

Rubenstein, S. (2008, September 22). Hospital employees fired for posting patient pics on MySpace. *Wall Street Journal.* Retrieved from http://bit.ly/4NfSUX

Russo, N. F. (2008). Personality tests. In L. T. Benjamin Jr. (Ed.), Favorite activities for the teaching of psychology (pp. 203–207). Washington, DC: American Psychological Association.

Ryder, R., & Hepworth, J. (1990). AAMFT ethical code: "Dual relationships." *Journal of Marital and Family Therapy, 16*(2), 127–132.

Safer, D. J. (1997). Adolescent/adult differences in suicidal behavior and outcome. *Annals of Clinical Psychiatry, 9*, 61–66.

Saltzman, J. (2007, May 31). Blogger unmasked, court case upended. *Boston Globe*. Retrieved from http://bit.ly/8HiUUX

Sanders, J. R., & Keith-Spiegel, P. (1980). Formal and informal adjudication of ethics complaints against psychologists. *American Psychologist, 35*, 1096–1105.

Sarason, S. B. (1974). *The psychological sense of community*. San Francisco, CA: Jossey-Bass.

Sarason, S. B. (1985). *Caring and compassion in clinical practice*. San Francisco, CA: Jossey-Bass.

Sarkar, S. P. (2009) Life after therapy: Post-termination boundary violations in psychiatry and psychotherapy. *Advances in Psychiatric Treatment, 15*, 82–87. doi: 10.1192/apt.bp.107.005108

Sarnat, J. (2010). Key competencies of the psychodynamic psychotherapist and how to teach them in supervision. *Psychotherapy: Theory, Research, Practice, Training, 47*, 20–27. doi: 10.1037/a0018846

Schank, J. A., & Skovholt, T. M. (1997). Dual-relationship dilemmas of rural and small-community psychologists. *Professional Psychology: Research and Practice, 28*(1), 44–49.

Schank, J. A., & Skovholt, T. M. (2006). *Ethical practice in small communities: Challenges and rewards for psychologists*. Washington, DC: American Psychological Association.

Schloendorf v. Society of New York Hospital, 211 N.Y. 125, 105 N.E. 92 (1914).

Schneidman, E. (1975). *Suicidology: Contemporary developments*. New York, NY: Grune & Stratton.

Schulyer, D. (1974). *The depressive spectrum*. New York, NY: Jason Aronson.

Scribner, C. M. (2001). Rosenhan revisited. *Professional Psychology: Research and Practice, 32*, 215–216. doi: 10.1037/0735-7028.32.2.215

Searight, H. R., & Searight, B. K. (2009). Working with foreign language interpreters: Recommendations for psychological practice. *Professional Psychology: Research and Practice, 40*, 444–451. doi: 10.1037/a0016788

Shapiro, D. L. (1990). *Forensic psychological assessment: An integrative approach*. Needham Heights, MA: Allyn & Bacon.

Sharfstein, S. (2006). Presidential address: Advocacy as leadership. *American Journal of Psychiatry, 163*(10), 1711–1715.

Sharkin, B. S., & Birky, I. (1992). Incidental encounters between therapists and their clients. *Professional Psychology: Research and Practice, 23*(4), 326–328.

Shedler, J. (2010). The efficacy of psychodynamic psychotherapy. *American Psychologist, 65*, 98–109.

Sher, L. (2006). Alcoholism and suicidal behavior: A clinical overview. *Acta Psychiatrica Scandinavica, 113*(1), 13–22.

Sher, L., Oquendo, M. A., Richardson-Vejlgaard, R., Makhija, N. M., Posner, K., Mann, J. J., & Stanley, B. H. (2009). Effect of acute alcohol use on the lethality of suicide attempts in patients with mood disorders. *Journal of Psychiatric Research, 43*, 901–905. doi: 10.1016/j.jpsychires.2009.01.005

Shuster, E. (1998). The Nuremberg Code: Hippocratic ethics and human rights. *Lancet, 351*, 974–977.

Simon, R. I., & Williams, I. C. (1999). Maintaining treatment boundaries in small communities and rural areas. *Psychiatric Services, 50*(11), 1440–1446.

Simpson, S. (2009). Psychotherapy via videoconferencing: A review. *British Journal of Guidance & Counselling, 37*, 271–286. doi: 10.1080/03069880902957007

Sinclair, C. M. (1998). Nine unique features of the Canadian Code of Ethics for Psychologists. *Canadian Psychology, 39*(3), 167–176.

Sinclair, C. M., & Pettifor, J. (2001). Introduction and acknowledgments. In C. Sinclair & J. Pettifor (Eds.), *Companion manual to the Canadian Code of Ethics for Psychologists* (3rd ed., pp. i–iv). Ottawa, Canada: Canadian Psychological Association.

Sinclair, C. M., Poizner, S., Gilmour-Barrett, K., & Randall, D. (1987). The development of a code of ethics for Canadian psychologists. *Canadian Psychology, 28*(1), 1–8.

Sinclair, C. M., Simon, N. P., & Pettifor, J. L. (1996). History of ethical codes and licensure. In L. J. Bass, S. T. DeMers, J. R. P. Ogloff, C. Peterson, J. L. Pettifor, J. R. P. Reeves, T. Retfalvi, N. P. Simon, C. Sinclair, & R. M. Tipton (Eds.), *Professional conduct and discipline in psychology* (pp. 1–15). Washington, DC: American Psychological Association.

Singer, J. L. (1980). The scientific basis of psychotherapeutic practice: A question of values and ethics. *Psychotherapy: Theory, Research, and Practice, 17*, 373–383.

Slater, L. (2004). Opening Skinner's box: Great psychological experiments of the twentieth century. New York, NY: Norton.

Slimp, A. O. C., & Burian, B. K. (1994). Multiple role relationships during internship: Consequences and recommendations. *Professional Psychology: Research and Practice, 25*(1), 39–45.

Slowther, A., & Kleinman, I. (2008). Confidentiality. In P. A. Singer & A. M. Viens (Eds.), *The Cambridge textbook of bioethics* (pp. 43–48). New York, NY: Cambridge University Press.

Smith, A. J. (1990). Working within the lesbian community: The dilemma of overlapping relationships. In H. Lerman & N. Porter (Eds.), *Feminist ethics in psychotherapy* (pp. 92–96). New York, NY: Springer.

Snook, B., Cullen, R. M., Bennell, C., Taylor, P. J., & Gendreau, P. (2008). The criminal profiling illusion: What's behind the smoke and mirrors? *Criminal Justice and Behavior, 35*(10), 1257–1276. doi: 10.1177/0093854808321528

Snowden, L. R., Masland, M., & Guerrero, R. (2007). Federal civil rights policy and mental health treatment access for persons with limited English proficiency. *American Psychologist, 62*, 109–117.

Sokol, D. K. (2009). Informed consent is more than a patient's signature. *British Medical Journal, 339*. doi: 10.1136/bmj.b3224.

Sonne, J. L. (1994). Multiple relationships: Does the new ethics code answer the right questions? *Professional Psychology: Research and Practice, 25*, 336–343.

Sonne, J. L. (2005). *Nonsexual multiple relationships: A practical decision-making model for clinicians.* Available at http://kspope.com

Sonne, J. L., Meyer, C. B., Borys, D., & Marshall, V. (1985). Clients' reaction to sexual intimacy in therapy. *American Journal of Orthopsychiatry, 55*, 183–189.

Spitz, V. (2005). *Doctors from hell: The horrific account of Nazi experiments on humans.* Boulder, CO: Sentient Publications.

Stanton, W. (1960). *The leopard's spots: Scientific attitudes toward race in America.* Chicago, IL: University of Chicago Press.

Statistics Canada. (2006). *The multicultural face of cities.* Retrieved from http://www41 .statcan.ca/3867/ceb3867_003_e.htm

Stenzel, C. L., & Rupert, P. A. (2004). Psychologists' use of touch in individual psychotherapy. *Psychotherapy: Theory, Research, Practice, Training, 41,* 332–345. doi: 10.1037/0033–3204.41.3.332

Sternberg, R. J. (2006). Evidence-based practice: Gold standard, gold plated, or fool's gold? In C. D. Goodheart, A. E. Kazdin, & R. J. Sternberg (Eds.), *Evidence-based psychotherapy: Where practice and research meet* (pp. 261–271). Washington, DC: American Psychological Association.

Stevens, N. (1990, August 25). Did I say average? I meant superior. *New York Times,* p. 15.

Stockman, A. F. (1990). Dual relationships in rural mental health practice: An ethical dilemma. *Journal of Rural Community Psychology, 11*(2), 31–45.

Stoltenberg, C. D., & Delworth, U. (1987). *Supervising counselors and therapists.* San Francisco, CA: Jossey-Bass.

Stone, A. A. (1978, March 19). Mentally ill: To commit or not, that is the question. *New York Times,* p. 10E.

Stone, M. T. (1982). Turning points in psychotherapy. In S. Slipp (Ed.), *Curative factors in dynamic psychotherapy* (pp. 259–279). New York, NY: McGraw-Hill.

St. Paul Fire & Marine Insurance Company v. Downs, 617 N.E.2d 33g (Ill. App. 1 Dist) (1993).

Stricker, G. (1992). The relationship of research to clinical practice. *American Psychologist, 47,* 543–549.

Stromberg, C. D., Haggarty, R. F., McMillian, M. H., Mishkin, B., Rubin, B. L., & Trilling, H. R. (1988). *The psychologist's legal handbook.* Washington, DC: Council for the National Register of Health Service Providers in Psychology.

Sturdevant, M. (2009, November 19). 1.5 million medical files at risk in Health Net data breach. *Hartford Courant.* Retrieved from http://bit.ly/8sXd7J

Sue, D. W. (1995). Multicultural organizational development: Implications for the counseling profession. In J. G. Ponterotto, J. M. Casas, L. A. Suzuki, & C. M. Alexander (Eds.), *Handbook of multicultural counseling* (pp. 474–492). Thousand Oaks, CA: Sage.

Sue, D. W., & Sue, D. (2003). *Counseling the culturally diverse: Theory and practice* (4th ed.). Boston, MA: Houghton Mifflin.

Sue, D. W., & Sue, D. (2008). *Counseling the culturally diverse: Theory and practice* (5th ed.). Hoboken, NJ: Wiley.

Suzuki, L. A., & C. M. Alexander (Eds.), *Handbook of multicultural counseling* (2nd ed., pp. 165–188). Thousand Oaks, CA: Sage.

Tallman, G. (1981). *Therapist-client social relationships.* Unpublished manuscript, California State University, Northridge.

Tavris, C. (1987, November 1). Method is all but lost in the imagery of social-science fiction. *Los Angeles Times,* Section V, p. 5.

Thieren, M., & Mauron, A. (2007). Nuremberg code turns 60. *Bulletin of the World Health Organization, 85*(8), 573. doi: S0042–96862007000800004 [pii]

Thomas, A., & Sillen, S. (1972). *Racism and psychiatry.* Secaucus, NJ: Citadel Press.

Thoreau, H. D. (1960). *Walden and civil disobedience.* Boston, MA: Houghton Mifflin. (*Civil disobedience* originally published 1849.)

Tolstoy, L. (1951). *The kingdom of God is within you* (L. Weiner, Trans.). Boston, MA: Page. (Originally published 1894.)

Tracy, M. D. (2005). Enhancing diversity in APA: Task Force members highlighted how APA can better serve diverse members and handle related conflicts. *Monitor on Psychology, 36,* 10, 66.

Triskel, N. (2009). Fortunately UK psychologists don't use the APA code of ethics. *British Medical Journal.* Retrieved from http://www.bmj.com/cgi/eletters/338/may14_1/b1972#213695

Truman v. Thomas, California, 611 P.2d 902, 27 Cal. 3d 285 (1980).

Truscott, D., & Crook, K. H. (2004). *Ethics for the practice of psychology in Canada.* Edmonton, Canada: University of Alberta Press.

Tsai, M., Plummer, M. D., Kanter, J. W., Newring, R. W., & Kohlenberg, R. J. (2010). Therapist grief and functional analytic psychotherapy: Strategic self-disclosure of personal loss. *Journal of Contemporary Psychotherapy, 40,* 1–10. doi: 10.1007/s10879-009-9116-6

Tschan, F., Semmer, N. K., Gurtner, A., Bizzari, L., Spychiger, M., Breuer, M., & Marsch, S. U. (2009). Explicit reasoning, confirmation bias, and illusory transactive memory: A simulation study of group medical decision making. *Small Group Research, 40,* 271–300. doi: 10.1177/1046496409332928

Tsuang, M. T. (1983). Risk of suicide in relatives of schizophrenics, manics, depressives, and controls. *Journal of Clinical Psychiatry, 39,* 396–400.

U.S. Bureau of the Census. (2003). Language use and English-speaking ability: 2000 (Report No. C2KBR–29). Washington, DC: Author.

U.S. Centers for Disease Control. (2010). Surveillance for violent deaths. *Morbidity and Mortality Weekly Report, 59,* SS-4, May 14.

U.S. Central Intelligence Agency, Inspector General. (2004, May 7). Special review: Counterterrorrism detention and interrogation activities, Appendix C: U.S. Department of Justice's August 1, 2002, Memorandum for Acting General Counsel of the Central Intelligence Agency, Retrieved from http://bit.ly/9CIARIZZO

U.S. Department of the Army. (2006, October 20). *Behavioral science consultation policy* (OTSG/MEDCOM Policy Memo 06–029). Washington, DC: Author.

U.S. Public Health Service. (1973). *Final report of the Tuskegee Syphilis Study Ad Hoc Advisory Panel.* Washington, DC: Author.

Van Horne, B. A. (2004). Psychology licensing board disciplinary actions: The realities. *Professional Psychology: Research and Practice, 35,* 170–178. doi: 10.1037/0735-7028.35.2.170

Vasquez, M. J. T. (1988). Counselor-client sexual contact: Implications for ethics training. *Journal of Counseling and Development, 67,* 238–241.

Vasquez, M. J. T. (2005). Independent practice settings and the multicultural guidelines. In M. G. Constantine & D. W. Sue (Eds.), *Strategies for building multicultural competence in mental health and educational settings* (pp. 91–108). Washington, DC: American Psychological Association.

Vasquez, M. J. T. (2007). Cultural difference and the therapeutic alliance: An evidence-based analysis. *American Psychologist, 62,* 878–885. doi: 10.1037/0003-066-X.62.8.878

Vasquez, M. J. T. (2009). Ethics in multicultural counseling practice. In J. G. Ponterotto, J. M. Casas, L. A. Suzuki, & C. M. Alexander (Eds.), *Handbook of multicultural counseling* (3rd ed) (pp. 127–146). Thousand Oaks, CA: Sage.

Vasquez, M. J. T., Bingham, R. P., & Barnett, J. E. (2008). Psychotherapy termination: Clinical and ethical responsibilities. *Journal of Clinical Psychology, 64,* 653–665. doi: 10.1002/jclp.20478

Vedentam, S. (2007, August 20). APA rules on interrogation abuse: Psychologists' group bars member participation in certain techniques. *Washington Post,* p. A3.

Velasquez, R. J., Arellano, L. M., & McNeill, B. W. (2004). *The handbook of Chicana/o psychology and mental health.* Mahwah, NJ: Erlbaum.

Vinson, J. S. (1987). Use of complaint procedures in cases of therapist-patient sexual contact. *Professional Psychology: Research and Practice, 18,* 159–164.

Vuorilehto, M. S., Melartin, T. K., & Isometsa, E. T. (2006). Suicidal behaviour among primary-care patients with depressive disorders. *Psychological Medicine, 36*(2), 203–210.

Walfish, S., & Ducey, B. B. (2007). Readability level of Health Insurance Portability and Accountability Act notices of privacy practices utilized by academic medical centers. *Professional Psychology: Research and Practice, 38*(2), 203–207.

Walker v. City of Birmingham, 388 U.S. 307, 18 L.Ed.2d 1210 (1967).

Walker, E., & Young, T. D. (1986). *A killing cure.* New York, NY: Holt.

Wallace, L. S., Keenum, A. J., Roskos, S. E., Blake, G. H., Colwell, S. T., & Weiss, B. D. (2008). Suitability and readability of consumer medical information accompanying prescription medication samples. *Patient Education and Counseling, 70*(3), 420–425.

Wampold, B. E. (2001). *The great psychotherapy debate: Model, methods, and findings.* Mahwah, NJ: Erlbaum.

Wampold, B. E. (2007). Psychotherapy: The humanistic (and effective) treatment. *American Psychologist, 62,* 857–873.

Wampold, B. E. (2010). *The basic of psychotherapy: An introduction to theory and practice.* Washington, DC: American Psychological Association.

Wang, C. (2009). Managing informed consent and confidentiality in multicultural contexts. Presentation at the annual meeting of the American Psychological Association, Toronto, Canada.

Ward, A. (2010). Confidentiality matters. In M. E. Heller & S. Pollet (Ed.), *The work of psychoanalysts in the public health sector* (pp. 113–123). New York, NY: Routledge/Taylor & Francis.

Weary, G., Vaughn, L. A., Stewart, B. D., & Edwards, J. A. (2006). Adjusting for the correspondence bias: Effects of causal uncertainty, cognitive busyness, and causal strength of situational information. *Journal of Experimental Social Psychology, 42*(1), 87–94

Weiner, M. F. (1978). *Therapist disclosure: The use of self in psychotherapy.* Boston, MA: Butterworths.

Weiner, M. F. (1983). *Therapist disclosure: The use of self in psychotherapy* (2nd ed.). Baltimore, MD: University Park Press.

Weisman, A. D., & Worden, J. W. (1972). Risk-rescue rating in suicide assessment. *Archives of General Psychiatry, 26,* 553–560.

Weisz, J. R., Hawley, K. M., & Doss, A. J. (2004). Empirically tested psychotherapies for youth internalizing and externalizing problems and disorders. *Child and Adolescent Psychiatric Clinics of North America, 13,* 729–815.

Werner, N. S., Duschek, S., & Schandry, R. (2009). Relationships between affective states and decision-making. *International Journal of Psychophysiology* [n.p.]. doi: 10.1016/j.ijpsycho.2009.09.010

Werth, J. L., & Blevins, D. (Eds.) (2006). *Psychosocial issues near the end of life: A resource for professional care providers.* Washington, DC: American Psychological Association.

Wessells, M. (2006, January 15). American Psychological Association Presidential Task Force on Psychological Ethics and National Security LISTSERV [Online forum comment]. APA PENS listserv correspondence, April 22, 2005 – June 26, 2006, Intelligence Ethics Collection, Hoover Institution Archives, Stanford University. Retrieved from http://s3.amazonaws.com/propublica/assets/docs/pens_listserv.pdf

Westen, D., & Bradley, R. (2005). Empirically supported complexity: Rethinking evidence-based practice in psychotherapy. *Current Directions in Psychological Science, 1*(10), 266–271.

Westen, D., Novotny, C. M., & Thompson-Brenner, H. (2004). The empirical status of empirically supported psychotherapies: Assumptions, findings, and reporting in controlled clinical trials. *Psychological Bulletin, 130,* 631–663.

Westermeyer, J. (1987). Cultural factors in clinical assessment. *Journal of Consulting and Clinical Psychology, 55,* 471–478.

Wetzel, R. (1976). Hopelessness, depression, and suicide intent. *Archives of General Psychiatry, 33,* 1069–1073.

Whaley, A. L., & Davis, K. E. (2007). Cultural competence and evidence-based practice in mental health services: A complementary perspective. *American Psychologist, 62,* 563–574.

White, H. (2009). Locating clinical boundaries in the World Wide Web. *American Journal of Psychiatry, 166,* 620–621. doi: 10.1176/appi.ajp.2009.08101464

Williams, J. R. (2008). Consent. In P. A. Singer & A. M. Viens (Eds.), *The Cambridge textbook of bioethics* (pp. 11–16). New York, NY: Cambridge University Press.

Williams, M. H. (1997). Boundary violations: Do some contended standards of care fail to encompass commonplace procedures of humanistic, behavioral, and eclectic psychotherapies? *Psychotherapy: Theory, Research, Practice, Training, 34*(3), 238–249.

Wilson, D. (2009, December 12). Poor children likelier to get antipsychotics. *New York Times.* Retrieved from http://www.nytimes.com/2009/12/12/health/12medicaid.html

Wingenfeld-Hammond, S. (2010). Boundaries and multiple relationships. In A. Allan & A. Love (Eds.), *Ethical practice in psychology: Reflections from the creators of the APS Code of Ethics* (pp. 135–147). Hoboken, NJ: Wiley-Blackwell.

Wise, E. H. (2008). Competence and scope of practice: Ethics and professional development. *Journal of Clinical Psychology, 64,* 626–637. doi: 10.1002/jclp.20479

Wong, J. P. S., Stewart, S. M., Claassen, C., Lee, P. W. H., Rao, U., & Lam, T. H. (2008). Repeat suicide attempts in Hong Kong community adolescents. *Social Science & Medicine, 66,* 232–241. doi: 10.1016/j.socscimed.2007.08.031

Woodward, H. E., Taft, C. T., Gordon, R. A., & Meis, L. A. (2009). Clinician bias in the diagnosis of posttraumatic stress disorder and borderline personality disorder. *Psychological Trauma: Theory, Research, Practice, and Policy, 1*, 282–290. doi: 10.1037/a0017944

Woody, R. H. (1998). Bartering for psychological services. *Professional Psychology: Research and Practice, 29*(2), 174–178.

Word, C., Zanna, M. P., & Cooper, J. (1974). The nonverbal mediation of self-fulfilling prophecies in interracial interaction. *Journal of Experimental Social Psychology, 10*, 109–120.

World Medical Association (2003, June 23). Physicians under threat, warns WMA president. [Press release]. Retrieved from http://www.wma.net/es/40news/20archives/20 03/2003_09/index.html

Wu, C., Liao, S., Lin, K., Tseng, M. M., Wu, E. C., & Liu, S. (2009). Multidimensional assessments of impulsivity in subjects with history of suicidal attempts. *Comprehensive Psychiatry, 50*, 315–321. doi: 10.1016/j.comppsych.2008.09.006

Wyatt, G. E. (1997). *Stolen women: Reclaiming our sexuality, taking back our lives.* New York, NY: Wiley.

Wyder, M., Ward, P., & De Leo, D. (2009). Separation as a suicide risk factor. *Journal of Affective Disorders, 116*, 208–213. doi: 10.1016/j.jad.2008.11.007

Wyman, A. J., & Vyse, S. (2008). Science versus the stars: A double-blind test of the validity of the NEO Five-Factor Inventory and computer-generated astrological natal charts. *Journal of General Psychology, 135*, 287–300. doi: 10.3200/ GENP.135.3.287–300

Yantz, C. L., & McCaffrey, R. J. (2005). Effects of a supervisor's observation on memory test performance of the examinee: Third party observer effect confirmed. *Journal of Forensic Neuropsychology, 4*(2), 27–38.

Young, C. (2007). The power of touch in psychotherapy. *International Journal of Psychotherapy, 11*, 15–24.

Younggren, J. (2002). *Ethical decision-making and dual relationships.* Available at http://kspope.com

Younggren, J. N., & Harris, E. A. (2008). Can you keep a secret? Confidentiality in psychotherapy. *Journal of Clinical Psychology, 64*, 589–600. doi: 10.1002/ jclp.20480

Zametkin, A. J., Alter, M. R., & Yemini, T. (2001). Suicide in teenagers: Assessment, management, and prevention. *Journal of the American Medical Association, 286*(24), 3120–3125.

Zavis, A. (2008, December 23). Former Cedars-Sinai employee held in identity theft, fraud. *Los Angeles Times.* Retrieved from http://articles.latimes.com/2008/dec/23/ local/me-cedars-sinai23

Zhang, Y., Conner, K. R., & Phillips, M. R. (2010). Alcohol use disorders and acute alcohol use preceding suicide in China. *Addictive Behaviors, 35*, 152–156. doi: 10.1016/j.addbeh.2009.09.020

ABOUT THE AUTHORS

KENNETH S. POPE, PHD, ABPP

Going to hear Dr. Martin Luther King, Jr., and the community organizer Saul Alinsky changed my life forever. Their words shook me awake, wouldn't let go.

By the time I graduated from college, their words had convinced me to delay a fellowship to study literature so that I could learn community organizing and try to make a difference. I worked in an inner-city area of severe poverty during the late 1960s and early 1970s. For the first time in my life, I lived where there were no neighbors of my own race.

Those years showed me how poverty, unmet basic needs, and injustice can assault individual lives. I also witnessed the power of people working together to bring about profound change.

A crucial lesson began one day in a cafe where the community gathered. A deacon in a church whose roots reached back to the days before the Civil War invited me to visit the church that Sunday.

I entered the church and a found seat at the back, looking forward to the minister's sermon. When the time came for the sermon, the minister walked up to the pulpit, looked out at us, and began, "We are most pleased that our neighbor, Mr. Ken Pope, agreed to visit us today, and we look forward to his sermon." This taught me not to assume that my understandings are always shared by others—and that life often calls for us to do more than just show up.

After my years living in that community, I began the delayed fellowship to study literature at Harvard. But the years between college and graduate school had changed me. When I received an M.A. at the end of the year, I did not want to continue studies in that field. I explained my change of heart, expecting to be shown the door. But they surprised me. They told me I could continue to study, taking whatever courses I found interesting in any fields. Some courses I took the next year were in psychology, and they felt like my home. I'll always be thankful to the university for their kindness in allowing me to delay my fellowship, letting me take courses in diverse fields, and in the professors' generosity with their time and support. Because Harvard lacked a clinical psychology program, I transferred to Yale for my clinical psychology doctorate.

What happened in these early years has continued happening throughout my life: Fellow students, colleagues (like my friend Melba Vasquez), patients, and others have made me realize that whatever beliefs I held at any given time could be rethought, that I needed to consider new perspectives, new possibilities, new ways of finding, creating, and using resources.

One example: Our faculty-intern discussions followed a predictable pattern: Asked to present a case, each of us interns would choose to describe that week's version of "my toughest case," making clear what overwhelming challenges we faced and how brilliant our insights and interventions. Midyear, an intern broke the pattern: "I feel awful this week. The situation was not that difficult, but I made some bad mistakes and ended up having to hospitalize the patient. I need help figuring out what's going on with this patient, why I did what I did, and how I can do things differently." Her honesty, courage, integrity, and clear concern for the person she wanted to help woke us from our complacent habits of thinking and feeling. We confronted how we approached learning and how we treated each other. We talked about how fear, envy, and competitiveness affected who we were, how we thought, and what we did. One person had changed our community.

In my early years as a licensed psychologist, I served as clinical director of a nonprofit hospital and community mental health center. My prior experiences led me to focus on the ability of the staff, the board of directors, and the surrounding community to work together identifying needs and creating ways to meet those needs. Working together, the diverse individuals in that array of groups created home-bound psychological services, a 24-hour crisis service, legal services for people who are poor or homeless, a program for people whose primary language is Spanish, and group homes allowing people who are mentally disabled to live independently. What the people in these groups accomplished showed again and again the decisive role that one person can play in the lives of others, the ways we can awaken each other to new perspectives and possibilities, and how people working together can bring about change.

Teaching the occasional undergraduate course in the UCLA psychology department, supervising therapy in the UCLA Psychology Clinic, chairing the ethics committees of the American Psychological Association (APA) and the American Board of Professional Psychology (ABPP), becoming a charter member and later fellow of what is now the Association for Psychological Science, and other experiences in those early years kept reminding me of the need to keep rethinking what I think I know and my ways of working, to ask: What if I'm wrong about this? Is there are better way to understand this? What else could I do that might be more effective?

Since leaving institutional work in the mid-1980s, I've been an independent clinical and forensic psychologist, but the themes of my work, just touched on, continue, even as they continue to take on new forms.

One question I've struggled with is: How can psychologists have better access to relevant information without it adding to their time restraints and financial burden?

Almost two decades ago, I started a Psychology News List via e-mail, free and open to all. I wanted to make it a little easier—especially for those in isolated areas or those who lack easy access to the relevant materials—to keep up with the new research, changing legal standards, controversial topics, and other trends that affect our work. Each day I send out 6 to 10 items, most of them excerpts from new and in-press articles from psychology and other scientific and professional journals, psychology-related articles from that day's newspapers, new court decisions affecting psychology, job announcements, and referral requests sent to me by list members. Although not a discussion list and now quite large, it has become a supportive community. From time to time members ask me to circulate a request for information or suggestions for dealing with an aging parent, a family emergency, a clinical or forensic issue, or a business-related problem with their practice. Almost all write me later to tell me how supported they felt to receive so many personal responses. Every year I've sent two questions to the list: Early in spring I ask what sources of joy, meaning, or hope recipients have that particular year that sustains them in hard times; and between the Canadian and U.S. Thanksgivings, I ask what they are especially thankful for that year. When I circulate a compilation of all the responses, members tell me how much the process makes them feel less alone and more connected to others.

Another way we can make information more accessible is through Web sites that provide articles and other resources without making access contingent on subscriptions, memberships, fees, or other restrictions. Two of mine are "Articles, Research, & Resources in Psychology" http://kspope.com and "Accessibility & Disability Information & Resources in Psychology Training & Practice" at http://kpope.com. A Web site also turned out to be a good way of sharing another part of my life: The wonderful family of special-needs dogs and cats who live in our home. That web site is at http://kenpope.com.

For 29 years APA was my professional home. As chair of the APA Ethics Committee and a fellow of nine APA divisions, I worked with many people who became close friends and gave so much to my professional and personal life. I was honored to receive the APA Award for Distinguished Contributions to Public Service "for rigorous empirical research, landmark articles and books, courageous leadership, fostering the careers of others, and making services available to those with no means to pay"; the Division 12 Award for Distinguished Professional Contributions to Clinical Psychology; the Division 42 Award for Mentoring; and other forms of recognition.

In 2008, with great regret and sadness, I resigned from the APA. My respect and affection for the members made this a hard and reluctant step. I respectfully disagreed with decisive changes that APA made in its ethical stance after the events of September 11, 2001. In my view, those changes moved APA far from its ethical foundation, historic traditions, and basic values and beyond what I could in good conscience support with my membership. The events of 9/11 cast all of us into a tangle of complex issues, dangerous realities, and hard choices. My decision to resign from APA reflected my effort to judge what was right for me. I respect those who saw things differently, held other beliefs, and took other paths. Chapter 12 discusses different perspectives on these complex issues.

We can each give so much to each other and to our communities. Sometimes just a word or gesture helps someone to keep going, overcome a baffling obstacle, or see new vistas. An example: During that second year at Harvard, I signed up for an advanced course in med school. The first day I was already lost. The professor kept asking if we saw various structures in our microscopes. Everyone nodded yes, but I had no idea what he was talking about. I was too embarrassed to admit I couldn't see any of them. Finally I raised my hand and confessed. He looked at me a long time, then came down the aisle, put his hand on my back, leaned down to the floor, and plugged in my electronic microscope. Sometimes that's all it takes.

MELBA J. T. VASQUEZ

Why am I interested in ethics? When I trace the path of my professional development, it becomes clear that themes of social justice, empowerment, and fairness have informed every step of those processes.

I was not destined for my career. I come from a working class Latino family from Texas. My first jobs were picking cotton, babysitting, and cleaning people's houses. During adolescence and young adulthood, my family and those of many in my community moved into the middle class, partly as a result of Lyndon Johnson's War on Poverty's initiatives. I was very much influenced by seeing that carefully designed and managed programs can make a positive difference in people's lives. I also witnessed the importance of dignity and integrity in people who often had little material wealth but who had so much to offer humanity through acts of kindness and compassion. As a first-generation college student coming from that rising middle class, I had never considered obtaining a doctorate but am grateful that my professor, Dr. Colleen Conoley, perceived me to be a "good fit" for the profession of counseling psychology. I obtained my doctorate from the APA-accredited, scientist-practitioner Counseling Psychology program at the University of Texas at Austin in 1978.

I am also grateful to have been in the first cohort of the American Psychological Association's Minority Fellowship Program, which supported the last three years of my graduate study and which served as a powerful socializing process into the profession. It taught me the importance of effective strategies for addressing injustices in psychology.

After receiving my doctorate, I worked for 13 years at two different university counseling centers and served as internship training director at both Colorado State University and the University of Texas at Austin. Then, in 1991, I entered full-time independent practice, initially planning to do so temporarily, with plans to return to university administration at some point. However, I found that I was able to continue active involvement in professional leadership, advocacy, and scholarship and enjoyed the work in independent practice.

Early in my career, I was encouraged to run for and was elected to the Board of Social and Ethical Responsibility for Psychologists (BSERP). I learned much in those days, as the BSERP led APA in divesting our investments in apartheid South Africa and raised awareness in the association about what was then a new disease, HIV/AIDS. This board, considered the social conscience of psychology, was later merged with the Board of Ethnic Minority Affairs, to become the Board for the Advancement of Psychology in the Public Interest, and I was the first chair of that new board. Thus, my first governance experience in APA was focused on ethics and social justice.

My interests led me to seek leadership roles in other areas of the APA. I served as a member of the Committee of Women in Psychology and of various task forces. After helping to found Division 45, the Society of the Psychological Study of Ethnic Minority Issues, I was its first council representative; I helped to organize and served as chair of the Ethnic Minority Caucus. I have also been a member of the Council of Representatives for Division 17 (and served as chair of the Public Interest Caucus) and for Division 42 (and served as chair of the Women's Caucus). The theme of engagement with social justice issues persisted as I became more involved in the inner workings of APA.

In the mid-1980s, I became interested in professional ethics and was elected to serve on the APA Ethics Committee. Ken Pope was a member of that group at the same time, and over the years, the two of us became coauthors on several ethics publications. I participated on the last two Ethics Committee Task Forces for revision of the Ethics Code (resulting in the 1992 and 2002 Ethics Codes).

I then went on to serve on both the Board of Professional Affairs, chairing it in my final year with that group, and on the Committee for the Advancement of Professional Practice. I was pleased to see the association so dedicated to developing services to meet the needs of psychologists to provide services to consumers in independent practice, Veterans Administration hospitals, community mental health centers, prisons, medical and hospital settings, and others. I have been involved in developing psychology's legislative advocacy through activities sponsored by the APA's Practice Organization and the Association for the Advancement of Psychology.

I was elected president of APA Division 35, Society for the Psychology of Women, the first Latina to hold that position. As my presidential project, I helped to cofound the 1999 National Multicultural Conference and Summit (with Rosie Bingham, Derald Wing Sue, and Lisa Porche Burke). The NMCS is now held every two years. I have also served as president of APA Division 17, Society of Counseling Psychology, and of the Texas Psychological Association, again being the first Latina in each of these roles. As I continued to experience a range of leadership activities, engaging in projects and events about which I felt passionate, I ran for and was elected to the APA Board of Directors (served 2007–2009). I became the first woman of color to be elected as APA president, to serve in 2011. The encouragement from others to seek higher levels of leadership contributed to my belief that I could perhaps do so. My passion for infusing psychology with social justice and fairness fueled my decision to do so.

Standing for candidacy of president of APA reflected love for and commitment to all the work I have just described. I believe in the ability of each person who chooses to be involved and provide input to have influence in shaping the policies and direction of the association and the profession. I also believe that together we can continue to identify concrete strategies to meet the needs of psychologists and to promote psychological knowledge and ethical strategies to address the challenges of society at a very critical time.

I truly enjoy providing keynote addresses, symposia presentations, and workshops in the areas of professional ethics, multicultural counseling, leadership, the ethics of self-care, and other related topics over the years. I continue to be amazed that I receive awards and honors for engaging in activities about which I feel strongly. Some of the more recent honors are listed next.

Honors

> Psychologist of the Year, American Psychological Association Division 42, Psychologists in Independent Practice, APA Annual Convention, August, 2008, Boston, MA
>
> Friend of the Asian American Psychological Association Award, Annual Conference, August 2008, Boston, MA
>
> Advocacy Award, Association for the Advancement of Psychology, August 2008, Boston, MA
>
> California Psychological Association Distinguished Contribution to Psychology as a Profession Award, California Psychological Association Annual Convention, April 2008, Anaheim, CA
>
> Alfred M. Wellner, PhD, Senior Career Award for Outstanding Service to Psychology, National Register of Health Service Providers in Psychology, November 2007
>
> Distinguished Professional Contributions to Independent or Institutional Practice in the Private Sector, American Psychological Association, August 2007

APA Karl F. Heiser Presidential Award for Advocacy, August 2007

APA Division 17 Presidential Citation for Outstanding Career Contribution to the Profession via Excellence in Mentoring, August 2007

Woman of the Year, American Psychological Association's Division 17, Society of Counseling Psychology Section for the Advancement of Women, August 2006

Honorary Doctorate, Phillips Graduate Institute, May 2005.

James M. Jones Lifetime Achievement Award, American Psychological Association, 2004

AUTHOR INDEX

SUBJECT INDEX

Abu Ghraib, 146, 152
Academic/teaching concerns, 103
Accountability, mechanisms for, 87–89
  civil statutes and case law, 106–108
  criminal statutes, 108–109
  ethics committees, codes, and
    complaints, 89–104
  licensing boards, 104–106
Adaptive Behavior Scale, 266
Ad Hominem/ad Feminam fallacies,
  20
Adopting the client's view, 223
Affirming the Consequent fallacy, 20
AIDS cases, 11–12
American Academy of Child and
  Adolescent Psychiatry Staff, 57
American Academy of Clinical
  Neuropsychology, 196
American Civil Liberties Union, 144
American Counseling Association, 65
American Medical Informatics
  Association, 57
American Mental Health Counselors
  Association, 57
American Psychological Association
  (APA):
  APA Critical Incident Study, 100–
    104
  approach to ethics code, 90–92
  assessment guidelines, 190–191
  Committee on Ethical Standards,
    91, 93, 96, 100
  Committee on Professional
    Standards, 195
  Committee on Psychological Tests

    and Assessment, 197
  Ethical Principles of Psychologists
    and Code of Conduct (2010), 199
  Ethics Code. See Ethics Code, APA
  membership, 89–90
  petition resolution, 131–132
  statements on torture, 148–149
  tradition of openness and
    transparency, 151–152
Americans with Disabilities Act, 319
American Telemedicine Association,
  57
Amnesty International, 144
Animals, treatment of, 147–148
Anxiety about work, 71
APA Presidential Task Force on
  Psychological Ethics and National
  Security (PENS Task Force), 140–
  142, 151
Appeal to Ignorance (ad Ignorantium)
  fallacy, 20
Argument to Logic (Argumentum ad
  Logicam) fallacy, 21
Assessment:
  awareness of basic assumptions in,
    197–198
  in child custody cases, 202
  client history and, 203
  competence in, 191
  culture and, 192, 266–267
  dual high base rates, 200–201
  Ethics Code on, 351–354
  forensics and, 202
  importance of feedback in, 204–205
  and insurance billing, 199–200

STUDY PACKAGE
CONTINUING EDUCATION
CREDIT INFORMATION

Ethics in Psychotherapy and Counseling: A Practical Guide

Our goal is to provide you with current, accurate and practical information from the most experienced and knowledgeable speakers and authors.

Listed below are the continuing education credit(s) currently available for this self-study package. *Please note: Your state licensing board dictates whether self study is an acceptable form of continuing education. Please refer to your state rules and regulations.*

COUNSELORS: PESI, LLC is recognized by the National Board for Certified Counselors to offer continuing education for National Certified Counselors. Provider #: 5896. We adhere to NBCC Continuing Education Guidelines. This self-study package qualifies for **6.75** contact hours.

SOCIAL WORKERS: PESI, LLC, 1030, is approved as a provider for continuing education by the Association of Social Work Boards, 400 South Ridge Parkway, Suite B, Culpeper, VA 22701. www.aswb.org. Social workers should contact their regulatory board to determine course approval. Course Level: All Levels. Social Workers will receive **6.75** (Clinical) continuing education clock hours for completing this self-study package.

PSYCHOLOGISTS: PESI, LLC is approved by the American Psychological Association to sponsor continuing education for psychologists. PESI, LLC maintains responsibility for these materials and their content. PESI is offering these self- study materials for **6.5** hours of continuing education credit.

ADDICTION COUNSELORS: PESI, LLC is a Provider approved by NAADAC Approved Education Provider Program. Provider #: 366. This self-study package qualifies for **8.0** contact hours.

Procedures:

1. Review the material and read the book.

2. If seeking credit, complete the posttest/evaluation form:

    -Complete posttest/evaluation in entirety; including your email address to receive your certificate much faster versus by mail.

    -Upon completion, mail to the address listed on the form along with the CE fee stated on the test. Tests will not be processed without the CE fee included.

    -Completed posttests must be received 6 months from the date printed on the packing slip.

Your completed posttest/evaluation will be graded. If you receive a passing score (70% and above), you will be emailed/faxed/mailed a certificate of successful completion with earned continuing education credits. (Please write your email address on the posttest/evaluation form for fastest response) If you do not pass the posttest, you will be sent a letter indicating areas of deficiency, and another posttest to complete. The posttest must be resubmitted and receive a passing grade before credit can be awarded. We will allow you to re-take as many times as necessary to receive a certificate.

If you have any questions, please feel free to contact our customer service department at 1.800.844.8260.

PESI LLC
PO BOX 1000
Eau Claire, WI 54702-1000

Ethics in Psychotherapy and Counseling:
A Practical Guide

PO BOX 1000
Eau Claire, WI 54702
800-844-8260

Any persons interested in receiving credit may photocopy this form, complete and return with a payment of $25.00 per person CE fee. A certificate of successful completion will be sent to you. To receive your certificate sooner than two weeks, rush processing is available for a fee of $10. Please attach check or include credit card information below.

Mail to: PESI, PO Box 1000, Eau Claire, WI 54702 or fax to PESI (800) 554-9775 (both sides)

CE Fee: $25: (Rush processing fee: $10)   **Total to be charged** _____

Credit Card #: _____   **Exp Date:** _____   **V-Code*:** _____
(*MC/VISA/Discover: last 3-digit # on signature panel on back of card.) (*American Express: 4-digit # above account # on face of card.)

	LAST	FIRST	M.I.

Name (please print): _____   _____   _____

Address: _____ Daytime Phone: _____

City: _____ State: _____ Zip Code: _____

Signature: _____ Email: _____

Date Completed: _____ Actual time (# of hours) taken to complete this offering: _____hours

Program Objectives After completing this publication, I have been able to achieve these objectives:

1. Describe and follow steps in ethical decision-making   1. Yes   No
2. Identify logical fallacies and other sources of ethical errors   2. Yes   No
3. Describe the fundamentals of the ethics codes of the American   3. Yes   No
Psychological Association and Canadian Psychological Association--their
basic approaches, how they are similar, and how they differ
4. Identify major causes of ethics complaints, licensing complaints, and   4. Yes   No
malpractice complaints for psychologists in the United States and Canada
5. Knowledgeably discuss ethical issues in such aspects of clinical   5. Yes   No
practice as informed consent, confidentiality, culture, assessment, suicide,
multiple relationships and other boundary issues, and supervision
6. Create a plan for self-care   6. Yes   No
7. Create a professional will   7. Yes   No

PESI LLC
PO BOX 1000
Eau Claire, WI 54702-1000

ZNT043015   CE Release Date: 9/01/2010

1. According to the book, ethical awareness is best described as:
a) a level of wisdom achieved on the basis of conscientiousness, study, and experience
b) a form of professional sensitivity best learned through mentoring
c) a continuous, active process that involves constant questioning and personal responsibility
d) a goal that we must always strive for though we never achieve it

2. According to the book, authorities and groups:
a) are examples of what the book calls "regressive ethical influences"
b) are the source of utilitarian but not deontological ethics codes
c) are the source of deontological but not utilitarian ethics codes
d) are valuable resources but when misused can block or short-circuit our ethical judgment

3. Consider the following statement: "People who are psychotic act in a bizarre manner; this person acts in a bizarre manner; therefore this person is psychotic." According to the book, this statement is an example of which of the following fallacies?
a) denying the antecedent
b) affirming the consequent
c) mistaking deductive validity for truth
d) post hoc, ergo propter hoc

4. The book discusses common language patters that can interfere with clear thinking about ethics. Which of the following is NOT one of those patterns?
a) substituting the general for the specific
b) using the active voice
c) replacing intentional unethical behavior with the language of accidents, misfortune, and mistakes
d) using the abstract language of technicalities

5. According to the book, the statement "It's not unethical as long as no law was broken":
a) was the primary foundation for the ancient Code of Hammurabi
b) is valid in only two specialty areas of psychology
c) is valid in only two clinical situations
d) is a common justification for unethical behavior

6. According to the book, the most recent version of the American Psychological Association's ethics code was published in what year?
a) 2010
b) 2007
c) 2005
d) 2004

7. The section on the detainee interrogation controversy was used to illustrate:
a) the slippery slope phenomenon
b) how people of good faith can reach different conclusions and respectfully disagree about important ethical issues
c) how the interaction of individual and organizational dynamics affects our attributions of responsibility
d) how MacGuffin's (2004) "5-step ethical resolution process" can be applied to complex issues

8. According to the book, which of the following is NOT one of the four basic ethical principles in the Canadian Psychological Association's Code of Ethics for Psychologists?
a) responsibility to the profession
b) responsibility to society
c) responsible caring
d) integrity in relationships

9. According to the book, informed consent is best viewed as:
a) a legally-binding obligation
b) an ethical responsibility involving 7 basic steps
c) a continuing or recurrent process
d) a habit

10. The book presents multiyear data on psychology licensing board disciplinary actions collected by the Association of State and Provincial Psychology Boards (ASPPB). The largest number of disciplinary actions occurred in which of the following categories?
a) incompetence
b) breach of confidentiality
c) nonsexual dual relationship or boundary violation
d) sexual misconduct

PESI LLC
PO BOX 1000
Eau Claire, WI 54702-1000

Made in the USA
San Bernardino, CA
05 April 2014